PSYCHOLOGY AND INDUSTRY TODAY

Fifth Edition

Psychology and Industry Today

An Introduction to Industrial and
Organizational Psychology

Duane P. Schultz
University of South Florida

Sydney Ellen Schultz

MACMILLAN PUBLISHING COMPANY
NEW YORK

Editor: Christine Cardone
Production Supervisors: Janice Marie Johnson and Charlotte Hyland
Production Manager: Alan Fischer
Text Designer: Leon Bolognese & Associates, Inc.
Cover Designer: Michael Jung
Cover illustration: E. Salem Krieger
Illustrations: Fineline Illustrations, Inc.

This book was set in ITC Garamond Light by Polyglot Ltd., and printed and bound by Arcata/Halliday. The cover was printed by Phoenix Color Corp.

Macmillan Publishing Company
866 Third Avenue, New York, New York 10022

Collier Macmillan Canada, Inc.

Library of Congress Cataloging-in-Publication Data
Schultz, Duane P.
  Psychology and industry today: an introduction to industrial and organizational psychology/Duane P. Schultz, Sydney Ellen Schultz. —5th ed.

      p.   cm.
Bibliography: p.
Includes index.
  1. Psychology, Industrial. I. Schultz, Sydney Ellen. II. Title. HF5548.8.S356   1990   158.7—dc20
  ISBN 0-02-407621-X   89-2572
                                                                                                 CIP

Printing: 2 3 4 5 6 7   Year: 0 1 2 3 4 5 6

Photo credits appear on page 668, which constitutes a continuation of the copyright page.

"...in industry you can make things happen. You put in a program, and you see some results. You might see better people selected, or job satisfaction go up, or turnover go down. But you've made something happen, and that's a very exciting kind of reward."

—Ann Howard, Ph.D.
Division Manager—Human Resources Research, AT&T

Preface

*T*he fifth edition of *Psychology and Industry Today* retains the theme and approach of the previous editions. The book is written as an introduction to the field of industrial/organizational (I/O) psychology and is designed as a text for courses in industrial, business, personnel, and applied psychology.

Our purpose in this book is not to train people to become I/O psychologists but rather to acquaint students—most of whom will work for some kind of organization—with the principles, practices, problems, and occasional pretenses of I/O psychology. In addition, we believe that it is important to show students how psychology will aid them in their careers and how the findings of industrial psychologists will directly influence their lives as job applicants, employees, managers, and consumers.

Research methods and findings are discussed within the framework of actual work situations and problems rather than as academic or theoretical exercises. The focus throughout the book is on contemporary on-the-job situations. We might describe the text as dealing with "applied" I/O psychology, that is, with the application of theories and research findings to the everyday problems the student is likely to encounter when he or she begins a full-time working career. Wherever possible, I/O psychology programs in action are discussed, showing their use in different kinds of workplaces.

Because *Psychology and Industry Today* is intended for undergraduate classroom use, it is written expressly for students. They are the ones who must read, underline, and study the text. We would like them not only to learn about I/O psychology, but also to enjoy reading about it. We have attempted, therefore, to combine readability with thorough and accurate coverage.

The material in this edition is written at a level suitable for students who are not psychology majors; these students often constitute a large portion of the enrollment in this course. The book is appropriate for use by departments of psychology and schools of business administration at the four-year college and university level as well as at junior and community colleges.

The fifth edition contains much new material, as befits a field that is growing so rapidly. The entire book has been revised and updated to deal with current practices, problems, and trends. Every chapter contains new topics as well as additional material on existing topics.

Throughout the book, much material has been added to reflect the impact of computer technology on the office and the factory, including electronic mail surveys, computer interpretation of selection tests, computerized performance appraisals and the automated monitoring of job performance, and training in computer literacy. We have also dealt with the effects of computers on the jobs of first-line supervisors and managers, on organizational structure, on physical working conditions, and on employee stress and health.

Some of the topics new to this edition are the problems of generalizing from laboratory studies to field settings, sources of error in survey research, examples of the conflicts between research and application, training and work experience (T&E) evaluation as a selection technique, AIDS and genetic screening in the workplace, cognitive processes in performance appraisal, characteristics of effective postappraisal interviews, leader match training, and the influence of locus of control on motivation in training programs. Also covered are self-assessments to determine training needs, additional leadership theories (cognitive resource utilization, vertical dyadic linkage, and situational), self-managing work groups, changing values of American workers, patterns of work and nonwork satisfaction, pay-for-performance programs, social loafing, focus groups in market research, and impulse buying.

Reflecting the substantial growth of the literature in I/O psychology, more than half of the references in this edition are research studies or review articles published since 1985. A complete reference list appears at the end of the book.

Each chapter includes an outline and a complete summary with important terms highlighted in boldfaced type. Key terms are listed alphabetically at the end of the chapter. The chapters also contain a short list of annotated readings for students who wish to pursue a topic in greater depth.

New to this edition are the case studies for Chapters 3–14. These are brief descriptions of actual investigations conducted on the job, and they have been chosen to represent specific topics from each chapter as well as the various research approaches I/O psychologists use to study worker behavior. The methods of data collection described in Chapter 2 (the experimental method, naturalistic observation, survey methods, and the correlational approach) are illustrated. The studies are drawn from recent articles in primary journals in the field.

The questions at the end of each example refer not only to the case problem and its methodology, but also to related aspects of the topic, requiring students to draw on material presented throughout the chapter. These questions are suitable for self-study, class discussion, or written assignments.

The photographs and many of the tables and figures are new to this edition. A test bank and student study guide are also available.

We would like to thank the many students and colleagues who took the time to write to us about the book and who offered suggestions for the new edition. In addition, several reviewers provided valuable and perceptive feedback on the material, and we are most appreciative of their efforts. They include Barbara A. Garwood, Lakeland Community College; Paul E. Spector, University of South Florida, Tampa; Jane A. Halpert, DePaul University; and Edward L. Levine, University of South Florida, Tampa. We also wish to thank Christine Cardone, our editor at Macmillan, for her continuing encouragement and enthusiasm about this project.

D.P.S.
S.E.S.

Contents

Chapter 4   Employee Selection 2: Psychological Testing *130*

Chapter 5   Performance Appraisal *171*

PSYCHOLOGY AND INDUSTRY TODAY

PART I

The Practice of Industrial/ Organizational Psychology

*I*ndustrial/organizational (I/O) psychology will affect your attitudes, behavior, and motivation, both on and off the job, whether you are seeking your first job, advancing in your chosen career, or planning for your retirement years. Chapter 1 examines the scope of I/O psychology as well as the goals and problems of I/O psychologists. Chapter 2 describes the research methods used by I/O psychologists to collect data, draw conclusions, and apply their findings to personnel and organizational problems.

Chapter 1

Principles, Practices, and Problems

Scope and Importance of Industrial/Organizational Psychology

Do you ever have fantasies about being rich? So wealthy that you could live in luxury for the rest of your days and never want for anything again? Suppose that you just won $10 million in the state lottery. Suddenly you're a millionnaire! Now ask yourself another question: Would you still look for a job after graduation? Would you ever want to work again?

The same question was asked of a sample of working Americans in a recent survey, and the results may surprise you. Two out of three employees said that, yes, they would continue to work, even if they no longer needed the money ("Would You Quit," 1988).

The response on this issue indicates the importance of work in our daily lives. Fortunately, because we spend a large portion of our waking hours at our jobs, employment provides us with much more than financial security. The nature of our work influences not only our economic well-being but also our emotional security and happiness.

First, a career offers us a sense of identity and status, telling us, and others, who and what we are. Work contributes to our sense of self-esteem and can satisfy our drive for fulfillment and accomplishment, for meaning and purpose in life.

Second, employment brings social rewards, meeting our need for belonging to a group and providing the security that derives from becoming an accepted and valued member of a team or community. Work furnishes opportunities to form friendships and meet types of people with whom we might not otherwise come in contact. At the least, work can prevent us from feeling lonely.

Thus, work can be good for you, but it can also be harmful to your health. In addition to physical hazards in the workplace itself, a job can contribute to a person's level of anxiety or frustration. If you are thwarted in your plans for advancement or dissatisfied with your boss, for example, you are likely to bring your discontent home with you at the end of the workday. Work-related stresses have been directly or indirectly associated with one's level of physical and emotional health. A long-term study found that the single greatest predictor of longevity is the degree of work satisfaction; satisfied workers live longer (*Work in America*, 1973). Ulcers, arthritis, and other psychosomatic illnesses have also been traced to stress and dissatisfaction in the workplace. In addition, much research suggests that a lack of job satisfaction is associated with heart disease (Howard, Cunningham, & Rechnitzer, 1986).

Choosing the most appropriate career and selecting the right kind of job may be the most important decision you will ever make. Perhaps you can already begin to understand why this course may be among the most personally relevant courses of your college career. Regardless of the kind of work you undertake, your future will be influenced by industrial/organizational (I/O) psychology, the branch of psychology that deals with the world of work. Because so much of your behavior and attitudes on and off the job will be shaped by industrial psychologists, you should become aware of the nature, approach, and activities of this field.

Your work helps define your identity and contributes to your sense of self-esteem, whether you are a surveyor at a construction site, a ground crew-member servicing an airliner, a business executive, a miner, or a television producer.

Your work helps define your identity and contributes to your sense of self-esteem, whether you are a surveyor at a construction site, a ground crew-member servicing an airliner, a business executive, a miner, or a television producer.

Most of you, on completion of college, will work for some sort of organization—a business corporation, a manufacturing concern, the federal or a state government, a hospital or university, or the military. No matter where you work, your entire career, from the day you approach the personnel office for your first interview until your retirement dinner, will be shaped and guided by the findings of I/O psychologists. Indeed, second to your own ability, I/O psychology will help determine the job you perform and the manner in which you perform it; your ultimate rank, responsibilities, and remuneration; and, most important, the kind of personal satisfaction you derive from your work.

I/O psychologists aid you initially in the difficult task of choosing a job because of their prominent role in employee selection. Your first formal contact with I/O psychology will probably be the application blanks, psychological tests, and the other selection measures used by a potential employer to determine if you are the right person for the job and, of equal importance, if the job is the most suitable one for you.

After you have satisfied an organization and yourself about the appropriateness of the job, the contribution of I/O psychology to your work life continues. Your advancement in the organization depends on several criteria, including your actual job performance (which will be periodically evaluated by using techniques devised by psychologists) and your performance on additional selection measures. In many businesses today, high-level promotions are never made without the recommendation of the company psychologist about a person's potential for handling increased responsibilities.

Because of your college training, you may obtain a management position at some level within the corporate hierarchy. This means that you must be aware of, and sensitive to, the diverse motivational and emotional factors that influence the people who work for you. To learn how best to lead and motivate your subordinates, you will be exposed to the research of I/O psychologists. Indeed, you will probably find yourself in a training program that was established by psychologists to teach you how to motivate your subordinates and how to be an effective manager of the work of others.

Even if you do not assume leadership responsibilities—if you are an engineer, an accountant, or a technician, for example, working in a staff capacity with no subordinates—you will still encounter problems of interpersonal relations. Whatever your job, most likely you will be working with other people, and a knowledge of human relations skills—how to get along with others—may mean the difference between success and failure.

The importance of getting along with others was recognized in a survey of more than 1,000 personnel department heads. The results showed that two common causes of employee turnover are being unable to get along with one's superior, and personal problems and conflicts on the job (Lawrence, 1988).

Interviews with personnel directors and corporate vice presidents at 100 of the largest corporations in the United States revealed that executives have to spend an average of 9.2% of their time dealing with personality conflicts among their employees ("When Managers Must," 1986). Thus, organizations today must devote a great deal of effort to improving interpersonal and human relations skills among their employees, training that you may well undergo yourself.

You will certainly be interested in seeing your employer grow and prosper because the more your company expands, the more opportunities there will be for you to advance within the organization. The company's output must be produced with as much efficiency and quality as possible. Therefore, the plant, equipment, and working conditions must foster a productive working climate. This is another responsibility of I/O psychologists; they participate in the design of machinery, the layout of assembly lines, and the arrangement of the working environment to assure maximum high-level production. The finished product of a manufacturing concern must be advertised and attractively packaged to entice people to buy it. Psychologists play a role in these activities too.

At all levels of modern organizational life, psychologists provide essential services to you and your employer. Psychology as applied to the world of work serves two masters, the individual and the organization. It cannot benefit one without benefiting the other.

A note of caution. As vital as the field of industrial/organizational psychology is, as influential as it will be in your career, it is primarily a tool. And any tool is only as valuable as the skill of the person who uses it. Improperly used by management, inadequately understood by employees, the findings of I/O psychology can do more harm than good. Proper use of this tool by competent managers and employees will profit everyone.

But there is more to I/O psychology. It also affects your daily life away from the job; its effects are not limited to the factory or office. I/O psychology influences your role as a consumer. We noted the use of psychology in packaging, marketing, and advertising a company's products. Advertising is an integral part of our society and a necessary cornerstone of our multibillion-dollar economy. On radio and television, in magazines and newspapers, on billboards, and even in the sky, we are continually bombarded by messages urging us to buy this and try that.

What governed your choice of a toothpaste, breakfast cereal, or car? Most likely it was the psychological image created for the product, the attractiveness of the package, or the emotional need satisfied by a particular brand. Advertising has told us, successfully, that we shall be more popular, nicer to be near, or more successful if we wear these jeans or use that cologne. And many of the professionals who create our needs and design the packages and slogans to satisfy them are psychologists.

The same kinds of psychological techniques designed to rid us of bad breath and heartburn are also used to sell political candidates. Psychology has entered the political arena to create images for candidates that will induce you to vote for them. Public opinion polls are widely used to inform political leaders about how people feel on various issues. Polling techniques are also used by psychologists in other areas. For example, the ratings that determine the television programs we watch are based on scientifically conducted polls of cross-sectional samples of television viewers.

Your driving behavior is influenced by the psychologists who assisted design engineers in the layout of the instrument panel so that knobs and controls are easy to use and visual displays (such as the speedometer) are easy to see and interpret. The shape and color of road signs are a result of research by psychologists on highway safety.

Every time you travel in a commercial airliner your safety depends on the work of psychologists who have designed aircraft instruments and controls so that they can be operated as quickly and efficiently as possible. At a more everyday level, psychologists have contributed to the design and layout of controls on such household items as kitchen ranges, microwave ovens, and telephones. The push-button phone is the result of research by psychologists who found that pushing buttons is easier, faster, and more accurate than the old-fashioned method of dialing.

The list of contributions of I/O psychologists to daily living both on and off the job is a long one but the point has been made. Because you are so affected by this field, no matter where you are or what you do, you should try to learn something about it, if only for self-defense.

Definition and Method of Industrial/Organizational Psychology

We can begin to define I/O psychology quite simply as *the application of the methods, facts, and principles of psychology to people at work*. As such, it is one of the many fields of the discipline of psychology. Now, as so often happens with definitions, we must define the term *psychology* to understand adequately our initial definition.

Psychology is the science of behavior and mental processes. Industrial/organizational psychology, then, involves *the application of the methods, facts, and principles of the science of behavior and mental processes to people at work*.

The fact that I/O psychology is a science tells us a great deal about its manner of operation. A science deals only with observable fact—that which can be seen, heard, touched, measured, and recorded. Hence, science is empirical, that is, it relies on verifiable observation, experimentation, and experience, not on opinions, intuitions, pet notions, or private prejudices. It follows that science is objective in its approaches and results. The observed facts must be public, that is, capable of being seen and confirmed by other scientists working independently. Chapter 2 examines the methods by which psychologists gather and analyze their facts or data.

One point to remember throughout this book is that I/O psychology in its methods and procedures attempts to be just as scientific as physics or chemistry; a science is known by its methods, not by its subject matter. When psychologists observe the behavior of people at work, they do so in the best time-honored traditions of science—objectively, dispassionately, and systematically.

Because the method of the science of psychology is objective, so must be the focus of its observation: human behavior. Overt behavior—our movements, speech, and creative works—are the only aspects of human existence that can be objectively seen, heard, measured, and recorded. Therefore, psychologists concentrate on overt behavior to understand and analyze the people they are studying. However, something more must be involved because psychology also is the science of mental, or cognitive, processes. Psychology deals with intangible human aspects such as motivations, emotions, perceptions, thoughts, and feelings. These facets of our inner or subjective life cannot be observed directly.

For example, we cannot see motivation. It is an internal driving force inaccessible to observation. How, then, can psychologists know anything about motives or drives? Although it is true that motivation itself cannot be seen, the *effects* of motivation can be observed. An angry person may openly exhibit this motivation in overt behaviors such as a flushed face, rapid breathing, or clenched fists. A person high in the motive or need to achieve will behave differently—on the job, in a social situation, or in a psychological experiment—than a person low in that motive.

We cannot see intelligence or cognitive ability directly, but we can see the overt behavioral manifestations of different levels of intelligence. Psychologists can observe objectively that one person performs, or behaves, at a higher level on an intelligence test than does another person. From these facts, it can be inferred that the first person possesses greater intelligence than the second.

Inference based on observed behavior enables us to draw conclusions regarding various human states or conditions even when these aspects cannot be seen directly.

This is how psychologists function. They observe the behavior of the worker on an assembly line, the secretary at a word processor, or the executive at a meeting under well-controlled and systematic conditions. They record the person's behavioral responses: the number of parts produced each hour, the number of words typed per minute, the quantity and quality of decisions made. They vary the conditions under which the job is performed and look for any resulting differences in performance. They use these and other techniques to seek a better understanding of human behavior, but, overall, the essence of the scientific method is simply that psychologists *observe*. Their goal is to look, listen, measure, and record with objectivity, precision, and dispassion.

A Brief History of Industrial/Organizational Psychology

I/O psychology was born of, and is continually nurtured on, necessity. The urgency of a practical problem needing a solution gave the initial impetus to the field, and the continuing demands of crisis and need have stimulated its growth and influence ever since.

Psychology itself is little more than 100 years old, and industrial psychology had its formal beginning only in the early years of the 20th century. It is sometimes difficult to determine the precise origin and founder of any field of study, but many accord the honor in this case to Professor Walter Dill Scott who, in 1901, spoke out on the potential uses of psychology in advertising. Responding to the urgings of the advertising industry, Scott wrote additional articles and, in 1903, *The Theory of Advertising*, a book generally considered to be the first dealing with psychology and an aspect of the world of work. In 1913, a second book appeared: *The Psychology of Industrial Efficiency* by Hugo Münsterberg, a German psychologist teaching at Harvard University who was an early advocate of the use of psychological tests to select employees. His book dealt more broadly with the field of industrial psychology.

These works generated a modest degree of interest, but it was the request of the U.S. Army for help during World War I that marked the emergence of industrial psychology as an important and useful discipline. Faced with the necessity of screening and classifying millions of recruits, the army commissioned a number of psychologists to devise a general intelligence test so that persons of low intelligence could be identified and eliminated from training programs. Two tests were developed: the Army Alpha for literates and the Army Beta for nonliterates.

That endeavor led to the preparation of additional tests for use in selecting candidates for officer and pilot training and for other military classifications that required special abilities. In addition, a group personality test, the Personal Data

Sheet, was developed to detect neuroses among army recruits. The formulation of these tests was an extremely difficult task because there were no precedents.

This military experience provided the basis for a dynamic proliferation of industrial psychology activities following the war. Businesses, school systems, and other organizations that required classifying and screening techniques became aware of the successful use of tests and eagerly clamored for more and better testing techniques. The tests that had been used by the army were adapted for civilian use and new ones were designed for a variety of situations. A broad and intensive program of psychological testing spread throughout the public schools, industry, and the military, a process to which we are now routinely exposed (perhaps overexposed).

Thus, the initial contributions of industrial psychologists centered around what is usually called *personnel psychology: the proper selection and placement or matching of the right individual for the right job.*

The scope of the field broadened considerably in 1924 with the commencement of the most famous series of studies ever conducted in industrial psychology. Called the Hawthorne studies, because they were conducted at the Hawthorne, Illinois, plant of the Western Electric Company, these research programs took industrial psychology beyond the selection and placement of workers to the more complex problems of human relations, morale, and motivation (Roethlisberger & Dickson, 1939).

The research began as a reasonably straightforward investigation of the effects of the physical aspects of the work environment on worker efficiency. The researchers asked such questions as, What is the effect on production of an increase in the level of illumination? Do temperature and humidity affect production? What happens if rest periods are introduced?

The results of the Hawthorne studies were astounding to both the investigators and the Hawthorne plant managers. It was found that social and psychological conditions of the work environment were of potentially greater importance than the physical work conditions. For example, changing the level of illumination from very bright to nearly dark did not diminish the level of efficiency of a group of workers. Other, more subtle, factors were operating to cause these workers to maintain their original production levels under almost dark conditions.

In another case, illumination was increased and production levels rose. Other changes were then introduced—rest periods, free lunches, a shorter workday—and with the introduction of each change, production increased. But the most startling result occurred when all the improvements were eliminated: production still increased. It was concluded that the physical aspects of the work environment were not as important as had been supposed.

These research studies opened up whole new areas of exploration, lasting more than a decade, into such factors as the quality and 'nature of supervision, informal groups among workers, employees' attitudes toward their jobs, communication, and a host of other social/psychological forces now recognized as capable of influencing, even determining, a worker's efficiency, motivation, and job satisfaction.

Although the Hawthorne studies have been criticized for their lack of scientific rigor, there is no denying their impact on the way in which the nature of work came to be viewed and on the direction of industrial psychology itself (Adair, 1984; Carey, 1967; Franke & Kaul, 1978; Parsons, 1974).

World War II brought more than 2,000 psychologists directly into the war effort. Their major contribution, as in World War I, was the testing, screening, and classifying of millions of recruits in various branches of the service. More complex human skills were required to operate the new and sophisticated planes, tanks, and ships, and the necessity of identifying persons who possessed the ability to learn these skills resulted in the development of many refinements in selection and training procedures.

The increasingly complex weapons of war also led to the development of an entirely new area of industrial psychology: *engineering psychology* (also called human engineering or human factors engineering). Working closely with engineers, engineering psychologists supplied information on human capacities and limitations for operating sophisticated equipment such as high-speed aircraft, submarines, and tanks and, therefore, influenced their design.

Industrial psychology achieved even greater stature and recognition as a result of its successful contributions to the war effort. Government and industry leaders were made aware that psychologists were well equipped to solve pressing practical problems. The experience also demonstrated to many psychologists, who before the war had worked in the isolation of their laboratories, that there were important and challenging problems in the real world and that they could effectively contribute to finding solutions to them.

The growth of industrial psychology since 1945 has paralleled the phenomenal growth of American business and technical enterprise. The size and complexity of modern business and government organizations have placed additional demands on the skills of psychologists to maintain and increase levels of industrial efficiency. New techniques and manufacturing processes mean that employees must be trained to develop new skills. In many cases, technical advances have led to entirely new occupations. The advent of computers, for example, generated the insistent need for computer programmers, and psychologists had to determine the abilities needed to perform computer programming successfully, the kind of person possessing these abilities, and the best methods for selecting and training such a person.

The demands made on engineering psychology today are more critical than ever before. Planes fly at supersonic speeds and weapons are so complex and dangerous that efficient and safe operation is of paramount importance. Engineering psychologists have also been called on to assist in the design of industrial equipment and consumer items. The increasing use today of robots, computers, and other means of automating jobs adds to the complexities of the proper design of the workplace.

Human relations skills are highly significant as industry leaders are made increasingly aware of the influence of motivation, leadership, and other psychological factors on job performance. The human relations aspect of management is of greater importance in the world of work as is the recognition of the impact of the organizational setting in which work takes place. Psychologists study the structure or climate of different types of organizations, their patterns and styles of communication, and the formal and informal social structures they produce to determine their effect on employee behavior.

So significant is this emphasis on organizational variables that the Division of Industrial Psychology of the American Psychological Association (APA) changed its name in 1970 to the Division of Industrial and Organizational Psychology, which, in 1982, became the Society for Industrial and Organizational Psychology. Indeed, the field is today referred to as industrial/organizational (I/O) psychology.

The Profession of Industrial/Organizational Psychology

The Professional Association

The success of I/O psychology in its contributions to business and government organizations has led to the development of a widely recognized and respected profession. The primary organization to which most members of this profession belong is the APA, the stated purpose of which is "to advance psychology as a science and profession and as a means of promoting human welfare."

The interests of psychologists as a group are so diverse that the APA includes 45 divisions representing various scientific and professional interests. Approximately 7% of the members of the APA work in the areas of industrial and organizational psychology (Turnage, 1988), and they are represented by four APA divisions: the Society for Industrial and Organizational Psychology; Military Psychology; the Society of Engineering Psychologists; and Consumer Psychology. Of these divisions, the Society for Industrial and Organizational Psychology has the largest membership (about 2,500) and represents most of the APA-affiliated psychologists working on problems of concern to both employers and employees. Many I/O psychologists, from both academics and business, also belong to the Academy of Management.

The purpose of the Society for Industrial and Organizational Psychology is to "promote human welfare through the various applications of psychology to all types of organizations providing goods or services, such as manufacturing concerns, commercial enterprises, labor unions or trade associations, and public agencies." Further, the society is concerned with scientific, professional, and ethical issues and specifies the following goals for its members (1983).

1. Improve the qualifications and usefulness of industrial and organizational psychologists through high standards of ethics, conduct, education, and achievement.
2. Advance the scientific status of the field, by such means as the encouragement and stimulation of sound research, the publication and communication of research findings, and the improvement of research methods and conditions.
3. Facilitate the exchange of information and experience among the members.

4. Improve opportunities and standards for training and development.
5. Facilitate the growth and development of the field.
6. Foster cooperative relations with allied groups and professions.
7. Strive to eliminate malpractices of untrained and unethical practitioners.
8. Contribute to the broad advancement of psychology.

Training Requirements for Industrial/Organizational Psychologists

It is an interesting phenomenon that although few people feel themselves to be qualified physicists, chemists, or biologists after taking one or two courses in those subjects, many people consider themselves expert psychologists even when they have had no formal training. Unfortunately, some individuals feel that the practice of psychology requires nothing more than common sense and a lot of experience with people. Merely interacting with other people, however, will no more make you a psychologist than years of taking medicines will qualify you as a physician.

Modern psychology is a complex and demanding profession that requires years of concentrated university work and a lifetime of continuing study to keep abreast of rapidly unfolding modern developments.

I/O psychologists are, first, psychologists and as such must have a solid background in the discipline before specializing in any one area. The four years devoted to an undergraduate degree in psychology are not at all sufficient to qualify you as an I/O psychologist because a BA or BS degree in psychology carries no professional recognition. This does not mean that an undergraduate degree in psychology is of no value for someone who is contemplating a career in industry. Indeed, the opposite is true, particularly for the person interested in a career in management. Many jobs in business are available to those with undergraduate degrees in psychology.

A minimal requirement for working as an I/O psychologist is an MA or MS degree, but the person who intends a career in the field might consider obtaining a PhD. The higher positions in terms of rank in the corporate hierarchy and salary typically go to those with the highest academic degree.

A survey of I/O psychologists employed as consultants identified several specific skills or areas of knowledge that they considered essential for a successful career. The purpose of the survey was to help psychology departments develop courses that will equip undergraduate and graduate students with the skills demanded by business and industry. The vital areas of study are listed, in order of importance, in Table 1-1 (Carducci et al., 1987).

Beyond the master's and doctoral degrees, I/O psychologists may also aspire to professional recognition for achievement. Members of the APA may be nominated to the status of Fellow on the basis of unusual and outstanding professional accomplishments.

The training and preparation of the I/O psychologist is long and difficult, but the rewards in terms of stimulating work, challenging responsibility, and continuing intellectual growth can be great. Career opportunities are excellent,

TABLE 1-1   Essential Skills for I/O Psychologists

Tests and measurements
Research methods and design
Statistics and statistical computer packages
Psychological report writing
Clinical and counseling skills, including listening and interviewing skills
Theories of organizational development
Personnel training and development
Performance evaluation
Legal issues, such as federal equal employment opportunity guidelines
Job analysis

Adapted from "Preparing Undergraduate Psychology Students for Careers in Business" by B. J. Carducci, et al., 1987, *Teaching of Psychology, 14*(1), pp. 16–20.

and the financial rewards may also be substantial. I/O psychologists have higher salaries than any other group of psychologists, including clinical psychologists. As a result, the number of graduate students choosing I/O psychology continues to grow each year, and the bulk of that increase is among master's-degree students.

Employment of Industrial/Organizational Psychologists

I/O psychologists usually work full time in business, industry, and government; in private consulting firms; and in colleges and universities. Many of those who teach courses in I/O psychology also conduct research or work as part-time consultants in business and for the government. The various employment settings of I/O psychologists are shown in Figure 1-1.

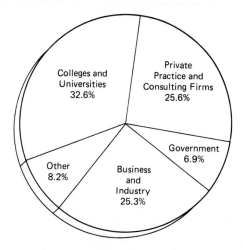

Figure 1-1 Employment settings of industrial/organizational psychologists. (Data from "Results of Society surveys" by N. Schmitt and M. DeGregorio, 1986, *The Industrial-Organizational Psychologist, 23*(4), p, 27.)

Colleges and Universities 32.6%
Private Practice and Consulting Firms 25.6%
Government 6.9%
Business and Industry 25.3%
Other 8.2%

Most psychologists who work full time in industry are employed by large organizations of practically every type. To give you an idea of the scope of employment opportunities for I/O psychologists, Table 1-2 contains examples of some of the companies that employ psychologists and their specific job titles. As you can see, the range of job responsibilities and titles is broad and impressive. Table 1-2 also provides an indication of the value of the contributions of psychologists to employing organizations.

A survey of personnel administrators revealed that they believe psychologists make important contributions in the following areas (Cederblom, Pence, & Johnson, 1984):

1. Management training.
2. Employee motivation.
3. Morale and job satisfaction.
4. Management selection.
5. Employee training.
6. Productivity.
7. Performance appraisal.
8. Employee selection.
9. Designing work conditions.
10. Designing organizational structure.

Many smaller organizations cannot afford a full-time psychologist and must rely on the services of consulting firms whenever they are faced with problems requiring an I/O psychologist. These consulting psychologists operate on a contract basis and perform activities such as assessing candidates for employment, developing a piece of equipment or an assembly line, establishing a training program, conducting a study on consumer acceptance of a new product, or determining why production efficiency is slipping. The value of consulting lies not only in the technical skills that can be applied to a problem but also in the freshness of approach and objectivity that an outside organization may possess. The number of such firms is increasing, and they are filling a vital need in business and government organizations.

The Practical Value of Industrial/ Organizational Psychology

The services of psychologists are used by so many organizations of different types and sizes for one very good reason: They more than pay for themselves in terms of reduced costs. The work of I/O psychologists adds directly to an organization's profits. One psychologist referred to this as a "contribution to the bottom line" and suggested that psychologists save money for an organization in four areas: absenteeism, turnover, job satisfaction, and personnel selection (Cascio, 1984).

Consider the problem of employee absenteeism. Employees who fail to show up for work cost their company money. The various techniques applied by psychologists to reduce absenteeism can lead to a savings of as much as $1,000

TABLE 1-2   Places of Employment and Job Titles of Selected I/O Psychologists

Bell Telephone Laboratories
  Business Systems Supervisor
City Government
  Assistant Personnel Director
Columbia Broadcasting System
  Director of Compensation
Continental Oil
  Director of Advertising
Dow Chemical
  Manager of Consumer Research
Executronics
  Vice President
General Dynamics
  Head of Human Factors Laboratory
General Electric
  Senior Staff Specialist
Harcourt Brace Jovanovich
  Executive Editor of Test Department
International Multifoods
  Director of Management Development
McGraw-Hill
  Regional Manager
Metropolitan Life Insurance
  Staff Psychologist
Port Authority of New York and New Jersey
  Supervisor of Test Development and Evaluation
Procter & Gamble
  Personnel Research Psychologist
Reynolds Metals
  Manager of Personnel Research
Sears, Roebuck
  National Director of Training and Development
Self-Employed
  Management Consultant
Standard Oil
  Manager of Psychological Services
State Department of Health and Welfare
  Program Planner, Bureau of Research and Training
Texas Instruments
  Personnel Director of Worldwide Operations
U.S. Naval Personnel Research and Development Center
  Research Engineering Psychologist
U.S. Steel
  Staff Supervisor of Testing and Counseling
Westinghouse Electric
  Manager of Employee Relations
Weyerhaeuser
  Industrial Psychologist
Xerox
  Manager of Information and Planning Services

per employee. One Canadian bank with 30,000 employees saved $7 million in one year by heeding their psychologist's advice and installing a computerized absentee reporting system. The psychologist's salary and the cost of the new system were considerably less than the amount saved.

Another costly problem faced by organizations is turnover. When employees quit, the company loses the money it spent in selecting and training them. Also, the organization must then hire and train replacements. At a large financial brokerage house, the cost for each employee who quit was $7,000. An I/O psychologist estimated that reducing the rate of turnover by 10% would save the company in excess of $100,000 a year.

Enhancing job satisfaction is another major concern of I/O psychologists. An increase in the number of contented employees can reduce grievances, strikes, absences, tardiness, and turnover. Improving the job attitudes of one group of 160 bank tellers saved the organization more than $125,000 in a single year.

Proper personnel selection methods can help to ensure that only the most highly qualified applicants are hired. This works to the benefit of both the individual employees and the organization. In one case—selecting 10 claims approvers for a life insurance company—the use of a psychological test as a selection device resulted in an annual gain in productivity estimated at $30,000 (Cascio, 1984).

Some psychologists believe that substantial economic gains could be made if more employers used tests of cognitive and mental ability as selection devices. Applying these tests to the entire U.S. work force could increase productivity at least $80 billion a year (Hunter & Schmidt, 1982). We shall examine this issue in greater detail in Chapter 4. In one instance, the police department of Philadelphia, Pennsylvania, introduced a test of cognitive abilities to select its rookie police officers. Over a period of 10 years, the city is expected to save more than $170 million (Hunter, 1979).

A study dealing with most of the white-collar jobs in the federal government compared those persons hired on the basis of intelligence or cognitive ability tests with those hired only on the basis of evaluations of their education and experience. The increases in productivity of those hired on the basis of test scores amounted to $600 million for each year they continued in government service. Because government employees remain on the job for approximately 13 years, the total gain in output for that period amounted to nearly $8 billion. In addition, the use of tests resulted in a 61.4% decrease in the number of poor performers hired (Schmidt, Hunter, Outerbridge, & Trattner, 1986).

Another study compared managers hired on the basis of their performance in an assessment center—a simulated job situation devised by I/O psychologists (see Chapter 3)—versus managers hired on the basis of personal interviews alone. The results showed a gain in performance valued at more than $2,000 per person for those selected by the assessment-center technique (S. Adler, 1987).

A research review of 11 approaches to improve employee productivity—such as improved selection and training, goal setting, performance appraisal, and revised work schedules—considered more than 200 programs initiated by I/O psychologists. These efforts yielded marked improvements in employee attitudes and 87% of the experiments resulted in significant gains in productivity (Katzell & Guzzo, 1983).

Psychologists employed by the Federal Aviation Administration (FAA) have also demonstrated the economic value of I/O psychology (Fisher, 1984). In the early 1980s, the FAA was forced to recruit and train thousands of air traffic controllers to replace those fired as a result of a strike. The administrators, faced with the necessity of getting new controllers on the job as soon as possible, wanted to eliminate the 3-month applicant screening process. Based on their research, however, FAA psychologists demonstrated that retaining the 3-month screening process would save $8 million for every 1,000 students in the training program.

Additional research by FAA psychologists showed that applicants up to the age of 35 could successfully be trained to perform the demanding work. The previous age limit had been 30. This greatly increased the pool of prospective candidates. The psychologists were also able to demonstrate that the training program for new air traffic controllers could be reduced from 4 to 2 years, with no detrimental effects.

These are only a few examples of the financial impact of the activities of I/O psychologists. However, as we noted, the practice of I/O psychology is also of enormous benefit to you, the employee. When the right person is matched with the right job and when work is meaningful and satisfying, everyone benefits. One psychologist summed up the goals of I/O psychology this way:

> We wish to enhance the quality of life for the individual at work and for the consumer as well as to make the organization more effective. We want to enhance the productive output of individuals, but we are also very much concerned with their ability to gain considerable satisfaction from their day-to-day activities (Thayer, 1983, p. 11).

Problems of Industrial/Organizational Psychology

No field of study is free of internal or external difficulties. I/O psychology as a science and profession has several problem areas, all aggravated by the very factor that has made it so successful—the demand for its services.

Quacks and Frauds

Certainly more than any other science, psychology has been bothered by quackery, that is, the illicit and invalid practice of psychology by persons with little or no professional training. This is particularly crucial in clinical and counseling psychology where untrained charlatans can do great harm to emotionally disturbed persons seeking help.

Quackery has also been practiced in I/O psychology; an uninformed business organization can be just as gullible as an individual. Unfortunately, there have been unethical consulting firms and individuals who have sold their services to industry and made quick money (and a quicker getaway) before the company realized it had been duped.

Not only is unethical behavior potentially dangerous to industry—consider, for example, the number of competent people who might not be hired because they did not perform well on the quack's phony test—but it is also harmful to psychology. If the company is damaged by the charlatan's services, psychology as a whole will frequently be blamed. The executives of a company that has been taken in the past may be reluctant to consider any psychological services or advice in the future.

The problem of the charlatan is lessening, however, because most states now license psychologists in the same way that professionals such as physicians are licensed. In these states, it is illegal for persons to call themselves psychologists or use any of the tools of psychology unless they have met the state's licensing requirements.

Other states have developed certification requirements which, although not as strong a control as licensing, do at least prevent unqualified persons from representing themselves as certified psychologists. However, a person or an organization must exercise care when seeking the services of a psychologist. It is not enough to consult the telephone directory. The educational and professional qualifications of anyone called a psychologist must be examined carefully.

Communication

All sciences develop a specialized technical jargon that its members use to communicate with one another. Unfortunately, this very specific vocabulary is not usually understood by those outside the discipline. Because I/O psychologists must work closely with supervisors, executives, workers, and other nonpsychologists, it is imperative that they be able to communicate with all these people. The research results and recommendations of psychologists will be of no value to a company if its executives cannot understand the language of the reports; they will be filed in the nearest wastebasket. Psychologists must know the terminology used by the organizations employing them and, in turn, must be able to present contributions in a form that will be easily understood.

The Reluctance to Try Something New

This section might be called, "I've always done it this way and I'm not about to change now!" Psychologists who work in industry often come across this attitude: an unwillingness to rock the boat, a resistance to change.

Frequently, a change in the usual way of performing a job is viewed as a threat to a worker's personal well-being. Employees who are told to change their work patterns to the more efficient system recommended by the psychologist may actively resist the change because they feel that the company is just trying to get them to work harder for no additional pay. If the workers are insecure, they may feel that the company is criticizing their past job performance. Whatever the reason, this resistance to change is a serious problem at all levels of industry, from the assembly-line worker to the company president.

If the recommendations of psychologists are to have any value, they must have the support of those who are affected. Psychologists must receive the active participation of those whose jobs will be affected by making the change. Consequently, psychologists must possess considerable human relations skills, patience, and persuasive abilities, in addition to a high level of technical competence.

Research or Application?

The question of research versus application continues to concern psychology in its relations with management. It is a problem that can often lead to unfortunate consequences for both the psychologist and the executive. Some executives complain that too little research in I/O psychology is oriented toward the practical, real-world problems with which they must deal. This so-called crisis of usefulness refers largely to academic research that has no immediate application. For psychologists who work directly for companies that have pressing problems to resolve, the two functions—research and application—are highly interdependent. Without research, there would be no knowledge to apply to the situations on the job. This point is often overlooked by organization leaders who demand immediate answers to highly specific questions and cannot understand the hesitation of the psychologist who tells them that the answer can come only from research on the problem.

For that reason, many I/O psychologists who work in nonacademic settings do conduct research. A survey revealed that they carry out research on most of the important topics in the field (see Table 1-3).

The conflict between research and application arises because executives often need prompt answers. Production schedules and contract deadlines will not always wait for the design and execution of a research study. Harried managers frequently become impatient when the company psychologist, the so-called expert on human behavior, cannot provide a quick answer.

The difficulty is that many human problems in industry are unique to a particular company or department or section within that company. The results of a research study conducted on absenteeism of spot welders at Company A may be irrrelevant when applied to spot welders at Company B. Of course, there are comparable situations where research results from one organization may be applied to another, but it is difficult to predict this transferability. An invalid solution applied to an industrial problem can be just as damaging as attempting no solution at all.

This is not to suggest that whenever psychologists are asked a question, they run to the laboratory to undertake a 2-month experiment. The 100-year history of psychology provides us with a wealth of data about human behavior in a variety of situations, and well-trained psychologists can often apply

TABLE 1-3   Research Topics of Nonacademic I/O Psychologists

Research topic	Percentage of respondents
Testing, selection, and validation	54
Performance appraisal	22
Opinions, attitudes, culture, and values	20
Assessment and assessment centers	18
Training and development	16
Job analysis and classification	14
Executive development and selection	12
Pay	10
Career development, promotion, and turnover	10
Employee assistance and family issues	10
Organization analysis and diagnosis	8

From "I/O Psychology Research Conducted in Nonacademic Settings and Reasons for Non-publication" by M. A. Campion, et al., 1986, *The Industrial-Organizational Psychologist, 24*(1), pp. 44–49.

this information to the specific problems of industry. The value of these data depends on the similarity of the settings of the past research and the current problem.

For example, learning studies conducted on chimpanzees or college sophomores have less relevance for a learning problem in a chemical company than will a learning study conducted in a steel company. The steel company research will probably provide the more useful results. But a learning study conducted in another chemical company might be even more applicable. And a study conducted on the very workers about whom the question was asked will be the most useful of all.

Compromise, patience, and understanding on both sides—the management and the psychologist—are called for. As an example of how one company handled the research-versus-application issue, consider the experience of the General Electric Company. Faced with a lack of applicability of social and behavioral science data to the company's problems, General Electric organized the Behavioral Research Service to conduct studies on their unique situations in their own work environment. Several features of the research approach are responsible for its success.

First, because research is conducted only on problems generated by specific company needs, employees and executives give their full interest and cooperation when they recognize the importance of the research for their own jobs. Such cooperation is vital because research efforts can be easily frustrated by executives who think the studies are a waste of time or by employees who may not understand how the research will benefit them.

Second, research is conducted only on problems that are generating current research in industrial and academic laboratories and for which a substantial body of data already exists. The greater the amount of available data that can be applied to the problem, the more directly and quickly that problem can be solved.

Finally, the Behavioral Research Service conducts its studies on the job—in the office or on the assembly line—rather than devising an artificial laboratory setting in which to pursue its investigations. Research conducted in the actual context of the problem stands a much greater chance of providing meaningful and useful results.

The experiences of General Electric and other business concerns demonstrate the necessary compatibility of research and application. Properly devised research can be of immense value to the productive efficiency of an organization as long as it is recognized that the fundamental question is not research versus application, but research plus application.

Areas of Industrial/Organizational Psychology

I/O psychology influences all levels and phases of the relationship between people and their work. We briefly note here specific aspects of this relationship, the professional interests of I/O psychologists, which are discussed in detail in later chapters.

Techniques, Tools, and Tactics

In every area in which psychology has an impact on human behavior, it does so through the judicious use of the tools and techniques of science. The findings of psychologists are offered within the context of carefully controlled scientific observation and experimentation. It would be difficult to comprehend fully the work of I/O psychologists without some understanding of the ways in which they perform their research and reach their conclusions. In Chapter 2, we consider the methods of science as they are used in I/O psychology.

Employee Selection

Perhaps the most important problem faced by any organization is to select qualified persons to perform the various jobs required in our complex society. The success or failure of any organization depends in large measure on the caliber of its employees. It was the critical nature of this problem for the U.S. Army in World War I, noted earlier, that gave such an impetus to the growth of industrial psychology.

Despite the opinion of some executives and personnel managers who still think they can judge job applicants by the strength of their handshakes, the steadiness of their gazes, or their clothing, employee selection is a complicated issue that requires detailed psychological knowledge and sound research.

Even before applicants reach the personnel office, considerable work must be done to determine the nature, requirements, and demands of the position for which employees are being sought. It is impossible to know who will be successful in a job without knowing exactly what the job entails, what skills, aptitudes, interests, or personality characteristics are basic to successful performance of the job.

Once the details of the job are known and the methods of selection have been chosen, it is necessary to determine if these selection measures are picking the best people. Employees selected and hired must be evaluated after they have been working for a period of time, and their job performance must be compared with their earlier performance on the selection devices. Only through such long-term research can selection procedures be evaluated objectively.

Selection and evaluation of employees continue long after the initial hiring. Throughout one's career, questions of promotion (or demotion) must be considered. Many of the same selection devices used in hiring are also used in making subsequent career decisions.

Properly executed, selection and evaluation procedures are of great value to an organization. Poor design and misuse of these techniques is costly, however, in terms of time and money.

Not only is appropriate selection important to the organization but it is also vital to you as an employee. Your initial job and subsequent advancement (or lack of it) will be determined in part by your performance in the selection situation. One of the most momentous days of your life is the day you apply for a job and undergo a battery of psychological selection measures. Your performance at that time influences the direction of your career.

It is beneficial, then, as you begin your career, to understand the selection techniques currently in use. It is also to your advantage that a potential employer use the most valid techniques possible. Improper matching of the person and the job can lead to unhappiness and dissatisfaction to you, your family, and your employer.

Performance Appraisal

One activity that will continue throughout your working career is the evaluation of the quality of your job performance. As with other areas of I/O psychology, performance appraisal is important to you and to your employer. How much responsibility should you be given? Should you be promoted? How great a salary increase should you get next year? Should you be fired?

Ideally, these questions will be answered on the basis of the quality of your work. Such decisions should be made as fairly, objectively, and precisely as possible. It is the responsibility of psychologists to devise adequate means of performance appraisal for all levels of employment.

For some jobs this is a straightforward task. The efficiency of workers on an assembly line can be assessed quantitatively and compared with co-workers by determining how many units they produce each hour or each day, how much spoilage they cause, or how many accidents they are involved in. A typist can be evaluated in similar quantitative terms.

But other jobs defy such objective measures of job performance. Should we assess the work of executives by counting the number of ideas they have each day? Obviously not. The scope of an executive's job is so broad that it cannot be evaluated in simple terms. Yet it is necessary that the work be appraised periodically and with as much fairness and objectivity as that of the lathe operator. I/O psychologists devote considerable effort to all levels of performance appraisal.

Training and Development

At any level of the organization for which you work—as apprentice, management trainee, or middle-aged executive—the training opportunities provided for you are important. Just as poorly selected individuals can cause frustration for themselves and their employers, so can poorly trained workers.

The goal of training programs in any organization is to develop specific skills, attitudes, and capacities to maximize the individual's job performance. Virtually every new employee in an organization undergoes some degree of training, either formal or informal. Inexperienced production workers must be taught the specific operations they are expected to perform. Experienced workers must learn, at the very least, the policies and procedures of a new employer.

Highly structured training programs are offered by many companies for new college graduates, who often spend up to 2 years in classroom instruction as well as on-the-job performance and training. Also, many organizations send their experienced executives to special institutes and seminars, usually at universities, to learn the latest techniques of management and administration. Career planning and development opportunities are increasingly being offered at all stages of working life.

I/O psychologists assume a large part of the responsibility for establishing, conducting, and evaluating training programs in industry. As the machinery of production and the dynamics of organizational life become more complex, the demands made on employees to learn and employers to teach increase in scope and significance.

Leadership

A key aspect of the worth of any organization is the quality of its leadership, from supervisor to president. One of industry's greatest challenges is selecting, training, and developing effective leaders at all levels. This problem is of concern to you for two reasons: (1) as an employee you will work under a supervisor and your efficiency and satisfaction will be affected by the style and nature of this leader and (2) because most business leaders today come from the ranks of the college educated, you will most likely find yourself, in time, at some level of leadership.

Psychologists have conducted much research on leadership in all kinds of organizational situations. They are concerned not only with the personal characteristics and abilities associated with effective leadership but are also continually experimenting with various styles of supervision to determine their differential effects on subordinates. Another area of interest is the kind of leadership that best inspires and motivates workers to produce at their optimal level in diverse work situations.

It is necessary to the continued growth and survival of any organization that the most competent people be placed in positions of leadership and that, once there, they exercise their influence in the most effective manner.

Motivation, Job Satisfaction, and Job Involvement

Factors that exert a considerable impact on the efficiency of any organization are the motivations of the employees, the kinds of satisfaction they receive from their membership in the organization, and the extent of their involvement with their jobs. Motivation, satisfaction, and involvement are strongly influenced by various aspects of the work environment, for example, the quality of leadership, advancement opportunities, level of job security, and physical and psychological work climate.

Because these factors can be manipulated to optimize motivation, satisfaction, and involvement, the employing organization should arrange them so that workers are efficient and content in their jobs. This is yet another task of I/O psychologists: to determine, through careful on-the-job research, what contributes to positive worker motivation, satisfaction, and involvement.

Intensive studies of the workers are required, through personal interviews and questionnaires, to elicit their concerns, gripes, and recommendations about how the job and work environment might be improved. If approached with consideration, openness, and fairness, the worker on the job is the best, sometimes the only, source of such information.

This research requires a high level of technical competence from the psychologist and the willingness of management to invest the time and money necessary to support the research. Negative aspects of a job environment can produce undesirable effects such as increased absenteeism and turnover, reduced production, higher accident rates, and grievances to the union. It is vital, therefore, that the company, through the work of its psychologists, find and correct factors that can impair the quality of working life before they have serious economic consequences.

Organizational Psychology

Few people work in isolation. Whether our work is in a classroom, a department store, or a steel mill, it takes place within the context of formal and informal organizational factors. The organization for which we work fosters a certain climate that includes, for example, the formal chain of command and the centralization or decentralization of power. These factors influence the way in which we perform our jobs and the satisfactions we may or may not find in them. The structures, policies, and resulting climate differ from one organization to another. Organizational psychologists study the impact of these structural aspects on productivity, motivation, and morale. Another dimension of the organizational structure, leadership, is part of the work climate as well, and the style and nature of leadership can have dramatic effects on the lives of the employees.

Because organizational psychology includes motivation, leadership, and the quality of working life, these topics as well as a chapter entitled, "The Organization of the Organization," are discussed in the "Organizational Psychology" section.

There is more to organizational psychology than the formal structural characteristics of an organization; informal climates develop that reflect the nature and characteristics of cliques or small groups of workers. Sometimes these informal groups set norms and standards of behavior that are at variance with those imposed by the organization, a situation that obviously affects production.

At all levels, from informal to formal, the organization of the organization represents a powerful source of influence on the worker, one that is receiving a great deal of attention from organizational psychologists.

Conditions of Work

The physical aspects of a job are obvious and visible; consequently, these were the first to be studied by psychologists in industry. Many research studies have been conducted on lighting, temperature, humidity, noise level, location of equipment, and working hours to determine their effects on production levels. Because of this vast amount of research, numerous guidelines are available to aid in the design and layout of the physical work environment. Additional research is needed, however, as new jobs and new methods of production are created.

Since the late 1940s, it has come to be recognized that the physical environment would have to undergo a drastic change to have any significant effect on production. Note the matter of temperature levels, for example. In most work environments, the temperature would have to become extremely cold or extremely hot for the workers' output to be greatly affected. The widespread use of air conditioning as well as improvements such as sound-proofing have reduced the extreme variations that used to mark many jobs. Modern technology has thus produced relatively stable physical conditions of work.

Attention has shifted, therefore, to less tangible and more complex social and psychological conditions of the work environment. The psychological climate of a job, including fatigue and boredom, is now recognized as more important than the physical climate because psychological conditions are subject to greater variation. However, just as features of the physical environment can be manipulated to produce more efficient and satisfying work, so can the psychological environment be controlled for optimum results once research has determined the desirable aspects of a job's psychological environment.

Engineering Psychology

The design of the equipment, tools, and vehicles used in work is directly related to the physical work environment, to motivation and morale, and to accidents. The machinery of the manufacturing and transportation industries has become increasingly complex; consequently, greater demands are placed on the human operators of this equipment.

Pilots of commercial jet airliners, for example, have only a limited time period in which to react in an emergency situation. Their equipment (the cockpit instruments and controls) must be designed and arranged so that needed information (altitude and speed, for example) can be read quickly and accurately and appropriate responses made as rapidly as possible. Operators of semiautomated rotary shears in a steel mill must be able to respond with as little delay as possible when something happens to the sheets of steel moving through the machine at 40 miles per hour. In your automobile, you want to be able to know as quickly as possible when your engine overheats.

All of these are examples of man-machine systems; it is the job of the engineering psychologist to provide the best functional relationship between the person and the machine. This is accomplished through proper design of the machine to compensate for the human operators' weaknesses and to capitalize on their strengths. New electronics and robot technology have drastically changed the nature of work today. Engineering psychologists are determining the most efficient and satisfying ways in which employees and the new technology can interact. This area of I/O psychology also has widespread application to consumer products.

Employee Safety and Health

All organizations are concerned about the safety records of their employees because accidents on the job cause suffering (sometimes death) to employees. Economic losses resulting from industrial accidents run into billions of dollars every year from lost hours of work, employee compensation, and the costs of hiring and training replacement workers.

Industry today devotes considerable energy and funds to accident prevention. Part of this effort is research by I/O psychologists who attempt to identify job-related factors and individual personality characteristics that may contribute to accidents. The research results have led to the development and installation of safety devices on potentially dangerous equipment, the selection and training of employees for safety awareness, and information programs designed to keep safety prominent in the minds of the employees. Because the majority of accidents are caused by the human element, not by equipment failure or bad luck, the application of psychology is crucial in reducing society's staggering accident toll.

Alcoholism has long been a problem among employees at all levels and in all kinds of organizations. It leads to excessive absenteeism, reduced productivity, poor quality of work, and increased accidents. Many companies are recognizing and accepting their responsibility for trying to help employees who have drinking problems, and psychologists, both in the company and in outside clinics, are called on to devise employee assistance programs.

Another problem in the world of work is the use of drugs on the job. Some companies, forced to screen for drug use as part of their selection program, now educate their employees on the effects of drugs and deal with those who are found using drugs while at work.

The disease AIDS is also a growing problem in the workplace. Many employers are developing educational programs to provide factual information about AIDS for their employees, and some companies are testing job applicants for the presence of AIDS-related viruses.

Stress at Work

Job-induced stress has serious effects on the mental and physical health of employees. Stress can interfere with production and efficiency on the job and can debilitate persons to the point of requiring medical or psychological treatment. Prolonged stress can lead to serious, even fatal, illness. An increasing number of organizations are dealing with the effects of stress through counseling programs and other psychological techniques. Psychologists are conducting

The proliferation of portable electronic office equipment, such as lightweight laptop computers, often means that employees are rarely free of the demands of the job, even while traveling. Such job-induced stress can interfere with productivity and efficiency and lead to a variety of physical complaints.

research to determine the aspects of work life that induce stress and how the job and job environment can be redesigned to be less stressful. The stress of being unemployed is also a concern of I/O psychologists.

Psychology and the Consumer

Consumer psychology is important to you for two reasons: (1) you are constantly being bombarded with advertising appeals to buy certain products, some of which you purchase and (2) if you work for a company that sells consumer products or services, its ability to do so successfully affects your economic well-being. Millions of dollars are spent annually by business organizations in an attempt to get you to notice their product, to want it, and, of course, to buy it.

The psychologist makes a unique contribution to the marketing of goods and services by studying the size and nature of the potential market for a product, the effectiveness of various advertising appeals and campaigns, customer reactions to different products, and the motivations and needs of the buying public.

The Future of Industrial/Organizational Psychology

The continuing growth of the U.S. economy, together with technological advances and population changes, will alter the nature of work in the future. And any changes in the way people work mean new demands and responsibilities for I/O psychologists. Several current modifications in the nature of work and the work force are already presenting challenges not only for psychologists but for employers and employees as well, challenges that will continue to have an impact throughout the 1990s.

One such change has to do with the kinds of jobs that are available. The heavy physical labor that supported several generations of blue-collar factory workers is rapidly disappearing. Job opportunities today and in the future will require more mental than manual effort. Consider the statistics. In a 10-year period, from 1973 to 1983, the number of workers in the steel industry dropped by 57%. Between 1978 and 1987, automobile industry employment declined by 23%. Among the nation's leading corporations, the Fortune 500, 2.8 million industrial jobs were lost between 1977 and 1988 (McCormick & Powell, 1988).

Almost 11 million American workers have lost their jobs in recent years, and more than 5 million of those positions were eliminated because the kind of work performed is no longer needed (Fraze, 1988).

Today, managers and other white-collar workers outnumber unskilled factory workers by 5 to 1. By the year 2000, almost 90% of the U.S. work force will be in service and information industries rather than in factories that produce goods. In the 1990s, according to the Bureau of Labor Statistics, 9 out of 10 new jobs created will be in such service fields as communications, finance, insurance, health care, real estate, and government. Also in the decade ahead

American business will need 98% more paralegal personnel, 72% more computer programmers, 69% more computer systems analysts, and 62% more medical technicians. There will be little need for unskilled factory workers (Whitney, 1988).

White-collar workers have not been immune from massive layoffs. In the 1980s, large numbers of middle-level managers lost their jobs as companies merged or reduced their management ranks in an effort to become more cost effective and competitive with foreign manufacturers. As a result, not even such large employers as AT&T and IBM can continue to offer the degree of job security that used to characterize management-level positions (London, 1987).

At the same time that the rate of growth in the number of middle-management jobs is declining, the number of people competing for them is increasing. Over the next 10 years there will be a 42% increase in the number of people in the 35–44 age group, the typical time for promotion to middle management, but the need for these managers is expected to grow by no more than 20%. The inevitable result is that opportunities for upward mobility at work for this generation may be severely limited. Many organizations will find themselves with well-educated, highly skilled employees who have no place to go, no higher jobs in the hierarchy to which to aspire (Levine, 1986b; Reilly & Diangelo, 1988).

As a result of this decline in both white- and blue-collar jobs, an erosion in worker power has occurred. Labor unions have been weakened and many employees have been forced to accept lower wages and a greater degree of management authority. The way that companies treat their employees has changed. "Clearly, large corporations no longer needed to pay much attention to workers' psychological needs, as the whip of unemployment and threat of foreign competition were frequently sufficient to keep them in line" (Bramel & Friend, 1987, p. 248). Obviously, this portends important differences in the workplace and in the needs and aspirations of employees.

Another change in the workplace stems from advances in microelectronics as manifested in computers, word processors, and industrial robots. More and more work environments have become automated, with machines and microchips assuming the functions once performed by human beings. More than half of all office workers in the 1980s used some sort of word-processing or data-processing equipment, thus eliminating many lesser-skilled clerical jobs. There are some 17 million video display terminals in offices throughout the United States, and up to 3 million are being added each year (Altman, 1988).

By the year 2000, it is estimated that more than 35 million workers will be affected by this electronic revolution in the workplace, causing major dislocations in the nature of work. Managers will have greater power while clerical and blue-collar workers will have less control over their work, adding to the stress and tension of all (see Figure 1-2). By reducing job complexity, the use of computer technology can make many jobs routine and oversimplified to the point of boredom (Gist, Rosen, & Schwoerer, 1988; Moos, 1986).

A third change in the workplace involves the decreasing job opportunities for unskilled, illiterate, and poorly educated persons. With the reduction in

TO CURE TECHNOPHOBIA YOU NEED A GOOD PSYCHOLOGIST.

A lot of people have a real phobia about new technology. At AT&T, we have someone who can help. In fact, we have over 150 of them.

Psychologists who observe people to test their reactions to new products. To find out what they're comfortable with. And what they're not.

And as we develop new products, we develop new ways of testing people's reactions to them.

You see, at AT&T we believe even the most advanced technology is of little use if people are afraid of using it.

AT&T. We're reaching out in new directions.

AT&T

Figure 1-2 AT&T recognizes the role of psychologists in the development of high-technology products for human use. (Courtesy AT&T.)

manufacturing jobs and the increase in the use of computers and industrial robots, there are fewer places in which undereducated men and women can find work. As many as 25 million Americans over the age of 17 are functionally illiterate. Many of them cannot read at all. Most read at no higher than the fourth-grade level, which means that they do not have sufficient reading and writing skills to fill out an application blank for a job (McGraw, 1987).

From the employer's standpoint, it is becoming increasingly difficult to recruit entry-level employees who have sufficient basic educational skills in reading, writing, and mathematics to learn how to perform many jobs. The New York Telephone Company, for example, had to interview and test 90,000 job applicants to find 2,000 who were qualified for a position that did not even require a high school diploma. Some 84% of the applicants could not pass a simple low-level test. The General Motors Corporation found that employees who lack basic skills have difficulty keeping up with the training programs that are required of their workers every 3 to 5 years to acquaint them with new technology ("Back to the Basics," 1987).

A fourth change in the nature of the work force relates to *demographics* (the statistical study of populations). The work force is getting older. The so-called baby boom generation, those born between 1946 and 1965, have been in the work force, some for more than 20 years. By the year 2000, the United States will have more older workers than at any time in its history. By then, half of the work force will be over the age of 35 (Blocklyn, 1987; H. E. Johnson, 1988).

At the same time, a decrease is forecast in the number of younger workers available to enter the work force. By the turn of the century there will be 12% fewer people between the ages of 18 and 31, which could lead to a serious labor shortage (Raynolds, 1987). Thus, we can foresee a situation in which the number of workers leaving the work force through retirement will be greater than the number entering it. This is true not only for the United States but also for West Germany, Italy, France, the Netherlands, and Britain (Goetschin, 1987).

Some companies are already feeling the effects of this shortage. The low-wage, low-skill service industries—fast-food outlets, grocery stores, and retail stores—are now finding it increasingly difficult to recruit teenage employees. Companies such as McDonald's are hiring greater numbers of older and retired workers to take up the slack. In the coming years, employers who depended on young workers to fill entry-level positions will be faced with the choice of changing the way their jobs are performed (using robots, for example), or retaining and retraining workers of retirement age (Kingson, 1988; Ryland & Rosen, 1988).

All of these changes in the workplace and the composition of the work force present challenges for I/O psychologists involved in selecting and training workers; designing jobs and evaluating their performance; determining how employees can best be managed and motivated; dealing with safety, health, and stress problems on the job; and marketing products and services. Thus, the needs for and demands on the skills of I/O psychologists are certain to grow.

Many formerly retired workers are taking jobs in service industries. By the year 2000 more than half of the U.S. work force will be over the age of 35.

Summary

Work is an important and meaningful aspect of life, affording more than just your means of livelihood. Work provides a sense of your identity, describes your social status, contributes to your self-esteem, and satisfies your needs for belonging and affiliation.

I/O psychology influences every aspect of your life at work and much of your life outside of work as well. It affects your initial hiring and training, the way in which your work is performed and evaluated, your motivations and the satisfactions you derive, and a host of other factors that determine your level of advancement and personal growth as well as the efficiency and vitality of the organization for which you work. As such, industrial psychology may be one of the most personally important courses of your college career.

I/O psychology is defined as **the application of the methods, facts, and principles of the science of behavior and mental processes to people at work**. As a science, psychology relies on the use of **observation** and **experimentation** and deals only with overt human behavior (that which can be observed objectively).

Industrial psychology began in the early years of the 20th century and grew rapidly, particularly under the impetus of the two world wars, which gave the field unique opportunities to demonstrate its value. A major change in industrial psychology was the recognition of the influence of social/psychological variables on worker behavior, as demonstrated in the **Hawthorne studies** of the 1920s and 1930s. A new area of industrial psychology, **engineering psychology**, emerged out of the development of increasingly sophisticated weapons in World War II. In the 1960s, another new area developed—organizational psychology—which is concerned with the setting or climate in which work takes place.

Most I/O psychologists are members of the **American Psychological Association**, which contains among its 45 divisions four that are devoted to the interests of I/O psychologists: the Society for Industrial and Organizational Psychology; Military Psychology; the Society of Engineering Psychologists; and Consumer Psychology. To work professionally as an I/O psychologist, a person needs at least a master's degree and will find a position of higher responsibility with a PhD degree. Diverse employment opportunities are available for I/O psychologists.

Psychology is of great practical value to organizations, contributing to profitability as well as to the satisfaction of individual employees. I/O psychology faces several problems that were brought about, in part, by the continuing demand for its services. These include (1) quackery, the practice of psychology by persons not professionally trained; (2) communication, the translation of technical jargon so that it can be understood by management personnel; (3) the reluctance to try something new, a resistance to change on the part of executives and employees often faced by I/O psychologists; and (4) research versus application, the necessary relationship between acquiring knowledge and applying it to specific problems.

Specific areas of I/O psychology are discussed in chapters on employee selection, performance appraisal, training and development, leadership, motivation and job satisfaction, organizational psychology, conditions of work, engineering psychology, safety and health, stress, and consumer psychology.

The future of I/O psychology calls for continued growth and new challenges, brought about by the changing age of the work force and the changing nature of work itself. Specific problems for the future include the declining number of factory and middle-management jobs, the electronic revolution, decreasing job opportunities for unskilled and illiterate workers, and the aging of the work force.

Key Terms

American Psychological Association (APA)
consumer psychology
demographics

engineering psychology
Hawthorne studies
industrial/ organizational (I/O) psychology

organizational psychology
personnel psychology
Society for Industrial and Organizational Psychology

Additional Reading

The Science and Practice of Industrial and Organizational Psychology. Survey of Graduate Programs in Industrial/Organizational Psychology and Organizational Behavior. Two brochures prepared by the Society for Industrial and Organizational Psychology, Division 14 of the American Psychological Association. The first describes the research and applied interests of I/O psychologists; the second lists selected graduate school programs. Free copies of the brochures can be obtained by writing to the Society for Industrial and Organizational Psychology, Department of Psychology, University of Maryland, College Park, MD 20742.

Birnbach, L. (1988). *Going to Work: A Unique Guided Tour Through Corporate America.* New York: Villard. Describes for college students life at work in some 50 U.S. companies in a dozen cities. Includes a range of occupations and organizations from a 6-person design firm to a 350,000-person automobile manufacturing plant. Presents first-person accounts of training programs, opportunities, and organizational climates.

Greenberger, E., & Steinberg, L. (1986). *When Teenagers Work: The Psychological and Social Costs of Adolescent Employment.* New York: Basic Books. Discusses the effects of part-time employment on grades, attitudes, drug use, and work habits of 10th and 11th grade high school students.

Chapter 2

Techniques, Tools, and Tactics

Why Study Research Methods?

In Chapter 1, we gained some appreciation of the importance of I/O psychology research to industry. Indeed, it can be said that psychology would be of little, if any, value to industry without the continuing application of research methods to the problems of people and their work.

Its value to industry, then, is beyond question, but what is its value to you in your future working career? How will you benefit from a knowledge of the methods used by psychologists to collect and analyze their research data?

Even though you may not be working as an I/O psychologist, most of you will be working directly with the findings of I/O psychologists. As potential managers, you no doubt will find yourselves interacting with psychologists to solve particular management problems and you will be faced with decisions based in part on the results and recommendations of your company's psychologists or of consulting psychologists your company has hired.

The problems confronting business managers and executives today are so complex and difficult that answers cannot be made on the basis of common sense, pet ideas, or past procedures. Suppose you are responsible for implementing a new manufacturing process in your department. A modern production facility must be developed, and part of your problem will be to facilitate the changeover from the old process to the new. How will the workers react to such an abrupt change in their jobs? Will they be able (and, more important, willing) to operate the new machinery to maintain high production levels? How will the new process affect morale, absenteeism, and safety? These are just a few of the questions you would be expected to answer. If you make an incorrect decision, the cost will be high to both you and your company.

Using information based on sound research, psychologists may be able to help you in this situation. However, if you are to evaluate properly their advice and recommendations, you must be aware of the methods they use to study the problems.

As a manager, you may also be called on to decide whether or not the research program recommended by the company psychologist is worth the time and money required. Again, a knowledge of the methods of research will enable you to make such a decision more wisely.

The purpose of this chapter is not to train you to do research yourself, but to acquaint you with the requirements, limitations, and methods of the scientific approach. The importance of understanding this information cannot be stressed too strongly. The application of the scientific method to problems too often dealt with by intuitive or subjective means may be psychology's most important contribution to better management and work practices. If you understand these research tools, you will be able to ensure their proper use.

Requirements of Psychological Research

One of the basic requirements and defining characteristics of scientific research in any discipline is *objective observation*. Researchers base their conclusions only on the objective evidence at hand and they view that evidence without preconceived ideas or biases.

It is well known in psychology that our perception of the world around us is subjective, that is, much of what we see is determined by our fears, values, attitudes, or prejudices. Thus, our observations are shaped not so much by what we are looking at as by our own psychological and emotional conditions at the time.

This is not the case with scientists. They must look on the data in an open and unbiased manner. The facts of the situation must speak for themselves and determine the conclusion. A psychologist's choice of a particular test, method of training, or work station design cannot be determined by private hunches, by the recommendations of prestigious authorities, or even by past research. Rather, the decision must be based on an objective evaluation of the facts at hand.

A second requirement of psychological research is that observation be *well controlled and systematic*. The conditions under which objective observations are made must be determined in advance so that every factor that could possibly influence the responses of the subjects is known to the researcher. If, for example, we are studying the effect of music on the typing efficiency of secretaries, the situation must be arranged so that no factors other than the music can affect typing efficiency.

The systematic control of objective observation also allows for the fulfill-ment of a third research requirement: *duplication and verifiability*. With careful control of conditions, a scientist working at another time and place can duplicate the conditions under which the earlier experiment was conducted. We can have more confidence in research findings if they have been verified by another investigator, and this verification is possible only under thoroughly controlled experimental conditions.

Psychological research in any setting, then, requires full and careful systematic planning, control of the total experimental situation so that findings can be duplicated and verified, and objective observation of the data. How these requirements are implemented by I/O psychologists is discussed in the following pages.

Limitations of Research in Industrial/Organizational Psychology

There are many challenges to the proper design and execution of psychological research when it is conducted in a university research laboratory. But when a study is undertaken in the real-life setting of a factory or office, the problems are magnified in scope and intensity.

One obvious limitation of psychological research in general is that its methods cannot be applied to every problem. In the area of social psychology, for example, psychologists cannot conduct carefully controlled observations of the behavior of people in riots; the situation is too complex and dangerous to prearrange. Similarly, in industry, it is not feasible to conduct systematic research on some procedures or devices designed to prevent accidents because subjects might be exposed to possible injury. There is a limit to what human beings may be exposed to in the interest of scientific research.

A second problem is that the act of observation may interfere with or change what the psychologist is trying to observe. If, for example, workers are given personality tests as a part of research into job satisfaction, they may fake or distort their test responses simply because they are aware that their personalities are being investigated.

Consider the matter of research on the effects of jet engine noise on the efficiency of engine mechanics. The mechanics, aware that they are part of a psychological study, may perform quite differently than they normally would on a routine workday when they are not being observed. Often people will behave in a changed manner when they know their behavior is being observed; however, ethical and technical considerations frequently dictate that subjects be informed that they are participating in a research study.

Sometimes, the behavior of workers on the job may change simply because something novel has been introduced into the workplace, either by the presence of the psychologist or by the experimental manipulation. This phenomenon was first observed during the Hawthorne experiments and so has come to be called the *Hawthorne effect*. Recall from Chapter 1 that one of the Hawthorne studies involved increasing the level of illumination in one work area. Production rose with each increase in lighting. However, production remained high even when the level of illumination was drastically reduced. Whether the lighting was increased or decreased, a novel situation had been introduced into the workplace, and that alone could help explain the increase in production. Of course, such a change does not remain a novelty for long. Workers will get used to it and, in time—a few days to several months, depending on the variable—production will decrease again. The psychologist must be able to determine whether the changes being observed in the workers' behavior are due to the actual changes made in working conditions or to the new stimulation of change itself, independent of working conditions.

Another weakness of psychological research is that some studies must be conducted in an artificial setting. For example, the management of a company may not allow the psychologist to disrupt production schedules by experimenting with various work procedures. As a result, the research may have to be conducted in a simulated job environment elsewhere in the plant. The research results, then, are based on performance in a setting that is not identical with the job environment in which the findings are to be applied. This artificiality may reduce the level of generalizability of the research findings.

The problem of artificiality is complicated further by the fact that much research in I/O psychology is conducted in university laboratories using college students as subjects. A review of five leading journals in the field for the period 1978 to 1983 showed that 87% of the studies published used students as subjects (Barr & Hitt, 1986). A majority of studies comparing student and nonstudent subjects revealed one or more important differences between these two groups (Gordon, Slade, & Schmitt, 1986). For example, a comparison of experienced business managers and college students performing the same task—evaluating applicants for a managerial position—showed that students rated the applicants much higher and recommended considerably higher starting salaries than did the managers (Barr & Hitt, 1986).

As for the larger issue of generalizing from academic research to the real world, some psychologists argue that research conducted in university laboratories can safely be generalized (Locke, 1986). Others, however, maintain that the differences between conditions in the world of work and in the laboratory are too great to permit more than the most cautious generalization (Guion & Gibson, 1988; Nichols, 1987; Raza & Carpenter, 1987).

Recognizing that there are weaknesses and difficulties in psychological research does not mean that research should not be attempted. For all its limitations, the results of carefully controlled and systematic research are infinitely superior to problem solving and decision making based on purely subjective considerations. The questions and problems investigated by industrial psychologists must be answered and only through objective observation can we have confidence in those answers.

Methods of Data Collection

Several procedures are available to the I/O psychologist to aid in conducting research. The problem of selecting the most effective technique is one of the first questions asked in any research program, and the answer is determined by the nature of the problem to be investigated.

The Experimental Method

The experimental method is simple in its basic concepts but difficult in its detailed operations. The purpose of an experiment is to determine the effect or influence of one variable on the performance or behavior of a group of subjects (the people being studied).

We are constantly bombarded by a wide range of stimuli in our environment, all of which may influence our behavior in one way or another. When psychologists want to investigate the effect of just one of these stimuli, they must arrange a situation in which only that stimulus is allowed to impinge on the subject. The operation of all the other stimuli in the environment must be eliminated or kept constant. Only in that way can we conclude that any change in the behavior of the subject is attributable to the stimulus in question.

Thus, two factors or variables are of importance in the conduct of an experiment: (1) the stimulus variable, the effect of which we are interested in determining, and (2) the resulting behavior of the subject. Both of these variables can be objectively observed, measured, and recorded.

The stimulus variable is called the *independent variable*, and the subject's behavior or response is called the *dependent variable*. The latter is called dependent for an obvious reason: It depends on the independent variable.

Consider the following experiment. The management of a company is concerned about the production level of a group of workers assembling television sets. The company psychologist is asked to find out how output could be increased. Many factors may be responsible for the workers' lowered production, for example, low pay, poor training, an unpopular supervisor, or faulty equipment. The psychologist, however, after inspecting the workplace, suspects that the problem is insufficient lighting.

The two variables in this experiment are easy to identify and measure precisely. The independent variable is the level of illumination (which will be increased in the experiment), and the dependent variable is the workers' resulting production rate.

The psychologist arranges for the lighting level in the workroom to be increased and compares the production level before the experiment with the production level 2 weeks after the lighting increase. Prior to changing the lighting, the workers each produced an average of 8 units per hour. Two weeks later, the individual production rate averaged 14 units per hour, a considerable increase.

Surely, then, we can conclude that the change in the independent variable (the increase in the level of illumination) brought about a change in the dependent variable (the increase in production). Wrong! We cannot draw this conclusion on the basis of the experiment described. How do we know that some factor other than the increased lighting did not bring about the higher production levels? Perhaps the usually grouchy supervisor was nicer to the workers during the 2-week experiment because he knew the company psychologist was around. Maybe the workers purposely produced more because they thought the presence of the psychologist meant that their jobs were in jeopardy, or because the weather turned better during that period. Perhaps production increased because of the novelty introduced by the brighter lights (the *Hawthorne effect*).

Many other factors could account for the increase in production, but the important point is that the psychologist must be certain that nothing operated to influence the subjects' behavior except the stimulus being manipulated, that is, the level of illumination.

An essential ingredient of the scientific method was omitted from our experiment, the element of *control*. Controlling the experimental conditions properly would assure us that any change in the behavior or performance of the subjects was solely because of the independent variable.

To provide this necessary control, two groups of subjects must be used in an experiment. The *experimental group* is exposed to the independent variable; the group discussed in our hypothetical experiment is an experimental group. The group that provides the element of control is called, not surprisingly, the *control group*.

In an experiment, the experimental and control groups are as similar as possible in every respect except that the control group is *not* exposed to the independent variable. Measures of productivity are taken from both groups at the beginning and end of the experimental period.

To conduct the experiment properly we must divide the workers into these two groups. Their performance is measured before and after the experiment, and the production level of the control group serves as a standard against which the resulting performance of the experimental group is compared.

If the groups of workers are similar and if the performance level of the experimental group at the end of the experiment is higher than that of the control group, we can conclude that the increased illumination (the independent variable) was, indeed, responsible for the increased production. Extraneous factors such as the weather or the supervisor's temper or the Hawthorne effect could not have influenced the subjects' behavior. If these factors had been influential, then the performance of both groups would have changed in the same manner.

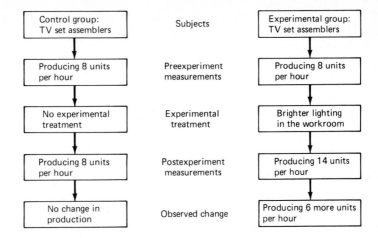

Figure 2-1 Design of lighting study.

The experimental design and results of this research study are shown in Figure 2-1.

Control Groups

The control group must be as similar as possible to the experimental group. There are two ways to bring this about.

One method, the *random group design*, involves the random assignment of the subjects to the experimental and control groups. In our experiment, if there had been 50 television set assemblers, they would have been assigned at random to the two groups, 25 to each condition.

The basis for dividing the subjects into the experimental and control conditions is random assignment, thus we may assume that the two groups are essentially similar. Any possible influencing variables such as age or length of job experience should be evenly distributed over the two groups because these factors were not allowed to influence the assignment of the subjects.

Another method of assuring similarity between experimental and control groups uses the *matched group design*. In this approach, the subjects in one group are evenly matched with the subjects in the other on the basis of characteristics that could influence the dependent variable. For example, in our experiment we could determine pairs of subjects who are identical in terms of length of job experience, age, level of intelligence, or supervisor's ratings, and assign one member of each pair to each group. In this way, the experimental and control groups would be evenly matched.

This approach, although desirable, is costly and difficult to put into practice. To find large enough numbers of evenly paired subjects, we need an even larger number of potential subjects from whom to choose. Further, it becomes extremely complex to equate pairs of subjects on more than one factor. Matching subjects on length of job experience alone presents little problem, but equating them on several factors at the same time becomes cumbersome. Finally, because many experiments in psychology involve more than one experimental group (such as studying the effects on production of several different levels of illumination), matching subjects becomes virtually impossible.

A Sample Industrial Experiment

An experiment conducted in a factory that produces lingerie was concerned with the influence of different levels of training on the turnover rate and productivity of sewing machine operators (Lefkowitz, 1970). The management had asked a consulting psychologist to determine why 68% of the workers had quit in 1 year. Based on the results of an attitude survey of the employees and the questioning of supervisors, the psychologist suspected that insufficient training for the job accounted for the high turnover.

Accordingly, it was decided to investigate the effects of increased training on both turnover and productivity. Note that the initial problem leading to the research was the high rate of job terminations. In the process of designing a study to investigate this factor, the psychologist saw that with little extra effort data could also be secured on another dependent variable, the level of production.

The subjects were 208 women employees hired in one year by the factory as trainees. The dependent variables were (1) job turnover, defined as the percentage of workers who quit in their first 40 days on the job, and (2) productivity, defined in terms of daily production figures in the first 40 days on the job. The psychologist chose the first 40-day period because the records of the company showed that most of the previous terminations had occurred within that length of time. The dependent variables are easy to observe, measure, and record with precision.

The independent variable is the level of training, and the consulting psychologist chose to investigate four different training periods. The company's standard practice was to provide 1 day of training for new employees, conducted in a training facility, not on the job. Thus, 1-day training was the control condition against which longer training periods would be compared.

Trainees assigned to Group I received the standard 1-day training, Group II received 2 days of training, Group III had 3 days of training, and Group IV also received 3 days of training but part of it was conducted on the job, whereas all the other training took place in the company's training facility.

The subjects were assigned to each of the four conditions on the basis of the date of their initial employment with the company. Those hired during the first month of the study were placed in Group I, those hired during the second month in Group II, and so on, repeating the cycle throughout the year the study was in progress. Statistical comparisons of each group's initial performance levels demonstrated their similarity.

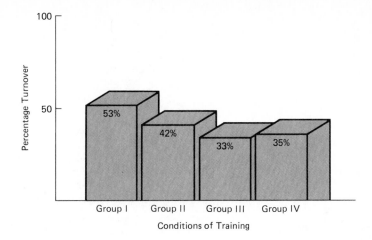

Figure 2-2 Turnover rates of four training conditions.

The results of the study concerned with turnover revealed that the longer the training received in the training facility (Groups I, II, and III), the lower the rate of turnover, as shown in Figure 2-2.

The 3-day training period combining on-the-job experience with the training facility (Group IV) did not reduce the turnover rate compared to the 3-day training period in the training room alone (Group III). Comparing Groups I and III, however, clearly shows that the two additional days of training greatly reduced the turnover rate from 53% to 33%.

The second part of the study, the effect of training on productivity, produced some unexpected complications. The data indicated that the longer a new employee remained in the training facility, the lower was the resulting level of production. Figure 2-3 shows a surprising finding. The 3 days of integrated training (Group IV) led to a higher level of productivity than the 3 days of training solely in the training facility (Group III).

This study demonstrates that the independent variable (different levels of training) produced conflicting results on the two dependent variables: greater time spent in the training room resulted in a lower turnover rate, but it also yielded a lower level of productivity.

It is at this point, the interpretation of the research results, that the training, wisdom, and experience of the psychologist are put to their most severe test. Experiments do not always, or even often, turn out as the researcher would like. Research results are not always clear-cut or consistent, and considerable interpretive skill is necessary to relate the data to the job or problem in question.

The psychologist in this study concluded that, considering both productivity and turnover, the 3-day integrated training condition (Group IV), was the most profitable. It yielded a close second-highest level of production and a close second-lowest rate of turnover.

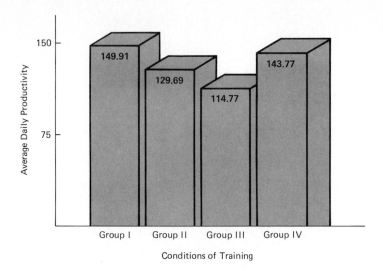

Figure 2-3 Production levels of four training conditions.

As we can see from this example, the research process proceeds at two levels of complexity: (1) designing the experiment and (2) understanding, interpreting, and implementing the results. Both steps depend on the cooperation of managers who are sensitive to the intricate nature of psychological research.

Naturalistic Observation

In the complicated study of human behavior, it is not always possible to bring the relevant variables under the precise control required by the experimental method. Also, it may be more appropriate to study some human behaviors as they occur naturally in real-life situations. We mentioned that one of the weaknesses of the experimental method is the artificiality it might introduce into the study of human behavior. To avoid this artificiality, it is sometimes preferable to observe behavior in its normal setting.

For these reasons, psychologists may be forced (and sometimes prefer) to observe behavior without introducing any manipulation of the independent variable. This is the essence of another method of data collection, that of naturalistic observation. As we shall see, however, not manipulating variables directly does not mean that the psychologist has no control over them.

One advantage of naturalistic observation is that the behavior being observed and the situation in which it is observed are more representative of what occurs in everyday life. Our ordinary daily activities take place in situations that are not under the stringent control necessary in the experimental method. Hence, advocates of naturalistic observation argue that the results of this method can be more readily generalized and applied to real life, for that is where the results were obtained.

This advantage is also a major source of weakness. Because researchers do not manipulate the independent variable, it is often difficult for them to conclude with any assurance just what brought about the resulting change in the subjects' behavior or performance. Another limitation is that the observation cannot be repeated; it is impossible to duplicate the exact conditions that prevailed during the initial observation.

The experimental method is not without its own limitations, as we saw earlier. Nevertheless, when it can be used, it is preferred over the method of naturalistic observation because the experimenter can control and systematically manipulate the independent variable. However, both tools, when used with precision and interpreted with caution and understanding, are valuable means of studying human behavior.

Sample Observational Studies

After a nationwide chain of convenience stores instituted a training program for its clerks on how to be friendly to customers, the company wanted to determine whether the friendly behaviors would, indeed, increase sales. Arranging an experiment would have been difficult and perhaps not very informative. For example, the company could have compared sales at two groups of stores, one of which had clerks trained to display the friendly behaviors and the other of which did not. But that might mean a loss in sales in the control group stores and the possible alienation of customers. The company could have designed a laboratory experiment in which subjects were asked if persons posing as clerks in one situation were more courteous than those in another situation, and if they thought they would buy more from the friendly clerks. But that would have been too artificial a setting and the persons posing as clerks would have known they were being observed, which might have influenced their behavior. Also, the results of such a study would not tell the company anything about the impact of the friendly behaviors on actual sales.

For these reasons, a naturalistic observation was conducted in which the behaviors of 1,319 clerks in 576 convenience stores were secretly watched by trained observers in 11,805 individual transactions with customers (Sutton & Rafaeli, 1988). Clerks were told that their level of courtesy would be monitored at some time, but they were given no idea when the observations would occur. The observers, chosen to fit the profile of a typical customer, and pretending to be customers actually making purchases, spent from 4 to 12 minutes in each store, depending on how many other customers were there. The more crowded the store, the longer the observers could stay without appearing suspicious. Observers reported that they thought clerks were suspicious of them in fewer than 3% of the observations; those data were excluded from consideration. The clerks' friendly behaviors recorded by the observers included smiling at customers, greeting customers, thanking customers, and maintaining eye contact with customers. Those behaviors, along with the sales figures for each store, were the dependent variables.

Although no independent variables were manipulated, factors that might have influenced sales and the clerks' behavior were controlled. The proportion of women to men clerks was considered, to control for variation in courteous behaviors by sex, because research suggested that women may be more courteous than men in any setting. The proportion of women to men customers was also recorded to control for differences in purchasing behavior between men and women. If some stores were patronized primarily by women, for example, and if women made more purchases than men, then sales figures for those stores would be higher, independent of the clerks' behavior.

The stores in which the observations were made were selected at random, but all were in heavily populated urban districts. None was from a suburban or rural area where the sales pattern might differ from an urban area, regardless of the training of the clerks. Finally, recognizing that people in different sections of the country might behave more courteously independent of the company's training program, the data from four regions—northeast, south, midwest, and west—were analyzed separately.

Thus, we can see that taking research out of the laboratory and conducting it in the real world still permits the psychologist to control relevant variables and make objective observations.

What did this study reveal? Did the clerks' courteous behavior result in higher sales? Surprisingly, the higher the level of courteous behaviors, the lower were the sales. The researchers called the findings "unexpected and confusing" (Sutton & Rafaeli, 1988, p. 470). People do not always behave the way psychologists think they will—or should.

Further analysis of the data showed that a store's level of sales may have caused the clerks to behave courteously, but the courteous behavior of the clerks, as we noted, did not lead to higher sales. The busier the store (the higher the sales), the less time the clerks had to be friendly. In stores with slower sales, clerks had time to behave in a more friendly fashion, and so did the customers. In addition, the results confirmed that women clerks were more friendly than men clerks and that clerks of both sexes in the western region of the United States were more friendly than those in the northeast.

Another example of naturalistic observation can be drawn from the work of an engineering psychologist for a company producing missile systems. The missile, a small surface-to-surface type launched from a truck, had already been built, and the customer, the U.S. Army, wanted to know if the procedures that had been established to assemble, aim, and fire the missile were the most efficient ones possible.

The launching of the missile required a sequence of several hundred small operations performed by a 10-person launching crew. These included aiming, assembling (attaching wings and fins), electronically checking out all components, and firing. The operating procedures were dictated by the engineering requirements of the system, and the purpose of the study was to determine if all the steps were necessary, if the sequence was correct, if there were possibilities of error, and if the total time taken could be shortened.

This study could have been conducted in a laboratory by having the subjects perform one operation and evaluating their performance before proceeding to the next step. However, if the research were conducted in as realistic a setting as possible, the results would be more directly applicable to the use of the missile in combat.

The observations were carried out under the naturally stressful conditions of the White Sands Proving Ground in New Mexico where, in the summer, the temperature often reached 120°F. The primary element of control was in the nature of the subjects used. Army troops trained in missile operation (the same kind of soldier who would eventually operate the system) followed the prescribed operating procedure. The subjects wore full military gear and worked under the pressure of time.

Observers with stopwatches carefully recorded each task, looking for potential sources of error and slowdown. The soldiers were interviewed periodically about their own suggestions for improving the operation of the missile system.

The subjects in this study knew that their performance was being observed and evaluated; they knew they were participating in an experiment. It would have been desirable if they could have been observed without their awareness, but the detailed nature of the required observations did not allow for this refinement.

The results of the research were an improvement in the procedures for launching the missile system and a considerable reduction in the time necessary to do so.

In both of these examples, the behavior being observed was not as well controlled as it could have been under laboratory conditions. However, the greater realism afforded by the use of real-life situations may offset this disadvantage. The nature and complexity of the phenomena under investigation often determine the most appropriate method. In other cases, the psychologist must decide on the relative merit of sacrificing some degree of control for greater realism, or vice versa.

Survey Methods of Research

Closely related to the method of systematic observation is the conduct of surveys and public opinion polls. These rely on the observation of behavior as revealed in the subjects' responses to personal interviews and questionnaires. Thus, the focus in the survey method is not on what subjects do (as in the experimental or naturalistic observation methods) but rather on what they say they do or will do. A survey of psychologists employed in the personnel departments of 31 leading American corporations revealed that 71% of the research in which they were involved related to surveys, making it their single most important research activity (Rassenfoss & Kraut, 1988).

Survey research has become a big business and is practiced throughout the world. One of the leading polling companies, the Gallup organization, is affiliated with 40 similar companies in other countries, making it possible to survey a large portion of the world's population (Gallup, 1988). Other polling organizations with a reputation for accuracy are the CBS News/New York Times poll and such academically affiliated groups as the Survey Research Center at the University of Michigan and the National Opinion Research Center at the University of Chicago.

Even the best polling organizations, however, have problems with the precise measurement of highly subjective personal opinions and attitudes. A major difficulty with surveys is that people may say they are going to do one thing and then do something else. Sometimes they simply change their minds. They may, for example, tell an interviewer in October that they will vote for the Republicans in the next national election and then vote for the Democrats in November.

People may say that they prefer a particular product or brand name because they believe this choice will make them appear sophisticated. For example, they may claim to drink an expensive imported European beer, but if the interviewer could look in their refrigerator or trash can, he or she might find an inexpensive domestic label instead.

Sometimes people express opinions in surveys even when they do not really have any because they do not want the interviewer to think they are stupid or uninformed. Take the case of a nationwide poll in which people were asked if they favored the new Monetary Control Bill. More than 25% of the respondents expressed an opinion (either pro or con). The rest said they had no opinion. There was no such bill—it had been made up by the poll takers—but 1 person in 4 responded as though it were real (Jaroslovsky, 1988).

Another problem with surveys, particularly those taken within a company, relates to the assurances given employees that their responses will be confidential or anonymous, that they will not be identified by name. In one study, 15% of the people questioned did not believe those assurances. Such disbelief could easily have biased their answers (Mischkind, 1986).

Another complication is the increasing difficulty in finding and getting people to respond, particularly to telephone surveys. More and more people are disturbed by so-called junk telephone calls pretending to be surveys when their real purpose is to sell land or dance lessons or something else. Also, because so many more organizations are now conducting polls, many people are no longer willing to devote the time necessary to respond properly, feeling themselves burdened by "survey overload" (Deutsch, 1987b). Further, some respondents may answer with the first thing that comes to mind out of a lack of interest, or boredom, or just because they are tired. Also, people may deliberately offer answers at variance with their true feelings or opinions because they enjoy the idea of invalidating the research results.

Finally, although it is usually easy to poll retired people and full-time homemakers, it is more difficult to reach an adequate sample of men and women in offices, young adults, and high-income people. Surveying such groups requires considerable time and effort on the part of poll-taking organizations.

Such problems and sources of error in surveys can account for lost elections and bankrupt companies. The problem lies not with the survey methods themselves but rather with the complex, vague, and often perverse nature of the object of study: human attitudes, preferences, and opinions. However, we have only to consider election results that were predicted accurately or products and television programs that have been successful to see the value of survey methods of research. They succeed more often than they fail.

Questionnaires and interviews to determine what people think, feel, like, and dislike have many uses in psychology. Within a company, psychologists use survey methods to ascertain those factors that contribute to job satisfaction and employee morale. Some large corporations, such as General Electric, have their own poll-taking staffs that are kept busy conducting employee surveys on a variety of work-related issues. Corporations have found that periodic polling serves several purposes, including giving employees the chance to air their gripes and complaints, assessing worker reaction to changes in work procedures and policies, and providing employees the opportunity to participate in policy-making.

These activities may lead to an increase in employee morale, a reduction in turnover, and the avoidance of costly union grievance procedures. Indeed, maintaining an open channel of communication between employee and employer has sometimes prevented unionization altogether. Workers who believe that their opinions are valued and acted on by management are less likely to feel the need for third-party representation, such as a union (Mischkind, 1986; Wright, 1986).

Advertising and motivation research firms also use survey techniques to uncover consumer preferences for specific products. Companies that manufacture consumer goods must constantly be aware of buying preferences, as we shall see in Chapter 14. To give one example, a few years ago the Campbell Soup Company questioned more than 100,000 consumers to determine their opinions on a variety of food and taste likes and dislikes. On the basis of the results, the company changed the seasonings in five of its frozen food dinners and introduced a line of low-salt soups (called, appropriately, Special Request) (Deutsch, 1987b).

Regardless of the use to which survey data eventually are put, the methods of gathering the information remain essentially the same. The three basic data-collecting techniques are personal interviews, mail surveys, and telephone surveys.

The *personal interview*, the most expensive and time-consuming technique, is widely used for all purposes of survey research. It requires a face-to-face meeting with the respondents who are asked not only to divulge information about themselves but also to give up a substantial amount of their time. Obviously, this requires cooperation and patience on the part of the persons being questioned and great skill in human relations on the part of the interviewers.

Finding and training capable interviewers is vital because their appearance, manner, dress, and general behavior can influence the way in which respondents will answer the questions put to them. For example, black interviewers asking white persons about their attitudes toward blacks might get different responses than would white interviewers asking the same questions.

There are also more subtle interviewer variables that can bias the results. If, for example, in asking questions about the use of drugs, interviewers show (by frowning or smiling) their agreement or disagreement with what respondents are saying, the respondents may modify their subsequent answers because of their perception of the interviewer's opinion about drugs.

Assuming a competent, well-trained interviewer, this method offers several advantages over telephone and mail surveys. It yields the highest percentage of returns—80% to 95%—and it can obtain greater accuracy in responses because the face-to-face situation establishes a rapport and encourages the respondent to answer more honestly. Also, it is usually possible to obtain more information in a personal interview than through the mail or over the telephone.

The major disadvantage of the personal-interview survey method is the high cost, in both time and money, of training interviewers and conducting the interviews. It is far more expensive and time consuming to contact 500 individuals in person than to telephone them or mail them a questionnaire. Additional problems involve the safety of interviewers in some neighborhoods, the difficulty of finding people at home, and the possible bias of the interviewer on the topic in question. Also, interviewers are generally not paid well and some have been known to make up answers to the interview questions rather than go to the time and trouble of actually conducting the interview.

A *mail survey* is a cheaper and more convenient method of obtaining information from large numbers of people over a wide geographical area. Those being questioned are able to remain anonymous, and this often encourages them to respond more freely and openly on sensitive or personal topics. Another advantage is that respondents are given more time in which to formulate their answers than in a personal interview situation.

The major disadvantage of mail surveys is the relatively small number of replies that are usually obtained. In one mail survey of 500 U.S. corporations having business operations in Europe, the companies could remain anonymous, the questionnaire was brief (one page), and a postage-paid return envelope had been included. However, only 45% of the companies responded. In a survey of the attitudes of one company's employees, the return rate was only 40%. This study suggested another disadvantage of mail surveys: The responses were influenced by the opinions of spouses, friends, and co-workers. Such influences are not possible in the personal-interview survey where the answers are given immediately and without consulting anyone else (Tagliaferri, 1988).

Research has shown that the source of a mail questionnaire can influence the rate of return. A questionnaire identified as coming from a university had a 52% return rate whereas one from a private research firm had only a 42% return rate (Albaum, 1987).

Follow-up procedures can be used to secure additional returns. A second letter can request cooperation and explain the importance of the survey. Letters sent by registered mail and follow-up telephone calls can also be used to solicit returns.

The rate of return can be increased by offering incentives. Some companies hold contests with the opportunity to win expensive prizes as an inducement to return questionnaires. Most organizations, however, offer only a token payment, such as a dollar bill enclosed with the questionnaire. "It's amazing what a nice crisp dollar bill in an envelope will do," a General Mills executive said. "People feel guilty if they take the dollar and don't fill out their questionnaires" (Deutsch, 1987b).

A recent high-tech method of conducting mail surveys uses electronic mail, in which questions are asked and answers obtained through the company's computer system. This approach is restricted to employees who have access to computer terminals and who use them in their daily work, but the number of such employees is increasing. A survey conducted in this manner in a research and development division of a major corporation brought a response rate of 73%, and the time required to receive the replies was less than a week, a high and rapid rate of return. In addition, there were no differences found in average response compared to a group of employees who answered a written question-naire sent through the mail (Sproull, 1986). However, because it is difficult to determine how those who did respond might differ on the issues from those who failed to respond, it can be unwise to generalize too broadly on the basis of the limited returns in most mail surveys.

Telephone surveys offer the advantage of a low cost per interview and the possibility of a single interviewer contacting several hundred people in the course of a day. Also, with perseverance, it is usually possible to reach almost every person in the sample by continuing to telephone until the person answers.

Telephone surveys are growing in popularity, aided in part by comput-erized dialing systems that considerably speed up the process. Recent research shows that telephone surveys cost about half as much as personal interviews and that comparable data are obtained. When only older respondents are consid-ered, however, a larger percentage of "I don't know" responses were obtained with the telephone approach (Herzog & Rodgers, 1988).

The major disadvantage of this technique is that it does not allow the researcher to contact a fully representative sample of the general public. There are still some people who do not have telephones, particularly in rural areas, and others who have unlisted telephone numbers.

With any survey method, two problems must be resolved: (1) the questions to be asked and (2) the people to be questioned.

In general, there are two basic types of question used in surveys—open-end questions and fixed-alternative questions. With the *open-end question*, respondents are allowed to present their answer freely in their own words without any limitations imposed by the interviewer or by the phrasing of the question. They are encouraged to answer in their own terms and to take as much time as needed.

An example of an open-end question is, What do you think about the proposed city bond issue? Because this kind of question has the advantage of eliciting answers in the respondents' own words, their complete thoughts on the issue can be recorded. Of course, this can also be a disadvantage; if there are many questions, the survey will be very time consuming. Also, the usefulness of the reply depends on how well respondents are able to verbalize or articulate

Telephone surveys offer the advantage of a low cost per interview and the likelihood that a single interviewer can contact hundreds of people in the course of the workday.

their thoughts and feelings. Finally, this kind of question places pressure on the interviewer to be accurate and complete in recording the answers.

The *fixed-alternative question* limits a person's answer to a fixed number of alternatives. The sample question might be phrased, How do you feel about the proposed city bond issue? Are you In Favor _____ Opposed _____ Undecided _____. Thus, the person is faced with a finite number of possible answers.

This type of question greatly simplifies and speeds up the survey being taken. More questions can be asked in a given period of time and the answers can be recorded more easily. A disadvantage is that the limited number of choices may not reflect accurately a person's feelings on the topic. For example, a person might be in favor of the proposed bond issue under certain circumstances and opposed to it under others. When he or she is restricted to yes, no, or undecided, these circumstances cannot be made known to the interviewer. If enough people questioned have such unexpressed qualifications, the results of the poll will be misleading.

No matter which type of question is used, it is desirable to pretest the questions on a small number of people to make sure they understand them. If respondents fail to understand a word that has been used in the question or if they interpret a question in a way that is different from what the interviewer intended, the results of the survey could be misleading. This happened with opinion surveys taken in 1973 about the possible impeachment of President Nixon. Many of the people questioned did not know the meaning of the word *impeachment* and interpreted it in various incorrect ways. This misunderstanding obviously affected the responses as well as the usefulness of the results of the survey.

The National Center for Health Statistics routinely surveys large samples of Americans about their health. One question asked annually relates to abdominal pain. It soon became clear that many people did not understand the phrase "abdominal pain" or know where the abdomen is located. The poll takers were given a diagram to show with that question, and they received quite different answers as a result.

The second problem in surveys is the selection of the sample of people who will be polled or questioned. This requires a great deal of careful attention.

Suppose that a researcher is assigned the task of determining the attitude of all automobile owners in the state of California toward a proposed change in the license fee. To question every car owner would be laborious and difficult, even if sufficient time and money were provided. It would not be feasible to locate and personally interview each automobile owner in the state.

Fortunately, it is not necessary to question every person in the population in which we are interested. With proper care, a representative sample of this population can provide the needed information. A sample of only several hundred, if it is truly representative of the larger population, can be used to predict accurately the responses of the total population.

To select a sample of automobile owners in California, we could question people wherever they are found—at a shopping center, a service station, or a busy intersection. However, this procedure would not guarantee that those questioned are representative of all automobile owners in the state; people found at a particular shopping center, for example, might only be from a suburban upper income bracket.

Two methods of constructing representative samples of the total population are probability sampling and quota sampling.

In *probability sampling*, each individual in a population has a known probability or chance of being included in the sample. By securing from the state department of motor vehicles a list of all automobile owners, the researcher can select, for example, every 10th or 25th name, depending on how large a sample is needed. Thus, every person in the population would have the same chance (1 in 10 or 1 in 25) of being included in the sample.

This method is satisfactory as long as there is a list of everyone in the population of interest. If you wanted to study every *eligible* voter in the United

States, however, this method could not be used because only *registered* voters are listed.

In *quota sampling*, the researcher tries deliberately to construct a duplicate, in miniature, of the larger population. If it is known from census data that in California 10% of all automobile owners are college graduates, 52% are men, 34% are of Hispanic origin, and so on, then these proportions must be included in the sample.

Interviewers are given quotas for people to interview in the various categories (level of education, sex, age, income, ethnic background) and must find appropriate respondents. Because the persons actually questioned are chosen by each interviewer, there is some opportunity for personal bias to enter into the selection of the sample. The interviewer may prefer to talk to those who live in nicer neighborhoods or who seem friendlier.

A Sample Survey

Three psychologists employed by a large business concern wanted to determine those factors that employees considered important to their own job satisfaction and work motivation (Wernimont, Toren, & Kapell, 1970). Cooperating with the firm's management, the researchers compiled a list of 17 variables thought to be relevant to job satisfaction and motivation. A questionnaire was developed that consisted of several questions related to employment history, the list of 17 variables, and a request to rank these factors in accordance with how much the worker thought they contributed to (1) job satisfaction and (2) motivation.

Constructing a sample did not present a problem in this case because the population—2,300 scientists and technicians employed by the company—was not too large to be reached with mailed questionnaires. Even though the responses were anonymous, only 41% of the employees returned completed questionnaires, approximately the same response rate as for other mail surveys, as we saw earlier. Anonymity also meant that it was not possible to use follow-up procedures to increase the rate of response because it could not be determined who had responded and who had not.

This low response rate is one disadvantage of surveys conducted by mail. There is no way of knowing if those who failed to respond did so because they were more or less satisfied or motivated in their jobs than those who did respond. In either case, the results would be biased and of limited value. Other reasons for not responding include carelessness or laziness, factors not necessarily related to the variables under study.

Another problem encountered by the psychologists with this survey was incomplete or incorrectly filled-out questionnaires. More than 150 of the returned forms could not be used for that reason, lowering the effective response rate to 34%.

If this survey had been conducted on a personal interview basis, it would not necessarily have yielded more useful results. Although a larger number of workers could have been sampled, they would not have been able to reply anonymously. They might not have answered as freely and honestly for fear that management might use their responses against them. Also, personal interviews would have been time consuming and disruptive of the work of many employees.

Keeping in mind these limitations, the researchers found that certain factors were considered more important than others by the employees in contributing to job satisfaction and work motivation. With information of this nature, the management was in a better position to arrange the working conditions to facilitate both satisfaction and motivation.

For any question that can be asked about the nature of human behavior at work, there is a psychological research technique available to explore the answer. The methods are not infallible—they have recognized weaknesses and limitations—but, for all their shortcomings, they do represent the best approach. Research can be difficult, expensive, and time consuming. Properly performed, however, research can provide results that will, if wisely applied, enhance the efficiency of any organization. The alternative to scientific research is a decision based not on facts but on opinion, prejudice, or habit.

Methods of Data Analysis

In research in psychology, as in any other science, data collection is merely the first step in the scientific approach to problem solving. If we have conducted a study on the production levels of 200 employees, we are left with 200 numbers, the *raw data*. It is necessary to evaluate and interpret these data, and that is the purpose of statistics.

The principles and concepts of the statistical analysis of data are not difficult to grasp. Statistics is a tool to help us summarize and describe large masses of data and to enable us to draw inferences or conclusions about the meaning of those data. The purpose of this discussion is to acquaint you with the nature and importance of statistical tools.

Descriptive Statistics

The first group of statistical techniques we shall cover are called *descriptive statistics*. You already know the meaning of the word *descriptive*. When you describe a person or an event in words, you try to convey a mental picture or image. Similarly, when psychologists use statistics to describe their data, they are trying to represent that raw information in a more meaningful fashion.

Let us examine some research data and see what statistical analysis can do to describe them. To evaluate a new test designed to predict the success of persons in life insurance sales jobs, a company psychologist administered the test to 99 applicants. The test scores are shown in Table 2-1. Just looking at this swarm of numbers should give you an understanding of why a method to summarize and describe them is so important. It is difficult to make any meaningful interpretation of these data as they now stand. You cannot get any useful idea about the performance of these job applicants as a whole by looking at the table of individual numbers.

**TABLE 2-1   Raw Scores of
99 Job Applicants on Life
Insurance Sales Test**

141	91	92	88	95
124	119	108	146	120
122	118	98	97	94
144	84	110	127	81
151	76	89	125	108
102	120	112	89	101
129	125	142	87	103
128	94	94	114	134
102	143	134	138	110
117	121	141	99	104
107	114	67	110	124
112	117	144	102	126
127	79	105	133	128
87	114	110	107	119
156	79	112	117	83
99	98	156	108	143
96	145	120	127	133
113	120	147	122	114
123	90	114	121	99
89	118	128	118	

One convenient way of describing the data is to present them in graphic form in a *frequency distribution*. To construct a frequency distribution, we plot on a graph the number of times each score occurs, that is, its frequency of occurrence. For convenience in dealing with many scores, we can group them into equal *intervals*. Grouping the data is not necessary, but it does make them

**TABLE 2-2   Frequency Distribution of Life Insurance
Sales Test Scores (grouped data)**

Interval	Tally	Frequency
65–74	|	1
75–84	卌 |	6
85–94	卌 卌 ||	12
95–104	卌 卌 ||||	14
105–114	卌 卌 卌 ||||	19
115–124	卌 卌 卌 ||||	19
125–134	卌 卌 ||||	14
135–144	卌 |||	8
145–154	||||	4
155–164	||	2

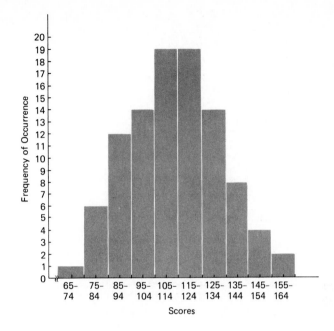

Figure 2-4 Histogram of life insurance sales test scores (grouped data).

easier to work with. Table 2-2 shows the frequency distribution of the 99 raw scores grouped into intervals, each interval comprising 10 possible scores.

By examining the frequency distribution we can get a much clearer idea of the performance of the job applicants as a group than we can by inspecting the individual raw scores in Table 2-1.

Two other ways of graphically portraying the raw data of a group of subjects are the *histogram* (Figure 2-4) and the *frequency polygon* (Figure 2-5).

All three of these graphic descriptions of the data enable us to see pictorially the performance of the group as a whole. Scientific analysis of the data, however, requires that the raw scores be summarized and described quantitatively; that is, we must be able to represent or summarize all the data with a single number. We must find the typical or average score on this test by measuring the *central tendency* of the distribution.

The most common measure of central tendency is the average or the arithmetic *mean*. The mean is found by adding up all of the raw scores and dividing the resulting sum by the total number of scores. The formula for the mean is

$$\bar{X} = \frac{\Sigma X}{N}$$

where $\bar{X}$ is the mean, X is the individual raw score, Σ is the process of adding, and N is the number of scores with which we are dealing. The mean of the raw

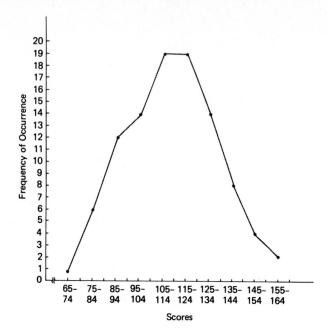

Figure 2-5 Frequency polygon of life insurance sales test scores (grouped data).

scores in Table 2-1 is

$$\bar{X} = \frac{11251}{99} = 113.6$$

We now know that the average score for this group of 99 job applicants is 113.6. Our raw data have been reduced to, and can be described by, this single number. The mean is the most useful measure of central tendency and provides the basis for many higher level statistical analyses.

Two other ways of measuring central tendency are the median and the mode.

The *median* is the score at the midpoint of the distribution. If we arrange our 99 scores in ascending order, the median is the score of the 50th person. Half of the job applicants scored higher than this, and half lower. In our sample of scores, the median is 114, which is quite close to the mean. The median is particularly useful when dealing with skewed distributions (as discussed in the following section).

The *mode* is the most frequently obtained score in the distribution. (A distribution may have more than one mode if two or more scores occur with the same highest frequency.) With our data, the mode is 114. The mode is seldom applied in analyzing data but is useful in certain practical situations. For example, a plant supervisor concerned with stocking an adequate inventory of machine parts would be interested in knowing which part was used more frequently than any other.

The Normal Curve of Distribution

In the three graphs showing the scores on the life insurance sales test, we can see that most of the applicants achieved scores in the middle of the distribution of scores and that only a few scored at either extreme end. Many measurements approximate this same kind of distribution. In general, this occurs when a large number of measurements are taken of a psychological or physical characteristic. Whether we are measuring height or weight or intelligence, a sample of sufficient size will produce a distribution in which most scores fall near the middle and few fall at the extreme low or extreme high end. This bell-shaped distribution is called the *normal curve*. Figure 2-6 depicts the normal curve of a distribution of a large number of scores on an IQ test.

The normal curve is predicated on the random nature and size of the sample tested. If the sample is not truly representative of the population but is biased in one direction or another, the distribution will not approximate the normal curve.

Suppose, for example, that we gave an IQ test to a group of the educationally disadvantaged, persons who have had insufficient schooling and little experience in taking tests. Obviously, this group is not representative of the general population, so the distribution of the test scores will not look like the normal curve (see Figure 2-7). When measurements are taken from specially selected groups of individuals, the distribution of their scores will most likely be *skewed* or asymmetrical.

In dealing with skewed distributions, the median is the most useful measure of central tendency. The mean (the arithmetic average) is seriously affected by a few extreme scores in either direction and may, thus, be misleading when dealing with skewed distributions. The median is less affected by such extreme scores.

A Note of Caution.   You have no doubt heard someone say, "Statistics lie!" Although it is true that statistics can be misleading, this is the fault of the person who misuses them, not of the techniques themselves.

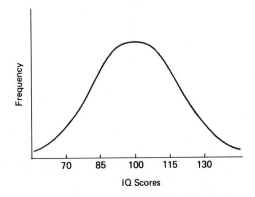

Figure 2-6 Normal curve of IQ scores.

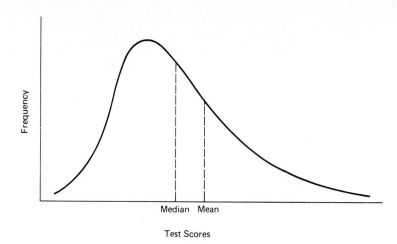

Figure 2-7 A skewed
distribution.

Consider the data in Figure 2-8, which represent median and mean awards in liability cases from 1960 to 1984. Clearly, the mean awards have increased sharply during those years, from about $60,000 each to $250,000 each. The median awards, on the other hand, have decreased slightly.

A controversy erupted in the pages of the *New York Times* over the interpretation of these data. Lawyers, who benefit from larger liability awards to their clients, argued that the liability awards have not increased over the 24-year period. Insurance companies, who have to pay those liability awards, argued that the awards had shown a fivefold increase ("When the Mean," 1986).

Figure 2-8 Median and mean liability awards, 1960–1984. (Data from the Institute for Civil Justice, Rand Corporation; *New York Times*, April 13, 1986.)

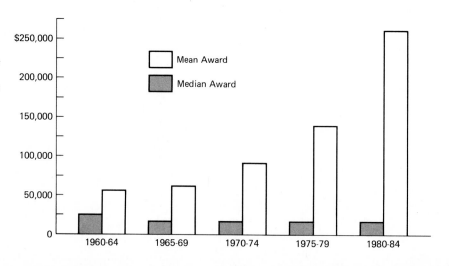

Lawyers were citing median liability awards; insurance companies were citing mean liability awards. Both sides are technically correct, although, as we noted, the median is the better measurement to use with a skewed distribution such as this one. The few extremely high liability awards affect the mean much more than they affect the median.

You can see that it pays to be skeptical when reading about average figures. Ask which average is being used, the mean or the median.

The Variability of a Distribution

Having proceeded to measure, pictorially and numerically, the central tendency of a distribution, you may not be happy to learn that still more analysis is needed to provide a comprehensive description of a distribution of scores. It is not sufficient to know only the central tendency of a distribution, we must also have a numerical indication of the spread of scores around the measure of central tendency. This spread is called *variability*.

Consider the two normal distributions in Figure 2-9. If we take the mean or the median as a measure of these distributions, we would conclude that the distributions are identical because the means and medians are the same for both curves. As you can see, however, the two distributions of scores are not identical. They differ greatly in their spread or variability.

There are several measures of variability. Two of these are the *range* and the *standard deviation*, but the range (the difference between the highest and lowest scores) is of so little value that it is seldom used.

Far more important as a numerical measure of variability is the standard deviation, a precise distance along the baseline of the distribution. Once we determine this distance, we can obtain a great deal of useful information about the data.

Let us examine the distribution of IQ scores in the United States. The data form a normal curve with a mean of 100 and a standard deviation of 15, as represented in Figure 2-10.

Figure 2-9 Normal curves with the same central tendency but different variability.

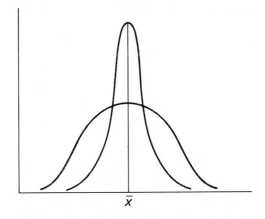

$\bar{x}$

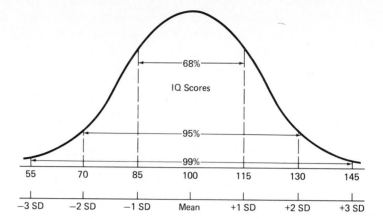

Figure 2-10 Normal distribution of IQ scores showing standard deviation units.

Knowing that the standard deviation (SD) is 15 tells us that an IQ of 115 is 1 SD distance above the mean of 100; an IQ of 130 is 2 SD units or distances above the mean. Similarly, IQ scores below the mean can be identified in terms of their SD equivalents. An IQ of 85 is 1 SD distance below the mean, or −1 SD.

With the standard deviation we can easily determine the percentage of scores in the distribution that fall above or below any particular raw score. Tables based on the mathematical formula for the normal curve give us the percentage of cases (or frequency of scores) that lie between standard deviation units or between a standard deviation unit and the mean.

For example, in Figure 2-10, 68% of the sample scores fall between −1 SD and +1 SD, 95% between −2 SD and +2 SD, and 99% between −3 SD and +3 SD. These percentages hold for any variable measured where the distribution of the data follows the normal curve. Thus, if we know the standard deviation of a distribution, we can determine precisely the meaning of any score; that is, we can tell where it falls in terms of the performance of the group as a whole.

Suppose we have developed a new aptitude test and a job applicant obtains a score of 60 on it. By itself, this figure tells us nothing about the aptitude level of this individual relative to all the others who applied for the job and took the same aptitude test. However, if we know that the distribution of test scores is normal, the mean of this distribution of test scores is 50, and the standard deviation is 10, the applicant's score of 60 (a distance of +1 SD from the mean) informs us that only 16% of the applicants in the sample scored higher than this person and that 84% scored lower. This can be verified by looking at Figure 2-10 and noting the percentage of cases above and below +1 SD.

There is a method by which any raw score in a distribution can be converted to a standard deviation score. In that way, we can interpret each raw score in the distribution. Also, the standard deviation allows us to compare the performance of individuals on two or more tests that utilize different scoring systems. By converting the distributions on all tests to standard deviation units, we can compare directly a person's performance on one test with his or her perform-ance on another test because the sets of scores will be expressed in the same terms.

The Relationship Between Two Variables: Correlation

Thus far, we have been concerned with the statistical treatment of one variable at a time, for example, a set of test scores from a group of job applicants. I/O psychologists are frequently concerned with the relationship between two or more variables. Any situation in which a prediction has to be made about whether a person is likely to succeed in a particular job involves matching two or more variables. We shall see many examples of this in the chapters on selection techniques. Any selection method must be matched with a later measure of actual job performance. That is the only way the personnel psychologist can determine if the selection method is picking the best person for the job. For instance, to determine if a particular test is of value in predicting the job success of crane operators, the psychologist would have to know how the test scores corresponded to a quantitative measure of success on the job. One statistical measure used to determine this relationship is the *correlation coefficient*.

The application of this statistical procedure tells the researcher two things about the relationship between variables: (1) the direction of the relationship and (2) the magnitude or strength of the relationship.

The direction of the relationship may be positive or negative, depending on whether high scores on one variable are accompanied by high or low scores on the other variable. To determine direction, both variables are plotted on a *scattergram*. The scattergram in Figure 2-11 shows the relationship between test scores of job applicants and their supervisor's ratings after some time on the job.

Figure 2-11 shows that as the test scores increased, so did the ratings; that is, those who had higher test scores as applicants consistently received higher ratings from their supervisors on actual job performance. This example illustrates a relationship that approaches a perfect positive correlation. A test score of 20 will likely be accompanied by a rating of 1, a test score of 100 by a rating of 5. By obtaining an applicant's test score, a personnel manager can predict with a great deal of accuracy the rating that person will later receive from a supervisor.

Through the use of a statistical formula for the correlation coefficient, it is possible to calculate in numerical terms the direction and the intensity or strength of this relationship. The correlation coefficient from the data in Figure 2-11 is +.95; a perfect positive correlation is +1.00. Positive correlations never exceed the value of +1.00. Thus, the magnitude of a positive relationship can be expressed by a number ranging anywhere from zero to +1.00.

Not all relationships are perfect or positive. Consider the scattergrams in Figures 2-12 and 2-13.

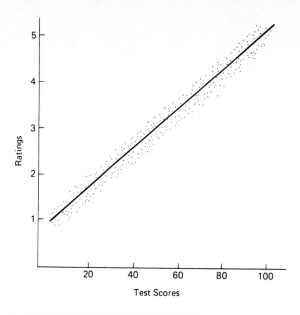

Figure 2-11 Positive correlation.

The negative correlation shown in Figure 2-12 indicates that as the test scores increase, job ratings decrease. Negative correlation coefficients range from zero to −1.00. It is important to remember that a correlation coefficient of −1.00 indicates just as strong a relationship or correspondence as a coefficient of +1.00. Only the direction is different. In both cases, performance on one

Figure 2-12 Negative correlation.

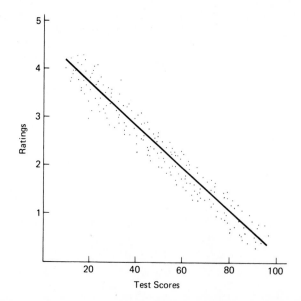

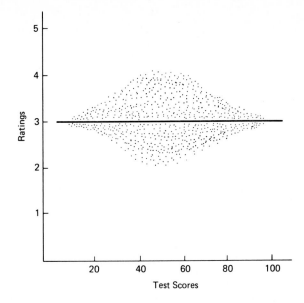

Figure 2-13 Zero correlation.

variable (for example, job ratings) can be predicted from performance on the other variable (for example, applicants' test scores).

Figure 2-13 depicts data with a correlation coefficient of zero; there is no predictive relationship between the two variables. Some people with low test scores received high ratings; some people with high test scores received low ratings.

The closer the correlation coefficient is to +1.00 or −1.00, the more accurately we can predict performance on one variable from performance on the other. Correlation is a valuable and widely used tool in psychology, and its applications in industrial psychology are numerous.

Inferential Statistics

In the typical psychological experiment, researchers are interested in comparing the performance levels of at least two groups: the experimental and the control groups. For example, in an experiment to test the value of a new method of training, the experimental group, which has had the training, is compared with the control group, which has not been exposed to the new method of training. An important decision rests on the basis of this comparison: Should this training method be recommended for the entire plant? The decision hinges on the size of the difference between the two groups on the dependent variable (job performance).

But how do psychologists know when the difference between the two groups is large enough to justify the cost of setting up a new training program? They must first determine the level of *statistical significance* of the difference between the means of the two groups. The answer is in terms of probabilities rather than certainties. The problem is this: Is the difference between the means of the two groups large enough so that it is unlikely that it could have occurred by chance?

Applying statistical techniques to the data from the experimental and control groups, we can calculate a probability value for the difference between the means. This figure represents the probability that this difference could have occurred by chance. Psychologists have arbitrarily established two levels of significance: a probability (p) of .05 and a p of .01.

Achieving a p value of .01 means that a difference as large as that obtained in the experiment would occur by chance only 1 time out of every 100. A difference of this level of significance can be attributed to the new training method used with the experimental group and not merely to chance. If the difference had reached a p value of .05, we would have a little less confidence in our results because this would indicate that there was a probability of 5 in 100 that the difference could have occurred by chance.

We can have greater confidence in findings that reach the .01 level of significance, but whatever level of significance is reached, this statistical tool gives the psychologist a firm basis on which to make the decision about the new training program. Note that statistical significance will not guarantee the success of the program, but it does allow the psychologist to make a more informed judgment. The use of statistics does not eliminate the need for decision making; it helps to guide the researcher in that task. Statistical tools are means to an end, not an end in themselves.

Summary

Knowledge of the **research methods** used by I/O psychologists is important to you in your working career. As a manager in an organization you will be working with the findings of psychologists and perhaps deciding whether a specific psychological research program should be supported. You can better understand the contributions of psychologists if you first understand how they work.

There are several requirements of psychological research: observations must be **objective, well controlled** and systematic, and capable of duplication and **verifiability**. These requirements are difficult to satisfy in psychological research, but their achievement is vital.

There are certain limitations to psychological research: Not every problem in human behavior can be investigated by psychological research (some are too complex or potentially dangerous); the act of observing some behaviors may interfere with or change them; the novelty of any change (the **Hawthorne effect**) may alter behavior more than the actual change itself; and some research must be conducted in artificial settings (this may limit the generalizability of the findings).

There are three methods of conducting psychological research in industry: the experimental method, the naturalistic observation method, and survey methods.

The essence of the **experimental method** is to investigate one influencing variable at a time while holding the other variables constant. The variable being investigated is called the **independent variable** and the resulting behavior is called the **dependent variable**. To conduct an experiment properly, the subjects must be divided into two groups: the **experimental group** and the **control group**. The groups must be as similar as possible. This similarity is brought about by random group design (subjects are assigned at random to the two groups) or by matched group design (subjects in the two groups are evenly matched on personal characteristics).

The method of **naturalistic observation** involves observing behavior in the real world. The experimenter has control over the independent variables but cannot manipulate them as can be done under laboratory conditions. Although not as desirable as the experimental method, naturalistic observation does offer the advantage of studying behavior under realistic conditions.

Survey methods of research focus on our attitudes and opinions. Three survey techniques are personal interviews, telephone surveys, and mail surveys. A new type of mail survey involves **electronic mail**, in which questions are asked and responses obtained through a company's in-house computer system. The personal interview is the most expensive and time-consuming method, but it offers the possibility of securing the most useful information.

Two styles of question are used in surveys: **open end** and **fixed alternative**. The latter restricts the respondents to a few choices rather than allowing them to answer the questions fully in their own words.

Representative samples of people to be questioned may be selected by **probability sampling** (each person in the population has a known probability of being included in the sample) or by **quota sampling** (constructing a duplicate, in miniature, of the larger population).

Once data have been collected, they must be analyzed and interpreted by means of statistical techniques. Large amounts of raw data can be summarized and described by **descriptive statistics**. Data can be presented in graphic form or reduced to a single number that adequately describes them. Three ways of measuring the central tendency of a distribution of data are the **mean, median,** and **mode**.

When sufficient data are collected from a representative sample of the population, they form a bell-shaped distribution, called a **normal curve**, in which most of the scores fall in the center or average range.

To measure the **variability** of a distribution, researchers use the **standard deviation (SD)**, a distance along the baseline of a distribution. The standard deviation provides information on the percentage of scores that lie above and below any raw score.

The **correlation coefficient** is a means of determining the direction and strength of the relationship between two variables. Correlation coefficients range from −1.00 (a perfect negative relationship) through zero to +1.00 (a perfect positive relationship) and enable us to predict performance on one variable from performance on another variable.

Inferential statistics are used to determine the level of **statistical significance** of the difference between the means of two groups by indicating whether the difference is large enough so that it is unlikely that it occurred by chance. Psychologists use two levels of significance: a probability of .05 (5 chances in 100 that the difference occurred by chance) and a probability of .01 (1 chance in 100 that the difference occurred by chance).

Key Terms

control group
correlation
correlation coefficient
dependent variable
descriptive statistics
experimental group
experimental method
fixed-alternative
   survey questions
independent variable
inferential statistics

mean
median
mode
naturalistic
   observation
normal curve of
   distribution
observational method
open-end survey
   questions
probability

probability sampling
psychometrics
quota sampling
sampling methods
scientific method
standard deviation (SD)
statistical significance
survey research
   methods
variability

Additional Reading

Gallup, G., Jr. (1988). Survey research: Current problems and future opportunities. *Journal of Consumer Marketing, 5*(1), 27–30. A review of past accomplishments, current problems, and future trends in survey research by the president of The Gallup Poll.

McCall, R. B. (1986). *Fundamental Statistics for Behavioral Sciences* (4th ed.). San Diego: Harcourt Brace Jovanovich. A clearly written introductory textbook on statistical methods and research design.

PART II

Personnel Psychology

T he areas of application that are generally called *personnel psychology* include the many activities involved in selecting, training, and evaluating new and current employees. Persons applying for a job undergo an extensive selection process; an organization may use techniques ranging from application blanks to sophisticated psychological tests. Once hired, new employees must be trained to perform their jobs efficiently.

The same selection and training principles and techniques are used when persons are being considered for promotion within the organization for which they work. The same process of matching employees' abilities and skills with the job's requirements and demands must be undertaken, and employees who are promoted to more responsible jobs must be trained for their new roles.

The performance of all employees—the newly hired and those who have been on the job for some time—must be objectively and fairly evaluated periodically. These appraisals serve three purposes, one of which relates to selection and training.

1. Performance appraisals provide information to the organization about the effectiveness of their selection and training procedures. In other words, the evaluations will indicate if the right kind of person is being hired and if he or she is being trained in the most appropriate way.
2. Performance appraisals provide information about how well an employee is doing the job. This information helps the organization make the difficult decisions about salary increases, promotions, demotions, and terminations.
3. Performance appraisals provide feedback to the employee about his or her progress on the job. By becoming aware of personal strengths and weaknesses, the employee can be guided in his or her growth and development as an individual and as an employee.

You can see how important selection, training, and evaluation activities are and how they can determine the kind of work we do and the way in which we do it. These are among the original activities of I/O psychologists and still form a substantial part of the field.

Chapters 3 and 4 are devoted to problems of selection. Chapter 3 discusses the general principles, processes, and problems of selection and basic selection techniques (application blanks, interviews, letters of recommendation, and assessment centers). Chapter 4 is concerned with the use of psychological tests for selection purposes. Problems and methods of evaluating work performance are discussed in Chapter 5, and principles and techniques of training are considered in Chapter 6.

Chapter 3

Employee Selection 1: Principles and Techniques

Introduction

When you leave college and take a job, there is a 50% chance that you will quit that job within 5 years. However pessimistic that may sound, it does reflect the reality of the employment situation. For a variety of reasons, fully half the students in your college graduating class will not find enough satisfaction in their work to stay with the first organization they join (Keller & Piotrowski, 1987; Nicholson & Glynn-Jones, 1987). They may find the job to be quite different from what they were told by a company recruiter, a fancy brochure, or a personnel department. Or they may find that their own abilities and characteristics are not what they had thought them to be or that they are temperamentally, intellectually, or socially unsuited to a particular kind of work.

Whatever the reasons may be for dissatisfaction with the job and irrespective of where the fault may lie, it is an unfortunate and disheartening situation in which both the individual and the organization are losers. And this situation emphasizes the importance of employee selection principles and practices. Improper matching of the person and the job, of the person's abilities and characteristics and the job's demands and requirements, leads to disharmony and unhappiness in the work situation. Much of this discontent may be unnecessary. Selection techniques are available that are capable of closely matching the person and the job, but these techniques must be used wisely and well by both participants in the selection process: the employing organizations and those who apply for work.

Selection is not limited to the world of work. Throughout our lives, from infancy to old age, we are involved in the process of selection. Sometimes we are the ones being selected; other times we do the selecting. We are selected as playmates, friends, teammates, lovers, and club members, and, at the same time, we select those with whom we choose to socialize or work or play.

In these everyday situations, selection is usually based on subjective factors—the way a person looks, acts, or dresses—without any attempt to make a systematic and thorough evaluation of the qualifications and abilities of the person being selected. Unfortunately, this kind of careless and haphazard selection process still occurs in some employing organizations. Some business leaders believe that they can size up candidates for a job by the strength of a handshake, manner of dress, or some other equally subjective and worthless criterion.

Because improper selection is so costly, management must make better use of all available psychological tools and techniques to ensure that the majority of those who are hired will work to the ultimate advantage of themselves and their organization.

However, even before you enter the personnel office of a potential employer, before you fill out an application blank or take a psychological test, certain preselection processes and problems will influence your choice of job. Some preselection factors are internal, for example, your own preferences and expectancies about what you want in a job and what a particular job or organization will be like. Other factors are external, such as the nature of the recruiting effort that brings you in touch with an organization and how much realistic information you are given about the job and the company.

The study of these highly influential preselection factors is a growing area of I/O psychology and may best be described as problems of *organizational entry*.

Organizational Entry

Your first job after college, your entry into that organization, is of immense importance to you not only for the immediate satisfactions it brings (or fails to bring) but also for long-term satisfactions. Just as the nature of your first love affair can influence your subsequent emotional relationships, so, too, your first job experience can influence your expectations for future jobs and your performance throughout your working career. An unfortunate first love affair or first job can affect all similar experiences for some time to come.

This effect has been demonstrated in the world of work by research on the amount of challenge in a person's first job. It has been shown that the degree of challenge in the first job has a significant impact on a person's career commitment and level of success (Arnold, 1986; McCall, 1988). The positive impact of the initial job challenge has been found to stimulate employees to perform at high levels throughout their careers. This, in turn, leads to greater success. Initial job challenge also causes employees to become more involved with their jobs, to have greater motivation, and to maintain a higher level of technical competence. This important relationship between the level of initial job challenge and later success has been demonstrated in a variety of organizations—government agencies, automobile manufacturers, and communications firms, among others—and in a variety of occupations (Super & Hall, 1978; Thayer, 1983).

Finding the right degree of challenge, then, is a major aspect of your own organizational entry. It is vital that the amount of challenge offered by your first job live up to your expectations and preferences. Indeed, it is important for both you and your employer that everything about your initial job comes close to satisfying your preferences; that is why employing organizations should try to learn something about the expectations of potential employees.

Employee Preferences

What will you be looking for in your first job? What aspects of the employment situation are important to you? Salary? Security? Fringe benefits? Working hours? The degree of challenge? Although there may be a single answer for you as an individual, there is no single answer for all employees. It is obvious that college graduates may have different job preferences from high school graduates, who, in turn, have different preferences and expectancies from those who did not complete high school.

Then, too, not all college graduates have the same preferences. Engineering majors differ from liberal arts majors and *A* students differ from *C* students. Employee preferences also change as a function of the general economic climate. In a time of economic hardship when jobs are hard to obtain, new employees may be interested primarily in job security. In better economic times when jobs are plentiful, factors such as meaningful work or opportunities to develop new skills may rank higher than security or pay.

Thus, preferences can change over time. Consider the changes that occurred over a 10-year period in what white male workers said they wanted from their jobs, as shown in Table 3-1 (Weaver & Matthews, 1987). As you can see, the preference for important and meaningful work, although the leading choice in both time periods, declined in importance in the 1980s. However, it declined among white-collar workers but not blue-collar workers. The importance of pay increased from the 1970s to the 1980s, superseding chances for advancement as the second most important job preference for both white- and blue-collar workers. As we shall see in Chapter 8, pay has become even more important for today's younger workers.

A different set of preferences was revealed in a survey of technical and managerial employees in a research laboratory at the DuPont Company, as shown in Table 3-2 (Nusbaum, 1986). Notice that pay, the second most important preference in the survey of white- and blue-collar workers (Table 3-1), was only fifth in importance with the higher-level technical and managerial employees. Yet, when the supervisors of these DuPont employees were asked what they thought was most important to their employees, they listed pay first, and interesting work fifth. Obviously, the supervisors were unaware of the job preferences and needs of their employees.

When personnel and training executives—people whose job it is to select and train new employees—were asked what they thought workers wanted from their jobs, they listed more job satisfaction (36%), job security (18%), more money (17%), better benefits (12%), and opportunities for promotion (6%) ("Job Satisfaction," 1988).

TABLE 3-1   Job Characteristics Preferred by White Male Workers (percentages)

	1973–1974	*1982–1984*
Important and meaningful work	53	48
High income (pay)	16	22
Chances for advancement	18	19
No danger of being fired	8	8
Short work hours and much free time	5	3

Adapted from "What White Males Want from Their Jobs: Ten Years Later" by C. N. Weaver & M. D. Matthews, 1987, *Personnel, 64*(9), p. 62.

TABLE 3-2   Job Preferences of Technical and Managerial Employees

Employee ranking (most to least important)	Preference
1	Interesting work
2	Appreciation
3	Feeling of being in on things
4	Security
5	Pay
6	Promotion and growth
7	Good working conditions
8	Personal loyalty from employer/supervisor
9	Sympathetic help on personal problems
10	Tactful discipline

Adapted from "The Career Development Program at DuPont's Pioneering Research Laboratory" by H. J. Nusbaum, 1986, *Personnel, 63*(9), p. 71.

Still other job preferences have been recorded in different cultures. A survey taken in the Soviet Union of people between the ages of 16 and 19, and another of male middle-aged managers in China, revealed the following preferences, from most to least important:

Russian adolescents: Interesting work, a friendly place to work, good pay, satisfaction from the job itself, and mastery of occupational skills (Phillips & Benson, 1983).

Chinese managers: Making a contribution to the company, having cooperative co-workers, autonomy, job training, and efficiency (Shenkar & Ronen, 1987).

Knowledge of job preferences is important to employing organizations and is an integral part of research on organizational entry. Unless the preferences and expectancies of potential employees are satisfied on the job, the work force is likely to become frustrated, bored, and unhappy. Research has shown that many people enter an organization with unrealistic or inflated expectations about the nature of the job and the organization. These findings help to explain why so many people leave their first job: The discrepancy between expectations and reality is too great (Greenhaus & Brenner, 1982).

The place where your expectancies begin to meet the realities of an organization, the point at which you have your first contact with a potential employer, is in your initial meeting with a company recruiter. This marks the first opportunity for each to size up the other, an extremely important step in the preselection processes of organizational entry.

The Recruitment Process

The number of recruiting sources available to organizations is varied. Surveys of the recruiting practices of large American corporations reveal that 85% use help wanted ads in newspapers, 70% use referrals from their own employees, and 52% use personnel agencies ("It's Not Who," 1988). Other sources include the placement services of professional associations, job fairs, and outplacement services of competitors who have had to lay off employees. Some companies offer cash bonuses and other incentives to workers who recruit job applicants. One company, American Tool and Die, found this procedure to be so successful that the turnover rate among new employees dropped from 27% to 4%. Other companies have found that using referrals from their employees to recruit new workers reduced the average cost of new hires by as much as 50% (Glickstein & Ramer, 1988). Research by personnel psychologists shows that the worst sources of job applicants are newspaper ads and employment agencies, neither of which, as a rule, supplies realistic information about the job (Schwab, 1982; Taylor & Schmidt, 1983).

Another popular source of recruiting is the college campus. Almost half of all large corporations conduct college recruiting programs, and approximately 50% of all managers and professional employees who have been working for fewer than 3 years were initially recruited at college (Blocklyn, 1988a; Rynes & Boudreau, 1986).

The college recruitment process is the most relevant to your own future career because this may well be the procedure through which you find your first postcollege job. The company recruiter is likely to be the first representative of the organization with whom you will meet. In a very real sense, then, that recruiter *is* the organization. You will likely judge the nature of the company by your image of and reaction to the recruiter.

College recruiting is of immense importance to employing organizations. Many thousands of dollars and hours of time are expended on it, and it is, as we noted, one of the most common recruitment sources for positions at beginning managerial and professional levels.

I/O psychologists have conducted much research on the characteristics and behavior of recruiters to determine how these influence college seniors in their choice of jobs. Those recruiter behaviors likely to induce graduating seniors to accept a job offer include nondirective counseling behaviors (smiling, nodding, and maintaining eye contact), empathy and warmth, thoughtfulness, perceived competence, and personableness (Harn & Thornton, 1985; Harris & Fink, 1987; Liden & Parsons 1986).

In addition, college senior job applicants who were interviewed by older recruiters, women recruiters, and representatives of personnel departments (instead of representatives of the department for which the new employee would work), were less likely to accept a job offer. College men showed the same likelihood of job acceptance whether their recruiters were men or women. Women applicants, on the other hand, were much more likely to accept a job offer when the company recruiter was a man rather than a woman (Taylor & Bergmann, 1987).

Almost half of all large corporations recruit employees on college campuses.

Some companies are questioning the effectiveness of their college recruiting programs, however. The cost of recruiting a new college graduate is equal to one third of his or her first year's salary, and research shows that many new employees recruited on college campuses perform at a lower level and hold more negative attitudes toward their job than graduates recruited in other ways (Bergmann & Taylor, 1984). In addition, it has been found that applicants tend to obtain more specific, accurate, and useful information about a prospective employer from friends who already work there than from a company recruiter (Anderson & Shackleton, 1986).

One reason why college recruiting may not be living up to its potential is that fewer than half of all company recruiters receive training in techniques of interviewing job applicants. Those who do receive training get, on the average, only 13 hours (Rynes & Boudreau, 1986). This may help explain another finding: Most recruiters reach a conclusion about a candidate's suitability for their organization within the first 2 or 3 minutes of an interview, hardly sufficient time to collect enough information about a person on which to base such an important decision (Seidel & Powell, 1983).

Other research on college recruiters shows that they seldom agree with one another about the topics that should be covered in an interview, and they consistently fail to discuss issues they consider to be important. Both of these tendencies reflect the lack of training in interviewing techniques (Taylor & Sniezek, 1984).

Despite the time, money, and effort companies devote to college recruiting, the activity generally has a low status within organizations and suffers from little involvement or interest on the part of upper-level executives. In addition, only 7% of companies involved in college recruiting make any effort to assess empirically the value of their recruitment programs. Thus, most companies have no objective indication of how well or how poorly their recruiting activities work (Rynes & Boudreau, 1986).

We have discussed what applicants prefer or expect in their first jobs, what they are looking for as they enter the world of work. What are employing organizations seeking in the college seniors they so actively recruit? What are the corporate preferences and expectations?

A survey of companies recruiting on college campuses revealed the 10 most important characteristics they look for among college seniors (Hafer & Hoth, 1983). These characteristics, in order of importance, are shown in the left column of Table 3-3. The right column shows the 10 characteristics college seniors *thought* the companies were interested in.

As you can see, except for the first two items, major disagreement exists between a company's needs and the students' opinions of those needs. Organizations place a greater emphasis on initiative, assertiveness, loyalty, and leadership than the students believed. On the other hand, the college seniors thought that the companies would be more interested in their enthusiasm, appearance, and previous work experience than was actually the case.

TABLE 3-3   Employee Characteristics Preferred by Organizations and College Students

Companies	*Students*
1. Oral communication skills	1. Oral communication skills
2. Motivation	2. Motivation
3. Initiative	3. Enthusiasm
4. Assertiveness	4. Appearance
5. Loyalty	5. Work experience
6. Leadership skills	6. Written communication skills
7. Maturity	7. Maturity
8. Enthusiasm	8. Initiative, assertiveness, loyalty
9. Punctuality	9. Punctuality
10. Appearance	10. Leadership skills

Adapted from "Selection Characteristics: Your Priorities and How Students Perceive Them" by J. C. Hafer & C. C. Hoth, 1983, *Personnel Administrator, 28*(3), p. 27.

The gap between these two sets of beliefs reflects a larger problem that college campus recruiters face: finding candidates who have a realistic view of the world of work. This is another reason why college recruiting does not produce the most desirable results. As noted, half of all college graduates leave their first job within 5 years.

Part of the reason for dissatisfaction on the part of new graduates can be traced to their initial contact with the company: the campus recruitment interview. Many students obtain a false picture of the company during this interview and of their possible role in it. This is sometimes attributable to the students' naïveté; they do not really know what questions to ask the recruiter because they have had no experience in corporate life. Also, students want to present the best possible image of themselves and may tend to hide weaknesses, attitudes, or ideals they think the recruiter may not like and to emphasize characteristics they think recruiters are looking for. Another reason for the misleading view, however, is the fault of the recruiters. Their job is to find people with promise for their company and, to accomplish this, they all too often paint an idealized picture of the organization and of the graduates' first job in it. "When I interview," one recruiter said, "I say good things about my job no matter how I really feel" (Sutton & Louis, 1987, p. 353).

Both sides, then, are guilty of presenting false images of what each has to offer, and the result is likely to be disaffection when each side turns out to be less than perfect. The obvious solution is greater frankness and honesty, with each party presenting both good and bad points. Some organizations have recognized this problem and are striving to present applicants with a realistic preview of the job as part of their organizational entry procedures.

Realistic Job Previews

Realistic job previews provide information that is as accurate as possible about all aspects of a job. Such information is supplied through a written description of the job, a film or videotape presentation, or a sample of the actual work itself to see if applicants can perform the required tasks. The purpose of realistic job previews is to acquaint prospective employees with both positive and negative aspects of the job that might not have been previously known to them. The idea behind this approach is that it will reduce overly optimistic or unrealistic expectations about what a job involves.

Beginning in the late 1970s, there was considerable excitement about the benefits of realistic job previews, and, for a time, it seemed that companies had found an easy and reliable technique for reducing turnover and job dissatisfaction among newly hired employees (Reilly, Brown, Blood, & Malatesta, 1981; Wanous, 1980).

One of the first companies to offer realistic job previews was Sears, Roebuck, which enlightened prospective employees about disadvantages as well as advantages of working for their company. Candidates were told bluntly about long and erratic work hours, frequent transfers, and the hectic pace. Nothing was hidden from potential employees. As a result, fewer of those recruited and offered jobs actually accepted them, but the management of the company believed that they were hiring better people than before. Recruits who did accept the positions knew what to expect. The less desirable aspects of their first job came as no surprise. Further, applicants who did not like working under the conditions described to them could turn down the job offer instead of accepting it and finding that they wanted to quit after a year or so. This is certainly to the advantage of both the employee and the employer. The college students recruited by Sears reported that they liked the procedure. One said, "They treat us with respect. That's a lot more than you get at most companies."

Another company to use realistic job previews was the Southern New England Telephone Company. Prospective telephone operators were shown a film in which current operators described the positive and negative aspects of their jobs as truthfully as possible. (There were twice as many negative comments as positive ones!)

More recent research has dampened the initial burst of enthusiasm about realistic job previews. The results of the technique may not be as impressive as they had once seemed (Meglino & DeNisi, 1987). However, realistic job previews are still a worthwhile addition to the recruiting phase of the personnel selection process. Research indicates that the technique only modestly influences job performance and job satisfaction, but it does seem to decrease turnover among new employees, particularly in more complex jobs (Guion & Gibson, 1988; Robertson & Makin, 1986).

Also, the effectiveness of such previews may vary with the method of presentation. Written material about a job's advantages and disadvantages seems to be more effective than an oral presentation of the same information (Dean & Wanous, 1984; Wanous, 1983).

Providing some form of realistic job preview is advantageous to both recruits and employers. Applicants know what they are getting into, their expectations about the job will more closely match reality, and they are much less likely to experience the disappointment and frustration that often result when people begin a job and find it quite different from what they were told. In recruiting, honesty is indeed the best policy.

After the recruiting process has been completed and applicants and organizations have each decided that the other may match their expectancies, it is time for the actual selection process to begin.

An Overview of the Selection Process

There is more to proper selection methodology than simply putting an advertisement in the newspaper, having those who appear in the personnel office fill out an application blank, and questioning them in a 10-minute interview. A proper selection program involves a number of additional steps between company and applicant.

Suppose a personnel manager (sometimes called a human resources manager) finds that 200 new employees must be hired to operate the highly complex machinery that will be required to produce a new product. How can these new workers be found?

First, the nature of the job for which employees are being sought must be thoroughly investigated. The company will not know what abilities to look for in potential employees unless it is known in detail what they will be expected to do to perform the job successfully. A process known as *job analysis* is undertaken to determine the specific skills and abilities necessary to the job. Then, from an analysis of the job, it is possible to develop an analysis of the potential worker.

Once the personnel manager knows the qualifications that must be sought in the applicants, the most effective means of identifying these characteristics must be determined. Does the job require the ability to read blueprints? Does it require experience with a particular type of machinery? Must the worker be a high school graduate? Does the work require excellent vision or a high level of intelligence or mechanical ability? What are the most efficient ways of finding out this information?

The necessary skill and background characteristics, determined from the job and worker analyses, must be assessed in each applicant. Cutoff scores or levels for the various abilities are established; that is, a minimal score on a test or a fixed number of years of experience is proposed, and no one is hired who falls below this level. It may be necessary to determine cutoff scores by conducting a research program to study current workers in the same or a similar job.

Recruitment decisions follow. How should the company recruit new employees: through ads in newspapers or trade journals, through an employment agency, or through referrals by its own employees?

How many potential employees are obtained by the recruiting program? This affects the caliber of those who are finally hired. For example, if there are only 250 applicants for the 200 jobs, the personnel manager must be less discriminating in hiring than if there are 400 applicants to choose from. Psychologists speak of this as the *selection ratio*, the relationship between the number of people to be hired and the number of people who are available to be hired. The available labor supply directly influences the stringency of the requirements established for the job. If there is a shortage of applicants and the jobs must be filled in a few weeks, some requirements (perhaps the cutoff score on an intelligence test or the level of education) will have to be lowered.

The actual selection from among the job applicants, classifying them as suitable or unsuitable, can be accomplished by a variety of techniques. This chapter considers, among others, interviews, application blanks, letters of recommendation, and assessment centers. As a rule, hiring decisions are not based on a single technique but on a combination of methods. For example, a large computer firm uses the following sequence of six steps to determine if an applicant should be offered a position:

1. *Preliminary interview.* An initial look at an applicant in a preliminary interview is a rough screening device that provides a general impression of the individual. From this, a decision is made whether the applicant has the general characteristics and qualifications to warrant further consideration.

2. *Application blank.* Those who pass the general screening complete a formal application blank that provides detailed background information on personal characteristics, employment history, and education.

3. *Employment tests.* Psychological tests are administered to those who appear from their application blanks to be qualified. The tests determine specific abilities, aptitudes, and characteristics that range from tests of typing ability for secretaries to tests of personality and cognitive ability for managers.

4. *Final interview.* Based on the considerable information now available on the applicant, detailed and insightful questions are prepared for an intensive structured interview. The applicant may be questioned by more than one member of the company so that several impressions can be obtained and compared.

5. *References.* If the person has successfully completed all these steps, the personal and business references named by the applicant are contacted. The purpose is to determine the level of performance in past jobs.

6. *Physical examination.* Because some jobs have demanding physical requirements, the applicant may be examined by a physician. Most companies have minimum medical standards for all jobs in their organization. In addition, because of the current concern about the use of drugs in the workplace, more companies are conducting drug tests of job applicants. Between 1986 and 1987 the number of companies requiring drug tests increased by 74%. (Drug testing is discussed in more detail in Chapter 12.) Also, because of the concern about AIDS in the workplace, some organizations are now requiring tests for the AIDS antibodies (Greenberg, 1988). Genetic screening, which can predict a person's likelihood of developing a certain disease, is expected to be commercially available by the mid-1990s and may be used, for example, to identify applicants who are sensitive to certain chemicals found in some work environments. Still in the research stage are tests based on brain waves that may be used to predict a disposition toward a certain illness (Office of Technology Assessment, 1987).

These selection procedures are complex and costly, but, in the long run, they are less complex and costly than selecting the wrong person for the job. It is better to find out before hiring who is not suitable for a position than to find out after that person has been hired, trained, and become an unhappy and unsatisfactory employee.

Next in the selection process is the testing of the selection procedures themselves. After the initial 200 workers in our example have been hired, the personnel manager must find out how many of them succeed on the job. Successful job performance is a major test of the worth of a selection program.

Every new selection program must be investigated to determine its predictive accuracy or validity. This can be done by evaluating the performance of the employees selected by the new procedures. For example, after 6 months, we can ask the supervisors of our 200 new workers to rate them on how well they do their job. We compare these ratings with their performance on the selection procedures to see how well the two measures correlate. Were the selection procedures capable of predicting who among the applicants turned out to be the better workers?

Suppose we learn that all those who received high ratings from their supervisors had performed very well on the psychological tests used for selection and that they all possessed similar background factors such as level of education. If those who received low supervisor ratings had performed poorly on those same selection measures, we then have evidence that our selection methods discriminate between potentially good employees and potentially poor ones. The selection techniques can be used with confidence in the future to find the right kind of person for this job. To evaluate the selection process, however, we must have some criteria of job performance to compare with performance in the selection situation. The ways of determining such criteria—methods of performance or work appraisal—are discussed in Chapter 5.

If the correlation between selection and job performance is very low, different selection procedures will be required, and the entire process must be begun again. The development of a sound selection system requires a great deal of skill on the part of the personnel psychologist and money and patience on the part of management.

The Challenge of Fair Employment

Successful selection has been rendered even more challenging in recent years by the requirements of the Equal Employment Opportunity Commission (EEOC). All job applicants, regardless of race, religion, sex, or national origin, must be given equal opportunities for employment. This problem has special relevance for members of minority groups. It has been alleged that some of the selection procedures used by employing organizations discriminate against educationally and culturally deprived individuals. Not only is such discrimination unethical and immoral, but it is also illegal. The Civil Rights Act of 1964 and the enforced guidelines of the EEOC (established in 1972) have declared it against the law to discriminate against job applicants.

Title VII, Section 703, of the Civil Rights Act states, "It shall be an unlawful employment practice for an employer to fail or refuse to hire or to discharge any individual, or otherwise to discriminate against any individual with respect to his compensation, terms, conditions, or privileges of employment, because of such individual's race, color, religion, sex, or national origin." The EEOC is empowered to bring legal action against any organization employing 15 or more persons that violates the provisions of Title VII.

Employment practices that have an *adverse impact* on any of the groups protected by Title VII are prohibited by law. When any minority group applying to an organization is treated markedly worse than the majority group then that minority group is said to be the target of adverse impact in the selection process. Any selection rate for a minority group that is less than 80% of the selection rate for the majority group is evidence of adverse impact. For example, say a company had 100 job applicants (50 whites and 50 blacks) and hired 50 persons

(40 whites and 10 blacks). In this case, 80% of the white applicants were hired but only 20% of the black applicants. Thus, the selection rate for blacks was one fourth of that for whites; this constitutes adverse impact. A company can be legally challenged for maintaining such a vastly different rejection rate for minority and majority groups.

As a result, employing organizations must try to ensure that all persons have equal access to job and training opportunities. Because of this legislation and increased social awareness, personnel departments have had to examine their screening procedures to ensure that a job applicant is not discriminated against because he or she is black, Hispanic, physically handicapped, or over a certain age, and, thus, may have had less opportunity to develop job and personal skills.

Suppose, for example, that a personnel department has established specific levels of arithmetic ability and verbal skill plus a high school diploma as requirements for a particular job. These requirements may disqualify certain minority-group members who may not have been able to complete high school for reasons having nothing to do with their mental ability. Similarly, some psychological tests may place a minority-group member at a disadvantage because he or she may have experienced cultural and educational deprivation.

To further equalize employment possibilities of minority groups, employers have been actively seeking minority job applicants. Recruiters are sent to predominantly black high schools and colleges, for example, instead of waiting for interested individuals to come to the personnel office.

The law requiring equal opportunity of employment has placed specific limitations on virtually all selection devices. Every method of selection should minimize adverse impact and be clearly related to performance on the job. The burden of proof rests on the employing organization. Personnel psychologists have put forth a great deal of effort to ensure that selection techniques are job related and that measures of job performance (against which selection techniques are validated) are as objective as possible. Later, we shall discuss the effect of this work on the use of psychological tests in selection (Chapter 4) and on the evaluation of job performance (Chapter 5). Interviews and application blanks are particularly affected. Psychologists and personnel departments are highly sensitive to what can and cannot be asked of a job applicant. Questions that might discriminate against minority-group members or women can result in lawsuits. Also, what is considered discriminatory varies among states, depending on the wording of each state's human rights laws.

To give you some idea of the kinds of questions that can no longer be asked of job applicants, consider the pre-employment questionnaire in Table 3-4 (Minter, 1972).

Only 3 of these 19 inquiries, numbers 6, 10, and 12, are considered to be lawful questions to ask a job applicant. A prospective employer can ask applicants if they are citizens of the United States (according to Title VII, they *must* ask this question), about their knowledge of foreign languages, and details of prior work experience. It is unlawful, at least in some states, to ask any of the other questions.

Let us examine some of these items to learn why they could be considered

TABLE 3-4   Pre-employment Questionnaire

Pre-employment inquiry	Lawful	Unlawful
1. Asking applicants if they have ever worked under another name.		✓
2. Asking applicants to name their birthplace.		✓
3. Asking for the birthplace of applicants' parents, spouse, or other close relatives.		✓
4. Asking applicants to submit proof of age by supplying birth certificate or baptismal record.		✓
5. Asking applicants for religious affiliation, name of church, parish, or religious holidays observed.		✓
6. Asking applicants if they are citizens of the United States.	✓	
7. Asking applicants if they are naturalized citizens.		✓
8. Asking applicants for the date their citizenship was acquired.		✓
9. Asking applicants if they have ever been arrested for any crime, and to indicate when and where.		✓
10. Asking applicants to indicate what foreign languages they can read, write, or speak fluently.	✓	
11. Asking applicants how they acquired the ability to read, write, or speak a foreign language.		✓
12. Asking applicants about their past work experience.	✓	
13. Requesting applicants to provide names of three relatives other than parents, spouse, or minor-age dependent children.		✓
14. Asking male applicants for their wives' maiden names.		✓
15. Asking applicants for their mothers' maiden names.		✓
16. Asking for the full names of the applicants' brothers and sisters.		✓
17. Asking applicants for a list of names of all clubs, societies, and lodges to which they belong.		✓
18. Asking applicants to include photographs with their applications for employment.		✓
19. Asking applicants to supply addresses of relatives such as cousins, uncles, aunts, nephews, nieces, or grandparents who can be contacted for references.		✓

Adapted from "Human Rights Laws and Pre-Employment Inquiries" by R. L. Minter, 1972, *Personnel Journal, 51*, p. 432.

discriminatory. Items 2, 3, 4, and 5 could easily identify the national origin, race, creed, or color of an applicant, as could items 7, 8, 13, 14, 15, and 16. Also, much of the information asked in these items has no bearing on the applicant's ability to perform the job for which he or she is being considered. Therefore, in addition to being possibly discriminatory, these questions serve no useful purpose in predicting the applicant's potential for success on the job.

It is considered unlawful to ask applicants if they have ever been arrested; minority-group members are much more likely to be arrested on suspicion, owing to the possible prejudices of arresting officers, and this should not be held against them. It *is* lawful, however, to ask applicants if they have ever been *convicted* of crimes. This could be relevant to job performance, for example, in the case of a person convicted of embezzlement who is applying for a job in a bank.

In addition to the discriminatory nature of some questions, there is the issue of personal privacy. Some authorities have suggested that job applicants leave blank any item on an application form that they consider to be irrelevant to the job for which they are applying, or to be an unfair invasion of their privacy (Harragan, 1983). Such behavior may be detrimental to their careers, however. In one study, managers viewed those applicants who did not answer application blank questions dealing with criminal convictions as being less suitable for employment than those who reported having no criminal convictions. The researchers noted that "a potential employer views a nonresponse to an application blank item as an attempt to conceal facts that would reflect poorly on an applicant" (Stone & Stone, 1987, p. 455).

Reverse Discrimination.   The impetus to hire and promote members of minority groups has sometimes resulted in discrimination against members of the majority group. For example, a company may be so intent on raising the number of women in its plant to meet federal guidelines that it denies job or promotion opportunities to men.

This phenomenon, known as *reverse discrimination*, has occurred frequently as organizations have tried to implement EEOC rulings. It has also occurred in graduate and professional schools, where white applicants have been denied admission in favor of minority-group applicants whose test scores or college boards may not have been as high as those of the white applicants.

The question of reverse discrimination is complex and controversial. The intent of Title VII was to prevent preferential treatment for *any* group. Yet, when any applicant, otherwise qualified, is denied educational or job opportunities because institutions must by law have more persons of a certain sex or ethnic background, those persons are also receiving preferential treatment, albeit of a negative kind.

The issue reached the U.S. Supreme Court in 1979, which ruled in favor of a company's racial quota for admission to a training program. A white employee who had been denied admission to the program sued the company, claiming that he had been discriminated against because of his race. He lost the case.

More recent Supreme Court decisions have sometimes upheld charges of reverse discrimination. These rulings have noted that the rights of majority groups must not be unnecessarily restrained in order to help minorities, and that minorities should not be hired or promoted simply on the basis of percentages or some other quota system. Rather, the Supreme Court ruled that only fully qualified minority employees should be hired or promoted (Greenlaw, 1988).

I/O research has consistently shown that disabled employees perform well on the job.

Other Types of Discrimination.   Discrimination in the job market does not involve only sex or race or national origin. Older workers and physically handicapped or disabled persons have also been treated unfairly in selection and promotion. Younger workers have traditionally been preferred, despite consistent evidence from I/O psychology research that older workers are at least as productive, and sometimes more so, as younger workers and have lower absenteeism and turnover rates (Giniger, Dispenzieri, & Eisenberg, 1984; Waldman & Avolio, 1986). A meta-analysis of 96 studies involving close to 39,000 employees found no relationship between age and job performance in both professional and nonprofessional jobs (McEvoy & Cascio, 1989). In addition, a survey of personnel managers showed that they reported older workers to be more loyal to the company and just as punctual as younger workers (Blocklyn, 1987). Other findings indicate that older workers do not, on the whole, suffer from poor health, diminished vigor, or declining mental abilities (H. E. Johnson, 1988).

The stereotypes of and discrimination against older workers persist. Older workers continue to receive more negative performance evaluations than younger workers, apparently more on the basis of age than actual work performance (Gordon, Rozelle, & Baxter, 1988). In one study, a group of hourly workers held a much more positive attitude toward older workers than did a group of supervisors. The supervisors viewed the older workers much less favorably, a finding that was identical to that of a similar study conducted 30 years earlier (Bird & Fisher, 1986). In other research, men interviewers gave older job applicants lower intelligence ratings and lower hiring recommendations, whereas women interviewers gave older job applicants lower ratings in attractiveness (Raza & Carpenter, 1987).

Older workers, like minorities, are now protected by law. The Age Discrimination in Employment Act of 1967 legislated against such discrimination against persons in the 40- to 65-year age bracket, a form of prejudice referred to as ageism. The act was amended in 1978 to raise the age at which employees could be forced to retire from 65 to 70. The argument in favor of the 1978 amendment was that depriving older people of the right to work was just as discriminatory as denying employment on the basis of sex or race. As a result of this legislation, the number of age-discrimination complaints filed with state and federal agencies has increased substantially. In 1979, over 5,000 such complaints were filed; by 1982, the number exceeded 19,000, and by 1986, it had risen to 27,000 (Faley, Kleiman, & Lengnick-Hall, 1984; Fritz, 1988a). In addition, the awards in age discrimination lawsuits have increased. Juries tend to be sympathetic to older workers who have been fired because of their age. The average award in such cases exceeds $300,000 (Marks, 1988).

Disabled employees are also protected by federal law against job discrimination. The Vocational Rehabilitation Act of 1973 made it mandatory for organizations to recruit, hire, and promote qualified handicapped persons. Some 36 million people in the United States have some mental or physical handicap, and many of them have found it difficult to secure employment because of the bias against them held by many employing organizations. The handicapped include not only persons with hearing, vision, motor, and mental disorders but also those with less visible conditions such as arthritis, diabetes, heart disease, cancer, and back problems. Together these groups constitute approximately 17% of all Americans of working age and some 7% of college freshmen (Asch, 1984; Feldman, 1988a). A study supporting the existence of this form of discrimination involved 50 employment agencies that were visited by a qualified job applicant (Johnson & Heal, 1976). In half of the visits, the applicant was in a wheelchair; in the other half, the applicant was ambulatory. The qualifications of the applicant were the same in both situations. The "handicapped" job applicant was given many fewer job interviews by the employment agencies and was actively discouraged from looking for routine employment.

This prejudice against hiring the handicapped worker is totally at variance with actual job performance. Research by personnel psychologists in a variety of organizations has consistently shown that handicapped employees perform at least as well as, and in many cases better than, nonhandicapped employees (Feldman, 1988a). Companies such as DuPont, 3M, McDonnell Douglas, Control Data Corporation, Sears, and Inland Steel have routinely hired handicapped workers because they make good employees (Pati & Morrison, 1982).

Great progress has been made in recent years in meeting the legal requirements of equal employment opportunity, but the problem remains a serious one. The social injustices committed by discrimination in hiring have not yet been fully eliminated, and they present moral, legal, and technical challenges for personnel psychologists.

The passage of the legislation described has reduced the amount of discrimination against certain well-defined groups in American society, but it has clearly not eliminated it. Research involving white men and women college students and managers in simulated employee selection situations showed that both groups gave higher evaluations to white candidates and recommended higher starting salaries for them than for black candidates. The managers in this research held middle- and upper-level positions with a variety of organizations and were actively involved in personnel selection. The students were junior and senior business administration majors (Barr & Hitt, 1986).

These students, but not the managers, also discriminated against women job applicants, offering them lower starting salaries than men applicants. Other studies confirm the existence of a hiring prejudice against women, particularly those applying for traditionally male jobs (Heilman, Martell, & Simon, 1988). However, overall, the research on sex bias has not produced *consistent* evidence of discrimination in hiring. The psychologists in one recent review of research noted that "there is marginal evidence of employment discrimination against females" (Olian, Schwab, & Haberfeld, 1988, p. 180).

No matter how much legislation is passed, however, it remains difficult to legislate changes in human attitudes or to prevent discrimination on the basis of personal characteristics or cultural stereotypes that are strongly ingrained.

Consider the attribute of physical attractiveness. Some job applicants have a more pleasing appearance than others in terms of generally accepted cultural standards. This type of judgment, referred to by some as "beautyism," also affects hiring and promotion decisions in the world of work. Many people believe that physically attractive persons also possess more desirable personal and social traits and will, therefore, be better qualified and more successful employees than less attractive persons (Hatfield & Sprecher, 1986). Research tends to support this idea. In one study, more attractive applicants were offered higher starting salaries than less attractive applicants, even though their qualifications, on paper, were identical (Dickey-Bryant, Lautenschlager, Mendoza, & Abrahams, 1986).

Another form of discrimination in hiring, which might be called "nationalism," occurs when one country's citizens are discriminated against by foreign-owned companies operating plants or offices in the host country. Japanese companies, such as Nissan and Honda, which have opened factories in the United States, are facing discrimination lawsuits from U.S. employees who claim that their nationality has prevented them from being hired for or promoted to upper levels of management. American companies in Japan face similar charges brought by Japanese employees (Fritz, 1988d).

Discrimination in hiring is also practiced between smokers and nonsmokers, liberals and conservatives, northerners and southerners, and against anyone whose manner of dress, speaking, or bearing may deviate from what the personnel office or the department head considers desirable.

Legislation cannot prevent all forms of discrimination. Only enlightened personnel practices and more objective selection procedures can do so. Personnel psychologists, as we shall see, have made substantial contributions to the solution of this problem.

Job Analysis

We have noted the steps involved in setting up a selection program. Let us now examine one of these steps—job analysis—more closely.

The purpose of job analysis is to describe, in specific terms, the precise nature of the component tasks performed by the workers on a particular job. Job analysis includes information on the kind of equipment or tools used, the operations performed, unique aspects of the job such as safety hazards, education or training required, pay scale, and so on. The value of job analysis in personnel selection has already been mentioned. Unless the company knows exactly what is required for the successful performance of a job, it will have no way of knowing what qualities to seek in applicants for that job.

Job analysis also has other important uses in organizational life (Grant, 1988b; Levine, Thomas, & Sistrunk, 1988). To establish a training program for a particular job, for example, the nature of the job must be known; a company cannot expect to train a person to perform a job unless the specific tasks, steps, and operations necessary for job success are known. Job analysis can aid in efforts to design a job so that it can be performed more efficiently. An analysis might reveal, for example, that a lathe operator has to walk 25 feet from the machine each time he or she needs to replenish the supply of raw material. This wasted time and effort can be easily eliminated, but it might never have been noticed by management had the job not been analyzed. Job analysis can also reveal safety hazards in equipment or operating procedures and suggest equipment-design changes for greater efficiency.

There are a number of techniques for conducting a job analysis (Ash, Levine, & Sistrunk, 1983; Levine, Sistrunk, McNutt, & Gael, 1988). An investigator might look for *published analyses* of similar jobs. There are limitations to this approach, however, because the other jobs, no matter how similar, will most likely not be identical to the one in question. A standard and comprehensive list of jobs is found in the *Dictionary of Occupational Titles* (DOT), produced by the Employment and Training Administration of the U.S. Department of Labor. This periodically revised work defines briefly some 22,000 jobs. The definitions are concise and not as detailed or comprehensive as a job analysis must be, but they do serve to familiarize researchers with the general form of any job. A few of these job definitions are listed in Table 3-5.

There are often additional job analyses already available on which investigators can draw. In a large organization, it is likely that the same or similar jobs have been analyzed in the past. Although such investigations cannot be applied directly to the current analysis, they can provide useful information.

Techniques for conducting job analyses include interviews, questionnaires,

---

TABLE 3-5   Sample Job Descriptions

Bowling-Ball Finisher
  Tends buffing machine that removes scratches and polishes surface of bowling balls.
Clip Coater
  Coats tips of sunglass clips with protective plastic and cures coated clips in oven.
Dog Bather
  Bathes dogs in preparation for grooming.
Maturity Checker
  Tends machine that mashes peas and registers force required to crush them to ascertain hardness (maturity) and grades peas.
Potato-Chip Sorter
  Observes potato chips on conveyor and removes chips that are burned, discolored, or broken.
Sequins Stringer
  Strings plastic sequins on thread for use as decoration on wearing apparel.
Squeak, Rattle, and Leak Repairer
  Drives automobiles of service customers to determine origin of noises and leaks, and repairs or adjusts components to eliminate cause of complaint.
Whizzer
  Tends machine that spins felt hat bodies to remove excess water.

From *Dictionary of Occupational Titles* (4th ed.). (1977). Washington, DC: Government Printing Office.

---

direct observation, systematic activity logs, critical incidents, and job elements. An investigation of organizations with exemplary job analysis programs found that most of the firms used questionnaires. Second in frequency of use was the interview, although interviews were sometimes conducted primarily to help construct questionnaires, which were then used for the actual job analyses. Fewer organizations used direct observation or the maintenance of a daily activity log (Levine, Sistrunk, McNutt, & Gael, 1988).

The same survey found that the primary sources of data on how jobs are performed are the workers on the job and their supervisors. Research has shown that when workers provide information on their jobs, it makes little difference whether they are good or poor workers. The resulting job analyses were found to be similar (Conley & Sackett, 1987).

Who conducts job analyses in the workplace? A survey of human resources or personnel managers in 142 companies showed that 39% used members of the personnel department, 22% used trained job analysts, and 13% hired outside consultants to undertake the task (Blocklyn, 1988a).

Let us now consider the specific techniques for conducting job analyses. The interview approach involves, as you might expect, extensive *interviewing* of those directly connected with the job, that is, the workers currently performing the job, their supervisors, and perhaps even the instructors who trained the workers for the job. This can involve either face-to-face interviewing of individuals or of a group of workers or the use of questionnaires.

Full cooperation and understanding on the part of those being questioned are required. The U.S. Employment Service suggests the following guidelines:

1. The person being questioned must be fully briefed as to who the interviewer is, why he or she is asking so many questions, and why it is important for the worker to answer fully and honestly. The workers, in short, must know what is required and why.
2. The questions must be thoroughly planned and worded in advance. This is where information from published job analyses is helpful. It can give the analyst some idea of what to look for.
3. The interviewer must secure the information as quickly as possible, recognize that the worker knows more about the job than the interviewer does, and express appreciation to the person being interviewed.

The interview approach has several advantages. Those who are directly concerned with the job are in the best position to know the details of the work. The face-to-face interaction between the worker and the job analyst provides the former with an understanding of what the latter is trying to accomplish. As a rule, workers who are fully informed of the importance of the project and of their vital role in it will be more helpful and cooperative than those who are not so informed, a point that applies to every job analysis technique.

Two types of questionnaire are used in job analysis: the *unstructured questionnaire* and the *structured questionnaire*. In the unstructured or open-end approach, the workers or their supervisors describe in their own words the details of the job and the tasks performed. Some respondents, however, may be unable or unwilling to describe all aspects of their jobs in sufficient detail. They may overlook operations that have become habitual, or they may be insufficiently articulate to analyze the tasks they perform. Others may find it boring to fill out such a questionnaire and, therefore, offer only a minimal amount of information to get finished as quickly as possible.

In the structured-questionnaire approach, workers or supervisors are provided with specific and detailed descriptions of a variety of tasks, operations, working conditions, and the like. They are asked to rate the items or to select those that best characterize their jobs.

The most frequently used questionnaire is the *Position Analysis Question-naire* (*PAQ*), which consists of 194 job elements related to specific human behaviors (Guion & Gibson, 1988; McCormick, 1979). These job elements are organized into six divisions, each representing a different facet of job behavior: information input, mental processes, work output, relationships with other persons, job context, and other job characteristics including any activities or conditions not found in the other five facets. From the ratings of each element in terms of its importance to the job in question, the judgments can be quantified. This is a considerable and obvious advantage over the information yielded by the unstructured-interview approach.

The PAQ has been described as "one of the most rigorously developed, well evaluated, and generally useful job analysis instruments available" (Harvey &

Hayes, 1986, p. 345). A modified British version of the PAQ, the Job Structure Profile (JSP), has also been developed. The JSP has demonstrated impressive levels of reliability in its application to nine different types of jobs including sales, clerical, secretarial, and managerial positions (Patrick & Moore, 1985). The PAQ has been used to establish the criteria for the cognitive and physical abilities needed for successful performance of 25 different jobs in the U.S. Navy (Carter & Biersner, 1987).

Some recent research suggests that for certain jobs, the PAQ may pinpoint nothing more than commonsense beliefs or stereotypes about the jobs. Studies have demonstrated that PAQ ratings obtained from expert raters correlated highly with those obtained from college students (naïve raters) who relied only on job titles or brief job descriptions. The implication is that if students who had never studied the requirements of a particular job could provide ratings similar to those of experts, then the PAQ may reflect only common knowledge about those jobs (DeNisi, Cornelius, & Blencoe, 1987). Thus, the PAQ may be less appropriate for some types of jobs than was previously believed. However, another study using naïve raters found that those who had more information about a job were significantly more accurate in their PAQ ratings than those who had been given only a job title (Harvey & Lozada-Larsen, 1988).

A third approach to job analysis is *direct observation* of the worker on the job. Sometimes this involves simply watching the workers perform their various tasks, but occasionally sophisticated methods of observation such as filming are used. It is well known from psychological research that persons may behave differently when they know they are being observed, so it is necessary for the analyst to remain as unobtrusive as possible. Also, the analyst must observe a sample of the workers (not just one) and must make the observations at various times during the workday to take account of changes caused by factors such as fatigue (for example, a worker may be more productive in the morning than in late afternoon).

A fourth technique of job analysis involves having the workers maintain a *systematic activity log* of everything they do in a given period of time. If these records are made with care, they frequently reveal details of the job not otherwise obtainable or observable.

Another approach is the *critical-incidents technique*, which records those behaviors (incidents) that are vital to the successful performance of the job. The goal is to identify from supervisors, co-workers, and others familiar with the job, behaviors that differentiate successful from unsuccessful workers. The critical-incidents technique focuses on the specific acts that lead to desirable or undesirable consequences on the job. A single critical incident is of little value, but hundreds of them can effectively describe a job task sequence in terms of the unique behaviors required for successful performance.

Another approach to job analysis is the *job-element method*, which is used extensively by the U.S. Office of Personnel Management to develop selection procedures, performance appraisal techniques, and curricula for training programs (Primoff, 1975). Experts on the job in question, including both supervisors and experienced employees, develop a number of specific job elements that are defined in terms of the knowledge, skills, abilities, and other personal characteristics required to perform the job. The experts rate every element on each of four scales (Ash, Levine, & Sistrunk, 1983, pp. 54–55):

1. What relative portion of even barely acceptable employees are good in the element?
2. How important is the element in picking out the superior employee?
3. How much trouble is likely if the element is ignored when choosing among applicants?
4. To what extent can job openings be filled if the element is required in all new employees?

Research comparing the effectiveness of the different approaches to job analysis has indicated that they vary in their usefulness. Therefore, the choice of a specific technique must depend on an organization's reasons for conducting the job analysis in the first place. In addition, research has shown that a combination of methods rather than just a single technique will ensure greater accuracy of job description (Levine, Thomas, & Sistrunk, 1988; Zedeck & Cascio, 1984).

Job analysis has always been an important part of the selection process, but today it is even more vital because of the equal employment opportunity legislation. Every employing organization must be able to justify each of its job requirements to show that whatever it asks of a job applicant is related to the ability to perform the job in question and is not being used as a tool to discriminate against certain kinds of people. A detailed job analysis helps provide justification for actual job requirements.

For example, if a company is charged with sex discrimination because its women employees are paid less than its men employees for what appears to be the same job, the company would have to prove that men are actually performing different tasks that justify the greater pay. If this is the case, a job analysis can provide that information.

For good reasons, then, organizations today take seriously the task of job analysis. Equal employment opportunity and successful selection programs would not be possible without it.

Methods of Selection: Biographical Information

The collecting of biographical information, or "bio data," on the backgrounds of job applicants is a common method of selection. The rationale for this selection technique is simple: A person's past experiences can be used to predict his or her future direction. For example, a job applicant whose biography includes exemplary performance in school or college, leadership in extracurricular activities, and summer employment would seem to be a promising candidate for a management-trainee position. Because many of our behaviors, values, and attitudes remain consistent throughout our lives, it is not unreasonable to predict a person's future behavior on the basis of how he or she behaved in the past.

We shall discuss three techniques for collecting biographical information: the standard application blank, the weighted application blank, and the biographical inventory.

Standard Application Blanks

Rarely is anyone hired by an organization at any level of employment without being asked to complete an application blank. Indeed, this is one of the most frequently used techniques in personnel selection and hiring. Even when other methods of assessment are used, the application blank is usually the initial step for the applicant to take. Not only does it provide useful information but it can also provide leads for subsequent interview questions.

The information solicited on an application blank includes routine biographical data such as name, address, education, and work experience as well as items such as criminal-conviction record, medical history, and special skills. For higher-level positions, applicants might be asked to describe their interests and hobbies, their reading habits, and their career goals. A sample application blank for a major publishing company is shown in Figure 3-1.

The most crucial problem in constructing an application blank involves deciding what information to ask of an applicant. What information does the employer need to know to find out if the applicant is suitable for the job in question? Beyond the routine biographical data, it is important that the company ascertain those facts about the candidate that correlate with subsequent success on the job.

In one company, for example, research demonstrated that successful executives were all college graduates who had achieved or exceeded a specific grade point average and had engaged in certain extracurricular activities while in college. Obviously, then, this is the kind of information the personnel department wants to know about an applicant as quickly as possible. If the application blank indicated that a candidate did not possess these qualifications, the company would not have to go to the time and expense of further selection procedures such as administering a battery of tests or flying the job applicant to the home plant.

Much valuable predictive information can be obtained from application forms. Knowledge of a candidate's financial history may provide an indication of responsibility for some occupations. Extracurricular activities may tell something of leadership ability or provide a clue to personality characteristics to be investigated in an interview.

Such predictive information can be obtained only through careful research. Each relevant item on an application form must be correlated with a later measure of job success. If a high positive correlation is found, that item can be used with confidence in selecting new employees.

PERSONAL DATA:

	LAST	FIRST	MIDDLE	Home Phone:
Name:				Business Phone:

	NUMBER	STREET	CITY	STATE	ZIP
Permanent Address:					

Social Security Number: _____   If under 18 years of age state your age: _____

If not a U.S. citizen, are you legally permitted to work?   Yes ☐   No ☐   If hired, proof will be requested.

WORK INTERESTS:

Position Desired: _____   Willing to Relocate?   Yes ☐   No ☐

Referred By: _____   Willing to Travel?   Yes ☐   No ☐

Salary Desired: _____   Typing Speed: _____ wpm   Other Business Skills: _____

EDUCATION:

	NAME & ADDRESS OF SCHOOL	MAJOR COURSE	LAST GRADE COMPLETED	GRADUATED/DEGREE	STILL ATTENDING
HIGH SCHOOL					
COLLEGE					
GRADUATE SCHOOL					
OTHER					

U.S. MILITARY SERVICE:

Have you ever served in the Armed Forces?   Yes ☐   No ☐   If Yes: Active Duty From _____ To _____

EMPLOYMENT

LIST BELOW YOUR FORMER EMPLOYERS, BEGIN WITH THE PRESENT EMPLOYER. NOTE ANY PERIODS OF UNEMPLOYMENT

1 EMPLOYER:	DATE EMPLOYED	POSITION:
ADDRESS:	FROM TO	MAJOR JOB DUTIES:
SUPERVISOR:		
MAY WE CONTACT?	SALARY	
REASON FOR LEAVING:	$ TO $	

2 EMPLOYER:	DATE EMPLOYED	POSITION:
ADDRESS:	FROM TO	MAJOR JOB DUTIES:
SUPERVISOR:		
MAY WE CONTACT?	SALARY	
REASON FOR LEAVING:	$ TO $	

3 EMPLOYER:	DATE EMPLOYED	POSITION:
ADDRESS:	FROM TO	MAJOR JOB DUTIES:
SUPERVISOR:		
MAY WE CONTACT?	SALARY	
REASON FOR LEAVING:	$ TO $	

Have you ever been convicted of a crime, offense, or violation, other than parking violations, within the last five years that was not sealed or annulled by a court?   Yes ☐   No ☐

If yes, list all convictions, showing date, court and name of offense. Conviction of a crime is not necessarily a bar to employment.

_____

I agree that the company may, as part of the verification of this application, contact the educational institutions and references above. I understand that falsification of any part of this application is justifiable grounds for immediate dismissal. If employed, I understand that the first ninety (90) days of my employment constitute a probationary period and, if employed, I understand that I am employed at the will of management and management retains the right to alter the terms and conditions of my employment at any time. Only a written agreement with management may alter these terms.

Date: _____   Signature: _____

Figure 3-1 Adaptation of a sample application blank. (Courtesy Macmillan Publishing Co.)

An application form should be limited to questions that provide useful guides for selection. Some companies use excessively long application blanks in an attempt to gather information on every conceivable facet of an applicant's life, whether or not the data are known to be useful. Surely, this is a wasted effort for the applicant (who may lose interest by the fifth page) and for the personnel manager (who may be burdened with considerable irrelevant information).

We noted in the section on fair employment the kinds of questions that cannot be asked of job applicants. Despite the publicity given to the problem of discrimination in hiring and the threat of legal action against companies that violate antidiscrimination measures, compliance with EEOC guidelines on application blanks is far from complete.

Another problem relating to application blanks involves the honesty of the applicant's response. Is the information he or she has provided correct? Did the applicant, for example, really supervise 50 workers in his or her last job, earn an annual salary of $30,000, or graduate from the college indicated?

A sizable number of applicants have been shown to provide misleading or fraudulent information. The greatest distortion occurs on questions dealing with previous job title, pay, and level of responsibility. As many as one third of the job applicants in one study misrepresented their college credentials, most of them claiming to possess a degree they had not earned. The degree most frequently claimed was the MBA (Vecchio, 1984).

The director of personnel research for the Port Authority of New York and New Jersey reported that one third of all job applicants lied about their past work experience, claiming to have had experience at certain tasks, which they did not, in fact, have. Other research has shown that as many as two thirds of applicants to other kinds of organizations may falsify some aspects of their background ("One Third of Applicants," 1987). It has been found that some of this faking can be reduced by follow-up interviews and by issuing advance warnings that all information provided on an application blank is subject to confirmation (Shaffer, Saunders, & Owens, 1986).

Many application forms carry a statement that applicants must sign noting that they agree to the employer's attempts to verify the information, and that false representation constitutes grounds for immediate dismissal. (Read the fine print at the bottom of the application form in Figure 3-1 for an example of this.)

It may appear to be a simple matter for an organization to check on the accuracy of the information supplied on an application form by contacting colleges and former employers. Surveys show that about 90% of all companies do check references named by applicants. Almost all of them contact former employers and approximately 50% contact the colleges listed on application blanks (Levine, 1984).

Although colleges will supply information about degrees granted, a problem arises with employing organizations. Companies are frequently reluctant to release information about former employees for fear of lawsuits, as we shall see in more detail later in this chapter. A former employee may sue a company for releasing unfavorable information, claiming libel or slander. For this reason, many employing organizations supply only limited factual data such as period of employment and job title. Few will give evaluative information such as why an employee left the company, what the person's actual responsibilities were, and whether the company would rehire the former employee. Hence, verifying certain kinds of information supplied on application blanks may be difficult.

Weighted Application Blanks

Once the correlation between each item of information and subsequent job success has been determined, it is possible to score an application blank with specific weights for each item.

For example, suppose a psychologist analyzed and weighted an application blank for a company and found the relationships that are listed in Table 3-6. Research showed that 80% of all married workers in the company were rated by their supervisors as successful in their jobs; a new job applicant checking married on an application blank would, therefore, be given a score of 8. A single candidate would get a score of 6 because only 60% of the company's single workers were rated as successful. The job applicant who would obtain the highest score is a married high school graduate who owns a home. The person least likely to be hired would be a divorced nongraduate who rents a home.

Research on each item of an application blank must be repeated periodically to check on the continuing predictive value of the information, particularly if there has been a change in job procedure or the overall labor supply. One way to ensure that all relevant personal history items are included on such an application blank is to conduct periodic job analyses. Assuming careful research and follow-ups, the weighted application blank can be as useful a predictive device as some psychological tests. Further, it can be graded or scored as objectively as a test, thus eliminating any personal bias in the selection procedure.

Weighted application blanks have been very successful in reducing turnover. The items that are usually of the greatest predictive value are age, marital status, level of education, and prior occupations (Lawrence, Salsburg, Dawson, & Fasman, 1982).

TABLE 3-6 Sample Results from Weighted Application Blank

Item	Characteristics of successful workers	Weight assigned
Married	80%	8
Single	60	6
Divorced	10	1
High School Graduate	70	7
Nongraduate	20	2
Owns Home	80	8
Rents Home	30	3

Biographical Inventories

Closely related to the weighted application blank is the biographical inventory or biographical information blank. The approach has been shown to be a valid predictor of success in a variety of jobs: scientist, office worker, middle-level manager, military officer, production worker, and salesperson (Owens & Schoenfeldt, 1979). Biographical inventories may have a greater predictive value than any other selection technique except for tests of cognitive or mental ability (Anderson & Shakleton, 1986; Childs & Klimoski, 1986; Hunter & Hunter, 1983).

Biographical inventories are typically much longer than application blanks and cover information on an applicant's life in greater detail. The rationale for this extensive probing is that on-the-job behavior is related to past behavior in a variety of situations as well as to attitudes, preferences, and values. Examples of the kind of information asked on biographical inventories are contained in Table 3-7. Such inventories are similar to some psychological tests in terms of the type of question asked and the multiple-choice format of the responses.

A great deal of research has been conducted on biographical inventories. The findings have generally supported the underlying theory that past behavior can be used to predict future behavior. There appears to be a stability over time in the different ways in which people with different early life experiences behave (K. R. Davis, 1984; Eberhardt & Muchinsky, 1982).

Biographical inventories usually are developed for a specific job and considerable research is necessary to determine the background experiences that correlate with success on the job. The process of item validation is essentially the same as for the weighted application blank—each item is correlated with some measure of job performance.

A pharmaceutical company used this approach to select research personnel with great success. They found that among other characteristics the more creative scientists were independent, overinvolved in their work, desirous of challenge, and had permissive parents. Of course, this same cluster of characteristics could be identified through a combination of interviews and psychological tests, but it is more efficient and less costly to elicit this information with one procedure.

Despite the high predictive validity of biographical inventories, there is concern with some of the problems inherent in this technique. First, there is the obvious problem of invasion of privacy. Some items on biographical inventories are of a most personal nature and some people (reasonably) object to being asked to reveal intimacies. Of course, not all people are bothered by being asked to reveal personal information. There are large individual differences in the questions people find objectionable. Some people are more bothered by questions dealing with family background, others object to questions about financial matters, and others do not like to be asked about social values.

Invasion of privacy is a sensitive and important issue and has an obvious bearing on the selection process wherein an organization is trying to learn as much as possible about an individual. How much personal information should we have to reveal to get a job? There is no easy answer, but it is a matter to which

TABLE 3-7 Sample Biographical Inventory Items

Habits and Attitudes

How often do you tell jokes?
1. *Very frequently.*
2. *Frequently.*
3. *Occasionally.*
4. *Seldom.*
5. *Can't remember jokes.*

Human Relations

How do you regard your neighbors?
1. *Not interested in your neighbors.*
2. *Like them but seldom see them.*
3. *Visit in each others' homes occasionally.*
4. *Spend a lot of time together.*

Money

How much of your yearly income would you plan to save as head of a family under normal conditions?
1. *5% or less.*
2. *6% to 10%.*
3. *11% to 15%.*
4. *16% to 20%.*
5. *21% or more.*

Personal Attributes

How creative do you feel you are?
1. *Highly creative.*
2. *Somewhat more creative than most in your field.*
3. *Moderately creative.*
4. *Somewhat less creative than most in your field.*
5. *Not creative.*

Self-impressions

Do you generally do your best
1. *At whatever job you are doing.*
2. *Only in what you are interested.*
3. *Only when it is demanded of you.*

Values, Opinions, and Preferences

Which one of the following seems most important to you?
1. *A pleasant home and family life.*
2. *A challenging and exciting job.*
3. *Getting ahead in the world.*
4. *Being active and accepted in community affairs.*
5. *Making the most of your particular ability.*

Work

How fast do you usually work?
1. *Much faster than most people.*
2. *Somewhat faster than most people.*
3. *At about the same pace as most people.*
4. *Somewhat slower than most people.*
5. *Much slower than most people.*
6. *Unable to tell.*

Adapted from *Biographical Data in Industrial Psychology* by W. A. Owens & E. R. Henry, 1966, Greensboro, NC: Richardson Foundation.

personnel psychologists, who design and administer biographical inventories and psychological tests, must be sympathetic.

Another problem with biographical inventories relates to equal employment opportunities. Many biographical inventory items deal with social and economic variables—homeowner versus renter, for example—and members of minority groups may be excluded from consideration because they have not had the economic advantages that are available to some others. All items in biographical inventories must be examined carefully to make sure they do not discriminate against any minority group.

We have seen that biographical inventories can be valid predictors of job success. For this reason, then, we might expect that biographical inventories would be used by nearly every organization that hires people. Unfortunately, the technique is currently used by only 7% of American companies, according to a 1988 survey of 248 personnel directors (Hammer & Kleiman, 1988). A survey conducted 9 years earlier found a 4% usage rate. Thus, during the time when the validity data on the technique was increasing, few organizations adopted it. Why is such a useful tool so seldom applied in the world of work?

The 1988 survey of personnel directors revealed several possible explanations. First, slightly more than half (52.2%) said they did not know much about biographical inventories. Second, 26.5% said they did not think biographical inventories were valid selection techniques. It appears that the company psychologists, and those who publish articles about biographical inventories, have not been effective in communicating the success of this selection technique to those in a position to implement it.

Additional factors suggest that even if personnel directors were fully informed of the high validity of biographical inventories, many still would not use them. For example, 62.5% of the personnel directors in the 1988 survey said that their organizations lacked sufficient time, money, and personnel to develop and update the inventories. Other reasons cited for failing to use biographical inventories included a lack of staff with statistical expertise, lack of support from top management, and concern that the questions would violate EEOC guidelines or constitute an invasion of privacy.

This situation illustrates the gap or conflict between research and application in I/O psychology. In this case, researchers have developed a highly successful employee selection tool that is seldom used in the workplace for a number of practical reasons. What is needed are data persuading executives that the use of such a valid procedure will save more money in the long run than it will cost to develop and implement it, and that such inventories comply with equal employment opportunity guidelines.

Training and Work Experience Evaluation (T&E)

Another method of selection which, like the application blank, is based on some form of self-report on the part of the job applicant, is *training and work experience evaluation*, known as T&E. It involves an attempt to predict job performance on the basis of systematic judgments of the information supplied through application blanks, résumés, and questionnaires designed to obtain data on the applicant's training and experience.

The information assessed in T&E includes performance on specific tasks in previous jobs; narrative descriptions of past jobs; accomplishments on such job-related behaviors as leadership; summaries of educational history and job training; and self-ratings on levels of knowledge, skills, and abilities (Ash, Johnson, Levine, & McDaniel, 1989).

The T&E approach differs from weighted application blanks and biographical inventories, in that information is assigned different weights on the basis of a judgment rather than being empirically determined by how highly each item of information correlates with a subsequent measure of job performance. The judgments in T&E are based on hypotheses formed by supervisors and other job experts about the degree of relationship between certain aspects of training and experience, and successful performance on the job. For example, an applicant might be assigned 3 points for each year of relevant job experience and 2 points for every year of college education in a specific field.

Five approaches to T&E have been described (McDaniel, Schmidt, & Hunter, 1988).

The point method. As in the preceding example, points are assigned for years of training and job experience.

The grouping method. Applicants are grouped into categories such as "well qualified" or "not qualified," based on judgments about their training and experience.

The task method. Applicants are evaluated on their experience with job-related tasks. In this method, which is based on self-ratings, the applicants rate their own experience levels on a given task.

The behavioral consistency method. In this approach, applicants describe their major achievements in areas related to a particular job, such as their leadership behaviors. These descriptions are evaluated on rating scales developed from supervisors' analyses of the degree to which they judge that these behaviors differentiate between good and poor workers already on the job.

The knowledge, skills, and ability (KSA) method. This approach involves the job-element method used in job analysis. Brainstorming sessions of experienced supervisors generate statements of KSAs that are relevant to the job in question. The KSAs are then rated in terms of how critical they are to successful job performance.

We noted that biographical inventories are seldom used on the job despite an impressive amount of research demonstrating their high levels of validity. Quite the opposite is true for T&E, which is used frequently in the workplace, particularly in the public sector, despite relatively little research support.

What research is available shows low overall validities, with the point and task methods having the lowest (.11 and .15) and the behavioral consistency method having the highest (.45). The T&E method can be described as "potentially promising," and at this point seems best suited to two purposes: establishing minimum qualification requirements and rank-ordering applicants (Ash, Johnson, Levine, & McDaniel, 1989; Ash & Levine, 1985).

Interviews

The personal interview is the single most frequently used selection technique both in the United States and in Britain (Karren & Nkomo, 1988; Robertson & Makin, 1986). Regardless of what other selection techniques are used, every prospective employer seems to want the chance to meet a job candidate in person. Interviews range in length from cursory meetings of five to ten minutes to elaborate affairs lasting two full days, even including questioning over dinner. Those who have been on both sides of the interview situation can attest to their often grueling and tiring nature.

The primary purpose of the interview is to provide a face-to-face meeting for evaluating an applicant's suitability for employment. A frequently overlooked

The personal interview is the single most frequently used selection technique.

point about the interview is that it can provide a two-way flow of information, allowing each party to assess the other. Not only do employers gain additional information about the candidates, but applicants can learn about the organization and the job under consideration. If applicants ask the right questions, the interview situation can be used to determine if the job and company are right for them. Some candidates do this so well that the interviewers feel *they* are being interviewed!

Personnel departments and managers rely heavily on the interview as a selection tool and are extremely reluctant to hire persons without the chance to meet and question them. Personnel psychologists, on the other hand, are considerably less enthusiastic and optimistic about the value of the interview for selection because the evidence shows consistently that the interview is not a good predictor of job success. The predictive validity of the interview remains embarrassingly low, a conclusion first demonstrated by Walter Dill Scott, a founder of industrial psychology whom we mentioned in Chapter 1 (Scott, 1915). Scott's conclusion is frequently corroborated in the psychological research literature in articles summarizing the findings on the utility of interviews (for example, Arvey & Campion, 1982; Mayfield, 1964; Schneider & Schmitt, 1986; Wagner, 1949).

An investigation in a high-tech company of how interviews are conducted revealed some of the reasons why the technique is such a poor predictor of job success (Harwood & Briscoe, 1987).

First, managers and supervisors were given no training in interviewing techniques. Because of this lack of training, they were not listening well during the interview situation. They often missed or ignored crucial information supplied by the job applicants. Further, there was little consistency in the questions asked. Many of the interviewers focused on factors that had no bearing on the job in question.

Second, the interviewers often collected too much or too little information. Sometimes, every interviewer asked the same question of a candidate, but at other times, key questions vital to assessing a candidate's suitability were not asked by anyone.

Third, too many people were involved in the interviewing. It was not unusual for an applicant to be interviewed by up to 10 people in the company.

The lack of structure, organization, and training in interviewing found in this study is not unusual. Indeed, interviews have been referred to by some personnel psychologists as "haphazard conversations" (Guion & Gibson, 1988, p. 367).

No matter how often personnel psychologists report a lack of research support for interviews, they will continue to be used for employee selection purposes. The major explanation for this may be overconfidence on the part of the interviewers. Over time, they come to develop a strong belief in their ability to make judgments about people and think that some unique combination of experience and intuition allows them to select successful employees (Karren & Nkomo, 1988).

As a result of the continued use of the interview, personnel psychologists are focusing on the mechanics and dynamics of this complex face-to-face meeting in the hope of coming to understand better its processes and problems. The more we learn about the personal and social interactions during an interview, the better chance there is of improving its usefulness. We shall see later that it is indeed possible to improve the interview technique.

Two traditional kinds of interview are the standard or unstructured interview and the patterned or structured interview.

The *unstructured interview* is characterized by a lack of structure or advance planning, as we saw in the preceding example of the high-tech company. The format and approach to questioning as well as the questions asked are left entirely to the discretion of the individual interviewer. Thus, it is possible that five interviewers conducting separate unstructured interviews with the same applicant could receive five different impressions of the person.

A basic weakness of the unstructured interview is its lack of consistency in assessing candidates. Interviewers may be interested in different aspects of a candidate's background, experience, or attitudes, thus the results of an interview may reflect more of the characteristics, biases, and prejudices of the interviewer than the objective abilities of the applicant. This lack of consistency among interviews causes this method to be extremely low in predictive accuracy. Despite its recognized limitations, the unstructured interview is heavily relied on in many organizations. Some companies use this approach as a preliminary get-acquainted technique and follow it up in the selection process by a more structured interview.

Following an unstructured interview, some organizations require interviewers to note their impressions of a candidate on an evaluation form. Figure 3-2 shows portions of a form designed to be filled out immediately on completion of the interview. Note the scope of the judgments called for in areas that range from physical appearance to ability to work with others, drive, and potential. These are extremely difficult characteristics to assess on the basis of a limited interview, and it is not surprising that such assessments are often deficient.

The opposite of the loose and haphazard unstructured interview is the patterned or *structured interview*. This approach uses a predetermined list of interview, and it is not surprising that such assessments are often deficient. Thus, the entire interview procedure is standardized so that the resulting assessment of candidates is less open to interviewer bias. Although subjective and personal factors can still influence the interviewer's judgment (no procedure can eliminate this factor entirely in an interpersonal situation), this is less of a problem in the structured interview.

In conducting a structured interview, the interviewer uses a printed form containing the questions to be asked of each applicant. The candidate's responses are recorded on the same form. So formalized is this approach that it has been characterized as an application blank that the interviewer fills out on the basis of what the applicant says.

These structured interview questions are typical of those used by a company to select college graduates for management positions. The questions deal with prior work experience and are intended for applicants who have had at least

PERSONAL PRESENTATION AND COMMUNICATIONS SKILLS—Consider the candidate's ability to communicate with others in relation to the requirements of the position applied for.

CIRCLE ONE

Appearance	Superior	Above Average	Average	Below Average	Unable to Rate
Poise/Polish	Unable to Rate	Below Average	Average	Above Average	Superior
Written Communication (clear, concise, logical, etc.)	Superior	Above Average	Average	Below Average	Unable to Rate
Oral Communication (clear, concise, logical, etc.)	Unable to Rate	Below Average	Average	Above Average	Superior

SKILLS IN PERSONAL RELATIONSHIPS—Consider the candidate's ability to deal effectively with subordinates, peers and superiors in relation to the requirements of the position applied for.

CIRCLE ONE

Tact	Superior	Above Average	Average	Below Average	Unable to Rate
Consideration for Others	Unable to Rate	Below Average	Average	Above Average	Superior
Ability to Get Work Done *With* Others	Superior	Above Average	Average	Below Average	Unable to Rate
Ability to Get Work Done *Through* Others	Unable to Rate	Below Average	Average	Above Average	Superior
Leadership	Superior	Above Average	Average	Below Average	Unable to Rate

DRIVE—Consider the candidate's ability in "getting on with the job" in relation to the requirements of the position applied for.

CIRCLE ONE

Initiative/Self-starter	Superior	Above Average	Average	Below Average	Unable to Rate
Enthusiasm	Unable to Rate	Below Average	Average	Above Average	Superior
Capacity for Work	Superior	Above Average	Average	Below Average	Unable to Rate

PERSONAL GOALS—Consider the degree to which the candidate has thought through goals and objectives.

CIRCLE ONE

Goals/Objectives (definite, well thought out)	Superior	Above Average	Average	Below Average	Unable to Rate
Career Plans (definite, well thought out)	Unable to Rate	Below Average	Average	Above Average	Superior
Consistency of Goals and Objectives with Capabilities (reasonable, realistic)	Superior	Above Average	Average	Below Average	Unable to Rate

POTENTIAL—Consider the degree to which the candidate is capable of assuming future responsibilities.

CIRCLE ONE

Growth—Can assume increasingly more responsible positions similar or related to the position applied for	Superior	Above Average	Average	Below Average	Unable to Rate
Flexibility—Can assume increasingly more responsible positions not necessarily similar or related to the position applied for	Unable to Rate	Below Average	Average	Above Average	Superior
Level Capable of Reaching— Supervisor	Superior	Above Average	Average	Below Average	Unable to Rate
Manager	Unable to Rate	Below Average	Average	Above Average	Superior
Director	Superior	Above Average	Average	Below Average	Unable to Rate
Officer	Unable to Rate	Below Average	Average	Above Average	Superior

OVERALL EVALUATION—Considering all of the preceding factors, assess the degree to which the candidate meets the total requirements of the position applied for.

CIRCLE ONE

Superior	Above Average	Average	Below Average

Figure 3-2 Postinterview evaluation form. (Courtesy Eastern Airlines, Inc.)

one job since graduation:

1. What was your first job after leaving college?
2. What would you say your major accomplishments were on that job?
3. What were some of the things you might have done less well, things that perhaps pointed to the opportunity for further development?
4. What did you learn about yourself on that job?
5. What aspects of the job did you find most stimulating and satisfying?
6. What are some of the things you look for in any job?
7. What are your thoughts about the future? What sort of work would you like to be doing 5 or 10 years from now?
8. Looking back over the past 10 years, what would you say were the most important ways in which you have changed in that time?

Because all applicants are asked the same questions in sequence, there is a firmer basis for the comparison of candidates than there is using the random questioning procedures of the unstructured interview.

Structured interviews represent a considerable improvement over unstructured interviews and have the potential for higher predictive validity. A number of studies verify this and have reported validities as high as +.56. Indeed, carefully prepared structured interviews have been shown to be as valid predictors of job success as a typical battery of employment tests (Arvey, Miller, Gould, & Burch, 1987; Campion, Pursell, & Brown, 1988).

Thus, the interview can be made a more useful selection device if it is formalized and structured. Unfortunately, the structured interview is not universally used. Most organizations still rely on the conversational, undependable, unstructured approach.

Another way of increasing the predictive utility of interviews is to have them conducted by a panel of some three to five interviewers instead of by a single interviewer. Combining the judgments about a prospective employee seems to improve reliability and validity and to temper the possible biasing effects of employee characteristics that are not job related (Arvey & Campion, 1982; Rothstein & Jackson, 1980). As many as 20% of all job interviews are now conducted by a panel (Weston & Warmke, 1988).

A recent innovation in interviewing is the use of videotape. This does not involve a traditional face-to-face, question-and-answer interview. Rather, it is the applicant's side of an interview that the personnel manager can see and hear but not respond to. Nevertheless, videotape can save time and money for both employers and applicants.

Employers may obtain much useful information by watching a tape of applicants describing themselves—their interests, abilities, values, and backgrounds. Clearly unsuitable candidates can be eliminated before undertaking the effort and expense of other selection procedures. An employment agency with a file of interview tapes can greatly speed up the initial screening process for a large organization.

Videotapes can work in the other direction as well. Some employment agencies maintain tape files of personnel managers describing the requirements and advantages of available jobs with their organizations. Applicants can quickly weed out jobs that are obviously unsuitable for them, saving them the time and expense of a personal visit to each company.

The use of the videotape interview seems to offer definite advantages in the selection process and is rapidly gaining in popularity.

It is fortunate that in at least some organizations the interview is not the sole selection technique because it is notoriously inaccurate by itself. There are a number of additional problems with its use that must be overcome.

(1) Failure of Interviewers to Agree.   A major problem with the interview is the difficulty of getting several interviewers to agree in their assessments of the same applicant, particularly with the unstructured interview technique. A classic study in the area (Hollingworth, 1929) involved having 12 interviewers independently rate 57 applicants on their suitability for a sales job. The interviewers were experienced sales managers who throughout their careers had conducted many interviews with job applicants. There was a total lack of agreement among the interviewers. Some applicants ranked first by one interviewer in order of suitability for the job were ranked last by another.

Figure 3-3 shows the ratings of one applicant by 12 interviewers. If the person responsible for making the final decision about hiring this individual was given this interview information, it would surely be of little help. It offers no firm basis on which to make the decision. Remember that these assorted ratings were all assigned to the same applicant; the differences are because of the interviewer, not the interviewee.

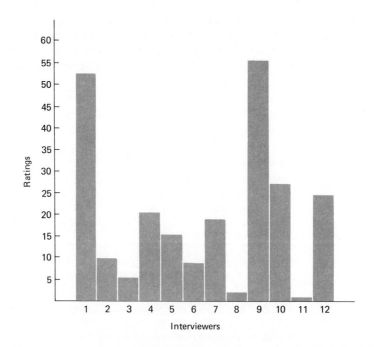

Figure 3-3 Ratings of one applicant by twelve interviewers. (Data from *Vocational Psychology and Character Analysis* (pp. 115–119) by H. L. Hollingworth, 1929, New York: Appleton.)

It is possible to overcome this lack of consistency. If interviewers are trained to follow standard patterns in their questioning (as in the structured interview technique) and to make their evaluations in standard objective terms, then consistency can be increased (Guion, 1987). In one study of three interviewers, marked differences were found in their judgments of applicants' suitability for employment. However, whereas two of the interviewers' judgments were invalid, those of the third were quite accurate. All three interviewers were given training in evaluating specific traits considered appropriate for assessment. Two of the interviewers, including the one with the valid pretraining judgments, improved in accuracy, as did the third, who could make valid predictions after the training but not as accurately as the other two. The point is that training reduced the differences among the judgments of the three interviewers so that they gave more consistent as well as more accurate judgments (Dougherty, Ebert, & Callender, 1986).

Thus, the more highly formalized or structured is the interview procedure, the greater will be the agreement among interviewers. Also, as we noted, interviews conducted by a panel of interviewers are more likely to yield a consistent judgment.

(2) Failure to Predict Job Success. Even if the problem of interviewer consistency were solved, there remain the difficulties with the predictive accuracy or validity of the unstructured interview technique. A major cause for the lack of predictive utility is that the interview is a subjective interpersonal process. The interviewer's assessment of a candidate can be distorted by personal prejudices as well as by the nature of the interview situation.

Research has also shown the importance of the first impression an interviewer receives of a candidate. In fact, the initial impression is so important that it is unlikely to be modified by information received later in the interview. Interviewers may be unaffected by significant aspects of a person's job qualifications if those aspects are not revealed until later in the interview situation. First impressions, no matter how misleading or incomplete they may be, seem to be what count in the interviewer's judgment. Interviewers often reach their decisions about whether to hire job candidates after no more than a few minutes of a 15-minute interview.

Another factor that may account for the failure of most interviews to predict job success is that interviewers tend to be affected much more by negative information about an applicant than they are by positive information. One or two negative items about a potential employee can cause an interviewer to overlook or ignore more positive information, no matter how important it is (Carlson, Thayer, Mayfield, & Peterson, 1971). Both of these biasing effects—first impressions and negative information—can be minimized by proper training.

(3) Stress of the Interview Situation. In an interview, it is natural to expect a certain amount of nervousness on the part of the applicants. They know that the impression they make on the interviewer will determine, at least in part, whether or not they will be offered the job. As a result, normally calm and composed persons may appear tense and unable to express themselves well. They may behave in a manner totally uncharacteristic of their subsequent behavior on the job, and this atypical behavior may mislead the interviewer.

A trained and experienced interviewer can do much to prevent or reduce applicants' nervousness by trying to establish a rapport early in the interview. How sympathetic, understanding, and friendly the interviewer appears can influence the applicants' behavior, which, in turn, influences the interviewer's assessment.

Stress in the interview situation can also operate on interviewers, particularly if they are behind in their quotas and are being pressured by the home office. In one study, three groups of managers evaluated descriptions of the same applicants: one group of managers was behind in its quota, another group was ahead, and the third group had no quota. The managers under the quota pressure perceived the applicants as having greater potential and said that they would hire more of them than did the other two groups of managers who were evaluating the same applicants (Feldman & Arnold, 1983).

(4) Interviewers' Standards of Comparison: The Contrast Effect. Interviewers see many job applicants, often one after another, and how they evaluate a particular applicant may depend on the characteristics of those persons whom they had interviewed previously. For example, after having interviewed three undesirable candidates, an interviewer may tend to see an average candidate in a more favorable light than that candidate's qualifications actually merit. That average candidate would be viewed less favorably by the interviewer if the previous applicants had all been highly qualified for the job (Wexley, Yukl, Kovacs, & Sanders, 1972).

In addition to pointing up the importance of your place in an interviewer's schedule, this situation means that interviewers often do not have any objective standard for the kind of person who is considered a suitable employee. Applicants are not evaluated on an absolute basis, but rather are judged relative to the other applicants on a particular day or week. How favorable an applicant appears depends on how good or poor the others are; in other words, the standard for the suitable employee is constantly changing, at least in the unstructured interview situation.

(5) Interviewers' Prejudices. Another characteristic of interviewers that can influence their judgment is their own likes and dislikes. An interviewer may dislike people who smoke, have foreign-sounding names, red hair, and do not meet the interviewer's gaze. Such an interviewer will not be kindly disposed toward a tall, shy, red-haired, chain-smoking job applicant whose name has five syllables. Men interviewers may believe that women are incapable of performing certain kinds of jobs. Studies show that interviewers are much more likely to hire women for so-called traditional female jobs than for so-called traditional male jobs. Older applicants and persons with handicaps tend to receive lower evaluations from interviewers (Arvey & Campion, 1982; Raza & Carpenter, 1987).

Biases can operate both ways. Just as interviewers may dislike people with certain characteristics and disqualify them for a job regardless of their qualifications, they may also hire others simply because they exhibit some characteristic the interviewer likes. For example, in the human factors department of one aerospace company, no employee was taller than the rather short department head. A short person had a definite advantage in being favorably assessed.

This phenomenon of generalizing from one trait or characteristic to the entire person, in either a positive or negative direction, is called the *halo effect*, and it is present whenever we fallible human beings make personal judgments about others. However, careful training of interviewers can reduce the effects of these prejudices, as well as of the other errors discussed in this section.

Situational Interviews

A different type of interview, the *situational interview*, is developed specifically to meet the needs of a particular job. The interview questions are not designed to inquire into general characteristics, traits, or abilities, but rather into the actual behaviors needed for the job in question. The job behaviors are determined by a systematic job analysis conducted by the critical-incidents technique.

The first step, therefore, in developing the situational interview is to prepare a list of critical incidents that differentiate between current successful and unsuccessful employees. These incidents are written by supervisors who have intimate knowledge of the job. The supervisors determine *benchmarks* for scoring the critical incidents, giving a score of 5 for those behaviors displayed by successful employees, 3 for behaviors displayed by mediocre employees, and 1 for those displayed by poor employees. Then, it is relatively easy to rephrase the incidents as questions, all of which are directly related to how the person would behave on the job for which he or she is applying. Because of the use of the benchmarks developed by persons who have detailed knowledge of the job, the scoring of the situational interview is objective.

The situational-interview approach has been used to select sawmill workers, first-line supervisors, salesclerks, and unskilled pulpmill workers, among others. In all cases, the interview results correlated highly with later performance on the job and were more valid than structured interviews (Maurer & Fay, 1988). The situational interview is quick to administer, once constructed. Also, it increases the motivation of job applicants because the questions are directly related to the job for which they are applying. Research has shown that situational interviews are also easier to administer and to interpret than unstructured and even structured interviews (Weekley & Gier, 1987).

As difficult, limited, and error prone as the standard interview approach is, it continues to be part of virtually every selection program in industry and government. The danger lies in placing too much emphasis on it. If used sparingly and wisely as an adjunct to more objective methods of selection, the interview can be of help to both the company and the applicant. And, as we have seen, predictive accuracy can be markedly improved by training and by developing structured or situational interviews.

References and Letters of Recommendation

A frequently used technique in the total selection process involves obtaining information about applicants from those who have known them, for example, former teachers, co-workers, employers, and perhaps friends. The purpose of this is to explore other people's impressions of the applicants and to verify the nature of the work experience the applicants report. It is not unreasonable to expect that the workers' performance, attitude, and general behavior in a past job will provide some indication of how they may behave in the job for which they are applying.

Reality has not matched that expectation. The predictive validity of letters of reference is, on the average, no higher than +.14, indicating a pronounced lack of accuracy in predicting job success (Paunonen, Jackson, & Oberman, 1987; Reilly & Chao, 1982).

The major limitation to the use of letters of recommendation is that they may present a misleading picture of the applicant. The person writing the reference may deliberately lie about a candidate's abilities for several reasons. A past employer may simply wish to be kind and will not say anything unfavorable about a former employee. Or an applicant's present employer may give an undesirable employee a glowing letter of reference in the hope that another company will hire the employee. Also, as we noted, many companies are no longer willing to supply evaluative information about former employees for fear of being sued for slander, defamation of character, or libel. Between 1982 and 1987, approximately 8,000 such lawsuits were filed against employers by former employees. In most cases, the verdicts went against the companies, with awards running as high as $2 million. "The mere threat of this type of lawsuit has chilled even ordinary reference checking," one attorney said ("Revenge of the Fired," 1987, p. 46).

Legal authorities now advise companies to adopt a policy of risk avoidance by refusing to reveal any information about former employees beyond dates of employment, job title, and final rate of pay. Any additional information supplied about ex-employees should be based on documentary evidence, not on opinion. For example, if a company chooses to describe the poor performance of a fired employee, it should, for its own protection, cite specific incidents—with dates, times, and places—and be prepared to document those incidents in a court of law. Supervisors are urged to assume that anything they put in a letter of reference may someday be scrutinized by a judge or jury (Dube, 1986; Essex, 1988).

Even though the amount and kind of information now received from references tends to be minimal, one survey of 115 personnel managers showed that 92% of them still checked references, if only to verify dates of employment and salaries (Blocklyn, 1988b).

There are also less sinister reasons for inaccurate letters of recommendation. A former employer may not have known the employee well enough to offer an evaluation but will nonetheless forward a general form letter that is likely to be of little value. Even if the employee was well known to the employer, the employer may lack the ability to describe and assess the worker adequately. In general, then, most letters of recommendation tend to be overly lenient.

There are several approaches to securing recommendations. The former employer may be asked to write a *letter* describing the job applicant's character and abilities. Sometimes a *questionnaire* is used or a *form* is provided, and the former employer is asked to supply detailed information where known.

Another way of checking references is to interview the persons over the *telephone*. A skillful interviewer can obtain a more accurate and thorough evaluation of a candidate in this manner than with a questionnaire or letter. People are often more willing to speak frankly when they are not committing their views to paper. Also, more specific as well as follow-up questions can be asked in a telephone conversation because it is a more flexible interview situation.

A costly and time-consuming approach is the *field investigation*. In this approach, references are interviewed in person. Research with this technique has shown that it can elicit a great deal of information not obtainable through letters. For example, in comparing the results of a questionnaire that had been sent with field interviews on the same applicants, it was found that unfavorable information (job incompetence, alcoholism, etc.) uncovered in the field interviews had not been mentioned by the references in their written recommendations (Lilienthal, 1980).

Because of legal difficulties, then, letters of reference are being used less frequently as a selection technique.

Assessment Centers: Selection by Simulation

The assessment center is a method of selection that places applicants in a simulated job situation so that their behavior under stress can be observed and evaluated. This approach, initially called situational testing, was developed and used by the German army in the 1920s to select officer candidates of high quality. It was first used extensively by American psychologists during World War II when it was adopted by the Office of Strategic Services (OSS).

The mission of the OSS was to send secret agents behind enemy lines. The selection procedures were deliberately designed to induce a high level of stress. How candidates reacted to these conditions, it was thought, would predict how they would react to the stress of behind-the-lines operations.

One test required the candidate to build a bridge across a stream in a fixed period of time. No plans were given, but the candidate was assigned a group of workers. In this way, the candidate's ingenuity, ability to improvise, and leadership skills could be appraised in a real-life setting. Further, to see how the candidate reacted to frustration, some of the workers assigned were stooges, instructed to do everything possible to prevent the building of the bridge. Many candidates broke down in tears when faced with such maddening frustration (OSS Assessment Staff, 1948).

The simulation techniques used by business organizations today are not as stressful as those of the OSS, but they are realistic enough so that it is possible to see how candidates work under pressure or how flexible they are in adapting to rapidly changing situations.

The use of situational testing in industry was pioneered by the American Telephone and Telegraph Company (AT&T) in the mid-1950s (Bray, 1964, 1982). It has since been adopted by more than 2,000 organizations, including IBM, Standard Oil of Ohio, the U.S. Department of Agriculture, Ford Motor Company, and Kodak. Assessment centers are also found in Britain, Brazil, Australia, Japan, and Western Europe. Over 21% of all business firms in Britain use assessment centers (Robertson & Makin, 1986). For the most part, assessment centers are used to select managers and executives, but they have also been used to predict job success for salespersons, police, pharmacists, stockbrokers, government workers, blue-collar workers, and women officers in the Israeli army (Gaugler, Rosenthal, Thornton, & Bentson, 1987; Tenopyr & Oeltjen, 1982; Tziner & Dolan, 1982).

Assessment centers usually involve 6 to 12 candidates at a time who are evaluated as they work through a series of exercises over several days. Candidates may be given psychological tests (particularly cognitive ability and personality tests) and are interviewed extensively, but most of the time is devoted to exercises designed to simulate the problems of high-level jobs. The candidates perform these work samples primarily using the in-basket technique or the leaderless group discussion. Both exercises attempt to reproduce the conditions of managerial-level work as a way of eliciting management-oriented behaviors.

The *in-basket test* presents each applicant with an in-basket such as that found on virtually every managerial or executive desk. The in-basket contains the typical problems, questions, and directives that managers would find when they returned to work from vacation. The applicants must process this material in a fixed period of time; that is, they must demonstrate how they would handle such questions and problems on the job. After the exercise, the applicants may be required to justify their decisions in personal interviews with the assessors.

AT&T's program relies heavily on the in-basket exercise. The candidate, acting as a supervisor, must process 25 items—memos, orders, and correspondence—in 3 hours. The assessors observe the candidates to see if they are systematic and establish priorities, delegate authority to subordinates, or become enmeshed in trivialities. Research shows that in-basket exercises can be scored with a high degree of reliability by the assessors (Smith & Tarpey, 1987). For most candidates, the in-basket exercise is their first taste of managerial responsibility. Some do not like it and refuse any forthcoming promotion. It certainly seems better for the employee and the company to come to this realization before rather than after an employee has spent an unsatisfactory and frustrating period on the job as a manager.

In the *leaderless group discussion*, the applicants meet as a group to discuss an actual business problem. For example, they might be given information about a group of subordinates from among whom they must select one for promotion. As the meeting proceeds, the behavior of the applicants is observed to see how each participant interacts with the others and what leadership and persuasive skills he or she displays.

In one leaderless group discussion exercise at AT&T, a group of five or six candidates were told that they were managers of a company and were directed to increase profits within a fixed period of time. They were given information about the company and the market, but no one was appointed leader and no rules were set forth as to how they should accomplish their goal. Typically, however, one candidate assumes the leader's role, and his or her abilities in fulfilling these responsibilities can be evaluated. The other group members are assessed on their cooperation in performing the tasks assigned by the leader.

To induce additional pressure, the participants are notified of changes in prices or costs every 20 minutes, sometimes immediately after the total problem has been solved. The new information must be considered and the planning renewed. All the while, the candidates are being watched by the assessors and the clock is ticking away. The situation is extremely stressful, and some participants become angry, disrupting the group or being obstructive. As the exercise progresses, the contrast between those who can function well under stress and those who cannot becomes obvious.

In addition to these two primary exercises, assessment centers often use *oral presentations* and *role playing*. In the oral-presentation exercise, candidates are given a packet of information on some aspect of a company's operations such as the development of a new product or a new sales campaign. The candidates must organize this material and present it to the group, a task similar to that executives often undertake on the job.

In the role-playing exercise, the candidate must act out or play the role of a manager in a simulated real-life situation from the world of work. For example, he or she may have to interview a job candidate, fire an incompetent employee, or deal with an angry superior.

Assessment centers can be a target of resentment and complaint, particularly from those who perform poorly in the exercises. Many persons believe that being evaluated unfavorably in an assessment center marks the end of their career, no matter how brilliant a record they may have compiled in their years on the job. Some candidates believe that success in an assessment center depends more on being outgoing, glib, or having a sparkling personality than on competence at managerial tasks.

There may be some truth to these charges. Several studies have demonstrated that interpersonal skills play a major role in the assessments given. Active and aggressive participation becomes an important criterion in the evaluations, perhaps to the point where quantity rather than quality of participation is rewarded. Of course, interpersonal skills are an undeniable part of executive functioning. Research does confirm, however, that the second criterion on which ratings are based is organizing and decision-making ability. This provides a more direct reflection of managerial competence.

Organizations using the assessment center technique believe that it is well worth their high costs because, as we noted in Chapter 1, assessment centers frequently more than pay for themselves. Studies have shown a gain in performance in excess of $2,600 per person per year when job candidates are selected by assessment centers instead of interviews. This represents an average gain of almost $12,000 per manager over the 4.4 years that their careers were followed, a gain considerably higher than the cost of sending them through the assessment centers (S. Adler, 1987).

Studies have shown that those persons selected for managerial jobs by means of assessment centers or promoted from within the organization to higher level jobs, perform as much as 50% better than those selected by traditional techniques. Other studies have shown that job candidates who received favorable assessments were significantly more likely to be promoted in the organization (even when their superiors did not have access to their assessment center evaluations) than were those who were assessed unfavorably. The latter were also much more likely to fail as managers (Bray, Campbell, & Grant, 1974; Cascio & Silbey, 1979).

Research has consistently shown high predictive validities for assessment centers, with validity coefficients ranging from +.30 to +.53 (Gaugler, Rosenthal, Thornton, & Bentson, 1987). Although we cannot yet say with complete certainty why assessment centers are such valid predictors, much research has been conducted on the way in which they operate. For example, validity has been shown to be highest under the following conditions: (1) when the group being assessed consists of a large proportion of women and a smaller proportion of minority candidates; (2) when a greater number of different types of exercises are used; and (3) when psychologists rather than managers serve as the assessors (Klimoski & Brickner, 1987).

Other research demonstrates that assessment centers measure primarily specific job performance factors rather than general managerial characteristics and abilities (Bycio, Hahn, & Alvares, 1987). Another study showed that men assessors rated women candidates higher than they did men candidates (Walsh, Weinberg, & Fairfield, 1987).

Participation in assessment centers can also lead to important changes in one's perception of interpersonal and administrative skills. Specifically, candidates who do well tend to believe they can develop more managerial skills. Those who do poorly tend to have lowered personal expectations for promotion. For that reason, it has been suggested that assessment centers serve an important function as realistic job previews, demonstrating to candidates what life as a manager would be like (Noe & Steffy, 1987).

Research also confirms important changes in candidates' self-perceptions as a result of being evaluated in an assessment center. In that sense, assessment center participation can be a valuable learning experience for candidates, increasing their self-insight even without receiving specific feedback from assessors. Self-assessments of planning and organizing ability are most affected by the in-basket exercise. Self-assessment of one's ability to influence others is most affected by group exercises such as the leaderless group discussion (Schmitt, Ford, & Stults, 1986).

There are other advantages of assessment centers. An unintended, but valuable, advantage is the development of behavioral observation, group dynamics, and problem-solving skills in the assessors. Assessors are typically managers from the organization who are sent to a center for a short period of time. Initially, their role was just to evaluate candidates, but the experience also provides them with extensive management-development training.

It is imperative that assessors be adequately trained in the evaluation of performance in assessment centers. Insufficient training of assessors can lead to unreliable and useless evaluations. So important an issue is this that the Task Force on Development of Assessment Center Standards has established an assessor certification program to ensure that assessors are able to observe precisely the behavior being measured.

The assessment center experience is also a training exercise for the candidates. Their management and interpersonal skills in addition to being assessed can be developed and refined by the feedback they receive from the assessors. Another advantage is that assessment centers do not conflict with legal requirements for equal employment opportunity. The exercises present realistic samples of the job for which a candidate is applying. Therefore, they are not open to the charge of irrelevance, as is the case with some psychological test and application blank information. The exercises are clearly job related.

Other Selection Techniques: Polygraphs, Honesty Tests, and Graphology

The *polygraph* or *lie-detector apparatus* is used in industry today to screen out potentially dishonest job applicants and to attempt to detect theft. It is estimated that American businesses lose $40 billion each year because of employee theft, embezzlement, espionage, the selling of corporate secrets, computer tampering, and other forms of employee dishonesty. It has been estimated that up to half of all employees steal at least one item every month from their employers (Cliff, 1986). Other estimates place the extent of employee theft at approximately 50% in manufacturing plants and offices, 58% in supermarkets, and 60% to 80% in other retail businesses. Further, fewer than 5% of all dishonest employees are caught and even fewer prosecuted and convicted (Taylor, 1986).

Surveys show that some 20% of U.S. corporations use polygraphs to test two million job applicants and employees annually (Fry & Fry, 1988). Polygraphs are used most frequently in the banking, securities, and retail industries. As many as 80% of those companies that use polygraphs refuse to hire applicants who fail the test. The rest will hire those who fail only on a probationary or trial basis (Greenberg, 1988).

The polygraph purports to measure deception, dishonesty, and lying by measuring changes in physiological functions such as heart rate, blood pressure, breathing rate, and the galvanic skin response (the electrical resistance of the skin).

Supporters of the polygraph claim accuracy of over 90% (Fry & Fry, 1988). A considerable body of research disputes such claims, noting results no better than chance. Accuracy can be reduced by tranquilizers, self-inflicted pain, the deliberate concentration on exciting or disturbing thoughts, and, of course, by the ability to lie without experiencing anxiety about it. Many people submitting to a polygraph test are judged to be lying when they are actually telling the truth (Murphy, 1987). A major U.S. government study concluded that the polygraph has no predictive value for personnel selection and screening ("Scientific Validity of Polygraph Testing," 1983). The British Psychological Society reached the same conclusion (Anderson & Shackleton, 1986).

The *voice stress analyzer* is a type of lie detector, a device that measures small tremors in the human voice. Like the polygraph, this machine essentially measures a person's state of nervousness or emotion rather than honesty or dishonesty. Unlike the polygraph apparatus, which is operated in full view and to which an individual is attached by electrodes, the voice stress analyzer can be used without a person's awareness. An interview may be tape-recorded for analysis at a later time. The device is even less accurate in detecting lying than the polygraph, and it is not considered by personnel psychologists to be a viable selection technique (Rice, 1978).

There are now laws restricting but not eliminating the use of polygraphs in 42 states and Washington, D.C. In 1988, the U.S. Congress passed a bill forbidding most private employers, but not the federal government, from using the polygraph to screen job applicants or to test current employees. The exceptions to the law are drug companies, private security firms, and organizations whose work involves public health, safety, or national security.[1] The legislation was supported by the American Psychological Association, which worked with the congressional staff and provided psychologists to serve as experts in hearings and briefings.

Another approach to detecting and predicting employee dishonesty involves *honesty tests*, paper-and-pencil tests that have been developed as more socially acceptable alternatives to polygraphs. Some 2.5 million tests are sold to American corporations every year (Bean, 1987). The tests are cheaper to administer and can be used in situations where the polygraph and the voice stress analyzer have been outlawed.

Most of the tests have been developed by security firms that specialize in the use of the polygraph, and little information has been published on reliability, validity, or norms for these tests. Some research suggests that they cannot

---

[1] It has been suggested that it makes little sense to use for jobs involving public safety and national security a selection device that has been outlawed for most other jobs on the grounds that it is invalid.

accurately identify employees who are stealing from their employers (Moore, 1987; Office of Technology Assessment, 1987). Thus, although these paper-and-pencil tests are popular with American businesses, they have not met the criteria for sound and useful psychological tests, as we shall see in Chapter 4.

Although most psychologists believe that *graphology* (the study of handwriting) is unscientific, it is being widely used as a means of employee selection in the United States and elsewhere. At least 3,000 American corporations use graphology, and in Europe it is being applied by an astounding 85% of all companies surveyed. In Israel, the technique is more popular than psychological testing (Fischman, 1987b; Nevo, 1987; Taylor & Sackheim, 1988). Further, the use of graphology appears to be increasing, a development two British psychologists have called "regrettable" (Anderson & Shackleton, 1986, p. 22).

Proponents and practitioners of handwriting analysis claim that the technique is a valid predictor of job success, but their evidence is primarily anecdotal. Most carefully controlled research has demonstrated consistently that graphologists perform no better than chance in making predictions of job success. The predictive validity of graphology as a selection technique is quite low (Ben-Shakhar, Bar-Hillel, Bilu, Ben-Abba, & Flug, 1986).

With graphology, and any other technique that is so strongly refuted by sound research, it is incumbent upon personnel psychologists to make their findings better known to those in industry who are responsible for employee selection. Here is another instance in which improved communication is needed between researchers and those who are in a position to apply the results of that research.

Standard Success Predictors for Managers

When a company is choosing from among a group of college graduates, it almost always considers the applicants' performance on several background success predictors such as college grades, quality of the college attended, and extracurricular activity participation. Regardless of the selection techniques used by a company, these items of biographical data will be determined early in the selection process. Often, a candidate with a poor showing on these items will be eliminated.

On the surface, this approach seems to make sense. It is reasonable to suppose that an applicant who graduated with top grades from a prestigious Ivy League university and who participated in a number of extracurricular activities may make a better manager than one with average or lower grades from a lesser known university.

But are such suppositions accurate? In an effort to determine the effect of college experiences on later managerial performance, psychologists at AT&T conducted two longitudinal studies of managers, comparing their performance in AT&T's assessment center, on a variety of questionnaires and psychological tests, and actual job behavior. The first study, called the Management Progress

Study, was begun in 1956; the Management Continuity Study was begun in 1977 (Bray, 1964; Howard, 1986). This comprehensive 30-year research program is described in a book entitled *Managerial Lives in Transition* (Howard & Bray, 1988).

The initial question the psychologists considered was whether there were job performance differences among managers between those who had attended college and those who had not. It was found that college attendance correlated positively with job success. Those who had gone to college showed much greater potential for middle and upper management when they were initially hired than did those who had not gone to college. Eight years later, these differences were even more pronounced, with the college sample rising faster and higher in the management ranks than the noncollege sample.

Grades attained in college correlated positively with assessment center ratings of management potential and with later advancement. Those who earned higher grades in college showed higher potential for promotion, achieved their first promotion earlier, and rose higher in management than those whose college grades were lower.

The quality of the college attended was found to be a less useful predictor of later job performance, although the assessment center ratings were higher for managers who had attended what was considered a higher quality college than for those who had attended a lower quality college.

A more valid predictor of both potential and actual promotion was one's major field of study in college. Those who majored in the humanities or the social sciences received superior ratings in assessment centers and in job performance, and moved faster and farther up the management ladder. Those who majored in business administration ranked second. Mathematics, science, and engineering majors were third.

The research showed that humanities and social science majors were superior in decision making, creativity in solving business problems, intellectual ability, written communication skills, and motivation for advancement. They, and the business administration majors, ranked higher than math, science, and engineering majors in interpersonal skills, leadership ability, oral communication skills, and flexibility.

Some extracurricular activities in college correlated positively with various measures of management potential, although they were not related to actual advancement. The significant extracurricular activities included student government, school newspaper, and debating team. Participation in sports showed no relationship to management potential.

The AT&T research provides ample evidence that the standard success predictors for managers, with the possible exception of the quality of the college attended, are valid predictors of a successful career in management.

As impressive and important as these findings are, however, two warnings are in order: (1) not all those who are high on these predictive variables will be successful on the job; and (2) some of those who are low on these factors will be successful on the job. Although the results of the research seem to favor selecting those persons who are high on the standard success predictor variables, it would be a waste of talent to reject automatically all persons who are low on these variables, without giving them the opportunity to demonstrate their abilities on other selection techniques.

No matter which selection technique is preferred, it should not be relied on exclusively. No technique is infallible. A personnel selection program should include a combination of techniques to maximize the chances of matching the right person with the right job.

Summary

The proper selection of employees—matching the right person with the right job—is a vital and complex process. Problems of **organizational entry**, which involve the applicant's preferences and expectancies as well as the nature of the recruiting efforts, are among the first to be dealt with in selection. A person's first job experience influences the rest of his or her working life; it is important that applicant expectancies match the realities of the job. This can be accomplished through a **realistic job preview**, an important aspect of recruiting. When both good and bad parts of a job are presented, applicants do not maintain unrealistic expectations about the work. The **recruitment** process has been aided by psychological research on the satisfactions job applicants desire in their work and the characteristics organizations are seeking among potential employees.

A selection program requires a sequence of specific operations, including (1) job analysis, (2) worker analysis, (3) establishment of minimal requirements and cutoff scores for the selection techniques, (4) recruitment of applicants, (5) administration of the chosen selection techniques, and (6) validation of the techniques (finding out how well they correlate with some measure of subsequent performance on the job).

The selection process has been affected by equal employment opportunity legislation. Selection techniques should be **job related** and should minimize **adverse impact** on minority groups in hiring decisions. Efforts must also be made to prevent discrimination against qualified majority-group members (**reverse discrimination**). Racism, sexism, ageism, prejudice against the handicapped, and factors such as "beautyism" and "nationalism" all affect the hiring process.

The first step in the selection process, **job analysis**, involves a highly detailed description of the component tasks performed on a job. The results are used not only for selection but also to set up training programs, to redesign jobs, and to reveal safety hazards in equipment design or work procedures. Job analysis can be undertaken by (1) referring to published job analyses such as the **Dictionary of Occupational Titles**, (2) interviewing in person or through questionnaires (structured or unstructured) those who are directly connected with the job, (3) directly observing the workers performing the job, (4) having the workers keep a systematic log of daily job activities, and (5) recording critical incidents that are vital to successful performance of the job. On the basis of the information collected in the job analysis, a **job specification** is written that defines the characteristics to be sought in those persons who apply for the job.

Specific techniques of selection are **biographical information** collected through standard application blanks and derivatives such as weighted application blanks and biographical inventories, **interviews, letters of recommendation, and assessment centers**.

Application blanks can provide much useful information about job candidates that can be directly related to the probability of success on the job. As an instrument of selection, the application blank first requires research to correlate each item of information with some subsequent objective measure of job performance. Weighted application blanks and biographical inventories have been successful in predicting success on the job and are not unlike some psychological tests in objectivity of scoring and the types of questions that are used. Some job applicants provide misleading information on application blanks, particularly with regard to college credentials and previous work experience. Many companies are reluctant to release information on ex-employees for fear of being sued. Hence, it can be difficult to check the accuracy of information supplied on application forms.

Training and work experience evaluation (T&E) involves the prediction of job performance on the basis of judgments of the information supplied by applicants about their training and experience. T&E information is assigned weights based on the hypotheses of supervisors and other job experts about the degree of the relationship between training and experience and successful job performance. Five approaches to T&E are the point; grouping; task; behavioral consistency; and knowledge, skills, and ability (KSA) methods.

The **interview** as a selection device, despite consistently unfavorable research findings, continues to be relied on by employing organizations. The weakest interview is the **unstructured** approach; the **structured** interview is a potentially more valid predictive device. Also, if interviews are conducted by a panel of interviewers, their predictive value increases. Basic weaknesses of interviews are (1) failure of interviewers to agree, (2) failure of interviews to predict job success, (3) pressure of the interview situation, (4) interviewers' subjective standards of comparison, and (5) interviewers' prejudices. In the **situational interview**, questions relating to actual job behaviors are developed from a job analysis using the **critical-incidents** technique. This may be the most valid interview predictor of job success.

Letters of recommendation, despite the recognized tendency of letter writers to be overly kind and the reluctance of employers to reveal only factual information for fear of being sued, are part of most selection programs. Four ways to secure recommendations on a job applicant are to (1) ask the person's former employer to write a letter or (2) fill out a questionnaire, (3) telephone the former employer, and (4) interview the former employer in person.

A technique used primarily for selecting managers and executives is the **assessment center**, where job candidates perform a series of exercises that realistically simulate problems found on the job. Using mainly the **in-basket technique**, the **leaderless group discussion**, **oral presentation**, and **role playing**, applicants are assessed by trained managers on their interpersonal skills and leadership and decision-making abilities. Although the assessment center approach has some problems, including the determination of criteria for success, these seem to be outweighed by advantages that include high predictive validity, compatibility with equal employment opportunity legislation, management-development training for both the candidates and the assessors, and changes in candidates' self-perceptions.

Polygraphs and **voice stress analyzers** (so-called lie detectors) are widely used in selection. However, neither device is an accurate measure of deception and their use has been restricted by federal and local legislation. Some firms are using paper-and-pencil **honesty tests** instead. **Graphology** (handwriting analysis) is used for selection by many employers in the United States and abroad, despite research showing its lack of validity.

Certain standard success predictors for managers are almost always considered in evaluating college graduates. They are based on assumptions made about the college experience. Longitudinal research on AT&T managers revealed that those who showed the greatest management potential in assessment centers, and who were more successful on the job, were college graduates who had earned high grades, participated in selected extracurricular activities, and majored in the humanities or social sciences. The quality of the college attended was a less useful success predictor.

Key Terms

adverse impact
application blanks
assessment centers
biographical
    inventories
critical incidents
Dictionary of
    Occupational Titles
    (DOT)
Equal Employment
    Opportunity
    Commission
    (EEOC)

fair employment
    practices
graphology
honesty tests
human resources
    management
in-basket technique
job analysis
job samples
job specification
leaderless group
    discussion
personnel psychology

polygraphs
realistic job previews
references
reverse discrimination
role-playing technique
situational interviews
structured interviews
training and work
    experience
    evaluation (T&E)
unstructured
    interviews

CASE STUDIES

Situational Interviews

The management of a major department store decided to lease its fine jewelry department to an outside company, which would operate the jewelry counters independently within the store facilities. As part of the lease agreement, the new company promised to evaluate for possible employment the salespersons currently working at the store's jewelry counters. The personnel manager had to determine which of the 54 present employees should be retained. To solve the problem, it was decided to use the situational interview approach.

The first step was to develop the questions to be asked in the interviews. A number of critical incidents were collected (behaviors that differentiate between successful and unsuccessful employees). These incidents were rephrased as questions that were then asked of each employee; how would he or she behave in or cope with the situation described? One question involved the best way to deal with a customer who was angry because the repair of his wristwatch was a week overdue. The applicants were given 3 alternative ways of handling the situation and asked to select one.

QUESTIONS

1. How would you go about collecting critical incidents for the job of jewelry salesperson?
2. How would you determine whether an applicant's answer represented the best way of handling a given situation?
3. What measure or measures of job performance could be used to validate the questions asked in the interview?
4. How do situational interviews differ from structured interviews?
5. What are the advantages of using situational interviews as a means of selecting employees?

Reference: J. A. Weekley & J. A. Gier (1987). Reliability and validity of the situational interview for a sales position. *Journal of Applied Psychology, 72*, 484–487.

Assessment Centers

Nearly 1,700 candidates for supervisory jobs in a large manufacturing company underwent 1 day of evaluation in an assessment center. Their participation in 5 exercises was observed. The exercises included (1) the in-basket technique, in which the candidates had 1 hour to respond to memos, reports, and other material, (2) the role-playing technique, in which the candidates played different roles to act out their solutions to on-the-job problems, (3) the human relations exercise, in which they evaluated a videotape of the interaction between a supervisor and an employee, (4) the problem-solving group exercise, in which individually and in small groups they tried to resolve job problems, and (5) a personal interview, in which each candidate was asked about work experience, job goals and preferences, and perceived skills and abilities.

The primary purpose of the assessments was to select those persons qualified for promotion to a first level supervisory position. A secondary purpose was to determine if performance on assessment center tasks would affect the candidates' perceptions of their own abilities. Would their behavior in the various exercises—even in the absence of feedback from the assessors—change the way they felt about their own supervisory skills?

QUESTIONS

1. How would you measure the self-perceptions of the candidates?
2. How would you determine whether any changes in perceived ability resulted from the assessment center experience?
3. In what ways would each of the 5 exercises influence your own self-perceptions?
4. Discuss other research showing that changes in

self-perceptions may result from being evaluated in an assessment center.

5. What are the advantages and disadvantages of assessment centers as a method of employee selection?

Reference: N. Schmitt, J. K. Ford, & D. M. Stults. (1986). Changes in self-perceived ability as a function of performance in an assessment centre. *Journal of Occupational Psychology, 59,* 327–335.

Additional Reading

Gatewood, R. D., & Feild, H. S. (1987). *Human Resource Selection*. New York: Dryden. A college textbook offering comprehensive treatment of fair employment practices, job analysis, application blanks, interviews, testing, and other issues in employee selection.

Grant, P. C. (1988). What use is a job description? *Personnel Journal, 67*(2), 45–53. Describes how job analysis data are used to prepare job descriptions, and how job descriptions can be used to recruit and motivate employees.

Hatfield, E., & Sprecher, S. (1986). *Mirror, Mirror: The Importance of Looks in Everyday Life*. Albany: University of New York Press. Reviews the phenomenon of physical attractiveness, with many examples from popular culture, and includes a chapter on the impact of physical appearance on hiring and job success.

Levine, E. L. (1983). *Everything You Always Wanted to Know About Job Analysis*. Tampa, FL: Workforce Dynamics. A clear, light-hearted, and informative guide to job analysis based on current research and practice.

Stevens, N. D. (1986). *Dynamics of Job-Seeking Behavior*. Springfield, IL: Chas. C. Thomas. Discusses the recruitment, selection, and training of new college graduates and examines effective approaches to career counseling.

Chapter 4

Employee Selection 2: Psychological Testing

CHAPTER OUTLINE

Introduction

What Is a Psychological Test?

Purposes of Psychological Tests

Characteristics of Psychological Tests
Standardization
Objectivity
Norms
Reliability
Validity
Validity Generalization

Fair Employment Legislation and Testing
Testing for the Handicapped

Establishing a Testing Program

Types of Psychological Tests: Administration
Individual and Group Tests
Computer-Assisted Testing
Speed and Power Tests
Paper-and-Pencil and Performance Tests
Objective and Subjective Scoring

Types of Psychological Tests: Characteristics Measured
Cognitive Ability
Interests
Aptitudes
Motor Ability
Personality

Advantages of Psychological Testing

Limitations and Dangers of Psychological Testing
The Uncritical Use of Tests
Unfair Rejection of Applicants
Faking Test Responses
Conformity
Quality of Psychological Testing Programs

Introduction

An important personnel selection technique is the psychological test. As you already know from your own experience, the use of psychological tests is widespread at all levels and periods of life.

Most public school systems give intelligence, aptitude, and interest tests to pupils at various stages in their education. If students are experiencing academic or social difficulties in school, they are likely to be referred to a school psychologist who will administer additional psychological tests to help diagnose the problem.

Nearly all those who attend college are admitted partly on the basis of their performance on an entrance examination. Those who want to continue their education in professional or graduate schools must take competitive examinations. In addition, persons headed for military service find that there is a test for almost every job and rank in the military. Indeed, one of their first few days in the service will be spent taking a comprehensive battery of tests.

In industry, tests are used to select employees for all levels of corporate responsibility, from apprentice to president. Many organizations administer tests not only to applicants but also to current workers to determine which ones have the ability to be promoted.

Some critics of testing believe that organizations rely too heavily on psychological tests. Others, including the U.S. Congress, argue that testing constitutes an unwelcome and unwarranted invasion of privacy. And, finally, the problem of providing equal employment opportunities offers a massive challenge to the use of tests as selection devices, a challenge so severe that the use of testing in industry underwent a sharp decline in the 1970s and early 1980s.

Many employing organizations stopped using tests during that period, despite their high predictive values, because of the threat of legal action arising from equal employment opportunity legislation. They turned instead to other selection methods (such as those we discussed in Chapter 3), which are less useful for predicting job success than the best psychological tests. Further, as we saw, some selection techniques permit greater possibilities for discrimination than do psychological tests.

There are indications that this trend away from the use of tests in employee selection has been reversed, especially with regard to tests of cognitive or mental ability. Beginning in the mid-1980s, there has been a marked resurgence in the use of psychological tests as selection devices in the United States (Burke & Normand, 1987; Taylor & Zimmerer, 1988). In Britain, where tests never lost favor because of the fair employment issue, surveys show that more than 70% of all employers use tests for selection purposes (Anderson & Shackleton, 1986). Some of the Japanese manufacturing plants now located in the United States rely heavily on tests. At Toyota's automobile plant in Georgetown, Kentucky, for example, job candidates undergo some 14 hours of testing, a screening procedure so rigorous that only 1 applicant out of 20 is accepted (Fritz, 1988d).

We shall see later in this chapter that growing numbers of personnel psychologists are suggesting that no other selection technique is superior to cognitive ability tests for selecting the best employees. These tests carry fewer opportunities for adverse impact in hiring decisions, and they are excellent predictors of performance both on the job and in training programs for all kinds of jobs (Hunter & Hunter, 1984; Schmidt & Hunter, 1981).

Thus, it may be even more difficult in the future than it is now to progress through life without being asked or required to take some kind of psychological test. In your working career, your performance on psychological tests may determine not only if you will be hired for a job but also what level you will reach by the time of retirement.

The technical and ethical questions involved in emphasizing test performance are constantly argued by psychologists in universities, government, and business. But as long as tests play such a prominent role in your life, it is vital that you have some understanding of what they are, what they can and cannot do, and what their dangers and benefits may be.

What Is a Psychological Test?

A psychological test is a measuring device, a yardstick applied in consistent and systematic fashion to measure a sample of behavior. Of course, the basic idea of a test is nothing new to you at this stage of your career. You have been taking them for many years.

The kinds of tests used to measure level of comprehension of the material in a college course are similar, in principle, to the psychological tests used to assess more complex abilities or characteristics. Your next quiz in this class represents a measuring device used by your professor to gauge your ability to learn this information. Each test in a course measures a sample of knowledge or behavior. For example, if your first test in a course in industrial psychology covers Chapters 1–4 of this book, you will be expected to know all of that material. The examination, however, will not question you on every item of information contained in the four chapters. Such a test would have to be almost as long as the chapters themselves. It is sufficient to question you on only a portion of the material to sample your knowledge. The same is true for psychological tests. On a test of cognitive ability or intelligence, it is impractical to question persons on everything they know to measure their level of intelligence, nor is it necessary. Useful measures of intelligence (or of personality, interest, or mechanical aptitude) can be obtained by asking only a sample of what persons know.

Thus, both a classroom test and a psychological test measure a sample of behavior, but here the resemblance ends. The psychological test is a more sophisticated and rigorous measuring device that has been developed through patient, thorough, and careful research.

Purposes of Psychological Tests

Two purposes are served by psychological tests: selection and placement. Both functions involve making a prediction about an individual's future behavior. The same kinds of tests are used for both purposes; the difference lies in how the results are applied.

For *selection*, the emphasis is on finding a person with the right qualifications for a particular job; the stress is on the job itself and on trying to select from among many applicants the ones who will succeed on that job. Selection is not limited to the initial hiring of an individual. The process is used at all levels, wherever an organization has a vacancy to fill. For example, if a sales manager quits, the company may have to decide who among their current sales force has the ability to be promoted. Selection at this level is more important for the company than at the level of initial employment; the wrong person in a higher level job can do more harm.

For *placement*, the emphasis is on the individual. The problem is to find the right kind of job for a particular person. This process is usually aided by a vocational or guidance counselor who attempts to diagnose an individual's capabilities to suggest the work in which he or she is most likely to succeed. Psychological tests are rarely used for placement purposes in industry but are usually given in schools and colleges.

Characteristics of Psychological Tests

Well-developed and soundly researched psychological tests have several characteristics that set them apart from the tests printed in the Sunday newspaper (the "Are You a Good Spouse?" or "What Is Your Sex Quotient?" variety). A good test involves much more than a list of questions that may sound relevant to the variable being measured. A proper psychological test is standardized, objective, based on sound norms, reliable, and valid.

Standardization

Standardization refers to the consistency or uniformity of the conditions and procedures for administering a test. If we expect to compare the performance of many job applicants on the same test, it is imperative that they all take that test under identical circumstances.

Each test must have its own standardized procedure that must be followed precisely each time the test is given. This means that every person taking the test reads or listens to the same set of instructions (with no variation), is allowed the same amount of time in which to respond, and is situated in a similar physical setting.

Any change in testing procedure may produce a change in individual performance on the test. For example, if the air-conditioning system breaks down in a plant on an extremely hot day, those persons who are unlucky enough to be taking a test may not do as well as those who took the test the day before at a more comfortable temperature. Or, if an inexperienced tester fails out of carelessness to read the complete instructions to a group of applicants, that group is not taking the test under the same conditions as had others.

The appropriate testing procedures can be designed into a test by its developers, but maintaining standardized conditions is the task of the persons actually giving the test. This is why it is so important that test administrators be properly trained. An excellent test can be rendered useless in the hands of an inexperienced or careless tester.

Objectivity

Objectivity, as a characteristic of psychological tests, refers primarily to the scoring of the test results. For a test to be scored objectively, it is necessary that anyone scoring the test be able to obtain the same results. In this way, the scoring process is free of subjective judgment or bias on the part of the scorer.

In the discussion of interviewing, we noted that a weakness of the interview was the subjective nature of the interviewer's judgments about an applicant's qualifications. Similarly, a subjective test is liable to misinterpretation because of a scorer's attitudes, prejudices, or momentary mood.

In your college career, you have no doubt taken objective and subjective examinations. With objective tests (such as multiple-choice or true-false), scoring is a mechanical process that requires no special training or knowledge. A clerk in a company's personnel department or an undergraduate grader in college or a computer can score an objective test as long as a scoring key with the correct answers has been provided. Scoring a subjective test (such as an essay exam) is more difficult and is liable to be influenced by personal characteristics of the grader, including a like or dislike of the person who took the test. To make fair assessments of job applicants as well as equitable compari- sons among them, objective tests are clearly the more desirable. Employers do use some subjective tests for selection purposes, as we shall see, but their results are questionable.

Norms

To interpret the results of a psychological test, a frame of reference or point of comparison must exist so that the performance of one individual can be compared with the performance of other, similar individuals. This is accomplished by means of test norms, the distribution of scores of a large group of people similar in nature to the job applicants being tested. The word *norm* in this context refers specifically to the average or typical performance on the test; this does not imply a level of "normal" or desirable behavior as we might use the term in everyday conversation.

The scores of this group, called the standardization sample, serve as the yardstick against which the applicants' scores are compared to determine their relative standing on the ability being tested. For example, if a high school graduate who applies for a job that requires mechanical skill achieves a score of 82 on a test of mechanical ability, the score alone reveals nothing about the degree of mechanical ability the person possesses. But if we can compare that score of 82 with the test norms, a distribution of scores from a large group of high school graduates, then we can ascribe meaning to the individual score. If the mean of the test norms is 80 and the standard deviation 10, we know immediately that an applicant who scored 82 possesses only an average or moderate amount of mechanical ability. With this comparative information, we are in a much better position to evaluate objectively this applicant's chances of succeeding on the job relative to the other applicants tested.

Some widely used psychological tests have sets of norms for different age groups, sexes, and levels of education. The adequacy of a test's norms can determine its usefulness as an aid to employee selection.

A survey of psychologists who conduct selection assessments of individuals found that nearly 38% of them used both published test norms and norms they or their company computed. Some 32% used only norms computed by themselves or their company, and 28% relied exclusively on published test norms. The important point is that almost all of these psychologists (98%) used normative data of some kind in evaluating test results (Ryan & Sackett, 1987).

Reliability

Reliability refers to the consistency of response on a test. If a group takes an intelligence test one week and achieves a mean score of 100 but then repeats the test a week later and achieves a mean score of 72, we would have to describe the test as unreliable because it yields inconsistent measurements. It is common to find slight variation in test scores when a test is retaken at a later date, but, if the fluctuation is great, it suggests that something is basically wrong with the test or the scoring method.

Before a test can be administered to the public, it is necessary to have a precise indication of the test's reliability. There are several methods for determining reliability.

The *test–retest method* involves administering a test twice to the same group of people and correlating the two sets of scores. The closer the correlation coefficient (called the reliability coefficient in this case) approaches a perfect positive correlation (+1.00), the more reliable is the test. There are several limitations to this approach. It is uneconomical to require workers to be away from their jobs to take the test twice; learning and other experiences between the two testing sessions may cause the group to score higher the second time; and the workers may recall some of the questions and, therefore, score higher on the retest.

The *equivalent-forms method* uses a test-retest approach. Instead of taking the same test a second time, a similar form of the test is given, and the two sets of scores are correlated. The disadvantage of this approach is the difficulty and expense of developing two separate equivalent tests. It is often costly enough to develop one good version of a test. For that reason, this method of establishing reliability is rarely used.

A third approach to the determination of the reliability of a test is the *split-halves method*. The test is taken once, divided in half, and the two sets of items are correlated with each other. This is less time consuming than the other approaches because only one administration of the test is required. Also, there is no opportunity for learning or memory to influence the second score.

Whatever method is used, the investigation of reliability is necessary in the development of a useful test. In choosing a test to be used for selection, the reliability coefficient ideally should exceed +.80, although a coefficient of approximately +.70 is considered acceptable.

Validity

The most important requirement in evaluating any psychological test is that it measure accurately what it is intended to measure. The technical term for this is *validity*. As with reliability, validity is a simple concept to understand but more difficult to attain.

Suppose that a psychologist working for the U.S. Air Force develops a test of radar operator proficiency. The test can be considered valid if it measures those skills needed for competence in this task. One way to determine this is to correlate the test scores with subsequent job performance. If persons who score high on the radar operator proficiency test also perform well on the job (and those who score low on the test perform poorly on the job), then the correlation between test score and performance will be high and the test will be considered a valid predictor of job success. (When the correlation coefficient is used to determine validity, it is called a validity coefficient.) Validity coefficients around +.30 to +.40 are considered acceptable for tests used in selecting employees. It is rare to find a test with a validity coefficient greater than +.50.

This definition of validity is not concerned with the inherent nature or properties of the test but only with the correlation between the score on the test and some subsequent measure of job performance. This approach to defining and establishing validity, which is called *criterion-related validity*, is the most frequently used approach.

Personnel psychologists are concerned with two approaches to criterion-related validity: predictive validity and concurrent validity. *Predictive validity* involves giving the test to all job applicants in a specific time period and then hiring them all, regardless of their performance on the test. At a later time, when some measure or criterion of job performance has been obtained on each worker, the test scores and criteria are correlated to determine how well the test actually predicted job success. Most managements are not in favor of this expensive practice because some of those hired will turn out to be poor workers.

The usual approach in industry to establishing the criterion-related validity of a test is *concurrent validity*, which is used much more often than the predictive approach. The procedure involves giving the test to employees already on the job and then correlating test scores with job performance measures. The major disadvantage of this method is that by using workers already on the job, the validation sample contains only the better employees. Poorer workers will have already been fired, demoted, transferred, or have quit. It is difficult, therefore, to determine with concurrent validity if a test can truly discriminate between good and poor workers.

The notion that predictive validity is superior to concurrent validity is now being challenged. Logically, the predictive approach appears to be the better because of the weaknesses of the concurrent approach we have discussed, but there is little empirical support for one over the other. Both methods have been shown to yield similar results.

The job performance criterion most often used in establishing predictive or concurrent validity is ratings by a supervisor of an employee's present level of performance. Such ratings are made routinely as part of employee performance appraisal, as we shall see in Chapter 5. When supervisor ratings of job performance were compared with quantitative measures of production for the purpose of validating 10 types of mental, perceptual, and motor ability tests, they were found to produce test validities that were highly similar. This suggests that subjective measures such as ratings can be as valid predictors of job success as more objective measures such as quantity of production (Nathan & Alexander, 1988).

Recent research also suggests that a longer range measure, called *promotional progress*, can provide an even more reliable and valid criterion measure of job performance and thus yield more accurate test validation data (Meyer, 1987).

Other research indicates that experienced personnel psychologists can make more accurate estimates of the validities of cognitive ability tests than are obtained by such empirical means as a criterion-related study. When the judgments of 20 experienced psychologists were averaged, the resulting estimate of validity was more accurate than was obtained in research correlating test scores and criterion measures of close to 1,000 subjects (Schmidt, Hunter, Croll, & McKenzie, 1983).

Additional research along this same line showed that less experienced judges (recent PhDs in I/O psychology) could provide estimates of validities as accurate as those obtained from smaller sample empirical studies. These psychologists' estimates were not as accurate, however, as those of the more experienced psychologist-judges cited earlier (Hirsh, Schmidt, & Hunter, 1986).

Personnel psychologists will be closely monitoring the situation to see whether validity estimates by experienced judges will be accepted as an alternative way to validate tests.

In recent years, psychologists have become interested in another aspect of validity, that which relates to the nature or content of the test, independent of its correlation with some external criterion. This kind of validity, called *rational validity*, focuses on the nature of the test itself rather than on the correlation between the test and job performance. In certain situations, it is not feasible to use empirical validation, perhaps because an organization is too small to support these expensive procedures or because the job in question is new. Consider the original selection of the U.S. astronauts, for example. For some years, until the first space flights, there was no measure of job performance that could be correlated with test scores.

Two approaches to establishing the rational validity of a test are content validity and construct validity. *Content validity* involves an attempt to assess the content of a test to assure that it includes a representative sample of all the questions that could be asked. This is accomplished by analyzing the requirements for the job and determining if the test is sampling the skills and abilities that are needed to perform that job. For example, in hiring secretaries, typing and shorthand tests are certainly related to job performance; tests or test questions pertaining to mechanical skills, however, might not be related. Ordinarily, content validity cannot be established by statistical means. Instead, content validity is usually based on the judgments of experts who must determine how appropriate the tests and test items are for the job. As such, establishing content validity has been called an "act of theorizing" (Guion, 1987, p. 208).

Construct validity is an attempt to determine the psychological characteristics measured by a test. How do we know, for example, that a new test that purports to measure intelligence does, in fact, do so? One way to determine this statistically is to correlate scores from the new test with scores on well-established intelligence tests. If the correlation is high, we can have some confidence that the new test is actually measuring the trait or ability it claims to measure.

A leading authority on psychological tests, Anne Anastasi, has argued that the term *validity* should be restricted to only construct validity because it, more than the other approaches, deals with the interpretation of the meaningfulness of a test (Anastasi, 1986). Other psychologists have also argued that all validity is really construct validity (Hogan & Nicholson, 1988). Anastasi supports an earlier argument that the other types of validity be given labels more descriptive of their actual functions (Messick, 1980). For example, content validity should be called "content relevance" and "content coverage." Criterion-related validity should be called "predictive utility." It seems unlikely, however, that these terms will be changed in the near future, if at all. Once a label becomes an accepted part of a discipline's vocabulary, scientists are reluctant to alter it.

Psychologists sometimes refer to a test's *face validity*. This is not a statistical measure but rather a subjective impression of how well the test questions appear to be related to the job for which the person is being tested. Experienced commercial airline pilots would not think it unusual to take tests dealing with the mechanics of flight or of navigation; these questions are directly related to the job they expect to perform. These pilots might balk, however, at being asked if they loved their parents or when they had their first date because they might not understand what such questions had to do with flying an airplane. Such tests may be said to lack face validity and may well cause the applicants to take them less seriously than they should. This, in turn, could lower their motivation to perform well on the tests. If their test performance is affected, it is certainly not in the best interests of the applicants or the company.

The best available psychological tests include in their manuals the results of validation studies. It is expensive and time consuming to establish a test's validity coefficient, but, without this information, a personnel department can have little confidence that the test is actually measuring the qualities and abilities being sought.

Validity Generalization

Until the late 1970s, psychologists following the doctrine of situational specificity recommended validating a test in every situation for which it was chosen as a selection device, whether for a different job or a different company. Tests were said to be differentially valid, that is, a test valid in one situation was not automatically considered to be appropriate in another. Therefore, no test could be suggested for selection purposes without first determining its validity in the given situation, no matter how valid the test had proven to be in other, perhaps similar, instances.

The idea of situational specificity or differential validity is now being replaced by *validity generalization*. On the basis of large-scale reanalysis of hundreds of previous validity studies (an approach known as *meta-analysis*), psychologists have concluded that tests that are valid in one situation may also be valid in another situation. In other words, the validity of a test, once established, can be generalized (M. J. Burke, 1984; Schmidt & Hunter, 1978, 1981).

If a test is valid for one job, it will be valid for others of the same or similar nature. A test valid in one company will be valid in other companies. And a test valid for one ethnic group will be valid for other ethnic groups. This generalizability has been verified by meta-analyses involving thousands of job applicants (Cornelius, Schmidt, & Carron, 1984). One study reexamined more than 500 validation studies conducted by the U.S. Employment Service, covering some 12,000 jobs (Hunter, 1980). The test in use measured three kinds of ability: cognitive, perceptual, and psychomotor. The results showed that all three abilities were valid predictors of success on the job and of success in training programs for all kinds of jobs.

Similar results were obtained from studies involving clerical, supervisory, computer programming, and law enforcement personnel in a number of organizations (Hirsh, Northrop, & Schmidt, 1986; Hunter & Hunter, 1983; Hunter & Schmidt, 1983). In one study, the same cognitive ability tests were used by 70 companies for six different jobs held by some 3,000 workers. The tests were found to be equally valid for the various kinds of jobs and for all of the companies (Dunnette et al. cited in Zedeck & Cascio, 1984).

In another study involving a meta-analysis of 80 criterion-related validity studies, cognitive tests showed validity generalization across a number of skilled and semiskilled technical jobs in a telephone company (Levine, Cannon, & Spector, 1985).

As impressive as these findings are, the notion of validity generalization is not without criticism and controversy, ranging from the feasibility of conducting meta-analyses in general, to the most appropriate procedures for carrying them out. Some psychologists have cast doubt on the conclusions drawn from certain procedures, as well as their accuracy. Others argue that earlier findings from validity generalization studies may have been overly optimistic (Bangert-Drowns, 1986; Kemery, Roth, & Mossholder, 1987; Spector & Levine, 1987).

The fact that psychologists are divided in their support for validity generalization must be kept in mind when considering the issue of the validity of psychological tests. However, the Society for Industrial and Organizational Psychology notes that "it now seems well established . . . that validities generalize far more than once supposed" (Society for Industrial and Organizational Psychology, 1987, p. 26).

The concept of validity generalization has important practical implications for psychological testing as an employee selection technique. The resurgence of interest in tests, particularly in cognitive ability tests, has been spurred by the validity generalization research. If tests no longer require expensive validation procedures for every job in every company, then employing organizations stand to save both time and money while improving their selection programs. Ideally, a personnel director could ascertain a test's validity from published sources of generalized validities that have been derived from meta-analyses of large samples.

Such an approach to test validation is, as we noted, quite different from the differential validity approach, that is, the practice of validating every selection test for each job and company as required by equal employment opportunity legislation. Until those legal requirements are modified, however, the practical value of validity generalization will not have its full impact on personnel selection in the workplace. Organizations using psychological tests must still establish validities for each situation.

Recent court decisions, however, stand 4 to 1 in favor of validity generalization. These rulings appear to indicate that it can eventually be widely applied in industry. In one court case, for example, the judge ruled that validity generalization "is a proper and accepted practice of generalizing the validity of one program by referring to a study made of another, similar program" (Sharf, 1987, p. 52).

Fair Employment Legislation and Testing

Validity has always been a requirement of psychological tests used for selection purposes. The passage of the equal employment opportunity legislation, however, dramatically increased the attention that psychologists paid to test validation. Psychological testing has come under close scrutiny to ensure that its use does not violate the 1964 Civil Rights Act (Heller, 1986). Section 703(h) of the Civil Rights Act dealing with testing states that, "It shall not be ... an unlawful employment practice for an employer to give and act upon the results of any professionally developed test provided that such test ... is not ... used to discriminate because of race, color, religion, sex, or national origin."

This federal legislation and the growing number of similar state laws have resulted in many investigations by the Equal Employment Opportunity Commission (EEOC) of organizational hiring and testing practices. In 1971, the Supreme Court ruled that tests used by employers must be directly related to the work to be performed.

Suppose, for example, that a company uses a test of cognitive ability to select applicants for a training program for skilled workers. If the records show that most blacks failed this test and most whites passed it, this may suggest that the test discriminates against blacks, not necessarily in terms of their ability to learn the skills, but rather because their educational background may put them at a disadvantage with respect to whites in passing the test. Intelligence tests are heavily weighted with verbal items. White applicants from better schools or home environments that encouraged learning may have an advantage over blacks from poorer schools or disadvantaged home environments. The test may not be measuring native intelligence as much as the available educational and cultural opportunities. Further, white applicants may fare better on selection tests because they may have had more experience in test taking and so do not react to it with as much anxiety. Thus, the test would result in a different validity coefficient for blacks than for whites, and this differential validity is clearly discriminatory.

Civil rights and equal employment opportunity legislation are directed against this kind of discrimination. What must be determined in this example is whether blacks' lower scores on the intelligence test have any relation to performance on the job. It could be the case that the applicants have ample ability to learn the skills necessary for the job but simply lack the background and preparation to pass the test. The burden of proof in demonstrating that a psychological test is job related is on the employing organization.

Of course, this is not a problem with all tests. Tests of specific skills such as typing are free of potential bias with regard to race or any factor other than typing ability.

One result of these legislative and judicial decisions is a marked increase in validity research. If studies clearly show, for example, that applicants of all races who score below a certain level on a test perform unsuccessfully on the job, then the test is not discriminatory by race. Validity research should be conducted anyway. If a test cannot choose among applicants in terms of ability to perform the job, it is worthless as a selection device. Nowadays, however, validity studies are required by law to show that a test is not being used as an illegal discriminatory device.

Criterion-related validation procedures (correlating test scores with actual job performance) are required by EEOC guidelines where feasible. Alternatively, rational validation procedures (content validity and construct validity) may be used. Indeed, EEOC guidelines now accord them equal status with criterion-related validity. Content validity is being increasingly used.

We noted in the last section that differential validity is no longer believed to apply to different ethnic groups. A test that is valid for white job applicants will also be valid for black job applicants. Research has also demonstrated that any differences that are found among average test scores for various ethnic groups are not the result of bias on the part of the test but rather arise from educational and social differences (Hunter & Hunter, 1983).

The National Research Council's Committee on Ability Testing conducted an extensive study of testing for employee selection (Yoder & Staudohar, 1984). Among the conclusions reached were the following:

1. Tests that are standardized do not discriminate against blacks.
2. Black and white applicants who achieve similar test scores generally perform equally well on the job.
3. There are no selection techniques better than tests, both in terms of validity and in reducing adverse impact on minority groups.

The empirical demonstration of validity, however, is no guarantee that a test will not be declared discriminatory and be barred from further use. That occurred with the Professional Administration and Career Exam (PACE), which was used as a selection test for more than 100 different occupations within the federal government. It was a highly valid test that correlated well with job performance.

Despite its impressive validity, PACE was banned for use after 1984 because, based on test scores, insufficient numbers of black applicants were being hired. Thus, adverse impact had been demonstrated and the test was declared illegal, even though it was valid. In 1988, the federal government further reduced its use of tests for selection, now relying instead almost exclusively on the college grade point average of applicants plus some job-related skills tests. There is still no test used for the more than 100 occupations in the federal civil service for which PACE had been used as a selection device (Hebert, 1988).

Another result of fair employment practices is the increasing importance of psychologists in employing organizations. I/O psychologists are needed more than ever before for their expertise in conducting validation studies and for their service as expert witnesses in the many court cases that have arisen out of alleged violations of equal employment opportunity legislation.

Testing for the Handicapped

Although the use of psychological tests has discriminated against minority-group job applicants, other applicants have sometimes been unable to take the tests at all. That form of discrimination has been reduced substantially as a result of EEOC regulations that require psychological tests to be adjusted or modified for handicapped or disabled applicants.

The federal civil service has been a leader in modifying psychological tests for job applicants with physical handicaps, particularly for those with partial to total visual or hearing defects. Obviously, some adjustment is necessary for applicants who are unable to see a written test clearly or to hear verbal instructions but who are otherwise capable of performing many jobs.

One such adjustment is in the administration of psychological tests. For visually handicapped applicants, the civil service presents test questions orally, in large print, or in braille, depending on the type and severity of the applicant's disability.

Another adjustment is in the time allotted to complete the test. Many psychological tests have a fixed time limit, but persons with visual defects will require additional time. Research conducted by personnel psychologists has established the amount of time required for various kinds of tests for visually handicapped applicants.

The content of psychological tests may also have to be changed for visually handicapped job applicants. For example, people who were born blind cannot be expected to answer questions pertaining to colors, shapes, and visual textures that they have never seen. Certain nonverbal and performance test items may also have to be modified or eliminated.

Job applicants with hearing disabilities also require modification of test content and administration. A government research program altered a general ability test by reducing the verbal content of the test, preparing written instructions to replace oral ones, and allowing an empirically determined amount of additional time in which to take the test. The verbal content was reduced because research had shown that persons with hearing disorders show poor verbal performance, not because of low intelligence but because of language deprivation (Nester & Sapinkopf, 1982).

Accommodating psychological tests to handicapped job applicants is time consuming and expensive, requiring much research before the modified tests can be used for selection purposes. It is being done through the efforts of psychologists in both government and private organizations.

Establishing a Testing Program

The basic steps in setting up a testing program are essentially the same as those necessary for any kind of selection program. The first requirement is to investigate the nature of the job for which testing is to be used as a selection device. Once job and worker analyses have been performed, the proper test or tests to measure the behaviors and abilities necessary for success on the job must be carefully chosen or developed. This is a crucial point: No matter how exhaustively a job has been investigated, if a poor test is subsequently used, the selection program is doomed.

Where do psychologists find suitable tests? They can use tests already on the market or can develop new tests specifically for the needs of the job and the company.

There are a large number of commercially available tests. No matter what kind of job is under study, there is probably a test that purports to measure abilities and predict success on that job. Unfortunately, testing is one area of I/O psychology in which the charlatan has been at work. Some prepared tests are little more than dozens of items (often borrowed from other tests) thrown together, given a professional-sounding title, and promoted as surefire ways to hire the right people. Such tests are worth little more than those that appear in popular magazines. Most of these test makers publish no information regarding reliability or validity studies for a very good reason: They did no research on their tests to determine these requirements. For the same reason, no norms are provided.

Trained personnel psychologists, who know what is important in selection devices, would never consider using these phony tests, but untrained personnel managers (having little, if any, background in psychology) might well be persuaded of the value of such tests by an impressive title or a glib sales representative. The tragedy of this situation is that it takes months or years before the company discovers that the test is worthless, before the poor quality of the workers selected on the basis of the bogus test becomes known to the management. In addition, well-qualified applicants might have been turned down by the company because of their score on the fraudulent test, and minority-group applicants may have been subjected to discrimination, thus making the organization a target for lawsuits.

This unfortunate experience is not only expensive for the companies involved but also acts to undermine confidence in psychologists and in legitimate psychological testing programs. Personnel managers stuck with a useless test that caused them to hire some poor employees may well conclude that all psychological tests are worthless and never consider using them again.

Only properly trained and qualified psychologists can set up worthwhile selection programs, especially ones that include the use of psychological tests. The personnel manager, who would not think of having an amateur diagnose chest pains, all too often calls on amateurs to diagnose selection problems. Psychologists can choose or develop the most appropriate selection tests and conduct the exacting research necessary to ensure the success of the complete selection program.

A sample of 163 consulting psychologists actively involved in developing testing programs and administering and interpreting psychological tests in the workplace were asked on what basis they chose the tests they used (Ryan & Sackett, 1987). The results are shown in Table 4-1. It is clear that each psychologist relied on more than one source of information, but the primary

TABLE 4-1 Sources of Information Influencing Choice of Tests

Information source	Percentage using source
Published research data	62.5
In-house research data	53.5
Test publisher information	45.1
Colleague recommendation	41.0
Trial and error	27.1
Other (for example, job analysis)	19.4
Client recommendation	9.7

From "A Survey of Individual Assessment Practices by I/O Psychologists" by A. M. Ryan & P. R. Sackett, 1987, *Personnel Psychology, 40*, p. 467.

source for all of them was the research data available on a test, whether from the published literature or from studies conducted at their own company. A survey of psychologists working in personnel research departments revealed that 45% of their research was concerned with test validation, making it their third most important research activity (Rassenfoss & Kraut, 1988).

When psychologists are searching for a published test to use, they know precisely for what to look and where to find it. The best tests include information on reliability and validity and make test norms available for public evaluation. In addition, there are several sources of information on the nature and statistical characteristics of psychological tests. The major source of information is the comprehensive and periodically revised *Mental Measurements Yearbook*. This reliable handbook contains critical reviews and evaluations of over 1,400 tests (Mitchell, 1985).

A leading journal in the field, *Personnel Psychology*, also publishes articles containing information on the validity of tests available for use in personnel selection. In addition, the general psychological research literature contains published reports of validity studies conducted on various tests. These can be found through the *Psychological Abstracts*. In 1988, the *Test Validity Yearbook: Organizational* began publication, focusing on criterion-related validity studies.

Psychologists know how to evaluate the information obtained and, thus, can learn much about the tests being considered for selection purposes. An intelligent choice among tests can only be made on the basis of full knowledge of the pertinent material.

There are several important factors to be considered in deciding whether to develop a new test or to use one already published. Cost is always important; it is considerably less expensive to purchase an existing test than to construct a new one, especially if only a small number of workers are to be selected.

Time is also important. The company needs qualified workers as soon as possible and may be unwilling or unable to wait for a useful test to be developed. A large-scale testing program may require months of research before the test can be used for actual selection purposes, whereas a published test can be used almost at once, assuming it meets the specific needs of the job in question. Some research will be necessary to determine the adequacy of an existing test and how well it meets EEOC requirements, but usually far less research than that required to develop a new test.

There are sound economic reasons, therefore, why management may prefer to use an existing test, but there are also situations in which available tests may not be appropriate. For example, if the job is entirely new, it may require new skills such as those needed to operate advanced and complex equipment. It is unlikely that an existing test will be able to measure the abilities needed for success in a new kind of work.

If a company decides to develop its own test for a particular job, the personnel psychologist must write or compile a list of suitable items or questions. Then, the psychologist proceeds to test the test, that is, to find out if the test really measures what it is supposed to measure. In other words, the test's validity must be determined. The psychologist also critically examines and evaluates each item in the test, conducting an *item analysis* to determine how effectively each item discriminates between those who scored high on the total test and those who scored low. In essence, this involves correlating a person's response on each item with the response on the test as a whole. A perfectly valid test question, then, is one that was answered correctly by everyone who scored high on the complete test and was answered incorrectly by everyone who scored low on the complete test. Only items with a high correlation coefficient are retained for the final form of the test.

The level of difficulty of each question must also be determined. If the majority of the test questions are too easy, most people will obtain high scores. The resulting small range of scores makes it difficult to discriminate effectively between those who are very high on the characteristic or ability being tested and those who are moderately high. A test on which most of the items are too difficult presents the opposite problem. It would be difficult to distinguish between those who possess extremely low ability and those who possess only moderately low ability.

Much of the research necessary to test a test involves the determination of reliability and validity by the methods discussed previously. Recall that the investigation of the test's validity usually requires the determination of some measure of job performance, a criterion with which the test scores can be correlated. Ideally, this assessment of a test's predictive validity is carried out by administering the test to a large group of applicants. All applicants will be hired on the basis of existing selection criteria without reference to their test scores. At this point in the research, the value of the test is unknown, so it makes little sense to base hiring decisions on level of test performance. Each worker's level of job success is later measured, after being on the job long enough to develop some job competence, and these ratings are compared with the test scores.

For reasons of economy, however, this approach remains more of an ideal than a reality. By far, the most common approach in use to establish a test's validity involves testing those already on the job (concurrent validity), which, as noted, may yield similar results to predictive validity.

An unfortunate management practice involves testing only the most superior workers. One psychologist described a company that had identified its best salespersons and planned to test only these and to use the results as the basis for selecting salespersons in the future. The rationale in this approach is that the characteristics of the top workers are the standard with which job applicants will be compared. The psychologist was able to convince the company's management of both the fallacy of this approach and the wisdom of testing all the salespersons, both good and bad. The reason for doing so when using a new test is simple: It could be the case that both good and poor workers would score alike on the test. This means that the test is not capable of discriminating between levels of competence—that it is not a valid test—perhaps because it did not measure the specific behaviors necessary for job success.

When the psychologist was able to administer the test to all of the company's salespersons, he found, as suspected, that both poor and good salespersons performed at the same level on the test. Had the company tested only its best workers and then hired applicants who scored at the same level, there would have been no improvement in the quality of employees hired by the company. The test could not distinguish between good and poor salespersons.

The importance of this point cannot be stressed too heavily. Psychological tests used for employee selection programs yield meaningful data only if they can discriminate between good and poor workers who have been rated on some criterion of job performance. A personnel manager who believes that we need only look at the best employees and use them as a standard is making a serious mistake. This admonition applies equally to existing tests and to those newly developed for a specific company. Both must be shown to correlate with success on the actual job in question.

One other point must be mentioned in our discussion of the problems of establishing the validity of a psychological test. It must not only discriminate between good and poor candidates but it must also deal with abilities directly related to the job in question, that is, it must have high content validity. A test of spelling would probably be a good device for discriminating between company presidents and janitors, but it does not follow that a psychologist can select company presidents by testing their level of spelling ability.

Why? Because all those eligible for the position of company president would most likely score high on this ability, such a test would be worthless for choosing from among the applicants. The test would not be valid for the specific purpose needed.

There are, then, many facets to the problem of test validity. The more effort expended on this crucial phase of test development, the greater the value of the test, and, of course, the better the workers selected. There are money-saving shortcuts, but in the long run they are self-defeating. A cheap testing program is a false economy.

Once validity and reliability of a test have been found to be satisfactory, the problem of setting a cutoff score (the score below which an applicant will not be hired) must be resolved. This depends partly on the available labor supply. The greater the number of applicants, the more selective a company can be. There are a number of procedures for establishing cutoff scores, most of which involve job analyses and criterion-related validity studies involving a minimally acceptable level of job performance.

In setting cutoff scores, we cannot assume that the better workers will always be those with the higher scores. For example, it has been found that quite intelligent people often do not work well in routine assembly-line jobs. It may be necessary, therefore, that both minimum and maximum cutoff scores be determined for an intelligence test that is part of this kind of company's selection program. The applicants must be intelligent enough to be able to learn the job but not so intelligent that they will be bored with it.

When the research has been completed and the test pronounced satisfactory as a predictive device, potential difficulties may arise in the actual administration of the test to job applicants, problems that may reduce the test's validity. Many people, particularly older ones who have been out of school for years, become anxious about the prospect of taking a test. It is in their best interest that the examiner attempt to establish rapport with all applicants and try to put them at ease as much as possible. The testing conditions must be standardized so that every applicant takes the test under identical circumstances. Also, the testing conditions must be as agreeable and comfortable as possible so that applicants are in the best personal condition to do well on the test.

In basic training in military service, for example, just two days after induction and feeling tired, confused, sick of inoculations and sergeants, and generally unhappy, a recruit may spend half a day in an extremely hot room taking a lengthy battery of psychological tests. Such conditions are not likely to induce a high level of performance. An army research study has shown that test performance of a group of trainees improved considerably when they were given the test again at a later time, after they were better adjusted to army life. Of course, a portion of the increase in scores might be attributed to greater familiarity with the test during the second testing session, but the primary reason for the better performance was the more agreeable conditions under which the test was taken.

This experience points up the need for well-trained test administrators. The task requires considerable technical skill plus sympathetic understanding of, and interest in, those being tested.

Types of Psychological Tests: Administration

There are two general ways to categorize psychological tests: (1) in terms of how they are constructed, administered, and scored and (2) in terms of the characteristics they are designed to measure.

Individual and Group Tests

Some tests are designed so that they can be administered to a large number of people at the same time. These *group tests* are advantageous in a situation that requires the testing of many people. The military, for example, tests thousands of people each year; it would be extremely expensive and time consuming if each recruit had to be tested individually. Many large-scale testing programs in industry involve a similar situation. A test designed for group administration can be given to 20, 200, or 2,000 applicants; the only limit is the size of the testing facility.

Individual tests, administered to one person at a time, are more costly and, therefore, are used to a lesser degree in industry than are group tests. Individual tests are used more frequently for vocational guidance and counseling, and for clinical and diagnostic work with emotionally disturbed persons. It is easier to establish rapport with the person being tested in the individual testing situation.

Because individual tests are costly and time consuming to administer, they are used mostly for vocational guidance and counseling and for selecting senior management personnel.

Also, it is usually possible to delve more deeply into the behavior being measured by using an individual test. One limitation is that the behavior of the individual being tested, and how well he or she performs on the test, is more dependent on the skill, sensitivity, and friendliness of the test administrator.

Computer-Assisted Testing

Designed for large-scale group testing, computer-assisted testing is nevertheless an individual testing situation in which the person taking the test interacts with a computer. The approach has sometimes been called tailored testing because the test is tailored or adapted to the individual taking it. The questions appear one at a time on the screen and the job applicant presses a key corresponding to the answer selected.

The advantages of computer-assisted testing are greater than just the mechanical presentation of questions. If you were to take, for example, a cognitive ability test in the usual paper-and-pencil format, you would be presented with many questions designed to sample the full range of your intelligence. Some questions will be easy for you because your level of intelligence is higher than the level at which these questions are aimed, whereas other questions will be more difficult because they are at or above your level of intelligence. To obtain a score on the test, however, you must take the time to answer all of the questions, even the simple ones.

In the computer-assisted testing situation, you do not have to waste your time answering questions that are below your level of intelligence. The computer begins the test by presenting a question of average difficulty, one that people of average IQ can answer. If you answer the question correctly, the computer proceeds to a question of greater difficulty because you have already demonstrated that your level of ability is at least average. Had you answered the question incorrectly, the computer would have given you a less difficult question.

Let us assume that a particular ability being measured ranges from 0 to 100. The first question is at the 50 level. If you answer this question correctly, the computer asks you a question at the 60 level. If you also answer this question correctly, the next question is at level 70, and if you answer this question incorrectly, the computer backtracks and asks you a question at level 65. And so the process continues, progressively focusing on your precise level of ability. Remember that on a traditional test you would have been required to answer all questions covering the full range of ability from 0 to 100. Computer-assisted testing thus reduces the time needed to take a test. Research has demonstrated that a precise measurement of a trait or ability provided by a 100-item conventional test can be provided by only 12 questions using the computer (Clark, 1975).

Computer-assisted testing can be done at any time a candidate applies for a job, not just when a qualified test administrator is available. A wide range of abilities can be measured in a short period of time, thus ensuring that the motivation and interest of the test-taker will not diminish, as sometimes happens when taking a conventional test. Studies show that the fatigue and boredom of test-takers is greatly reduced with computer-assisted testing (Burke & Normand, 1987). Also, immediate feedback is available to the personnel department because the computer provides the applicant's scores in a matter of seconds.

Research shows that most people who take tests at computer terminals react favorably to the experience. In addition, with personality tests, candidates tend to give more accurate information about sensitive personal topics than they would on a paper-and-pencil test or in a face-to-face interview (Burke & Normand, 1987).

Computer-assisted testing is, however, still a relatively expensive procedure that may be suitable only for larger organizations that regularly test great numbers of people.

In some selection situations, particularly those involving high-level managers and executives, a psychologist will administer a battery of tests and write a narrative description of the person's abilities based on the scores, instead of simply reporting the scores without comment. Computers can now be programmed to produce similar reports by drawing on a set of sentences and phrases, each of which interprets a score on a test or on one of its subscales.

A large retail company developed such a system, basing the narrative descriptions and interpretations on the recommendations of a panel of testing experts. Comparing the computer-generated reports with those written by personnel experts about the same examinees showed that the computer narratives were the more accurate and thorough and were just as readable. The person-generated narratives, on the other hand, presented the more coherent and integrated summaries of the applicants' personalities (Vale, Keller, & Bentz, 1986).

Computerized test interpretation offers several advantages. It is more efficient and less costly, and it provides standardized reports. Two psychologists analyzing the same set of scores will not necessarily produce identical interpretations, but the computer is programmed to do so. Computers also eliminate all personal biases and errors of interpretation and are unaffected by feelings of fatigue, boredom, or burnout. Also, computers do not decide to take the day off, go on vacation, quit, or retire, taking their expertise with them.

Speed and Power Tests

The difference between speed and power tests is in terms of the time allotted for completion of the test. A *speed test* has a fixed time limit at which point everyone taking the test must stop. A *power test* has no time limit—the examinees are allowed as much time as they feel they need to finish the test. A power test often will contain more difficult items than a speed test.

A large-scale testing program is facilitated by the use of speed tests because all test forms can be collected at the same time. Also, there are cases in which working speed is a vital part of the behavior being measured. Tests of clerical ability, for example, contain relatively easy items and most people, given enough time, would be able to respond correctly. The important predictive factor in clerical jobs such as typist or factory jobs such as mail sorter is the quality of work that can be performed in a fixed period of time. A power test would not be able to evaluate this ability properly.

Paper-and-Pencil and Performance Tests

Paper-and-pencil tests are the kind with which you are most familiar. The questions are in printed form and the answers are recorded on an answer sheet. Most of the standard group tests of intelligence, interest, and personality are paper-and-pencil tests.

Some behaviors or characteristics do not lend themselves to evaluation by paper-and-pencil means. Mechanical ability, for example, is tested better by having the applicants perform a series of mechanical operations than by having them answer questions about the nature of these operations. Consider again the evaluation of typing ability. The best way to assess this skill is to observe the typist in operation. For the evaluation of more complex skills, expensive equipment may be required. *Performance tests* may take longer to administer than paper-and-pencil tests and also may require an individual testing situation.

Objective and Subjective Scoring

We have discussed the importance of *objectivity* in testing. For the reasons noted, the majority of the tests used for industrial selection purposes are objective.

Subjectivity in test scoring, as in interviewing, allows personal prejudices and attitudes to enter into the testing situation. This can lead to distortion of the evaluation. The use of subjectively scored personality tests for selection purposes is discussed later in the chapter.

Types of Psychological Tests: Characteristics Measured

Perhaps the most useful distinction among psychological tests for selection purposes is in terms of the characteristics or behaviors they are designed to measure. The basic types are tests of cognitive or mental ability, interest, aptitude, motor ability, and personality.

Cognitive Ability

Several tests of cognitive ability (better known as intelligence tests) are used frequently in employee selection. A survey of psychologists involved in selection found that 78% of them used such tests (Ryan & Sackett, 1987). Group intelligence tests, the kind used most often, are primarily a rough screening device. The tests are short, take little time to complete, and can be administered to large groups. They can be rapidly and easily scored by a clerk or a machine.

We noted that personnel psychologists have found that tests of cognitive ability are highly valid for predicting success in training programs as well as actual job performance (Colarelli, Konstans, & Dean, 1987; Guion & Gibson, 1988). Indeed, such tests are the "most valid way known of identifying the workers or trainees who will be the most productive workers" (Hawk, 1986, p. 413). Consider, for example, the validity coefficients for both on-the-job proficiency and success in training programs for eight diverse occupations (Table 4-2). The data represent the results of validity studies conducted during the years 1949 to 1973. Recall that a validity coefficient of +.30 to +.40 is considered acceptable for selection tests. Many of the validities shown in Table 4-2 are higher than that.

We shall now discuss some of the intelligence tests commonly used in industry.

The *Otis Self-administering Tests of Mental Ability*, a frequently used selection test, has proven to be useful for screening applicants for a wide variety of jobs, including office clerks, assembly-line workers, and lower level supervisors, that is, jobs not requiring an extremely high level of intelligence. The test is group administered and takes little time to complete. It is less useful for professional or high-level supervisory positions because it does not discriminate well at the upper ranges of intelligence.

The *Wonderlic Personnel Test*, a 50-item version of one of the Otis series of tests, is particularly popular in industrial selection because it takes a mere 12 minutes to complete, making it an economical screening device. This group test includes verbal, numerical, and spatial content items and has been useful in predicting success in certain lower level clerical jobs.

The *Wechsler Adult Intelligence Scale-Revised* (WAIS-R) is a lengthy, individually administered test that is used in industry primarily for the selection of senior management personnel. The administration, scoring, and interpretation of the WAIS require much training and experience on the part of the examiner.

TABLE 4-2   Validity of General Cognitive Ability for Job Proficiency and Training Success

Occupation	Job proficiency	Training success
Salesperson	+.61	—
Clerk	.54	.71
Manager	.53	.51
Service worker	.48	.66
Trades and crafts	.46	.65
Protective professions	.42	.87
Elementary industrial	.37	.61
Vehicle operator	.28	.37

Adapted from "Cognitive ability, cognitive aptitudes, job knowledge, and job performance" by J. E. Hunter, 1986, *Journal of Vocational Behavior, 29*, p. 343.

The test includes 11 subtests in two sections, verbal and performance. The verbal subtests are Information, Comprehension, Arithmetic, Similarities, Digit Span, and Vocabulary; the performance subtests are Digit Symbol, Picture Completion, Block Design, Picture Arrangement, and Object Assembly. Two separate measures of intelligence, therefore, can be obtained as well as a full-scale IQ score by combining the verbal and performance measures. Computer-assisted interpretation is available.

Interests

Interest inventories are of greater value in vocational guidance and career counseling than in industrial personnel selection. Nevertheless, some companies do include measures of interest as part of their total testing program. (You are probably familiar with interest inventories. Many high schools routinely administer them to help students choose the kind of work for which they seem best suited.) Basically, interest tests include items about many daily activities and objects from among which the test-takers select their preferences. The rationale is that if a person exhibits the same pattern of interests and preferences as those who are successful in a given occupation, the chances are good that the individual will find satisfaction in that occupation.

It is important to note that just because a person possesses a high degree of interest in a particular occupation, it is no guarantee that he or she has the ability to succeed in that job. All it suggests is that the individual's interests are compatible with the interests of people who are successful in that career. Of course, if the test shows that a person has absolutely no interest in an occupation, his or her chances of succeeding in it are limited.

Two widely used interest inventories are the *Strong–Campbell Interest Inventory* (SCII) and the *Kuder Occupational Interest Survey*.

The SCII is a group-administered test composed of 325 questions that deal with occupations, school subjects, activities, leisure pursuits, and social contacts, some of which are to be ranked in order of preference and others rated as like, dislike, or indifferent. The SCII groups occupations in six areas: realistic, investigative, artistic, social, enterprising, and conventional. Scoring is done by computer.

The *Kuder Occupational Interest Survey* consists of a large number of items arranged in groups of three. Within each triad, examinees must indicate which activity they most prefer and which they least prefer. They are not allowed to skip any group if they do not like any of the alternatives or to check more than one as the most preferred activity. It can be scored for 126 occupations.

Here are two sample sets of items (Kuder & Diamond, 1979).

Visit an art gallery.	Collect autographs.
Browse in a library.	Collect coins.
Visit a museum.	Collect butterflies.

Both of these interest inventories are primarily for use in vocational counseling, where the focus is on trying to select the right kind of work for an individual. One difficulty with their use as a selection tool is the problem of faking responses; the success of any such inventory rests largely on the honesty of a person's answers. Presumably, when taking an interest inventory for vocational counseling, a person will answer honestly because the results are used to help the person find a suitable area of employment. In a selection situation, however, the person's answers may determine whether he or she is hired for a particular job, thus the motivation to falsify answers may be great.

Aptitudes

For many jobs, aptitude tests must be created especially to measure the skills required by that job, but there are published tests that measure general aptitudes for mechanical and clerical skills. Often, as part of the testing for skilled jobs, the applicant's keenness of vision and hearing will be tested, primarily by mechanical means. These are sometimes called aptitude tests and in a very general sense they are. We limit this discussion, however, to the measurement of more complex abilities by means of psychological tests. We also note that some of these tests, although widely used, are being legally challenged on the grounds of discrimination and adverse impact.

Several tests measure *clerical aptitude* and are useful in the prediction of success for clerical workers. These tests are concerned primarily with speed and accuracy of perception.

The *Minnesota Clerical Test* is a group test consisting of two parts, number comparison and name comparison, examples of which are given in Figure 4-1. The test is a speed test to determine the individual's accuracy when working in a limited time period. The test instructions urge the examinees to work as fast as they can without errors. The number comparison consists of 200 pairs of numbers, each of which contains 3 to 12 digits. The name comparison section is similar but uses proper names instead of numbers. These tasks are analogous to work required in clerical jobs.

The *General Clerical Test* is a group speed test published in two booklets: *A—Clerical, Numerical* and *B—Verbal*. Booklet *A* contains items on checking, alphabetizing, numerical computation, error location, and arithmetic reasoning and is suitable for testing job applicants for accounting or payroll clerk positions. Booklet *B* contains items on spelling, reading comprehension, vocabulary, and grammar and is suitable for applicants for secretarial jobs.

Figure 4-1 Sample items from Minnesota Clerical Test. (Reproduced by permission. Copyright 1933, renewed 1961 by The Psychological Corporation, New York, N.Y. All rights reserved.)

When the two numbers or names in a pair are *exactly the same,* make a check mark on the line between them.

66273894 _____ 66273984

527384578 _____ 527384578

New York World _____ New York World

Cargill Grain Co. _____ Cargil Grain Co.

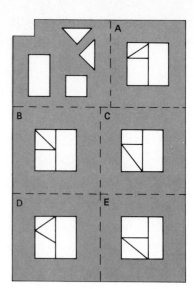

Figure 4-2 Sample items from Revised Minnesota Paper Form Board Test. The subject must pick the figure (from A to E) that shows how the parts will look when assembled. (Reproduced by permission. Copyright 1941, renewed 1969 by The Psychological Corporation, New York, N.Y. All rights reserved.)

Tests to measure *mechanical aptitude* focus on the abilities of mechanical comprehension and spatial visualization.

The *Revised Minnesota Paper Form Board Test* is a measure of spatial relations or visualization and the manipulation of objects in space, necessary abilities for occupations such as drafting. The applicant is presented with drawings of figures cut into two or more segments and must be able to picture how the total figure would appear if the pieces were put together. Sample items from this test are shown in Figure 4-2.

Research conducted with this test has demonstrated some degree of validity in predicting successful performance in mechanical work, engineering shopwork, and power sewing machine operation as well as classroom performance of art and dentistry students.

Another widely used test of mechanical aptitude, in both the military and private industry, is the *Bennett Mechanical Comprehension Test*. This test employs pictures with questions about the mechanical principles involved in them and provides norms for various levels of training and background. Sample items are shown in Figure 4-3. Both written and tape-recorded instructions are available, the latter for use with applicants who have difficulty reading. Both forms are available in Spanish as well as English.

Motor Ability

Many jobs in industry and the military require a high degree of motor skill involving muscular coordination, finger dexterity, or precise eye-hand coordination.

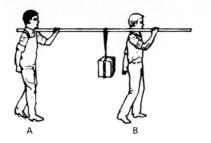

X
Which man carries more weight?
(If equal, mark C.)

Figure 4-3 Sample items
from Bennett Mechanical
Comprehension Test.
(Reproduced by permission.
Copyright 1940, renewed
1967; 1941, renewed 1969;
1942, renewed 1969; ©
1967, 1968 by The
Psychological Corporation,
New York, N.Y. All rights
reserved.)

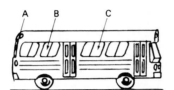

Y
Which letter shows the seat where
a passenger will get the smooth-
est ride?

The *MacQuarrie Test for Mechanical Ability* is one of the few tests of motor ability in paper-and-pencil form. The seven subtests include:

1. *Tracing*—a line is drawn through very small openings in a number of vertical lines.
2. *Tapping*—dots are made on paper as quickly as possible.
3. *Dotting*—dots are made in circles as quickly as possible.
4. *Copying*—simple designs are copied.
5. *Location*—specific points must be located in a smaller size version of a stimulus figure.
6. *Blocks*—the number of blocks in a drawing must be determined.
7. *Pursuit*—the visual tracing of assorted lines in a maze.

Some of these tasks are pictured in Figure 4-4.

The *Purdue Pegboard* is a performance test that simulates conditions on an assembly line and measures finger dexterity as well as gross movement skills of fingers, hands, and arms. The task is to place pins in a series of holes as rapidly as possible, first with one hand, then the other, then both. Each of these tasks takes 30 seconds.

The *Purdue Pegboard* also includes a 1-minute test involving the simultaneous use of both hands to assemble pins, collars, and washers in each hole.

The *O'Connor Finger Dexterity Test* and *O'Connor Tweezer Dexterity Test* measure how fast a person can insert pins into small holes, both by hand and by the use of tweezers. This is a standard measure of finger dexterity, and the test has proven to be useful in predicting success among sewing machine operator trainees, dentistry students, and a variety of other tasks requiring precise manipulative skills.

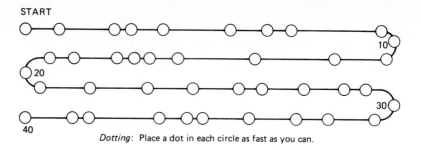

START

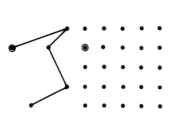

Dotting: Place a dot in each circle as fast as you can.

Copying: Copy figure in dotted space.

Blocks: How many blocks touch each block with an X on it?

Figure 4-4 Sample items from MacQuarrie Test for Mechanical Ability by T. W. MacQuarrie. (Reproduced by permission of the publisher, CTB/McGraw-Hill, Monterey, Calif. 93940. Copyright © 1925, 1953 by T. W. MacQuarrie. All rights reserved. Printed in the U.S.A.)

Pursuit: Follow each line by eye and show where it ends, by putting the number in the correct square at the right.

The *Minnesota Rate of Manipulation Test* consists of two parts. The examinee's task in the first part is to place 60 cylindrical blocks in 60 wells in a board. The second task is to turn all the blocks over. The score is the amount of time taken to complete each task.

There are other tests of motor ability that measure coordination. The most common ones utilize the pursuit rotor, a test in which the testee uses a stylus to follow a dot on a revolving disk.

One variation of this procedure is the *Purdue Hand Precision Test*. As an upper disk with a hole revolves, the person being tested must touch target holes in a plate underneath the disk by using a stylus. The score is kept electronically as the stylus activates a counter.

Occasionally, special devices are developed to measure motor skills—sophisticated machines on which the examinee performs highly complex motor activities in response to visual signals. Such equipment is considerably more costly than the standard motor ability tests.

Personality

Research shows that certain personality characteristics, at least for some occupations, are important for job success. For example, traits of affiliation and nurturance are important for a successful career as a counselor, autonomy and persistence are vital to an investigative reporter, and orderliness and precision are needed by an accountant. Ratings of job applicants' personalities have been found to correlate with proficiency in a number of other jobs, such as police officer and stockbroker. Further, personality may influence not only job performance, but also job satisfaction (Paunonen & Jackson, 1987).

Thus, the influence of personality on job performance can be considerable. The problem lies not so much in demonstrating that relationship as in measuring personality variables with accuracy. Personality tests are frequently used for the purpose of employee selection despite research evidence that casts doubt on their predictive validity.

Two approaches to the measurement of personality are self-report inventories and projective techniques. The *self-report inventory* presents a variety of items that deal with specific situations, symptoms, or feelings. Examinees are asked to indicate how well each item describes themselves or how much they agree with each item.

A major problem with the self-report personality test is the honesty of the people taking the test. Those who wish to appear in a certain manner or who may want to hide some bothersome facet of their personality can do so quite easily on most of these tests. The questions are frequently transparent and reasonably intelligent applicants (say salespersons who wish to appear extraverted) can make themselves seem qualified with little difficulty. Some personality inventories are designed to detect such faking. Because most of these tests can be easily distorted, however, their predictive efficiency is less than desirable. They do offer the advantage of being easy and economical to administer and score. Some 78% of psychologists involved in selection use personality inventories (Ryan & Sackett, 1987).

The *projective-technique approach* to personality testing presents the individual with an ambiguous stimulus such as an inkblot. The task is to give some structure and meaning to this stimulus, in other words, to tell what is seen in the figure. The theory behind this approach is that an individual will project personal thoughts, desires, wishes, and feelings onto this amorphous structure in an effort to give it some meaning.

These tests cannot be faked because there are no right or wrong answers. They are time consuming and must be administered individually. Extensive training and experience are required to interpret them properly. Because there are usually no objective scoring keys, there is ample opportunity for the examiner's subjective feelings to influence the interpretation. Some psychologists have said that the examinee's responses become a projective technique to the examiner, who projects his or her own thoughts and fears onto the responses of the person being tested! Although projective techniques are used in personnel selection, particularly at the executive level, considerable research consistently reports low or no validity (Anastasi, 1988; Reilly & Chao, 1982). The survey of psychologists conducting selection assessments showed that 34% use projective techniques (Ryan & Sackett, 1987).

Self-report Inventories.   The *Guilford–Zimmerman Temperament Survey* is one of the more widely used paper-and-pencil personality inventories. The items are in the form of statements rather than questions, and the examinee responds by checking Yes, ?, or No. Three sample items from this test are the following:

You start work on a new project wth a great deal of enthusiasm	YES	?	NO
You are often in low spirits	YES	?	NO
Most people use politeness to cover up what is really "cutthroat" competition	YES	?	NO

The test yields separate scores for ten independent personality traits: General Activity, Restraint, Ascendance, Sociability, Emotional Stability, Objectivity, Friendliness, Thoughtfulness, Personal Relations, and Masculinity. As a check against deliberate faking or carelessness in responding, the test has three falsification scales based on the answers to selected test items.

The *Minnesota Multiphasic Personality Inventory* (MMPI), probably the best known and most influential of all the self-report inventories, contains 550 statements classified by the respondent as true, false, or cannot say. Its excessive length limits its usefulness for selection purposes; a high level of motivation is required to respond to each item with care. One advantage of the MMPI is the use of three scales that can be scored to determine if the examinee was faking, careless, or misunderstood the directions. Typical items are the following:

I believe I am being plotted against.
When I get bored I like to stir up some excitement.
Most people will use somewhat unfair means to gain profit or an advantage rather than to lose it.

There are other self-report inventories that measure a variety of traits, and there are also tests that measure specific personality traits such as introversion-extraversion, sociability, emotional maturity, or emotional security.

Self-report inventories are usually used for selection at the executive or managerial level. As to the question of their usefulness, the record is largely a poor one (with some notable exceptions). However, these tests continue to be used enthusiastically by many personnel departments and executive recruitment firms.

Projective Techniques. Projective tests of personality were developed primarily for use in clinical psychology for work with emotionally disturbed individuals. However, they are also used to assess candidates for high-level executive positions. Because the tests were originally intended to distinguish between psychotic and "normal" persons, it is not surprising that they usually fail to discriminate among "normal" persons in a selection situation.

The best known projective technique is the *Rorschach*, popularly called the inkblot test, which was first published in 1921 by Hermann Rorschach, a Swiss psychiatrist. Examinees are shown, individually, 10 standardized inkblots and asked to report what they see in the figures. Five of the inkblots are in colors and five are in shades of black and gray. After all 10 cards have been seen, the examiner reviews each card and asks the applicants specific questions about what the inkblots represent to them. The process of interpreting the responses is complicated and is based on whether the applicants reported seeing movement, human figures, inanimate or animate objects, and so on. The scoring is subjective and depends on the training, skill, and personality of the examiner. However, a set of standardized procedures for administering, scoring, and interpreting the *Rorschach* has been developed (Exner, 1978, 1986).

Research conducted on the value of the *Rorschach* for personnel selection consistently indicates low predictive validities.

Another well-known projective test is the *Thematic Apperception Test* (TAT), developed by the American psychologist Henry Murray in the late 1930s. Nineteen ambiguous pictures that show two or more persons in different situations are presented. Applicants are asked to make up a story about each picture. The stories are analyzed by a subjective, unstandardized process that is open to the biases of the analyst. The TAT is used primarily in clinical psychology and research but also in the industrial selection situation.

Several other commercially available projective tests use various kinds of pictures to be interpreted or arranged sequentially by applicants. Some tests also use the sentence completion method: The beginning of a sentence is presented (such as, "My ambition...") and the person is requested to complete it.

Advantages of Psychological Testing

The primary advantage of psychological tests as a selection technique and the only valid reason for using them, is that some types of tests can improve the selection process. A well researched and developed testing program can be of great value to any organization. As we noted in Chapter 1, the use of tests of cognitive ability for the entire U.S. work force could save $80 billion a year.

Psychological tests offer specific benefits over the other selection devices we have discussed. One advantage (excluding, of course, projective tests) is their objectivity. Compared to interviews or letters of recommendation, objective tests are less susceptible to biased interpretations on the part of the examiner. Also, it is somewhat easier to conduct evaluative research on psychological tests than on other methods of selection. In part, this is because of the precise quantification of test results, something that is more difficult to achieve with, say, interview results. Psychological tests also offer the advantage of providing a great amount of information about an individual in a short period of time.

As noted, tests are only as good as the quantity and quality of the research preceding and accompanying their use. Continuous supporting research is required if psychological testing is to be a positive addition to a selection program.

In terms of predictive value, tests of cognitive ability are valid predictors of performance on the job and in training programs for all jobs in a variety of settings. We have also seen that tests of cognitive ability are equally valid for job applicants of different ethnic groups.

As is the case with the other selection techniques, the usefulness of an organization's psychological testing program depends on the amount of time and money the management is willing to invest in the necessary psychological research.

Limitations and Dangers of Psychological Testing

The Uncritical Use of Tests

A continual danger with psychological tests is their uncritical use by gullible personnel managers who may be taken in by slick promises of instant success in solving their employee selection and equal employment opportunity problems. All too frequently, a personnel manager will choose a test just because it is new, without making any attempt to investigate the test's reliability and validity. Sometimes a test will continue to be used even when information about it is negative, usually because the personnel manager is unaware of the research. Often, there are no data to support a test because no research was ever conducted on it. In general, the more long-term data available on a test, the more effective that test will be.

Given a trusting and naïve personnel manager and a greedy or fraudulent test developer, we can begin to understand the reasons for the uncritical use of tests (at least of the wrong kinds of tests). The harm generated by improper testing affects not only the personnel department and the company but also you, the applicant, when an ineffective test disqualifies you unfairly from a job.

Unfair Rejection of Applicants

Even the best psychological tests are not perfectly valid. No validity coefficients for tests reach a perfect positive correlation of $+1.00$. There is always, therefore, some margin of error in the prediction of job success. Sometimes unqualified people will be hired, but the reverse is also true, that is, sometimes otherwise qualified persons are rejected on the basis of their test performance. In fairness to psychological tests, this error of prediction also exists with other selection techniques.

Chiefly for this reason, a selection program should not be based on a single device. The use of several techniques allows for the gathering and evaluating of as much information as possible on an applicant.

Human behavior is so complex that it is difficult, if not impossible, to predict success with complete accuracy. There will always be some unfair rejections for that reason, but they can be minimized when a competent person uses a competent test. The more carefully researched the testing program, the smaller is the number of applicants rejected unfairly.

The uncritical use of tests and the problem of unfair rejections point again to the need for qualified psychologists to be actively involved in developing and administering a testing program. The pitfalls of such a program are magnified when it is run by someone untrained in the proper use of psychological tests.

Faking Test Responses

We mentioned the problem of deliberately distorting responses on a psychological test in such a way as to maximize the possibility of appearing in a favorable light. This is a crucial problem with some tests used for personnel selection. If the applicant does not answer honestly, any prediction of future job performance is likely to be inaccurate.

With certain kinds of tests, faking is not a problem. It is not possible, for example, to improve your score on an intelligence test or a test of mechanical comprehension by deliberate faking. However, with objective personality tests and interest inventories, it is easy to distort the answers. Faking may be the greatest possible liability in the use of personality and interest tests. The motivation to lie is frequently strong.

Suppose you are in desperate need of a job and apply for a sales position. The company's test includes questions such as:

I enjoy meeting new people.	YES _____	NO _____
I get along well with most people.	YES _____	NO _____
I find it easy to talk to people.	YES _____	NO _____

If you really want the job, you can easily answer in the way you think the company expects salespersons to answer, indicating that you enjoy meeting people, get along well with them, and find it easy to talk to them. Unless these characteristics truly apply to you, however, your answers will provide the company with a false picture. You may be hired, but you probably will not succeed or be happy in the job because it requires characteristics you do not, in truth, possess.

In the long run, therefore, faking test responses may work to your disadvantage—but it is hard to convince an avid job-seeker of this in advance.

It cannot be assumed that all applicants will answer personality and interest tests honestly. What can be done, however, is to detect faking when it occurs and discard the test results of those found to be deliberately dishonest. A number of tests (including the MMPI and the *Kuder Occupational Interest Survey*) have lie detection scales built into their design.

There is an interesting moral dilemma here, in that applicants willing to lie may be rewarded with a job. They may later find themselves unsuited for the job, but, most likely, they will not blame themselves for having misrepresented their abilities in the first place.

On the other hand, persons who respond honestly, admitting perhaps to low-level neurotic behaviors (which most of us possess), may be punished by not getting the job. Everyone—the honest and the dishonest applicants, the psychologist who sets up the testing program, and the company—may lose in the long run. The company may be hiring skilled and practiced liars and losing the honest and perhaps better qualified applicant.

Conformity

One frequent criticism of the use of psychological tests for employee selection is that they lead to the hiring of the same type of person, someone who is unimaginative, disinclined to rock the boat, and interested only in preserving the status quo. The argument is that the truly exceptional and questioning individual is penalized, particularly by personality tests, which gauge everyone by a certain standard of normality.

Companies using personality tests do establish a profile of personality patterns to define the kind of individual they are seeking. Those whose test results match the profile are hired whereas those who show extreme deviations are not. As a result, after several years of selecting people on the basis of their test results, the employees will exhibit similar personality patterns, leading to a kind of corporate inbreeding.

Two points can be made against the argument that testing leads to conformity. First, some conformity may not be negative. A company could, for example, establish a profile that identifies the creative, imaginative, and innovative individual. In this case, the unimaginative person would not match the profile and would not be hired. Thus, the company would still be looking for those who conform to a norm, but it is a norm of dynamic, creative talent. Second, even if the company's profile does reward the person whose test results show him or her to be unimaginative and conventional, there is always the expectation that creative people may be hired anyway (perhaps because they faked the test results in the direction in which they felt the company was looking).

At any rate, most organizations need both kinds of people, the conservative and the exceptional, some to perform the routine work (even at the executive level) and others to lead and challenge. We should not minimize the negative aspects of conformity that can be brought about by personality testing. Where the situation exists, however, it is more a fault of the organization and less of the tests it uses.

Quality of Psychological Testing Programs

Another weakness and danger of testing, independent of the quality of the tests themselves, is the lack of care paid to the everyday business of giving the tests in an employment situation, that is, the problem of sloppy test administration.

One study investigated the testing practices of 28 government and industrial organizations that used psychological tests. The results were not encouraging. Although most organizations provided sufficiently large testing facilities, two thirds of them failed to keep the testing room free of interruptions while testing was underway. Any interruption of the testing procedure violates the condition of standardization, which is vital to the reliability and validity of the test results. Many organizations lack sufficient concern for this important condition of proper testing.

Only 13% of the organizations surveyed required any kind of training for the persons who administered the tests. In terms of overall quality of the testing program, most were judged moderate. None was rated excellent or superior.

This is a strong indictment of the testing programs of these organizations. Such shoddy administrative procedures can negate the years of sound research devoted to developing the program. One untrained or careless clerk can virtually destroy the effectiveness of the most expensive and thorough selection testing system.

Attitudes Toward Psychological Testing Programs

Psychological tests (indeed, any kinds of tests) have never been popular with those who are required to take them and who find their future dependent on the outcome. But most people have little choice about taking tests, either in school or in business and industry. True, we can refuse to take the tests a company wants to give us as a selection device, but this may mean that we shall not be considered for the job. One survey of personnel managers found that 52% reported that their companies had a policy of automatically rejecting any applicant who refused to take any kind of test. The remainder of the personnel managers indicated some degree of flexibility and would consider the individual merits of each case of refusal (Blocklyn, 1988b).

Many people react with uneasiness, anxiety, or even fear to test taking, and this reaction may be mixed with suspicion and hostility. Labor unions also view tests negatively and have rarely encouraged the use of testing programs in industry. They believe that testing serves only the company, never the employee. We have seen, however, that a carefully researched and administered testing program can be of tremendous value to employees by guiding them into the kind of work for which they are best suited. Whether or not their attitude is well founded, unions remain distrustful of testing programs and any company developing such a program must consider this factor.

The American Psychological Association (APA) is justifiably concerned about the ethical practices of all psychologists, whether engaged in research in a university or selecting persons for jobs in business. Principles for proper conduct argue that psychologists must protect the dignity, worth, and welfare of individuals at all times.

Unfortunately, the spirit of this credo is sometimes violated and many of these violations occur with the use of psychological tests for selection purposes. Some tests have been used for selection in the absence of adequate validity data.

This is harmful to the applicants and surely does not represent a concern for their dignity and worth.

The ethics code of the APA discusses proper safeguards for the distribution and use of psychological tests (American Psychological Association, 1985):

1. *Test users*. Those who administer and interpret tests should be aware of the principles of psychological measurement, of validation, and of the limitations of test interpretation. They must avoid any discrimination and bias in their work and should always consider more than one means of assessment. They must adhere strictly to the standardized procedures for administering a test and make every effort to achieve accuracy in the scoring and recording of test results.

2. *Test security*. Actual questions from tests should never be reprinted in any public medium such as a newspaper or magazine. It is permissible to publish sample questions—those resembling the real questions—but not items used in the actual scoring of a test. (The test items reproduced in this chapter are sample questions.) Tests should be sold only to professionals who will safeguard their use. The specific test in question will determine the qualifications necessary for proper use of the test. Several lawsuits have challenged this notion of test security and have demanded that organizations provide copies of tests as well as answers and test scores to applicants. Federal courts have upheld the right of organizations and psychologists to maintain the security of test questions and answers.

3. *Test interpretation*. Test scores should be given only to those qualified to interpret them. The scores should not be given to anyone outside of the personnel department such as the applicant's potential supervisor unless he or she has the training necessary to interpret the scores. This point is sometimes violated, however. One survey revealed that 21% of the companies questioned provided test results to the applicant's supervisor. Only 27% of the companies had established guidelines for the confidentiality of test data (Blocklyn, 1988b). The person being tested has the right to know his or her score and what it means.

4. *Test publication*. Tests should not be released for use without adequate background research to support the claims of the test. Fully informative and current test manuals containing data on reliability, validity, and norms should be made available with all tests. Advertisements should describe the tests accurately and not use emotional or persuasive claims.

One aspect of psychological testing that has come under attack in recent years is the use of personal or intimate questions. Critics charge that such personal probing is an unwarranted and unnecessary invasion of privacy and that individual freedom is violated by requesting information not directly relevant to the specific job for which the person is applying. The primary target of this criticism is the personality test questions that range from sex life to the condition of one's digestive tract.

Few people question the right of an organization to investigate job applicants. The company must know something of an applicant's background, training, and abilities to determine whether to hire the individual. The issue is the relevance of the information sought by the employer to the job. Critics of personality testing argue that the generally low validities of personality tests in terms of predicting job performance as well as the ease of faking responses suggest that such information is of little value in selection. Certainly, personal characteristics that have been shown to be directly related to job performance must be investigated, but personal questions that have no known relevance constitute an unnecessary invasion of privacy and must be avoided. Even if such questions could be used to predict job performance, however, there remains the issue of how much of ourselves we have to reveal to a potential employer.

Summary

There has been a marked resurgence of interest in **psychological tests** as selection devices, largely as a result of research showing that tests of cognitive ability are excellent predictors of success on the job and in training programs.

Psychological tests are measuring devices that are used to assess a sample of behavior consistently and systematically. Tests serve two purposes: placement and selection. **Placement** is concerned with determining what kind of job is suitable for a particular person; **selection** is concerned with determining what kind of person is suitable for a particular job.

Psychological tests must meet and satisfy the following characteristics. **Standardization** refers to the consistency of procedures and conditions under which people take a test. **Objectivity** involves the accurate and consistent scoring of a test, unbiased by the personal characteristics of the scorer. All tests must have one or more sets of **test norms,** scores of a group of people who are similar to those taking the test, which serve as a point of comparison for individual scores. **Reliability** refers to the consistency of responses on a test and can be determined in three ways: the **test-retest method,** the **equivalent-forms method,** and the **split-halves method. Validity** of a test is concerned with how well it measures what it intends to measure.

Validity is of two types. **Criterion-related validity** is determined by the methods of **predictive validity** or **concurrent validity. Rational validity** is established by either **content validity** or **construct validity.** There is also the concept of **face validity**—how valid or relevant the test appears to the person taking it.

Tests are no longer considered to be differentially valid. Researchers are investigating the concept of **validity generalization.** A test valid for one job will be valid for other jobs. Therefore, tests may no longer need to be validated every time they are applied to a different job or company.

Fair employment legislation has had a strong impact on the use of psychological tests in selection, making it illegal to use any test that discriminates against applicants because of their race, color, religion, sex, or national origin. The Equal Employment Opportunity Commission (EEOC) has prescribed the kinds of validation studies that must be conducted on all tests used for selection to ensure that they are measuring characteristics that are clearly related to the job in question. The concept of validity generalization suggests that a test that is valid for one ethnic group may be valid for others. However, a test can be valid and still be declared discriminatory if adverse impact is demonstrated.

A number of steps are required to establish a testing program: (1) conducting a job and worker analysis, (2) finding or developing a suitable test, (3) conducting an item analysis of each question on the test, (4) determining the level of difficulty of each question, (5) establishing the reliability and validity of the test, and (6) setting the cutoff scores.

Psychological tests can be categorized by the ways in which they are constructed, scored, and administered or in terms of the behavior they measure. Categories of tests include **individual** or **group tests, speed** or **power tests, paper-and-pencil** or **performance tests** and **objectively** or **subjectively scored tests. Computer-assisted tests,** designed for large groups, involve one person at a time interacting with a computer. Tests can also be interpreted by computer programs that produce a narrative description of a person's abilities based on sentences or phrases keyed to individual scores.

The kinds of behavior measured include **cognitive ability, interest, aptitude, motor ability,** and **personality.** Personality testing is particularly controversial. Personality characteristics are measured by **self-report inventories** and **projective techniques**.

There are advantages to the use of psychological tests for selection. Tests (particularly cognitive ability tests) can aid the selection process, they are objective measures, and their effectiveness is easier to evaluate than some other selection devices. There are no alternatives better than tests in terms of high validity and reducing adverse impact.

The limitations and dangers of psychological testing include uncritical use, unfair rejection of applicants, faking of test responses, conformity, and poor quality of test administration. In recent years, the public has become more critical of tests and there are serious ethical issues involved in their use as selection devices, including invasion of privacy and the confidentiality of test questions and answers.

Key Terms

aptitude tests
cognitive ability tests
computer-assisted
    testing
concurrent validity
construct validity
content validity
criterion-related
    validity
equivalent-forms
    reliability
face validity
fair employment
group tests

individual tests
interest tests
meta-analysis
motor skills tests
objectivity
paper-and-pencil tests
performance tests
personality tests
power tests
predictive validity
projective techniques
psychological
    assessment
psychological testing

rational validity
reliability
reliability coefficient
self-report inventory
speed tests
split-halves reliability
standardization
subjectivity
test norms
test-retest reliability
validity
validity coefficient
validity generalization

CASE STUDIES

Personality as a Predictor of Job Performance

To investigate the relationship between specific personality variables and job performance, 43 accountants employed by a medium size accounting firm were studied. Based on a job analysis, conducted by means of interviews and critical incidents, 6 dimensions were identified as being important for job success. These dimensions included (1) potential for becoming a manager, (2) technical ability, (3) timeliness of work, (4) client relations, (5) cooperation, and (6) work ethic.

To measure these dimensions, a paper-and-pencil, self-report inventory called the Personality Research Form was given to all applicants for the job of accountant until data had been collected on 43 persons. All of these persons were hired. The test scores were not used to make the hiring decisions because it was not yet known whether they would correlate with success on the job. To obtain measures of actual job performance, 7 partners in the accounting firm provided performance ratings on the 43 subjects.

Three of the personality scales—work orientation, ascendancy, and interpersonal orientation—were found to be significantly related to the dimensions identified as important for job success. In addition, ascendancy correlated negatively with the job performance ratings, indicating that persons who scored low on this scale (who were cooperative and worked easily with others) rated high in job performance.

The results suggest that specific personality scales may be related to important dimensions of job performance and therefore may be useful in predicting job success.

QUESTIONS

1. Do these results suggest that personality tests alone can be used to select accountants? Why or why not?
2. What is the major problem with the use of self-report inventories for employee selection purposes?
3. If a personality test were shown to be a valid selection device for accountants, would it also be valid for related occupations such as Internal Revenue Service (IRS) agents?
4. How has the concept of validity generalization contributed to a resurgence in the use of psychological tests for employee selection?

Reference: D. V. Day & S. B. Silverman. (1989). Personality and job performance: Evidence of incremental validity. *Personnel Psychology, 42*, 25–36.

Using Measures of Performance to Validate Tests

Data from applicants for jobs with two small high-tech companies were analyzed to compare two performance criteria: (1) ratings by supervisors (the most frequently used measure of job performance in validity research), and (2) promotional progress (performance on the job over time that results in an increase in rank or pay). One company administered the Wesman Personnel Classification Test to its applicants. The other company used the SRA Computer Programmer Aptitude Battery.

Two measures of job performance were obtained: a current performance appraisal by supervisors and a measure of promotional progress. To determine promotional progress, one company calculated a "career progress index," which showed how much each person's salary deviated from the average salary of other workers in his or her age group. In the other company, promotional progress was measured by the time served in the status of trainee.

The correlation coefficients between the test scores and the performance appraisal ratings were +.09 and +.11. The correlation coefficients between the test scores and the promotional progress measures were +.42 and

+.40. Thus, for both companies, the criterion of promotional progress showed a significant positive correlation with the test scores whereas the criterion of supervisors' ratings did not.

QUESTIONS

1. Name and define the type of validity being measured in these studies.
2. What other kinds of validity may be used to determine the usefulness of a psychological test for employee selection?
3. What have I/O psychologists learned about *estimating* the validities of cognitive ability tests as compared to conducting empirical validation studies of cognitive ability tests?
4. Describe the methods used to establish the reliability of a psychological test.

Reference: H. H. Meyer. (1987). Predicting supervisory ratings versus promotional progress in test validation studies. *Journal of Applied Psychology, 72,* 696–697.

Additional Reading

Anastasi, A. (1988). *Psychological Testing* (6th ed.). New York: Macmillan. Reviews the origins and uses of psychological testing; social and ethical issues in testing; problems with norms, reliability, and validity; and specific tests for employee selection.

Burke, M. J., & Normand, J. (1987). Computerized psychological testing: Overview and critique. *Professional Psychology, 18,* 42–51. Describes the technology of several types of computerized testing systems and examines potential advantages and disadvantages of each.

Guion, R. M., & Gibson, W. M. (1988). Personnel selection and placement. *Annual Review of Psychology, 39,* 349–374. Covers the current literature on issues in personnel selection including fair employment, job analysis, interviews, and assessment centers as well as psychological tests and validity generalization.

Yoder, D., & Staudohar, P. D. (1984). Testing and EEO: Getting down to cases. *Personnel Administrator, 29*(2), 67–74. Discusses U.S. Supreme Court decisions on employment testing and their impact on employee selection procedures.

Chapter 5

Performance Appraisal

Introduction

The frequent, continuous, and impartial appraisal by an organization of the performance of its employees is vital not only for the growth of the organization but also for the growth of the individual employees. A company must know who are its outstanding workers, who needs additional training, and who is not contributing to the efficiency and welfare of the company. Figure 5-1 indicates the extent to which different kinds of jobs are subject to periodic performance appraisal (Dunham, 1983). As you can see, most types of employees undergo some evaluation, either formally or informally. Survey results show that 94% of employers now use some formal system of performance appraisal, an increase from 89% in 1977 ("Appraisal Trends," 1988). Half of all research conducted by psychologists employed in company personnel research departments is related to performance appraisal (Rassenfoss & Kraut, 1988).

At all levels of employment, personnel decisions relating to promoting, retaining, or firing workers are made daily and, ideally, such decisions are based solely on the merit or ability of the employees. The quality of a worker's performance on the job must be assessed in some way, and such assessments will be more fair and useful if they are based on objective and systematic criteria. These criteria must involve factors relevant to the person's ability to perform the job.

In your own organizational career, your performance will be monitored and appraised periodically, and your level of salary, rank, and responsibility will depend on how well you satisfy the established criteria of job performance.

Performance appraisal is not practiced only in business. Indeed, it has been taking place throughout your academic career. Classroom examinations, term

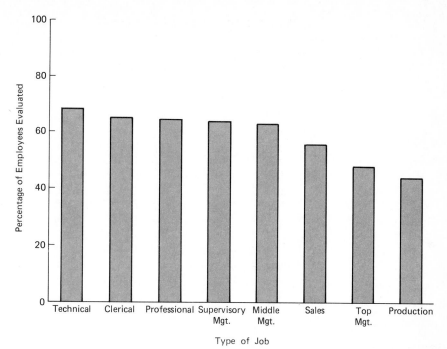

Figure 5-1 Frequency of performance appraisal programs by job type. (Adapted from "Organizational practices" by R. B. Dunham, 1983, *The Industrial-Organizational Psychologist, 21*(1), p. 46.)

papers, and special reports are all techniques of performance appraisal used by educational institutions. In principle, they are similar to the techniques used in the world of work, that is, they are methods of gauging or assessing the quality of your work. And, as in industry, the results of these evaluations have an important bearing on your future. They may well determine whether you will be promoted to the next grade level or will graduate.

Although you may not take formal examinations in your working career, performance appraisals in industry are just as difficult and important. Whether or not you are considered qualified for a pay raise or promotion will have an obvious and direct bearing not only on your income and standard of living but also on your self-esteem, emotional security, and general satisfaction with life. In a sense, then, you are never finished passing tests of one kind or another. Once you have passed the various selection criteria used by a company and been hired, you will continue to be tested, although in a different manner.

It is important to remember that performance appraisal is as beneficial to you as to your company. Just as classroom examinations tell where you stand and show where you need improvement, so the well-run performance appraisal program will enable you to gauge your rate of development on the job. Performance appraisal will point up strengths and weaknesses so that you may strive to improve your performance on the job.

Performance appraisals, like psychological tests and other selection devices, serve you by enabling you to find the right job and perform successfully in it. It is important, therefore, that you understand the principles and procedures of performance appraisal. Also, it is vital that the procedures used by your company be as objective and systematic as possible, which is another task of personnel psychologists.

Fair Employment Legislation and Performance Appraisal

For the reasons discussed, performance appraisal has always been important in the world of work. Under the impact of fair employment legislation that requires selection methods to be related to job performance, performance appraisal has become even more vital to employing organizations.

Equal Employment Opportunity Commission (EEOC) guidelines apply to any selection procedure that is used for making employment decisions. Such decisions include not only initial hiring but also promotion, demotion, and transfer. Therefore, performance appraisal is an employee selection procedure because its results are used to select employees for such career events. As such, performance appraisal procedures must be validated like any other selection technique. Failure to do so invites legal complications.

We shall see that most performance appraisals are based on supervisors' ratings, subjective human judgments that can be influenced by personal factors and prejudices. Some early research suggested that people of different races tended to evaluate the performance of members of their own racial group more favorably than those of other racial groups (Schmitt & Lappin, 1980). More recent research does not support any such consistent racial bias, although experts in the field do not deny that discrimination on the basis of race does continue to exist in performance appraisal (DeMeuse, 1987; Ford, Kraiger, & Schechtman, 1986; Guion & Gibson, 1988).

Sex bias in performance appraisal has been reported in laboratory studies but not in most research conducted on the job. In the workplace, appraisal ratings usually do not differ for men and women working at the same level (Drazin & Auster, 1987; Shore & Thornton, 1986). Nevertheless, there is sufficient inconsistency in the research findings to suggest that the gender of the employee being rated does have some effect on his or her evaluation.

The evidence with regard to age bias is clearer. Research shows that older workers receive significantly lower ratings than younger workers, particularly in self-development and interpersonal skills as well as on overall job performance. As we noted in Chapter 3, job proficiency does not necessarily decline with age. Thus, we must infer that the lower ratings given to older workers on the job are a function of age bias (DeMeuse, 1987; Waldman & Avolio, 1986).

Performance appraisal systems, then, which depend on one person evaluating another, provide opportunities for discrimination and unfair treatment in terms of salary, promotions, and other rewards of employment. A number of organizations have lost lawsuits brought by employees against their performance appraisal programs. The cost to these companies can be calculated in millions of dollars, not including the negative publicity that is generated when a company is shown to be discriminating against its minority employees.

Performance appraisal programs have been found to be in violation of EEOC guidelines on several points (Barrett & Kernan, 1987; Martin, 1986; Romberg, 1986).

1. Persons doing the appraising were not given specific written instructions on how to conduct the appraisals, nor were they trained in techniques of evaluation. As a result, they used vague and subjective criteria that were open to bias and to different interpretations.
2. Job analyses were not used to develop the appraisal criteria; EEOC guidelines require a job analysis for a performance appraisal system.
3. Appraisals were made in terms of personality traits instead of specific, objective, job-related behaviors. Appraising traits instead of behaviors is subjective and is open to bias.
4. The results of the appraisals were not reviewed with the employees. Thus, employees received no feedback on their behavior or on how it might be improved.
5. Appraisers were not in a position to observe the employees' job performance on a daily basis.
6. Appraisers did not provide counseling or corrective guidance to help poor performers improve.

For employing organizations to ensure compliance with fair employment legislation, performance appraisals should be based on job analyses, focus on behaviors rather than on traits, be reviewed with the employees being evaluated, and offer counseling to those not performing well. The persons conducting the appraisals should be trained in their duties, observe the employees on the job, and receive specific written instructions on how to conduct the evaluation.

As a result of the pressures of fair employment legislation, many companies have revised their performance evaluation programs, and personnel psychologists have attempted to increase the rigor and objectivity of performance evaluation.

Purposes of Performance Appraisal

The overall purpose of performance appraisal is to provide an accurate measure of how well a person is performing the job. On the basis of this information, decisions will be made affecting the future of the individual employee. A survey of 106 psychologists employed in industry found that performance appraisals had the greatest impact on salary decisions, job performance feedback to employees, and the identification of employee strengths and weaknesses (Cleveland, Murphy, & Williams, 1989).

TABLE 5-1 Uses of Performance Appraisal Programs

Rank	Function for which appraisal is used
1.	Merit increases
2.	Performance results, feedback, and job counseling
3.	Promotion
4.	Termination or layoff
5.	Performance potential
6.	Succession planning
7.	Career planning
8.	Transfer
9.	Manpower planning
10.	Bonuses
11.	Development and evaluation of training programs
12.	Internal communication
13.	Criteria for validating selection procedures
14.	Expense control

Adapted from "Strategic issues in performance appraisal: Theory and practice" by C. J. Fombrun & R. L. Laud, 1983, *Personnel, 60*(6), p. 28.

Performance appraisal can fulfill a number of functions for both management and employees. A survey of more than 250 companies revealed 14 functions or uses of performance appraisal programs (Fombrun & Laud, 1983). These functions and their frequency of use are shown in Table 5-1.

Let us consider a few of the functions of performance appraisal in greater detail.

Validation of Selection Criteria

As noted in Chapters 3 and 4, selection devices must be correlated with some measure of job success to establish their validity. Whether we are dealing with psychological tests, application blanks, or interviews, we cannot determine the usefulness of a technique until we examine the subsequent performance of the workers who were hired on the basis of that technique. We can have no confidence in a selection technique until we can compare a measure of the performance of successful and unsuccessful workers on the job with scores on a test or on other selection techniques. Ideally, then, the goal of validating selection techniques should be a major application of the results of performance appraisal programs. However, as shown in Table 5-1, it is next to last in actual use in the workplace. Few companies routinely collect satisfactory criterion data as part of an appraisal program.

Training Requirements

A careful evaluation of an employee's performance may uncover weaknesses or deficiencies in a specific job skill, knowledge, or psychological attitude that, once identified, may be remedied through additional formal training. Assuming that the employee's service has been otherwise satisfactory, it may be worth the cost to the company to enable the employee to improve on a weakness.

Occasionally, an entire work crew or section is found deficient in some aspect of job performance. Information of this sort can lead to the redesigning of the training program for new employees and the retraining of current workers to correct the shortcomings in job performance.

Performance appraisal can also be used as a means of measuring the worth of a training program by determining how much job performance may have improved after the training has been completed.

Employee Improvement

Performance appraisal is important to employees because it tells them how they are doing. This factor—knowledge of personal progress or performance— appears to be crucial to maintaining high morale. It is not sufficient for only the supervisor to be made aware of the strengths and weaknesses of individual workers. The employees must also be informed.

The results of a performance appraisal, communicated tactfully and constructively to employees, can indicate to them how they might alter behaviors or attitudes to improve their job efficiency and value to the company. This purpose of performance appraisal is similar to that of improving training requirements, except that in this case a worker's deficiencies can be changed through self-improvement rather than through a formal training program. As noted earlier, this reviewing of the results of an appraisal with the employee is important in meeting EEOC requirements.

Promotions, Wages, and Transfers

Most people feel, justifiably, that they should be rewarded for above average or superior performance. Surely in your college work, fairness dictates that if your performance on examinations or term papers is superior to that of someone else, you should receive a higher grade. If differential recognition and reward were not practiced—if, for example, everyone in a class received a *C* regardless of his or her academic performance—there would be little motivation or incentive for hard work.

In industry, the rewards are in the form of salary increases, promotions in rank, or transfers to a more desirable opportunity. To maintain initiative and morale, these changes in status must not be based on personal bias or prejudice, but on objective evaluation of an employee's merit. Performance appraisals should provide the basis for these career decisions.

It must be noted that many labor unions require that seniority, not performance appraisal, be used as the basis for promotion. However, length of employment alone is no indication of ability to perform a higher level job. An assembly-line worker with 12 years of experience may know everything about that job, but, without a more formal and objective evaluation of the worker's competence, there is no basis for concluding that he or she would be a good supervisor. Senior people should be given the first opportunity for promotion, but they should be qualified for that promotion on the basis of ability, not just length of service.

Reductions in Force

An unfortunate, but seemingly ingrained, aspect of our economic system is the periodic recession, sometimes in a single industry and sometimes over the entire economy. During these times, it often becomes necessary to lay off a portion of the working force, a procedure sometimes called a "rif," for reduction-in-force.

In such critical times, a company will benefit by dismissing the least competent of its employees and retaining as long as possible those who have proven themselves to be better workers. Such decisions should be made in terms of objective analyses of actual job performance.

However, labor union requirements again may dictate that seniority determine any such dismissals, that is, those who have been with the company the shortest period of time should be the first dismissed. As with promotion, seniority does deserve consideration, but many argue that it should be weighed against the worker's job performance as measured by objective techniques of performance appraisal.

Thus, there is no single aspect of a working career that cannot be influenced directly by performance appraisal. Despite its recognized importance, however, there are still those who actively resist the installation and implementation of work appraisal programs.

Opposition to Performance Appraisal

As noted, labor unions are not overly enthusiastic in supporting performance appraisal programs. As a rule, they have been the greatest source of opposition to such programs. The source of their resistance stems from their understandable motivation to provide the greatest degree of job security possible for their members. Unions traditionally have been committed to the principle of seniority as the determining factor in welfare and status decisions of the worker (for example, promotions and pay increases).

Of course, if all such decisions were made on the basis of seniority alone, there would be little need (and even less hope) for a system of merit or ability rating such as is provided by performance appraisal. Fortunately, it is only in a minority of cases that union contracts dictate seniority as the determining factor in personnel decisions.

Most unions do recognize the need for considering the ability of the worker, but, even then, seniority remains the ultimate context within which personnel decisions must be made. In practice, this means that even where ability is evaluated, it remains secondary. Workers who have been at their jobs the longest time are given the advantage over short-term employees, even though some of the latter may be better qualified.

Union opposition affects only those jobs covered by union contracts. This does not include the majority of job holders in the United States; only 19% of U.S. workers belong to a labor union. Bowing to reality, many companies concentrate their performance appraisal programs on nonunion job categories.

Another source of opposition to performance appraisal can be the individual employee. Few of us enjoy being tested or evaluated, particularly if we feel we might not receive a favorable rating. Few of us are so confident of our abilities that we consistently expect to receive glowing comments from our superiors. Further, few of us suffer criticism gladly, regardless of its objectivity, truth, or the tact with which it is presented to us. So because many people would rather not be assessed and told of their weaknesses or deficiencies, they often react with suspicion and hostility to the idea of performance appraisal. Psychologists suggest that the majority of employees dislike the whole idea of performance appraisal. A survey of the Fortune 500 companies revealed that 45% report that performance appraisal had brought about no improvement in employee attitudes (Taylor & Zawacki, 1984).

Sometimes, particularly when a performance appraisal program is being introduced, an entire section or department of employees will band together to protest to their supervisor. First-line supervisors, who must work closely with employees and maintain their loyalty, are placed in a difficult situation when faced with such opposition. They are under pressure from superiors to implement the program and under equally strong pressure from subordinates not to implement it. Sometimes the result is that supervisors merely go through the motions of the program without giving anyone a bad rating, to maintain peace and harmony among the employees.

When individual opposition is combined with resistance from a labor union, the company is usually on the losing side of the battle, but so are the employees in the long run.

Another source of resistance to programs of performance appraisal are members of management who may oppose such appraisals because of unfavorable experiences with them. As with psychological tests or other selection methods, a poorly designed and inadequate performance appraisal system can do more harm than good. Unfortunately, industry has all too often introduced these programs without adequate preparation and care, which sometimes has given performance appraisal a bad reputation.

In addition, many managers dislike performance appraisal systems because they are required to assume the role of judge. Managers may look on worker evaluation as playing God, and they are unwilling or unable to accept the burden of directly affecting the future of their subordinates.

Even those managers who believe that performance appraisal programs are necessary are often reluctant to evaluate the performance of their subordinates when they know they will have to discuss the evaluations with them. Many supervisors dislike providing feedback to employees, particularly if it involves criticism. Some managers give lenient evaluations to avoid having to criticize their subordinates in the postappraisal interviews. These negative feelings on the part of managers reduce the effectiveness of performance appraisal systems and can also lower a manager's own level of job satisfaction.

Despite the resistance to performance appraisal, it remains a necessary activity in organizational life. Its critics often overlook the point that some form of performance appraisal is inevitable. Some basis must be established for deciding on pay raises, transfers, promotions, or training requirements. These determinations cannot be made haphazardly or by the toss of a coin; neither should they be based on subjective factors such as a supervisor's likes and dislikes. Evaluations of performance must be made, and they can be either objective and accurate or subjective and error filled. Surely, employer and employee alike would prefer, even insist, that ability be appraised in a manner that reflects, as objectively as possible, the qualifications and abilities to do the job.

Techniques of Performance Appraisal

A number of techniques to measure job performance have been developed. In general, the specific technique chosen varies with the type of work. The work performed in a routine, repetitive assembly-line job differs from sales work or the duties of an advertising account executive or department head, and the performance measure used must reflect the nature and complexity of the job. Assembly-line job performance can be assessed more easily and objectively than the daily activities of the executive.

There are two categories of performance measure: those for production jobs and those for nonproduction jobs, although some measures can be used for both categories. Some sample performance measures for both kinds of work are listed below.

Production Jobs:

1. *Quantity of output*—the number of units assembled or produced in a given period of time.
2. *Quality of output*—assessed by inspection standards or the number of faulty units produced.
3. *Accidents*—accident record of the worker.
4. *Salary*—earnings history of the worker, rate and frequency of increases.
5. *Absenteeism*—number of days lost from work.
6. *Rate of advancement*—record of promotion.

Accidents, salary, absenteeism, and advancement may also be used in assessing performance on nonproduction jobs.

Nonproduction Jobs:

1. *Assessment by supervisors*—appraisal of level of proficiency.
2. *Assessment by peers*—co-workers' judgments of performance level.

3. *Self-assessment*—appraisal of one's own performance level.
4. *Performance in an assessment center.*

As you can see from these sample performance measures, the criteria used differ greatly for the two job categories. Production jobs readily lend themselves to more objective measures of performance and output (although subjective factors can still enter into the assessment), whereas nonproduction jobs require more judgmental and qualitative assessments.

Performance Appraisal for Production Jobs

The measurement of performance on production jobs is relatively easy in principle; it usually involves a simple recording of the number of units produced in a given period of time. This measure of quantity is widely used in industry, partly because records of production are readily available.

In practice, however, performance appraisal of production jobs is sometimes not so simple, particularly for nonrepetitive jobs. The quality of the work produced must also be assessed. Consider the example of two secretaries: one types 70 words per minute and the other types 55 words per minute. If we use quantity as the sole measure of job performance, the first secretary receives the

Some routine production jobs can be evaluated in terms of the number of units produced in a given period of time.

higher evaluation. However, if we appraise quality of performance, we find that the first secretary averages 20 mistakes per minute and the second makes none. The performance ratings reflecting these quality considerations should now be reversed and the second secretary should receive the higher evaluation.

There are additional complications in measuring performance on some production jobs. Even when the quantity of output data have been corrected for quality, there is still the possibility that other factors may contaminate or distort the resulting performance measure.

In the case of the two secretaries, perhaps the one who made so many typing errors works in a noisy office filled with distractions and the other works in quiet and peaceful surroundings. The quantity and quality of the work produced by each may be seriously influenced by the office environment. This factor also must be considered in the fair assessment of the typing ability of both secretaries. Note that this contaminating factor is extraneous to the task itself. It is a condition that is not a part of the actual job, but one that nonetheless affects job performance.

Another contaminating factor may be found in differences in the nature of the same job from one worker to another. For example, one secretary types only short business letters and the other types complex technical engineering reports. It would be unfair to determine the level of performance without in some way correcting for the difference in level of difficulty of the work.

A final contaminating factor is length of job experience. Usually the longer employees are on a job, the greater is their productivity. Hence, the performance appraisals of two otherwise identical workers on the same job, say, one with 20 years of experience and the other with 2 years of experience, may be expected to differ. It does not necessarily follow, however, that the lower performance evaluation of newer workers indicates that they are not good employees. They may be quite efficient considering their amount of job experience.

Thus, several factors have to be recognized in evaluating the performance of a production job. The more contaminating factors that are taken into account, the less objective is the final appraisal. Personal judgments must be made on the nature and extent of extraneous influences and some modification applied to the measure of production. Therefore, even with some production jobs in which there is a tangible product that can be counted, performance appraisal may not be completely objective. Whenever any judgment is required, an opportunity is provided for personal factors to bias the evaluation.

However, in repetitive jobs, such as much assembly-line work, such personal factors would have less of an impact. A straightforward recording of the quantity and quality of production may suffice as a means of performance appraisal.

Computerized Performance Appraisal

A relatively recent kind of production job involves a form of electronic assembly line in which the work is conducted at computers. This type of job characterizes

In computerized performance appraisal, the worker's data entries are continuously monitored and evaluated.

the work environment of more than 17 million employees in the United States who currently operate video display terminals (VDTs). Many companies that rely heavily on data processing operations have programmed their computers to automatically monitor their employees' on-the-job activities. Every time these employees produce a unit of work—for example, a keystroke on the keyboard—it is counted and filed, providing an objective measure of job performance.

In addition to recording the number of keystrokes per unit of time (say, per minute), computers can automatically record the incidence of errors, the pace of work over the course of a worker's shift, and the number of times the worker takes a break. This continuous monitoring and evaluating of performance by an "electronic supervisor" who sees and remembers everything already affects some 6 million workers.

Computers are also being used to assess workers whose jobs involve telephone communications, such as airline and hotel reservations agents and telephone operators. Reservations agents for Pacific Southwest Airlines in San Diego, California, are electronically evaluated from the moment they plug in their headsets until the end of their work period. They are expected to spend no more than 109 seconds responding to each call and are allotted 11 seconds between calls for paperwork. If employees are disconnected from their VDTs for more than 12 minutes during a shift or take longer than 109 seconds to deal with a call, they receive demerits and unfavorable evaluations.

TABLE 5-2   Computerized Performance Measures of Selected Jobs

Job	Measures	How measures are obtained
Word processors	Speed, errors, time working	Keystrokes counted by computer
Data-entry clerks	Speed, errors, time working	Keystrokes counted by computer
Telephone operators	Average time per call	Calls timed by call distribution system
Customer service workers	Time per customer, number and type of transaction	Calls timed by call distribution system, transactions counted by computer
Insurance claims clerks	Number of cases per unit time	Time spent on each form tabulated by computer

From *The Electronic Supervisor: New Technology, New Tensions* (p. 29), by the Office of Technology Assessment, 1987, Washington, DC: Government Printing Office.

Computerized performance appraisal will no doubt become more widespread as more jobs are automated, and the practice may soon apply to managerial and professional jobs as well. Table 5-2 shows some office jobs that are currently being monitored in this fashion, indicating what is measured and how these measures are obtained.

Computerized performance appraisal offers a thorough and accurate technique for evaluating performance on some types of jobs. Some employees favor it because it ensures that their work will be evaluated objectively, but others object to the approach and see it as stressful. Workers are constantly aware that every action is being monitored, and preliminary research shows that this pressure causes them to focus more on quantity of output than on quality (Grant, Higgins, & Irving, 1988). Labor unions have expressed opposition to electronic performance appraisal and have asked the U.S. Congress and several state legislatures to ban it.

Job-Related Personal Data

Items of personal data such as absenteeism, earnings history, accidents, and rate of advancement, are also used in assessing performance. These factors are considered primarily for production jobs, but they are also used for some nonproduction jobs.

It is usually simpler to acquire job-related personal information than it is to measure production. The information can usually be obtained from personnel office files. This availability is, of course, an advantage, but what do personal data tell us about an employee's actual job performance?

The evidence shows that such factors may tell little about a worker's ability on the job, but they can be used to distinguish good from poor employees if we make the semantic distinction between employees and workers. Consider a highly skilled and experienced machine operator who is prone to excessive absenteeism and tardiness. This person could be considered an excellent worker when actually on the job but a poor employee, in that the company cannot rely on him or her to contribute consistently to the efficiency of the organization.

Job-related personal data have a definite use in assessing the relative worth of employees to the organization, but they do not substitute for measures of job performance.

Performance Appraisal for Nonproduction Jobs

A nonproduction job is one in which competence or efficiency is measured in qualitative terms because these employees do not produce a countable product, or one that it makes sense to count. How would you evaluate the performance of firefighters? Should we count the number of fires they put out in a day? How would you judge brain surgeons? Should we count the number of brains they operate on each week? Or, in evaluating business executives, do we count the number of decisions they make each month?

In each of these cases, we must find some way to assess and judge the merit or ability of the person's work, not by counting, but by observing work behavior over a period of time and rendering an opinion as to its quality. Thus, to determine how good or effective a nonproduction worker is, we have to ask someone who is familiar with the person and his or her work—usually the supervisor.

For a nonproduction job such as architect, performance appraisal involves assessing the quality of the work over time.

Some companies use written narratives—brief essays describing employee performance—as the sole means of performance appraisal. Others supplement the written narratives with some type of numerical rating procedure.

Although both the narrative and the rating approaches are subjective, the narrative technique is more prone to bias. The descriptive phrases in an essay can often be imprecise or ambiguous in meaning when used to characterize someone's job performance. Many common phrases are so vague as to be useless. Others may be misused, inadvertently or deliberately, and thus distort the appraisal, usually to avoid giving a negative impression. Table 5-3 presents a humorous look at standard phrases found in performance appraisals together with their probable intended meaning (Jackall, 1983).

Let us now turn to the rating procedures used in performance appraisal.

Merit-Rating Approaches

A worker's performance level is often judged through the procedure known as merit rating.

Throughout our lives, we make judgments about the people with whom we come in contact. We assess them in terms of their intelligence, personality, humor, agreeableness, and the like. Based on these informal judgments, we decide whether to like or dislike these people, invite them to join our club, or marry them. Of course, while we are busy judging others, they are likewise judging us and making the same kinds of decisions. Our judgments are sometimes incorrect—the would-be friend becomes an enemy or the spouse becomes an adversary in divorce court. The reason for errors in judgment lies in the fact that the process is subjective and unstandardized; we judge on the basis of false and misleading criteria, on superficial and meaningless factors.

The process of judgment used in merit rating is more formal and specific; relevant criteria are established to serve as standards for comparison. The fallible human beings who are the raters can still inject their own biases or prejudices into the judgment process, but that is not the fault of the technique.

TABLE 5-3   Common Phrases in Performance Appraisal and Their Probable Meaning

Phrase	*Probable meaning*
Exceptionally well qualified	Has committed no major blunders to date
Tactful in dealing with superiors	Knows when to keep his or her mouth shut
Quick thinking	Offers plausible excuses for errors
Meticulous attention to detail	A nitpicker
Slightly below average	Stupid
Unusually loyal	Wanted by no one else

Adapted from "Moral mazes: Bureaucracy and managerial work" by R. Jackall, 1983, *Harvard Business Review, 61*(5), p. 127.

The merit rating is designed to be an objective evaluation of work performance compared with established standards.

Several merit-rating techniques are rating, ranking, paired comparison, forced distribution, forced choice, behaviorally anchored rating scales (BARS), behavioral observation scales (BOS), and management by objectives (MBO).

Rating Technique

The most frequently used method of performance appraisal is the rating technique. The supervisor's task is simply to specify how or to what degree each relevant characteristic is possessed by the worker. In rating the quality of work, based on observations of the worker's performance, the supervisor might express a judgment in terms of the following scale and decide at what point the work quality falls. The worker in this example has been judged as producing at slightly above average quality.

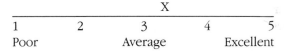

Not all firms use this numerical scale format, but the principle applied is the same: the individual receives a rating or score at some point along a dimension ranging from low to high, or poor to excellent.

Figure 5-2 shows part of a performance appraisal rating form used by a large textile company. Instead of a numerical rating scale for each characteristic, this company uses verbal designations to describe the range from exceptional to poor. In the column at the right of the form, the rater is asked to compare the current evaluation with the worker's last appraisal and to indicate whether the worker has shown improvement, slipped back, or shown no change on each characteristic. Space is provided for additional comments on each characteristic, an opportunity to explain extenuating circumstances that may have adversely affected a worker's performance or to add praise beyond that indicated in the formal rating.

Once supervisors have carefully judged a worker on the seven characteristics noted, this company then asks them to answer general questions about the employee in their own words (Figure 5-3).

The questions noted on the employee evaluation form in Figure 5-3 require written answers, the content of which exceeds the relatively simple ratings required in Figure 5-2. Of course, supervisors' comments are expected to be based on their ratings but should be more elaborate.

Ratings are a popular way of evaluating performance for two reasons: (1) they are relatively easy to construct and (2) they attempt to be as objective as possible. We know by now, however, that no procedure that depends on one person judging, assessing, or forming an opinion of another can be totally objective or free of personal bias, but well-designed rating scales attempt to keep biasing factors to a minimum.

PERFORMANCE REVIEW

NAME	POSITION
COMPANY	DEPARTMENT
DATE	DATE OF LAST REVIEW

INSTRUCTIONS

Evaluate the employee on the job now being performed. Circle the dot in the space above the horizontal line which most nearly expresses your over-all judgment on each quality. The care and accuracy with which this appraisal is made will determine its value to you, to the employee and to the organization.

Consider the employee's performance since the last appraisal and show by a check (√) whether he/she has gone back, remained stationary or gone ahead in each of the qualities listed to the left.

						HAS IM-PROVED	LITTLE OR NO CHANGE	HAS GONE BACK
KNOWLEDGE OF WORK: Consider knowledge of job gained through experience; general education; specialized training.	● Well informed on all phases of work.	● Knowledge thorough enough to perform without assistance.	● Adequate grasp of essentials. Some assistance.	● Requires considerable assistance.	● Inadequate knowledge.	COMMENTS		
QUANTITY OF WORK: Consider the volume of work produced under normal conditions. Disregard errors.	● Rapid worker. Unusually big producer.	● Turns out good volume.	● Average.	● Volume below average.	● Very slow worker.	COMMENTS		
QUALITY OF WORK: Consider neatness, accuracy and dependability of results regardless of volume.	● Exceptionally accurate, practically no mistakes.	● Acceptable, usually neat, occasional errors or rejections.	● Seldom necessary to check work.	● Often unacceptable, frequent errors or rejections.	● Too many errors or rejections.	COMMENTS		
ABILITY TO LEARN NEW DUTIES: Consider the speed with which he/she masters new routine and grasps explanations. Consider also ability to retain this knowledge.	● Exceptionally fast to learn and adjust to changed conditions.	● Learns rapidly. Retains instructions.	● Average instruction required.	● Requires a great deal of instruction.	● Very slow to absorb. Poor memory.	COMMENTS		
INITIATIVE: Consider the tendency to contribute, develop and/or carry out new ideas or methods.	● Initiative resulting in frequent saving in time and money.	● Very resourceful.	● Shows initiative occasionally.	● Rarely shows any initiative.	● Needs constant prodding.	COMMENTS		
COOPERATION: Consider manner of handling business relationships.	● Goes out of the way to cooperate.	● Gets along well with associates.	● Acceptable.	● Shows reluctance to cooperate.	● Very poor cooperation.	COMMENTS		
JUDGMENT AND COMMON SENSE: Does he/she think intelligently and make decisions logically.	● Thinks quickly, logically. Outstanding.	● Judgment usually logical.	● Fairly reliable.	● Inclined to be illogical.	● Poor. Unreliable.	COMMENTS		

Figure 5-2 Performance rating form.

INSTRUCTIONS: Based on the appraisal you have made on the reverse side please answer the following questions in your own words.

IS EMPLOYEE WELL SUITED FOR TYPE OF WORK HE/SHE IS NOW DOING? ☐ YES ☐ NO (If "no" indicate type of work for which he/she is suited)

WHAT CONTRIBUTION HAS EMPLOYEE MADE TO COMPANY, DEPARTMENT OR DIVISION BEYOND NORMAL REQUIREMENTS OF POSITION?

ALONG WHAT LINES DO YOU FEEL THAT HE/SHE NEEDS TO IMPROVE SELF?

WRITE HERE ANY ADDITIONAL COMMENTS GOOD OR BAD, WHICH YOU FEEL HAVE NOT BEEN COVERED.

WHAT WOULD BE YOUR OVERALL EVALUATION OF EMPLOYEE? (Place check (√) above horizontal line)

1	2	3	4	5
EXCELLENT	GOOD	SATISFACTORY	FAIR	POOR

	REVIEWED BY		DATE

Figure 5-3 Employee evaluation form.

Ranking Systems

In the ranking technique, supervisors list or rank their workers in order from highest to lowest or best to worst on specific characteristics or in terms of overall job effectiveness. There is a major conceptual difference between ranking and rating. In ranking, each employee is compared with all the others in the unit or section; rating compares the individual with his or her own past performance or a company standard. Ranking is not as direct as rating (although raters may unconsciously compare one individual with another in their judgments).

One advantage of the ranking technique is its simplicity. No elaborate forms or complicated instructions are required. Ranking can be accomplished quickly and is usually accepted by supervisors as a routine sort of task to perform. Further, supervisors are not being asked to judge workers on a variety of characteristics, such as initiative or cooperation, some of which they may not be competent to judge.

The ranking method has limitations when working with a large number of employees, however. A supervisor would be expected to know all the employees in the unit quite well to make comparative judgments of their efficiency. With a group of 50 or 100 subordinates, it is difficult and tedious to rank them in order of merit from best to worst.

Another limitation is that because of its simplicity, ranking supplies much less evaluative information on each employee than does rating. For example, specific strengths and weaknesses of workers cannot be readily determined. Hence, the ranking method may provide less useful feedback to employees about how well they are doing or what they might do to improve performance.

The use of the ranking method to evaluate employees makes it difficult to indicate similarities in efficiency among workers. For example, in ranking 10 workers, a supervisor may feel that three of them are equally outstanding and two others equally poor, but there is no way to specify this. The workers must be ranked in order from highest to lowest. Only one of the three outstanding workers can receive the highest performance appraisal, even though all three deserve it.

Another problem concerns the magnitude of the differences between the ranks. These differences may appear equal but may not be so in practice. For example, is the difference between the workers ranked fourth and fifth the same as the difference between the workers ranked fifth and sixth? As they are only one number apart, the tendency is to think that the differences are equal, but there is no way of being certain because the estimate is subjective.

These limitations make the ranking method a crude measure of performance appraisal at best. It should be applied where only a small number of workers are involved and where little information is desired beyond an indication of the relative standing of the workers as a unit.

Paired-Comparison Systems

The paired-comparison technique requires that each worker be compared with every other worker in the work unit. It is similar to the ranking technique, and the result is a rank ordering of workers, but the comparative judgments are more rigorously controlled and systematic.

Comparisons are made between two people at a time and a judgment made as to which person within the pair is superior. If specific traits or characteristics are judged, the comparisons must be repeated for each item. When all possible comparisons have been made, an objective rank ordering is obtained based on the person's score in each comparison. For example, suppose that a supervisor is asked to evaluate six workers by the paired-comparison technique. This means that 15 paired comparisons must be made because there are 15 possible pairs obtainable with six people, based on the formula

$$\frac{N(N-1)}{2}$$

where N is the number of persons to be evaluated.

A major advantage of the paired-comparison approach over the ranking procedure is that the judgmental process is simpler. The supervisor only has to judge one pair of workers at a time instead of an entire section or department. Another advantage is that it is possible to give the same rank to those of equal ability.

The disadvantage of this technique lies in the large number of comparisons required when dealing with many employees. If a supervisor has 60 employees in a department, he or she would be required to make 1,770 comparisons, a task that would not only be monotonous but would leave the supervisor little time to supervise. Further, if the performance evaluation calls for the ranking of workers on, say, five separate traits, each of the 1,770 comparisons would have to be made five times. The use of this technique, therefore, is restricted to small groups and usually to a single ranking in terms of overall effectiveness.

Forced-Distribution Technique

The forced-distribution technique, useful with somewhat larger groups, rates employees in terms of a predetermined distribution of ratings. The supervisor must rate the workers in certain proportions. In other words, a fixed percentage of the workers must be placed in each of several categories. The standard distribution used is as follows:

Superior	10%
Better than average	20%
Average	40%
Below average	20%
Poor	10%

Employees must be assigned in accordance with this distribution on whatever characteristics or abilities are being evaluated. If, for example, 100 persons are being rated, 10 must be assigned to the superior category, 20 to the better-than-average category, and so on.

If you have taken a test that was graded on a curve, then you are already familiar with this approach. The top 10% of the class received a grade of *A*, regardless of their specific score. The next 20% received *B*s, and so on, until all the grades were forced into a distribution resembling the normal curve, as in the preceding example.

The judgments of ability are made on a relative rather than an absolute basis, that is, workers are assessed as poor, for example, relative to their performance in the particular group in which they work. On an absolute standard of performance, these employees may not be the least effective workers, but, relative to their particular work group, they are so rated.

A disadvantage of the forced-distribution approach is that it compels a supervisor to use predetermined rating categories that might not represent a particular group of workers. Suppose, for example, that all the workers in a department are well above average in job performance. They all deserve good ratings. The forced-distribution technique, however, would dictate that 30% of these workers receive below average or poor ratings; this is obviously unfair. The Xerox Corporation abandoned a forced-distribution rating system for that reason and replaced it with written narratives, which are then discussed with each employee (Deets & Tyler, 1986).

Forced-Choice Technique

One difficulty with the rating techniques we have discussed is that the raters are fully aware of whether they are giving good or poor ratings to the employees. This awareness may allow personal bias or favoritism to influence the ratings. The forced-choice technique eliminates this knowledge on the part of the supervisors. It prevents raters from knowing how favorable or unfavorable a rating they are giving an employee.

With the forced-choice technique, raters are presented with a series of descriptive statements (in pairs or groups of three or four) and are asked to select the phrase that best describes an employee and/or the phrase that least describes that employee. The phrases within each group are designed to appear equally favorable or equally unfavorable.

For example, raters are asked to choose one statement in each of the following pairs of statements that best describes a worker.

1. Is reliable.   1. Is careful.
2. Is agreeable.   2. Is diligent.

Next, raters pick one statement in each of the following pairs that is least descriptive of that worker.

1. Is arrogant.   1. Is uncooperative.
2. Is not interested in the job.   2. Is sloppy on the job.

Given a number of these sets of statements, it becomes difficult for supervisors deliberately to give good or poor ratings to a worker. How would they determine which of each pair of statements represents a desirable or an undesirable characteristic? The pairs appear to be equally favorable or equally unfavorable.

In the development of statements for the forced-choice technique, each phrase is evaluated by personnel psychologists to determine how well it correlates with a measure of job success. Thus, although the statements seem equal in terms of their favorable or unfavorable nature, they are not equal in fact. One statement in each pair has been found to discriminate between more efficient and less efficient workers.

An advantage of this technique is the prevention of the possible influence of personal bias on the performance appraisals. However, this is more than offset by several disadvantages so that the forced-choice technique is not very popular in industry.

First, a considerable amount of research is necessary to determine the predictive validity of each item. Thus, the forced-choice technique is considerably more costly to develop than other methods of performance appraisal. Second, it is a difficult technique for many raters to understand and perform. The task of choosing one of a pair of equally favorable or unfavorable statements is tedious and raters often experience difficulty in making their choices. Third, despite the useful information provided to the organization, the technique yields little information on the strengths and weaknesses of the employees. Finally, research has failed to establish any clear superiority of this technique over the others we have discussed (King, Hunter, & Schmidt, 1980).

Behaviorally Anchored Rating Scales

The behaviorally anchored rating scales (BARS) approach attempts to evaluate performance in terms of specific behaviors that are critical to success or failure on the job rather than in terms of general traits or attitudes such as aggressiveness, ambitiousness, or diligence. These broad personal characteristics are subject to varying interpretations by different raters. In contrast, it may be easier and more precise to judge an employee on the specific behaviors he or she displays in the performance of the job.

The usual way of developing specific behavioral criteria is through the critical-incidents technique described in Chapter 3 as a method of job analysis. Typically, supervisors familiar with the job observe the performance of their employees and record those behaviors that are critical to success on the job. Through these observations, a series of critical incident behaviors are established, some associated with superior performance and others with poor or unsatisfactory performance. These behaviors are then used as standards for judging the efficiency of individual workers, standards developed on the basis of actual job performance.

The incidents that deal with the same behaviors are then grouped in clusters from which items for the BARS are constructed. Each item can be scored objectively by either checking it if the employee displays that behavior or selecting, on a scale, the degree to which the employee displays that behavior. An example of a BARS scale developed to appraise checkout clerks in a supermarket is contained in Figure 5-4 (Fogli, Hulin, & Blood, 1971).

You may also be interested in the BARS performance appraisal form contained in Figure 5-5, which was developed by an I/O psychologist with a sense of humor.

Much of the success of this approach depends on the observational skill of the supervisors in determining the kinds of behavior that are truly critical to successful or unsuccessful performance on the job. If the list of critical incidents is inadequate, any performance appraisal based on these behaviors may be misleading.

The effective compilation of a list of critical incidents requires a great deal of time and effort. Supervisors must be continually alert to the specific behaviors of their subordinates and must record each instance. It is not sufficient to wait until

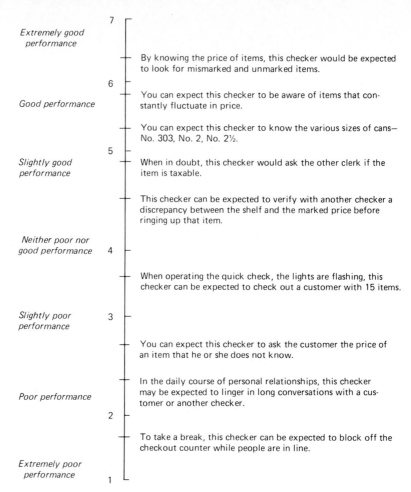

7 — Extremely good performance

By knowing the price of items, this checker would be expected to look for mismarked and unmarked items.

6 — Good performance

You can expect this checker to be aware of items that constantly fluctuate in price.

You can expect this checker to know the various sizes of cans—No. 303, No. 2, No. 2½.

5 — Slightly good performance

When in doubt, this checker would ask the other clerk if the item is taxable.

This checker can be expected to verify with another checker a discrepancy between the shelf and the marked price before ringing up that item.

4 — Neither poor nor good performance

When operating the quick check, the lights are flashing, this checker can be expected to check out a customer with 15 items.

3 — Slightly poor performance

You can expect this checker to ask the customer the price of an item that he or she does not know.

In the daily course of personal relationships, this checker may be expected to linger in long conversations with a customer or another checker.

2 — Poor performance

To take a break, this checker can be expected to block off the checkout counter while people are in line.

1 — Extremely poor performance

Figure 5-4 Critical-incident behaviors associated with job performance for supermarket checkout clerks. (From "Development of first-level behavioral job criteria" by L. Fogli, C. L. Hulin, and M. R. Blood, 1971, *Journal of Applied Psychology, 55,* p. 6.)

a performance appraisal is required to try to remember specific behaviors. Supervisors should be prepared to meet with each subordinate and point out examples of desirable and undesirable job behaviors that have occurred since the previous evaluation. This requires supervisors to keep what may have to be a daily log of the critical events they have observed. In some applications of this technique, behaviors are listed in terms of what an employee is expected to do at different performance levels, rather than in terms of actually observed behavior. In this case, the BARS is called a behavioral expectation scale (BES).

One advantage of the BARS and BES approaches to performance appraisal is that they meet EEOC guidelines for fair employment practices. The criteria on which workers are assessed are job related because they derive from actual job performance.

Area of Performance	Degree of Performance				
	Far Excels Job Requirements	Exceeds Job Requirements	Meets Job Requirements	Needs Improvement	Does Not Meet Minimum Requirements
Quality of work	Leaps tall buildings in a single bound	Leaps tall buildings with running start	Can leap over houses, if prodded	Often stumbles into buildings	Is often knocked down by buildings
Promptness	Is faster than a speeding bullet	Is as fast as a speeding bullet	Would you believe a slow bullet?	Misfires frequently	Wounds self when handling a gun
Initiative	Is stronger than a locomotive	Is as strong as a bull elephant	Almost as strong as a bull	Shoots the bull	Smells like a bull
Adaptability	Walks on water	Strong swimmer	A good water treader	Favorite haunt is the water cooler	Passes water in emergencies
Communication	Talks with God	Talks with the angels	Talks to self	Argues with self	Loses most of these arguments

Figure 5-5 Behaviorally anchored rating scale (BARS) for hypothetical "superman" or "superwoman" job. (Adapted by Hurd Hutchins from *The Industrial-Organizational Psychologist*, 1980, *17*(4), p. 22.)

Considerable research has been conducted on the effectiveness of the BARS approach compared with other techniques, but the results are mixed. Some research shows that the BARS approach is no more objective or free of bias than scales that do not have behavioral anchors (Murphy & Constans, 1987).

Behavioral Observation Scales

In the behavioral observation scale (BOS) approach to performance appraisal, employees are also evaluated in terms of critical incidents of behavior on the job. In that respect, it is similar to the BARS. Unlike the BARS, however, the BOS appraisers rate subordinates on the frequency of these critical incidents as they are observed to occur over a given period of time (Latham & Wexley, 1977).

The ratings are assigned on a 5-point scale such as the one shown here. This particular example is of a critical incident for the job of supermarket checkout clerk.

Item: Knows the price of competitive products:

Never	Seldom	Sometimes	Generally	Always
1	2	3	4	5

The evaluation yields a total score for each employee determined by adding the scores or ratings for each critical incident. The behavioral incidents are developed in the same way as in the BARS approach, through their identification by supervisors or other experts on the job. Like BARS, the behavioral observation scales meet EEOC guidelines because they are clearly related to the behaviors required for successful performance on the job.

Research comparing the BOS and the BARS techniques is inconclusive. Some studies claim superiority for one technique, others fail to confirm it (Kane & Bernardin, 1982; Latham & Wexley, 1981).

A survey of managers who conduct performance appraisals revealed that the BOS was preferred over BARS, and that BARS were considered to be no more effective than scales that measure traits. After using BOS for a year, these managers reported that the technique allowed them to justify low ratings, improved the quality of the feedback they gave employees, and resulted in more comprehensive appraisals. The same study also questioned lawyers who specialize in EEOC litigation. They believed that the BOS approach was more defensible in court than BARS or the trait rating systems (Wiersma & Latham, 1986).

Management by Objectives

Management by objectives (MBO) involves a mutual agreement between employees and supervisors on goals to be achieved in a certain period of time. The MBO technique has been used by a variety of organizations to increase motivation, and it is also a means of appraising performance. Instead of focusing on traits as in merit rating or on job behaviors as in BARS and BOS, management by objectives focuses on job results, on how well people accomplish the goals they set for themselves. Thus, the emphasis is on what employees do rather than on what their supervisors think of them or perceive their behaviors to be.

The MBO technique not only provides a measure of performance, it also challenges employees to increase their productivity in the future. Unlike the other methods we have discussed, MBO actively involves the employees in their own performance evaluations; they are not simply graded or rated by superiors.

In practice, MBO consists of two phases: goal setting and performance review. In the *goal setting phase*, employees meet individually with supervisors to determine the goals they will strive for during the period before the next appraisal, usually one year. The goals must be realistic, specific, and as objective as possible. It is not sufficient for salespersons to say that they will try to sell more products in the coming year. A specific number of items or dollar volume must be established as the goal. In addition, employees and supervisors discuss ways of reaching the goals in terms of specific prescriptions for job behavior.

In the second phase, *performance review*, employees and supervisors meet to discuss and evaluate how effectively the goals were met. Again, this is a mutual process; both parties participate in the appraisal. The results are based on actual results, not on general traits such as "cooperation" or "initiative."

Employees have expressed satisfaction with the MBO approach. In a study conducted at a large oil company, 91% of the employees said they were much more satisfied with MBO evaluations than with the more traditional trait-rating approach that the company had used previously (Murray, 1981).

One potential problem for employees is that they may feel pressured to set increasingly unrealistic goals in successive appraisals to show evidence of progress or improvement. A supervisor may not accept last year's quota for next year. Thus, higher goals may have to be set from one year to the next.

The implementation of MBO requires time, patience, and training on the part of managers who must be willing to allow employees to participate in establishing their own objectives or goals. Also, MBO is not appropriate for jobs that do not permit quantification. It would be inappropriate, for example, to expect research chemists to say that they will develop five more scientific breakthroughs this year than they did last year.

The MBO technique became popular in both private industry and the federal government beginning in the 1970s. Part of this popularity stemmed from the fact that MBO satisfies EEOC guidelines relating performance appraisal programs to job requirements. Surveys indicate that as many as 50% of organizations use some form of MBO to assess performance, usually for managers (Licker, 1987).

Sources of Error in Performance Appraisal

Regardless of the sophistication of the techniques, performance appraisal remains basically a subjective procedure. The information it provides for employer and employee may be inaccurate or incomplete. No matter how much research is conducted to develop rating or ranking devices, the process still involves one human being judging, assessing, or estimating the characteristics or performance of another. This means that human frailties and prejudices can affect the evaluations. All of us tend to judge people and things in our life in terms of our own preferences or fears. One person's assessment of another's abilities can be influenced by the other person's religion, race, mode of dress, attractiveness, attitude, and personality as well as by more objective characteristics and abilities.

Some common sources of error that can distort performance appraisals include the halo effect, constant bias, most-recent-performance error, inadequate-information error, average-rating error, and the rater's cognitive processes.

Halo Effect

The halo effect involves the familiar tendency to judge all aspects of person's behavior on the basis of a single attribute or characteristic. If we find a person to be extremely likable, friendly, and easy to get along with, we tend to evaluate that person favorably on all other personality characteristics. Or, if we find a person to be extremely unlikable, unfriendly, and hard to get along with, we may tend to evaluate that person unfavorably on all other personality characteristics. There are, then, both positive and negative halo effects.

A supervisor who finds an employee high on one factor of a rating scale may tend to rate that person high on all other factors. This distorting effect is particularly likely to occur when a high rating is given on one or two traits and the other traits to be rated are difficult to observe or define, are unfamiliar, or involve vague or ambiguous personality characteristics.

One method of attempting to control the halo effect is to have more than one person rate a worker on the assumption that the biases and prejudices of different raters will tend to cancel each other out. This method can only be used when the raters have had experience with, and the opportunity to observe, the worker being evaluated.

Another way of countering the halo effect is to have supervisors rate all subordinates on one trait or characteristic at a time instead of rating each person on all traits at the same time. When workers are compared on only one characteristic, there is somewhat less opportunity for an individual's rating on this trait to be carried over to another trait.

Some psychologists have argued that earlier research on the halo effect may not have been accurately measuring it. They suggest a distinction between true halo and illusory halo. The latter, also called halo error, refers to a systematic bias in the ratings that is falsely identified as a halo effect but which actually results from other sources.

These other sources of bias can include a lack of adequate job knowledge on the part of the rater, lack of rater familiarity with the employees, similarities in wording among the categories or characteristics to be rated, carelessness, and cognitive distortion produced by the raters' own information-processing capacities (Becker & Cardy, 1986; Kozlowski, Kirsch, & Chao, 1986; Lance & Woehr, 1986).

Because of these potential difficulties in accurately measuring the true halo effect, some psychologists have suggested a moratorium on further research until the problem of accuracy has been resolved (Guion & Gibson, 1988). The halo effect is an influence on performance appraisal, but the real extent of the problem remains to be determined.

Constant or Systematic Bias

Constant or systematic bias as a source of performance appraisal error has its basis in the standards or criteria used by the raters. Some supervisors may expect more than others from their employees. A similar phenomenon exists in college; some professors have reputations as easy graders and others are known to be hard graders. The constant biasing error means that a top rating given by one supervisor may not be equivalent to a top rating given by another supervisor, just as an *A* in one course may not mean the same (as an evaluation of merit or ability) as an *A* in another course.

One possible means of correcting this constant bias is to require supervisors to distribute their ratings in accordance with the normal curve of distribution. This introduces another potential problem, however, in that some workers will receive low ratings that may be undeserved. The method is unfair to a group of outstanding workers who all happen to be employed in the same unit and, consequently, are evaluated together. Similarly, in a class where all students performed well on an examination, the forcing of the distribution (grading on a curve) dictates that some students would have to receive lower grades than their ability warranted.

Most-Recent-Performance Error

Performance appraisals are usually made periodically, every 6 or 12 months. As a result, there is an understandable tendency to base the rating on the most recent behavior of the workers, not taking into account or being able to remember their performance throughout the period since the last appraisal.

It is natural for memory to be clearer about events that occurred more recently, but recent behavior may be atypical or distorted by extraneous factors. A worker could, because of illness or marital problems, for example, perform poorly in the weeks prior to the evaluation even though previous job behavior was exemplary. Or, if a worker is aware that an evaluation is forthcoming, he or she may work more efficiently just prior to the rating. In either case, the performance being evaluated is not typical of overall job performance and a falsely high or low rating would result.

One way of reducing this problem is to require more frequent appraisals. By shortening the time between appraisals, there might be less tendency to forget a worker's typical behavior. Informing supervisors of the possibility of the most-recent-performance error has also been found to be useful.

Inadequate-Information Error

When it is time for performance appraisal, supervisors are required to rate employees whether or not they know enough about them to do so fairly. To admit to their superiors that they lack adequate knowledge of their employees might be construed as a personal failing, so supervisors rate the workers anyway.

The resulting appraisals are worthless to the organization because they cannot reflect accurately the abilities and characteristics of the employees. Further, considerable harm can be done to the workers in terms of the false picture presented of them.

The best solution to this problem is to train supervisors on the value of performance appraisal and the harm committed by ratings based on inadequate knowledge. Supervisors should be given the opportunity to refuse to rate employees about whom they have little information, and the assurance that such refusal will not be met with disapproval.

Average-Rating Error

Some people, when placed in the position of judging others, are reluctant to give extreme scores in either direction whether very good or very poor. The result is the tendency to be lenient, to assign average ratings to all workers. When examining the ratings of a small number of workers, it is not unusual to find them clustered around the middle of the scale with no more than 1 or 2 points separating them.

Thus, the range of abilities indicated is restricted and the ratings so close together that it becomes difficult to distinguish between good and poor workers. This error in performance appraisal does not result in a true reflection of the range of differences among the workers, and such ratings provide no useful information to the company or to the employees.

Cognitive Processes of Raters

Performance appraisals can also be affected by the cognitive processes that underlie the raters' judgments of performance. Psychologists have conducted considerable research on how the information used to evaluate performance is processed, that is, how it is encoded, stored in our memory, categorized, recalled, and integrated into a judgment. We shall discuss four cognitive variables: category structures, beliefs, interpersonal affect, and attribution.

The *category structures* used by managers in evaluating their employees can influence their assessments. When a manager mentally assigns a worker to a particular category, the recall of information about that worker will be biased toward that category. Suppose that an employee is perceived to be a team player. That becomes a category in the manager's mental evaluation of that person. This means that the person's performance on the job is likely to be observed, interpreted, stored, and recalled in terms of how a typical team player is expected to behave, rather than in terms of how that employee actually behaves. We can hold many such categories, all of which can influence our judgments about human behavior.

The notion of categories has also been invoked to explain the halo effect, which may arise from behavior patterns that are considered to be equivalent when placed in the same category. The halo occurs when the ratee's behavior is seen as consistent with the category structure the rater has formed.

Leniency in ratings can be explained in a similar way in that only information consistent with the category structure will be recalled and used in appraising an employee's performance. Inconsistent information will not be recalled. Research has demonstrated support for this suggestion. In one study, ratings were much more accurate when the behavior of these being rated was consistent with the expectations of the rater (Mount & Thompson, 1987).

A related cognitive variable capable of influencing performance appraisal involves the raters' *beliefs* about human nature. These beliefs lead them to give ratings in terms of how they view people in general, instead of in terms of the behavior of the worker being assessed. Studies have shown that raters' personal beliefs can influence the accuracy of their ratings of their employees. For example, raters who believed that people are basically altruistic and trustworthy tended to give more lenient ratings than those who did not hold such beliefs. Also, raters who believed that there are broad individual differences among people gave less lenient ratings (Wexley & Youtz, 1985).

Another cognitive variable, *interpersonal affect*, refers to one person's feelings or emotions toward another. Common sense suggests that except for those raters who are able to maintain strict impartiality and objectivity toward their employees, ratings would have to be influenced by the nature of the relationship between rater and ratee. Research supports this idea and demonstrates that raters with positive emotion or affect toward their workers gave higher ratings than did raters with negative affect. This finding held true for ratings made by superiors, peers, and subordinates. In all cases, the degree of liking or not liking influenced the ratings.

The halo effect was also influenced by interpersonal affect. Raters with either positive or negative affect toward their employees exhibited significantly more halo effect (in the expected direction) than did those who were more neutral in their affect. Further, the halo effect was significantly greater with negative affect than with positive affect. In other words, negative feelings influenced raters more strongly than did positive feelings (Tsui & Barry, 1986).

The concept of *attribution*, another cognitive influence on the performance appraisal process, derives from research in social psychology where it was found to have an effect on the way in which we form impressions of other people (Kelley, 1973). Performance appraisal involves a situation in which one person forms an impression of the abilities and characteristics of another. As part of this process, a supervisor attributes or assigns causes and reasons to the subordinate's behavior. These beliefs about why an employee behaves in a particular way can affect the rating or evaluation the supervisor gives. For example, two employees whose job performance is identical could receive different appraisals if their manager attributes different explanations to their behavior.

Psychological research on attribution shows that a person's behavior can be attributed to external factors such as luck or the difficulty of the task, or to internal factors such as a person's ability and effort. An employee's evaluation will depend, in part, on what factors the supervisor thinks account for the level of job performance.

In one study, some employees who performed well were rated higher than other employees who performed equally well because supervisors believed that the performance of the first group resulted from effort rather than from inherent ability. In general, supervisors rated high performers higher and low performers lower when they attributed the causes of the given level of job performance to internal rather than external factors (Steers & Porter, 1983).

Not surprisingly, interpersonal affect influences attribution. One study found that managers were more inclined to attribute poor performance to internal factors when they disliked the person being rated than when they liked the person. Thus, the poor performance of those employees the managers did not like was seen to be the employees' own fault, whereas the poor performance of employees the managers liked was attributed to external factors (Dobbins & Russell, 1986).

The attribution error can be reduced by having the supervisors spend time performing the job being evaluated. This experience can help persuade supervisors of the importance of external factors in job performance (Mitchell & Kalb, 1982). Supervisors must also be shown how their perception of the causes of an employee's performance may differ from the employee's own view. For example, a supervisor may believe that poor performance is the result of a worker's laziness, whereas the worker may attribute his or her performance to an exceptionally heavy work load (Smither, Skov, & Adler, 1986).

Improving Performance Appraisals

The fact that performance appraisals can be so easily biased by the characteristics of the raters and the ratees is no reason to abandon hope of achieving objective evaluations. We have discussed various steps that can be taken to reduce some of the sources of error in performance appraisal. In addition, two techniques are being used in industry today to attempt to reduce error and increase accuracy. These involve better training for raters and providing feedback to raters on the quality of their evaluations.

Training of Raters

Almost two thirds of all employing organizations in the United States provide training to those who conduct performance appraisals (P. King, 1984). Training can involve two steps: (1) creating an awareness that abilities and skills are usually distributed in accordance with the normal curve so that it is perfectly acceptable to find large differences among a group of workers, and (2) developing the ability to define appropriate criteria for the behaviors being evaluated, a standard or average performance against which employees may be compared.

A number of recent studies have compared the effects of different types of training with the ratings given in performance appraisals (Latham, 1988; Wehrenberg, 1988). The results support the suggestion that some kinds of training may reduce errors in ratings, particularly errors of leniency and the halo effect. This reduction was still evident 6 months after the training program, but it had dissipated markedly a year after the training (Bernardin & Bulkley, 1981; Fay & Latham, 1982).

Other studies have found that even a brief period of training (no longer than 5 minutes) reduces rating errors, but these positive effects diminish over time. Further, although training reduces halo and leniency errors, it may lead to less accurate ratings if no feedback is provided on the ratings (Edwards & Goodstein, 1982).

The type of training given to raters is important because not all training methods are equal in improving performance appraisal. The more actively involved the raters are in the training process, the greater will be the beneficial effects of the training, particularly in reducing leniency errors. Giving raters the opportunity to participate in a group discussion, along with practice sessions and exercises in providing feedback to ratees, produces better results than presenting the same material to the raters in a lecture. Practice and feedback exercises have been shown to be particularly valuable in increasing the accuracy of ratings (D. E. Smith, 1986).

Training programs that focus on increasing accuracy rather than on avoiding errors seem to be the more effective. An approach called *frame-of-reference* (FOR) *training* emphasizes the establishment of a common frame of reference or context within which to evaluate performance. It has been shown to be effective in increasing the accuracy of ratings and in reducing the halo effect. The FOR training approach includes practice and feedback and is superior to programs that provide the same information but without the opportunity for practice and feedback (Athey & McIntyre, 1987).

Training of supervisors not only influences the ratings they give but also their subordinates' reactions to the evaluation process. In one study, supervisors were trained to provide feedback and to set goals during the postappraisal interview. Their employees felt that the appraisals were more fair, accurate, and clear than when no such training had been given (Ivancevich, 1982).

Teaching raters how to conduct postappraisal interviews with their subordinates can also reduce the raters' own dislike of this part of the evaluation process. Observing and practicing proper interview procedures have been shown to lead to a greater willingness to undertake performance appraisals promptly and efficiently (Fisher & Thomas, 1982).

Much additional research is needed to determine the most effective type of training to reduce rating errors. Because the effects of training diminish over time, refresher courses may be necessary. Personnel psychologists have suggested that allowing raters to participate in the development of rating scales may facilitate training in their proper use.

Providing Feedback to Raters

As we noted, the frame-of-reference (FOR) training approach includes providing feedback to raters. Feedback by itself, without the other aspects of a training program, can also improve performance appraisals. In one study, marketing managers in a large high-technology company received feedback from trained raters about the evaluations they had given to their subordinates. This feedback consisted of information about how the ratings of each manager differed from those of other managers. Specifically, the feedback was designed to deal with the halo effect and the leniency error.

When the marketing managers evaluated the same employees approximately 1 year later, they assigned significantly lower ratings than did a control group of managers that had received no feedback on the quality of their earlier appraisals. Thus, the leniency error had been markedly reduced. There was no reduction in the halo effect, however. A majority of the managers, some 93%, reported that they had taken into account the feedback they received on their initial ratings when making the second ratings. All of them said that the feedback program should be continued (Davis & Mount, 1984).

Other experiments with feedback to raters suggest that it can help make raters aware of their systematic biases (whether favorable or unfavorable) toward specific employee groups such as women and minorities (Edwards & Goodstein, 1982). Recognition of such biases is often a first step toward modifying them.

Performance Appraisal of Managers

The performance appraisal of managerial personnel presents problems not faced in the assessment of lower level workers. Although the traditional rating and ranking systems discussed previously are often used in the evaluation of low- and mid-level supervisory personnel, higher level managers usually require other methods of appraisal.

One difficulty in assessing the performance of managers and executives is the diversity of responsibilities, tasks, and skills found among them. An assembly-line supervisor has a fairly homogeneous group of workers to rate, that is, the job each worker performs and the skills required are similar from one worker to the next. A company vice president faced with the task of assessing several department heads, however, may find no common job requirements or responsibilities among them. The head of the research department, for example, is subject to demands and duties quite different from those of the head of the marketing department. This means that it is virtually impossible to define standards or behavioral criteria against which all managers at the same level may be compared. Further, this heterogeneity makes comparison of one executive with another most difficult.

Thus, performance appraisal of managerial personnel is complex, and it can have important implications for the continued success of an organization. Just as the effects of a poor selection program are more harmful to an organization at the executive level, so, too, is a poor appraisal system of managerial performance on the job. For this reason, great emphasis is placed on assessing how well executives perform. Some 65% to 75% of the organizations in the United States use some form of management appraisal for executives in middle- and top-management positions.

Performance appraisal for management personnel is undertaken in assessment centers, by the MBO technique, and by having superiors, colleagues, managers, and subordinates conduct evaluations.

The Assessment Center Technique

We discussed assessment centers as a selection device in Chapter 3. They are used similarly as a means of performance appraisal. Managers participate in a variety of simulated tasks such as management games, group problem solving, leaderless discussion groups, the in-basket test, and interviews. The staff of the assessment center evaluates each person on how well these tasks are performed, and the evaluation is provided to the person's superior.

Assessment centers do not assess actual behavior on the job but rather in a variety of activities that are like those encountered on the job. The results of assessment center evaluations for performance appraisal purposes have been positive. The reliability of assessments among raters is high, as is the validity of the assessments (Borman, 1982; Hinrichs, 1978; Schmitt, 1977). Thus, not only do different appraisers agree in their assessments of individuals but their assessments can also be used to predict future job performance with a moderate degree of accuracy.

Evaluation by Superiors

The most frequently used means of executive appraisal is assessment by the person's superior in the organization. In actuality, an assessment by the immediate superior is often supplemented by the judgments of higher level superiors. The latter step of appraisal presents a problem. The greater the distance between the executive and superiors in the hierarchy of the organization, the less intimate and detailed will be the latter's knowledge of the former. To provide an example from the academic community, a department head is able to give a better evaluation of a professor in the department than is the dean or chancellor. The chairperson works closely with the professor and is in a better position to assess personal strengths and weaknesses.

It is rare for an executive evaluation to be carried out using a standardized rating sheet. Usually, the executive's superior writes a description of the individual's level of job performance.

Evaluation by Colleagues (Peer Rating)

Peer rating, developed during World War II (then known as buddy rating), requires that all executives or managers at the same level rate or assess each other in terms of general ability to perform the jobs or on specific traits or characteristics. This approach is used extensively for the evaluation of officers in the military and is also used in industry and business to identify those with the potential for promotion. Although peer ratings tend to be somewhat higher than ratings given by superiors, there is a positive correlation between high ratings from one's peers and subsequent promotion. Peer ratings also show high interrater agreement, only a slight error from the halo effect, and a greater focus on job-related abilities (Imada, 1982; L. Siegel, 1982). Some psychologists believe that peer rating has the potential for providing the most accurate judgments of any method of performance appraisal (Wexley & Klimoski, 1984).

Of course, there is the potential for bias whenever a person is asked to express judgments on colleagues who may be close friends—or rivals for the next promotion. The situation offers the temptation to slant the evaluation favorably or unfavorably. It is also possible for colleagues to get together and agree to assign only good ratings or, at least, not to give bad ones.

Studies indicate that employees generally favor the peer rating approach to performance appraisal. Their attitudes, however, are significantly more favorable when the results of the ratings are used only for developmental rather than evaluative purposes (McEvoy & Buller, 1987).

Self-evaluation

Another approach to executive evaluation is to ask individuals to assess their own performance and abilities. The usual procedure is for managers and their superiors to establish mutually a set of objectives such as new skills to be developed or weaknesses on which to improve. After a period of time, the managers meet with their superiors and discuss how well they feel they have attained the objectives, a procedure that is similar to MBO.

It is not surprising that the results of self-evaluations tend to be higher or more favorable than those given by superiors and to show greater leniency effects and fewer halo effects (McEnery & McEnery, 1987; Thornton, 1980). However, leniency was reduced in one study in which the raters were told that their self-evaluations would be validated against more objective criteria (Farh & Werbel, 1986). Self-ratings also tend to emphasize different aspects of job performance than ratings given by superiors. Whereas ratings by superiors stress initiative and job skills, self-ratings focus more on interpersonal skills.

One study investigated the effects of incorporating self-ratings with the more traditional supervisor ratings. The results showed that self-ratings were highly congruent with supervisor ratings and that both employees and supervisors liked the self-rating approach. In addition, the use of self-ratings reduced defensiveness in employees during the postappraisal interviews and helped to resolve disagreements between subordinates and superiors over the evaluation results (Farh, Werbel, & Bedeian, 1988).

A study of 357 male recruits for the Israeli army found that self-appraisals had a low but statistically significant validity for predicting success in a training program. The self-ratings were also significantly related to ratings made by peers and superiors (Fox & Dinur, 1988).

Although self-ratings can be useful supplements to a performance appraisal program, their value as the sole technique of evaluation is questionable. They are, however, useful as a means of helping to identify areas in which employees can improve their job performance.

Evaluation by Subordinates

A still little used but apparently effective approach to the performance appraisal of managers involves evaluation by subordinates. There are three advantages to this approach.

1. Subordinates are in a better position to observe and evaluate some aspects of their managers' behavior than are peers or superiors.
2. Because such appraisals are conducted by a number of people, more information is provided than in assessments performed by one person, typically the manager's superior.
3. Providing the opportunity to participate in the evaluation of their superiors can enhance worker satisfaction and morale.

Subordinate appraisals have been found to have higher validities than assessment centers in predicting subsequent managerial performance. Further, the combined use of subordinate ratings and assessment center results was found to be superior to either technique used alone. Subordinate ratings have also been shown to correlate positively with both supervisor ratings and self-ratings (Bernardin, 1986)

The strongest support to date for subordinate appraisal comes not from the research literature but from companies that use it. These include IBM, RCA, and the Ford Motor Company. At IBM, subordinates periodically rate their managers on how well they handle disciplinary problems, provide feedback on job performance, anticipate employee workloads, explain business decisions that affect their jobs, and emphasize quality.

In all subordinate appraisal programs, the raters are not identified. A survey of RCA employees found that 88% of them said they would not be as open and candid in their evaluations of their superiors if they had to put their names on the evaluation forms. As noted, employees doing the appraising like this approach, and so do most of their superiors. At RCA, 94% of the managers evaluated by their employees indicated that they approved of the technique (Bernardin, 1986).

Combined Ratings

Because ratings by superiors, subordinates, colleagues, and the managers themselves are relatively easy to obtain, it seems logical to combine the evaluations on each person into one overall appraisal. This may also reduce sources of bias. If all parties know that their ratings will be compared with those given by others, they may be more inclined toward objectivity in their assessments.

We have already mentioned several successful combinations of ratings, such as self and supervisor ratings, and subordinate ratings with assessment center results and with supervisor and self-ratings. Other research, however, demonstrates generally low correlations between different raters. Exceptions include the correlations between self and peer ratings (+.36), between self and supervisor ratings (+.35), and between peer and supervisor ratings (+.62). The amount of agreement between ratings varies as a function of type of job. For example, the correlations for self/supervisor and for self/peer ratings were lower for managerial and professional employees than for blue-collar and service workers (Harris & Schaubroeck, 1988).

In cases in which all ratings are consistent, decisions about a manager's future can be made with greater confidence. Further, the manager may be more willing to accept critical evaluations when they come from a source other than the immediate supervisor. If the ratings greatly disagree, however, the individual may be reluctant to accept a negative assessment and recommendations for improvement.

In general, the combined approach to executive assessment promises to provide useful information to both the organization and the individual.

The Postappraisal Interview

As noted at the beginning of the chapter, performance appraisal serves two purposes: (1) supplying information to management for personnel decisions, and (2) diagnosing strengths and weaknesses of employees to enable them to improve their specific job performance and to provide them with sufficient motivation for doing so. The latter function is not fulfilled by conducting the appraisal alone. The results, interpretations, and recommendations of the appraisal must be communicated to the employees if the assessments are to be of any personal value. This is usually accomplished through an interview between the worker and the supervisor, a situation that can easily become antagonistic. When an appraisal contains criticism, the stage is set for the interview to be trying, frustrating, or even hostile. As the amount of criticism in a postappraisal interview increases, defensiveness on the part of the subordinate is likely to increase, along with the tendency to reject the criticism.

We noted in the section on self-appraisal that employees tend to have a high perception of their level of performance. A person's self-appraisal may not be matched by his or her superior's appraisal. In other words, a discrepancy will exist between how well employees think they are doing their job and how well their superiors think they are doing it.

During the postappraisal interview, the extent of this misconception is revealed. Studies have shown that the larger the discrepancy, the more defensive the employee becomes. He or she may try to shift the blame for the alleged shortcomings in job performance by minimizing the importance of the appraisal, downgrading the job itself, or criticizing the supervisor.

In the postappraisal interview, the supervisor should be positive and supportive and should focus on specific job problems rather than on the worker's personal characteristics.

The primary purpose of telling employees how they fared in a performance appraisal is the hope that they will improve their behavior on the job. For example, if an employee is told that he or she asks the supervisor too frequently how a task should be performed, perhaps in the future the employee will show some personal initiative in finding the answer.

The expectation of behavioral improvement may be naïve on the part of management. Some workers when criticized react by behaving in a contradictory manner as an imagined means of revenge. A worker may never again ask a supervisor for assistance, for example, and may make many more mistakes on the job as a result. Far from helping subordinates, criticism can lead to a deterioration in job performance and motivation.

Perhaps it is also unrealistic to expect that a brief meeting every six months or so will be sufficient impetus for employees to want to change their behavior. Behaviors and attitudes are deeply ingrained by adulthood, and a postappraisal interview may not provide enough motivation to produce behavioral changes lasting more than several days.

Finally, it may be unwise to believe that supervisors, in the absence of special training, have the insight necessary to diagnose properly the reason for a worker's unsatisfactory job performance and to prescribe means of improvement. Lacking these skills, many supervisors are reluctant to make the judgments necessary to the success of a performance appraisal program.

If feedback on employee performance were provided more competently and frequently, the motivation to alter job behavior and to persist in the new behavior might be enhanced.

The postappraisal interview can also serve as a way of rewarding or praising workers for better-than-average job performance in the hope that such praise will spur them to even more efficient behavior. Unfortunately, this goal, too, remains more ideal than real. When criticism as well as praise is presented, many workers focus unduly on the criticism and minimize or ignore the praise.

We might legitimately ask, then, if there is any diagnostic value in the postappraisal interview. The answer is yes, but only under certain conditions. Criticism must be offered with the utmost tact and understanding. To most of us, our jobs are vital, not only in terms of financial security but also in psychological terms. A job provides us with much of the basis of our sense of self-worth, esteem, and pride.

Even a rating of average or satisfactory can be damaging to an employee's self-esteem. A study involving employees of the National Aeronautics and Space Administration (NASA) and the Department of Defense found that those who received an average rating in their performance appraisal evidenced a significant drop in their attitudes and in organizational commitment within 2 months of the evaluation. That decline in organizational commitment occurred with both managerial and nonmanagerial personnel and was still evident 1 year later (Pearce & Porter, 1986). Attacking the way we do our work affects more than our on-the-job behavior. It influences our whole self-image.

Despite these limitations and problems with postappraisal interviews, they can be made to fulfill the purposes for which they are intended. Considerable psychological research has identified several factors that can influence the success of these interviews. Specifically, subordinates are more likely to be satisfied with postappraisal interviews and to follow supervisors' suggestions about how to improve job performance under the following conditions (Anderson & Barnett, 1987; Dorfman, Stephan, & Loveland, 1986; Greenberg, 1986):

1. When employees have been allowed to participate actively in the whole appraisal process.
2. When the interviewer takes a positive, constructive, and supportive approach.
3. When the interviewer focuses on specific job problems rather than on the employee's personality characteristics.
4. When specific goals to be achieved are established jointly by employee and supervisor.
5. When the employee has the opportunity to question, challenge, and rebut the interviewer's evaluation without fear of retribution.

A Sample Performance Appraisal Program

The top management of a division of the General Electric Corporation concluded that their performance appraisal program was a failure. Managers thought so poorly of the program that no more than half of them used it. Employees criticized it as inaccurate, unreliable, and a waste of time. Two major complaints were identified: (1) appraisals were conducted only once a year and were based on traits rather than on actual job behavior, and (2) employees had little opportunity to participate in the appraisal process.

An appraisal task force, assisted by personnel psychologists, was established to devise a better approach (Butler & Yorks, 1984). The new appraisal system they proposed offers a continuous process of planning and reviewing the work of the entire division. The following goals were established.

1. All work is planned jointly by employees and supervisors. Specific objectives, and the best ways of meeting them, are mutually determined, providing employees ample opportunity to participate in the appraisal process.
2. Formal appraisals are given annually, but interim evaluations and coaching are provided as needed. The focus in these informal sessions is on monitoring employee progress toward achieving goals and on devising changes in behavior where appropriate.
3. In the annual formal appraisals, employees and managers discuss the ways in which objectives have or have not been accomplished. They are evaluated in terms of their outcomes and new goals are set mutually for the future.

According to follow-up research, the system is working well. A high degree of satisfaction among both managers and employees has been reported. Some

85% of the employees like the program. Nearly 60% believe that the evaluations reflect actual performance, even though the ratings tend to be lower than under the previous system. Only 5% of the employees thought that their appraisals were unfair. In addition, a mere 6% of the employees reported that the postappraisal interviews were characterized by conflict and stress. Among managers, 86% believed that the new system was superior to the old one, and only 2% reported conflict in the postappraisal interviews.

The major ingredients for the success of this program are mutual goal setting, frequent feedback, and an emphasis on behavior rather than on personal traits. Overall, perhaps the best explanation for the acceptance of this performance appraisal system is that it was designed not solely to judge employees but also to help them.

Performance Appraisal: A Poor Rating?

It is possible to develop effective and worthwhile programs of performance appraisal that will benefit both employees and management. Unfortunately, innovative programs such as General Electric's are rare. Most organizations evaluate their workers by traditional methods that, as we have seen, have disadvantages and limited success. As a result, both parties to the appraisal may view it with suspicion, and the gap between worker and supervisor often widens. Performance appraisal may be one of the least popular programs currently in use in the world of work. Few people like them in spite of the recognition that appraising job performance in some fashion is necessary.

We noted that performance appraisals may cause a decrease in performance and motivation and lead to employee defensiveness. In one survey of a large number of business organizations, a staggering 90% of the corporate officers indicated that their performance appraisal programs were ineffective. When asked why, the executives pointed to the discrepancy between employee and supervisor perceptions of the employees' level of job performance. An industrial psychologist reviewing performance appraisal methods concluded that most companies do not know what their evaluation programs are doing for them. Another described performance appraisals as "a bad joke" (Edwards & Goodstein, 1982; Winstanley, 1980).

Why do performance appraisal programs get such a poor rating? We have already discussed the many opportunities for error with these evaluation techniques. There are other reasons as well. Consider the supervisor, the person responsible for making periodic evaluations. Performance appraisal systems demand much time and conscientious effort from supervisors who, in many cases, are already subject to stresses and demands. A supervisor must spend many hours observing subordinates to develop sufficient knowledge of their capabilities and be able to assess them fairly. Additional hours are needed to complete the performance appraisal forms. In practice, supervisors often resist performance appraisal programs to the point of filling out the forms only when pressured to do so by superiors. Also, evaluations are often hastily compiled, a situation that is not conducive to thorough and systematic appraisals. Many supervisors do not like the idea of judging employees, of being in a position to affect their future adversely, so they may be reluctant to give their subordinates low ratings, even for poor performance.

Supervisors may also deliberately delay providing feedback and may distort the evaluation results. Research shows that delays in communicating with subordinates are widespread, particularly when the evaluation is negative. Distortion of appraisal findings is common and results in suppressing unfavorable information or inflating the ratings given. By pretending that the employee is performing at a higher level than his or her job performance would justify, the supervisor can eliminate any potential confrontation and reduce the negative impact of an unfavorable appraisal (Benedict & Levine, 1988).

In general, employees also do not seem to like the idea of performance appraisals. They fear the effect of the assessment on their career. They are apprehensive that their supervisor will use the opportunity for evaluation against them for misunderstandings or personality clashes unrelated to their work ability. Often, employees do not know the criteria by which they are being judged or even precisely what is expected of them on the job.

In many organizations, the results of a performance appraisal program are filed in the personnel department and are never used for their intended purposes: to help make decisions about promotions and pay increases or to assist employees in their personal development. And this simply reinforces negative attitudes toward the whole idea of performance appraisal.

In sum, the system of performance appraisal, as generally practiced in industry today, is unsatisfactory, which may help to explain why the correlation between ratings and results-oriented job performance criteria (such as sales or output data) is relatively weak (+.27) (Heneman, 1986). However, new approaches and techniques such as better training for raters are being developed because performance appraisal, in some fashion, must be carried out. Judgments and appraisals of job ability at all levels of employment are necessary. The question is not whether to use an employee appraisal system, but rather which is the most effective approach to take. This can be determined only through additional research.

Summary

Performance appraisal programs are vital to employer and employee for several reasons. They are used to validate selection criteria; to determine the need for, and success of, training programs; to improve individual employee behavior; to determine promotions, wages, transfers, and reductions in force; and to identify workers with promotion potential.

Fair employment legislation has made performance appraisal more important because selection techniques must be validated against job performance. Performance appraisal is considered to be a type of selection procedure because the results are used to select employees for promotion, demotion, and transfer. Because some ratings of job performance have been found to be discriminatory, employers and personnel psychologists must pay close attention to EEOC guidelines. To ensure compliance, performance appraisals must be based on job analyses, must focus on behaviors rather than traits, and must be reviewed with the person being evaluated. The appraisers must be trained, must be able to observe the employees, and must have written instructions about evaluation procedures.

Despite the importance of performance appraisal programs, there are several sources of opposition. Labor unions do not favor performance appraisal because of their commitment to seniority as the basis for personnel decisions. Employees (the persons being evaluated) dislike performance appraisal because few of us like being judged or criticized. Supervisors (the persons doing the evaluations) do not like to make appraisals that directly affect the future of their subordinates.

However, evaluations of performance on the job are necessary in some fashion—informally or formally, subjectively or objectively, carelessly or systematically. It will surely benefit all concerned if performance appraisal is conducted in the most objective and systematic way possible.

There are two approaches to performance appraisal: that designed for **production jobs** in which a tangible product can be counted and that designed for **nonproduction jobs** in which there is no tangible product. In general, production jobs lend themselves more readily to objective measures of performance than do nonproduction jobs although, in both cases, objectivity in evaluation is the goal. Computerized performance appraisal, used with jobs involving computers, provides continuous monitoring of quantity and quality of output. Computers can monitor and assess workers whose jobs involve telephone communications, such as airline reservations agents.

Production jobs can be evaluated by considering the quantity and quality of output, accidents, salary, advancement history, and absenteeism. Nonproduction jobs are more difficult to evaluate and must be done in more qualitative terms by having supervisors assess the workers' ability to perform on the job. These assessments are usually made through written narratives and the process of **merit rating**, which includes several specific techniques: rating, ranking, paired comparisons, forced distribution, and forced choice. These techniques are subjective, in that they involve one person judging the ability or characteristics of another.

Two other approaches to merit rating, **BARS** and **BOS**, attempt to evaluate performance in terms of specific behaviors critical to success or failure on the job. These approaches meet EEOC guidelines and have the potential for reducing rating errors. The **MBO** technique involves mutual agreement between subordinates and supervisors about specific goals and how to achieve them. Appraisal is in terms of how well the goals are satisfied.

Sources of rater error include the halo effect, systematic bias, most-recent-performance error, inadequate-information error, average-rating error, and the rater's cognitive processes (category structures, beliefs, interpersonal affect, and attribution). Two ways of improving performance appraisals are (1) **rater training**, with periodic retraining, active involvement of raters in the training process, and focus on increasing accuracy rather than on avoiding errors, and (2) providing **feedback** to raters.

The evaluation of **managerial** performance is difficult but may be accomplished through assessment centers, or evaluation by supervisors, by colleagues, by the executives themselves or by their subordinates. Of particular value may be the combination of superior, colleague, self and subordinate ratings into one overall appraisal.

Once a performance appraisal has been completed, it must be communicated to the employee to provide him or her with an evaluation of job strengths or weaknesses. This feedback must be given with tact and sensitivity, particularly when criticism is involved, for it can cause defensiveness on the part of the employee and may even lead to a decline in job performance. Employee defensiveness can also be caused by an unrealistically high perception of one's performance level that is not matched by the supervisor's perception. To be maximally effective, feedback sessions should be frequent, informal, focus on setting specific goals, and allow for the subordinate's participation. A model performance appraisal program conducted by General Electric stresses helping employees develop rather than judging them.

In practice, performance appraisal is often ineffective and is not popular with those who have to do the rating or with those who are rated. However, the fact remains that, in some way, job performance must be assessed.

Key Terms

attribution

average-rating error

behavioral expectation scales (BES)

behavioral observation scales (BOS)

behaviorally anchored rating scales (BARS)

cognitive processes

constant bias

fair employment practices

feedback

forced choice

forced distribution

frame-of-reference (FOR) training

halo effect

inadequate-information error

interpersonal affect

management by objectives (MBO)

merit rating

most-recent-performance error

paired comparison

peer rating

performance appraisal

ranking techniques

rating techniques

self rating

CASE STUDIES

A Flawed Performance Appraisal System

A major division of the Xerox Corporation had been using the same performance appraisal system for more than 20 years. It required annual appraisals in which employees documented their own accomplishments for the previous year. Managers then assigned a numerical rating to each accomplishment. The ratings ranged from *1* (unsatisfactory performance) to *5* (exceptional performance). At rating of *3* indicated that the employee met and sometimes exceeded the expected level of performance.

The performance appraisal ratings for each work group had to conform to a forced distribution. The amount of the merit pay increase the workers received was related directly to the work group's ratings. When supervisors met with each employee to discuss the results of the performance appraisal, they also provided information on the merit pay raise.

Surveys of supervisors and employees revealed a high level of dissatisfaction on the part of both groups with the performance appraisal system. A major complaint was that 95% of the ratings were either *3* or *4*; few people received *5*s. Also, merit increases varied no more than 2% among all employees. No one received a raise of a larger amount. Finally, those who received a rating of less than *4* (showing that they did not consistently exceed the expected level of performance) believed themselves to be failures at their jobs. Largely because of these complaints, a new performance appraisal system was implemented.

QUESTIONS

1. Are there any aspects of the Xerox performance appraisal system that you find unsatisfactory? Why?
2. In what ways would you change this performance appraisal system?
3. How would you determine the effectiveness of your approach to performance appraisal?
4. What safeguards would you introduce to avoid violating EEOC guidelines?

Reference: N. R. Deets & D. T. Tyler (1986). How Xerox improved its performance appraisals. *Personnel Journal*, 65(4), 50–52.

Peer Appraisals

In 1982, the Utah plant of a nationwide food processing company established a peer appraisal system for its hourly employees. The system, developed with the cooperation of labor and management, called for each employee to be evaluated at least once a year for the purpose of making decisions about wages, and twice a year for growth and development purposes. Each employee was rated by 5 co-workers, including 1 with extensive seniority and job experience. The ratings encompassed 7 factors: attendance, attitude, safety, adaptability, cooperation and teamwork, sanitation, and work performance. The same rating forms were used for wage and for growth and development evaluations.

When supervisors received the rating forms, they eliminated the high and low ratings for each factor and averaged the remaining ratings for each employee. In feedback sessions, supervisors informed employees of their average performance scores. Employees were not told about the highest and lowest ratings they had been given by their co-workers, and they could not determine how their individual co-workers had rated them.

These peer evaluations were only 1 of 3 dimensions the company used for wage decisions. The other dimensions were absenteeism and tenure. Thus, one third of the information on which wage increases were based came from peer appraisals.

QUESTIONS

1. What criticisms would you make of this company's approach to peer appraisals?
2. How would you determine the workers' reactions to this method of performance appraisal?
3. How does the accuracy of peer ratings compare with that of other performance appraisal techniques?
4. What sources of error might influence a peer appraisal system?

Reference: G. M. McEvoy & P. F. Buller. (1987). User acceptance of peer appraisals in an industrial setting. *Personnel Psychology, 40,* 785–797.

Additional Reading

Anderson, G. C, & Barnett, J. G. (1987). Characteristics of effective appraisal interviews. *Personnel Review, 16*(4), 18–25. Identifies 5 components of the successful post-appraisal interview: employee participation, a positive and supportive interviewer, specifying job performance problems, setting goals, and emphasizing the worker's performance rather than his or her personality.

Benardin, H. J. (1986). Subordinate appraisal: A valuable source of information about managers. *Human Resource Management, 25,* 421–439. Discusses advantages and disadvantages of having subordinates rate managerial performance. Offers guidelines for the implementation of a subordinate appraisal system that will enhance job satisfaction and morale.

Electronic Supervisor: New Technology, New Tensions. (1987). Washington, DC: Government Printing Office. [Office of Technology Assessment, OTA-CIT-333] Deals with the use of computer technology to monitor employee performance in clerical, telephone sales, and data-entry jobs.

McEvoy, G. M., Buller, P. F., & Roghaar, S. R. (1988). A jury of one's peers. *Personnel Administrator, 33*(5), 94–101. Describes a peer appraisal system designed jointly by employees and managers.

Smith, D. E. (1986). Training programs for performance appraisal: A review. *Academy of Management Review, 11,* 22–40. Evaluates research on the effects of rater training on the quality of performance appraisals.

Chapter 6

Training and Development in Organizations

Introduction

Regardless of the sophistication and predictive validity of a selection program, it is almost always necessary to expose newly hired employees to some kind of training before they can be maximally effective on a new job. Even if the company is fortunate enough to find employees who are experienced with the machinery or equipment they will be operating, it may still be necessary to teach them operating procedures or company policies that may be unique to the organization. However informally such information may be presented, it does constitute a kind of training, the purpose of which is to increase the employees' productive efficiency and to enhance organizational goals.

Training requirements are made more complicated when the workers have had little actual job experience or are being hired for a type of work they have never performed. The organization's selection procedures ideally ensure that new employees have sufficient intelligence, aptitude, and attitude to learn the job, but, once hired, the organization must then properly train these employees in the specific skills required for successful performance of the job.

Thus, proper training is certainly as important as proper selection in the delicate relationship of matching the right person to the right job. The two activities are complementary; as a rule, one cannot succeed fully without the other. The best *potential* lathe operators, for example—those who possess the proper degree of mechanical aptitude and an eye for spatial relations—will not be able to realize their potential without adequate formal training. On the other hand, the most sophisticated training program is of limited value if used to train persons who possess little ability to be lathe operators.

Some form of training seems always to have existed in the world of work. Historical records tell of formalized apprentice programs in which a young person became indentured to a skilled craftsman for a number of years, during which time the apprentice learned the skills of the trade.

In modern, complex work environments, ironically, we often find much less systematic training methods. New employees may be assigned to more experienced workers and told simply to watch them and imitate what they do. Fortunately, this informal, and often unsatisfactory, kind of training differs sharply from other types of organizational programs in which new employees attend lectures, watch movies, and practice the job under the watchful eyes of skilled instructors, people who have been trained to train.

I/O psychologists have devoted considerable effort to exploring ways of imparting information and skills to new employees. Since the 19th century, much research on human learning has been conducted by psychologists. Applying what is known about the learning process to the world of work, however, where questions of money and management support are paramount, has not always been easy or successful. Indeed, the gap between research and application is wide. One psychologist wrote of the "gap between the psychologists who conduct research on training, and the training practitioners who appear unfazed by this research" (Latham, 1988, p. 546). In cases in which learning principles and research have been applied with the support of management, organizations have often realized great returns on the time and money invested. It is not unusual for overall job efficiency or production to increase as much as 40% as a result of proper training. Also, training can lead to greater job satisfaction and morale, reduced accident rate, and decreased employee turnover, all factors that make for a more efficient organization.

Training does more than serve the organization, however. It also serves the employee. Employees recognize that training can increase their feeling of job security, provide greater opportunities for advancement, and enhance their sense of status, self-worth, and prestige. Indeed, the provision of a good training program is regarded by many employees as an important fringe benefit, an inducement to work for that company.

As a result of the impact of fair employment legislation, many organizations are placing special emphasis on training programs for minority-group workers to assure them a responsible place in the economy. When people can be trained to become contributing members of society, the entire social and economic system benefits. Companies have also come to recognize the importance of long-term career development programs for all employees and are increasingly offering various kinds of training to match employee needs throughout their careers.

Training needs in industry have always been important, but even greater demands will be placed on them in the future. Methods of manufacturing are undergoing drastic and rapid changes. Wholly automated machinery is being designed, much requiring little in the way of human work. New developments in nuclear energy, laser technology, and computers have created a growing demand for large numbers of skilled workers, all of whom must be trained to work with this equipment. A survey of American and British companies showed that of all employee-relations activities, training will be the one most affected by new technologies (Helfgott, 1988).

As we noted in Chapter 1, many blue-collar jobs in basic industries such as steel are being eliminated as automated equipment takes over functions that used to be performed by humans. By the year 2000, more than 4 million factory jobs may be assumed by robots and almost 90% of all jobs will be in service and information industries. Labor unions have been increasingly demanding and getting contracts that require companies to retrain workers displaced or laid off by automation.

One group of potential workers that needs extensive training before they can become productive are the 25 million Americans whose reading skills are so poor that they are considered to be functionally illiterate. They cannot read or comprehend the simplest written instructions. They cannot even read ads in the newspaper for jobs or fill out application blanks. They must be taught to read before they can be trained to perform a job as must the large number of recent immigrants to the United States who must first be taught the English language. Organizations such as General Motors, Dow Chemical, and Phillip Morris have been sponsoring reading improvement training for their employees and for public school students who might become employees in the future. Southland Corporation, parent company of the 7-Eleven stores, offers free English courses to its immigrant employees. American Express currently spends $10 million a year training entry-level employees in basic reading and writing skills (Hollie, 1987).

Your training and growth as an employee will continue throughout your working career, in many cases with formal instruction at least as difficult as your college-level courses. And both you and your employer will benefit from the training opportunities offered by the organizations for which you work. Through training programs, you will be able to advance as far as your ability and motivation permit.

The Scope of Organizational Training

From high school dropout to college graduate, from hard-core unemployed to seasoned executive, in industry today, all of these people are involved in some form of training program. So extensive is organizational training that a chemical company executive is said to have exclaimed, "When I look at the money we spend on education and training, I wonder whether we're running a chemical business or a damned college!"

Training programs actually begin at a much more elementary level, teaching new employees basic mathematics and English skills. A survey of personnel managers at 115 companies revealed that 26% of them had hired entry-level employees who were seriously deficient in those fundamental skills. In addition, 30% of the companies established training programs to counteract the deficiencies (Blocklyn, 1988a).

Other sources put the proportion of entry-level workers who require basic skills training as high as 75% (McGraw, 1987). The number of remedial education programs for new employees is predicted to double by the year 2000.

Some companies are trying to teach basic skills to potential employees while they are still in high school. In Alabama, for example, General Electric donated $1 million to the county in which its plant is located for the purpose of upgrading the public schools. In Boston, Massachusetts, the John Hancock Life Insurance Company and a number of banks and law firms have given huge sums of money to the city's school system to improve instructional programs. Other companies offer tutorial and enrichment programs for high school students, in the hope of recruiting employees with sufficient math and language skills to be able to complete the organizations' job training programs (Fritz, 1988e).

Training for skilled jobs in technology is a high priority in industry, government, and the military. The military services, for example, offer more than 8,500 courses in specialized skill training for jobs ranging from fire fighting to nuclear engineering. On any given day, some 200,000 military personnel are involved in formal training activities (Halff, Hollan, & Hutchins, 1986).

Aerospace and other defense-related industries that use computer-assisted manufacturing and design techniques must train employees to use this sophisticated high-tech equipment. A number of companies located in California, including Northrop, Hughes Aircraft, General Dynamics, and Lockheed, have joined with local community colleges to operate apprenticeship programs leading to academic degrees in manufacturing technology. The programs are used to train both new employees and current employees who need to update their job skills ("Aerospace Labor Crunch," 1988).

When the Polaroid Corporation installed computers and computer-operated machinery at its plants, management also established training programs for the employees. In the first 3 years of these programs, one third of Polaroid's 10,000 employees went back to school. When General Motors changed from building standard automobile carburetors to more complex fuel-injection systems, it, too, had to set up a retraining program for its workers. Retraining workers to operate updated equipment now constitutes a major part of industrial training ("Business Teaching," 1988).

Training programs for other types of skilled workers have been established in fields in which there are shortages of trained personnel. The 1980s saw a 30% decline in the number of apprentice pipefitters, a 63% drop in apprentice brickmasons, and a 50% fall in apprentice machinists, all high-paying occupations vital to industrial productivity (Hicks, 1988).

Training is also prevalent at the professional and managerial levels, where it is both more extensive and more expensive. Consider the example of the Western Electric Company's Corporate Education Center, a company college devoted to instruction in engineering and business management. With more modern and elaborate instructional equipment than many colleges, this facility offers more than 300 courses on its 190-acre campus. A dormitory is maintained where employee-students can live while taking courses. Some courses last as long as 22 weeks.

Almost all of the engineers hired by Western Electric participate in 6-week orientation programs, one during the first 6 months of employment and a second during the next 6 months. Engineers already employed by the company may attend 4-week courses in their specialty areas, classes designed to keep them informed of the latest developments in their field. Engineering supervisors may choose among a variety of courses intended to update their technical knowledge and make them more competent as supervisors of other engineers.

One part of Western Electric's educational program is the opportunity for engineers to earn an advanced degree while employed full time. In conjunction with Lehigh University in Bethlehem, Pennsylvania, the Corporate Education Center offers a master of science degree in several fields.

If employees cannot come to the Corporate Education Center, the center will come to them in the form of more than 100 correspondence courses. Thus, widespread opportunities are provided for Western Electric engineers to improve their knowledge, obtain advanced degrees and, in the process, become more valuable to themselves and to the company.

The Corporate Education Center also offers management training at four levels, from first-line supervisor to manager. Attendance at these training courses is by invitation. Only the most promising candidates for promotion are given the opportunity to enroll. Courses range from planning and interdepartmental relationships to urban affairs and industrial psychology. The management training is not conducted by the lecture methods widely used in the engineering program but by group techniques, role playing, and business games.

This ambitious venture of Western Electric's is not atypical in American business. Industry has assumed an ever-increasing share of the responsibility of education. Sophisticated training centers have been established by many large firms. IBM offers a 4-week school for rising executives; General Electric conducts a 9-week general management course; and Avis Rent A Car trains 100 employees a month at its educational center in a variety of job tasks.

Motorola spends more than $44 million per year on training programs and has 800 employees assigned to full-time training activities. In 1986, it opened the $10-million Center for Continuing Education in Illinois, which is so busy that it operates on two shifts daily. In addition to classrooms, an auditorium, lounge areas, and a learning resources center, it houses the manufacturing management and engineering management institutes. These facilities are equipped with personal computers, computer-aided design and manufacturing equipment, robots, and other high-technology tools for learning and practicing the skills required in today's manufacturing and engineering environments.

Student-employees at the center can also take courses, via a satellite delivery system, from the National Technological University in Colorado, the only degree-granting university developed to transmit courses electronically from 21 U.S. colleges to businesses throughout the country. Motorola employees can

In one major bank in Philadelphia, new college graduates find themselves back in the classroom to learn about company policies and practices.

earn a master's degree in electrical engineering in 3 years while working full time (Wagel, 1986c).

The Xerox Corporation built a $55-million International Center for Training and Management Development on a 2,200-acre site outside Washington, D.C. Designed to house and train as many as 1,000 employees at a time, the center offers courses ranging from machine repair to sales and management. Students live in suites of private rooms in the strikingly modern buildings and study in classrooms filled with the latest audiovisual instructional equipment. When not studying, employees are free to use the gymnasium and swimming pool or relax in luxuriously appointed lounges.

So do not be surprised if during your first month on the job, and many other times throughout your career, you find yourself back in the classroom. Although you may not welcome that prospect now, it can provide you with the key to job advancement in the future.

Some of you may already be involved in industry-related and sponsored training while you are attending college. *Cooperative education programs*, in which students alternate between being full-time students on a college campus and full-time employees in an organization, are increasingly popular, involving some 1,000 U.S. colleges and more than 200,000 students, an increase from only 35,000 students in 1970 (Reed, 1988b).

Cooperating companies in these earn-while-you-learn programs hire the students to work a portion of each year in their field of study. This gives the students not only money to pay their college expenses, but also valuable job experience. Many are offered a job after graduation with the same company with which they already have experience and personal contacts. General Motors, for example, hires 95% of the students enrolled in its cooperative education program when they graduate.

Some of the organizations that participate in such programs are IBM, Texas Instruments, Exxon, Duke Power, Xerox, and Eastman Kodak, as well as many agencies of the federal government. The colleges involved range from small liberal arts colleges to large universities such as Cornell, Columbia, and the University of California at Berkeley.

To find a cooperative education program that involves a college or business in your area, you may write to the National Commission for Cooperative Education, 360 Huntington Avenue, Boston, MA 02115.

Fair Employment Legislation and Training

It is possible for training programs to have an adverse impact on minority-group employees. As a result, some training programs have become targets of lawsuits. Training programs are subject to equal employment opportunity legislation because decisions on promotion, firing, and transfer are often based on employee performance in a training program. And, as we have seen, any approach or technique that results in personnel decisions carries with it the opportunity for discriminating against minority, women, older, or handicapped workers. Therefore, training techniques are subject to the same basic requirement of any selection technique: They must be clearly related to job performance before they can be used as the basis for any personnel decision.

Several aspects of training are potential sources of discrimination:

1. *Selection for training.* If employees of an organization are selected for training on the basis of any kind of selection procedure such as those described in Chapter 3, it is possible that there will be discrimination against some employees. It is not sufficient for the organization to show that the selection techniques are related to success in training; that is not appropriate as a validation criterion. The selection techniques must be related to actual performance on the job.
2. *The training program.* The kind of training offered may have an adverse impact on minority groups if they enter the program with lower level skills or aptitudes. Such workers may be at a disadvantage because of insufficient preparation and so may not be able to benefit as much from the training as people with higher level skills and aptitudes. If minority groups perform noticeably poorer than the majority group in a training program, equal employment opportunity legislation requires that the program be modified. For example, additional training time may be provided for minority employees.
3. *Retention and progress in training.* If minority trainees perform at lower levels in the training program and are, thus, not allowed to remain in the program or are evaluated in a discriminatory fashion, the employing organization may be in violation of EEOC guidelines.
4. *Job placement after training.* If better jobs are given to those who did better in the training program and if there was a differential level of performance for minority- and majority-group employees, then training performance must be validated against job performance measures to alleviate adverse impact and ensure the legality of the program.

Specifying Training Objectives

The first step in establishing a formal training program is the precise formulation of objectives. These objectives must be in terms of particular behavioral criteria, that is, the acts or operations employees must perform on the job and the way in which they should perform them to maximize job efficiency. It is impossible to determine what the training should involve without knowing what it is intended to accomplish. In other words, what must employees be taught to maximize their level of job performance?

The objectives of the training program, then, must derive from the specific needs of the organization and of the employee. A *needs assessment* must be conducted to determine the company's and the individual's goals and how a training program would help to achieve them. The specific nature of each job and the skills and abilities required to perform it must be determined, a requirement that often is not met. For example, a survey of 1,000 large U.S.

companies revealed that fewer than one third of them systematically assessed the training needs of their managers (Saari, Johnson, McLaughlin, & Zimmerle, 1988).

The investigation of training objectives is usually difficult, but there are situations in which the need for a training program is obvious. A company that automates a manufacturing process, thereby eliminating a number of jobs, may, if vacancies exist elsewhere in the organization, retrain its employees to fill these positions. Rapid expansion creating a number of new jobs requires a training program to fill the vacancies. A high accident rate in a department or operation may call for training in safe job skills.

In the absence of a clear indication that training is needed, the responsibility falls on an enlightened management to analyze periodically its entire operation to determine if any part might benefit from additional training. This is where the difficulty occurs: A deficiency or poorly performed operation must first be noticed and, then, analyzed to determine if the problem can be corrected by training. It may be, for example, that substandard performance is caused by faulty equipment, not by the way the workers are performing their tasks.

This kind of general organizational analysis can suggest broad training needs that can be translated into the specific needs of the individual employees, a task accomplished by job analysis, critical incidents, performance-appraisal techniques, and self-assessment.

Job analysis, which was discussed in Chapter 3, is the most frequently used technique for determining training needs and objectives. The job analysis yields a detailed list of the characteristics needed to perform a job successfully and the precise sequence of operations that are required. From this analysis, it is possible to determine how performance might be improved by new training procedures.

The *critical-incidents technique*, which focuses on particularly desirable or undesirable behaviors on the job, can provide valuable information on how employees are equipped to cope with critical events that occur from time to time. For example, how well do assembly-line workers cope with jammed machinery, or how do supervisors fare with personal disputes among their subordinates? An examination of such critical incidents can tell a training director where instruction is needed.

The third source of information on training needs is the periodic *performance appraisal* that most workers receive. These can point up an employee's weaknesses and strengths and often lead to a recommendation for training to correct a specific deficiency.

Self-assessment, based on the assumption that the person performing a job is the best source of information about what skills are needed for that job and, hence, in what areas he or she may need training, is being used more frequently, particularly for managerial positions. Little research has been conducted on this technique, however. One study showed that a person's managerial level influenced self-perceived training needs with higher level managers reporting higher needs for conceptual training and lower level managers reporting higher needs for technical leadership skills (Bernick, Kindley, & Pettit, 1984).

Another study found that the managers who believed that training was a worthwhile activity tended to report higher training needs, particularly for quality control skills. In addition, the results showed, in agreement with the earlier study, that lower level managers felt they needed more technical training in such leadership areas as union guidelines, safety matters, and inventory control than did middle-level managers (Ford & Noe, 1987). Self-assessment of training needs thus appears to vary with the level of management and belief in the value of training.

By whatever method, the determination of a training program's needs and objectives is important and can decide if the entire training program will be worth the effort.

The Training Staff

The quality of an instructor can have a tremendous influence on your performance as a student. Some teachers are able to bring the subject matter to life, to organize and present it with enthusiasm, and to inspire interest in the class. Other instructors teaching the same material can make the classroom experience frustrating, tiring, and boring. The important factor in teaching anything at any level seems not to be the level of competence or expertise in the subject matter. Competence is a necessary, but not sufficient, condition for success. You have observed that some professors possess a comprehensive knowledge of their subject but lack the ability to communicate it to others. Success in instruction depends on something more. It is for the purpose of teaching that something more—the ability to teach—that colleges of education were established. And this is true for organizational training also: The trainers must be trained. A program designed to teach job skills may never achieve the desired success if the teachers are not capable of communicating the material to their students and motivating them to learn. Consequently, a crucial task in establishing a training program is finding educated and experienced instructors. Unfortunately, training in organizations is too often conducted by persons widely experienced in the task or skill to be taught but who have had no formal instruction in how to teach that task effectively to others.

It is also customary in industry to use first-line supervisors to instruct new employees in their jobs. Like experienced workers as instructors, supervisors may know a great deal about the job, but, without preparation to teach, they may well provide inadequate training.

The solution is to use professional teachers, people trained both in the skills to be taught and in methods of teaching. Some large companies have full-time teaching staffs, persons equipped to teach a number of subjects, as in the public schools. Not only does this provide maximally effective instruction but it also prevents interference with the ongoing operations of the plant, as is the case when supervisors or co-workers must take time from their jobs to instruct new employees.

Also, job trainees may be affected by the trainer's behavior, particularly by his or her expectations about how well the trainees will learn. If an instructor expects some trainees to learn faster or better than others, he or she may then behave differently toward the two groups of trainees. This may lead to precisely the results the trainer expects: Trainees thought to be faster learners, will be. This has been demonstrated in considerable research, including a study done in a combat command course in the military. Although all trainees possessed approximately the same level of ability, instructors were led to believe that some trainees were better learners than others. By the end of the course, those who were expected to perform better did so (Eden & Shani, 1982).

Of course, the degree of competence of a professional training staff rests on the familiar problem of the willingness of management to pay the price necessary to develop a truly effective training program. As we saw with selection programs, a company usually gets what it pays for. If it wants a cheap program, it will get just that—a shoddy, second-class effort that may not even be worth the low price paid for it.

Psychological Principles of Learning

Psychologists have devoted considerable effort to the experimental study of learning. The literature contains thousands of human and animal research studies on a variety of factors and conditions that are capable of influencing the learning process. This should not suggest that psychologists know all the answers about this complex activity, but certain factors that can facilitate or hinder learning have been uncovered, some concerned with characteristics of the learner (motivation and ability to learn) and others with how the training program and material to be taught should be organized and presented.

Despite years of research and theorizing on learning, it is still difficult to apply the findings to specific organizational training problems. Most of the research is conducted on rats running mazes or college sophomores memorizing nonsense syllables. These experiences do not directly relate to the skills needed to perform most jobs. Therefore, any generalization of research findings and principles must be made with caution. The principles of learning can serve as general guidelines, but not as specific rules.

Individual Differences in Ability. People differ in their ability to profit from instruction. Those with higher levels of mental ability may be capable of learning to perform a job task in a short time, whereas others are still struggling with the fundamentals. Some may drop out because of failure to grasp the basics. The rate of instruction, then, must be geared to the ability levels of the trainees, some of whom will be capable of learning faster than others. Ideally, the training staff will be given some advance indication of the individual differences in ability.

Individual differences in training ability can be predicted through tests of cognitive ability, life-history measures, attitude tests, and performance in initial training. In addition, some research on individual differences in learning ability has shown that trainees with greater seniority (presumably, older trainees) required longer training periods than workers with less seniority (Gordon, Cofer, & McCullough, 1986). Therefore, once trainees have been selected, instruction should be individualized as much as possible so that the fast learner in a class is not held back or the slow learner is not expected to improve too rapidly. Either situation can lead to a trainee's frustration and disappointment. We shall see that some training methods provide for differential and individualized rates of learning.

Education and training will often benefit the brighter person more than the less bright one. If two individuals are far apart in ability before entering a training program, this gap may increase by the end of the program. The slower learner will learn to perform the task, given sufficient time, but the brighter one will usually learn to perform it faster and at a more efficient level. Training does not always equalize differences in ability; it may well magnify them.

Motivation.   The motivation or desire to learn is of utmost importance in training. Learning will not take place unless the person really wants to learn, and this is true regardless of ability. To some degree, a high level of motivation can compensate for a lower level of ability. Every profession or trade includes people who have attained their position with less than the usual levels of intelligence required, but who possess great drive and motivation to succeed.

Some people are driven to achieve whatever they attempt to do because the attainment of success satisfies a basic need in their personality. (This need to achieve is discussed in Chapter 8.) They seem to have an inherent motivation, and need no other impetus to perform well in a training program. Others must be inspired by the trainer or by other external means to do well in any training endeavor. If the trainees can be persuaded that the training program will have a definite influence on their future and if the material presented is meaningful to them and to the job, then the chances are good that they will be sufficiently motivated to learn.

A good trainer is aware of individual differences in motivation among the trainees and gears the level of instruction accordingly. Thus, motivation can be affected by the interaction between employees and the organization. The company's trainer or instructor needs to create and foster adequate motivation in the trainees so that they will want to learn the material.

Other factors can influence the motivation of trainees. For example, in one study trainees who agreed with the assessment of their skill weaknesses, on which the assignment to training had been based, were more likely to perceive the training program as useful than those who disagreed with the assessment. In addition, those trainees who were more involved in their jobs and careers were more motivated to learn the behaviors emphasized in the training program than those less involved.

Long-term career plans on the part of the trainees were particularly important in improving actual job behavior as a result of the training. This suggests that training opportunities may be wasted on workers with low job involvement and a lack of career interest because their motivation to learn may be low. Perhaps pretraining programs to increase job and career involvement should be offered (Noe & Schmitt, 1986).

Another factor influencing motivation to learn in a training program is the personality trait called "locus of control" (Rotter, 1966). Persons said to possess an *internal locus of control* believe that their performance on the job, and their work-related rewards such as promotions and salary increases, are dependent on their own behavior and are, therefore, under their personal control. Persons thought to possess an *external locus of control* believe that everything that happens to them at work is dependent on external factors such as luck, chance, or whether their supervisor likes them. Events on the job, and in everyday life, are seen as beyond their personal control.

Internally oriented persons are much more likely to exhibit high levels of motivation in training programs because they believe that mastering the content of the training is under their own control. They are also more likely to accept feedback during training and to take action to correct deficiencies and weaknesses. In addition, internals show higher levels of job and career involvement, which are associated with higher motivation to succeed in training (Noe, 1986).

Trainees' beliefs or expectations that they can learn the material presented in a training program and that something positive will result from it (a promotion or a bonus, for example), can also influence their motivation to learn the behaviors and skills presented in the program.

These general factors—individual differences in ability and in motivation—are internal characteristics of the individual. Other variables capable of influencing learning are external and are concerned with the arrangement or manipulation of the methods of learning and with the materials to be learned.

Active Practice of the Material.   Practice may not always make perfect, as the saying goes, but it is a great help. For learning to be maximally effective, trainees must be actively involved in the learning process, not merely passive recipients of information. It is not sufficient to read about the operation of a machine or to watch someone else, on film or in person, operate it. These presentations can provide basic principles of operation, but they cannot train persons to become proficient at a task. The training program must provide sufficient opportunity to practice actively the skills required on the job.

Imagine trying to learn to drive an automobile by listening to a lecture, memorizing highway regulations, and watching a film of someone driving. This can help make you a better driver, but you cannot learn how to drive the car until you actually sit in the driver's seat and start practicing.

This principle also holds for learning academic material. Actively taking notes in class, outlining the material from the textbook, or discussing it with classmates facilitates learning much more than simply sitting in the classroom soaking up lectures like a sponge. (Fully soaked sponges, you may have noticed, become soggy, heavy, and useless.)

It is not desirable for workers to start to practice a complex task without prior instruction. They could easily absorb incorrect or unsafe work procedures. The practice must be guided so that trainees perform the task in the most efficient and safest manner. Until they have achieved a certain degree of proficiency, they must work under close supervision.

Massed Versus Distributed Practice. What is the best way of scheduling practice sessions? How long should they be? For some tasks there should be a few relatively long sessions (massed practice). For others, a large number of shorter sessions (distributed practice) is preferred. In general, the distributed practice method is usually, but not always, the better approach to learning, particularly for teaching motor skills. One British company compared massed and distributed practice sessions for training workers to operate word processing equipment. Both groups were given a total of 60 minutes of training time. The massed practice group was exposed to the training in one uninterrupted session whereas the distributed practice group received its training in two sessions (35 minutes and 25 minutes with a 10-minute break). On tests of performance given immediately after the training and again 1 week later, the distributed practice group worked significantly faster and more accurately than the massed practice group (Bouzid & Cranshaw, 1987).

The evidence is somewhat less clear for learning verbal skills, although research suggests that massed practice may be the more useful technique. Much depends on the nature and complexity of the task and the material to be learned (Goldstein, 1986).

Short, simple material can be learned quite well by massed practice because the sessions will not have to be excessively long for trainees to learn this type of material. Difficult, lengthy material often must be broken up into shorter units and is learned better by distributed practice.

The optimal practice schedule for the task to be learned must be determined. If massed practice periods are too long, trainees may become tired or bored. If the breaks between distributed practice sessions are too long, trainees may forget too much information from one session to the next. If practice periods are too short, they may not hold the trainees' interest and their motivation may wane. Determining the better approach to training sessions requires careful evaluation of the material to be learned.

Whole Versus Part Learning. Whole versus part learning refers to the relative size of the unit of material to be learned. Should the material be divided into small parts, each of which is learned individually, or should it be learned as a whole? Which approach is better depends on the nature and complexity of the material and the levels of ability of the trainees. Neither method is superior in all situations, and each offers advantages and disadvantages.

More intelligent trainees are capable of learning larger units of material that might confuse or frustrate slower learners. The latter, presented the material in smaller doses, may be able to learn it better and faster than if dealing with it as a whole.

Some tasks and skills adapt themselves well to whole learning; indeed, some require it for efficient learning. Recall the example of learning to drive a car. It serves no useful purpose to break down driving skill into component parts (turn on the ignition, shift from neutral to first gear) and to practice each part separately. Driving is an interdependent flow of movements and actions (for example, take one foot off the gas pedal and simultaneously apply the other to the brake) and can more efficiently be learned as a whole.

Where a task does require the initial learning of several subskills, the part method is the more efficient. The various parts are mastered at a certain level before being integrated into the total behavior pattern or operation.

The trainer must decide on the basis of the trainees' abilities and the nature of the material whether whole or part learning is more efficient.

Transfer of Training. Organizational training often takes place in an artificial setting, a training facility that may use equipment similar to that used on the job but that differs from the actual job environment in several ways. Even in cases where training does occur on the job, differences between the training situation and the actual work situation may still exist. For example, a supervisor may be more friendly and helpful during the training sessions than after training.

The discrepancy between the training and job environments must be bridged. The training program must ensure that there will be a transfer or carryover of the skills learned during training to the job itself. The question is one of relevance: Is everything taught during training relevant and meaningful to job performance? How accurate is the correspondence between behaviors and attitudes taught during the training sessions and those required on the job? Will everything the employee learns in a training situation be used on the job? Will the information be used in the same way? In many cases, the answer to these questions is no. It has been estimated that no more than 10% of the money spent on training results in transfer to the actual job, a dismal record of achievement (Baldwin & Ford, 1988).

If there is a close correspondence between the requirements of the training and the work situations, *positive transfer* is likely to develop. This means that information learned during training aids or facilitates actual job performance. The opposite may also occur. If there is little similarity between job and training situations or if a behavior or attitude stressed during training is downgraded by co-workers or supervisors on the job, *negative transfer* will occur. In this case, the learned behavior hampers or interferes with performance of the job. In negative transfer situations, learned behaviors must often be unlearned or changed before employees can successfully perform the work in question.

Psychologists and managers who design training programs must ensure that the conditions of training accurately reproduce the conditions of the job to avoid negative transfer and maximize positive transfer. Another way to facilitate positive transfer is by setting specific goals for the trainees to reach.

In addition, the organizational climate must be favorable to new practices learned in a training program. It does no good for a manager to learn a new technique for motivating subordinates, for example, if his or her department head or supervisor is unwilling to accept such an approach. In this case, there would be no positive transfer because it would not be allowed.

Knowledge of Results. People learn more readily when they are given a clear idea of how well they are doing. Feedback, or knowledge of results, indicates to learners the level of progress being made and can be very important in terms of maintaining motivation, as we saw in Chapter 5 on performance appraisal.

Knowledge of results contributes directly to proper training, in that it tells trainees what they are doing wrong. If they were not provided with this information, they might continue throughout the entire training session to learn and practice inadequate or inappropriate behaviors and methods of job performance.

Classroom examinations in college are aimed at providing you with a means of gauging your progress. The knowledge of your results, given periodically throughout a semester, may enable you to correct faulty study habits or to improve your understanding of the material.

To be maximally effective, feedback must occur as soon as possible after the behavior. If a behavioral operation is incorrect and must be performed another way, the desired change is more likely to be brought about if trainees are told immediately, rather than, say, a week later. Training proceeds most rapidly where provision is made for fast and frequent knowledge of results.

This has been demonstrated many times in industry. For example, in a program to train employees to follow safety procedures in their work, their behavior did not change until they were provided with feedback on the job. Training by itself was ineffective. Training plus feedback achieved the desired results (Komaki, Heinzmann, & Lawson, 1980).

Also, learning may be facilitated by the specificity of this feedback. The more detailed the knowledge of results, the more useful it will be to trainees in correcting or changing their behavior. However, if too much information is given, it may confuse the trainees.

Reinforcement. Reinforcement refers to the consequences of behavior. Those behaviors that lead to, or result in, a reward of some kind tend to be learned; behaviors that do not lead to a reward (or that lead to punishment) usually are not repeated and, hence, not learned.

The greater the reward or successful consequence that follows a behavior, the more readily and rapidly that behavior will be learned. The reward can take many forms—a good examination grade, a gold star for good conduct, a pat on the back and a smile from a supervisor, or a promotion for successful completion of the training program. The reward, whatever its nature, is controlled and manipulated by the trainer. By introducing a series of reinforcements or rewards, a trainer can establish and maintain high morale and motivation and can effectively shape the trainees' behavior by rewarding only those acts that are intended to be learned. (Most of what is known about reinforcement derives from the work of the eminent behaviorist psychologist B. F. Skinner.)

To be maximally effective, reinforcement should be given immediately after the desired behavior has occurred. The longer the delay between behavior and reinforcement, the less effective the reinforcement will be, primarily because the connection between displaying a particular behavior and being reinforced for that behavior will be less clear.

Reinforcement should be given every time the desired behavior is displayed in the early stages of training, but it is not necessary to continue constant reinforcement once some level of learning has taken place. The behavior can be maintained and strengthened by providing only partial reinforcement. For example, trainees could be reinforced every 3rd or every 10th time they display the desired behavior. That schedule of reinforcement, called a *fixed ratio schedule*, is an effective means of facilitating learning.

Reinforcement as a means of changing behavior, a process known as *behavior modification*, has been used with great success in prisons, mental hospitals, schools, and with individuals who have behavior problems such as stuttering or bedwetting. Behavior modification has also been applied to organizational problems, as we shall see.

The use of punishment as an aid to learning has little to recommend it. Punishment may eliminate an undesirable behavior, but it may leave in its place anxiety, hostility, or anger on the part of the trainee. The use of reward or reinforcement is a much more positive aid to learning.

Training Methods for Nonsupervisory Employees

Now that we have seen how general psychological principles can be used to facilitate learning, let us consider specific techniques used in organizational training today. Each technique offers unique advantages, and the training psychologist must determine the best method for a particular training program.

In general, there are two types of training methods, each having different goals and designed for different levels of employees. In this section, we discuss methods appropriate for training nonsupervisory and nonmanagement personnel. The next section discusses techniques used for training managers and executives. However, it should be kept in mind that sometimes the same methods can be used for all levels of employees.

On-the-Job Training

One of the oldest and most widely used training methods in industry takes place directly on the job for which the worker is being trained. Under the guidance of an experienced operator, supervisor, or, occasionally, a trained instructor, trainees learn while working. For example, they operate the machine or assembly process in the actual production facility and develop proficiency while they work.

This approach offers certain advantages, not the least of which, it is argued, is economy. The company does not have to establish a separate training facility with duplicate or simulated equipment. If workers or supervisors can serve as trainers, then, not even the cost of a professional instructor is necessary. However, this technique may be expensive in the long run. Workers or supervisors must take time from their regular jobs to train new employees. As a result, some reduction in their productivity is inevitable. An additional cost is in the form of slower production or damage to the equipment or product because of the new and inexperienced operators. For these reasons, it is recommended that trainees be moved through the training process as quickly as possible and that the best and most experienced employees not be involved in the training.

In this on-the-job training program in a window screen factory, new employees practice the job tasks under the supervision of an experienced worker.

Supervisors or, preferably, staff from the training department, should conduct the training (Kainen, Begley, & Maggard, 1983).

The costs of on-the-job training are hidden and not easily determined by management whereas the cost of establishing a separate training facility is not only visible but also formidable. Because on-the-job training appears economical to many organizations, it is generally considered to be a cheaper training method than other approaches.

Another advantage (and this is more real than apparent) is the provision for positive transfer of training. The workers do not have to carry over their performance in a training situation to the actual work situation because the training and the job are conducted at the same place.

On-the-job training implements several other psychological learning principles. Active practice on the task is provided from the outset. The learning situation is obviously relevant to the job, which can help to ensure a high degree of motivation. Knowledge of results is immediate and visible—an error can lead to the production of a faulty unit.

The disadvantages of on-the-job training can outweigh the benefits, however. In practice, it is often carelessly planned and poorly implemented (Goldstein, 1986). There is the danger that production facilities can be damaged, that production rates can be slowed, or that finished products fail to pass inspection. In certain jobs, allowing untrained persons to operate machinery may be hazardous not only to the trainees but also to others working nearby. Accident rates among trainees on the job are usually higher than among experienced workers. Another disadvantage is in the use of current workers as trainers. Just because a person performs a job competently does not mean that he or she has the ability to teach that job to someone else. Unless closely and professionally supervised, this kind of training can be haphazard, erratic, and generally inadequate. Often, such training amounts to no more than the supervisor saying to the trainees, "Go ahead and start. If you have any questions, come see me."

Another potential problem is that when skilled workers are told to break in the new worker, they may look on the assignment as a chance to get away from their own job for a while and goof off. As a result, the trainees are neglected and do not receive the attention and guidance they need and deserve. Also, skilled workers may resent new employees, feeling that the latter are being trained to take over their job. This insecurity can have obvious and detrimental effects on the kind of instruction the workers give to newly hired trainees.

The problems with using current workers as trainers can be overcome by training them in proper techniques of instruction, emphasizing the importance of their role as trainers, and trying to change their attitudes toward the new employees. Unfortunately, this effort is rarely made in industry.

Despite these difficulties, on-the-job training sometimes works quite well if proper care is taken in the development of the training program. With the necessary safeguards, on-the-job training can be effective, particularly in teaching relatively simple skills such as those required for clerical, production, or retail sales positions. However, little empirical research has been performed to compare the effectiveness of on-the-job training with other methods.

Vestibule Training

As noted, on-the-job training can interfere with the production process. Partly for this reason, many companies prefer the vestibule training method in which a simulated work space is set up in a separate training facility. Using the same kind of equipment and operating procedures as in the actual work situation, trainees learn to perform the job under the guidance of skilled instructors, not experienced workers.

There are several advantages to vestibule training. Because its purpose is solely to train workers, there is no emphasis or pressure on production. This and the use of professional trainers means that more personalized attention can be given individual trainees. Also, trainees do not have to worry about making costly or embarrassing errors in front of future co-workers. Nor do they have to be concerned about damaging actual operating equipment or slowing down the production process. They are free to concentrate on learning the skills necessary for successful performance of the job.

The greatest disadvantage of vestibule training is the expense. The organization must equip a facility and maintain a staff of instructors. The cost may seem particularly burdensome when there are not enough new employees to make full use of the training facility.

If the training situation does not closely match the actual working situation, there will be the problem of transfer of training. Without a close correspondence between the two situations, trainees may need informal on-the-job training when they actually begin work.

The problem of transfer can be aggravated by the common practice of using obsolete equipment, retired from the production floor, in the training program. This false economy could result in negative transfer if the equipment in actual use is sufficiently different from the training equipment. If properly conducted, however, vestibule training can be a very effective technique.

Apprenticeship

Probably the earliest recorded training method still in existence is the apprenticeship program for skilled crafts and trades. Conducted today both on the job and in the classroom, apprenticeship involves extensive background preparation in the craft and actual work experience under the guidance of experts.

Apprenticeships average 4 years, although in some skills they last as long as 7 years. The standard procedure is for trainees to agree to work for a company for a fixed period of time in return for a specified period of training and a salary, usually about half that earned by skilled craftspersons.

Trainees usually must complete their apprenticeship successfully before they are allowed to join a trade union, membership in which is vital to secure employment. Apprenticeship programs thus represent a joint effort by industry and labor to try to maintain an adequate supply of trained workers.

This combination of classroom instruction and actual work experience can provide excellent training in highly complex skills. If it is sometimes unsuccessful, that is not the fault of apprenticeship itself but of those who misuse it. Sometimes a company provides inadequate formal training, exploiting apprentices as a cheap supply of labor, expecting them to learn a job quickly by providing a slapdash version of on-the-job training. Such a company is not truly concerned with training but only with increased production.

Labor unions can also be criticized for the conduct of apprentice programs. Some apprenticeships seem much longer than necessary to learn the job. Unions may have a vested interest in maintaining lengthy programs. If there are too many craftspersons in a particular job category, there might not be enough jobs or sufficient scarcity of qualified personnel to maintain high wage rates.

The rapidly changing nature of manufacturing techniques sometimes renders a job obsolete by the time apprentices have finished the required period of training. For example, automation has completely altered the printing industry in recent years and has totally revised the skill requirements. Also, there is pressure on the housing industry for factory-produced homes as an alternative to on-site construction. The skills required of a carpenter working on an assembly line to build one part of a house are different from those required of the on-site carpenter.

Apprenticeship programs must be flexible and capable of modifying their requirements and procedures in line with changes in modern industry. Apprenticeship is generally a most effective training method and is likely to remain useful for many years.

Programmed Instruction

Programmed instruction is popular in the military, industry, the federal government, schools, and universities. Many major business organizations use programmed instruction, including AT&T, IBM, DuPont, Raytheon, Dow Chemical, Monsanto, Zenith, Exxon, and Maytag. Some of the basic jobs now being taught by this method include blueprint reading, air traffic control, tax return analysis, basic electronics, insurance sales, bank teller procedures, and computer programming.

There are several techniques for carrying out programmed instruction, ranging from paper-and-pencil book-type formats to costly computer-assisted electronic equipment. All means of programmed instruction involve self-instruction: Trainees proceed at their own pace.

In essence, detailed (programmed) information is presented to the trainees who must make frequent and precise responses to the material. The instructional material begins at a very easy level and gradually becomes more complex. The steps of increasing difficulty are designed to be small so that slower learners can progress with relative ease. On the other hand, faster learners are allowed to proceed more rapidly through the material. The trainees' rates of learning are determined solely by their own motivation and mental ability.

Two approaches to programmed instruction are *linear programming* and *branching programming*. In the linear program, all trainees follow the identical program in the same sequence. The learning steps are so small and simple that trainees rarely make incorrect responses. Therefore, they receive frequent positive reinforcement.

Branching programs are designed to conform more to individual differences in level of ability. Trainees are allowed to skip steps if they are learning the material well or to go back for remedial work if they are not learning it well. If trainees respond incorrectly to a set of questions at any point, they are directed to a new set of questions dealing with the same material. If trainees are proceeding well, they are directed to move on to the next section. If they are doing extremely well, they may be directed to skip intervening sections and to move on to more difficult material.

In terms of general psychological learning principles, there are certain advantages to programmed instruction.

1. Programmed instruction provides for continuous active participation on the part of the trainees, who must record their answer to one item before proceeding to the next. In machine-assisted programmed instruction, it may be impossible to move on to the next item until the current one is answered.
2. Programmed instruction provides constant and immediate feedback or knowledge of results. After each item, the trainees are informed of the adequacy of their response.
3. Positive reinforcement is provided. The items are purposely constructed to increase the probability that the trainees will be able to learn the correct response.

Proponents of programmed instruction suggest additional advantages.

1. Programmed instruction eliminates the need for an instructor. Especially with the book form, trainees may learn where and when they choose. They do not have to be assembled at one time and place.
2. Because programmed instruction caters to individual differences, brighter trainees may complete a course of instruction more quickly than in a group-teaching situation, which would have to be geared to the average level of the class. (This is particularly true with branching programs.)
3. The course of instruction is standardized. All trainees are exposed to the same material. This may not be the case if groups of employees are taught by several instructors, each of whom may emphasize, change, or omit different areas of the material to be learned.
4. A complete record is provided of the progress of each trainee that could aid in the future counseling of those who might experience difficulties.

This method may seem ideal for organizational training, but certain disadvantages must be considered. The kind of material that can be taught by programmed instruction is limited. It is not effective in teaching certain complex job skills, but it is capable of teaching items of knowledge, particularly those requiring rote memorization. In general, it is more useful for training blue-collar workers than managers and executives.

Programmed instruction techniques can be costly to develop and operate. Even when expensive equipment is not involved, the cost of writing the program is still high. Therefore, programmed instruction in organizations is usually restricted to training programs that involve very large numbers of trainees. Some trainees become bored and restless using programmed instruction. Initial acceptance is usually enthusiastic, but, as the small steps continue in robotlike fashion, a number of trainees develop a dislike for the experience.

Most of the research comparing the learning effectiveness of programmed instruction with traditional training methods has shown that programmed instruction is an effective approach, although this statement must be qualified. Programmed instruction has been shown to be a faster method of training but the level of learning is not higher than with traditional teaching methods. Thus, programmed instruction does not seem to improve the quality of learning, but it does provide for faster learning, which could be an asset to an organization that needs trained workers within a short period of time (Nash, Muczyk, & Vettori, 1971).

Programmed instruction is an important organizational training tool that is being used for a wide variety of jobs.

Computer-Assisted Instruction

A logical derivative of programmed instruction is computer-assisted instruction (CAI), or computer-based training, now being used successfully by military, government, and business organizations. A survey of Fortune 500 companies showed that 54% of them use some form of CAI and that 81% planned to introduce it or expand their use of it in the near future (Madlin, 1987).

In CAI, a computer, which stores an entire program of instruction, becomes the teacher and interacts with each trainee on an individual basis. Each answer provided by the trainee is instantly recorded and analyzed by the computer. The next item that is presented to the trainee is based on this continuing analysis of the trainee's progress. In a variation of this form of instruction, CAI can be used in conjunction with a training instructor who introduces the material and then directs the trainee to the computer for specific topics.

One of the most popular examples of computer-based training is the software package that comes with many personal computers and is used to teach the person how to operate the computer. IBM has sold more than 4 million copies of its training course on floppy disk called "Exploring the IBM Personal Computer." The course covers basic topics such as how to use the keyboard, the printer, and the disks. The lessons appear on the video display terminal. The trainee types in responses on the keyboard and receives immediate knowledge of results, such as when the word "good" appears on the screen. If the trainee makes an error, the program presents more detailed instructions on the topic and gives the trainee another chance to type in the correct response (Hassett & Dukes, 1986).

A computer consultant trains older employees at a large medical center complex in the use of a new computer system.

Computer-assisted training is being used to teach many skills involving the use of computers and other automated office equipment. One of the most extensively developed CAI programs is PLATO (Programmed Logic for Automated Teaching Operations). It is capable of presenting such a variety of displays and touch-panel graphics that it can be used to simulate virtually every button, switch, dial, and signal light in the cockpit of a Boeing 767 airliner. American Airlines uses PLATO for flight crew training and has found that it reduces the number of hours pilots and co-pilots need to spend in a more expensive flight simulator. This saves the airline approximately $4,000 per trainee. The military uses PLATO to teach remedial mathematics in a straightforward drill-and-practice program.

An advantage of CAI is the greater amount of individualized instruction it offers, compared to programmed instruction. Using CAI is not unlike being privately tutored by an excellent teacher who has complete command of the subject matter and who never becomes impatient or annoyed with the student. The computer instantly responds to the progress of each trainee without sarcasm, prejudice, or error. Because CAI also assumes record-keeping functions and maintains an up-to-date performance analysis of each trainee, instructors are free to devote more time to individual learning problems.

In terms of the psychological principles of learning, computer-assisted instruction allows the trainee to participate actively in the learning process. It also provides positive reinforcement and immediate knowledge of results.

CAI can deal with large numbers of trainees at the same time and in different locations. The PLATO system in operation at the University of Illinois encompasses 950 terminals for students on the campus itself and as far away as California. AT&T reduced both training time and travel costs by mailing 1,600 copies of a software training program to its employees instead of bringing them from around the country to training sites in New Jersey and Colorado and paying hotel bills and meals for a week.

The major disadvantage of CAI is the expense. The hardware as well as the software programs are costly, and the annual budget for management and maintenance of such a system is estimated at $200,000. Thus, most small companies are not yet able to afford this approach to training.

There has not been a great deal of research comparing the effectiveness of CAI with other methods of instruction, but what has been published is mostly favorable. Studies indicate that CAI-trained students perform at the same level or higher than those who were trained by traditional methods or by programmed instruction, and that learning took place in 30% less time (Dossett & Hulvershorn, 1983; Orlansky & String, 1981). Whether faster learning is worth the expense of a CAI system is the question that most organizations must answer for themselves.

Training for Computer Literacy. We have seen how computers are being used to train workers in a variety of skills—including how to use a computer—and have noted the inroads being made in the workplace by computer-operated office and manufacturing equipment. We said that 17 million American workers currently use VDTs on the job, and that up to 3 million jobs each year are being automated. Obviously, then, the development of computer skills, or computer literacy, is becoming increasingly necessary in the modern workplace.

A survey of major American corporations reported that 86% of them offer computer skills training. Another 7% expect to offer such training soon. The survey also showed that there are three methods currently in use to teach computer literacy: (1) the traditional classroom lecture method, used by 44% of the companies surveyed; (2) self-training using written manuals, preferred by 29% of the companies; and (3) some form of computer-assisted instruction, used by 19% (Kleinschrod, 1988).

It has been suggested that much of the training offered in computer skills is less than satisfactory. Too many workers are presented with computerized equipment and given unstructured on-the-job training or inadequate classroom lectures, and insufficient opportunity for hands-on practice before being required to use the machines in their work (Majchrzak, 1987).

In addition, there has not been a great deal of research on how best to teach computer literacy. One study compared a computer-assisted training approach with behavior modeling. In the CAI condition, trainees were given floppy disks containing step-by-step interactive instructions, which they used to complete exercises and solve problems. The trainees responded to questions with each exercise and received immediate feedback on the correctness of their responses.

Behavior modeling as a training technique will be discussed in more detail later, but in this experiment it involved having trainees watch a videotape of a man demonstrating the use of the instruction program. Seated in front of a computer terminal, he described each step and made the appropriate responses. After each step in the demonstration, the videotape was stopped and the trainees were allowed to practice the procedure on their computers before proceeding to the next step.

The results of the experiment showed that behavior modeling (watching the "model" on the videotape) was superior to CAI for teaching computer literacy. Further, younger trainees (those under the age of 45) attained greater mastery of the computer equipment than older trainees, suggesting that older workers may need additional training to be able to use computers competently. However, older trainees achieved greater computer literacy in the modeling condition than in the CAI condition, perhaps because the model was also middle-aged (Gist, Rosen, & Schwoerer, 1988).

As computers become even more prevalent in the workplace, the need for evaluative research on the development of computer skills will grow.

Behavior Modification

In the discussion of reinforcement as a learning principle, we mentioned behavior modification and its use in the world of work. The idea behind the application of behavior modification in industry is simple. An assessment, known as a performance audit, is conducted periodically in an organization to determine the existence of specific problems or employee behaviors that should be changed. Then, a program of positive reinforcement is introduced whereby employees are reinforced when they display the desired behavior. Punishment is not used. Instead of being punished for displaying undesirable behaviors, trainees are rewarded for displaying desirable behaviors. Productivity increases as high as 52% and improvements in product quality up to 64% have been reported for behavior modification programs with various industrial jobs (Luthans, Maciag, & Rosenkrantz, 1983).

An impressive demonstration of behavior modification in organizations was conducted at Emery Air Freight, where the behavioral changes induced were directly connected with job performance (Feeney, 1972). A performance audit revealed two problem areas: (1) despite the employees' belief that they were responding within 90 minutes to 90% of the customer telephone inquiries, they were actually responding to only 30% of customer inquiries; (2) employees were combining packages into containers for shipment only 45% of the time, whereas management thought that containers were being used almost 90% of the time. The goals in the behavior modification training program were to get the employees to respond faster to customer inquiries and to use containers for shipment whenever possible.

All managers at Emery were given instruction, through programmed-instruction techniques, on positive reinforcement and the importance of feedback. A workbook for managers discussed 150 different recognitions and rewards to bestow on employees, ranging from a smile and a nod to highly specific praise for a job well done (the latter turned out to be the most effective). Managers were taught to reinforce desirable behaviors as soon as possible after they had occurred and to shift gradually from constant to partial reinforcement.

In terms of feedback, Emery required employees to keep a detailed record of what they had accomplished each day so that they could compare their performance with the desired standard of performance (for example, the standard of responding to customer requests within 90 minutes). Note that in this program of reinforcement and feedback, bonuses or pay increases were not used to try to change behavior. Praise and recognition proved to be sufficient incentives to improve job performance. The company saved $3 million in 3 years, considerably more than the cost of instituting the program, and has since expanded the program into other departments.

Organizations as diverse as Scandinavian Airlines, Ford Motor Company, Upjohn, Bethlehem Steel, Chase Manhattan Bank NA, Westinghouse, Procter & Gamble, and various city governments, have used behavior modification techniques. Overall, however, the use of behavior modification in the workplace is limited, as is the research on its effectiveness (Goldstein, 1986; Wexley, 1984).

Training Methods for Managers

As we move up the organizational ladder to the level of supervisor, manager, or executive, the need for adequate training becomes more crucial. The cost to a company of an incompetent department head can be far greater than that of an incompetent assembly-line operator. Industry devotes considerably more money, time, and effort to management training than to the training of nonsupervisory employees.

It is generally recognized that few people are born leaders. Many may possess good leadership characteristics—certain levels of intelligence, personality, aptitudes, for example—but they still must be trained in the development and exercise of their capacities before they can function as effective managers and executives. Assuming that an organization's selection procedures find good potential managers, they will remain only potential until they are trained in specific leadership skills and abilities.

Interest in management training began during the early 1940s, and it has become a major focus for personnel psychologists. It is estimated that more than 75% of businesses and government agencies operate some form of management training program. In addition, as a consequence of rapidly accelerating technological advances, a growing number of executives need retraining during their careers. Although they may not be required to operate new high-tech equipment, they must understand its features so as to maximize their usage of it. In the coming decades, up to 90% of all executives will require some form of retraining to keep current with technological change (Mintz, 1986).

Before discussing specific management training techniques, let us briefly examine the training provided by the Western Electric Company in its Corporate Education Center (described earlier). One part of Western Electric's ambitious training program is designed for low-level managers who have exhibited strong potential for promotion to top management. Approximately 30 candidates each year are selected to attend a 22-week program that uses a variety of instructional techniques. For example, trainees are assigned a program of independent reading, ranging from management practices to ancient Greek philosophers.

In addition, trainees attend lectures and discussions. Frequently, they are formed into groups of 4 to 6 for intensive discussions called buzz sessions. Role-playing techniques in which actual job situations are presented to the trainees are also used, and the trainees must assume various managerial roles in attempting to solve the problems. Most of the discussions and role-playing exercises are recorded on videotape so that trainees and instructors can later watch and criticize. Many trainees consider this experience more demanding and challenging than their college work.

Overall, there are two goals in management training. First, there is training in the general skills required for leadership roles: decision making, problem solving, delegation of responsibility, and other abilities necessary for managerial success. Second, there is human relations training directed toward optimizing the interpersonal relations vital to manager-employee harmony. Today's executives must possess more than the technical skills of leadership. To carry out their leadership roles, they must learn to interact effectively with subordinates as well as colleagues and superiors. Simply stated, managers must be able to get along with people if they are to become successful leaders.

Much of the management training for promising upper-middle and top-level executives at larger corporations is conducted on university campuses, typically at graduate schools of business administration. In these programs, managers live on the campus for 2 weeks or more and focus their attention on decision making and organizational planning activities. Some universities have responded to the increasing demand for on-campus training by building separate facilities to house the programs. The University of Pennsylvania's prestigious Wharton School of Finance, for example, built a $23-million executive training complex that includes 100 guest rooms, a health spa, and scores of classrooms equipped with personal computers.

These programs are becoming so popular that they constitute the fastest growing segment of higher education in the United States. Some 15,000 executives attend such programs every year at a cost to their companies of up to $30 billion, a figure that includes their salaries while they attend school. Many schools have now established executive training programs that are geared to the needs and problems of specific companies. Training programs for low- and middle-level managers, however, are usually conducted within a company's own training facilities (Wells, 1987).

One problem with management training involves transferring the results of that training to actual on-the-job performance. We noted that there can be no positive transfer from any training program if the trainee's superior is not in favor of the application of the newly acquired skills.

This has been a persistent difficulty in many organizations. Management trainees quickly come to understand—picking up subtle and not-so-subtle cues—whether or not their superiors value the skills and abilities acquired in the management training program. For example, in contrast to lower level employees who receive technical skill training, many management trainees are not tested or graded at the end of the course to determine how much they have learned. As a result, some of these trainees may fail to take the training seriously enough to produce any meaningful changes in their behavior.

When the trainees return to their jobs following their training, they are apt to find that their superiors express little interest in what they have learned. In one survey of large U.S. corporations, more than 70% of the management trainees said that their superiors never inquired about their training or how they intended to use it on the job (Pattan, 1983). This lack of interest on the part of the trainees' superiors, who are also supposed to serve as their role models in the organization, sends a clear signal that management training is not considered to be very important.

Not all organizations are characterized by such attitudes. Those that are, however, are wasting the money they spend on management training. Such training programs will be useless without a supportive and reinforcing attitude on the part of higher management.

A number of specific techniques are useful for both leadership training and human relations training. Some of the approaches used for nonsupervisory employees can also be applied to management training. On-the-job training and programmed instruction are used at the managerial level, as are traditional lecture, classroom, and discussion methods. Other techniques are used almost exclusively for management training. These include job rotation, the case study method, business games, in-basket training, role playing, behavior modeling, and sensitivity training. There is little use of computer-based training techniques at the managerial level.

Also, it must be remembered that despite the emphasis organizations place on formal training for managers, most executive development occurs primarily through informal, unstructured on-the-job experiences. When we consider that managers spend 98% to 99% of their time on the job and no more than 1% or 2% in formal training programs, it follows that most learning must occur on the job (McCall, 1988).

Job Rotation

Job rotation, a popular management-training technique, involves exposing trainees to different jobs and departments within the organization to acquaint them with all facets of the business. This is frequently used with new college graduates who are just beginning their working career. Trainees gain a useful perspective on various aspects of the organization, have the opportunity to see and be seen by higher management, and learn through direct experience where they might best apply their talents, abilities, and interests. Job rotation also offers the continuing challenge of adapting to, and learning about, many kinds of operations and responsibilities. Trainees often complete their job-rotation program with a clearer idea of the positions in which they are likely to be successful and, of equal importance, which jobs they may be unsuited for.

The rotation phase of a new manager's career may last several years and carry the person not only from one department to another but also from one plant or office to another. Frequent changes can lead to the development of flexibility, adaptability, and a growing sense of self-confidence as new challenges (and superiors) are successfully dealt with.

There are, of course, disadvantages to job rotation. An organization with branches throughout the United States or overseas requires significant adjustments on the part of the trainee's family and may also disrupt a spouse's career. If the rotation period is too short in each job, there may not be sufficient time for the trainee to learn it before it is time to move on. Further, if top management is more interested in the trainees as some sort of temporary office help instead of rising managers in need of their guidance and example, the purpose of the rotation program is not being served. The trainee may not have the chance to acquire the necessary skills to transfer to higher levels of management.

Case Study Method

The case study method, developed by the Harvard School of Business, is frequently used in executive training programs. In this approach, a complex problem, of the kind faced daily by managers and executives, is presented to the trainees prior to their general meeting. The trainees are expected to familiarize themselves thoroughly with the case and to find, on their own, additional relevant information.

When the trainees meet as a group, each member must be prepared to advance and discuss an interpretation of, and solution to, the problem. Through the presentation of diverse viewpoints, the trainees ideally come to appreciate the fact that there are different ways of looking at a problem and, consequently, different ways of attempting to resolve it.

Usually, the case studies chosen have no one correct solution. The leader of the group discussion does not suggest a solution; the group as a whole must resolve the issue.

The purpose of the case study method is to teach trainees the skills of group problem solving and decision making, the ability to analyze and criticize their own assumptions and interpretations, and the ability to be amenable to points of view other than their own.

One criticism of the case study method is that it often does not relate the trainee's behavior in the classroom to the requirements of the job. There may be a discrepancy between the theoretical solution to the case study and the solution that is practical for the organization, a situation not conducive to positive transfer.

A modification of the case study method involves the presentation of a brief incident in a management situation rather than a complex, larger scale problem. This approach—the *incident process*—is a more formalized training procedure, in that the instructor takes an active role in the discussion. The incident is investigated by the trainees in question-and-answer fashion; the instructor supplies the answers. Then, the trainees record and debate their solutions to the incident. Finally, the instructor tells the group how the incident was actually handled on the job and what the outcome was. Such definitive solutions are not supplied in the case study method.

Business Games

Another popular approach to executive training involves the gaming process in which a complex, real-life situation is simulated. Like the case study method, this approach is intended primarily to develop problem-solving and decision-making skills and to provide practice in exercising these skills in a situation in which mistakes will not harm the organization.

Teams of trainees compete against one another, each team representing a separate business organization. The team companies are given detailed information on all aspects of the operation of their organization such as data on finances, sales, advertising, production, personnel, and inventories. Each group must organize itself, that is, assign various responsibilities and tasks to its members and proceed to handle the problems that face the company. As decisions are made, instructors (usually aided by computers) evaluate their results. The group may be required to make additional decisions on the basis of these results.

The problems presented to the trainee teams are realistic, and most trainees become emotionally involved with their company and its problems. The

In a typical business game, a group of trainees operates a fictitious company and makes decisions about personnel, production, and finances.

trainees gain experience in making decisions on a variety of real problems under the pressures of time and competing organizations.

One of the better business games is called "Looking Glass, Inc." (McCall & Lombardo, 1982). Trainees spend an entire workday managing a fictitious glass manufacturing company, beginning by reading a thick pile of annual reports, financial statements, job descriptions, and memos. Throughout the day they must respond to some 150 management problems, and they do so in an office setting in which they hold meetings, make telephone calls, and write memos, all activities required on the job. And, as in a real work situation, there are more problems to contend with than there is time.

At the end of the game (or sometimes at intervals throughout the game), instructors conduct critiques of the decisions made. Discussion is encouraged about other approaches to the problem that might have been taken.

Several hundred business games are available. They differ in terms of their complexity and how realistically they simulate the operation of a business organization. Basically there are two types: (1) *top-management games* dealing with the decision-making problems faced by high-level corporate officers and (2) *functional games* dealing with the operation of a single aspect of a company such as production control or marketing.

In-Basket Training

The in-basket technique was discussed in Chapter 3 as a method of selection. The same procedure is used to train prospective managers in the principles of executive leadership. When used for training, the in-basket technique is conceptually a business game, in that it simulates the job of a manager. Unlike the business game, however, the trainee usually operates alone in the in-basket technique rather than as part of a group. (There is a variation of the in-basket technique in which trainees operate in groups of four.)

Trainees are given a stack of letters, memoranda, customer complaints, requests for advice from subordinates, and other similar items, presenting them with the problems faced by managers on the job. The trainees must take action on each item within a certain period of time, indicating exactly how they would handle it. After completing the tasks, each trainee reports on the decisions to a small group of other trainees and the trainer, and individual actions are discussed and criticized. This kind of training focuses on decision-making skills rather than on interpersonal skills or the learning of factual material.

Role Playing

In role playing, management trainees project themselves into a particular role and act out the behavior they believe is appropriate in that situation. For example, trainees may be asked to imagine themselves to be a supervisor who must discuss with an employee a poor performance evaluation. This role playing is often conducted in front of other trainees and instructors. Also, the trainees may play a variety of roles. In the previous example, one trainee plays the supervisor and another the employee. Then, they may be asked to reverse roles and replay the situation. Usually, a critique is offered by other trainees or the trainer, and trainees may be shown a videotape of their role-playing performance.

Many people feel awkward or foolish about acting out a role in front of others, but, once begun, most trainees develop a feeling for the role and try to become the person they are pretending to be.

At this point, the procedure can be a valuable learning device. It enables trainees to get a feel for the various roles they will be expected to play on the job. Not only do they gain practical experience in the role but also, through the analyses of other trainees and instructors, they learn how to improve their behavior. Further, they are able to practice these job-related behaviors in a situation in which mistakes will not interfere with production or jeopardize on-the-job interpersonal relations. In one study, role playing improved the ability of sales managers to set goals in their interviews with subordinates, a behavioral change that was still evident 3 months later (Ivancevich & Smith, 1981).

Role playing can provide the trainees with a greater sensitivity to others, particularly subordinates. Many management trainees, by assuming the role of a worker in relation to a supervisor, gain an appreciation of the worker's viewpoint, which they would otherwise not experience. Role playing is not used as frequently as other management training techniques, however.

Behavior Modeling

The behavior modeling approach to management training involves having trainees model their behavior on examples of exemplary management performance. (We saw earlier that behavior modeling is effective in teaching computer literacy.) Four features of behavior modeling (or applied learning) are modeling, behavior rehearsal, feedback, and transfer of training (Sorcher, 1983).

Modeling is the core of the training. Trainees watch a film or videotape of a manager who is effectively handling a particular job situation with a subordinate. The situation might involve poor job performance, excessive absenteeism, or poor morale. Whatever the problem, the manager in the film displays a number of important behaviors that lead to a successful resolution of the problem.

Having seen the film, trainees engage in *behavior rehearsal*, practicing the behaviors performed by the model. Trainees are not role playing in this case; they are rehearsing the actual behaviors they will use on the job, the behaviors they witnessed in the film.

These behaviors are rehearsed in front of the trainer and the other trainees who provide *feedback*, telling each trainee how well he or she was able to imitate the behavior of the model. Trainees become increasingly confident in displaying the modeled behaviors under the social reinforcement conditions provided by the feedback. Note that throughout the training the emphasis is on actual managerial behaviors, not on broad attitudes, traits, or general characteristics.

The fourth feature of the behavior modeling approach, *transfer of training*, refers to a variety of techniques designed to assure that what is being learned in the modeling sessions transfers or carries over to the job. The problems between manager and subordinate viewed on the tape or film are real situations that managers must confront every day. The high degree of relevance of this training technique to the actual job increases the trainees' motivation to accept and apply the training.

The training program proceeds from simple problems to more complex ones. Trainees learn behaviors and solutions in a sequence of increasing difficulty and can master the beginning steps before moving on to higher level ones. The training schedules allow for distributed rather than massed practice. (We saw that distributed practice is more effective when the material to be learned is difficult and lengthy.) Also, follow-up activities and additional reinforcements are given for the learned behaviors.

Behavior modeling is usually conducted with groups to 6 to 12 trainees, people already working as supervisors or managers. Each 4-hour training session is given once a week for 4 weeks. In the intervals between training sessions, the trainees are on the job applying what they have learned and receiving additional feedback.

Reports from the more than 300 companies using behavior modeling are enthusiastic. The technique has been successful in raising employee morale; improving communication with, and sales to, customers; decreasing absenteeism; enhancing supervisory skills; improving work quality and quantity; and overcoming employee resistance to change. Some of the companies with behavior modeling programs are General Electric, IBM, Westinghouse, Union Carbide, Exxon, AT&T, and Federated Department Stores. A review and analysis of 70 management training studies showed that behavior modeling was among the more effective techniques (Burke & Day, 1986).

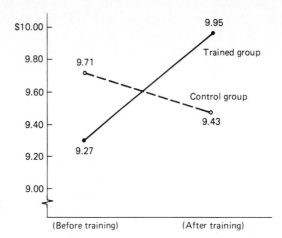

$10.00

9.80

9.60

9.40

9.20

9.00

9.95

9.71

9.27

Trained group

Control group

9.43

(Before training)   (After training)

Figure 6-1 Per-hour commissions before and after training. (From "An objective evaluation of a behavior modeling training program" by H. H. Meyer & M. S. Raich, 1983, *Personnel Psychology*, *36*, p. 759.)

In a behavior modeling training program for employees of the home appliance and radio/television departments of a chain of 14 stores, sales increased an average of 7% in the 6 months following the training (Meyer & Raich, 1983). The salespersons in the control group showed a 3% decrease in average sales. The commissions earned by the two groups before and after training are shown in Figure 6-1.

Sensitivity Training

Another technique of management training is sensitivity or T-group training (also known as laboratory training, encounter groups, or action groups), designed to develop an understanding of interpersonal communication and interaction. Originating in the late 1940s at the National Training Laboratories in Maine, the technique shows individuals how others react to or perceive them and what effect their behavior has on others. In this way, it is hoped that the trainees will develop a clearer and more accurate picture of themselves.

Trainees usually meet in groups of 12 a few hours a day for a number of weeks, although some sessions are marathons lasting 8 to 10 hours a day over a weekend. Often, the training course takes place at a comfortable retreat, far removed from the pressures, strains, and securities ot everyday life and work. Before the sessions begin, trainees are given lectures on the sensitivity process and on the elements of learning and growth in social situations.

After these introductory lectures, the trainers assume a passive role in the T-group process, stressing that the responsibility for discussion and growth lies with the individual group members. There is no agenda or format for the discussion; in the beginning, it tends to be vague and formless. The topic of discussion also seems immaterial. The important thing is that something be discussed and that everyone be actively involved in the discussion. Ideally (although sometimes prodding by the trainer is necessary), the members begin to discuss themselves and each other, pointing out weaknesses and strengths. The conversations become frank and open, highly emotional, and often hostile, and it is these feelings of anger or hostility that become the main focus of discussion.

Sensitivity training reached its peak of popularity in the early 1970s and has since been declining in use. It has been offered throughout the United States by consulting organizations, religious groups, universities, and, unfortunately, by a large number of poorly trained practitioners. There is increasing fear that the intimate frankness and personal attacks may hurt people more than they help. Studies of the aftereffects of participation in sensitivity training show psychological casualty rates of up to 50%. Whatever the incidence of harmful effects, it is clear that some people are damaged emotionally by sensitivity sessions (Hartley, Roback, & Abramowitz, 1976).

On the positive side, there is evidence (although it is mostly anecdotal) that some managers develop greater tolerance and acceptance of others, increased self-insight, greater self-control, and a more cooperative and tactful attitude toward others. There is little research support for these conclusions, however, and some research indicates that any changes induced by sensitivity training may be only temporary (Smith, 1975).

Whether these possible changes make any real difference in the trainees' productive capacities and decision-making leadership abilities (their worth to the company) is questionable. Further, required attendance at such programs raises important ethical questions. Does an organization have the right to compel employees to participate in such an emotionally revealing and potentially harmful process? If managers perform well at their jobs, is not that sufficient? Even if there were indisputable evidence that sensitivity training produced greater leadership skills, this ethical question would still be paramount. In the absence of such evidence, this issue must be considered by every organization using this training technique and by every person who may be asked or required to participate in it.

Leader Match Training

A newer method of management training, leader match training, derives from the contingency theory of leadership, developed by Fred Fiedler, which will be discussed in Chapter 7 (Fiedler, 1967). It is difficult, however, to understand the leader match training technique without some introduction to the theory. Briefly, the contingency theory of leadership states that a leader's effectiveness will be contingent upon, or depend upon, the interaction between (1) the leader's motivational and personality characteristics and (2) the control or influence the leader has over the situation he or she manages. In other words, leadership depends on the match between the manager's motivation and the management situation.

The motivation of managers can be measured by the Least Preferred Co-worker (LPC) Scale shown in Figure 6-2. In responding to this scale, managers are asked to describe, in terms of the characteristics listed, the one

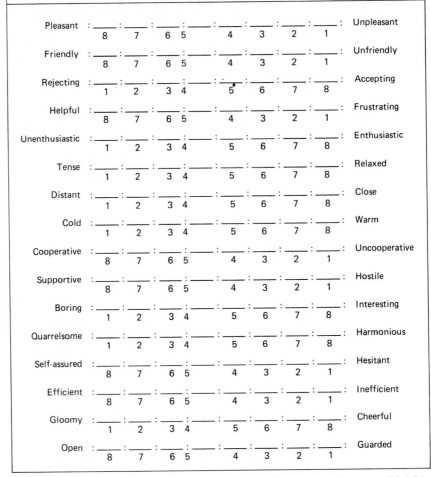

Think of the person with whom you can work least well. He or she may be someone you work with now, or someone you knew in the past. He or she does not have to be the person you like least well, but should be the person with whom you had the most difficulty in getting a job done. Describe this person as he or she appears to you.

	8	7	6	5	4	3	2	1	
Pleasant									Unpleasant
Friendly									Unfriendly

	1	2	3	4	5	6	7	8	
Rejecting									Accepting

	8	7	6	5	4	3	2	1	
Helpful									Frustrating

	1	2	3	4	5	6	7	8	
Unenthusiastic									Enthusiastic
Tense									Relaxed
Distant									Close
Cold									Warm

	8	7	6	5	4	3	2	1	
Cooperative									Uncooperative
Supportive									Hostile

	1	2	3	4	5	6	7	8	
Boring									Interesting
Quarrelsome									Harmonious

	8	7	6	5	4	3	2	1	
Self-assured									Hesitant
Efficient									Inefficient

	1	2	3	4	5	6	7	8	
Gloomy									Cheerful

	8	7	6	5	4	3	2	1	
Open									Guarded

Figure 6-2 Least preferred co-worker scale. (From "The leadership game: Matching the man to the situation" by F. E. Fiedler, 1976, *Organizational Dynamics,* (Winter), p. 10.)

person in their entire career with whom they worked least well—their least preferred co-worker.

High scorers on the LPC rate even their least favorite co-worker in positive or relatively acceptable terms, which indicates, according to Fiedler, that they view close interpersonal relationships (being pleasant, helpful, and friendly, for example) as necessary for the accomplishment of any management task. Low

LPC managers, on the other hand, show a strong negative reaction to people with whom they have difficulty working ("If I can't work with you, you are no damn good!"). Low LPC managers focus on the needs of the task first and place less emphasis on interpersonal skills (Fiedler, 1976).

On the situation side of the leader/situation match we have what Fiedler calls "situational favorableness," which refers to the degree to which leaders have control over, and therefore believe they can influence, group interaction. Control and influence are high when managers (1) have the support of the members of their group; (2) know exactly what do to and how to do it (the degree of precision of the task structure); and (3) have the means to reward and punish subordinates (the degree of position power).

Research on the contingency theory of leadership has shown that low LPC leaders (those who are task motivated) function best in situations in which their control and influence are either very high or very low. High LPC leaders (those who are relationship motivated) function best in situations in which their control and influence are moderate.

Leader match training involves teaching managers that they can alter the situation so that it will better match their type of motivation. They can do so by assessing how supportive their subordinates are, the degree to which their task is structured, and the amount of position power they have.

The training uses a programmed workbook supplemented by lectures, feedback sessions, group discussions, and films. Trainees complete the LPC scale, which they score themselves, to determine their motivational style. They fill out additional scales to measure the three components of the situation: subordinate support, task structure, and position power. Trainers offer guidance on developing the leadership situation in which the trainees will be most successful, that is, the one that will most closely match their motivational style. Detailed step-by-step instructions are provided on how to change the management situation. For example, depending on whether the leaders are high or low on the LPC scale, they may be advised to request more routine or less structured tasks, or to develop more or less formal relationships with their subordinates.

The workbook explains how the contingency theory can be applied to the job and gives examples of leadership problems, which trainees are asked to solve. Feedback is offered on their responses. Short tests are interspersed throughout the workbook and a final examination appears at the end, so that trainees receive frequent feedback on their progress.

Leader match training has been used with more than 40,000 managers, and Fiedler claims positive results for the method in nearly two dozen studies (Fiedler & Chemers, 1984). A good deal of additional research has been conducted on it, but the results are mixed (Burke & Day, 1986; Fiedler & Mahar, 1979; Frost, 1986; Jago & Ragan, 1986). One study showed that leader match training plus behavior modeling increased productivity and decreased accidents in the mining industry, an effect still evident 5 years after the training (Fiedler, Wheeler, Chemers, & Patrick, 1988).

Career Development and Planning

We have discussed specific training programs designed to correct some deficiency such as problem-solving ability or interpersonal relations. The goal of such training is to enhance a person's performance in a particular area, say, job skills or attitudes. Most of these training programs are oriented toward a specific stage in an employee's career—new workers, for example, or managers who have reached a certain level in the corporate hierarchy—or toward a specific job.

In addition, many organizations offer training and development opportunities throughout an employee's career. This approach, *career development and planning*, may be described as a lifelong learning approach oriented toward specific skills and abilities as well as personal development.

Corporations with career development and planning programs include General Electric, AT&T, 3M, Merrill Lynch, Dow Jones, Traveler's Insurance, and TRW. The Xerox Corporation has a Career Information Center where an employee at any level in the company can find information, including videotapes, on the various career paths offered by Xerox. Material is provided on career self-analysis so that the employee can plan his or her own working life in line with personal needs and goals.

A great many companies routinely offer counseling and training workshops to assist employees in personal career planning at every stage of their career. Employees are encouraged to set goals for their own development both in terms of job progress and personal growth. Opportunities are provided for periodic review and evaluation of each employee's progress.

Organizations also offer tuition refund plans for employees who want to return to college or graduate school to update their job skills or to learn new skills that could be applied to their work. Home-study courses are offered by many companies as well as in-house training programs to enhance technical skills. Minority employees are especially encouraged to participate in career development programs. Some companies require their participation as an affirmative action tool to prepare minority workers for advancement (Gooding, 1988).

Theoretically, career development is open to all employees, but surveys show that in practice it is used primarily by managerial, professional, and technical employees (Gutteridge & Otte, 1983). Further, the likelihood of participation seems to be directly related to the employees' perception of some desirable outcome, such as obtaining a promotion. Also, participation in a career development program may decrease job satisfaction and organizational commitment if participants discover, or believe, that the organization's plans for their future do not match their own. In general, employees are most satisfied with programs that offer a close contact with management, such as periodic career reviews given by supervisors, and personal mentoring and coaching (Portwood & Granrose, 1986).

Career development and planning programs are growing in popularity. A survey of 142 firms in Philadelphia, Pennsylvania, revealed that 65% had career development programs. The survey also suggested that the motivation for instituting career development was not entirely altruistic. Some companies started their programs because of government pressure to bolster affirmative action efforts. The strongest motivation, however, may be economic, that is, the belief that career development can produce financial returns. One large bank reported a savings of almost $2 million in 1 year which they attributed to increased productivity on the part of employees who had participated in a career development program (Kleiman, 1984). A year after Dow Jones introduced its career development program, a survey found that the company had developed a vaster pool of highly qualified workers to draw from in filling job vacancies. Communication between managers and employees had improved, as had employee morale (Broszeit, 1986).

Organizations recognize that adults change and grow throughout their careers, that they do not have the same values, goals, needs, and fears at age 20 as at age 40. The job or lifestyle that was appropriate just after college may be inappropriate in middle age. Both employer and employee should admit to these changes (because they will affect job performance) and make the necessary adjustments in career planning.

Psychologists have identified three career stages that you will pass through in your working life, and your needs will probably be different during each of them (Hall, 1976; Super & Hall, 1978).

1. *Establishment*. During this stage, which lasts approximately from age 20 to 40, people are first getting established in their careers. After the initial selection and training they are adjusting to their work routines. Toward the middle of this period they begin to learn whether or not they are going to be successful in their chosen path, through promotions and the promise of personal satisfaction or by being terminated or transferred into a dead-end position. If unsuccessful, they may try another career, so self-analysis and counseling become necessary. If successful, they develop feelings of competence and confidence and an increasing commitment to the organization.
2. *Maintenance*. This phase lasts from about age 40 to 55 and is often described as the time of the midlife crisis. People become aware that they are getting older; death is no longer viewed in the abstract. They know by this stage that they have either reached (or are likely to reach) the goals they set for themselves or that they have failed to reach them. It is a time of self-examination and planning for the remainder of life. The outcome of this self-exploration may be a change in lifestyle and values. People may want new challenges and satisfactions and so change jobs, careers, or spouses. Many organizations offer counseling and personal growth workshops to help employees through this difficult period.
3. *Decline*. During this time, from age 50 or 55 to retirement, employees face the end of the career to which they may have devoted their entire adult life. They face the prospect of living on a reduced income and of having diminished physical capacity. Retirement suddenly brings losses—no job, no work to go to every day, no co-workers with whom to socialize. Both federal

and private agencies and an increasing number of companies are offering courses, workshops, and counseling on coping with the emotional, financial, and physical traumas of retirement.

A number of studies have shown that one's career stage is related to job attitudes, work perception, job performance, and job satisfaction. A study of 466 salespersons found that job satisfaction and performance levels increased during the maintenance stage and fell during the stage of decline (Cron & Slocum, 1986). Other research on salespersons reported that those in the establishment stage were more concerned with promotion than were those in the later stages. Those in the maintenance stage were the most productive (using objective measures of sales volume). Those in the decline stage had low sales volumes and the lowest level of belief in future promotions. In addition, decline stage persons evidenced high interest in such activities as "developing easier ways of doing their work," "attempting to cut down on work hours," and "developing more hobbies to replace work interests." Obviously, then, their career was no longer central to their life (Cron, Dubinsky, & Michaels, 1988). An investigation of restaurant managers in the establishment stage showed a strong positive correlation between length of time on the job and objective measures of performance, that is, job performance improved with greater experience (McEnrue, 1988).

Separate career stages have been documented for many occupations including highly educated and highly paid professionals. A study of 115 engineers, lawyers, chemists, and other scientists, 53% of whom held master's degrees and 20% of whom held doctoral degrees, found three career stages that roughly parallel those described earlier (Raelin, 1985).

1. *Establishment or finding a niche (ages 25–34).* In this initial stage young professionals seek challenge and variety in their work and an organization with which they can identify. These intrinsic job benefits are more important to them than salary. They prefer a management style that shows interest in their career and their personal development.
2. *Maintenance or digging in (ages 35–44).* Professionals at this stage are intensely committed to their work, put in long hours, and perform at the peak of their abilities. They exhibit a strong desire to be left alone by management, to work in small autonomous groups, and to be highly paid.
3. *Decline or entrenched (ages 45–65).* In this stage, professionals have lowered their organizational and professional aspirations and commitments. They have accepted, however reluctantly, the realities, limitations, and politics of organizational life and believe that they are not being paid as much as they deserve.

Career planning and development at each stage of working life involve responsibilities shared by employer and employee. The organization must offer the facilities and opportunities for the personal growth and development of its employees. The individual must make effective use of these counseling and development programs and be willing to engage in the self-analysis that is necessary for growth at any stage of life.

A Sample Career Development Program

The Zale Corporation of Dallas, Texas, owns and operates more than 1,000 retail jewelry stores throughout the United States, most of them located within shopping centers or malls. Under pressure from increasing competition, a growing sophistication among customers, and the company's own accelerated growth needs, Zale established a comprehensive career development program available to employees at all levels (N. Kelly, 1982).

The program, which took 2 years to develop, includes several important restrictions brought about by the need to implement it in each of the stores over a wide geographical area. Because the company management did not want to bear the expense of periodically assembling large numbers of employees at a single site, each store manager had to be responsible for carrying out the program directives for his or her employees. Thus, each manager had to become a training expert.

The company stipulated that managers could not spend a great deal of time teaching the trainees because their own productivity would suffer. Trainees would learn at their own pace as much through on-the-job experience as through the self-study materials that were made available. Also, career development activities were not permitted to disrupt the regular work routine. Instead, they became an integral part of the job.

Zale's career development program consisted of three phases, each composed of six to nine projects that would teach new skills. Phase I was for new employees such as stockpersons or salespersons, Phase II for experienced employees and management trainees, and Phase III for more experienced management trainees and assistant managers. Once a person had mastered the learning projects in one phase, he or she was permitted to begin the next phase. The employee and the store manager together determined the degree of proficiency achieved in each project and each phase, and where additional study and practice might be needed.

Completion of all three phases qualified employees to become managers, and they were allowed to undertake the actual management of the store for up to 2 weeks. If their performance was considered satisfactory, they were recommended for attendance at a 6-day Management Candidate Seminar at a corporate facility in Dallas. For these trainees, the program offered an additional year of management training involving both self-study and on-the-job learning.

As you can see, the goals of the program were oriented toward individual employees as well as toward the organization. Employees were provided with the training necessary to perform their present job at a high level of efficiency and also to develop the skills and abilities that would qualify them to advance to more challenging and better paid positions.

In satisfying these goals for their employees, top management was also satisfying additional corporate goals. First, the career development program proved to be an effective recruiting incentive. Second, store employees became skilled in more than one job function. Third, the program identified and produced a continuous stream of qualified candidates for higher management positions. Fourth, it provided objective performance appraisal data.

The results of Zale's program have been highly gratifying to management. Offering the career planning and development program at all levels of employment has resulted in lower turnover, greater productivity, better trained managers, and a system of performance appraisal based on actual job performance rather than on personal traits.

Training the Hard-core Unemployed

In Chapters 3 and 4, we noted that organizations are making efforts to recruit and hire persons labeled hard-core unemployed. Hiring these people, however, is not enough; because of their impoverished background, they require a heavy investment in training opportunities before being able to realize their potential. As a result of this need, business and government organizations are devoting much time and effort to training those who had once been considered unemployable.

Who are the hard-core unemployed? On the average, they are almost always members of minority groups with no job skills, have dropped out of school, have not worked for at least 6 months, have never worked regularly, and live below the poverty level (Goldstein, 1986).

One of the earliest programs to train the hard-core unemployed was conducted by Boeing Aircraft in 1968. It still serves as a model of thoroughness. Many problems never before encountered by trainers were discovered when the program began. There were serious problems in communication, not just in communicating ideas or concepts, but the more basic problem of understanding spoken words. If the trainers were white, there was hostility and fear on the part of the trainees. Many trainees had mannerisms, habits, and dress styles that trainers found unorthodox and even offensive. A rapport had to be established before the actual job training could begin. The trainees needed to be convinced that the program was genuine and that the training was geared directly to a job and to correcting their deficient abilities. Only in this way did trainees develop any real motivation to learn.

Research on the Boeing program suggested that the training must contain the following five elements:

1. Basic education and remedial work in areas such as English and mathematics and communications skills.
2. Prevocational training involving the establishment of the relevance and meaning of vocabulary, arithmetic, and other skills basic to the actual job as well as proper attitudes toward work such as punctuality, reliability, and mode of dress.
3. Characteristics of the job itself (preassignment training), involving a simulated work environment in which specific job skills were taught.
4. On-the-job training under the supervision of a working supervisor.
5. Supportive services such as personal and job counseling, medical help, and aid with transportation and finances (these elements were present throughout the training program).

Experience from other hard-core unemployed training programs has demonstrated the necessity of dealing with motivational and attitudinal factors as well as with actual job skills. Several paper-and-pencil tests and behavioral rating scales have been developed to assess the concept of work maturity, a measure of factors such as initiative, responsibility, and acceptance of authority (Love & O'Hara, 1987).

Training programs for the hard-core unemployed have pointed up the importance of the first-line supervisors to whom trainees are assigned after completing their training. The supervisors may also need training to understand the backgrounds, fears, and anxieties of the new employees. One of the most important factors affecting the job behavior of hard-core unemployed persons is the support, tolerance, and understanding they receive from their supervisors once they undertake the job. In fact, supervisor support may be more influential than job-skill training in determining how well these employees perform and how long they stay on the job.

Several studies have been conducted on the factors that determine whether the hard-core unemployed will remain on the job once training is completed (Goodman & Salipante, 1976; Salipante & Goodman, 1976). Supervisor support is critical, as we noted. Other factors include the availability of personal counseling during and after training and the pay and status of the first job. Not surprisingly, the higher the pay and status of the initial job, the lower the termination rate of hard-core unemployed persons. Also, the number of persons of the same minority group employed by the organization has a significant effect on whether the hard-core unemployed stay on the job after training. Particularly important is the number of minority supervisors. The more of these, the lower the quitting rate of the hard-core unemployed.

Training is a complex task with all levels of employee, but it is much more difficult when dealing with disadvantaged persons. Business and government organizations are making major efforts to bring the hard-core unemployed into the economic mainstream.

Evaluating Training and Development Programs

Regardless of how impressive and sophisticated a training program or facility may appear, it is necessary that the effects or results of the training be evaluated in systematic and quantitative fashion. Unless evaluative research is conducted, an organization that has devoted large amounts of money and time to the program will have no idea of how worthwhile the effort has been. Are employees learning the skills needed for their jobs? Does production increase after training? Are accidents and wastage declining? Have interpersonal skills and leadership abilities improved? To answer these questions adequately, the psychologist must compare the performance of trained with untrained workers in the same job or compare the same workers before and after training with a comparable control group that was not exposed to training. In this way, the organization can determine if a training program should be modified, eliminated, or extended for use throughout the plant.

With such a large investment at stake, one would expect executives and training directors to be eagerly and constantly examining the utility of their training programs. This is not often the case, however. Most programs are evaluated, if at all, on subjective or intuitive terms.

A survey of nearly 100 corporate training directors revealed that 90% of them used no definite method of evaluating their training programs (Olivas & Inman, 1983). Thus, most companies in the United States do not have a clear idea whether the millions of dollars they are spending on training is worthwhile (Fisher, 1988; Goldstein, 1986).

Further, of the few organizations that do attempt to evaluate their training programs, most of them do so poorly. A review of the published literature in the 1970s on the evaluation of management training programs found that only 68% of the evaluations produced meaningful data. The other 32% of the studies had no control groups and used only posttraining measures as a basis for comparison. Only 19% of the studies compared the effectiveness of different training methods and only 8% attempted to measure the effect of individual differences on the outcome of the training (Clement, 1981; Wexley, 1984).

Aside from the cost of such research, other factors contribute to the lack of training evaluation. Many nonpsychologists involved in corporate training do not have the proper training to conduct this research, and many training directors overestimate the effectiveness of the programs they initiate and oversee.

Also, a number of organizations are involved in training, not because they are convinced of its worth, but because their competitors are doing it. Given that motivation to institute a training program, it is easy to see why the firm would be reluctant to spend even more money to test the effectiveness of its program.

Another reason for the scarcity of evaluative research has to do with the nature of the behavioral changes that result from training, that is, some are more easily evaluated than others. It is simple, for example, to determine the effectiveness of training to operate a machine or assemble a part. The training goal and the measure of the behavioral change are straightforward. The number of items produced per unit time by trained and untrained workers, or workers trained by different techniques, can be determined objectively and compared. At this work level, training programs have been shown to be quite effective. But in dealing with the behaviors involved in human relations, problem solving, or other aspects of management training, it is more difficult to evaluate the effects of these programs. Management training is definitely favored by many top executives in American industry, but is it truly worthwhile?

The only way to answer this question is with considerable and thorough research. A review and analysis of 70 managerial training studies showed that the training was, on the average, only moderately effective (Burke & Day, 1986). The face validity of management training is high—everybody says it is good, and it looks good for an organization to have such a program. Many training directors defend management training by pointing out that a large number of the graduates of management training programs are subsequently promoted to higher levels of responsibility. This in itself is not a valid measure of the worth of the training because only the most capable and promising individuals are usually chosen to participate in management training programs initially. In other words, the trainees are the most promotable candidates even without the training programs. Training directors also defend the worth of their programs by indicating how much the participants liked the training. Although it is nice when trainees enjoy a training session, that in itself is no indication that the experience will result in better performance on the job. Yet, many organizations evaluate their human relations training *only* in terms of the trainees' subjective reaction rather than in terms of behavioral changes.

One way to evaluate the effectiveness of a training program is to permit employees to respond anonymously to an evaluation questionnaire. Ideally, the data sought by the questionnaire will be directly related to the specific objectives of the training program. As we noted, a favorable response to or an expressed liking for a training program does not necessarily mean that the program will be effective in changing employee behavior. However, the information thus obtained can assist the training staff in planning future

Figure 6-3 A sample trainee reaction questionnaire. (Adapted from *Developing and Training Human Resources in Organizations* (pp. 79–80) by K. N. Wexley & G. P. Latham, 1981, Glenview, IL: Scott, Foresman. Reprinted by permission.)

Considering everything, how would you rate this program? (Check one)
Unsatisfactory ___ Satisfactory ___ Good ___ Outstanding ___
Please explain briefly the reasons for the rating you have given.
_____
_____

Were your expectations exceeded ___ matched ___ fallen below ___ ?
Are you going to recommend this training program to other members of your department? Yes ___ No ___ If you checked "yes," please list the job titles of the people to whom you would recommend the program.

_____
_____
_____

Please rate the relative value to you of the following components of the training program (1=very valuable; 2=moderately valuable; 3=of little value):
Videocassettes _____   Role-playing exercises _____
Workbooks _____   Reading assignments _____
Small group discussions _____   Lectures _____
Please rate the trainer's presentation in terms of (1=not effective; 2=somewhat effective; 3=effective):
Ability to communicate _____   Use of visual aids _____
Emphasis on key points _____   Quality of handout materials ___
How would you evaluate the activities required of you?
Overall workload: Too heavy ___ Just right ___ Too light ___
Homework assignments: Too much ___ Just right ___ Too little ___
Classroom participation: Too much ___ Just right ___ Too little ___
What suggestions do you have for improving the program? _____
_____
_____
_____

programs. Examples of trainee reaction questionnaires are shown in Figure 6-3 and Figure 6-4 (Wexley & Latham, 1981).

A major challenge faces psychology and industry today. Organizations must be encouraged to expend the resources necessary to appraise their elaborate training and development programs. It makes little sense to continue to support an activity in the absence of firm knowledge about its value. Psychologists, both industrial and academic, must focus research attention on the specific behaviors involved at the various levels of training (particularly management training) so that they can determine the best means of modifying those behaviors effectively for job success.

Figure 6-4 A sample questionnaire for evaluating trainers. (From *Developing and Training Human Resources in Organizations* (p. 83) by K. N. Wexley & G. P. Latham, 1981, Glenview, IL: Scott, Foresman. Reprinted by permission.)

TRAINING COURSE: _____

DATE STARTED: _____

LOCATION: _____

TRAINER: _____

NOTE TO TRAINERS: To keep conditions as nearly uniform as possible, it is important that *no instructions* be given to the trainees. The rating scale should be passed out without comment.

NOTE TO TRAINEES: Following is a list of qualities that tend to determine if the trainer (instructor) is effective or ineffective. Of course, nobody approaches the ideal in all of these qualities, but some do so more than others. You can provide information that will be used in improving subsequent training programs by rating your trainer on the qualities shown below. Please circle one of the 10 numbers along the line at the point which most nearly describes him or her with reference to the quality you are considering.

This rating is entirely confidential. Do not sign your name or make any other mark on your paper that could serve to identify yourself.

	10 9 8	7 6 5 4	3 2 1
Interest in Subject	Always appears full of the subject.	Seems mildly interested.	Subject seems irksome to him or her.
Considerate Attitude toward Trainees	Always courteous and considerate.	Tries to be considerate, but finds this difficult at times.	Entirely unsympathetic and inconsiderate.
Stimulating Intellectual Curiosity	Inspires students to independent effort; creates desire for investigation.	Occasionally inspiring, creates mild interest.	Destroys interest in subject; makes work repulsive.
Presentation of Subject Matter	Clear, definite and forceful.	Sometimes mechanical and monotonous.	Indefinite, uninvolved and monotonous.
Relevance	Ties ideas and facts back to the job.	Occasionally goes off onto irrelevant tangents.	Is too academic and school-like.
Depth of Knowledge . .	Knows the area thoroughly.	Sometimes has to look things up to answer questions.	Knows little more than trainees.

Summary

Training and development takes place at all levels of employment, from unskilled ghetto youngsters who need remedial training in basic math and English skills to seasoned corporate vice presidents, from the first day on a job to the final months before retirement. Training is a continuing organizational activity, particularly at the management level, on which a great deal of money and effort are expended. Training is not restricted to specific job skills. Much training activity is directed toward changing attitudes, motivations, and interpersonal skills. At any level of employment or type of training, the goal is to improve performance on the job and, in the process, to increase the value of individual employees to themselves and to their organization. **Cooperative education programs**, in which students alternate college course work with jobs, are increasingly popular.

Fair employment legislation can affect training programs because decisions on promotion, firing, and transfer are often based on performance during training. As such, training has the potential to be discriminatory. Discrimination can occur in selection for training, the training program itself, retention and progress in training, and job placement after training.

The first step in establishing a training program is to specify the training objectives, in other words, to determine specifically the objectives that the training is intended to accomplish. These can be determined by several techniques: **job analysis, critical incidents, performance appraisal**, and **self-assessment**.

Also of importance in a training program is the selection and training of the **training staff**, those persons who will conduct the formal teaching. Those who are knowledgeable in the subject matter, in communicating effectively, and in interpersonal skills have been shown to be the best instructors. Trainers' expectations can also influence trainee behavior.

Psychological principles of learning relate to training in organizations. These derive from the vast amount of psychological research that has been conducted on the human learning process. Two principles—**individual differences in ability** and **motivation**—deal with characteristics of the learner. Motivation to learn can be influenced by the trainee's level of involvement in the job and career, **locus of control** (internal or external), and beliefs and expectancies. Other principles deal with various ways in which the subject matter can be organized and presented: **active practice of the material, massed versus distributed practice, whole versus part learning, transfer of training, knowledge of results,** and **reinforcement.**

Specific training techniques used for nonsupervisory employees and for managers are presented. Techniques used for nonsupervisory employees include (1) **on-the-job training**, in which trainees learn while actually working at the job; (2) **vestibule training**, in which training takes place in a simulated work space away from the actual job; (3) **apprenticeship**, in which trainees undergo both classroom experience and work experience under the guidance of skilled craftspersons; (4) **programmed instruction**, in which the material is presented in easy steps, for each of which the trainees must indicate if they are comprehending the material; (5) **computer-assisted instruction (CAI)**, in which trainees interact with a computer that contains the course content; and (6) **behavior modification**, in which trainees are reinforced or rewarded for displaying the desired behaviors. Advantages and disadvantages of these techniques are presented along with examples of actual use. Millions of workers are being trained in **computer literacy**.

Some of the techniques used for training nonsupervisory employees are also used for training managers, although most executive development still occurs through informal on-the-job experience. In addition, the following techniques are used for management training: (1) **job rotation**, in which trainees are rotated among different jobs; (2) the **case study method**, in which trainees analyze, interpret, and discuss a complex problem faced by managers on the job; (3) **business games**, in which a group of trainees interact in a simulated business situation; (4) **in-basket training**, another simulated business situation, in which trainees respond individually; (5) **role playing**, in which trainees play the roles of workers or managers; (6) **behavior modeling**, in which trainees model their behavior on that of successful managers; (7) **sensitivity training**, in which groups of individuals develop skills in relating to one another; and (8) **leader match training**, in which managers learn how to change the situation to match their motivational style.

Career development and planning is a lifelong learning approach oriented toward job skills and abilities and personal development throughout a person's working career. Through employee self-analysis and company counseling and training workshops, the individual is assisted during three career stages of adult working life: the establishment stage, the maintenance stage, and the stage of decline. Employee attitudes, behaviors, and job performance differ at each stage.

Special training for the hard-core unemployed is offered by a number of organizations. It is necessary to focus on motivational and attitudinal training as well as specific job-related skills.

Perhaps the weakest point in the overall training process is the evaluation of training. This has rarely been carried out on a systematic and quantitative basis. Many training programs remain in use because of subjective judgments about their worth. It is important to evaluate the actual behavior changes that result from training.

Key Terms

apprenticeship
behavior modeling
behavior modification
business games
career development
case studies
computer-assisted
   instruction (CAI)
computer literacy

cooperative education
   programs
fair employment
in-basket technique
individual differences
internal/external locus
   of control
job rotation
leader match training
on-the-job training

positive reinforcement
programmed
   instruction
reinforcement
   schedules
role-playing technique
sensitivity training
transfer of training
vestibule training

CASE STUDIES
Training in Self-Management

State government employees who had a history of taking excessive sick leave were offered the opportunity to volunteer for an 8-part training course designed to enhance their self-regulatory or self-management skills. The objective was to increase their attendance at work. The training program consisted of weekly 1-hour group meetings followed by 30-minute sessions in which each trainee met individually with an instructor.

In the first session, principles of self-management were explained. In the second session, trainees discussed the reasons for their unusual amount of sick leave. The reasons were assigned to appropriate categories as follows: legitimate illness, medical appointments, job stress, job boredom, difficulties with co-workers, alcohol- and drug-related matters, family problems, transportation problems, and the feeling that taking sick leave was an employee's right whether or not he or she was ill. The most frequently cited reasons for taking sick leave were family problems, difficulties with co-workers, and transportation problems, none of which was related to an actual illness.

The trainees were taught to develop descriptions of their problem behaviors, such as getting along with co-workers, to identify the conditions that led to those behaviors, and to devise alternative ways of coping with those behaviors other than taking time off from work. Thus, this aspect of the training program focused on self-assessment.

Other sessions focused on goal setting. Each trainee was encouraged to set a specific goal for reducing sick leave and increasing attendance on the job within a given time period. Employees were also encouraged to adopt as goals the coping behaviors described in earlier sessions.

The importance of monitoring one's own behavior was dealt with next. The trainees learned to keep attendance records and to note the reasons for missing a day of work as well as the steps taken to cope with the problem and return to work. Emphasis was placed on the importance of this daily feedback obtained from keeping such records.

Trainees were encouraged to identify activities or events that would serve as self-administered reinforcement or punishment for achieving or failing to achieve their goals. These activities had to be powerful yet easy to administer, such as buying a candy bar as a reinforcer or performing an odious chore as a punishment.

In a review session, the trainees reexamined the work of the previous sessions by writing a personal behavioral contract, specifying the goals they hoped to achieve, the time period within which to achieve them, the reward or punishment consequences, and the specific behaviors necessary to reach the goals. The final session focused on maintaining the new behaviors and dealing with any relapses.

Follow-up measures revealed that the trainees' perceived self-efficacy (the belief that they could control their own behavior) had increased, as had their level of attendance on the job. The training program was judged to be a success.

QUESTIONS

1. Identify the dependent variable and the independent variable in this research.
2. What psychological principles of learning are involved in this research?
3. What other training methods could be used to increase attendance?
4. Do you think such a training program would be effective with the so-called hard-core unemployed? Why or why not?
5. In general, which is more effective in modifying behavior, reinforcement or punishment? Why?

Reference: C. A. Frayne & G. P. Latham. (1987). Application of social learning theory to employee self-management of attendance. *Journal of Applied Psychology, 72,* 387–392.

Additional Reading

Goldstein, I. L. (1986). *Training in Organizations: Needs Assessment, Development, and Evaluation* (2nd ed.). Monterey, CA: Brooks/Cole. Examines the basic issues involved in the establishment of training programs in organizations and the variety of instructional techniques available to teach different skills. Considers special training needs of the hard-core unemployed workers and the older workers.

Latham, G. P. (1988). Human resources training and development. *Annual Review of Psychology, 39*, 545–582. Discusses the psychological literature on major topics in the field including the identification of training needs, the training of raters, and the evaluation of training programs.

Leibowitz, Z. B., Farren, C., & Kaye, B. L. (1986). *Designing Career Development Systems*. San Francisco: Jossey-Bass. Reviews the design and implementation of corporate career development programs and the problems in balancing employee career needs with organizational effectiveness.

Meyer, H. H., & Raich, M. S. (1983). An objective evaluation of a behavior modeling training program. *Personnel Psychology, 36,* 755–761. Describes a behavior modeling training program for salespersons in the large appliance and radio/television departments of a major retailing chain.

PART III

Organizational Psychology

Organizational psychology includes those functions and processes that define the social and psychological climate within which we work. Few people work alone. Most of us work in small groups such as a crew on one unit of an assembly line or a department in a corporate office, and here we form cliques, influential informal groups that generate their own values and attitudes, which may not be compatible with those of the organization.

We are also affected by the formal structure of the organization for which we work—the company, government agency, or university that employs us. Like the informal groups, formal groups generate a psychological climate of ideals and attitudes that influences our feelings about our job and the way in which we perform it.

Formal organizations range from rigid and hierarchical bureaucracies to more loosely structured and flexible companies in which employees participate in decision making at all levels. The participative organization is the modern approach; it is distinguished by a focus on the intellectual, emotional, and motivational needs and characteristics of the individual employees. The older bureaucratic style focuses solely on the form of the organization with no regard for the psychological characteristics or needs of the workers.

Employee attitudes and work behavior are affected by both the social factors of the organization and the psychological factors of the individual members of the organization. Organizational psychology (Chapters 7–9) is concerned with the relationships between these two sets of factors.

Leadership (Chapter 7) is a major source of influence on worker attitudes and behavior. Various styles of leadership, from dictatorial to democratic, create different social climates. Organizational psychologists are concerned with the influence of leadership styles and the psychological characteristics of the leaders, their motivations, stresses, and job duties.

Chapter 8 deals with the motivations that employees bring to their work and the ways in which organizations can satisfy (or fail to satisfy) these needs. The chapter also discusses the nature and extent of our involvement with our jobs and how this affects our performance and satisfaction.

Chapter 9 is devoted to formal and informal organizations and the psychological climate fostered by each. It covers the movement to humanize work through participatory democracy, ways in which organizations can adapt to social and technological innovations, the socialization of new employees to the organization, and efforts to improve the quality of working life in the United States and abroad.

Organizational psychology directly affects your working career. Your motivations, the style of leadership under which you function, the style you may exercise yourself, and the form of organization for which you work determine the quality of your working life. This, in turn, influences your satisfaction with life in general.

Chapter 7

Leadership in Organizations

Introduction

Organizations today place great emphasis on finding and training leaders at all levels, from supervisor to president. Indeed, a major portion of all selection and training activity is devoted to leadership. Business leaders and I/O psychologists understand that the success or failure of any organization depends, in large measure, on the quality of its leaders. Some analysts believe that the basic difference between a successful and an unsuccessful organization is its leadership. All types of organization—business and industry, government and military agencies, universities and hospitals—recognize the importance of the leadership function. They must do so to remain viable.

Half of all new businesses fail within their first 2 years and only one third survive 5 years. In most cases, the business failures are caused by poor leadership. It is not surprising, then, that organizations engage in extensive searches for new methods of selecting and developing their managers and executives and for making the best use of their leadership abilities once they are on the job. Because executives are so highly valued, they are offered inducements to join and remain with a company, benefits such as stock options, insurance policies, liberal expense accounts, and lavishly decorated offices.

Psychologists play an important role in leadership. In addition to direct efforts in selection and training, they have conducted considerable research on aspects of leadership such as characteristics of successful and unsuccessful leaders, effects of different styles of leadership behavior, and techniques for maximizing leadership abilities. The quality of organizational leadership today reflects the research activities and practical applications of psychologists.

Anything that affects the fortunes and future of the organization for which you work also affects you, the employee; leadership is no exception. Regardless of the level of your job, the quality of leadership in your place of employment will influence you daily. Unless (or until) you are the company president, you will take orders from someone else. Much of your motivation, enthusiasm, hope for the future, and even ability to perform your job, will depend on how well your leader performs his or her duties.

Also, as college graduates, most of you will fill positions of leadership. Most organizations develop their leaders from among the ranks of the college educated. How well you perform your job as a leader will influence your salary, rank, and sense of self-worth.

Changing Views of Leadership

The ways in which leaders behave, the specific acts by which they play out their leadership roles, are based on certain assumptions about human nature. Consciously or unconsciously, leaders function on the basis of some theory of human behavior, a view of what their subordinates are like as people. Managers who closely watch subordinates to make sure they are performing the job exactly as told hold a different view of human nature than managers who allow subordinates to accomplish their work in whatever way they think best.

These concepts have been changing throughout the 20th century, partly because of the growth in the size of business organizations since 1900, changing social forces such as the rise to power of the labor unions, and widespread psychological research and theory on the nature and motivation of people at work.

In the early years of the 20th century, foremen, the most immediate supervisors of the workers, were promoted from the ranks of the workers and had little formal training for a leadership role. These turn-of-the-century supervisors exercised virtually complete control over subordinates. Foremen hired and fired, controlled production levels, and set pay scales. Obviously, this approach left much room for abuse. All too often foremen were dictators, not truly leaders in the modern sense of the term. There were few reins on their authority—no labor union, no personnel or industrial relations department, no one to whom a worker could complain. They functioned by what a congressional committee in 1912 called the "driving method," a combination of authoritarian behavior, combativeness, and physical intimidation to get workers to put forth their maximum effort (Zuboff, 1988, p. 35).

The philosophy of management at that time was *scientific management*. This approach, established by an engineer, Frederick W. Taylor, was concerned solely with ways to maintain or increase production levels (F. W. Taylor, 1911). Through the use of time-and-motion studies, representatives of scientific management were interested in standardizing the production process, getting the machines and the workers who ran them to work faster and faster.

Scientific management regarded workers as nothing more than extensions of the machines, and, thus, the relationship between workers and the organization was highly impersonal. No consideration was given to employees as human beings, as people with needs, fears, and values. Indeed, workers were looked on unfavorably, as lazy, dishonest, shiftless, and possessing a low level of intelligence. This view of workers was reinforced by the research that was then being conducted in the United States on intelligence testing. One of the pioneers in this field was the psychologist H. H. Goddard, who argued persuasively that people with low intelligence required close supervision by people of more superior intelligence. "We must learn," Goddard said, "that there are great groups of men, laborers, who are but little above the child, who must be told what to do and shown how to do it.... There are only a few leaders, most must be followers" (quoted in Broad & Wade, 1982, p. 198). Thus, workers were regarded as little more than extensions of their machines. It is understandable, then, that the goals of scientific management were to increase production and efficiency, and it was believed that the only way to accomplish this was for workers to submit to the needs of the machinery and to a dictatorial style of leadership.

Nowadays, it is difficult to imagine people working under such a system. Instead of a lack of concern for their workers, many modern organizations regard the needs of their employees as a major concern. This is the *human relations* approach to management, which began in the 1920s and 1930s under the impact of the Hawthorne studies that focused on the workers instead of on production.

Part of the change introduced into the work situation in the Hawthorne studies was the style of leadership. Women workers had been treated harshly by their bosses. They were shouted at and severely disciplined for dropping parts, for talking while working, and for taking breaks. Some of the workers were so routinely singled out for abuse that they were reduced to tears. They were treated like children who had to be constantly watched and punished by an autocratic leader.

In the Hawthorne experiments, the workers were exposed to a different style of leadership, one that allowed them to set their own production pace and to form social groups. They were no longer criticized by their supervisors, they could talk to one another while working, and their views on the work itself were solicited. In short, the leader treated them like fellow human beings. Since the time of these experiments, the human relations style of leadership has influenced the management practices of growing numbers of organizations.

The human relations movement brought about a recognition of workers as human beings, no longer interchangeable cogs in a giant production machine. It made organizations alert and responsive to the personal and social needs of employees and to the interpersonal relations that develop within the organization. In this view, the task of leaders should not be solely to maintain or increase production but also to facilitate cooperative goal achievement among subordinates, enhance their personal growth and development, and improve the quality of work life.

These two approaches to management behavior were given formal theoretical expression by psychologist Douglas McGregor as *Theory X* and *Theory Y* (McGregor, 1960). McGregor's views became influential in the world of work and encompassed divergent images of workers and the ways in which they can be managed.

Underlying the Theory X approach to management are the three following assumptions about human nature:

1. Most people have an innate dislike of work and will avoid it if they can.
2. Therefore, most people must be "coerced, controlled, directed, threatened with punishment" to get them to work hard enough to satisfy the organization's goals.
3. Most people prefer "to be directed," wish "to avoid responsibility," have "relatively little ambition," and want "security above all."

Theory X provides a most unflattering image of human nature. According to this view, people would not work at all at their jobs without a dictating and demanding leader. Like children, workers must be led, scolded, threatened, and punished; they are basically irresponsible and lazy.

Theory X is compatible with scientific management and with the classic form of organization called *bureaucracy*. However, Theory X is incompatible with current views of human motivation, particularly the influential work of psychologist Abraham Maslow (see Chapter 8). Maslow argued that the ultimate and overall goal of human beings is to self-actualize, that is, to realize all of their distinctly human capabilities. This conception of human nature is reflected in McGregor's Theory Y, which assumes

1. "The expenditure of physical and mental effort in work is as natural as play or rest." Most people do not have an innate dislike of work. Indeed, work may be a "source of satisfaction."
2. "External control and the threat of punishment are not the only means for bringing about effort toward organizational objectives." Most people will display self-discipline in working for goals to which they are committed.
3. "Commitment to objectives is a function of the rewards associated with their achievement."
4. Most people, under proper conditions, are capable not only of accepting responsibility but of seeking it.
5. "The capacity to exercise a relatively high degree of imagination, ingenuity, and creativity in the solution of organizational problems is widely… distributed in the population."
6. "Under the conditions of modern industrial life, the intellectual potentialities of the average human being are only partially utilized." (McGregor, 1960, pp. 33–34, 47–48).

In the radically different image of human nature that Theory Y presents, people are industrious, creative, need and seek challenge and responsibility, and are not at all averse to work. These persons need and function best under a different type of leader than do Theory X persons. Rather than a dictatorial leader, Theory Y persons need a leader who will allow them to participate in the achievement of personal and organizational goals. The Theory Y view of leadership applies to the human relations movement and to modern organization theory that calls for worker participation in management decisions. An example of the application of Theory Y is the management by objectives (MBO) approach to performance appraisal, discussed in Chapter 5. As we saw, MBO involves a high degree of participation on the part of employees in setting their own goals for performance on the job and for personal growth.

Approaches to the Study of Leadership

Academic and organizational psychologists have been studying the nature of leadership for decades. Their goal is to determine the nature of leadership and the factors that cause some people to be effective leaders and others to be ineffective leaders.

Initially, the problem of delimiting leadership characteristics seemed to be simple. After all, in most situations it is not difficult to determine which persons are good leaders and which are poor. All that appeared necessary was for researchers to measure the traits of good leaders and poor leaders and see how they differed.

This *trait approach* sought those characteristics that good leaders possessed in much greater degree than did poor leaders. For example, if it were found that good leaders consistently scored high on a scale that measured extraversion and poor leaders consistently scored low (the introverted end of the scale), it might be concluded that effective leaders are persons who are extraverted. It would then be possible to predict leadership potential on the basis of a person's score on the extraversion scale in combination with scores on scales that measured additional traits that differentiate good from poor leaders.

Thus, the emphasis in the trait approach is on the personal characteristics of leaders. No consideration is given to the circumstances or the situation in which leadership occurs. It follows that there is no need to consider the leadership situation; if leadership ability is a function of personal traits, the person possessing the right combination of traits will be a good leader in all situations.

The trait approach to leadership has a commonsense appeal because it agrees with a popular notion that some people are born leaders; they possess unique characteristics that induce others to want to follow them. However, psychological research has not fully supported the trait approach. In general, the most consistent finding from more than 50 years of studies on the trait approach is that there does not seem to be a universal set of traits that distinguishes good from poor leaders in all situations. The person who is a good leader in one situation may fail dismally as a leader in another situation. Thus, what may determine effective leadership is not so much the characteristics of individual leaders but rather the nature of the situation in which they are expected to lead and the characteristics and needs of the followers.

When psychologists realized this, they turned from the trait approach to the *situational approach* in their investigation of the nature of leadership. This conception of leadership focuses on the dynamic interactions between leaders and followers. It is concerned with the needs of followers and with the problem or task confronting the group. Viewing leadership in this way (as a function of a particular situation) means that leadership is a dynamic, not a static, process. That is, the abilities, characteristics, and behaviors necessary for effective leadership may change in response to changes in the tasks and goals of the group or in the needs of the followers. For example, a newly established business may require a different kind of leadership than a long-established, smoothly running organization. The abilities required for success in one situation may not suffice in others. In some cases, these abilities might even be counterproductive.

Leadership requirements may also change in the same situation over a period of time as new values or outlooks are needed such as the change from the scientific management approach to the human relations approach to management and the movement toward increased worker participation that occurred from the 1900s to the 1990s.

This necessity for flexibility is another factor that may preclude the possibility of uncovering a single set of characteristics with which to predict leadership performance in all situations.

Psychologists are also interested in leadership *behavior*, investigating what leaders do in addition to what they are. Do good leaders behave differently from poor leaders? What do they do on the job that makes them so effective?

Leadership behavior is examined in the following way. The psychologist collects, usually by means of interviews, examples of effective and ineffective leadership that actually occurred on the job. Each specific behavioral example is then judged by a panel of experts as to how good or poor it is. Based on these expert ratings, the examples are scaled in quantitative terms and a behavioral questionnaire is developed. The questionnaire is administered to subordinates who indicate those behaviors that have been exhibited by their supervisors.

One research program using this approach detailed 1,800 examples that were reduced to a leader-behavior questionnaire of 150 specific behaviors. Table 7-1 contains sample items from such a questionnaire.

Once the questionnaire has been developed and validated, it simplifies the evaluation of a particular leader's behavior and allows for the comparison of the behavior of different leaders. The scale also indicates which behaviors are the most desired or effective for a particular job, department, or work group. Current and future leaders can then be trained to develop effective behaviors and to eliminate ineffective ones.

An underlying assumption of the behavioral approach to the study of leadership is that leaders can be trained to function well. This contrasts with the trait approach, which holds that leaders are born with traits that cause them to be effective and that those who do not possess these traits are incapable of becoming good leaders.

The trait approach to the study of leadership has not been abandoned, however. Psychologists are continuing to investigate the personal traits of leaders in specific situations. Thus, the search for leadership traits is conducted within the context of the situation and the nature of the followers. This restricted trait approach has revealed characteristics and abilities that distinguish successful leaders from less successful ones, as we shall see.

TABLE 7-1   Sample Items from Supervisory Behavior Description Form

1. Supervisor expresses appreciation when one of us does a good job
2. Supervisor is easy to understand
3. Supervisor demands more than we can do
4. Supervisor insists that everything be done his or her way
5. Supervisor treats subordinates without considering their feelings
6. Supervisor is friendly and can be easily approached
7. Supervisor rules with an iron hand
8. Supervisor offers new approaches to problems
9. Supervisor stresses being ahead of competing work groups
10. Supervisor emphasizes the quantity of work

Adapted from "The description of supervisory behavior" by E. A. Fleishman, 1953, *Journal of Applied Psychology, 37,* pp. 3–4.

In addition, some recent research suggests that the conclusion drawn earlier about the failure of the trait approach may have been too pessimistic. Further, it may have been wrong to generalize from these studies—which involved perceptions of leadership effectiveness—to actual on-the-job effectiveness. None of the earlier trait studies used task performance or observer ratings of effectiveness as the dependent variables. They all involved, instead, the relationship between perceptions of leadership effectiveness held by group members and the various measured traits of the leaders.

Judgments of a leader's effectiveness made by his or her subordinates are, however, relevant to the leadership process. Being perceived as a competent leader can allow that leader to exert a greater influence on the work performance of his or her subordinates than can someone perceived to be an incompetent or ineffective leader. Meta-analyses to reexamine the earlier research on the relationship between personality traits of leaders and perceived leader effectiveness have pinpointed three characteristics that significantly discriminate between effective and ineffective leaders (Lord, DeVader, & Alliger, 1986). These characteristics are intelligence, masculinity/femininity, and dominance. Perhaps there is reason for psychologists to continue the once-abandoned search for leadership traits that might operate in all kinds of situations.

In sum, there are several separate but interacting elements in the leadership process: the characteristics and behaviors of leaders, the characteristics of followers, and the nature of the situation in which leaders and followers interact. To analyze and understand fully the nature and requirements of leadership, all these elements must be studied.

Theories of Leadership

We have noted that there are several ways of discussing leadership, several theoretical viewpoints from which to approach the topic. We considered three such approaches: traits, situations, and behaviors. Each assumes a different definition of the nature of leadership.

Other, more specific, theoretical views of leadership relate to these broad approaches. They take the position that effective leadership is dependent or contingent on a particular alliance or combination of leader traits and behaviors plus the characteristics of the situation in which the leadership is required. We shall describe six of these explanations of leadership: contingency theory, cognitive resource utilization theory, path-goal theory, normative decision theory, vertical dyadic linkage theory, and situational leadership theory.

Contingency Theory

Perhaps the best known and most thoroughly researched of the contingency theories is the one proposed by Fred Fiedler (1978), which we summarized in

Chapter 6 in our discussion of leader match training, which derives from this theory. In contingency theory, a leader's effectiveness is determined by the interaction between the leader's personal characteristics and some aspects of the situation. Leaders are classified as primarily person oriented or task oriented. The kind of leader who will be the more effective depends on the leader's degree of control over the situation.

In turn, control of the situation depends on three factors: the relations between the leader and the followers, the degree of task structure, and the leader's position power or amount of authority. If a leader is popular, is directing a highly structured and routine task, and has the power or authority to administer punishment, he or she is said to have a high control of the situation, a highly favorable condition. An army sergeant, for example, who gets along well with the members of his or her squad is a high-control and effective leader. An unpopular president of a social club that has no formal goals or tasks and who has no authority to maintain discipline is a low-control leader in a highly unfavorable situation.

According to the contingency theory, in extreme situations (highly favorable or highly unfavorable), the task-oriented leader will be more effective. When the situation is moderately favorable, the person-oriented leader will be more effective.

The theory has generated a great deal of research, much of which is supportive (House & Singh, 1987; Peters, Hartke, & Pohlmann, 1985). However, most of the research that supports this theory was conducted in laboratory settings and not in actual work situations. Therefore, it has not yet been determined whether, or to what extent, the findings are generalizable to the workplace.

The major criticism of contingency theory involves the Least Preferred Co-worker Scale, the purported measure of a leader's personality and motivation. Critics contend that it is not clear just what characteristics or constructs this scale really measures. In addition, its reliability and construct validity have been called into question.

Because of these and other criticisms of the contingency theory over the last decade, Fiedler has proposed a new theory of leadership that has grown out of his earlier work.

Cognitive Resource Utilization Theory

Fiedler's new leadership theory focuses on the cognitive resources of leaders, that is, their intelligence, technical competence, and job-related knowledge (Fiedler & Garcia, 1987). It is the leader's intellectual or cognitive abilities that provide the plans, decisions, and strategies that guide a group's actions. The better a leader's cognitive abilities, the more effective his or her plans, decisions, and strategies will be. Those decisions are presented to the group through the leader's directive behavior, and they will be acted upon if the group supports the goals of the leader and of the organization, and if the leader is not distracted by stress.

Fiedler offers several hypotheses as part of the cognitive resource utilization theory.

1. When leaders are under stress, their cognitive abilities are diverted from the task at hand and they will focus on problems and activities that are not relevant to the task. Therefore, group performance will suffer.
2. The cognitive abilities of directive leaders correlate more highly with group performance than do the cognitive abilities of nondirective leaders.
3. Unless the group complies with the leader's directions, the leader's plans and decisions will not be implemented. Therefore, the correlation between a leader's cognitive resources and group performance is higher when the group supports the leader than when it does not.
4. The leader's cognitive abilities will contribute to group performance only to the degree to which the task requires those abilities, that is, the degree to which the task is intellectually demanding.
5. The directive behavior of the leader is determined in part by elements of the contingency theory such as the leader's task and relationship motivations (as determined by the Least Preferred Co-worker Scale) and the leader's control over the situation.

The theory details the interaction between cognitive resources, work performance, and stress. The findings on stress have practical implications because it is a variable that can be partially controlled by the leader (see Chapter 13). Through stress management techniques, the leader's cognitive resources can be applied more effectively.

According to Fiedler, a major source of stress on leaders arises from their own leaders. When managers have a stressful relationship with their boss, for example, they tend to depend on their previous job experience (what behaviors worked for them in the past) rather than on their intelligence. When leaders are free of stress, they rely on their intelligence rather than being constrained by prior job experience.

Fiedler has presented impressive research support for the cognitive resource utilization theory, with correlations ranging well above +.50. Much of this research was conducted in the laboratory and not in the field, so the problem of generalizability to the world of work remains an issue. This theory, together with the contingency theory, is, however, an attempt to combine both personality and situational variables to explain leadership behavior.

Path-Goal Theory

The path-goal theory of leadership focuses on the kinds of behaviors a leader should exercise to allow subordinates to achieve their goals (House, 1971; House & Mitchell, 1974). Specifically, the theory states that leaders can increase their subordinates' motivation, satisfaction, and performance by giving rewards that depend on achieving particular goals. In other words, effective leaders will help subordinates by pointing out the paths they must follow to obtain the rewards or goals and by providing them with the means to do so.

House proposed four styles of leader behavior. (1) In directive leadership, the leader lets subordinates know what they should do and how they should do it; (2) in supportive leadership, the leader shows concern and support for subordinates; (3) in participative leadership, the leader allows subordinates to participate in decisions that affect the work; and (4) in achievement-oriented leadership, the leader sets challenging goals for subordinates and emphasizes high levels of performance.

The leadership style that will be most effective depends on the nature of the situation and on the subordinates. Thus, leaders must be flexible and adopt whichever style is called for. For example, subordinates who rank low in the ability required to perform the job might function best under directive leadership, whereas those high in ability need less direction and so might function best under supportive leadership. For unstructured jobs, directive leadership would be effective. Leaders must be able to perceive the nature of the situation and recognize the characteristics of their subordinates and respond with the most appropriate style of leadership.

Considerable research has been conducted on the path-goal theory, but the results are contradictory (Fulk & Wendler, 1982; Hornstein, Heilman, Mone, & Tartell, 1987). Overall, the research support is weak. It is a difficult theory to test experimentally because certain basic concepts, including "path" and "goal," defy reduction to operational definitions.

Normative Decision Theory

Normative decision theory focuses on one aspect of leadership: decision making. It attempts to prescribe behaviors for leaders in decision-making situations. The word *normative* refers to a norm or standard of behavior considered to be the correct one. The most crucial part of the theory involves the extent to which a leader invites or allows his or her subordinates to participate in decisions (Vroom & Yetton, 1973).

The theory postulates five styles of leadership behavior, ranging from complete autocracy at one extreme, in which decisions are made solely by the leader, to complete participation at the other extreme, in which decisions are reached through consensus.

The most effective leader behavior depends on the three components of the situation: the quality of the decision, the degree of its acceptance by subordinates, and the time needed to make the decision. For example, a decision reached through participation might be better accepted by subordinates than a decision made for them by their leader, but participation will require more time. Leaders must be flexible and adaptable in selecting the decision-making approach that produces the highest benefits in terms of quality, acceptance, and time.

Normative decision theory provides an objective means for leaders to choose the best approach by answering several diagnostic questions relating to the situation. The theory is a promising one with some degree of empirical support behind it (Field, 1982; Jago & Vroom, 1980). However, one replication of the original research conducted in seven field settings found results suggesting that the normative decision theory may not be descriptive of how managers actually make decisions in the workplace (Pate & Heiman, 1987).

Vertical Dyadic Linkage Theory

Vertical dyadic linkage theory, developed by Graen and several colleagues, deals with the ways in which the relationship between leaders and followers affects the leadership process (Graen, 1976; Graen & Schliemann, 1978). Graen criticized other leadership theories for focusing on average leadership styles or behaviors and for ignoring individual differences among subordinates. He suggests that the relationship or link between each leader-subordinate pair, or dyad, must be considered separately. The dyads range across two levels of the organizational hierarchy, from subordinate to superior, and so are described as vertical dyads.

The theory divides subordinates into two groups: (1) the in-group, whom the supervisor views as competent, trustworthy, and highly motivated; and (2) the out-group, who are viewed by the leader as incompetent, untrustworthy, and poorly motivated.

The theory also distinguishes between supervision (leadership based on formal authority) and leadership (in which influence is exerted through persuasion) as styles of behavior. With members of the out-group, leaders use supervision and assign them tasks requiring low levels of ability and responsibility. Also, there is little in the way of a personal relationship between a leader and the members of the out-group of subordinates.

With members of the in-group, leaders practice leadership rather than supervision and assign members important, responsible tasks requiring high levels of ability. In this case, personal relationships are established between leaders and subordinates, in which the subordinates provide support and understanding.

Research, most of it conducted in actual work settings, has been generally supportive of the theory, both in the United States and in Japan, and at various levels of management from low to high (Crouch & Yetton, 1988; Graen, Novak, & Sommerkamp, 1982; Graen & Wakabayashi, 1986; Vecchio & Gobdel, 1984).

Other research has shown that the quality of the leader–subordinate relationships (called the leader–member exchange or LMX) can be improved through training, resulting in the display of more leadership than supervision as well as significant improvements in satisfaction and productivity among subordinates (Scandura & Graen, 1984). Another study found a 54% improvement in productivity along with decreases in errors following training (Graen, Scandura, & Graen, 1986).

Such findings give the vertical dyadic linkage theory a practical advantage over most other leadership theories.

Situational Leadership Theory

The situational leadership theory is concerned with two kinds of managerial behavior: (1) task behavior, the extent to which managers organize and direct the work of subordinates, telling them what to do and how to do it; and (2) relationship behavior, the extent to which managers develop and maintain a personal relationship with subordinates by providing social and emotional support and by developing two-way communication channels (Hersey & Blanchard, 1982).

The theorists argue that managers can display either high or low task behavior and high or low relationship behavior resulting in four possible combinations: high task/high relationship, high task/low relationship, low task/high relationship, or low task/low relationship.

According to the situational leadership theory, managers must choose one of these combinations in dealing with their subordinates. That choice is based on the employee's level of task-related maturity, which is defined as the capacity and willingness to perform at a certain level.

Thus, leaders should behave in different ways toward workers who have different degrees of task-related maturity. In dealing with immature subordinates, high task behavior is more important because these employees need greater guidance in performing their work. For employees with high task-related maturity, managers would be urged to display low task/low relationship behaviors because those subordinates need little in the way of job direction or personal support. As workers' levels of task-related maturity rise with more experience on the job, the manager's behavior toward them should shift from an emphasis on task behavior to more relationship behavior.

Little research has been conducted to date on the situational leadership theory, but some studies provide support for the low task-related maturity condition (Blank, Weitzel, & Green, 1986; Hornstein, Heilman, Mone, & Tartell, 1987; Vecchio, 1987).

Leadership Styles

Much research focuses on what leaders do: their style of leadership and the behaviors by which it is manifested. This section describes several dimensions that distinguish various styles of leadership.

Appointed Versus Elected Leadership

A basic distinction between leadership styles is the source of the decision about who will be the leader. Are leaders appointed by sources outside the group they lead or are they chosen by members of the group itself? In the first situation, sometimes called *headship* or nominal leadership, leaders are imposed on the group, appointed by higher management. In the second situation, *elected leadership* or effective leadership, the members of the group select those whom they wish to lead them.

You can find examples of both kinds of leadership in your own experience. Elected representatives at state and federal levels of government are chosen by the people. The same is true for clubs, fraternities and sororities, and other social groups. In most large organizations, however, leaders are usually imposed on the group. Workers rarely elect their supervisors, and enlisted personnel do not elect their officers (although this did occur during the Civil War).

Persons appointed to leadership positions are automatically given the trappings, status, and authority of superiors. With sufficient authority such as the power to reward and punish possessed by an army officer or a manager, appointed heads are able to direct the activities of a group and gain compliance, but they may not necessarily be able to *lead* the group in the larger sense of the term.

Appointed leadership usually guarantees that leaders can direct or dominate the actions of followers, and such leaders are given the power to punish followers if the latter do not obey. Followers may not willingly or loyally cooperate with imposed heads, however, or give them their full support, unless the heads are also effective leaders. Indeed, group members may only perfunctorily carry out commands from appointed leaders. True leaders are able to enlist the cooperation of a group and enhance its solidarity and cohesion so that the members willingly work with the leaders to perform the job.

Thus, although appointed heads may begin their roles armed with the perquisites of leadership—the symbols, title, and office—their ability to work with their followers determines how effectively they will be able to lead. No appointed heads truly lead their followers and receive their active cooperation without first gaining their support, confidence, and trust.

Table 7-2 presents some of the differences between appointed and elected leadership.

Appointed heads face special problems not shared by elected leaders. Because the majority of organizational leaders are appointed, it is important to consider the limitations and difficulties these leaders face.

Appointed leaders have a dual, sometimes conflicting, set of obligations and responsibilities. First, they are responsible to those who appointed them, that is, their superiors in the organization. If they are to retain their position, they must satisfy the company's demands and goals. Supervisors, for instance, must reach and maintain the production levels set by their superiors.

Second, appointed leaders must also try to satisfy the needs and wishes of subordinates. Supervisors must, for example, secure the support of their workers if they hope to meet established production quotas. Supervisors must arrange for satisfactory physical and psychological work conditions and adequate pay scales, and they must represent the subordinates to higher management, passing along grievances and suggestions.

In contrast, elected leaders have a single set of responsibilities. They must answer only to those who put them in their position of leadership. Although they may have obligations outside the group, their responsibility is to their followers.

TABLE 7-2 Differences Between Appointed and Elected Leadership

Personal and situational variables	Headship	Leadership
Power exercised by	Appointed head	Elected or chosen leader
Source of authority	Delegated from above	Accorded from below
Basis of authority	Legal or official	Personal competence
Authority vested by	Values institutionalized in formal contract	Recognition of contribution to group goals
Relationship of superior to subordinates	Domination	Personal influence
Responsible to	Superiors	Superiors and subordinates
Social gap with followers	Wide	Narrow
Behavior pattern	Authoritarian	Democratic

Adapted from "Leadership and headship: There is a difference" by C. R. Holloman, 1968, *Personnel Administration*, 31(4), p. 38.

Another difficulty often faced by appointed heads is a limited flexibility in their own methods of leadership. In a large business or government organization, they have to operate within established guidelines about how to accomplish various aspects of the job. The rigidity of these rules varies among organizations, but appointed leaders cannot operate too innovatively without running afoul of organizational policy.

Elected leaders are not so constrained. Because they are responsible only to their followers, they are free to lead in any way they believe will satisfy the wishes of their followers.

Leadership competence of the two types of leaders varies. It can be assumed that elected leaders have already displayed qualities necessary to satisfy the group before they are chosen to lead. If not, the group would not have made them leaders. No such assumption can be made about appointed heads. We have seen that it is difficult to assess management potential. Promotions and leadership appointments are often based on proficiency in a person's current job. However, the fact that a person is best in sales for the district, for example, is no guarantee that he or she will make a good sales manager.

Although there are disadvantages and limitations to leadership by appointment, it seems unlikely that industry will alter this basic management procedure. The ideal situation is where appointed leaders are able to assume the characteristics and interpersonal relations of elected leaders. This can be difficult, but two factors may facilitate this change.

First, the complexity of modern production processes necessitates a close working and consulting relationship between line supervisors and various staff specialists. For example, supervisors often meet with members of the personnel department before making promotion decisions. Years ago, supervisors made such decisions on their own. The dependence of managers on other high-level personnel has decreased their autonomy and caused them to be more flexible in considering the opinions of others, including subordinates. If managers begin to listen to subordinates, they are well on the way to becoming effective leaders.

Second, the emphasis on human relations skills and participatory democracy encourages managers to be concerned with developing motivation, with setting mutually agreeable goals, and with personal and group satisfaction among subordinates.

These two factors, then, foster the positive trend toward fusing the characteristics of appointed and elected leadership.

Authoritarian Versus Democratic Leadership

The words *authoritarian* and *democratic* are familiar to you as forms of government. An authoritarian government is dictatorial and tyrannical, and its leaders exercise absolute political, economic, and social power. A democratic government places a large measure of power in the hands of the people who are able, through the vote, to influence the major issues affecting the country. The leaders in a democracy—elected, not appointed—must be responsive to the needs and wishes of the people or they may not be returned to office at the next election.

In fire fighting, a stressful situation that requires rapid and efficient job performance, authoritarian leadership is preferred. The nature of the work does not allow time for a more democratic approach.

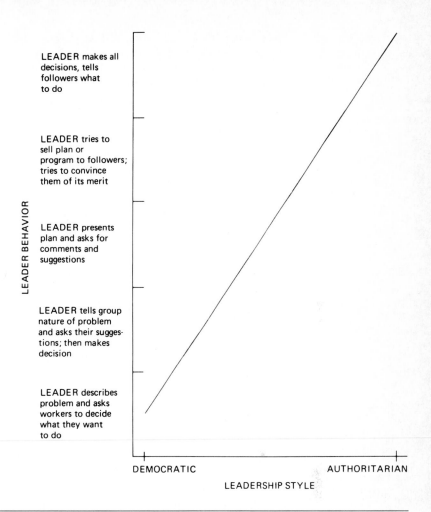

LEADER makes all
decisions, tells
followers what
to do

LEADER tries to
sell plan or
program to followers;
tries to convince
them of its merit

LEADER presents
plan and asks for
comments and
suggestions

LEADER tells group
nature of problem
and asks their sugges-
tions; then makes
decision

LEADER describes
problem and asks
workers to decide
what they want
to do

LEADER BEHAVIOR

DEMOCRATIC   AUTHORITARIAN

LEADERSHIP STYLE

Figure 7-1 Authoritarian-
democratic leadership
continuum.

Leadership situations usually involve some modification or combination of these extremes. Think of a continuum ranging from a totally autocratic situation to one of participatory democracy in which the group as a whole must agree on any decision that affects them. There is room on this continuum, then, for considerable variation in leadership style. (A parallel is often drawn between appointed leadership and authoritarianism and between elected leadership and democracy.)

Figure 7-1 presents the authoritarian-democratic continuum with representative leader behaviors. There is a broad latitude in leader behavior and responsibility between the two extremes.

Which leadership style is the more effective depends on the nature of the situation and the needs and characteristics of the followers. Some workers prefer to be told what to do and how to do it and would find it frustrating to operate in a democratic situation where they would be required to make frequent decisions affecting their lives. Others could not tolerate an authoritarian organization (or society) where they would have no say in the important decisions that affect them. Because many employees are of the latter type, participatory democracy and Theory Y leader behavior have become prominent in the workplace.

Studies show that participatory democracy is conducive to higher job satisfaction among a majority of employees. An analysis of studies comparing the two styles of leadership indicated that 60% found the democratic approach to be superior to the authoritarian approach, whereas 30% found no difference between the two. Only 9% showed higher satisfaction with the authoritarian approach; there are, as we noted, some people who are happier when they are told what to do and who do not want to have any say about the nature of their work.

For actual job performance rather than job satisfaction, research results do not favor the democratic style of leadership quite so strongly. Some 22% of the studies showed performance to be higher under the democratic style, but no differences in performance were reported between the two leadership styles in 56% of the studies. Job performance was found to be higher with authoritarian leadership in 10% of the studies (Locke & Schweiger, 1978).

In work situations that are highly stressful and require unusually rapid or efficient work, both productivity and satisfaction are more likely to increase under authoritarian leadership. Psychologists suggest that employees recognize that the nature of the work does not allow enough time for a democratic approach (Rosenbaum & Rosenbaum, 1971).

On both measures, job satisfaction and job performance, the participatory or democratic style of leadership is generally more desirable than the authoritarian style. This superiority, however, is not universal. The nature of the followers and the characteristics of the situation are important variables in determining the most effective leadership style.

The Role of Power in Leadership

It is difficult to discuss leadership without referring to the role of power on two levels: (1) the power that leaders have over their subordinates and (2) how leaders are motivated by power.

Obviously, leaders exert varying degrees of power over their followers. Also, leaders have different kinds of power, depending on the situation, the nature of the followers, and the leaders' personal characteristics (for example, how self-assured the leaders feel). Psychologists have identified five kinds of power in terms of their derivation (French & Raven, 1959; Kipnis, 1976):

1. *Reward power.* Organizational leaders possess the ability to reward their subordinates (with pay raises or promotions, for example). This gives leaders

a means of tremendous control over followers and can influence employee behavior in many ways.

2. *Coercive power*. An equally strong source of power is the ability to punish subordinates by firing them, failing to give them promotions or pay raises, or keeping them in undesirable jobs.

3. *Legitimate power*. This refers to the formalization of the power structure by the rules of the organization (as in headship). The hierarchy of control in an army unit, a government agency, or a classroom legitimizes the right of the leader to control or influence followers and the duty of the followers to accept that power.

These three sources of power are derived from, and are defined by, the formal organization to which leader and subordinates belong. It is power dictated or prescribed by the organization. The next two sources of power derive from the leaders themselves. In a sense, they are earned or merited by the unique qualifications and characteristics of an individual leader as perceived by his or her followers. They might be thought of as respect rather than power.

4. *Referent power*. This relates to the extent to which followers identify with their leaders and the leaders' goals. It is similar to true leadership, in which followers accept the leaders' goals as their own and work with, rather than for, the leaders to achieve the goals.

5. *Expert power*. This refers to the extent to which leaders are perceived to be knowledgeable in an area that is necessary to the attainment of group goals. Followers recognize the benefits for them of their leaders' expertise and, therefore, become more willing and supportive subordinates.

The possible and likely outcomes of the application of these five types of power on the employee variables of commitment, compliance, and resistance are shown in Table 7-3.

The effects of these five kinds of power were investigated in a study of 251 male middle-level managers in the United States. The dependent variables were the following: (1) overall job satisfaction, (2) satisfaction with their supervisor's

TABLE 7-3 Outcomes from Exercise of Different Types of Power

Power source	Commitment	Compliance	Resistance
Legitimate power	Possible	Likely	Possible
Reward power	Possible	Likely	Possible
Coercive power	Unlikely	Possible	Likely
Expert power	Likely	Possible	Possible
Referent power	Likely	Possible	Possible

From "The effective use of managerial power" by G. Yukl & T. Taber, 1983, *Personnel, 60*(2), p. 39.

technical skills, (3) satisfaction with their supervisor's human relations skills, and (4) organizational commitment.

The results showed that legitimate, referent, and expert power correlated positively with all four measures. Reward power correlated positively with the first three measures but not with organizational commitment. Coercive power showed a strong negative correlation with all four measures of satisfaction and commitment. Obviously, then, coercive power was viewed negatively and the other forms of power were viewed positively. This suggests that leaders who rely primarily on coercive power are likely to be less effective than leaders who exercise the other kinds of power (Hinkin & Schriesheim, 1988).

The type of power exercised can vary with the situation, as demonstrated in a study of 125 bank managers in Holland (Mulder, de Jong, Koppelaar, & Verhage, 1986). At times of crisis, the managers were viewed by their subordinates as exerting more legitimate power, referent power, and expert power than in noncrisis situations. The more effective of the managers were viewed by their superiors as exerting more legitimate power in crisis situations than did the less effective managers.

What is the role of power in motivating organizational leaders? How important is the desire to influence and control others? With high-level executives and many middle-level managers, the personal need for power is great. It has been shown that effective managers demonstrate a greater need for power than do less effective managers (McClelland & Burnham, 1976).

Other studies indicate that managers high in the need for power are more partial toward subordinates who are ingratiating or who flatter them than are managers low in the need for power. Also, high-power-need managers are more prone to inhibit group discussions. They show greater physiological activation or arousal levels when they are involved in supervision than do low-power-need managers. Further, managers high in the need for power tend to be impulsively aggressive and more likely to drink heavily. Not all people high in the need for power undertake business careers. Some choose careers in psychology, teaching, or journalism, jobs that also afford the opportunity to influence others (Fodor, 1984; Fodor & Smith, 1982; McClelland, 1985).

The most effective managers do not seek power for personal gain. Rather, their power need is directed toward the organization for which they work and the achievement of organizational goals. As a result, they are successful in establishing and maintaining a good work climate, high morale, and high team spirit among their subordinates.

Managers who are motivated by the need for personal power, on the other hand, serve themselves rather than their organization. They are capable of creating loyalty and team spirit among their subordinates, but it is a loyalty directed toward themselves and not toward the organization. They are more effective managers than those who have no motivation for power, but they are not as effective as those whose power is oriented toward the organization.

Power plays an influential role in organizational leadership, both in leader-follower interactions and in the motivation of the leaders themselves.

Functions of Leaders

Let us now turn to a consideration of leadership functions, the activities and processes in which leaders engage. There are several views of the functions of leaders, determined by factors such as level of management and type of organization.

One way in which psychologists describe leadership functions is in terms of the two dimensions known as *consideration* and *initiating structure* (Fleishman & Harris, 1962). Considerable research has demonstrated that most management activities can be classified under one of these two headings.

The functions in the consideration dimension involve the awareness of, and sensitivity to, the personal feelings of subordinates. This has grown out of the human relations approach to management. In this approach, leaders must understand and accept subordinates as individuals, each of whom possesses a unique set of motivations, feelings, and needs. Leaders, if they are to be effective, must relate to each subordinate by being considerate of his or her personal characteristics. This places a great demand on the sympathy, warmth, and understanding of managers because they must, at the same time, maintain production levels and deal with the technical details of the plant's operation.

In sum, managers operating under this dimension display consideration for their subordinates, a characteristic capable of enhancing the quality of working life. Effective managers display four elements of consideration (Strauss, 1977): (1) creating a feeling of approval, (2) developing personal relations, (3) providing fair treatment, and (4) enforcing rules equitably.

Consideration is an obvious and important function of organizational leaders. Ideally, it enhances employee morale and job satisfaction and may also improve productivity.

There is a degree of similarity between the consideration function and some of the leadership styles or behaviors described by the leadership theories we discussed earlier. Consideration relates, for example, to the person-oriented leader proposed by the contingency theory, participative leadership in the path-goal theory, complete participation in the normative decision theory, leadership in the vertical dyadic linkage theory, and relationship behavior in the situational leadership theory.

The functions in the initiating-structure dimension include the tasks traditionally associated with a leadership role, that is, organizing, defining, and directing the work activities of subordinates. At times, this aspect of a manager's job may run counter to the demands of the consideration dimension. To get the job done (to initiate structure), managers must assign specific tasks to employees, direct the manner and speed at which the tasks are performed, and monitor the work to make sure it is being done properly.

These activities may call for some authoritarian behavior, and there may not always be time or opportunity for managers to consider subordinates' personal feelings about a task. A certain amount of work must be performed at a specified level of quality in a fixed period of time and the company's survival may depend on meeting these standards consistently. Managers are often forced to walk a thin line between the demands of consideration and initiating structure.

The leadership function of initiating structure is, in general, similar to the task-oriented leader described by the contingency theory, directive leadership in the path-goal theory, autocracy in the normative decision theory, supervision in the vertical dyadic linkage theory, and task behavior in the situational leadership theory.

How do managers balance the two often conflicting demands between consideration and initiating structure? As we noted, because of the impact of the human relations movement on organizational life, the manner in which growing numbers of leaders carry out their functions has changed. Successful managers must create an environment or work climate in which subordinates are able to satisfy their individual needs and attain personal goals in such a way as to contribute to the attainment of the organization's standards and goals.

Instead of issuing orders, modern managers must influence or persuade subordinates by exercising appropriate managerial skills. Some techniques by which this may be accomplished are the following (Miljus, 1970):

1. *Managers must determine realistic objectives.* In all aspects of a job—production levels, safety, maintenance schedules, turnover—managers must establish goals that are realistic in the light of the company's objectives, resources, funds, and equipment as well as the workers' capabilities and level of competence. Without short-range and long-range objectives for which to strive, there is an inevitable waste of time and energy. Also, realistic goals provide the reinforcement or feedback of accomplishing an objective; this is a rewarding experience for managers and subordinates.

2. *Managers must provide the necessary resources.* If goals are to be reached, managers must supply the proper tools, equipment, and trained manpower to make the attainment of the objectives possible. To expect subordinates to produce at a certain level without providing the physical means to do so is stressful and frustrating for all.

3. *Managers must make their expectations known.* Through formal and informal communications, managers must make known to subordinates precisely what is expected of them to satisfy organizational goals. Subordinates must be informed about policies and procedures that affect their work and about actual work techniques. It is unfair for managers to expect workers to proceed in the absence of clear guidelines and instructions.

4. *Managers must provide an adequate reward structure.* This is basic to any job, and to the needs of the employees. Rewards include salary, fringe benefits (such as company-paid insurance and retirement pension plans), good working conditions, and opportunities for promotion.

   Effective managers also provide less tangible rewards such as challenge and responsibility, praise for outstanding job performance, and intrinsically satisfying work. These rewards can satisfy individual needs and (assuming an adequate salary) bring about higher levels of motivation and production. Individuals vary greatly in their need for praise or challenge; effective managers know their subordinates well enough to be aware of their differential reward needs.

5. *Managers must delegate authority and invite participation.* To motivate and challenge subordinates and to train them to assume a greater responsibility, managers must delegate some of their functions. This can enhance subordinates' morale and ease some of the managers' burden so that they will be able to perform their job more efficiently.

   The human relations movement involves a trend toward democratic participation by all those connected with a particular work function. We discuss in Chapter 9 the benefits of allowing subordinates to participate in making decisions that were formerly the responsibility of the managers. For example, workers will more actively support changes in work procedures or working conditions if they have been allowed to have some say in the shaping of the new policy rather than having the final decision announced and imposed on them by management.

6. *Managers must remove barriers to effective performance.* Anyone or anything that may impede effective job performance should be removed so that the workers and the company may obtain their goals. It is the managers' responsibility to see that faulty equipment is replaced, slow delivery of materials speeded up, ineffective subordinates retrained, closed channels of communication opened, and negative attitudes overcome.

7. *Managers must periodically appraise their subordinates' performance and inform them of the results.* It is vital that employees know how they are performing their jobs. Managers must evaluate each subordinate and communicate the results in an understanding and positive manner so that employees will be motivated to improve their weaknesses and will know that their strengths are appreciated.

What leaders do on the job varies among organizations and from one part of the same organization to another part. However, virtually all leadership functions can be grouped in the two dimensions of consideration and initiating structure. The functions deal, as we saw, with people or with the goals and tasks of the organization. Ideally, effective managers are able to integrate these overall dimensions, and their ability to do so may be the most important leadership function of all.

What specific tasks do managers perform as they carry out the functions of consideration and initiating structure? I/O psychologists have studied this by observing managers at work and by questioning them about their tasks. The results of one such analysis are shown in Table 7-4 (Carroll & Gillen, 1987).

You can see that although much of a manager's time (41%) is spent interacting with other people, almost as much time is devoted to paperwork, and only a small amount of time is spent on thought and reflection. This may indicate that managers are kept quite busy tending to the demands of everyday activities and problems.

Another approach to the study of managerial behavior on the job involves the use of the Operant Supervisory Taxonomy and Index (OSTI), which

TABLE 7-4 Daily Work Activities of Managers

Work activity	Percentage of total work time
Conversing with others	41
Preparing and writing reports, letters, etc.	19
Reading and reviewing reports, letters, etc.	18
Minor clerical duties (filing, sorting, etc.)	5
Operating equipment	5
Engaging in personal activities	5
Thinking and reflecting	3
Walking and traveling	2
Inspecting products and procedures	1
Performing mathematical computations	1

Adapted from "Are the classical management functions useful in describing managerial work?" by S.J. Carroll & D.J. Gillen, 1987, *Academy of Management Review*, *12*, p. 41.

includes seven categories of leadership behavior that describe most daily management activities (Komaki, Zlotnick, & Jensen, 1986). These categories are the following.

1. *Performance consequences*: indicating and providing knowledge of performance to subordinates.
2. *Performance monitoring*: collecting information about the performance of subordinates.
3. *Performance antecedents*: providing instructions, goals, and expectations about the performance of subordinates.
4. *Own performance*: gathering and discussing information about one's own performance.
5. *Work related*: involving work, but not subordinate performance.
6. *Nonwork related*: activities having no bearing on work, such as talking about one's family or telling jokes.
7. *Solitary activity*: not involving social interaction.

One study used the OSTI to compare the behavior of effective and ineffective managers at a large medical insurance company (Komaki, 1986). No differences were found between the two groups of managers on six of the seven categories of leadership behavior. Effective and ineffective managers engaged in essentially the same daily activities. Where the two groups differed was in performance monitoring. Effective managers spent significantly more time collecting information about their subordinates' performance, especially by direct observation of the workers and by inspection of their output. Ineffective managers tended to rely on reports from subordinates or from other sources.

Much research focuses on the specific tasks and events that fill a manager's days, and it is coming to be recognized that some managerial tasks differ from what their superiors expect them to do or believe they are doing (Hales, 1987).

Effective managers balance the leadership functions described as "initiating structure" and "consideration." These managers create a work environment in which both organizational goals and employees' personal goals can be satisfied.

Characteristics of Leaders

We turn now to an investigation of the behaviors and characteristics of successful leaders. The trait approach to the study of leadership has proven generally unproductive because leadership characteristics vary greatly from one situation to another. However, within one situation, it does seem possible to identify characteristics that distinguish effective from ineffective leaders.

The characteristics required for successful leadership vary with the person's level in the organization. The president of a large automobile manufacturing plant performs different functions and needs different abilities than a supervisor on the assembly line. In general, the higher the leader on the corporate ladder, the fewer consideration functions and the more initiating-structure functions he or she performs. It follows that a high-level executive needs fewer human relations skills than a supervisor because the executive controls and interacts directly with fewer subordinates. A corporate vice president may directly manage only a half dozen department heads, whereas a first-line supervisor may have 50 or more employees.

It is necessary, therefore, to consider the level of leadership when dealing with the characteristics of successful leaders. We shall discuss behaviors and characteristics of first-line supervisors and, then, those of higher level managers and executives.

First-line Supervisors

One study compared successful and unsuccessful first-line supervisors for the Prudential Insurance Company and found the following differences (Sartain & Baker, 1978):

1. *Person centered.* Successful supervisors (defined as those whose work units were more productive) were much higher in consideration than were unsuccessful supervisors. Successful supervisors were much more concerned with the needs, hopes, goals, and problems of their employees. Less effective supervisors were more concerned with job-related matters—quotas, deadlines, and costs. Despite the greater concern of less effective supervisors for the initiating-structure function, their work units were less productive.
2. *Supportive.* Effective supervisors were much more supportive and helpful of subordinates than were less effective supervisors. Good supervisors were more willing to defend their employees against criticism from higher management.
3. *Loyal to both company and employees.* Poor supervisors gave their primary allegiance and loyalty to the company. Good supervisors shared their loyalty between their subordinates and the company.
4. *Democratic.* Effective supervisors held many more meetings with their employees in which they encouraged participation. Less effective supervisors were more authoritarian.
5. *Flexible.* By explaining the goals of a job and the guidelines for achieving them in a general or loosely structured way, the effective supervisors left their employees free to accomplish the goals in their own way. Poor supervisors dictated precisely how each job was to be handled and allowed no deviation or flexibility on the part of their subordinates.

Good supervisors rank high on the dimension of consideration of their subordinates. Although they stand no higher on initiating structure than do less effective supervisors, they are able to lead their subordinates to considerably higher job performance. These results confirm the importance of consideration at the first level of supervision. One's amount of technical ability in facilitating the work may be unable to compensate for poor interpersonal skills.

Another study compared effective and ineffective managers at two manufacturing plants: one that operated in an authoritarian manner and the other that functioned in a more participatory manner (Klein & Posey, 1986). Thus, the organizational climates in which the supervisors functioned were quite different, yet the data showed that the best supervisors exhibited the same characteristics, independent of the leadership style they might have been expected to show, based on the type of organization for which they worked.

Effective managers in both plants were found to be more competent, caring, and committed to their work and to their subordinates than ineffective managers. The effective managers emphasized quality in the work, provided clear directions, and gave timely and accurate feedback to their workers. They functioned more as coaches than directors, sharing with subordinates information about policies, procedures, and the reasons for their decisions.

Executives

At higher levels of the corporate hierarchy, executives engage in fewer consideration behaviors and more initiating-structure behaviors, in other words, executives are less people oriented and more work oriented. One study of the skills and characteristics displayed by middle-level to upper-level executives divided these skills into three categories: conceptual, human, and technical. Conceptual and technical skills are the ones most concerned with initiating structure. High-level executives needed these skills more than twice as much as did first-line supervisors. Some of the specific skills within each category are the following (Guglielmino, 1979):

1. *Conceptual skills*—making decisions, identifying opportunities, innovating for the good of the organization, understanding and monitoring the business environment, and structuring the organization.
2. *Human skills*—writing and speaking effectively, handling grievances and disturbances, leading and motivating others, and negotiating and controlling change.
3. *Technical skills*—understanding a balance sheet and budgeting, writing a computer program, preparing a cost-benefit analysis, and searching for information.

Of the four human skills, only handling grievances and leading others fit the dimension of consideration. Thus, as we noted, this aspect of leadership, so vital at the supervisory level, diminishes in importance at higher levels of management.

An investigation of the background characteristics of 425 highly successful executives in top jobs found that 98% of them had attended college and 89% had graduated (Ross & Unwalla, 1988). The factor of college attendance ranked higher with this group than with a similar study of executives conducted in 1952. At that time, 24% of the executives had never attended college, and 13% had not completed high school.

The proportion of successful male executives whose fathers had been executives or owners of large businesses, and thus in a position to help their sons' careers, declined slightly from the 1950s to the 1980s, from 31% to 28%. However, the number of successful executives who reported having friends who were also influential business connections increased sharply from 15% to nearly 40%.

A study of the characteristics of 165 effective and innovative managers in five corporations showed that they shared the following characteristics: These managers tended to be tolerant of change; to have clear future directions; to be extremely thorough, persistent, and persuasive; to be able to share rewards and recognition with their subordinates; and to exercise a highly democratic style of leadership (Kanter, 1982).

In an analysis of executives who once showed great potential but were later retired early or fired, it was found that the primary explanation was related to personality rather than to poor job performance. Specifically, those who failed were judged by their superiors to be insensitive to others, to exercise an abrasive and domineering leadership style, to be arrogant and aloof, and to be overly ambitious for the attainment of personal rather than corporate goals. Clearly, they were lacking in consideration behaviors (McCall & Lombardo, 1983).

Missing from these lists of executive characteristics is power, which, as we noted, seems to be an important drive in successful executives. Psychologist David McClelland, who has studied this issue for many years, has proposed a pattern of motives that he informally labels "empire building," but which is more formally known as the *leadership motive pattern* (LMP). Executives who possess a high LMP are thought to be effective high-level managers. The LMP consists of a high need for power, a lower need for affiliation with other people, and a great amount of activity inhibition or "self-control." Thus, effective managers have a greater need to influence people than to be liked by people (McClelland, 1975; 1985).

Long-term studies involving follow-ups of managers, at 8- and 16-year intervals after their LMPs were first determined, show that this particular personality pattern is highly predictive of success for managers in nontechnical jobs. However, these characteristics were not found in successful managers in more technical jobs that involved engineering. The managers' level of the need to achieve (to perform well in one's work) was also predictive of success in nontechnical managerial jobs (McClelland & Boyatzis, 1982).

This was confirmed in a large-scale study of 1,700 managers and blue-collar workers in which those at higher levels of management scored higher in both the need for achievement and the LMP than those lower in management. Managers, in general, scored higher on both variables than did blue-collar workers. About one third of the blue-collar sample scored low on the need for achievement and the LMP and one fourth scored high, whereas none of the managers scored low (Stahl, 1986).

Other research has shown that managers high in the LMP tend to gravitate toward occupations and jobs that are high in prestige and status. Of the three components of the leadership motive pattern—power, affiliation, and self-control—the need for power and the willingness to exert it emerges as vital for success as a manager, at least in nontechnical positions (Cornelius & Lane, 1984).

Research on the LMP reinforces the point we made earlier, that the traits or characteristics of leaders may vary with the situation. Persons high in the LMP are excellent managers in nontechnical work situations, not in technical situations.

Stability of Managerial Characteristics.   We have discussed a number of characteristics possessed by successful managers and have described how these characteristics differ as a function of the specific work situation. Are these traits stable over a manager's working life? Do they change with age or as the manager advances to a higher level within the organization? Do the potential leadership traits of the 22-year-old management trainee continue to define that person when he or she is a 55-year-old department head or corporate vice president?

The best way to answer these questions is to conduct a longitudinal study, to investigate the nature and behavior of the same people at different ages. I/O psychologists at AT&T have been doing this since 1956. Their Management Progress Study was designed to determine and analyze personal characteristics as managers progressed through their careers (Bray, 1982; Howard & Bray, 1988).

The primary means of studying the AT&T managers has been the assessment-center technique. In addition, each manager has been interviewed extensively. The managers' superiors have also been interviewed. The findings to date indicate that success in management is highly predictable and is based on seven general factors: administrative skills, leadership skills, advancement orientation, general mental ability, stability of performance, work motivation, and independence of others.

Six personality factors were also identified as being highly related to success as a manager: leadership motivation, ambition, impulsivity, affability, self-esteem, and optimism. "The most promising managers are those who want to lead and advance, who reject dependency on others, who are self-confident and optimistic, energetic, and work oriented. Thus, motives and traits are important ingredients of success in management" (Bray, 1982, p. 186).

How stable and enduring were these personality characteristics over a period of 20 years? Four of the six traits changed significantly during that time. Although leadership motivation increased, ambition decreased. This is not as contradictory as it might seem at first glance. The decline in ambition was related to a similar decline in one of the general factors, that of advancement orientation. The managers had lost interest in further promotions either because they had reached a satisfactory level or because they had accepted the fact that they were unlikely to receive additional promotions. However, they were still interested in taking charge and in achieving on the job, perhaps more so than 20 years earlier.

Two other personality characteristics that changed over the period of the study were affability, which declined, and impulsivity, which rose. The managers had become somewhat more cynical and selfish.

Self-esteem and optimism remained unchanged during the period of the research and were strongly related to job satisfaction and general happiness.

The Management Progress Study is expected to continue into the 1990s, following the manager-subjects to retirement. This research is a monumental, although all-too-rare, undertaking that has provided practical benefits for the organization while adding to our knowledge and understanding of the nature of people at work.

A New Breed of Manager.   Another situational variable in the world of work that affects leadership behavior relates to generational characteristics. Changing economic and social conditions can markedly affect the values, motives, and personality traits of the members of different generations. The generational change has been particularly abrupt and massive for the so-called baby-boom generation born in the early and middle 1950s.

When they entered the work force in the 1970s, they were dubbed the new breed of worker, an idea we shall examine in greater detail in Chapter 8. Unlike their parents' generation, the new workers were less motivated for success, less optimistic, and less inclined to obey orders and to heed authority. In contrast, they expressed a strong desire for challenging work and for the right to participate in decisions that would affect their work.

Many of these employees have now entered the ranks of middle management. Do their personal characteristics differ so clearly from those of the previous generation that we are dealing with a new breed of manager today? A second AT&T study, the Management Continuity Study, began to investigate the baby-boom generation that enrolled in management training programs in 1977, comparing them with the company's new managers of 20 years earlier (Howard & Bray, 1988; Howard & Wilson, 1982).

On measures of ability, no differences were found between the two generations, nor did they differ in terms of the need for achievement, that desire to do well and to accomplish something of significance. What surprised the researchers, however, was the sizable difference in motivation between the two groups.

Today's manager does not appear to possess the traditional motivation or behavior expected of managers, the characteristics expressed by managers of the previous generation. For example, the current group of managers evidenced no interest in personal advancement, in becoming upwardly mobile toward high-paying, high-status, and powerful positions. This lack of motivation to climb the corporate ladder was matched by a decline in their level of expectation. They did not believe the future had as much to offer them as the previous generation did. Only 45% of the 1970s managers thought that in 5 years they would have a challenging job that would give them the opportunity to learn and to accomplish something. Among the 1950s managers, 60% held such a belief.

Race and sex differences were noted with the 1970s managers, although a comparison could not be made with the 1950s group, which consisted solely of white male managers. Blacks and women in the 1970s sample scored much higher than white men in both motivation to advance and expectations for the future. The major motivation for blacks and women was higher pay, not the power and challenge that also come with top management positions.

The 1970s managers scored lower on measures of dominance than did the 1950s generation. This indicated less interest in the traditional leadership tasks of leading, directing, and influencing others. In addition, the new breed of manager exhibited less willingness to defer to and follow those in higher positions as well as less need for approval of their superiors. It would seem that today's younger managers do not really want to be leaders, but neither do they wish to be followers.

One personal characteristic on which the 1970s group scored significantly higher than the 1950s group involved the need to give and receive emotional support. This quality may help them in exercising the consideration function of leadership, but it is of little aid in initiating structure, a prime requisite for success and effectiveness in higher management.

Additional research involving more than two dozen managerial groups studied between the 1960s and 1980s confirms the AT&T findings about current managers. The data point to a sharp decline in managerial motivation and in the characteristics required for successful management. The greatest decreases have been in attitudes toward authority, identification with an organization, importance of work in one's life, competitiveness, assertiveness, and the willingness to engage in routine communications and decision making (Howard, 1986; Miner & Smith, 1982).

All of these items are important components of managerial jobs. The fact that they are not being found in the ranks of younger managers today suggests that there may soon be a shortage of managerial talent in American business, industry, and government. As managers of the previous generation retire, to be replaced by men and women who lack or have not expressed the motivations and personal characteristics necessary for executive success, the future competitiveness of American industry may be in jeopardy.

Organizational psychologists are finding some indication that the generation of recent college graduates just beginning their organizational careers may bring a return to more traditional managerial motivations and abilities. The downward trend in leadership qualities may have begun to stabilize. Although still low compared to generations prior to the baby boom, they are no longer declining (Bartol, Anderson, & Schneier, 1980). If the 1980s group does possess effective managerial motives and traits, the impact on the middle-management ranks of industry will be felt in the 1990s.

Pressures and Problems of Leadership

Just as leader characteristics vary with the level of leadership, so do the pressures and problems. We deal with two levels of organizational leadership: the first-line supervisor and the executive. Each faces unique stresses and conflicts.

First-line Supervisors

In most organizations, a distinction is made between first-line supervisors (foremen) and higher level managers. In terms of responsibilities, obligations, and background, there are many differences between these two levels. In some ways, supervisors have more difficult and demanding jobs, yet, paradoxically, they often receive less formal training in how to manage others. Indeed, in some cases, they receive no training at all, nor are they selected as carefully as those entering higher management positions. Often, the best worker is chosen to be a supervisor, with little or no attention to his or her leadership abilities.

A survey of 100 American corporations found that almost 88% had no formal procedure for selecting first-line supervisors (Rendero, 1980). Those companies with specific selection procedures relied on the use of interviews and a review of the candidate's performance appraisals. They used none of the more sophisticated selection techniques we discussed.

Almost all of the companies indicated that they provided some form of on-the-job training for new supervisors. Much of that training, however, involved simply watching another supervisor on the job. Only about half of the companies provided any more structured training, a finding confirmed in several surveys (Levine, 1982).

In some cases, supervisors have college degrees. Many company training programs place new graduates in first-line supervisory positions in one or more departments for several months to several years, the job-rotation training technique described in Chapter 6. The purpose is to familiarize them with various aspects of production while providing leadership experience. For college graduates, the job of supervisor is a stepping-stone to higher levels of executive responsibility.

As many as three fourths of all first-line supervisors, however, are promoted from the ranks (Bittel & Ramsey, 1983). The level of supervisor may be their ultimate goal. At a time when a college education is considered increasingly necessary for a management position, the first-line supervisory position is about as high in management as less well-educated persons may be allowed to rise. This is an unfortunate and unwise use of talent. Many people who lack college degrees nevertheless possess the intelligence and ability to be trained for higher levels of responsibility.

Supervisors promoted from the ranks are often placed in a difficult position because of conflicting demands and loyalties. Before their promotion, they were accepted as co-workers by those who shared not only the job but also their attitudes and values as well. They may have had many friends among their co-workers, people with whom they socialized off the job. They had an identity as a member of a particular group and a sense of belonging that provided a measure of emotional security.

What happens when they suddenly become supervisors? They can no longer enjoy the same relationship with former co-workers and friends—they are no longer one of them. Even if they should try to remain one of the gang, the others will no longer react to them in the same way because they are now the boss. The emotional security from group affiliation and identification is lost.

New supervisors become part of a new group, that of management, and begin working with people whose levels of education, background, values, and lifestyles are usually vastly different. New supervisors can try to emulate them, and many succeed, but it is difficult. They may have to learn new modes of dress, behavior, or conversation.

Despite their promotion, first-line supervisors do not have the prestige or status symbols of executives. Supervisors do not get fancy offices, secretaries, reserved parking places, or private dining rooms. Also, supervisors are often paid only a little more money than those they supervise. Workers receiving overtime pay, which supervisors rarely get, can earn more than their supervisors. Thus, in economic, social, and status terms, first-line supervisors are closer to their subordinates than to higher management.

New first-line supervisors are, thus, in an unenviable position. They may not be accepted by either world, workers or management. Some workers have been known to reject promotions to this level. In a survey of more than 7,000 supervisors, only 40% said they felt themselves to be part of management. Also, 29% of the supervisors who had been promoted from the ranks expressed unhappiness at having accepted the promotion (Bittel & Ramsey, 1982).

Supervisors must also confront the demands of the new job. Regardless of the competence and sophistication of a company's executives, the efficiency of the plant's organization, or the quality of the management's decisions, the success or failure of any program frequently rests on the shoulders of the first-line supervisor.

Like sergeants in the army, supervisors are responsible for getting things done, for example, implementing the department head's decision on monthly production quotas. They are the point of contact between management and workers, trying delicately to maintain their own balance between the often conflicting needs of both sides.

Not only do they present management's needs and decisions to the workers but they must also represent the workers to management if they expect to establish or retain the loyalty and cooperation of the workers. They must serve not only as a buffer between management and workers but also as a channel of communication.

Overall, of course, first-line supervisors must be responsive to the demands of their superiors if they expect to keep their jobs. One investigation of 160 first-line supervisors in a large pharmaceutical plant showed that pressure from higher management to exercise strict supervision resulted in harsh and punitive behaviors toward subordinates (Hammer & Turk, 1987). First-line supervisors usually are not in a position to use their own discretion in managing their workers.

What specific tasks are they expected to perform? They are responsible for introducing new employees to their jobs and teaching them company policies, procedures, and regulations. They may have to train or monitor the training of new workers and the retraining of current workers.

First-line supervisors must ensure that safety procedures are being followed properly and instruct workers on new safety methods and devices, be alert for unsafe practices, and explain to superiors the reasons for any accidents that may occur.

As representatives of the workers to higher management, supervisors must handle any grievance on the part of their subordinates. How diplomatically and effectively they deal with complaints can mean the difference between satisfied workers and a wildcat strike or work slowdown. If a grievance is not resolved in a manner that is satisfactory to the workers, they will take it to the union and it then becomes more serious in terms of morale and production.

A first-line supervisor at an automobile plant in Tennessee meets with subordinates before work to discuss problems and hear grievances.

First-line supervisors also act as purveyors of rewards and punishments. For good work to continue, supervisors must provide incentives in the form of verbal praise to the workers, feedback through performance evaluation reports, and salary increases. To keep their best workers, they must convince their superiors to raise their pay. They must also act as disciplinarians in cases of sloppy work, tardiness, absenteeism, or drinking on the job. In unionized plants, they must exercise a somewhat gentle and totally impartial discipline because the union shop steward is constantly watchful for the welfare of union members.

First-line supervisors must exercise great care in disciplining or firing subordinates (Klotchman & Neider, 1983). Fair employment legislation was designed to protect minorities in firing as well as hiring decisions, and supervisors must be alert to any possible violations of EEOC regulations.

The more mundane and routine activities include scheduling work, arranging for equipment maintenance, answering memos from superiors, and attending meetings. Thus, first-line supervisors must exercise both the consideration and the initiating-structure functions.

When workers become supervisors, they assume a heavy responsibility that they are expected to carry out without the status and authority of higher levels of management.

The job of the first-line supervisor is becoming more difficult, demanding, and stressful as a result of three major changes in the nature of work: participative management, self-managing work groups, and computer-automated offices and factories (Kerr, Hill, & Broedling, 1986).

In participative management, supervisors lose much of their power and autonomy as they are forced to share leadership and decision-making powers with their subordinates.

Self-managing work groups, which we will discuss in Chapter 9, also represent a threat to supervisory power and autonomy. Instead of sharing leadership functions with subordinates, first-line supervisors are called upon virtually to abandon their traditional responsibilities, remaining available as resource persons, not as leaders. Initial reports on self-managing work groups show that they can be effective, but that supervisors receive the blame when things go wrong, and no praise or recognition when things go well. In the latter case, top management is likely to attribute the favorable results to the groups themselves and not to the first-line supervisors.

The introduction of computer technology in the workplace has had an extensive impact on the sort of work managed by the first-line supervisor. Increasingly, supervisors are directly responsible for equipment they may not understand, and that takes the control and monitoring of the quantity and quality of production out of their jurisdiction. Computers make it possible for higher management to obtain information about individual employees, production levels, and other aspects of the office routine or manufacturing process without consulting the first-line supervisor.

Computers, self-managing work groups, and participative management are expected to continue to influence the workplaces of the 1990s, perhaps to the point of redefining the job of the first-line supervisor and his or her role in the modern organization.

Executives

The problems faced by executives vary as a function of their level in the corporate hierarchy. A department or section head faces different strains and stresses than the head of the company. We can distinguish two levels of executive: middle level and top level.

Middle-level managers, despite comfortable salaries and a host of fringe benefits, often face a great deal of discontent in their lives. One of the most frequent complaints voiced by middle managers is their lack of influence in the formulation of company policy, policy that they are expected to implement without question. Middle managers also complain about not having sufficient authority or resources to carry out company policy. They must constantly fight for recognition from their superiors and compete for support for their ideas and projects. As a result, there is often a great deal of frustration and tension among middle managers as they vie for position in their race for the few available slots in the hierarchy above them.

Another long-standing source of discontent is the almost universal feeling of obsolescence that characterizes middle managers when they reach their late 30s and early 40s. Most employees of that age have reached their limit, the plateau from which they will rise no further in the corporate hierarchy. The realization that there will be no more promotions is part of the general midlife crisis that affects most people; it is a time when each person takes stock of his or her life. This painful period of self-examination is especially difficult for middle-level managers. They feel threatened by younger subordinates, new managerial and cultural values, and new organizational goals (such as worker involvement in decision making). As a result, their productivity, creativity, drive, and aggressiveness often wither and die, and they may retire on the job, making no further contribution to the organization.

A relatively recent source of discontent for middle managers is the trend toward democratization of organizations. Although middle managers remain without influence in decisions affecting their own jobs, they see that assembly-line workers, for example, can now participate in such decisions and design their own jobs, new rights that are denied the middle managers. Participatory democracy results in drastic changes in the ways that managers can direct their subordinates. When this occurs, middle managers must share leadership with subordinates, which results in a loss of their authority, status, and power.

Democratization in some organizations has also resulted in the discarding of traditional management perquisites such as reserved parking spaces, separate dining rooms, and private offices. The more democratic an organization becomes, the fewer visible signs of class distinction are allowed. Some companies have eliminated private offices for all but top management, insisting that middle-level managers work side by side with their subordinates. When managers must compete with their subordinates for parking spaces, eat in the employee cafeteria instead of the executive dining room, and give up their carpeted offices for a desk on the factory or office floor, it is understandable that they feel that their position of superiority is threatened.

In the 1980s, many middle managers were faced with another threat, not just to their authority, autonomy, and power, but to their jobs themselves. As a result of domestic and foreign competition in the marketplace, and the large number of mergers, acquisitions, and buyouts of hundreds of companies, many thousands of middle-level managers found that their positions had been eliminated. Organizations tried to become leaner in their administrative structures, and they did so by slashing at the middle of the organization chart. A survey of 100 personnel directors found that more than half of their companies had fewer layers of management today than in the 1970s (Levine, 1986b).

Some companies, recognizing the increasing pressure on their middle managers, are attempting to provide them with new opportunities for job and personal growth. Some examples are shown in Table 7-5.

Frustration has led some middle managers to quit their jobs and take management positions with other organizations, but other managers have left corporate management altogether. An investigation carried out at a large electronics company compared 140 former managers who had accepted

---

TABLE 7-5 Opportunities for Job and Personal Growth of Middle Managers

Opportunities	*Percentage of companies offering opportunity*
Encouraging managers to gain new knowledge through attending seminars and conferences	76
Expanding managers' scope of responsibility	73
Including managers in strategic planning	66
Assigning managers to special projects	66
Changing the breadth, depth, and type of managers' assignments	64
Helping managers set and attain ambitious professional goals for their staff	61
Exposing managers to the newest techniques and technology in their fields, related fields, or potential areas of responsibility	56
Encouraging managers to participate in public and community affairs	53
Varying managers' assignments	49
Offering managers the opportunity to serve with and lead inter- and intraorganizational committees and task forces	41
Encouraging managers to discuss their frustrations with supervisors or others in the organization	37
Helping managers practice time- and stress-management techniques	37
Making mobility assignments among staff and line functions and units	34
Giving managers speaking and writing assignments	25
Having a team approach to problem solving	2

From "The squeeze on middle management" by H. Z. Levine, 1986, *Personnel, 63*(1), p. 63.

---

nonmanagerial jobs with 143 people who were still managers (Campion & Mitchell, 1986). The psychologists found no differences between the two groups in age, sex, or race, or in their recent performance appraisals. The performance appraisals indicated that the former managers who quit management altogether did not do so because of poor job performance but for other reasons: (1) a lack of sufficient satisfaction and motivation with their management job, (2) difficult adjustment and socialization problems on the job, (3) a lack of fulfillment of their expectations, and (4) a feeling that they were under stress. Some top executives have taken early retirement from their jobs because they can no longer cope with the stress.

A frequent source of stress facing managers (particularly high-level managers and top executives) is the intense commitment of energy and time to the organization. It is not uncommon for executives to work 50 to 60 hours a week. Most of this time is spent in the office, but many executives bring work home with them; home becomes not a haven from work but just another place to work. Many evenings are occupied with work at home or at the office and executives often visit the plant on weekends. With the advent of portable electronic equipment—car telephones, personal computers, portable fax machines—executives now work while traveling to and from business appointments. It is increasingly difficult for them to escape contact with the office.

In addition, companies expect their executives to involve themselves actively in the community, for example, in civic organizations or charity drives. Despite the long working hours, it is not the time that executives devote to the company that is the real problem. Rather, it is the sheer physical exhaustion of such a schedule and the limited attention they can devote to their families.

Children who grow up seeing too little of a parent are a common consequence of life in the executive suite. Also, executives often feel guilty over this neglect and wish they had more time for their families. Their energy and commitment are directed almost exclusively to the job, and relegating their family to a secondary status causes them great concern. Some organizations attempt to deal with this problem by sending executives and their spouses to counseling seminars.

The potential rewards for an executive position—power, money, status, challenge, and fulfillment—are great, but so are the stresses. There is a price to be paid for success, but so is there for failure.

A word should be said about the positive aspects of life at the top of the corporate hierarchy. Although middle managers are not a particularly happy group, upper-level executives seem to be more content with their work. Surveys have shown that 66% of high-level executives would continue with their jobs even if they suddenly found themselves financially independent and no longer needed their executive salary. Their work provides more than financial satisfaction.

This conclusion is supported by studies of executive job-changing behavior. The major reasons for such changes are the desire for greater responsibility and the need for more potential for promotion. Few executives change jobs for more money (Zippo, 1982).

There are problems and pressures for many people at all levels of management, but it should be remembered that many nonmanagerial jobs are also stressful. We will deal with this topic in Chapter 13.

Women in Management

One result of fair employment legislation and practices has been a noteworthy increase in the number of women in management positions. From 1979 to 1986, the number of women in management positions rose from 22% to nearly 40% (Powell, 1987; 1988). Most women still hold jobs in the beginning to middle-management level. Fewer than 2% are found in top management positions. However, the percentage of companies with at least one woman on their board of directors has increased from 10% in the 1970s to more than 40% in the 1980s (Kirk & Maddox, 1988). Although affirmative action programs have greatly increased the number of women in management, some psychological costs have been reported. Women who believe that they were hired solely because of their gender rather than their qualifications or abilities tend to be less satisfied with their job and less committed to the organization than women who do not believe they were hired solely because they are women (Chacko, 1982).

The increase in the number of women in management positions is impressive, but there is ample evidence that business-oriented women are still at a disadvantage. Women graduates with MBA degrees are paid higher starting salaries than men with the same degrees, but men outdistance women in salary after only a few years of experience. Many women managers believe they are not getting the opportunities for promotion they feel they deserve.

Also, many women are restricted to management positions in clearly defined areas of responsibility, notably those dealing with personnel, public relations, consumer affairs, and social responsibility. These women managers are confined to velvet ghettos in the corporate world, limited to work that calls more for social sensitivity and interpersonal relations skills than for general leadership abilities. These jobs are usually of a *staff* rather than a *line* status such as heading a production department.

A common sex stereotype is being applied in this case, discriminating against women managers by keeping them in "women's" work, that is, jobs requiring so-called "feminine" abilities such as empathy and sensitivity. The reverse side of this sex stereotype is that "masculine" characteristics are better suited to line functions such as production and sales. The real power is to be found in line positions, and these are the traditional stepping-stones to top management jobs.

Sex stereotypes hold that men are tougher, more aggressive, forceful, self-reliant, ambitious, and less emotional than women, characteristics that many people believe are necessary for the difficult job of being a corporate leader. Many top executives, most of whom are men, do not think women are tough enough to function effectively as line managers.

When women managers are successful on the job, their superiors (usually men) are likely to attribute that success to luck or to other external factors, and not to personal ability. When men succeed, it is typically attributed to their own ability.

Appearance may work to a woman's disadvantage in the eyes of higher level male executives. When choosing between men and women managers for promotion, equally qualified women were judged less suitable when they were perceived to be attractive. Physically attractive men, on the other hand, were judged to be more suitable. Thus, the same physical attribute—attractiveness—had different values when applied to women and to men (Devanna, 1987).

Women are also judged differently on behavior. Research comparing men and women managers showed that when women displayed the same level of assertiveness as men, they were judged as being too pushy (Bozzi, 1987). It is interesting to note that these judgments were made by other women, not by men. The men judges seemed less bothered by the demonstrated assertiveness.

Other research shows that men managers expect women managers to be assertive and aggressive, but only up to a point. Men did not expect women to "forfeit all traces of femininity because that would make them too alien" (Morrison, White, & Van Velsor, 1987, p. 20). That study also found four other contradictory sets of expectations held by men toward women in management. The men surveyed expected women managers to take risks but always be outstanding; be tough but not macho; be ambitious but not to expect equal treatment; and take responsibility but follow the advice of others. Thus, research shows that women managers are expected to perform better than men managers, but they should not expect better, or even equal, treatment.

Do women managers actually behave differently from men managers on the job? The evidence shows a few differences.

One study compared 2,000 men and women managers and found no important differences between them in the ways in which they performed their jobs. Out of 43 specific comparisons made, only two differences appeared. Women managers displayed greater motivation for achievement than men, and men were more candid in dealing with their co-workers than were women (Donnell & Hall, 1980).

On tests of intelligence, personality, and problem-solving abilities, no significant differences were found between men and women managers (Morrison, White, & Van Velsor, 1987). Nor did they differ on assessment-center exercises in their ability to lead, influence, and motivate subordinates. Managers of both sexes were found to exhibit equal amounts of the leadership functions of consideration and initiating structure, and to attain equal performance appraisal ratings. In other ratings of leadership effectiveness, men were rated as being more effective, but only in laboratory settings. There were no differences reported between men and women managers in studies of effectiveness conducted in field settings (Dobbins & Platz, 1986; Drazin & Auster, 1987).

Other research has reported results showing significantly less assertiveness on the part of women managers, along with a higher drive to succeed (Ottaway & Bhatnagar, 1988; Rizzo & Mendez, 1988). A survey of 100 men and women managers in a variety of industries showed that women were rated high in three areas in which they are traditionally held to be inferior to men: decision making, controlling emotions, and being able to take criticism. The men managers reported that, in their experience, women managers controlled their emotions better than men. These results suggest that women in management may be expending additional effort to dispel "feminine" stereotypes. The survey clearly indicates that sex has no effect on ability and performance in management positions.

The men participating in the survey also thought that women in management positions represented a positive step for the organization as a whole. Women were not so steeped in traditional management approaches and values, and they brought new insights and viewpoints to management problems.

Additional studies of women managers show that they are, in general, happy with their jobs. Their level of job satisfaction is much higher than that of women in nonmanagerial positions. This high level of job satisfaction has not been diminished by the fact that most women managers feel they have been subjected to discrimination at some point in their careers and the belief that they need to work much harder than men colleagues to achieve the same level of success. Indeed, women managers may be more career oriented than men, and many are able to make a more intense commitment to their careers (Rice, 1984). The Management Continuity Study at AT&T found that women managers were higher than men managers on positiveness, affability, poise, flexibility, and self-confidence (Howard & Bray, 1988).

The research discussed thus far was conducted on women who currently hold managerial positions. Studies have also investigated the characteristics of women managers in training, those majoring in business administration at the undergraduate and graduate levels. There has been a great increase in the number of women studying for academic degrees in business. The number earning MBA degrees increased a staggering 344% over the 10-year period from 1976 to 1986. The increase for men during this time was 25% (Raynolds, 1987).

Women business students were found to score significantly higher on career commitment but significantly lower on motivation to manage than men business students (Bartol & Martin, 1987; Gutek, 1988). The attitudes and concerns of women business students appear to vary with age. One comparison of 260 women students, ages 18 to over 34, found that those over 34 expressed less interest in a management career and more reservations about their own suitability for such a career than did women students younger than 34 (Russell & Rush, 1987).

Women business students ages 22 to 34 were more concerned about the possibility of meeting resistance from subordinates in their future jobs than were either the older or younger students. The youngest group (ages 18–22) was most concerned about reconciling the conflicts between career and family, an issue also of importance to the younger women managers in the AT&T Management Continuity Study (Howard & Bray, 1988). This group was also the most interested in the availability of day-care services and counseling.

In countries other than the United States, the situation for women managers is different. In Britain, only 11% of managers at all levels are women, compared to almost 40% in the United States. Women managers in Britain usually have to be more highly qualified than men, and they encounter considerable prejudice and discrimination. Further, most women managers in Britain are limited to so-called feminine businesses such as retailing. Despite these obstacles, growing numbers of younger women are preparing for management careers. More than 40% of the business school students in British universities are women, compared to only 10% in 1973 (Davidson & Cooper, 1987).

In Japan, one of the most productive industrialized nations, opportunities for women in management are restricted, despite an equal opportunity law that became effective in 1986. (The law provides no penalties for violations such as discriminating against women in employment.) Although women constitute 40% of Japan's work force, they are relegated to lower level nonmanagerial jobs (Carney & O'Kelly, 1987).

The lack of opportunity for women in management holds true for most Asian countries. Paradoxically, American women managers assigned to the Far East by their American companies report that they are generally well received by male executives in the host countries. One survey of American women managers working in Asia found that 97% of them thought that their overseas assignments had been successful (N. J. Adler, 1987). Apparently, the Asian men managers perceived the American women managers more as foreigners than as women, and behaved accordingly.

The problems of women managers are many, but in the United States at least, more women are being accepted as competent executives.

Blacks in Management

Not so many years ago, black employees were excluded from executive positions because of stereotyping and prejudice. Today blacks have access to management positions in increasing numbers. Like women in management, however, the current generation of black managers faces unique problems, pressures, and challenges (Henderson, 1986).

Blacks frequently have to work harder than their white colleagues to prove themselves, and their performance may be evaluated more strictly. Many blacks find that they must adapt and conform to a different culture and value system to achieve success. On the job, they may find that white employees resent their presence and believe that they were hired and promoted with fewer qualifications just so the organization could meet equal employment opportunity requirements. Also, racist attitudes expressed more directly can make everyday dealings with superiors, colleagues, and subordinates difficult.

A survey of 107 black managers with MBA degrees from leading universities revealed some disturbing perceptions about their working climates (Jones, 1986). For example, 98% of the black managers believed that American businesses did not offer equal opportunities for black managers. Further, 90% thought they were treated unfairly in performance appraisals compared to white managers at the same level, and 98% of the black managers felt that subtle racial prejudice pervaded their company. The black managers were asked to check a list of words and phrases that best described the organizational climate for black managers. The results are shown in Table 7-6.

American corporations need to do more to enable blacks to see that they are truly being offered the opportunity to rise as high in the business world as their abilities warrant.

Results of the AT&T Management Continuity Study demonstrated that black managers scored lower than white managers on such traits and characteristics as positiveness, impulsivity, poise, and flexibility. Black managers scored higher than white managers on affability. As noted, blacks also scored higher on motivation for advancement (Howard & Bray, 1988).

Conflict may arise when a black manager is promoted over equally qualified white managers. The common reaction of those passed over for the promotion is that the black person got the job only on the basis of race. This attitude can lead to a great deal of animosity.

Black managers not only have problems with white subordinates but also with

TABLE 7-6 Organizational Climate for Black Managers

Description	Percentage agreeing
Indifferent	59
Patronizing	41
Reluctant to accept blacks	40
Encouraging	24
Psychologically unhealthy	21
Unfulfilling	20
Whites are resentful	20
Supportive	11
Open in its communication	10
Negative	7
Unwholesome	7
Trusting of blacks	4

From "Black managers: The dream deferred" by E. W. Jones, Jr., 1986, *Harvard Business Review, 64*(3), p. 86.

other minorities on the job such as Hispanics or Asian Americans. These groups, too, may believe that blacks receive preferential treatment and may openly express their prejudices. The black manager must be sensitive to cultural differences when dealing with other minorities and must be careful to avoid personal prejudice, particularly when conducting performance appraisals of subordinates.

All minority employees, including blacks, may expect a black manager to be more lenient than a white manager. Black managers have come under pressure from black and other subordinates to protect them or give them special consideration on the job such as excusing lateness or poor performance. Managers of any race would jeopardize their jobs if they showed such favoritism, but not showing it may create animosity among a black manager's minority-group subordinates, which, in turn, can affect the performance of the work unit.

Studies show that black managerial candidates expect more than white managerial candidates do from their jobs and that they have a higher motivation to manage. Black management trainees and candidates are more upwardly mobile than whites, have a greater preference for working independently, and show a stronger need for recognition. Blacks also evidence a great preference for clear-cut rules and procedures and are more concerned with long-term career objectives (Brenner & Tomkiewicz, 1982).

Summary

Because of the importance of leadership in organizational life, it has long been the subject of extensive study by psychologists. How psychologists view leadership and how leadership functions are carried out are based on assumptions about human nature that have changed over the last several decades.

An early view of leadership was based on **scientific management**, which was concerned solely with production. Workers were believed to be mindless adjuncts to their machines. This idea was replaced in the 1920s and 1930s by the **human relations** approach, which is concerned with satisfying workers' personal needs and enhancing their growth and with maintaining production.

McGregor's **Theory X** and **Theory Y** give formal expression to these two extreme views of leadership. Theory X holds that people dislike work and need strong, directive, and punitive leadership. Theory Y takes a more flattering view of human nature. It holds that people are creative, industrious, personally responsible, and function best under leaders who allow them to participate in decisions that affect their work.

There have been several approaches to the study of leadership. The **trait approach** sought traits and characteristics that distinguish leaders from followers. When it became apparent that universal leadership traits did not appear to exist, attention turned to the **situational approach**. This focused on the nature of followers and their interactions with leaders. The **behavioral approach** investigated what leaders do rather than what they are like.

Six leadership theories were discussed. **Contingency theory** argues that a leader's effectiveness is determined by the interaction between his or her personal characteristics and aspects of the situation. **Cognitive resource utilization theory** focuses on leaders' cognitive resources—intelligence, technical competence, and job-related knowledge. In **path-goal theory**, the emphasis is on the behaviors leaders should exercise to allow subordinates to achieve their goals. **Normative decision theory** deals with the extent to which leaders allow subordinates to participate in making decisions. **Vertical dyadic linkage theory** is concerned with ways in which leaders behave toward subordinates. **Situational leadership theory** is concerned with the task-oriented or relationship-oriented behaviors of leaders.

Another way of studying leadership is to investigate leadership styles such as **appointed** versus **elected leadership** and **authoritarian** versus **democratic leadership**. They differ essentially in the degree of participation they allow subordinates to have in the leadership process.

Leaders display five kinds of **power**. These differ in terms of their base of derivation: (1) reward power, (2) coercive power, (3) legitimate power, (4) referent power, and (5) expert power. Power has been identified as an important need of leaders.

Much research has been undertaken to identify the functions of leaders, all of which can be subsumed under two general categories: **consideration** and **initiating structure**. Consideration functions are concerned with the personal feelings of subordinates and include four critical elements: creating a feeling of approval, developing personal relations, providing fair treatment, and enforcing rules equitably. Initiating-structure functions are concerned with how the work of the organization can best be accomplished. Several lists of specific duties are presented—everyday activities by which leaders carry out their consideration and initiating-structure functions.

The **characteristics of leaders** vary with the level of leadership in the organization. In general, the higher the level of leadership, the fewer consideration functions and the more initiating-structure functions are displayed. Good **first-line supervisors** are person centered, supportive, loyal to the company and the employees, and exercise a democratic and loose style of supervision. Effective **executives** need decision-making and technical skills more than human relations skills.

A longitudinal study of the stability of managerial characteristics found that leadership motivation increased over 20 years while ambition decreased. Characteristics such as impulsivity, affability, self-esteem, and optimism remained stable over time. Studies of younger managers (members of the baby-boom generation) show that they have less interest in personal advancement and upward mobility than older managers. They also score lower on measures of dominance.

Problems of leadership also vary as a function of level. **First-line supervisors** are often poorly trained for the job and are caught between the demands of superiors and subordinates. Fair employment legislation has complicated supervisory jobs, and their work has been made more stressful as a result of participative management, **self-managing work groups**, and computers.

Middle-level managers often find themselves losing authority and status as a result of the democratization of organizational life and becoming obsolete at midcareer. **High-level executives** face the problem of extremely long working hours, yet they seem to derive greater satisfaction from their jobs than persons at other levels of leadership.

Women managers are often restricted to staff positions because of sexist stereotypes about their abilities. They have been found to perform at least as well as men but must work harder to prove themselves. Women business students score higher on career commitment but lower on motivation to manage than men business students. **Black managers** also perform well but face similar problems of prejudice and stereotypes and often have to work harder to prove themselves. Whites often believe that blacks are given preferential treatment. Black managers may have problems with black and other minority subordinates and sometimes experience guilt about their present success.

Key Terms

appointed leadership
authoritarian
  leadership
bureaucracy
cognitive resource
  utilization theory of
  leadership
consideration functions
  of leadership
contingency theory of
  leadership
democratic leadership
elected leadership

first-line supervisors
headship
human relations
  management
initiating structure
  functions of
  leadership
labor/management
  relations
line jobs
normative decision
  theory of leadership

path-goal theory of
  leadership
power need
scientific management
self-managing work
  groups
situational leadership
  theory
staff jobs
theory X/theory Y
vertical dyadic
  linkage theory of
  leadership

CASE STUDIES

The Use of Power by Leaders

The leadership behaviors of 125 managers in a European bank were investigated by means of the Influence Analysis Questionnaire (IAQ), which was completed by the managers' subordinates and superiors. The IAQ measures relevant aspects of a leader's influence on others, and the kinds of power on which that influence is based. The questionnaire covered both crisis and noncrisis situations. The types of influence and power assessed included sanction power, formal power, referent power, expert power, reciprocal open consultation (in which both leader and subordinate are willing to be persuaded by the other's argument), expertise (a quality that may be possessed by either the leader or the subordinate), upward influence, and outward influence (in which a person's influence may extend beyond his or her work unit).

The results showed that in noncrisis situations, leaders were judged by their subordinates to exhibit reciprocal open consultation much more frequently than they did in crisis situations. In crisis situations, formal power, sanction power, and expert power were displayed more frequently. Managers judged by their superiors to be more effective were seen to be using more formal power in crisis situations than in noncrisis situations. For managers judged by their superiors to be less effective, no differences were found in the kind of power they displayed in the two types of situations.

QUESTIONS

1. Discuss the potential problems in using a questionnaire to measure the kind of power a leader exerts.
2. Describe the different kinds of power found among corporate leaders.
3. How do managers who are high in the need for power differ from those who are low in the need for power?
4. What do you think the results of this research would be if the leaders studied were U.S. Army officers instead of bank managers?

Reference: M. Mulder, R. D. de Jong, L. Koppelaar, & J. Verhage. (1986). Power, situation, and leaders' effectiveness: An organizational field study. *Journal of Applied Psychology, 71,* 566–570.

Leadership in Traditional and Participatory Situations

First-line supervisors in two industrial plants were interviewed and their behavior was observed during regular work shifts. One plant operated in a traditional, hierarchical, bureaucratic manner. The other functioned as a participatory democracy. The supervisors studied were classified as either "outstanding" or "average" on the basis of their superiors' evaluations of job performance. The purpose of the investigation was to determine the differences in behavior of the outstanding and the average supervisors working in situations

that required traditional and participatory managerial styles.

The interviews and observations of the outstanding supervisors found no differences in their behavior. In both traditional and participatory situations, these supervisors displayed similar characteristics and behaviors. The supervisors who were outstanding in one type of plant would presumably be outstanding in the other type.

Supervisors of average ability in both leadership situations also showed similar characteristics, abilities that rendered them less effective. According to this research, then, the traditional and participatory leadership situations in these two plants did not require leaders to exhibit different characteristics.

QUESTIONS

1. This investigation was based on interviews and observations. What weakness in these two methods might have influenced the results?

2. How would you have designed an experiment to study these supervisors?
3. What do the results of this research suggest about the situational and the trait approaches to the study of leadership?
4. What are some of the problems first-line supervisors experience on the job?

Reference: J. A. Klein & P. A. Posey. (1986). Good supervisors are good supervisors—anywhere. *Harvard Business Review, 64*(6), 125–128.

Additional Reading

House, R. J., & Singh, J. V. (1987). Organizational behavior: Some new directions for I/O psychology. *Annual Review of Psychology, 38,* 669–718. Reviews research and theory on several management topics including leadership behaviors, decision making, the needs for achievement and for power, and health concerns of executives. Discusses these issues within the context of the total organization.

Howard, A., & Bray, D. W. (1988). *Managerial Lives in Transition: Advancing Age and Changing Times*. New York: Guilford Press. An account of 30 years of longitudinal research at AT&T on personal and work-related characteristics of managers.

Jones, E. W., Jr. (1986). Black managers: The dream deferred. *Harvard Business Review, 64*(3), 84–93. Assesses the lack of progress of black managers in reaching senior executive positions in U.S. corporations.

Luthans, F., Hodgetts, R. M., & Rosenkrantz, S. A. (1988). *Real Managers*. Cambridge, MA: Ballinger. An account of what 44 managers actually do on the job; managers who advanced rapidly in the corporate hierarchy were designated as "successful" and managers who promoted high job performance and job satisfaction among their employees were designated as "effective."

Morrison, A., White, R. P., & Van Velsor, E. (1987). *Breaking the Glass Ceiling: Can Women Reach the Top of America's Largest Corporations?* Reading, MA: Addison-Wesley. Discusses obstacles facing women trying to advance their careers and attain high-level corporate positions. Identifies personal and job performance factors involved in success and failure.

Chapter 8

Motivation, Job Satisfaction, and Job Involvement

Introduction

One of the most pressing problems facing organizations today is how to motivate employees to work more productively and to increase their feelings of satisfaction, involvement, and commitment. All around us we see examples of shoddy and imperfect work in consumer products such as new cars with faulty parts or in careless mistakes made in government offices. It is a troublesome list that grows with each passing year. Department stores, manufacturers, and the postal service all echo the same complaint: Too many employees do not seem to care about doing a good job.

Tremendous strides have been made in recruiting, selecting, and training workers, and in providing the most effective kinds of leadership. But none of these functions can improve the quality of the work being done if workers are not sufficiently motivated to do the best job possible.

The study of motivation should be of great personal concern to you. As a consumer you are often the victim of dissatisfied workers who produce faulty products or improperly process your requests. Even more important is the fact that the research of I/O psychologists on motivation, job satisfaction, and job involvement can make your future work satisfying and fulfilling instead of dull and disappointing. Most of us will spend at least one third of our waking hours each week at work for 40 or 45 years. That is a long time to be frustrated and unhappy, especially when unhappiness at work carries over into other aspects of life, can disrupt relationships with family and friends, and can influence physical and mental health.

The concepts of motivation and job satisfaction and involvement are interrelated—satisfaction and involvement can result from the fulfillment of motivations, and new sources of satisfaction and involvement can generate other motivations. From an academic and theoretical standpoint, however, we can separate these three aspects of work and discuss them individually. First, it is important to consider the changing values that characterize American workers today.

The Changing Values of the American Worker

The values and needs of a significant portion of the American work force changed dramatically in the 1970s. A new generation of American workers—the so-called new breed—estimated to include more than 50% of the population, had different motivations from their parents' generation.

Their different values included a declining interest in pay as an incentive, a need for more challenging work as a result of higher education, increasing resistance to authority, and a decline of the Protestant ethic. Early signs of the emergence of these ideas appeared with the student protest and women's rights movements in the 1960s. Both groups were demanding a greater control over their lives and a greater sense of participation in the organizations and the culture of which they were part.

These ideas spread into the workplace with alarming speed as large numbers of young people and women entered the work force. The result was a change in what the new worker wanted from his or her job and a significant decline in the traditional values of the world of work. (These older values still held for older workers and for workers with little formal education.)

The values that formerly characterized employees are the following (Yankelovich, 1979):

1. A strong loyalty to the company for which they worked.
2. A strong motivation or drive for money and status.
3. A strong motivation for promotion in the organization.
4. A strong need for job security and stability.
5. A strong identification with work roles rather than with personal roles off the job.

The values of the newer generation focused on self and emphasized job characteristics that led to self-development and self-fulfillment. Their work-related values and needs included the following (Donovan, 1984; Jackson & Mindell, 1980):

1. Little loyalty or commitment to an organization.
2. A need for recognition of one's accomplishments.
3. Little concern with job security and stability.
4. Leisure considered more important than work.
5. Desire for work that is challenging, that provides opportunities for personal growth and development, and that calls for creativity.
6. Desire to participate in decisions that affect one's job.
7. A stronger identification with one's personal role in all facets of life rather than with one's work role.

As you can see, the values of the new breed of worker differed sharply from those of the old breed. They were sometimes referred to as "expressivism" because they focused on personal self-expression or expressing one's full human potential.

As we noted in Chapter 7, however, the latest generation entering management positions appears to be showing some return to more traditional managerial motives and abilities. That revival of earlier values, including a rediscovery of the work ethic, may signal yet another new breed, those born in the 1960s who have now embarked on their working careers.

Overall, the attitudes of working Americans of all ages (including members of the new breed generation) changed during the middle and late 1980s. This may reflect the severe erosion in worker power experienced during that time, to which we referred in Chapter 1. As we saw, the decline in white-collar and blue-collar jobs, and the transition in the U.S. economy from manufacturing to service industries, brought about reductions in job opportunities and in wages, and an increase in employer authority over workers.

The nature of these altered values is clear. Surveys taken in the 1980s revealed that American workers of all ages show a declining concern with self-fulfillment as their primary goal. This finding was strongest among workers under the age of 30, where the desire for self-fulfillment from work declined more than 13% from the 1970s. Although workers of the 1980s still expressed an interest in having important and meaningful work, this was not as central to their lives as it had been during the 1970s, particularly for white-collar workers. While their interest in meaningful work declined by 5%, the desire for higher income increased by nearly 6% (Kahle, Poulos, & Sukhdial, 1988; Weaver & Matthews, 1987).

The increased concern with pay, with material rewards from work, is evident among high school and college students, who are the next generation of workers and managers. For first-year college students, the goal of being financially well off almost doubled from 39% in 1970 to 73% in 1986. In contrast, the goal of developing a meaningful philosophy of life, so important to college students in the 1970s (77%), fell by almost half (to 40%) in 1986 (Conger, 1988).

It is interesting to note that although the college students of the mid-1980s were largely interested in being financially secure, they also expressed concern with self-fulfillment, self-expression, and self-realization. These were also the predominant values of the new breed of worker in the 1970s. However, today's interest in self-expression does not include the sense of commitment to the betterment of society that characterized the social activism of the student movements of the 1960s and 1970s.

Thus, research shows how workers' values can change dramatically from one generation to the next. The values and goals workers cherish most highly will define the factors that will motivate them at work and the aspects of the job that will bring them satisfaction. For this reason, then, employing organizations must be sensitive to these changing values.

Motivation

Why do people behave as they do? How can we account for the workers who are always on time, exceed production quotas, and are polite to the boss, whereas other workers at the same plant who perform the same job under the same conditions for the same pay behave in the opposite way?

We may say that the motivation of some workers to do a good day's job is higher than that of others, but what does this really tell us? Unfortunately, very little. It is easy to say that we must increase the motivation of employees, but unless we know precisely what factors constitute motivation in this specific instance, we shall be unable to change anything.

Human motivation is most complex. We seldom behave or respond to a particular situation because of a single motive. We are driven by a variety of needs and desires, some complementary and others conflicting.

The question why people behave as they do has fascinated and frustrated seekers of knowledge for centuries and psychologists are no exception. Although we do not fully understand our motivational structure, we do know, from psychological research and theory, quite a bit about the forces that drive us.

Several theories of work motivation have been advanced. These motivational theories are provocative, seemingly plausible, and the research they have generated has led to new ways of thinking about why people behave as they do on their jobs.

Need-Achievement Theory

In discussing characteristics of successful executives (Chapter 7), the need for achievement was included. This desire to accomplish something, to do a good job, to be the best typifies many people in our society, not only successful business executives. Those who possess this need derive great satisfaction from their achievements and are motivated to excel in everything they undertake.

Since the early 1950s, this motivational factor has been studied intensively by the Harvard psychologist, David McClelland, and his colleagues. They measured the need for achievement *(n Ach)* by asking people to write stories about a series of ambiguous pictures. The theory behind this projective technique is that people will project their innermost thoughts, feelings, and needs onto an ambiguous stimulus to give it meaning and structure. Accordingly, those with a high need to achieve will make up stories that focus on achieving or accomplishing a goal. For example, one picture shows a man at a worktable, and on the table is a photograph of his family. Persons with a low *n Ach* may write a story in which the man is daydreaming about his family or reminiscing about a pleasant family experience. Such a story contains no suggestion of achievement or accomplishment (Atkinson & Feather, 1966; McClelland, Atkinson, Clark, & Lowell, 1953).

Persons with a high need for achievement, however, would write a different kind of story. They may describe a problem on which the man is working. For example, one story told how the man solved a problem, and it gave the steps in his decision-making process. The focus was on work and how best to accomplish it; the family photograph was mentioned only in passing.

Successful business managers in the United States and other countries have been tested in this way; all consistently show a high *n Ach*. In Poland, a Communist country, the level of concern for achievement was almost as high as in capitalist countries such as the United States. Evidence also shows that the economic growth of private companies and of whole societies is related to the level of the need for achievement among managers in these private companies and members of these societies (McClelland, 1961).

Successful business managers generally score higher in need for achievement than do those who are less successful. Once high *n Ach* persons have been identified, it is possible to determine what they want and need in their work to satisfy this high level of achievement motivation.

The organization for which high *n Ach* persons work does not have to generate the motivation; these persons already possess the motivation. What the company must do is provide working conditions that will allow them to achieve. If they cannot satisfy their high drive for achievement, they will become frustrated and probably look for another job. If they can satisfy this drive, however, they will become happy and productive members of the organization.

McClelland's research identified three characteristics of high need-achievement persons.

1. They favor a working situation in which they are able to assume personal responsibility for solving problems. If they were not solely responsible for finding the solutions to problems, they would not have any sense of achievement. They are not happy when the solution depends on chance or on external factors beyond their control. It must depend on their own efforts and ability. This is a desirable characteristic for an executive as long as the working situation affords the opportunity for personal responsibility. The organization must provide these persons with challenging responsibility and a degree of personal autonomy.
2. They have a tendency to take calculated risks and set moderate achievement goals. By assuming tasks of moderate difficulty, high *n Ach* persons are able to satisfy their achievement needs. If the tasks or goals were too easy, there would be little sense of accomplishment. If they were too difficult, they might not succeed and would again have no sense of accomplishment. They must arrange the job and working conditions to face new problems or goals of moderate difficulty constantly.
3. High *n Ach* persons must have definite and continuing feedback about their progress. If they did not receive recognition for their work, they would not have a clear idea of how well they were doing. Fortunately, companies provide continuing feedback in periodic sales, cost, and production figures. High *n Ach* persons feel a greater sense of accomplishment if they have personal feedback from superiors in the form of congratulatory memos, pay raises, promotions, or a pat on the back.

Many studies support the need-achievement theory. Research has shown a high correlation between the *n Ach* scores of executives and the financial success of their organizations. In other words, the higher the *n Ach* scores of the executives, the more successful were their companies. Other studies show that managers high in *n Ach* display a number of desirable managerial characteristics. They tend to have more respect for their subordinates and to be receptive to new ideas and new ways of doing things. Also, they are more open to participatory democracy than are managers low in *n Ach*. High *n Ach* managers appear to be better than low *n Ach* managers to lead and motivate the new breed of employee.

Studies have also been conducted on the need for achievement in nonmanagerial employees. In an investigation of 141 salespersons for a retail furniture chain, it was found that their behavior at work varied as a function of their level of achievement motivation (Puffer, 1987). Those high in *n Ach* were also high in prosocial behavior, that is, in performing tasks beyond their formal job duties that would benefit the organization—assisting other salespersons, for example, or keeping display areas tidy.

In contrast, those salespersons low in *n Ach* exhibited noncompliant behaviors such as excessive lateness, frequent breaks, complaints about the company, and taking sales away from colleagues, behaviors that obviously are harmful to the organization. Those highest in *n Ach* were also the most effective salespersons. Thus, the need for achievement has been shown to influence many aspects of job performance.

A study of 268 telephone reservation agents working for an airline, a routine sort of job, found that those high in achievement motivation performed less well the longer they stayed on the job (Helmreich, Sawin, & Carsrud, 1986).

There are unresolved questions about the need-achievement theory of motivation, and not all research has been supportive. However, it does seem to be a useful theory of behavior and a plausible explanation for the motivation of some employees. The theory is judged to be high in scientific validity and in its usefulness in application to the world of work.

Needs-Hierarchy Theory

Abraham Maslow, a founder of humanistic psychology, developed a theory of motivation in which human needs or wants are arranged in a hierarchy of importance (Maslow, 1970). According to Maslow, people constantly desire better circumstances; they always want what they do not yet have. Consequently, needs that have been satisfied are no longer capable of motivating behavior and a new need rises to prominence. Lower level needs must be satisfied before attention can be paid to higher level needs. The five categories of needs (from lowest to highest) are

1. *Physiological needs.* The basic human needs, including food, oxygen, water, sleep, and the sex and activity drives.
2. *Safety needs.* Security, stability, order, and physical safety in one's environment.
3. *Belonging and love needs.* Social needs involving interactions with other people such as affection, affiliation, and identification.

4. *Esteem needs*. Self-respect, self-esteem, prestige, and success.
5. *Self-actualization needs*. The highest need level, self-fulfillment, involves achieving one's potential, realizing one's full capabilities.

The needs must be satisfied in the order presented. Persons who are hungry or fear for their safety are too busy satisfying these needs to be concerned about higher needs such as self-esteem or self-fufillment. In times of great economic hardship, most people are so intent on survival that they cannot be concerned with esteem or self-actualization needs. But, when the society or the individual has reached a sufficient level of financial security, people must move on to satisfy the next level of needs.

The social or love needs can be important motivating forces on the job—workers can find a sense of togetherness and a feeling of belonging through relations with co-workers. The human relations emphasis in organizations recognizes the sense of social security that can be provided by the work environment.

Most working people today are able to satisfy physiological and safety needs. Through interpersonal relationships on the job, we may also be able to satisfy belonging and love needs. The esteem needs—prestige, success, self-respect—can be satisfied in our personal life by buying a bigger house or on the job by status indicators such as the manager's plush carpeting, a private secretary, or a reserved parking space.

With the lower order needs satisfied, the focus shifts to self-actualization, the highest need. To satisfy this need, to be properly motivated, people must be provided with opportunities for growth and responsibility, the chance to exercise their capabilities to the utmost. A routine, boring, nonchallenging job will not satisfy this high-level need, no matter how high the salary.

Maslow's theory has received little research support and is judged to have low scientific validity and low usefulness in application (Miner, 1984a; Wahba & Bridwell, 1976). However, it must be recognized that the complexity of the theory makes it difficult to test adequately. Also, the theory continues to be popular among many managers and executives who have accepted a need for self-actualization as a motivating force to be reckoned with on the job. It has also influenced McGregor's Theory X/Theory Y formulation.

ERG Theory

Closely related to Maslow's theory is the ERG theory developed by Clayton Alderfer. Instead of postulating five types or levels of need, Alderfer suggests three basic human needs: Existence needs, Relatedness needs, and Growth needs. They encompass Maslow's needs and can be satisfied by some aspect of the job or work environment (Alderfer, 1972).

Existence needs are the lowest level needs and are concerned with physical survival. They include the obvious needs for food, water, shelter, and physical safety. An employer can satisfy these needs through salary, fringe benefits, a safe working environment, and some measure of job security. Existence needs relate to tangible environmental goals such as being able to buy food and shelter.

Relatedness needs involve interactions with other people and the satisfactions they can bring in the form of emotional support, respect, recognition, and a sense of belonging. These needs can be satisfied on the job by social relationships with co-workers and off the job by friends and family.

Growth needs focus on the self and include the need for personal growth and development, which can be satisfied only by using one's capabilities to the fullest. This conception includes Maslow's self-esteem and self-actualization needs. Both aspects, esteem and growth, must be satisfied. A job can provide satisfaction of the growth needs if it involves challenge, autonomy, and creativity.

Although Alderfer's theory is concerned with the same needs as Maslow's, it views the needs as operating in different ways. The ERG needs are not rigidly hierarchical. More than one of the ERG needs can operate at the same time. Satisfaction of one need does not lead automatically to the emergence of a higher need.

Another difference between Maslow's theory and Alderfer's theory is that frustration of one of Alderfer's higher needs (relatedness and growth) may lead to a reversion to a lower need. Maslow stated that a person will persevere to satisfy a need. For example, in Alderfer's theory, if a worker's relatedness need is not being satisfied, he or she may give up on it and focus instead on existence needs. In practical terms, this means that the worker may demand higher pay or fringe benefits as compensation for failing to satisfy the relatedness needs.

Maslow believed that once a need is satisfied it no longer motivates the individual. Alderfer suggests that satisfaction of a need may increase its intensity. If, for example, a job affords a great deal of challenge, autonomy, and creativity, the growth needs, instead of being fulfilled, might become stronger, necessitating additional autonomy and challenge for satisfaction.

Alderfer's theory is appealing on intuitive and logical grounds and is seen as more directly applicable to the motivation of people at work. Despite its promise, however, relatively little research has been conducted on it. The theory does have more empirical support than Maslow's theory, but not all the studies, not even those by Alderfer himself, have been positive (Wanous & Zwany, 1977).

Motivator-Hygiene Theory

The motivator-hygiene theory, combining motivation and job satisfaction, was proposed by Frederick Herzberg in 1959. Although controversial, the theory is a simple one and has stimulated vast amounts of research yielding important implications for the structure of some jobs. It also had ramifications on actual job design, the way in which various jobs are performed (Herzberg, 1966, 1974).

Herzberg's theory is similar, in part, to Maslow's needs-hierarchy formulation. The premise of the motivator-hygiene theory is that lower level needs have generally been satisfied in contemporary society. Where they have not, job dissatisfaction is the result. However, the reverse is not true: The fulfillment of basic needs does not produce job satisfaction. Only higher order needs such as self-actualization are capable of producing satisfaction. But, failure to find self-actualization in a job does not necessarily lead to dissatisfaction.

Thus, there are two sets of needs: those that produce job satisfaction and those that produce job dissatisfaction. They are separate; the presence or absence of one set of needs does not produce the opposite condition.

Herzberg calls the factors that produce job satisfaction *motivator needs*— they motivate the worker to the highest possible level of performance. These motivators are intrinsic to or inherent in the work itself and include the nature of the work and the person's sense of achievement, level of responsibility, and personal development and advancement. Notice the similarity between these factors, Maslow's self-actualization needs, and Alderfer's growth needs. The motivator needs can be satisfied only by stimulating, challenging, and absorbing work.

The factors that produce job dissatisfaction are the *hygiene* (or maintenance) *needs*. They have little power to produce satisfaction. They have nothing to do with the nature of the work itself but rather involve features of the work environment such as company policy and administrative practices, type of supervision, interpersonal relations, company benefits, and working conditions. Thus, they are extrinsic to or outside of the actual job tasks.

The hygiene needs are roughly analogous to Maslow's lower order needs (physiological, safety, and love needs). Just as Maslow's needs-hierarchy theory postulates that lower order needs must be satisfied before one is affected by higher order needs, so in Herzberg's theory, hygiene needs must be satisfied before attention is paid to motivator needs. It is important to remember, however, that satisfaction of hygiene needs will not produce job satisfaction, merely an absence of dissatisfaction.

Herzberg's theory is controversial. Although it was influential in the world of work in the 1970s and led to the redesign of many jobs, it has also been criticized. Research by I/O psychologists both supports and contradicts the theory, but overall its scientific validity is low and it is declining in popularity in both academic and applied circles.

The primary criticism of Herzberg's theory is directed against the alleged mutual independence of the two factors or needs, motivator and hygiene. In Herzberg's view, only motivator needs can produce job satisfaction and only hygiene needs can produce job dissatisfaction. Critics suggest that some of Herzberg's hygiene factors—for example, praise from a supervisor—could also act as motivators because they provide recognition for achievement. And, as we discussed, achievement is a motivator need. It is possible, therefore, that the distinction between motivator and hygiene factors is not as rigid as Herzberg indicated. Some extrinsic aspects of work may serve as motivators in addition to the intrinsic aspects of the job.

There is ample evidence to suggest, for example, that at least one hygiene factor, physical working conditions, is related to job satisfaction. The physical environment in which a job is performed—plus the variety of environmental factors such as lighting, temperature, and noise level—have been shown to be capable of affecting job satisfaction (Sundstrom, 1986).

As we shall see, pay, an extrinsic factor, has been positively related to job satisfaction. Thus, it can be suggested that the changing values of the American worker have rendered Herzberg's theory less appropriate today. "The assumption that intrinsic satisfactions are better than extrinsic ones is one that varies with current social mores. In times of social commitment such as the 1960s, extrinsic motives were frowned upon, and the predominant value of the time was to pursue your true self in your work. In more materialistic periods such as today, extrinsic motives seem to be more important and desirable to many people" (Osipow, 1986, p. 144).

Despite these criticisms, Herzberg's theory did help to focus interest on the importance of the intrinsic aspects of the job and their ability to motivate workers. It also spawned the concept of job enrichment.

According to Herzberg, much of a person's satisfaction and motivation derive from the intrinsic nature of the work. It follows that a job could be redesigned to maximize the motivator factors. This effort, known as *job enrichment*, was a major impact of Herzberg's theory.

Herzberg suggested the following ways of enriching a job:

1. Remove some of the controls over employees and increase their personal accountability or responsibility for their own work.
2. Provide employees with complete or natural units of work where possible. For example, instead of having them make one component of a unit, let them produce the whole unit.
3. Give employees additional authority and freedom in their work.
4. Provide reports on production on a regular basis directly to the workers instead of to their supervisors.
5. Encourage workers to take on new and more difficult tasks.
6. Assign highly specialized tasks so that workers can become expert in a particular task or operation.

All of these proposals have the goal of increasing personal growth and advancement, enhancing the sense of achievement and responsibility, and providing recognition; in other words, they all facilitate the satisfaction of the motivator needs.

Initial reports on the application of job enrichment told of impressive increases in production and morale and decreases in turnover and absenteeism. Unfortunately, many of these accounts were misleading and were based on poorly designed research, which often did not utilize control groups. Sometimes, changes said to have occurred on the job did not, in fact, take place. Also, some reports omitted mention of other changes introduced in the workplace that could have been responsible for any improvements in job performance.

Because it provides an example of the pitfalls of unscientific research, let us consider one of the most frequently cited cases of the successful implementation of a job enrichment program, that involving the janitorial employees at the Texas Instruments Company (*Work in America*, 1973). The company fired the firm that had been contracted to provide maintenance services and hired its own janitorial staff instead.

Texas Instruments enriched the jobs of its new employees by giving full responsibility and accountability to each worker. Instead of having a supervisor delegate and oversee the work, the janitors decided among themselves how the work would be divided and scheduled. They were also responsible for setting and maintaining the quality of their work. As a result of this job enrichment approach, it was reported, the facilities were kept cleaner than before and the work force was reduced from 120 to 71 persons. Also, turnover declined from a staggering 100% to a mere 10%.

However, the research report neglected to mention two important changes that were made in the working conditions at the same time, changes that had nothing to do with job enrichment. The company raised the starting pay for the janitorial jobs by 46% and added fringe benefits such as health insurance, sick leave, paid vacations, and profit sharing, benefits that had not been available to the previous workers. These employee benefits were worth one third of the workers' pay. Further, by providing such incentives, the company was able to recruit more qualified workers (Fein, 1974).

We cannot conclude that the ways in which the janitorial jobs were enriched contributed nothing to the increase in performance and the reduction in turnover. But neither can we ignore the possible impact of the extrinsic factors, that is, the better pay and fringe benefits. Because the research did not control for these additional variables, we cannot be certain that the changes in employee behavior resulted solely from the job enrichment program.

Herzberg maintains that job enrichment is "the key to designing work that motivates employees" (Herzberg, 1987, p. 120). In the workplace today, his approach to redesigning jobs is rarely applied, but the principles on which it was based can be seen in newer attempts to change the nature of work (see Chapter 9). Also the motivator-hygiene theory has led to consideration of the question, What specific characteristics of the job are being enriched?

To help answer this question another theory of motivation was proposed. It is called the job-characteristics theory and it focuses on job characteristics and individual differences in growth needs among workers.

Job-Characteristics Theory

The job-characteristics theory was developed by two psychologists, J. Richard Hackman and G. R. Oldham, and grew out of research on objective measures of job characteristics that would correlate with worker satisfaction and attendance (Hackman & Oldham, 1976; 1980). Evidence suggested that certain job characteristics influenced both behavior and attitudes at work, but these characteristics did not affect all workers in the same way.

The research pointed to individual differences in the need for growth, that is, some people have more of it than others. Those individuals higher in the need for growth seem to be more influenced by changes in these job characteristics than are persons lower in the need for growth.

Also, changes in job characteristics do not directly influence job behavior.

Any such influence comes about through the workers' subjective or psychological experiences in reaction to the job changes. These psychological experiences lead to changes in work motivation and behavior.

The presence of positive job characteristics causes employees to feel a positive emotional state when they perform well on the job. This internal state motivates employees to continue to perform well, based on the expectancy that good performance leads to good feelings—the positive emotional state. In addition, the strength of employee motivation depends on the strength of a need to grow and develop. The stronger the need, the more the person will value the positive emotional state that results from good job performance.

Thus, we have a theory stating that specific job characteristics lead to psychological conditions, which, in turn, lead to increased motivation, performance, and job satisfaction if one's need for growth is strong to begin with. The theory is shown schematically in Figure 8-1.

To understand the theory fully, we must briefly define the five core job dimensions or specific characteristics of jobs.

1. *Skill variety.* This refers to the number and variety of skills and abilities required to perform a job. The more challenge a job entails, the more personally meaningful it is for the worker.
2. *Task identity.* This refers to the unity of a job, whether it involves doing a whole unit of work or completing a product or making just a part of that product, as on an assembly line. Making a whole product is experienced as more meaningful than making a portion of it.
3. *Task significance.* This refers to the importance of the job to the lives and

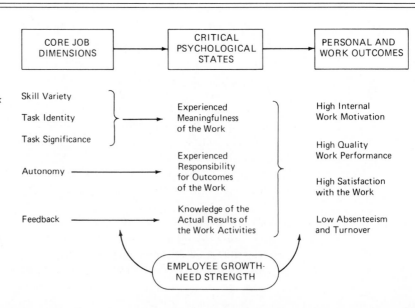

Figure 8-1 The job-characteristics theory of work motivation. (From "Motivation through the design of work: Test of a theory" by J. R. Hackman & G. R. Oldham, 1976, *Organizational Behavior and Human Performance,* 16, p. 256. Reproduced by permission.)

well-being of others. The job of aircraft mechanic, for example, directly affects the lives of other people and so is experienced as more meaningful than a job that has little or no impact on others.

4. *Autonomy.* The amount of independence an employee has in scheduling and organizing work is important. The more a job depends on employees' efforts and initiatives, the greater their sense of personal responsibility. They know that successful performance depends more on them than on their supervisor.

5. *Job feedback.* This obvious job characteristic refers to the amount of information employees receive about the quality of their job performance.

Five specific ways in which jobs may be redesigned or enriched to enhance the core job dimensions and, thus, performance and satisfaction are the following:

1. *Combining tasks.* Combining small specialized tasks to form new and larger units of work influences skill variety and task identity.

2. *Forming natural work units.* Arranging the work into meaningful groups in which the worker is responsible for an identifiable unit of work enhances task identity and task significance.

3. *Establishing client relationships.* Putting the worker into direct contact with the client or recipient of his or her work and making the worker responsible for directing the relationship with the client increases skill variety, autonomy, and feedback.

4. *Vertical loading.* Giving the worker more authority, responsibility, and control over the work increases autonomy, skill variety, task identity, and task significance.

5. *Opening feedback channels.* Enabling the worker to learn how well he or she is performing the job increases feedback.

Hackman and Oldham developed the Job Diagnostic Survey (JDS) to measure the three major variables in the theory: (1) the respondents' perception of the job characteristics, (2) the respondents' level of growth needs, and (3) the respondents' job satisfaction (Hackman & Oldham, 1975). A revision of the JDS was developed in 1987, but preliminary research suggests that the revised items do not improve the usefulness of the instrument in predicting job satisfaction, internal motivation, and productivity (Idaszak & Drasgow, 1987; Kulik, Oldham, & Langner, 1988).

Research support for the job-characteristics theory is mixed. One study of 509 employees working at four different types of organizations found a positive relationship between the job characteristics as they were perceived subjectively and the amount of effort put forth by the workers (Glick, Jenkins, & Gupta, 1986). A meta-analysis of almost 200 studies confirmed the existence of a positive relationship between actual and perceived job characteristics, and provides support for the notion that job characteristics consist of different dimensions and are related to both satisfaction and performance (Fried & Ferris,

1987). However, that analysis also suggests that not all of the five core dimensions of the job-characteristics theory are equal in their effect.

For example, improvements in productivity were related mostly to the dimensions of task identity and job feedback. Reduced absenteeism was related to skill variety, autonomy, and job feedback. Attitudes toward the job were related to skill variety, task significance, autonomy, and job feedback. Overall, then, job feedback was the only dimension related to both satisfaction and performance.

Another meta-analysis involving almost 7,000 workers in 876 jobs in 56 organizations investigated variations in job characteristics across the different job categories (Fried & Ferris, 1986). The results challenge the existence of some of the core dimensions. The authors suggest that task identity and job feedback are legitimate dimensions but that the other three could be grouped into a single factor. However, the study also found that the number of dimensions varied with age, educational level, and job level. Thus, the five core dimensions of the job-characteristics theory may not be applicable to all workplaces and all types of workers.

A study of more than 1,500 workers found that the core dimensions could serve as a basis for the development of a taxonomy of jobs (Naughton & Outcalt, 1988). Specifically, 10 relatively homogeneous clusters of jobs were found. A meta-analysis of 57 jobs in Hong Kong found that all of the core dimensions, except task significance, successfully described the characteristics of the jobs (Birnbaum, Farh, & Wong, 1986).

Thus, we can see that the job-characteristics theory continues to generate a great deal of research and seems to be a useful way of investigating the nature and structure of jobs. It also provides a basis for redesigning jobs, and reports indicate that such attempts have been at least moderately successful (Kulik, Oldham, & Hackman, 1987; Thayer, 1983).

There is a similarity among the need-achievement, needs-hierarchy, ERG, motivator-hygiene, and job-characteristics theories: All focus on the importance of the work itself and the challenges, growth opportunities, and responsibilities provided for the worker. If these theories have any validity, then studies of job satisfaction should also identify the same factors as being the most rewarding to people at work. We shall examine this issue in a later section.

Another point of similarity among these theories is that they are concerned with what might be called the *content* of motivation, the specific needs that arouse and guide behavior. Even the job-characteristics theory, which stresses the characteristics of jobs and experienced psychological states, still invokes an internal need for growth as the basic driving force.

Not all theories of motivation are of the content type. Some are *process* theories, so-called because they focus on the psychological processes involved in making decisions and choices about work, usually about how hard to work. We shall briefly consider three process theories of motivation: expectancy theory, goal-setting theory, and equity theory.

Expectancy Theory

The expectancy theory, originated by Victor Vroom, which may be the most popular motivational theory of the workplace, states that people make choices based on their perceived expectancy that certain rewards will follow if they behave in a certain way (Vroom, 1964). In the work situation, this means that people will choose to perform at the level that results in the greatest payoff or benefit. They will work hard if they expect this effort to lead to desirable rewards such as higher pay or promotion.

A person is motivated to obtain a particular outcome, the importance of which varies with the individual. The person's perception of the psychological value of the outcome, the *valence* of the outcome, determines its motivating strength. Of course, the outcome may not be as satisfying as expected. Nevertheless, it is the degree of expectancy that determines whether or not the person will work hard to obtain it.

There are several methods an organization can use to raise the expectancies of its employees and thereby increase their motivation to perform well on the job. For example, a company may state clearly exactly how good performance will lead to rewards such as higher pay or more rapid promotions. Informing employees about the level of production that must be achieved to earn higher wages is thus one way of establishing formal expectancies. A company can also institute a fair and objective performance appraisal system so that worker performance is not assessed subjectively and thus influenced by factors unrelated to how well the job is done.

Financial rewards should be based on some sort of commission or incentive system so that pay directly reflects effort. A seniority system, in which pay raises are given solely because of the passage of time on the job, sets up no expectancies about the rewards of working hard. A company should not discourage employees who perform well by unfairly raising the performance level needed for the promised commission, incentive, or bonus, once that level of production has been achieved.

The expectancy theory has generated a great deal of research, most of which has been highly supportive. In addition, it seems to agree with personal experience and common sense; the higher our expectation of receiving some reward, whether a good grade or a promotion, the harder we shall work for it (Mitchell, 1974; Porter & Lawler, 1968a).

Goal-Setting Theory

Developed by Edwin Locke, goal-setting theory also has a commonsense appeal and is clearly relevant to the world of work. Locke argues that our primary motivation in a work situation can be defined in terms of our desire to achieve a particular goal (Locke, 1968). The goal represents what we intend to do at a given time in the future. For example, we may have as a goal graduating from college with honors or achieving the highest sales recorded in the company or getting a pay raise to buy a new house.

Goals are important in any endeavor, motivating and guiding our behavior so that we perform in the most effective way. Studies of work behavior have shown how goals influence our motivation. For example, having goals results in higher performance than not having goals. Specific goals are more motivating than general goals. Goals that are difficult to obtain are more motivating than easy goals. On the other hand, goals that are so difficult as to seem impossible to achieve are worse than having no goals at all as far as motivation and performance are concerned.

A meta-analysis of 72 studies found that the motivating effects of goal-setting were strongest for easy tasks and weakest for more complex tasks (Wood, Mento, & Locke, 1987). These effects were found to generalize across a variety of organizations, jobs, and specific tasks. Thus, the results were not specific to the situation, that is, valid in only one or a few settings and not in others.

Goals facilitate job performance in four ways: (1) they direct attention and action, (2) they mobilize energy and effort, (3) they increase persistence, and (4) they motivate the development of behaviors that are necessary and appropriate to attain the goals.

A key aspect of the goal-setting theory is a person's commitment to a goal, that is, the strength of our determination to try to reach a goal. Locke identified three types of determinants of goal commitment: external factors, interactive factors, and internal factors (Locke, Latham, & Erez, 1988).

Three external factors that influence goal commitment are authority, peer influence, and external rewards. Complying with an authority figure (a boss, for example) has been shown to be an inducement to goal commitment in both laboratory and field studies. Also, it has been found that goal commitment is increased when the authority is physically present, supportive, and trusted. Peer group pressure and external rewards such as pay also induce goal commitment.

The interactive factors that influence goal commitment are participation in the setting of the goal and competition, which can induce people to set higher goals and work harder than those not in a competitive situation.

An internal factor facilitating goal commitment is the person's expectation of success. Commitment to the goal declines as the expectancy of achieving it declines. Another possible internal factor is self-administered reward or feedback, which has been linked with high commitment and performance.

Other researchers have suggested additional factors, both personal and situational, that may affect goal commitment (Hollenbeck & Klein, 1987). Personal variables include high need achievement, endurance (the ability to work long and hard), Type A behavior (which includes aggressiveness and competitiveness), a record of success in achieving difficult goals, high self-esteem, and an internal locus of control (the belief that events are under one's control and not a function of luck or fate). The situational variables related to goal commitment are "publicness" (the extent to which others are aware of one's goals), and information about the performance of others in relation to the same or similar goals.

The goal-setting theory may be the most thoroughly researched of all the motivational theories we have discussed. The evidence is highly supportive.

In case after case, goal setting has been found to produce substantial increases in employee output. Further, the theory is among the highest in both scientific validity and in usefulness on the job (Hunter & Schmidt, 1983; Locke, Latham, & Erez, 1988; Locke, Shaw, Saari, & Latham, 1981; Miner, 1984b).

Equity Theory

The notion that our motivation is influenced by our perception of how equitably we are treated at work was proposed by J. Stacy Adams (Adams, 1965). In any work situation, be it a classroom or an office, we assess both our *inputs*—how much effort we are putting into the work—and our *outcomes*—how much reward we are receiving for the work. We then, perhaps unconsciously, calculate the ratio of outcome to input and compare our ratio with what we perceive are the ratios of fellow students or co-workers.

Are we getting equal outcomes as a function of our inputs or are we getting less than other people? If we are getting less, a state of *inequity* exists, which creates tension and motivates us to create a condition of equity. If we are getting the same, a state of *equity* exists. Research shows (and personal experience confirms) that people do make such comparisons. You may have felt unfairly or inequitably treated in a course for which you worked harder than someone who, ultimately, received a higher grade. Did you work even harder as a result of this inequity?

An extension of the equity theory suggests that people react in three consistent but different ways to their perceived equity or inequity. These behavioral responses have been labeled benevolent, equity sensitive, and entitled (Huseman, Hatfield, & Miles, 1987). The level of reward received by these different types will influence their motivation, job satisfaction, and performance.

Benevolent persons are described as altruistic. They are satisfied when they are underrewarded in comparison with others, and feel guilty when they are equitably rewarded or overrewarded.

Equity-sensitive persons represent the traditional equity theory. As such, they believe that everyone, including themselves, should be rewarded fairly for the work they do. They experience distress when they are underrewarded and guilt when overrewarded.

Entitled persons believe that everything they receive is their just due. Hence, they feel satisfied only when overrewarded and distressed when underrewarded or equitably rewarded.

It is generally accepted that a sense of being treated fairly (in accordance with our expectations) with respect to others can influence work motivation, either by increasing or reducing it. The equity theory as originally formulated is fairly well supported by primarily laboratory research but has a limited application to specific situations at work (Middlemist & Peterson, 1976; Miner, 1984b).

Job Satisfaction: A Measure of the Quality of Working Life

It is sometimes difficult to distinguish between motivation and job satisfaction because of their high degree of interrelationship. There is also such a relationship between job satisfaction and morale; many writers use these terms interchangeably. Basically, job satisfaction refers to a set of attitudes that employees have about their jobs. We may describe it as the psychological disposition of people toward their jobs—how they feel about the work—and this involves a collection of numerous attitudes or feelings. Thus, job satisfaction or dissatisfaction depends on a large number of factors, ranging from where employees have to park their cars and whether the boss calls them by their first name to the sense of achievement or fulfillment they may find in their work.

Additional factors can influence job satisfaction, personal factors that are not directly part of the job or work climate. For example, job satisfaction varies as a function of age, health, number of years worked, emotional stability, social status, leisure and recreational activities, family relationships, and other social outlets and affiliations. Also, personal motivations and aspirations and how well these are fulfilled can influence the attitude we have toward our work.

Recent research also suggests that for some employees, job satisfaction may be a stable, enduring, individual characteristic, independent of the features of the job. For these workers, changes in job status, pay, or working conditions may have little or no effect on their level of job satisfaction. Their tendency to be happy (satisfied) or unhappy (dissatisfied) may vary little over time and circumstances (Staw, 1984).

Other research suggests the possibility that different satisfaction profiles, involving both work and nonwork satisfaction, may characterize different people. A study of 390 male college graduates, tested after they had been out of college and working for 5 or 6 years, revealed the existence of five such satisfaction profiles (Shaffer, 1987).

1. *Generally satisfied*—high in both work and nonwork factors.
2. *Nonwork compensators*—high in nonwork satisfaction, low in work satisfaction.
3. *Work compensators*—generally dissatisfied with both work and nonwork activities, satisfied with the job and the pay.
4. *Materially dissatisfied*—low in satisfaction with pay and environment.
5. *Generally dissatisfied*—low on all work and nonwork factors.

The generally satisfied employees were found to be more likely to remain with their present employers, but the work compensators were more likely to leave their present jobs because of dissatisfaction with the work.

Job satisfaction—and satisfaction with all aspects of one's life—is not a simple or unitary concept. It is a highly complex variable that encompasses a wide range of individual differences and presents continuing challenges for I/O psychologists.

Job satisfaction is related to personal characteristics, the nature of the work, and the conditions of the workplace. For some employees, a well-run cafeteria is a source of job satisfaction.

Background and Uses of Job Satisfaction

Organizations today focus much attention on measuring and improving their workers' attitudes, but this was not always the case. In the scientific management era when the worker was considered to be just another machine, there was no interest in job satisfaction—after all, a machine does not have attitudes or feelings. The way in which industry tried to improve production during that time was almost exclusively through the development of more efficient selection techniques.

The human relations focus drastically changed this view. It became apparent that workers' productivity was not solely a function of their skills and abilities. During the Hawthorne studies in the 1920s, some 20,000 interviews conducted with workers convinced management that their employees did indeed have feelings and attitudes about their jobs that could affect their productivity.

As soon as industry realized this, frantic efforts were undertaken to measure attitudes and to train supervisors to be sensitive to employee feelings. It was thought that if job satisfaction and morale could be improved, job performance would improve as well. By the mid-1950s, however, it became clear that the relationship between performance and job satisfaction was much more complex than originally supposed.

Workers' attitudes must still be measured, however, because they are of great value to organizations. For example, if negative attitudes toward a particular job feature are uncovered, it is possible to institute corrective procedures. Without attitude measurement, management might know something was wrong—that morale was low—but would not be able to pinpoint the problem.

Measurements of employee attitudes can also be used to benefit employees. Some organizations consider attitude surveys a form of upward communication for their employees, a chance for employees to express their feelings about positive and negative aspects of the workplace. Such attitude surveys are only beneficial when the communication channels operate in both directions. It is not enough to allow employees a chance to air their gripes through an attitude survey. To make the survey an effective means of two-way communication, employees should be given the chance to help design the questionnaire so that it focuses on their employment problems and concerns. Once a survey is completed, employees should receive feedback from the company. They should be informed of the results and be permitted to participate in formulating solutions to the problems uncovered by the survey.

An analysis of companies on their use of surveys found that 35% of them conducted surveys on an annual basis and 45% had conducted at least one survey in the previous 5 years (Lo Bosco, 1986a). The approach used most often, by 93% of the firms, was the anonymous questionnaire. The major issues investigated in the company surveys are listed in Table 8-1.

More than half of these companies reported that they took corrective action as a result of the responses to their survey questions. The changes included retraining and disciplining of managers, modifying personnel policies, and adjusting wages and benefits. By making such changes, the companies demonstrated the high value they placed on their employees' opinions.

Periodic attitude surveys can be of immense practical importance to both employers and employees, providing both an ongoing analysis of the organization and a sense of employee participation in shaping the organization's policies and practices.

TABLE 8-1   Major Issues Addressed in Company Surveys

Issues	Percentage
Working conditions	90
Pay	77
Immediate supervision	77
Management	74
Training and development	71
Benefits	68
Obstacles to doing the job	61
Physical work environment	58

From "Employee attitude surveys" by M. Lo Bosco, 1986, *Personnel, 63*(4), p. 67.

Measuring Job Satisfaction

There are several techniques for measuring job satisfaction, all of which involve, in essence, asking workers how they feel about various aspects of their jobs.

The most popular technique is the questionnaire, either distributed to workers in the plant or office or mailed to their homes. Usually, questionnaire responses are voluntary and anonymous. This means that not all workers will complete a questionnaire, and there is no way of knowing which employees responded and which did not. It might make a difference, for example, if more good than poor workers responded.

Two questionnaires that are popular in industry today are the Job Descriptive Index and the Minnesota Satisfaction Questionnaire. The Job Descriptive Index contains scales to measure five aspects of a job: pay, promotion, supervision, the work itself, and one's co-workers. It can be completed in 15 minutes or less and has been published in English and several other languages (Smith, Kendall, & Hulin, 1969). An updated version was prepared in 1987.

The Minnesota Satisfaction Questionnaire also measures individual aspects or facets of a job. The long form (30 minutes) assesses 20 facets, including advancement, independence, recognition, social status, and working conditions. The short form (10 minutes) measures overall or general job satisfaction (Weiss, Dawis, England, & Lofquist, 1967).

A technique sometimes used in conjunction with questionnaires is the personal interview in which employees discuss various aspects of the job with a supervisor or an interviewer from the personnel department. In Chapter 3, we discussed the low reliabilities and validities of the interview procedure; it is also time consuming and expensive.

Another method of measuring job attitudes is the sentence-completion test. Workers are presented with a list of phrases that they are asked to complete: for example, "My job is _____" or "My job should be _____."

The critical-incidents technique is also used. Employees are asked in a personal interview to describe job incidents that occurred at times when they felt extremely good or extremely bad about their jobs. A high-tech way of conducting a survey uses electronic mail. In this approach, questions are asked and answers given through the company's in-house computer system.

Extent of Job Satisfaction and Dissatisfaction

Every year since 1949, the Gallup poll has asked a representative sample of American workers the following question: On the whole, would you say you are satisfied or dissatisfied with the work you do? The poll has shown consistently that 10% to 13% of the workers questioned each year say they are dissatisfied with their jobs.

If approximately only 10% to 13% of the work force is dissatisfied, why is so much attention paid to job satisfaction? We mentioned in Chapter 2 that the results of an opinion poll are strongly influenced by the wording of the questions. When more sophisticated and specific questions are asked about job satisfaction, different results are obtained.

For example, when blue-collar workers were asked if they would like to change jobs, substantial numbers of them said yes, even though they had indicated that they were satisfied with their present jobs. Apparently, when many people say they are satisfied, they really mean that they are not dissatisfied. Although pay and external working conditions may be satisfactory, it does not follow that the jobs themselves are challenging, rewarding, or stimulating. Satisfaction is defined for many people, then, as the absence of negative factors rather than the presence of positive factors.

There can be widespread differences in reported job satisfaction, depending on how the issue is investigated. When more sophisticated questions are used, the proportion of those sampled who express dissatisfaction with their jobs tends to rise. When examining statistics on job satisfaction, it is, thus, necessary to find out the kinds of questions asked.

A great many studies have been conducted on job satisfaction. Some have questioned a representative national sample of workers. Others have dealt with more specific and narrowly defined populations, such as the workers in a particular industry. A nationwide survey of 5,000 employees reported that most American workers, more than 60%, say they are satisfied with their jobs. However, only 40% are even moderately satisfied with their salaries ("Jobs OK," 1988).

These assembly-line workers at a computer manufacturing plant may be less satisfied with their jobs than workers who are not on assembly lines. I/O psychologists have suggested that routine, repetitive work offers little opportunity for personal growth and fulfillment.

Job satisfaction appears to vary with one's level and type of work. An anonymous questionnaire survey of 209 women in nonmanagerial positions in a food processing factory found that those on the assembly line were significantly less satisfied with their jobs than those not on the assembly line (Clegg, Wall, & Kemp, 1987).

A survey of more than 800 senior U.S. Civil Service executives found extremely low morale and satisfaction. Almost 70% said they would advise intelligent young people not to work for the federal government. When the executives were asked if they would seek work elsewhere if they could start over again, 66% answered yes. Some 75% reported that they would never fulfill their ambitions in the civil service, and more than 88% did not see any prospect of improvement in government employment (Posner & Schmidt, 1988).

Other surveys comparing job satisfaction in government service with that in private industry also revealed pessimistic results with regard to public sector work. A survey of 240 high-level managers in a variety of private and public organizations in Israel found significantly higher levels of satisfaction for the private sector managers (E. E. Solomon, 1986).

Job Facet Satisfaction

The survey results we discussed in the preceding section dealt with global or overall satisfaction with one's job. Many I/O psychologists have come to recognize that this may not be an adequate measure of how people feel about their work. Employees may be satisfied with one or two aspects or facets of the work situation and totally dissatisfied with other facets. A person may find the working conditions to be ideal, but the supervisor, co-workers, or company policies to be terrible. A general measure of job satisfaction fails to represent such differences clearly. Therefore, in recent years, organizational psychologists have focused their attention on the measurement of *job facet satisfaction* (Stagner, 1982).

The Job Descriptive Index and the Minnesota Satisfaction Questionnaire measure facets of job satisfaction. To derive a measure of global satisfaction, the scores for each facet are added. This simple summation technique may not reflect, or even encompass, all possible elements of which a job is composed.

In one study, 185 employees were given the short form of the Minnesota Satisfaction Questionnaire, interviewed about their satisfaction with their jobs, and asked two single-item questions about overall satisfaction (Scarpello & Campbell, 1983). The results showed low correlations between the sum of the facets on the Minnesota Satisfaction Questionnaire and the overall measures of satisfaction. The researchers concluded that the facets on the questionnaire may not measure all the variables that can affect job satisfaction.

This was confirmed in the interviews, which uncovered five facets not measured by the questionnaire: flexibility in scheduling work hours, tools and equipment, work space, co-workers facilitating of work, and pleasantness of interactions with other people at work. These facets correlated highly with the global measures of satisfaction both on and off the job.

TABLE 8-2   Facets or Conditions of Job Satisfaction

Source	*Effect*
Events or Conditions	
Work itself: Challenge	Mentally challenging work that the individual can successfully accomplish is satisfying.
Work itself: Physical demand	Tiring work is dissatisfying.
Work itself: Personal interest	Personally interesting work is satisfying.
Reward structure	Just and informative rewards for performance are satisfying.
Working conditions: Physical	Satisfaction depends on the match between working conditions and physical needs.
Working conditions: Goal attainment	Working conditions that facilitate goal attainment are satisfying.
Agents	
Self	High self-esteem is conducive to job satisfaction.
Supervisors, co-workers, subordinates	Individuals will be satisfied with colleagues who help them attain rewards.
	Individuals will be satisfied with colleagues who see things the same way they do.
Company and management	Individuals will be satisfied with companies that have policies and procedures designed to help the individual attain rewards.
	Individuals will be dissatisfied with conflicting roles or ambiguous roles imposed by company or management.
Fringe benefits	Benefits do not have a strong influence on job satisfaction for most workers.

From *Psychology of Work Behavior* (p. 399) by F. J. Landy, 1985, Homewood, IL: Dorsey Press. Copyright 1985, Dorsey Press. Based on "The nature and causes of job satisfaction" by E. A. Locke, 1976, *Handbook of Industrial and Organizational Psychology* (pp. 1297–1349), Chicago: Rand McNally.

This study and others demonstrate empirically that job satisfaction is highly complex. Continuing research on job satisfaction must investigate all facets of the work environment. Psychologists believe that the number of job facets will vary from one job or kind of work to another. Also, some facets will be more important to some employees than to others. Some aspects of job satisfaction will be found only in certain jobs, whereas others will be common to all jobs. Ten facets thought to contribute to employee satisfaction for all jobs have been identified, as shown in Table 8-2.

Personal Characteristics and Job Satisfaction

As we have seen, characteristics of the work itself and of the context or situation in which the work is performed strongly influence job satisfaction. By redesigning the job and the working conditions, it is possible to increase job satisfaction and worker productivity. Situational factors, then, are important in job satisfaction. Consider, for example, two different situational factors: job complexity and working spouses. Research has shown that both factors affect job satisfaction. The greater the job complexity (assuming that it does not exceed the person's capacity), the higher the job satisfaction (Gerhart, 1987). Having a wife who is employed outside the home has, for married male employees, a significant negative effect on job satisfaction and overall life satisfaction (Staines, Pottick, & Fudge, 1986).

In addition to such situational factors, personal characteristics can influence job satisfaction. Satisfaction in work can be affected by age, sex, race, level of intelligence, use of skills, and length of job experience. Although these factors cannot be changed by employing organizations, they can be used to predict the relative levels of satisfaction to be expected among different groups of workers.

Age

In general, job satisfaction increases with age; the least job satisfaction is reported by the youngest workers. The relationship holds for both blue-collar and white-collar employees and for women as well as men (Bourne, 1982; Rhodes, 1983). Research has shown, however, that the increase in job satisfaction with age is reliable only until about the age of 60, at which point the evidence becomes less conclusive. Many young people are disappointed when they begin to work because they fail to find sufficient challenge and responsibility.

Why does job satisfaction increase with age when the initial reaction to work is one of such great disappointment? There are three possible explanations. First, the most strongly dissatisfied young workers may drop out of the labor force or change jobs so frequently in their search for fulfillment that they are no longer included in surveys. This would mean that the older the workers studied, the fewer dissatisfied people are likely to be among them. Second, a sense of reality (or resignation) sets in as workers grow older. They may give up looking for fulfillment and challenge in work and, so, become less dissatisfied (although not necessarily fully satisfied) with their jobs. Perhaps they are making the best of a bad situation, realizing that for family and financial reasons they must remain on the job. Perhaps they also realize that they have fewer alternatives to their present jobs as they get older. Younger workers are more mobile in that they can more easily find other jobs elsewhere. Third, older workers may have more opportunities to find fulfillment and self-actualization in their jobs than do workers who are just starting out. Age and experience on the job usually bring greater competence, self-confidence, esteem, and a higher level of responsibility in which a person may feel a greater sense of accomplishment.

Sex

In the United States, more than half of all women of employable age (18–64) are currently in the work force. The majority, however, still work at routine white-collar jobs, such as telephone operator, keypunch operator, and clerk.

Large numbers of women also hold factory assembly-line jobs. Because women constitute a significant portion of the work force, it is important for employing organizations to have some understanding of their level of job satisfaction.

The evidence, however, is inconsistent and unclear. Some studies show that women are satisfied on the job, whereas other studies show the opposite. Some research shows women to be far more dissatisfied than men with their jobs. There are also indications that women are concerned with different aspects of the job. For example, disadvantaged women evidenced a greater need to like their work and to have a fair boss; disadvantaged men were more concerned with the opportunity to prove themselves and to have a steady job (Forgionne & Peeters, 1982; Sauser & York, 1978).

It is reasonable to expect different sources of job satisfaction for women who willingly choose a career in the business world as compared to women who are forced to work to support their families. The motivations and satisfactions of career women more closely parallel those of men executives. Women in management report a high level of job satisfaction. Working mothers, on the other hand, often do not look on outside work as the major focus in their life, deriving satisfaction instead from the jobs of homemaker, wife, or mother (Weaver & Holmes, 1975).

Researchers suggest that it is not gender that relates to job satisfaction but rather a group of factors that varies with sex. For example, women are paid less than men for the same work and their opportunities for promotion are fewer. Women executives believe they have to work harder and be more outstanding in their work than men executives before they can expect to receive the same rewards and recognition.

Race

White employees generally report greater job satisfaction than nonwhite employees, although the differences are not usually statistically significant. Among managers, however, whites are significantly higher in job satisfaction than nonwhites (Forgionne & Peeters, 1982; Weaver, 1978). Of course, before a person can be concerned with job satisfaction, he or she must first have a job. For some minorities, finding a job may be the more basic issue.

Approximately one third of the employable members of minority groups in the United States are currently unemployed, employed irregularly, or too discouraged to continue to seek employment. Another one third of minority-group members hold full-time jobs, but these typically are low-level jobs that offer marginal pay and little opportunity for advancement. Thus, the problem for many nonwhite workers may not be fulfillment, achievement, or responsibility, but simply finding a job that pays a decent wage.

Intelligence

By itself, a person's level of intelligence does not appear to be of major importance in influencing job satisfaction. However, intelligence considered in relation to the kind of work being performed may be an influential factor.

For many occupations and professions, there is a range of intelligence associated with efficiency of performance and job satisfaction. Persons with IQs beyond this range (either too high or too low) are likely to experience boredom or frustration and dissatisfaction with the job. Persons who are too intelligent for the work—for example, a bright college graduate in a routine assembly-line job—may find insufficient challenge and become bored and dissatisfied. Likewise, those in jobs that require a higher level of intelligence than they possess may be frustrated if they are unable to handle the demands of the job. The problem of matching job level with intelligence can be eliminated by the use of adequate selection procedures.

A factor usually, but not always, related to intelligence is level of education. A number of studies have shown that education is slightly and negatively related to job satisfaction (Glenn & Weaver, 1982a, 1982b). One explanation for this finding is that persons with more education may have higher expectations, believing their work should bring greater fulfillment and responsibility. Most jobs will not satisfy these expectations. However, employees with college degrees are somewhat more satisfied with their jobs than those who attended college but did not graduate. This finding may be due to the fact that many higher level positions are open only to those who have earned degrees.

Job Experience

The relationship between job satisfaction and number of years on the job is complex. During the early stages of employment, new workers tend to be satisfied with the job. This early period involves the stimulation and challenges of developing skills and new abilities. Also, the work may seem attractive because it is new. Early satisfaction wanes unless employees receive evidence of their progress and growth. After a few years on the job, discouragement is common, brought on by the feeling that the worker is not advancing as rapidly as he or she would like. Also, in times of inflation and rapidly rising starting salaries, employees with a few years of experience find that they are making little more than beginning employees, despite the salary increases they have received over the years.

A study of 124 salespersons from seven companies showed that those with greater time on the job were significantly less satisfied. In addition, those with more experience did not believe that job performance led to rewards. They were not as challenged or involved with their jobs or as committed to their company as those with less experience (Stout, Slocum, & Cron, 1987).

In general, however, job satisfaction increases after a number of years of experience and improves steadily thereafter. The relationship between job satisfaction and length of experience closely parallels that with age. Perhaps they are the same phenomenon under different labels.

Use of Skills

A common complaint, particularly among engineering and science graduates, is that employees are not called on to exercise the skills and knowledge developed in their college training. Surveys of engineers, for example, show extremely high levels of job dissatisfaction with many facets of their work such as pay, working conditions, supervisors, and chances for promotion (Rynes, Tolbert, & Strausser, 1988). Other studies have shown that people are happier in their work if they have the opportunity to use abilities they believe they possess (Andrisani & Shapiro, 1978; Forgionne & Peeters, 1982). The use and exercise of personal abilities are part of what Maslow meant by self-actualization, which refers to the all-important needs for personal growth and development.

Another study investigated the relationship between job satisfaction and person-environment congruence, that is, the fit or match of a worker's personality with the job or work environment. The subjects were 792 men and 1,077 women who were tested initially in their first year at college and again 6 years after graduation. All subjects were employed at the time of the second testing. Those at the highest level of congruence had aspired to their present jobs early in their college career and had majored in a field leading directly to those jobs. It was assumed that these employees were using the skills and knowledge they had acquired and developed in college.

Those at the lowest level of congruence, on the other hand, had not aspired to their present jobs in college and had not majored in a field leading to those jobs. The results showed that both men and women at the highest level of congruence were more satisfied with their income, fringe benefits, and promotion opportunities (extrinsic aspects of the job) than those at the lowest level of congruence (Elton & Smart, 1988).

Personality

There may be a positive relationship between chronic job dissatisfaction and poor emotional adjustment. Although not entirely conclusive, evidence suggests that those who are more satisfied in their work are also better adjusted and more emotionally stable.

The fact of such a relationship seems reasonably clear, but the cause and effect sequence is not clear. Which comes first, emotional maladjustment or job dissatisfaction? Either is capable of causing the other. Emotional instability can cause discontent in every sphere of a person's life, including one's job; prolonged job dissatisfaction can lead to poor emotional adjustment.

Regardless of which one might cause the other, the result is likely to be the same. Some companies have instituted personal counseling programs, particularly for managerial and executive personnel, and some maintain clinical psychologists and psychiatrists on the staff or have them available as consultants to deal with emotional disturbances of high-level personnel.

Two facets of personality that have been related to job satisfaction are alienation and internal versus external control. Employees who feel less alienated and who have a strong sense of internal control (that is, who believe that rewards are a function of their own behavior rather than fate or luck) are reported to be high in job satisfaction (King, Murray, & Atkinson, 1982). Internals are also higher in job involvement and organizational commitment (Stout, Slocum, & Cron, 1987).

Occupational Level

The higher the occupational or status level of a job, the higher is the job satisfaction. Executives express more satisfaction with their jobs than do first-line supervisors, who, in turn, are more satisfied than their subordinates. In general, the higher the level of the job, the greater is the opportunity to satisfy the motivator needs (described by Herzberg) and the greater is the autonomy, challenge, and responsibility. In a study of more than 1,000 managers, satisfaction of the needs for esteem, autonomy, and self-actualization increased with each level in the organizational hierarchy (King, Murray, & Atkinson, 1982; Roach & Davis, 1973).

Job satisfaction has also been found to vary with different kinds of occupation. For example, those with the highest satisfaction scores are either in business for themselves or in the construction industry. Chances of dissatisfaction in these two areas are only 1 in 20. Persons in technical, professional, and managerial jobs report a 1 in 10 chance of being dissatisfied. The least satisfying occupations are manufacturing, service occupations, and wholesale or retail businesses, where the chances for dissatisfaction are almost 1 in 4 (Sheppard & Herrick, 1972).

Job Satisfaction and Productivity

It is reasonable to assume that a high level of job satisfaction is directly related to positive behavior on the job, specifically to high performance, low turnover, and low absenteeism. In noting the history of job satisfaction, we mentioned that organizational leaders once thought that increasing job satisfaction would result in greater production. The relationship turned out to be neither direct nor simple. The issue of motivation and job performance is complicated and involves a wide range of job and personal characteristics. Although the relationship between satisfaction and job behavior is still recognized, it is no longer looked on as the simple answer to production problems.

Production

Level of production is certainly a major concern of any organization. If job satisfaction were not at all related to performance improvement, management would be understandably reluctant to support research in this area. Although the evidence suggests a positive relationship between satisfaction and performance, it has not been demonstrated conclusively. The correlations do not tend to be high, and some studies show a lack of correlation. Part of the problem is the difficulty of conducting the research. How can successful performance be measured? Some jobs lend themselves more readily than others to objective assessments of performance level. Thus, different measures of success must be used for different jobs, and this in itself can produce varying results.

Despite the research problems, inconclusive findings, and general lack of strong positive correlations, a weak though consistent relationship apparently exists between satisfaction and performance.

Organizational psychologists have offered an interesting interpretation of this relationship (Lawler & Porter, 1967). Instead of considering job satisfaction as leading to improved performance, we should think of performance as causing satisfaction. Satisfaction presumably derives from the fulfillment of our needs. If our work provides us with this fulfillment, then we can in effect administer our own rewards by improving our levels of performance. If, for example, a job satisfies our need for achievement, by performing at a higher level we can better fulfill this need.

It has been suggested that this formulation may be more applicable to managers or executives than to lower level workers. Managers have greater opportunities to express their needs for self-actualization, achievement, and personal growth than do workers on an assembly line. The latter have little control over their jobs and little opportunity to fulfill higher order needs. Most of their rewards are determined by factors beyond their control; executives can operate with greater autonomy. Because most workers are unable to fulfill these needs through work, they cannot derive any satisfaction from the job. This plus the fact that most research on satisfaction and performance has been conducted on lower level workers could easily explain the lack of a strong positive relationship between the two variables.

To test this theory, 148 managers in five organizations were studied. It was found that high-performing managers did not receive greater external rewards (such as pay) than did low-performing counterparts. However, high performers reported many more rewards from satisfying needs such as autonomy and self-realization. Further, high-performing managers reported higher levels of job satisfaction than did low performers, providing strong support for the idea that need fulfillment from a job leads to satisfaction, which, in turn, leads to higher performance (Porter & Lawler, 1968b).

This study also supports the theories of motivation that discuss the importance of fulfilling higher order needs, and it confirms the necessity of designing challenging and stimulating jobs that allow for growth and self-actualization.

The theories are also supported by research on four of the core dimensions in the job-characteristics theory of motivation. Satisfaction with the dimensions of autonomy, skill variety, task identity, and job feedback was strongly related to increased productivity.

Counterproductive Behavior

If high levels of job satisfaction lead to positive behaviors, does it follow that job dissatisfaction leads to behaviors that are counterproductive to organizational goals? Negative behaviors can interfere with production and lead to faulty products, sabotaged equipment, theft, or destructive rumors and gossip. Employees may view these kinds of behaviors as a way of striking back at a company because of real or imagined grievances.

Studies have shown a positive relationship between job dissatisfaction and counterproductive behavior. However, this relationship held only for workers over the age of 30. This does not mean that employees over 30 engage in more negative behaviors. Indeed, the opposite is true; the frequency of such behaviors is much higher for employees under age 30. It was only in older workers, however, that the behaviors could be related to job dissatisfaction.

Absenteeism and Turnover

The first point to note about absenteeism is that it is rampant and is extremely costly to organizations. On any given workday in the United States, some 16% to 20% of employees do not show up for work. So widespread is absenteeism that it accounts for more time lost from work than strikes and lockouts. The cost of this lost time to business has been estimated at $30 billion a year.

Absenteeism has plagued industry since the invention of machines (Zuboff, 1988). In textile mills in Wales in the 1840s, absenteeism was commonly at a rate of 20%, and during the 2-week period following each month's payday, absenteeism often reached 33%. In England, throughout the 19th century, workers typically took off on Mondays—"Saint Monday," it was called—following weekend drinking bouts. Nothing factory owners did, from fining workers to firing them, made any difference.

Not all employees have the same rate of absenteeism. A relatively small percentage of employees account for a disproportionate share of absences. The primary excuse is illness (Johns, 1987). Not surprisingly, the more liberal the sick-leave policy of an organization, the higher its absenteeism rate. For example, absenteeism is very high in companies that do not require proof of illness, such as a doctor's certificate, and that permit sick leave to be taken for many days with no loss of pay. Tightening such policies has been shown to reduce absenteeism. Also, high-paying industries have higher rates of absenteeism than low-paying industries. The more a worker makes, the more likely he or she is to feel able to afford to buy some time off.

Other factors contribute to what has been called an "absence culture," a climate in which informal rules and shared beliefs encourage and support taking time off from work (Dalton & Enz, 1987). Societal values may foster absenteeism, as is evident in the wide variations in absentee rates in different countries. Japan and Switzerland, which consider job attendance to be almost a sacred duty, have low levels of absenteeism. Italy, France, and Sweden report very high levels of absenteeism. In Italy, which is particularly permissive in societal attitudes toward attendance at work, companies have been forced to hire nearly 15% more workers than needed to make sure they have enough workers present to remain in operation every day.

Situational factors are also important. Absenteeism declined in the United States during World War II because it was considered unpatriotic to miss work.

Management often contributes to the formation of an absence culture by not enforcing company rules about absenteeism and so appearing to condone it. If management is believed to be lenient and unconcerned about absenteeism, then some employees will take advantage of the situation. The nature of the job may also contribute to absenteeism. Workers in routine, low-status jobs have a higher absence rate than those in more interesting and challenging jobs. Not surprisingly, research generally supports a relationship between high job satisfaction and low absenteeism (Cotton & Tuttle, 1986).

Turnover is also costly to organizations. Every time someone quits, his or her replacement must be recruited, selected, trained, and given sufficient time on the job to gain experience. A number of factors, in addition to general job dissatisfaction, contribute to turnover. These include low organizational commitment, low job involvement, poor promotion opportunities, and dissatisfaction with supervision and with pay (Blau & Boal, 1987).

The general economic climate is also a factor. Turnover is much higher in times of low unemployment and expanding opportunities than it is in times of high unemployment and limited opportunities. Thus, the relationship between job satisfaction and turnover is strong in periods of economic prosperity when there is low unemployment, but weak during economic downturns when there is high unemployment (Carsten & Spector, 1987).

There is one crucial difference between absenteeism and turnover. Absenteeism—taking time off from a job—is almost always harmful to the organization, but turnover is not necessarily detrimental. Sometimes it is the poor job performers who leave. A distinction has been made between functional turnover (when low performers quit), and dysfunctional turnover (when high performers quit) (Watts & White, 1988). A study of 143 salespersons in a big-city department store found that more than half of the turnover was functional, that is, those who quit their jobs had been rated as marginal or unsatisfactory employees in their performance appraisals (Hollenbeck & Williams, 1986). The result of this turnover was potentially beneficial to the company.

A meta-analysis involving more than 7,000 employees in a variety of jobs and organizations found that good performers were significantly less likely to leave than poor performers (McEvoy & Cascio, 1987). It must be remembered, however, that many good employees do also quit their jobs, and their loss is expensive for their organizations. Thus, it is especially important for companies to identify their better employees through performance appraisal programs, and if these employees show low satisfaction, commitment, and involvement, to try to remedy the situation.

Pay As a Source of Motivation and Satisfaction

Frederick Taylor, the father of scientific management, believed that money was what workers wanted more than anything else. If managers wanted to increase production, all they had to do was to increase pay. After many years, that simple idea lost favor. As we saw in our discussion of the changing values of American workers, the concern with pay fell during the 1970s. However, since then, pay has once again become important as a motivator and satisfier. For this reason, organizational psychologists are reemphasizing the value of money, especially for blue-collar workers (Locke, 1982; Thayer, 1983).

One group of psychologists analyzed studies that had been conducted in industry to compare four methods of motivating performance among blue-collar workers. The four techniques were money, goal setting, participation in decision making, and job enrichment. The greatest increase in performance, 30%, was brought about by an incentive-pay system. None of the other methods approached this figure. Goal setting showed an increase of only 16% (Locke, Feren, McCaleb, Shaw, & Denny, 1980).

Many surveys and studies have demonstrated a positive relationship between income and job satisfaction; the higher the pay, the higher the satisfaction (Adelmann, 1987). Among the more important determinants of satisfaction with one's pay is not so much the actual amount but rather its perceived equity. A survey of 248 employed men found that the more strongly they believed they were receiving the salaries they deserved, and the smaller the gap between their actual pay and what they thought they were worth, the more satisfied they were with their income. The survey also showed that older men were more satisfied with their pay than younger men. Employees with more education and higher level jobs were less satisfied with their pay than those with less education and lower level jobs (Berkowitz, Fraser, Treasure, & Cochran, 1987).

Most employees at the managerial, white-collar, and blue-collar levels have become increasingly dissatisfied with their pay in recent years and believe that their employers' pay practices are unfair. Further, they believe that their pay increases bear no relation to how well they perform their jobs (Schiemann, 1987). Although the majority of companies surveyed consider job performance to be the single most important factor in determining pay raises for managerial and white-collar employees, the majority of those employees do not see a relationship between their effort and their salary increases.

Part of the reason for this attitude is that most pay raises are small, which results in barely perceptible differences in rewards for good and poor workers. Reviews of company pay practices show that the pay differential is usually no greater than 2% between raises for good and poor workers, hardly an adequate reward for having performed one's job well or an incentive to work harder in the future (Kanter, 1987a, 1987b; Teel, 1986).

Thus, the notion of pay for performance, or *merit pay*, is fine in theory but does not translate well into actual use in the workplace. A survey of the human resources directors of 805 companies revealed that 70% of them thought their pay-for-performance systems were unsuccessful, even though more than half (54%) said that such systems were a high priority with top management (Fritz, 1988c). The major reasons for the general lack of success of merit-pay systems include poor training of managers in appraising performance and lack of objective performance appraisal measures. Here is further evidence of the importance of performance appraisals in the world of work.

There are other reasons for dissatisfaction with merit-pay plans (Rollins, 1988). First, it has been suggested that the more pay depends on job performance, the lower is the inherent interest of that job to the employee. In other words, when the task is focused on as a means of getting more money, then the managers' focus shifts from the task itself to the goal or reward for performing the task well.

Second, the amount of salary increase depends solely on the judgment of the manager's superiors and their ability to discriminate among various levels of competence. And, as noted with performance evaluation, most people are not very good at making such subjective judgments. For this reason, labor unions rarely agree to merit-pay plans for their members.

Third, the key role of superiors in determining salary constantly reminds managers of how directly dependent they are on their superiors for rewards. This fosters efforts by managers to please their superiors, which can be demeaning.

Fourth, merit-pay programs put managers in a situation of competing with other managers for a portion of the limited rewards. If one manager is to get a large raise, another one must get a smaller raise because a fixed amount of money is available for salary increases. By forcing this competition, managers tend to see their colleagues as enemies. This has harmful effects on working relationships.

Overall, the merit-pay plan is viewed as a threat to the managers' self-esteem. Most people believe that they are above average in their abilities, and to be told that they are below average (evidenced by a small pay increase) is damaging (Cumming, 1988). Instead of motivating them to work harder, such a judgment can have a negative effect, causing managers to feel that their true worth is not recognized.

Ironically, when surveyed, most managers say they want their pay to be determined by merit. In practice, however, the feeling of managers is extremely prevalent that their salaries are influenced by factors other than how well they perform their jobs.

I/O psychologists have conducted research on factors that may influence the size of pay increases in merit-pay plans. One of the most striking findings involves the large-scale differences among managers within the same organization as to the relative importance they attach to certain characteristics of their subordinates in determining pay increases. In one study, some managers relied heavily on length of service in making their recommendations for pay increases. Others ignored that factor. Some managers emphasized consistency of performance, whereas others considered this a negative factor (Sherer, Schwab, & Heneman, 1987). The important point is that there was a lack of agreement among the managers about what aspects of employee job behavior were important in deciding on the size of a pay raise. A worker in one department might receive a large raise for the same behavior that might bring no raise in another department.

Other research has shown that supervisors who themselves receive large pay increases tend to give larger increases to their subordinates. Further, larger increases were given to younger workers who had high performance ratings and who were considered to be low in their salary grade (Heneman & Cohen, 1988). It has also been suggested (though not yet confirmed by much research) that the size of the pay increases given by managers is influenced by their degree of dependence on their subordinates and the existence of threats to that dependence. If, for example, a manager is low in self-esteem, he or she may depend on subordinates for praise or positive feedback and thus may be reluctant to give them low pay increases. The low self-esteem manager may fear that the subordinates will no longer offer praise or support if they do not receive sufficient raises (Bartol & Martin, 1988).

There are also problems with the primary pay determination system used for lower level production workers. Large numbers of production workers are paid on the basis of a *wage-incentive system*, usually in terms of number of units produced in a given period of time. Through a time-and-motion analysis of the job, the average or standard for producing a unit is determined and the wage-rate incentive is established accordingly. Theoretically, this system should provide the incentive to work hard—the more units produced, the higher the wage. But this seldom works in practice.

Most workers will not work to full capacity under a wage-incentive system, partly because they distrust management. They fear that the standard production rate will be set too high, forcing them to work unusually hard for a small bonus. Also, if the production rate is set too low (so that it is easy to exceed the standard and make more money), they believe that the company will then raise the rate. One survey of workers on a wage-incentive system showed that 75% of them felt strongly that they should not work too hard for fear of a reduction in their rate of pay per unit.

Many groups of workers establish their own standard of what constitutes a good day's work and will not produce more regardless of the wage incentive offered. They will spread out the work so that it comfortably fills the number of hours on the job. For these reasons, most workers seem to prefer a straight hourly payment system (Lawler, 1971).

Another aspect of pay that can lead to job dissatisfaction, particularly at the managerial level, is the secrecy of salaries within an organization. In most organizations, it is a standard policy to keep everyone's salary confidential so that no one knows how much one's colleagues or superiors earn. This is particularly widespread at management levels and results in the prevalent phenomenon of managers overestimating the salaries of other managers. Studies show that managers also consistently overestimate the amount of the salary increases that their colleagues receive (Geis, 1987).

As a result, many managers tend to believe that no matter how well they are performing their job, they are getting less than average raises. Not surprisingly, this results in a lowering of their motivation. In other words, they come to believe that their salary is not based on worth. Also, when managers do not know what other managers earn, they find it difficult to judge their own worth relative to their peers. They cannot tell if their superiors perceive them to be better, worse, or the same as other managers.

The same problem occurs at other levels of employment. A survey of approximately 11,000 hourly employees in 37 companies revealed that two thirds of the employees believed that there were major inequities in the pay scales in their organization and that other workers were being paid sub-stantially more than they were for the same job. As a result, pay was a major source of discontent (Rabinowitz, Falkenbach, Travers, Valentine, & Weener, 1983).

Although pay is intended to spur employees to higher levels of performance and to increase their job satisfaction, the way in which pay is determined can have the opposite effect.

Because of the dissatisfaction often associated with traditional pay-for-performance plans, and because the challenges of the marketplace are forcing many organizations to reduce their labor costs, growing numbers of companies are trying approaches to pay that might increase motivation and satisfaction. Some of these include bonuses, profit sharing, stock ownership, and extra pay for extra jobs. All of these programs are based on the same idea: The more productive the employees and the organization become, the more money the employees will make (Grant, 1988b; Horn, 1987).

A survey of 108,000 workers showed that profit sharing and stock purchase plans were favored by more than 75% of the sample (Schiemann, 1987). A study of 2,804 workers participating in stock ownership programs in 37 companies found that such plans increased organizational commitment among the workers and lowered their turnover intentions when three conditions were met: (1) the financial benefits were generous, (2) management was highly committed to the program, and (3) the company maintained extensive communication with the employees about the program (Klein, 1987).

There are more than 8,000 employee stock ownership programs in the United States today. Advocates of the approach suggest that it leads to higher productivity and morale, although there is, as yet, little empirical support for this claim.

Many companies offer year-end bonuses to all employees, if the company profits have increased sufficiently during the year. Individuals who devise money-saving schemes are also given bonuses. High-tech firms are particularly generous with financial incentives. Although they tend to pay lower base salaries than other organizations, they offer greater pay-for-performance awards through profit sharing, stock options, and bonuses. A survey of 64 high-tech firms found that more than half of them provided financial incentives to innovative employees (Kanter, 1987b). For example, individual cash bonuses for money-saving or money-making ideas have been reported as high as $100,000. Now that's an incentive!

Job Involvement

Closely related to motivation and job satisfaction is the notion of *job involve-ment*, defined as the intensity of a person's psychological identification with his or her work. How important is your job? How central a part of your life is it? The higher one's identification or involvement with a job, the higher one's job satisfaction. Because of its strong contribution to job satisfaction, it is important for organizations to understand the nature of job involvement.

What causes a person to be intensely involved with a job? Studies show that it depends on the personal characteristics of the employee and on the characteristics of the job itself.

The personal characteristics important in job involvement are age, strong growth needs, and belief in the Protestant ethic value of hard work. Today the Protestant ethic characterizes primarily older workers who cling to traditional work values. It is not surprising, then, that age is a related factor in job involvement; older workers are usually more involved with their jobs than younger workers. It may be, however, that older workers have more opportunities to be involved with their job because they are working at higher levels of responsibility and challenge and so can more easily satisfy their growth needs. Younger employees, in beginning positions, often have less stimulating and challenging jobs. The strong positive correlation between age and job involvement has been found for workers in the United States as well as in England, Turkey, Mexico, Thailand, and Japan (Morrow & McElroy, 1987; Rhodes, 1983; Saal, 1978).

No significant sex differences have been reported in job commitment. Women appear to be just as involved with their jobs as are men at the same working level (Chusmir, 1982).

A study of 325 accountants showed that professionalism, the degree of commitment to one's profession, bore no relation to job involvement (Morrow & Goetz, 1988). Apparently, it is possible to be intensely committed to a profession but feel no corresponding sense of involvement with one's job.

Because strong growth needs are important in job involvement, it follows that the characteristics of jobs related to involvement are those that allow for the satisfaction of the growth needs. Research has shown that stimulating jobs—those high in autonomy, variety, task identity, feedback, and worker participation—are the ones that invite a strong sense of involvement.

Social factors on the job can influence job involvement. People who work in groups display a much stronger job involvement than those who work alone. Participation in decision making is also related to job involvement, as is the extent to which employees have accepted and internalized the organization's goals. In addition, success on the job and a feeling of achievement enhance job involvement (D. C. Feldman, 1981; Lodahl & Kejner, 1965).

We might expect job involvement to correlate positively with job performance, but the evidence is inconsistent and unclear. It is impossible to state that workers who are more involved with their jobs are more productive than those who are less involved. Studies do show, however, that those high in job involvement are more satisfied with, and successful at, their jobs. Also, their turnover and absenteeism rates are lower than those of less involved workers.

A study of 128 employees in a variety of jobs found that after their return from vacation, their job involvement decreased significantly and their turnover intentions increased (Lounsbury & Hoopes, 1986). Unfortunately, the subjects were not questioned again after being back on the job for longer than a week, so it is not possible to know if their prevacation levels of job involvement eventually reappeared.

Organizational Commitment

Another variable closely related to employee motivation and job satisfaction is the degree of the employee's attachment to, identification with, or commitment to the organization for which he or she works. Research suggests that *organizational commitment* consists of three components: (1) accepting the values and goals of the organization, (2) being willing to exert effort for the organization, and (3) having a strong desire to remain with the organization (Mowday, Porter, & Steers, 1982). Other research has identified three underlying dimensions of one's psychological attachment to an organization: internalization of the organization's values, identification, and compliance (O'Reilly & Chatman, 1986).

Both personal and organizational factors have been found to increase organizational commitment. Older employees who have been with a company for more than 2 years and who are high in achievement motivation are likely to be strongly committed to their organization. However, a study of 119 bank employees in New Guinea showed that organizational commitment developed as early as 6 months after joining the company and that such commitment was positively related to job satisfaction (O'Driscoll, 1987). Commitment to management goals is positively related to organizational commitment, according to a study of employees of a community mental health agency (Reichers, 1986).

Employees with more education and who work as scientists, engineers, or personnel specialists have been shown to have little organizational commitment. Also, employees who have reached a career plateau—who have held the same position for 5 years and so feel they are less marketable and have lower promotional chances—exhibit a significant decline in organizational commitment (Stout, Slocum, & Cron, 1988).

Organizational factors associated with high commitment include job enrichment, autonomy, opportunity to display skills and abilities on the job, and positive attitudes toward the work group. Other factors that may contribute to organizational commitment are pension plans, number of children in school, owning one's home, and friendships in the community.

A study of clerical and other white-collar personnel showed that employee commitment to the organization is strongly influenced by their perception of how committed the organization is to them. The greater the perceived commitment to the employees, the higher the employees' expectation that greater effort on their part in meeting organizational goals will be fairly rewarded (Hutchison & Sowa, 1986).

As with job involvement, organizational commitment does not correlate positively with job performance. It has been suggested, however, that it is related to reduced absenteeism and turnover.

There are two additional points to make about organizational commitment. First, there may be two kinds of commitment: affective or attitudinal commitment and behavioral or continuance commitment (Meyer & Allen, 1984). In affective commitment, the employee identifies with the organization, internalizes its values, and complies with it. This is the kind of personal commitment we have been describing.

In behavioral commitment, the employee is bound to the organization only through peripheral or extraneous factors, such as pension plans and seniority, which would be lost if he or she left. In behavioral commitment, there is no personal identification with, or internalization of, organizational goals and values. Research supports the distinction between these two kinds of commitment (McGee & Ford, 1987). A study of managers in the food service industry found that affective commitment was positively related to job performance and that behavioral commitment was negatively related to job performance (Meyer, Paunonen, Gellatly, Goffin, & Jackson, 1989).

Second, we have assumed that organizational commitment is beneficial to employees. Indeed, it is related to motivation and satisfaction, and can lead to promotions and pay raises as rewards. However, intense organizational commitment can also bring negative consequences to employees.

By limiting their mobility, their freedom to move from one company to another, intense organizational commitment can stifle individual growth. The dedication to one's organization's norms and values can also inhibit personal creativity and innovation and lead to a bureaucratic resistance to change (which can also be disadvantageous to the organization). Strong commitment to an organization can lead to stress in family relationships as the employee focuses more and more time and energy on the company. Social relationships and personal development may also suffer (Randall, 1987).

The Laid-off Worker: No Job Satisfaction

It is fitting to close a chapter on the motivations and satisfactions of work by considering the state of those whose work has been taken away from them. There are many instances of workers who have been dismissed because an automated process has rendered their jobs obsolete or a company reorganization or merger has closed a department or a plant. In periods of economic downturn, whole segments of industry can slow down or close altogether, as happened to many companies in the 1980s. As we saw in Chapter 1, millions of employees, from managers to assembly-line workers, have lost their jobs in recent years, so many that the plight of the laid-off worker has become a nationwide problem. Thus, many workers find themselves without jobs through no fault of their own, that is, they were not fired for poor job performance.

Studies confirm the obvious; this is a time of great stress for the individual who has been laid off. One characteristic frequently observed is the development of guilt on the part of the dismissed workers—the feeling that it is somehow their own doing. This was even observed during the Great Depression of

Unemployment brings
feelings of tension, anxiety,
and resentment that may
persist even when a new job
has been found.

the 1930s. Despite massive unemployment, many people felt personally responsible for being out of work.

There is also a feeling of rootlessness or lack of connection and an increase in mental and physical illness and in suicide. The suicide rate in communities hit by widespread layoffs is 30 times the national average (DeFrank & Ivancevich,

1986). Unemployed workers experience considerable tension, anxiety about the future, and feelings of resentment. For every 1% increase in the unemployment rate, some 36,000 people are believed to die from heart attacks, homicides, or suicides related to their unemployed status. Increases in alcoholism, drug abuse, divorce, child and spouse abuse, and juvenile delinquency are also linked to unemployment. Children of laid-off parents may suffer developmental difficulties, digestive problems, and chronic irritability (Liem & Rayman, 1982; Riegle, 1982).

Higher level employees may suffer even more from unemployment. They become more defensive and self-critical, whereas lower level workers are more adaptable. Among managers, executives, and professionals, there is a deep and long-lasting transformation that affects lifestyle, expectations, goals, and values. For probably the first time in their lives, the unwritten psychological contract they thought they had with their employer had been breached. The terms of that agreement specified that if the employee worked hard and showed loyalty, the company would remain loyal by providing the security of steady employment and periodic pay raises and promotions. Now, such security can no longer be relied upon, and many managers who lost their jobs in the 1980s experienced a sense of betrayal.

The trauma of unemployment may last even when a new job has been found. One study of unemployed men showed that those who found new jobs regained some level of self-esteem, but it did not match the level of self-esteem of a control group who had not lost their jobs (H. G. Kaufman, 1982). Although many jobs may bring feelings of dissatisfaction, being without a job may be the most dissatisfying state of all.

A survey of laid-off workers found that almost half of them found other jobs within 14 weeks, but fully 30% did not find other work for more than a year. In general, it took blue-collar workers a considerably longer time to find a new job than white-collar and service workers. In all three categories, women were unemployed for longer periods than men (Podgursky & Swaim, 1987).

Although not as severe as losing one's job, receiving a demotion or a loss in status or level of work can also be traumatic. A study of professional social workers whose jobs were reduced to nonprofessional status for budgetary reasons showed that the loss of the professional work role resulted in lower job satisfaction and work-related self-esteem. The social workers also expressed higher turnover intentions (Schlenker & Gutek, 1987).

The unemployment of large numbers of people in the 1980s spawned the growth of *outplacement services* for those who had been "placed out" of their jobs. Combining psychological assessment, career counseling, emotional support, job-seeking skills, and, if necessary, retraining, outplacement services are offered mostly to managers and executives, but some companies provide them for lower level employees as well (Duffy, O'Brien, Brittain, & Cuthrell, 1988; Foxman & Polsky, 1988; Piccolino, 1988).

So strong has been the demand for outplacement services that the number of companies providing them rose from 43 in 1980 to 154 in 1986. Typically, the services are paid for by the company that let the manager or executive go, at a fee of 15% of the person's annual salary. Some companies that periodically lay off large numbers of workers have established their own in-house outplacement services.

When Alcan Rolled Products Company downsized a plant in Ohio, it gave employees 3 months' notice and provided counseling and job retraining for more than a year, during which time over 60% of the employees were able to find new jobs (Fraze, 1988). It is significant, however, that even with the company's extensive assistance, almost 40% of its former employees were still jobless a year later.

General Motors, which has had to lay off thousands of workers in recent years, offers employees the choice of a transfer to another location, early retirement for those who qualify, or the use of outplacement services. Those services include career counseling, aptitude testing to assess skills, and the development of job search skills and strategies (D. Feldman, 1988b).

What about the effects of large-scale company layoffs on those who remain with the company? A study of 105 engineers who worked for companies that had experienced mild layoffs (2% to 4% of the work force over the previous 2 years) and for companies with severe layoffs (25% to 70%) found that those who were high in the work ethic retained their higher levels of job involvement as compared to those low in the work ethic, but only in the mild layoff condition. Apparently, a high work ethic was not a sufficiently strong resource or buffer to protect those in the severe layoff companies from the stress caused by the layoffs (Brockner, Grover, & Blonder, 1988). Thus, economic conditions that produce large-scale layoffs can affect even those who retain their jobs.

Summary

The problem of employee **motivation** is crucial in all kinds of organizations today and is responsible for the shoddy products we buy and the careless service we receive. Traditional employee values involved a loyalty to the company and a strong drive for money, status, promotion, and security. The new breed of worker focused on self-fulfillment and self-actualization and demanded jobs that were challenging and that allowed the chance to participate in decision making. They had little loyalty to the organization and less concern with money, status, and security. In the 1980s, workers' values changed again, showing a declining concern with self-fulfillment and an increased concern with pay.

Psychologists have proposed several theories of motivation. The **need for achievement** (McClelland) posits the existence in certain people of a need to accomplish, to do a good job, and to be the best in whatever they undertake. Studies show that good executives are higher in *n Ach* than poor ones. High *n Ach* people like working conditions in which they have responsibility and take calculated risks and set moderate achievement goals. These individuals constantly need feedback on their progress.

The **needs-hierarchy** theory (Maslow) proposes a hierarchy of five needs—physiological, safety, love, esteem, and self-actualization—each of which must be satisfied before the next one becomes prominent. Self-actualization, the highest need, involves using one's capabilities to the fullest, and it can be satisfied by jobs that allow autonomy, challenge, and responsibility.

The **ERG** theory (Alderfer) suggests three basic human needs: existence, relatedness, and growth. The growth needs include Maslow's concept of self-actualization. The ERG needs are not as rigidly hierarchical as Maslow's needs. The satisfaction of a need may increase its intensity.

The **motivator-hygiene** theory (Herzberg) proposes two sets of needs: motivator needs (the nature of the work and its level of achievement and responsibility) and hygiene needs (aspects of the work environment such as pay and supervision). Motivator needs produce job satisfaction; hygiene needs can produce job dissatisfaction if the working conditions are inadequate. However, even if the working conditions are outstanding, hygiene needs cannot produce job satisfaction.

An outgrowth of the motivator-hygiene theory is **job enrichment**, the redesign of a job to maximize the motivator factors. Job enrichment involves (1) removing controls over employees and increasing their personal responsibility for their work, (2) providing employees with full and natural units of work, (3) giving employees more authority and freedom in their jobs, (4) providing feedback on production directly to workers, (5) encouraging workers to assume new and more difficult tasks, and (6) allowing workers to become experts or specialists in a particular task. Initial reports on the success of job enrichment programs were often misleading and based on poorly designed research.

The **job-characteristics** theory of motivation (Hackman and Oldham) posits individual differences in the need for growth and suggests that the workers' perceptions of job characteristics influence their motivation. The five **core job dimensions** are skill variety, task identity, task significance, autonomy, and feedback. These lead to critical psychological states, which, in turn, lead to high motivation, satisfaction, and performance.

These theories deal with **content** of motivation, with internal needs that arouse and guide behavior. **Process** theories of motivation focus on the psychological processes involved in making decisions and choices about work. Process theories include **expectancy** theory, which focuses on a person's perceived expectancy that certain rewards will follow certain behaviors; **goal-setting** theory, which argues that employee motivation is defined by our intention to achieve a particular goal; and **equity** theory, which deals with our perceived ratio of outcome to input and how equitably that ratio compares with those of co-workers.

One way to determine the quality of working life is to measure the attitudes that constitute **job satisfaction**. This is usually accomplished through questionnaires, personal interviews, and electronic mail.

Estimates of job dissatisfaction are strongly influenced by the kinds of questions asked, by personal characteristics of the respondents, and by the level and kind of work. Psychologists today recognize that global measures of job satisfaction may not accurately reflect how people feel about their work. Attention is now being focused on **job facet satisfaction**, individual aspects of the job that can influence the employee's attitude toward it. Much research has been conducted to determine the influence on job satisfaction of factors such as age, sex, race, level of intelligence, length of job experience, personality characteristics, and occupational level.

Job satisfaction seems to increase with age, length of job experience, and occupational level. Sex differences in job satisfaction are, to date, inconsistent and unclear. Race differences have not been found to be statistically significant except at the managerial level, where whites score higher in job satisfaction than do blacks. Satisfaction appears to be unaffected by intelligence, assuming the job is challenging enough but not too challenging for a person's level of intelligence. Job satisfaction is higher for those who feel less alienated and who have a strong sense of internal control.

The relationship between job satisfaction and job behavior is complex. The relationship between job satisfaction and production is inconsistent. It may be that high levels of performance cause job satisfaction instead of the other way around. Perhaps high performance fulfills internal needs, which, in turn, produce a feeling of satisfaction with the job. Job dissatisfaction also can produce **counterproductive behavior** that may interfere with organizational goals. Such behavior includes verbal and physical sabotage, shoddy work, and theft.

Absenteeism is higher in companies with liberal sick-leave policies, high pay, and low-status jobs. It varies among cultures and is higher when management appears lenient. **Turnover** is related to low job involvement and organizational commitment, poor promotion opportunities, and dissatisfaction with supervision and pay. In functional turnover, low performers quit; in dysfunctional turnover, high performers quit.

The value of **money** as a motivator and satisfier has once again assumed importance. A positive relationship has been found between income and job satisfaction. An important determinant of satisfaction with pay is its perceived equity and relationship to job performance. The way in which one's salary is determined, however, is a potential source of dissatisfaction. Blue-collar workers whose pay is determined by a **wage-incentive system** and managers whose pay is determined on a merit basis report dissatisfaction with salary. **Merit-based pay**, in particular, seems to lower motivation to work harder and is perceived by employees as inequitable, in that their true abilities may not be sufficiently rewarded.

Keeping salaries confidential in an organization is also a cause of job dissatisfaction because it can lead to overestimation of what employees think their peers are being paid. As a result, people feel they are being paid less than they are worth and are unable to judge their own performance relative to their peers. Other approaches to pay-for-performance include bonuses, profit sharing, and stock ownership.

Job involvement, the intensity of a person's psychological identification with his or her work, is related to job satisfaction. Involvement results from personal characteristics (belief in the Protestant ethic, age, and a strong need for growth) and from job characteristics (jobs that are stimulating and allow for worker participation).

Organizational commitment is also related to motivation and satisfaction. Commitment to the organization for which a person works is higher in employees who are older and who are high in achievement motivation. Other factors contributing to organizational commitment are job enrichment, autonomy, opportunity to display skills and abilities, and a positive attitude toward the work group. Two kinds of organizational commitment are affective and behavioral commitment.

Perhaps the most dissatisfied workers are those who, through no fault of their own, have been dismissed from their jobs. **Unemployment** is a traumatic experience that is damaging to self-esteem and health. It also leaves emotional scars even when new employment is found. Large-scale layoffs are also harmful to those still on the job. Many companies provide **outplacement** counseling for laid-off workers.

Key Terms

absenteeism	job facet satisfaction	needs-hierarchy theory
equity theory of	job involvement	of motivation
motivation	job satisfaction	organizational
ERG theory of	merit pay	commitment
motivation	morale	outplacement
expectancy theory of	motivation	counseling
motivation	motivator-hygiene	turnover
extrinsic factors	theory	unemployment
goal-setting theory of	need-achievement	wage-incentive
motivation	theory of motivation	systems
intrinsic factors		
job-characteristics		
theory of motivation		

CASE STUDIES

Equity Theory and Status in the Workplace

Because of a program of extensive renovations to the offices of a large insurance company, 198 employees were moved to temporary office spaces for a period of 2 weeks. A psychologist took this opportunity to test the equity theory of motivation. The employees were assigned randomly to offices that were either of higher, lower, or the same status as their regular offices. Four characteristics defined office status: the number of employees sharing an office, the presence or absence of a door, the amount of space per employee, and the size of the employee's desk. High-status offices were private with solid doors and large desks. Low-status offices housed up to 6 people at small desks; these offices had no doors.

Job performance was measured by the number of insurance cases completed during the 2-week period. The results supported the equity theory. The performance levels of employees assigned to high-status offices increased, whereas the performance levels of those assigned to low-status offices declined. No changes in performance were recorded for employees given offices of equal status. Also, the size of the change in job performance was directly related to the magnitude of the increase or decrease in office status.

QUESTIONS

1. What other factors might have produced these changes in performance levels?
2. Is it likely that these status-based differences in performance levels would persist if the employees remained in their new offices for a longer period than 2 weeks?
3. How might employees identified as "benevolent," "equity sensitive," and "entitled" react to such changes in their status?
4. What other theory of motivation might account for these findings?

Reference: J. Greenberg. (1988). Equity and workplace status: A field experiment. *Journal of Applied Psychology,* 73, 606–613.

Job Satisfaction on the Assembly Line

Research on the effects of assembly-line work on job satisfaction, mental health, and absenteeism was conducted at a food processing factory in England. Subjects were more than 200 women employees working at various jobs throughout the plant. Based on preliminary discussions, observations, and interviews about the nature of the work, a questionnaire was developed to measure 4 variables. This preliminary research showed that the 4 variables appeared to be related to the dependent variables (job satisfaction, mental health, and absenteeism).

The 4 independent variables were (1) personal factors such as age, marital status, and length of time on the job, (2) job design dimensions such as job complexity, decision latitude, and attentional demands, (3) psy-

chological reactions such as workers' self-perceptions and their feelings about their jobs (taken as an indication of mental health), and (4) potential moderating variables such as amount of social support on the job and amount of time spent daydreaming.

The results showed that the women on the assembly line were significantly less satisfied with their jobs than were the women in nonassembly jobs such as mixing foods and cleaning equipment. The major cause of dissatisfaction with assembly-line jobs was the low perceived complexity of the work. Despite low job satisfaction, however, assembly-line workers did not have a significantly higher absenteeism rate than workers in other jobs at the factory, a finding at variance with other research on this topic. Assembly-line workers who reported a lot of daydreaming and who believed that their jobs made poor use of their skills measured lower on mental health. Social support on the job was found to have no effect on job satisfaction, mental health, or absenteeism.

QUESTIONS

1. Do you think the results of this investigation would have been different if the subjects had been (1) men, (2) older workers (men or women) in their 50s, (3) employees high in the need for achievement, or (4) new employees on the job fewer than 6 months?
2. Does the job-characteristics theory explain any of the research findings?
3. What other factors have I/O psychologists identified as influences on absenteeism?
4. How is job satisfaction usually measured?

Reference: C. Clegg, T. Wall, & N. Kemp. (1987). Women on the assembly line: A comparison of main and interactive explanations of job satisfaction, absence, and mental health. *Journal of Occupational Psychology, 60,* 273–287.

Additional Reading

Goodstein, L. D. (1988). The social psychology of the workplace. In S. I. Cohen (Ed.), *The G. Stanley Hall lecture series* (Vol. 8, pp. 7–46). Washington, DC: American Psychological Association. Discusses the social/psychological climate of the workplace and how it affects both the functioning of the organization and the satisfaction of the employees.

Herzberg, F. (1987). One more time: How do you motivate employees? *Harvard Business Review, 65*(5), 109–120. A reprint of a classic article on the motivator-hygiene theory of motivation and job satisfaction first published in 1968. Includes a retrospective commentary by the author to relate his earlier work to current quality-of-work-life issues.

Kanter, R. M. (1987). The attack on pay. *Harvard Business Review, 65*(2), 60–67. Describes challenges to traditional pay systems and discusses options such as profit-sharing and gain-sharing programs, employee performance bonuses, and employee ownership schemes.

London, M., & Mone, E. M. (1987). *Career Management and Survival in the Workplace.* San Francisco: Jossey-Bass. A guide to helping managerial and professional employees enhance their motivation, reduce stress, and make decisions about changing jobs or careers.

O'Brien, G. E. (1986). *Psychology of Work and Unemployment.* New York: Wiley. Discusses the nature and importance of work (and the lack of it). Describes the effect of meaningful work (the utilization of one's skills) on job satisfaction, job performance, health, personality, stress, and feelings of personal control.

Chapter 9

The Organization of the Organization

Introduction

All of us live and work within the framework of some kind of organization, a context that provides written and unwritten, formal and informal rules and guidelines about how its members should conduct themselves. As an everyday example, recall your childhood when you were growing up in an organization called a family. A climate was established by your parents that defined the rules by which the family functioned; acceptable attitudes and values and behaviors blended to make your family a unique organization that was different from the families of your friends. Perhaps a family up the street had a personality based on orthodox religious beliefs and strict standards of behavior, whereas a family down the street was moderate in its religious beliefs and raised its children permissively. These families operated within different styles of organization. They established their own climate, characterized by a unique set of expectations, fears, and values for the family members.

Various organizational styles are also evident in your classes. One professor may be stern, even dictatorial, allowing no student participation. Another may operate in a more democratic manner in which students participate in deciding how the course is to be conducted.

Differences in organizational style also occur in the workplace. Some companies are rigid, hierarchical bureaucracies (such as the military) in which detailed rules and regulations prescribe what workers do and how they do it; no deviation is tolerated. In fact, virtually all businesses were once organized along these tight bureaucratic lines.

In recent years, however, a new organizational style has developed as part of the general trend toward the humanization of work. This new look in organizational life is much less rigid and hierarchical. It treats workers as integral members of the organization and allows them to participate in the planning of the work that takes place. This is a radical shift in organizational structure, and it has brought about monumental changes in the ways in which work is organized and performed. Indeed, the movement might well be called a revolutionary one, and it is geared to improving the quality of work life.

To investigate these trends in organizational style and to determine their impact on individual workers (and vice versa), the field of organizational psychology was begun. We have seen that leadership and motivational factors are important aspects of the organizational influence. In this chapter, we discuss the factor that most influences leadership and motivation—the organization of the organization.

Classic Versus Modern Organizational Styles

The two extremes in organizational style have previously been noted: the older bureaucratic style and the newer participatory style. There are many organizations that incorporate aspects of both styles, but we discuss the extremes because the differences between them indicate clearly the radical changes that are currently taking place in the organization of work life. You should be aware of the influences of both styles for a practical reason. You will be working in one climate or another or some variation. As noted, most organizations are bureaucratic at least to some degree, but a rapidly growing number of companies are experimenting with worker participation (often called participatory democracy) as a part of the quality-of-work-life movement so popular in the United States and Western Europe.

The Classic Organizational Style: Bureaucracy

Nowadays we think of bureaucracies in derisive terms, as bloated, inefficient, grossly overorganized, highly structured, and wrapped in miles of red tape that prevents the accomplishment of anything creative or original. These bureaucracies represent a kind of system that exists everywhere but for which no one wants to work. And there is some truth to this attitude as we well know from our everyday experiences trying to deal with bureaucracies.

Yet, it is important to remember that the introduction of the bureaucratic style of organization was once just as revolutionary as today's participative approach, and it was considered just as humanistic in its intentions. Bureaucracy was devised to improve the quality of work life, which it did.

As a movement of social protest, bureaucracy was designed to correct the inequities, favoritism, and downright cruelty that marked organizations at the beginning of the Industrial Revolution. Companies were owned and managed by their founders, and there were a great many abuses in the lives of the workers. The owner-managers had absolute control over the workplace, and employees were at the mercy of the owners' whims, biases, and subjective judgments.

To attempt to correct this deplorable situation, the German sociologist, Max Weber, described a new organizational style that would operate in a manner that was free of social and personal injustice (Weber, 1947). Bureaucracy was to be a rational, formal structure in which the roles of managers and workers were rigidly defined. It would operate along impersonal and objective lines rather than personal and subjective ones: an orderly, predictable system in which all members knew their roles and their rules and abided by them. Like a machine, the bureaucratic organization would operate with precision and efficiency, uninfluenced by personal prejudice. Workers would have the opportunity to rise in the organization on the basis of their ability rather than as a result of social class or favoritism. Compared with the prior situation of workers, bureaucracy was a tremendous improvement and served, in its day, to humanize the workplace.

Although the concept and nature of bureaucracy was first described by Weber in the early years of the 20th century, the practical application of this organizational style was seen in the United States in the mid-19th century with the development of bureaucracy's most famous symbol, the organization chart. In the 1850s, a general superintendent of the New York & Erie Railroad, Daniel McCallum, prepared such a chart for his company and insisted that all workers abide by its structure (Chandler, 1988). McCallum's idea of formalizing the position and status of all employees in a hierarchical structure spread rapidly. By 1910, it had been adopted by most American corporations. The first record of an organization chart in England is in 1919. Thus, in formally defining bureaucracy, Weber was describing a system already in widespread use.

Basically, the change in organizational style represented on the organization chart and formalized by Weber involved breaking down or decentralizing the organization into its component parts and operations, each of which is linked to the others in a rigid hierarchy of control. Weber described four dimensions by which the bureaucratic organization functioned: (1) division of labor, (2) delegation of authority, (3) span of control, and (4) structure.

Recall that the essence of the bureaucratic organization is its reduction to a number of component units. This specialization characterizes the administration of the organization as well as the actual work performed. Different work units were established to manufacture different products or different parts of the same product. Thus, *division of labor* entered the world of work, a concept later fostered by scientific management and technological developments, notably the assembly line. Jobs tended to become simpler, requiring less skill and training, and more highly specialized. Therefore, a new system of managing or coordinating work had to be developed. With increasing specialization of functions, no individual could hope to oversee it all, so leadership and management also needed to become specialized. Authority had to be delegated to a series of interconnecting smaller units.

Delegation of authority meant that for each activity in the organization, one person had to be responsible, and this responsibility was not to be shared or overlapped with anyone else's area of responsibility. Also, every member of the organization would report to only one superior. All communication would flow to, through, and from that superior, effectively cutting the worker off from contact with other levels of the organization. Communication, like management and the performance of the job itself, became specialized or fragmented.

Division of labor and delegation of authority can be seen clearly in the *organization chart* shown in Figure 9-1. In Figure 9-1, the delegation of authority is represented by the vertical dimension. Level *A* (the top position) has four subordinates, each of whom has five subordinates. Authority is delegated downward and, in this example, each step down in the hierarchy is accompanied by a larger number of subordinates. The degree of specialization or division of labor is represented by the horizontal dimension. Each unit of five positions in Level *C* is separate (administratively and in terms of function) from the other units on that level.

The chart shows the organization reduced to its component parts, each administered separately, with each higher level of management responsible for coordinating the activities of larger numbers of component parts. Lines of communication are clear. Employees in Level *C* can communicate upward only through their supervisor in Level *B*, and they receive communications downward in the same way.

An organization chart also portrays the other bureaucratic dimensions: span of control and structure. *Span of control* refers to the number of people a

LEVEL A

LEVEL B

LEVEL C

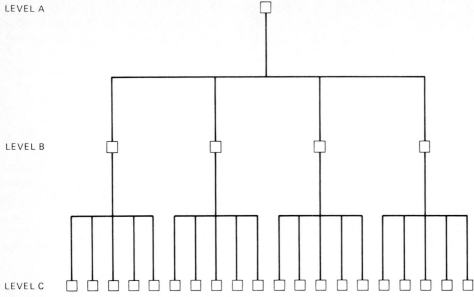

Figure 9-1 A typical bureaucratic organization.

supervisor controls. There is, of course, a limit to how many subordinates a supervisor can effectively manage directly. One individual cannot personally direct the work of 200 people meaningfully, not without an intervening level of managers, each of whom is responsible for a much smaller number of subordinates. Organizational theorists have focused a great deal of effort on determining the optimum span of control, and, although the issue is not fully settled, 5 to 7 subordinates seem to be the most satisfactory, depending on the task and the skills of the workers.

Structure refers basically to the relative height and width of an organization. The organization in Figure 9-1 is wide in structure but not very tall, that is, its span of control is wide and the levels of authority in it are few. A different structure is shown in Figure 9-2. In this case, the span of control is narrow (no one manages more than two subordinates), and there are many levels of authority. Obviously, organizations with different purposes, such as a manufacturing plant and a research laboratory, lend themselves to different structures. However, the principles of the bureaucratic organization were meant to apply to all organizations to maximize their productive efficiency.

Organization charts look nice and give some managers the feeling that everyone is in his or her proper place and the mechanism of the organization is running smoothly. However, neat lines and boxes on paper do not always characterize the daily operations on the job. There is an organization within the organization, an uncharted complex of informal social groups of workers that can sabotage the most rigid rules of the most dictatorial and hierarchical

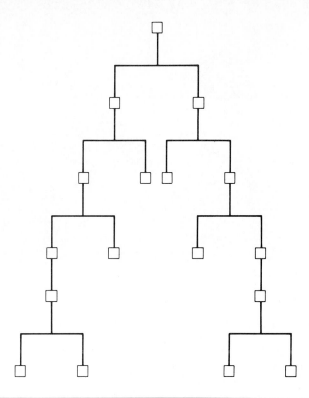

Figure 9-2 A tall organizational structure.

organization. Often, it is through these informal links that the real work of an organization gets done (or undone).

The major problem with a bureaucratic organization, then, is that no matter how rationally it is designed, how ideal its span of control and structure, how specialized the work, and how well delegated the authority, human beings do not always abide by the formal structure. To explain why they do not, let us examine the criticisms that have emerged over the years against this classic form of organization.

Criticisms of Bureaucracy

The major complaint about bureaucratic organizations is that they ignore human values and needs. They treat employees as blocks on an organization chart, as interchangeable as the machinery they operate. As a result, bureaucracy allows no opportunity for personal growth, self-actualization, or participation in decision making, all of which are important motivators. Perhaps this accounts for the differences in job satisfaction as a function of occupational level, which we discussed in Chapter 8. We noted that the lower the level of a job in the bureaucratic hierarchy, the lower was the job satisfaction of the employee holding the job. Conversely, the higher the job within the hierarchy, the higher

The few executives at the top of the organization chart have little contact with the employees at lower levels.

was the job satisfaction. This relationship has been found for employees in the United States as well as in Israel, Italy, and Yugoslavia (Tannenbaum, Kavačič, Rosner, Vianello, & Wieser, 1974).

Bureaucracies can affect job satisfaction in another way. Research has shown that an inverse relationship exists between the workers' perceived degree of the bureaucratization of their organization and their level of job satisfaction. The more heavily bureaucratic they believe their company to be, the less satisfied they are with their jobs. One such study investigated government employees' perceptions of change in division of labor and hierarchy of authority (the number of discrete levels in the hierarchy) in their organizations over a 5-year period. Those who felt that these two characteristics of bureaucracies had increased in their organization reported a significantly lower level of job satisfaction than those who thought their organization was not so highly bureaucratic (Snizek & Bullard, 1983).

Individual employees within a bureaucracy have no separate identities. In addition, they have no control over any aspect of work or of the organizational policies that affect the quality of their work life. The ideal employees in a bureaucratic system are docile, passive, and dependent, rather like children in relation to their parents. Decisions are made for them for their own good because they are not considered capable of deciding for themselves.

This kind of attitude has become increasingly unpopular with employees, who demand jobs in which they participate actively in decision making and that afford them opportunities for personal growth and development. Bureaucracies in their present form cannot meet these needs.

We said earlier that workers in a bureaucracy are cut off from contact with all levels of the organization above their immediate superior. This not only isolates the workers from higher management but also prevents them from participating in decisions that affect their jobs and well-being. This barrier to communication also means that higher management is deprived of the suggestions, advice, and recommendations of employees about how best to perform their jobs. This can be valuable information that is usually not known by others in the organization.

There is another problem with bureaucracies. Not only are bureaucracies criticized for their stultifying effects on workers but also for their harmful effects on themselves. Just as they prevent personal growth, so bureaucracies prevent (or minimize) the growth of the organization, in part by the barriers to upward communication. Bureaucracies represent and foster stability, rigidity, and permanence. Therefore, they do not adapt well or quickly to changing social conditions or to technological innovations. New developments are viewed as threats to the orderly structure of the organization, which is more interested in preserving the existing conditions.

Of course, bureaucracies can and do change, but the process of change is slow and difficult. The only way in which change can be introduced is from the top, initiated by the highest leaders. And this change is then imposed by absolute authority from each level of management to the one beneath it. There is no possibility of input from those most directly affected—the workers.

In sum, the bureaucratic style of organization, for all of its revolutionary fervor and humanistic intentions, has not been an overwhelming success in terms of satisfying human and organizational needs, yet it continues to characterize most business and government organizations today.

The Modern Organizational Style: Participatory Democracy

The classic style of organization was seen as a system running automatically and uninfluenced by individual employee-members. The focus was on the functioning total organism (the system) with no consideration of the individuals who made up the system. It may be analogous to considering the human body solely as a global system, taking no account of the organs of which the body is composed.

The modern style of organization focuses on the individual workers who make up the corporate body. This approach believes that the organization is a reflection and composite of its members and that it is necessary to understand their behavior before attempting to understand the behavior of the organization as a whole. This focus, on the intellectual, emotional, and motivational aspects of human beings, was missing from the classic organizational approach. Thus, topics such as attitudes toward work, job satisfaction, motivation, and psychological aspects of leadership are recognized as being capable of influencing the form and functions of the organization.

This does not mean that the more modern organizational style ignores the characteristics and needs of the organization as a whole. Rather, these organizational factors are believed to arise from and reflect the psychological aspects of the employees (their abilities, characteristics, and needs).

Some organizational psychologists go so far as to suggest that the nature of the employees determine the character of the organization, that the people make it what it is. Employees with different personal characteristics are attracted to different kinds of organizations, and these organizations select and retain them as employees because of the compatibility of their interests and personalities. "Over time, persons attracted to, selected by, staying with, and behaving in organizations cause them to be what they are" (Schneider, 1987, p. 445). It follows that if there are changes in the values, needs, interests, motivations, and satisfactions of potential employees, then the kinds of organizations for which they work will change. We described in Chapter 8 some of the changes in workers' values from one generation to the next. These changes are reflected in the modern organizational style.

How does today's organizational style apply to the world of work? We noted that a major criticism of bureaucratic organizations is their tendency to dehumanize workers, to treat them as docile, passive, and dependent. The more modern organization theory takes quite a different view of human nature, which is perhaps best summarized by the Theory Y position in McGregor's Theory X/Theory Y formulation (see Chapter 7).

Theory X described a view of human nature that is compatible with the rigid requirements of a bureaucracy. Workers needed a controlling, dictatorial kind of leadership because they were seen as incapable of doing anything on their own. Theory Y, on the other hand, assumed that human beings are highly motivated on their own to seek and accept responsibility in their work. Theory Y also assumed a high level of creativity, commitment, and need for personal growth.

In the Theory Y viewpoint, bureaucratic organizations stifle the individual's high level of motivation and potential for growth. The work of McGregor and others holds that the organization must decrease worker dependency, subordination, and submissiveness to take full advantage of human potential. Jobs and organizations must be designed less rigidly, allowing opportunity for the workers themselves to determine how best to perform the work. Jobs must be expanded and enriched to increase the workers' sense of challenge and responsibility. Leadership must become less autocratic and more responsive to input from workers. All members of the organization must be allowed to participate in decision making. Organizations, as a whole, must become more flexible, altering in form and function in response to worker needs and social, technological, and economic forces.

This participative style of organization has been called "high-involvement" management, which is based on three categories of assumptions about people, participation, and performance (Lawler, 1986).

1. *Human relations:* people should be treated fairly and with respect; people want to participate and when they are allowed to do so, they accept change and are more satisfied and committed to the organization.
2. *Human resources:* people are a valuable resource because they have ideas and knowledge; when people participate in decisions, better solutions to

problems are developed; organizations must foster the development of their employees because it makes them more valuable to the company.

3. *High involvement:* people can be trusted to make important decisions about their work; people can develop the knowledge to make the important decisions about the management of their work; when people are allowed to make decisions about their work, the result is greater organizational effectiveness.

In short, the modern organizational style calls for active worker participation in policy making at all levels resulting in greater opportunity for individual expression, creativity, and personal fulfillment and for increased organizational effectiveness. All of these are found in the popular quality-of-work-life movements that have spread throughout the United States, Europe, and other parts of the world, and have led to major changes in the organization of work.

The Changing Organization of Work: Quality-of-Work-Life Programs

We have seen that the contemporary organizational style differs sharply from the older bureaucratic style. The structure of employing organizations and of the nature of work itself is being altered by programs designed to focus on worker participation, and by the recognition that personal growth needs must be satisfied on the job.

Let us examine some applications of this participative organizational style, which is part of a larger movement to improve the quality of work life (QWL) in the United States and Western Europe.

In 1970, Denmark's Federation of Trade Unions signed an agreement with the Employers Confederation that gave employees the opportunity to participate in the organization of their own work. As a result, many Danish companies changed dramatically the way in which work is performed. An ink-manufacturing company setting up a new plant invited its employees to participate in the design of the facility. They were given the chance to tell the planners how their individual work stations should be designed for greater efficiency, safety, and attractiveness.

In the first 2 years of operation, productivity in the new facility more than doubled. It rose 20% at the old plant before the move was made, even though much work time was being devoted to planning the new facility instead of making ink. Turnover in the new plant was cut from 80% to 10%, and absenteeism, previously as high as 30%, dropped to almost zero.

One problem resulted from the employees' participation—they wanted more of it. Once they moved to the new facility, the workers wanted to be consulted by management on all company decisions. When the company arbitrarily introduced some new equipment, the employees resented not being asked for their advice. An executive said, "Once you start with industrial democracy, there is no way of going back." The company now lets workers decide work scheduling and other matters without management control.

In France, the QWL movement enjoys government support through the National Agency for the Improvement of Working Conditions. The agency's function is to assist companies in modifying their organizational structure and the ways in which jobs are performed.

Volvo of Sweden is another pioneer in the movement. For more than 20 years, Volvo automobiles have been built by autonomous teams in factories especially designed to facilitate team organization and cohesion. The teams control their own work and are responsible for manufacturing the entire product. Volvo's experiments in humanizing work have paid off handsomely for the company. Although the output is lower, the quality of the product has improved considerably. In addition, turnover was cut to one fourth what it had been and absenteeism to half its previous rate (Gyllenhammer, 1977).

Many American companies have instituted participative programs intended to improve the quality of working life. LTV Steel Company established labor-management participation teams in the early 1980s to break down the barriers between union and management and to involve employees in efforts to solve work-related problems (Wagel, 1986b). Each team consists of 8 to 10 members, with 2 co-leaders chosen by the team. In addition, each team has a facilitator, a consultant trained in group problem-solving techniques. All team members are trained by the facilitator in team building, problem solving, and communication skills. The teams meet for 1 hour a week to deal with problems that have developed in their areas of responsibility.

LTV has reported a number of benefits from this participative approach to problem solving, including reduced production costs and improved product quality. Some LTV teams have worked with teams from their customers, such as Ford Motor Company, in an attempt to increase the quality of the steel supplied. An LTV team composed of hourly workers designed a system to improve the flow of paperwork within the company, resulting in an annual savings of $72,000. In addition to such tangible benefits, the company reports increased satisfaction among its employees.

At Honeywell's systems research center, teams of managers make decisions that affect the operation of the entire company, from the distribution of funds to designing work facilities to hiring new managers. Each manager hired is chosen by the consensus of a 10-member team. The teams recruit, screen, and interview the job applicants. Managers hired by this team approach have been highly effective, in part because they begin the job with the trust and support of their colleagues (Kizilos & Heinisch, 1986).

When United Technologies Corporation got a new president in 1985, he stated that his first priority was to introduce a participatory management style throughout the company. He planned to delegate responsibility for decision making to all levels and to encourage every employee to participate in and take responsibility for these decisions.

Recognizing that managers are sometimes reluctant to share power and authority with their subordinates, the United Technologies president initiated training programs in participative management from the top down. Some managers could not adapt to this organizational style and either left the company voluntarily or were asked to leave. Those who remained were fully committed to the idea of participative management. Without this total support from management (however autocratically the president instituted the change), the program could not have been implemented successfully among the employees (Furtado, 1988).

One of the most ambitious QWL programs is that undertaken by General Motors Corporation. Enjoying the full support of top management and the United Auto Workers union, the program began in 1973 when company and union officials agreed to form a joint labor/management committee on QWL projects (E. C. Miller, 1978).

Since that time, teams of psychologists, managers, and employees have been involved in redesigning jobs, production facilities, and the basic organizational structure. When a new plant is scheduled for construction, an I/O psychologist is involved in the planning stages to ensure that the facility offers the most satisfactory working conditions. Both the physical work environment (extrinsic factors) and employee involvement and satisfaction (intrinsic factors) are considered as being important in defining a QWL program.

Consider the example of the GM assembly plant in Fremont, California. The company closed the plant in 1982 because of its dismal record. The quality of the cars built there was exceptionally poor, absenteeism was at 20%, on-the-job use of alcohol and illicit drugs was rampant, and more than 800 grievances had been

Under the quality-of-work-life program instituted at this automobile plant, small teams of workers are responsible for mastering a variety of tasks and for solving problems relating to productivity.

filed by the workers against the company. Clearly, this was not a happy or productive place to work. The plant reopened 3 years later, in 1985, as New United Motors Manufacturing Inc. (Nummi), a joint venture of GM and Toyota, committed to the participative style of management.

Employees at Nummi work in small teams of 4–6 members and perform different tasks throughout the workweek, although the cars are still built on the assembly line. Each person rotates from one job to another, mastering new skills in the process. All employees participate in solving problems and in devising new and better ways of accomplishing the work.

Status barriers have been eliminated. Workers and managers eat in the same cafeteria, and they all start the workday with 4 minutes of group exercises. Initial reports show that a majority of the employees, most of whom had worked in the old plant, like the new organizational style and that the quality of the cars produced there has improved noticeably. Labor productivity is reported to be at least 50% higher than at other GM plants and nearly as high as at a typical Japanese Toyota manufacturing plant (Parker & Slaughter, 1988).

There is no single model, approach, or technique for improving the quality of work life that will succeed in all organizations. What is effective at Volvo may not be appropriate at GM; what is successful at one GM plant may not be applicable to another. There are few broad rules to follow to ensure a more effective organizational structure and improved work life quality. Flexibility is vital. Each company, and each department within the company, must be willing to experiment until it finds the approach that works best.

There are many reports of successful outcomes of QWL programs, but it should also be noted that some have failed. Analyses of the reasons for these failures suggest that some employees do not want to participate in decision making and may prefer—or even need—more rather than less direct supervision from managers. Also, QWL efforts can fail when managers try to control their subordinates instead of working with them in a situation of shared authority and power (Muczyk & Reimann, 1987; Ronco, 1988).

Overall, I/O psychologists do not yet have a great deal of data on the success rate of QWL programs because not many of these programs have been studied systematically or over a long period of time. In addition, some of the programs known to be successful have not been publicized. Procter and Gamble, for example, closed a plant that had been redesigned to improve the quality of work life to outside observers so that competitors would not copy the program. Apparently, however, their QWL program works well; since its inception, Procter and Gamble has built more than 20 new plants to emulate the organizational style of the initial plant.

An analysis of 20 plants that had redesigned the structure of their work led one psychologist to conclude that QWL programs can result in increased employee well-being and satisfaction, increased quantity and quality of output, improvements in work methods and procedures, and a better ability to attract and retain workers. QWL programs have also been shown to lead to reductions in the number of grievances filed and in the level of staff support and supervision needed (Lawler, 1986).

Until empirical data become available that might challenge these findings, we may suggest that QWL programs appear to be of substantial benefit to both employees and organizations.

A vital component of these QWL programs is, of course, worker participation and involvement at all stages and levels of decision making. Let us examine this in more detail.

The Nature of Worker Participation

For worker participation to be maximally effective, several psychological and social conditions must be satisfied.

1. Employees must fully understand the meaning and the implications of worker participation and must deal with the changes and processes in a realistic and objective fashion.
2. Employees must agree with the idea of worker participation. Employees who believe that the boss always knows best or that they have no business being involved with decision making will not be highly motivated to participate.
3. Employees must understand that the kinds of decisions being considered are personally important and relevant. They must know how their own jobs and the quality of their everyday working lives will be affected by the decisions in which they are invited to participate.
4. Employees must be able to express themselves effectively and must believe that they are contributing to the decision-making process. They must have some relevant experience on which to draw when considering a work-related problem.

External conditions also influence the implementation of a worker participation program.

1. Sufficient time must be made available to permit group decision making. Employee participation in decision making is time consuming, more so than having a manager make the decision for the group. If a decision must be reached immediately, there may not be sufficient time for the mechanics of group participation.
2. The financial cost of employee participation must not be so high that it will cancel out the advantages. Because employee participation takes time from actual work, the cost of that lost production must enter into the decision to institute or expand worker participation.
3. Employees must feel safe from retribution for their participation. It must be made clear to them that no matter what they say, their rank, salary, and job will not be jeopardized.
4. Effective channels of communication must be opened through which employees can participate in decision making. These communication channels must be convenient and easy to use.
5. Effective employee participation requires some training so that employees understand the format and purpose of the participative process.

A survey of 100 personnel directors showed that 42% of their companies had initiated some form of participative management (Levine, 1986b). A year later, a survey of 1,598 companies reported that 50% had at least one employee participation program (Horn, 1987). Other surveys have revealed that unionized workers are much more likely to favor participation programs than are nonunionized workers, and that the idea has spread rapidly among industries threatened by competition or by general economic conditions (Zalesny, 1988).

The widespread growth of worker participation programs has sparked renewed interest in a traditional form of participation already found in most organizations, that is, the regularly scheduled meeting of a work group. Depending on the receptivity of supervisors, such meetings can provide employees with the opportunity to contribute ideas and suggestions about their work and about company policies. Although meetings are no substitute for the kinds of participation programs we have described, they nonetheless provide some similar benefits.

An analysis of employee participation programs grouped them in six categories, ranging from high to low degrees of involvement (Cotton, Vollrath, Froggatt, Lengnick-Hall, & Jennings, 1988).

1. *Participation in work decisions*. These are formal, long-term participation programs in which employees have a great deal of influence, including the power to make final decisions on all aspects of the work.
2. *Consultative participation*. This approach is similar to participation in work decisions with one difference: Here, workers have less influence. They may offer their opinions but they are not permitted to make final decisions.
3. *Short-term participation*. These programs are of limited duration, but they offer workers the power to make final decisions about a particular issue or problem.
4. *Informal participation*. In this case, the company has not established a formal participation program, but worker involvement in decision making occurs informally, depending on the nature of the relationship between employees and their managers.
5. *Employee ownership*. In employee-owned organizations, every employee has the right, as a stockholder, to participate in decision making. The form of participation tends to be indirect because managers make all decisions relevant to the daily work. Those decisions can be influenced, however, by inputs from the employee-owners.
6. *Representative participation*. In this approach, as in a democracy, employees participate through their elected representatives, who serve on some form of governing council. Individual participation is thus less direct than in the other approaches, and the power of the representatives ranges from high (such as having a vote in management meetings) to low (such as serving in an advisory capacity only).

Research has been conducted on the effectiveness of employee participation and on various aspects of the process. A meta-analysis of 47 studies of the effects of participation on satisfaction and productivity found that participation influenced both variables but that its effect on satisfaction was stronger than its effect on productivity. Also, the organizational climate of a participation program had a more substantial effect on satisfaction than did actual worker participation in making specific decisions. In other words, having the opportunity to participate may be at least as satisfying, and perhaps more so, than actually participating (Miller & Monge, 1986).

A study of 73 managers in two electronics firms in Canada investigated factors influencing their desire for employee participation and found that the greatest determinant was the belief that worker involvement would improve the quality of the decisions reached. Thus, the managers' desire for worker participation was based on a practical matter and was not affected by personalities, job involvement, or organizational commitment. Two job-related factors were found to have influenced the managers' personal interest in worker participation. First, the more dissatisfied managers were with their superiors, the stronger was their desire for employee involvement. Second, the higher the degree of the managers' feelings of job security, the weaker was their desire for worker participation (Long, 1988).

Participation is favored and fostered not only in Western countries and technologically advanced Eastern countries such as Japan, but also in a less developed Communist society, the People's Republic of China. Since 1949, worker committees in China have been consulted by the government in decision making on medical care, housing, child care, welfare, and other social programs. Since 1960, these committees have participated in management decisions affecting the nature of work. Workers at all levels of industry and agriculture play an active role in setting production goals and determining how to meet them (Shenkar & Ronen, 1987).

There are still questions about employee participation. Will workers, given some degree of participation in decision making, insist on even greater power? Will the movement lead to a struggle for organizational control or some sort of shared management? Or will the changing values of new generations of workers, and changing economic conditions, reduce the desire and need for employee participation? Remember that the entire QWL movement originated in the 1970s in response to (1) worker demands for increased challenge and personal fulfillment in work, and (2) the problems of low productivity and high absenteeism and turnover that plagued industry when jobs were plentiful.

Thus, there were both moral and practical reasons for industry's attempts to eliminate boring and routine jobs and to redesign work so that it would offer the chance for self-actualization. The economic climate and sustained unemployment among blue-collar and managerial employees have eased absenteeism and turnover somewhat today, and have replaced the desire for a fulfilling work life with a concern for any kind of work life. We noted that today's young workers are more interested in pay than in personal growth. Self-actualization may be giving way to more basic concerns.

Still, employee participation and involvement remain dynamic components of working life. Two additional ways of organizing work to enhance participation are quality circles and self-managing work groups.

The Quality-Control Circle Movement

The quality-control circle movement came into being as a result of Japanese applications of ideas from American social and behavioral science that were prevalent in the 1950s. Within a relatively short period of time, Japan progressed from being a producer of inexpensive, low-quality goods to a manufacturer and exporter of a variety of high-quality, reasonably priced products. We have only to look around at the large numbers of Japanese automobiles, television sets, stereo equipment, cameras, and business machines to see the truth of that. When the U.S. economy began to suffer from the influx of these Japanese goods, American industry looked for reasons why the Japanese were producing such superior products. They concluded that a major factor was the use of quality circles, an idea that had originated in the United States but had been ignored by business leaders.

Quality circles are not concerned with the overall quality of work life but rather with ways to improve the quality of the finished product and the level of production. In the process, quality circles may raise employee satisfaction and morale and contribute to personal growth and development. These, however, are by-products of quality-control circles. Their goal is a higher quantity and quality of production.

The quality-control circle, based on the work of Maslow, McClelland, and Herzberg, is the notion that a worker must be given greater responsibility for his or her work and be allowed to participate in decisions about the work and the way in which it is performed.

Each circle consists of 7 to 10 employees working in the same organizational unit. Membership is voluntary, and hour-long meetings are usually held once a week. In the initial meetings, led by a supervisor, members of a circle are trained in human relations skills and problem-solving techniques. Research has shown that the extent and nature of the training is critical to the success of quality circles (Smeltzer & Kedia, 1987). Once trained, the groups can tackle specific problems relating to production and decide how these problems can best be resolved.

The quality-control circle is a simple idea and a classic example of worker participation. Who knows better the problems of a specific job than the employees who do the work? It is important to note that quality circles, although they afford the opportunity for employee participation in decision making, do not affect the majority of decisions made in organizations. The hierarchical structure remains in place, and managers do not share their power with quality circles as they do in large-scale worker participation programs. Quality circles have no formal authority. Because they advise but do not direct, they offer only a limited form of participation. Their purpose is, as we noted, to bring about enhanced quantity and quality of production.

Not all employees eligible for quality circles volunteer for them. One survey showed that in more than half of 800 firms that had quality circles, fewer than

15% of the workers were involved (Horn, 1987). A study of 47 quality circles in a Tennessee factory found that less than 7% of the work force had volunteered (Tang, Tollison, & Whiteside, 1987). Other research showed that those who joined quality circles wanted a greater degree of involvement in their work and believed that quality circles would satisfy that need and would also improve their jobs and their organizations. No differences were reported between those who joined quality circles and those who did not in terms of age or length of time on the job (Marks, 1986).

Companies using quality circles have reported substantial savings in money and time, increases in production and satisfaction, and decreases in absenteeism and turnover. An analysis of 33 studies dealing with the effectiveness of quality circles found that 49% of them reported positive results (Barrick & Alexander, 1987). However, there are still not sufficient data available from which to draw overall conclusions about the effectiveness of quality circles. Some quality circles are successful and others are not. Organizational psychologists are conducting research which is oriented toward determining the factors that may account for the differential results.

Initial research does show that the longer a quality circle is in operation, the greater the likelihood that it will produce benefits. Further, management-initiated quality circles solve more problems and solve them faster than worker-initiated programs. Quality circle groups whose members are high in self-esteem are more successful than groups whose members are low in self-esteem (Barrick & Alexander, 1987; Brockner & Hess, 1986; Tang, Tollison, & Whiteside, 1987). Other research comparing participants and nonpartici-pants in quality circles found no differences in QWL attitudes as a function of participation in quality circles, but the quality circles did lead to higher quantity and quality of production and to reduced absenteeism (Marks, Mirvis, Hackett, & Grady, 1986).

Some quality circles disband after a period of time. Reasons for these terminations include lack of support from senior managers and resistance from middle managers, who may find it difficult to accept suggestions from their subordinates. Also, any failure to implement the workers' ideas can lower their motivation and their willingness to remain in the program. Some quality circles fall victim to their own success. Having solved the major problems, there is no longer any reason to continue to meet (Hill, 1986; Lawler & Mohrman, 1987).

Quality circles are popular in many organizations in the United States and in Japan, where it is estimated that at least 3 million workers are involved. More than 90% of the Fortune 500 companies in the United States use quality circles. American organizations that have instituted quality circles include Boeing, General Electric, the *Los Angeles Times* newspaper, Honeywell, Lockheed, and the Department of Defense, among others.

Self-Managing Work Groups

A newer form of worker participation, self-managing work groups, allows the members of a work team to manage, control, and monitor all facets of the work, from recruiting, hiring, and training new members to deciding when to take breaks. A growing number of American and British companies have adopted this approach, including TRW, Procter and Gamble, Johnson & Johnson, Jaguar, and Wedgwood. Typically, self-managing work groups have been introduced in new plants rather than existing plants.

According to one analysis, successful self-managing work groups share five characteristics (Hackman, 1986).

1. Employees assume personal responsibility and accountability for all outcomes of their work.
2. Employees constantly monitor their own performance and actively seek feedback on how well they are accomplishing their task and meeting organizational goals.
3. Employees manage their own performance, taking corrective action when necessary to improve that performance and the performance of other group members.
4. Employees assertively seek guidance, help, and resources from the organization when they do not have what they need to do their job.
5. Employees help the members of their work group as well as employees in other areas of the organization to improve job performance so as to increase production for the company as a whole.

Self-managing work groups require a degree of maturity and responsibility not called for in traditionally managed groups. They also must have clear directions from the organization about the quantity and quality of production needed. In addition, a highly supportive staff must provide expertise and direction when needed, and adequate material resources (raw materials, tools, and equipment) are obviously necessary. In traditional working groups, production goals, guidance, and material resources are supplied by a supervisor or manager. In self-managing work groups, the workers themselves must make sure these are available.

The experiences of a chemical plant in Texas point to one potential problem with self-managing work groups: Not all employees like them. The facility was organized to operate without any level of supervisor or manager. The members of each work team were trained in a variety of skills so they could each perform a number of jobs. The more tasks they could master, the higher were their wages.

The teams managed and monitored all aspects of their work and conducted performance appraisals of one another in face-to-face meetings. However, during the first 2 years of this restructured work program, half of the employees—all of whom had previously worked under a traditional management system—quit. Improved selection procedures later reduced turnover to less than 5% but production remained low until the work force stabilized. Since this initial period, the company has reported improvements in production, and operating costs have declined (Wagel, 1987).

More than 100 telephone operators in one office of the Mountain Bell Telephone Company in Arizona ran the facility full time without direct supervision. The operators were responsible for training, service quality, productivity improvements, office procedures, discipline, and expenses and overhead. The work teams experienced lower absenteeism, fewer grievances, fewer customer complaints, and increased productivity after changing to this self-managing system (Taylor, Friedman, & Couture, 1987).

Self-managing work groups in a British confectionery plant were studied for a period of 30 months and compared with traditionally managed groups performing the same jobs with the same equipment. The results showed a substantial and long-lasting positive effect of the self-managing condition on job satisfaction, but no effect on organizational commitment or work performance level. However, because of reduced labor costs in the self-managing groups, overall productivity showed an improvement. Although the employees claimed to like the new working arrangement, turnover increased after it was introduced (Wall, Kemp, Jackson, & Clegg, 1986).

I/O psychologists will continue to observe and evaluate self-managing work groups to determine their effects on the quality of work life.

The Introduction of Change in Organizations

The programs we have discussed called for radical changes in organizational style, and, as we noted, the classic bureaucratic organization is highly resistant to change. By emphasizing stability and permanence, bureaucracies are not able to adapt quickly or easily to social and technological changes. Yet organizations, like biological species, must adapt to survive. Companies that produced long-playing vinyl records, for example, had to adapt to the new technology of compact discs, or they soon went out of business. Therefore, organizations must be able to change. How is such change best brought about and how can resistance to change be handled?

When a change is to be introduced into an organization, it is often met with a variety of negative reactions: slowdown in productivity, strikes, hostile and sullen worker behavior, and increased turnover and absenteeism. Whether the change is new equipment, an altered work procedure, revised location and layout of work space, new job titles, or reassignment of personnel, it will usually be met, at first, with some resistance.

This need not always be the case, however. Some organizations are able to introduce changes with the full cooperation and support of the employees. The factor that most determines whether a change will be received positively or negatively seems to be the manner in which the change is introduced. If the workers are simply told of the change and given no further explanation or chance to participate in the formulation of the change, they may react negatively.

In one study, changes designed to improve the quality of work life were presented to employees of a large insurance company (Gardner, Dunham, Cummings, & Pierce, 1987). The workers affected by the changes were not given the opportunity to participate directly in the decisions to implement the changes. Three months later, their performance on several measures was compared with that of a control group of employees whose jobs had not changed. Although no severe negative responses were reported, neither were there any of the beneficial effects that management expected would result from the changes. Measures of job satisfaction, performance, absenteeism, and turnover intention revealed no differences between the change group and the control group.

If management makes an effort to explain the nature of a change, the reasons for it, and the benefits that may accrue from it—for both the employees and the organization—then the workers are more likely to react in a positive and accepting manner (Hinkin & Schriesheim, 1988). However, the most positive and accepting reaction can be expected when a company allows the employees who will be affected by the change to participate actively in making decisions about it.

In a classic study of the introduction of change in an organization, machine operators in a clothing factory were studied for their reaction to a small change in work procedures. The experimenters divided the workers into four groups who differed in terms of how the change was to be introduced to them. Group I was the no-participation group: The workers were told about the new work procedures but were given no say in the process. In Group II, representatives of the workers met with management to discuss the change. In Groups III and IV, workers were allowed to participate fully with management in implementing the change.

The reaction of Group I to the change was quite negative. Production by the members of the group dropped immediately by one third, there were marked expressions of hostility and resentment, and 17% of the group quit within 40 days. There was no hostility in Groups III and IV, and none of the workers quit. Production in these groups dropped initially but quickly rose to a level higher than before. Allowing participation through representatives (Group II) was not as effective as full participation by all the workers involved. Clearly, participatory democracy was the best method of overcoming resistance to change, a finding that has been subsequently verified by other studies (Coch & French, 1948).

Are these positive effects permanent or do they disappear after the researchers leave? To investigate this question, two psychologists visited a plant $4\frac{1}{2}$ years after it had undergone a radical change from a centralized, authoritarian, classic bureaucratic organization to a flexible, innovative, fully participative one. The change had been guided primarily by the company president (also a psychologist) and was very successful in terms of productive efficiency and employee satisfaction. The effort is considered a model of how to change an organization effectively.

The visiting psychologists found that the benefits were visible $4\frac{1}{2}$ years later. In fact, on a number of variables, the effects were even greater than during the period right after the change was first introduced. Table 9-1 shows employee attitudes measured in 1962 before the change was introduced, in 1964 after the change was made, and in 1969 during the follow-up study.

Only two factors (satisfied with supervisor and plan to stay indefinitely)

TABLE 9-1 Employee Attitudes Before and After Organizational Change

	Percentage of employees giving favorable responses		
Questionnaire topics	Before change (1962)	After change (1964)	5-year follow-up (1969)
Company is better than most	22	28	36
Satisfied with work	77	84	91
Satisfied with pay system	22	27	28
Company tries to maintain earnings	26	44	41
Satisfied with supervisor	64	54	54
Like fellow employees	85	86	85
Work group is cohesive	25	25	30
Plan to stay indefinitely	72	87	66
Expect the situation to improve	23	31	43

Adapted from "Durability of organizational change" by S. E. Seashore & D. G. Bowers, 1970, *American Psychologist, 25*, p. 229. Copyright 1970 by the American Psychological Association. Reprinted by permission.

showed a decline from 1962 to 1969, although these factors are still at high levels.

Other items showed that the general increase in job satisfaction was accompanied by an increase in the workers' concern with production. Also, the company rose from a position of loss in 1962 to one of substantial return on investment by 1964. By 1968 (the last year of record), the company's profits were still increasing (Seashore & Bowers, 1970).

An organizational change, then, can have long-lasting effects. Positive benefits can continue to accrue as a result of the new organizational climate.

Organizational Development

The examples we described illustrate both change in one part of an organization and change in an entire organizational structure. I/O psychologists have focused a great deal of attention on total organization change. This effort is known as *organizational development (OD)*.

OD involves a combination of techniques, including several we have discussed in previous chapters: sensitivity training, role playing, group discussion, and job enrichment. Two additional techniques of OD are survey feedback and team building.

In the *survey-feedback technique*, periodic surveys are conducted throughout an organization to assess employee feelings and attitudes. The results of the surveys are then communicated to individuals and work groups at all levels of the organizational hierarchy. The tasks of these individuals and groups is to interpret the findings and to develop procedures for correcting the problems identified in the surveys. These survey techniques are becoming increasingly popular.

The *team-building technique* of OD is based on the fact that much organizational work is performed by people in a group or a team. To enhance a team's morale and problem-solving ability, an OD consultant works with the group to develop their self-confidence and self-sufficiency and to break down any barriers to their working effectiveness. The task is to build the team's effectiveness and sense of unity and purpose (Shea & Berg, 1987).

OD takes a global or systems approach to an organization. It is usually a long-range effort and operates under a set of assumptions about human nature that resemble those of McGregor's Theory Y. Some psychologists believe that OD programs are similar to QWL programs, which also often involve total organization change. Indeed, one psychologist has referred to QWL programs as "OD under a new name" (W. W. Burke, 1980).

The introduction of OD to a company is often carried out by consultants called *change agents*. Because they are usually outsiders, the change agents have the advantage of not being biased by the company's existing social climate and are therefore able to view the organization with greater objectivity. However, in-house managers are increasingly responsible for carrying out OD. Change agents' first task is diagnosis, to find out the organization's present and future problems through questionnaires and interviews. They evaluate the organization's weaknesses and strengths and then work out in considerable detail strategies and techniques designed to solve the problems. However, as we noted, it can be harmful for change agents to introduce changes without allowing the affected employees to participate in the restructuring of the organization.

Next in the OD process is the implementation of the recommended strategies, a process known as *intervention*, which begins at the highest management level. Experience has demonstrated that unless organizational changes enjoy the full support of top management, their chances of succeeding are slim.

In actual application, OD techniques vary as a function of the nature of the change agent, the problems facing the organization, and the nature of the organization itself. In other words, OD is flexible in its operation, adapting to the needs of each organizational situation. One generalization can be made: Because most organizations are still classic bureaucracies, OD may serve to free the total organization from rigidity and formality of structure, thereby allowing more flexible and open participation.

Today, OD techniques are used by many organizations such as private companies, public school systems, hospitals, police departments, and the military. The research results with regard to OD demonstrate significant increases in worker productivity. At the same time, the research shows negative effects on job satisfaction, perhaps because of increased pressure for greater productivity (Goodstein, 1988; Sashkin & Burke, 1987).

Socialization: The Introduction of New Employees in Organizations

One way in which organizations are frequently undergoing change is through the addition of new employees at all levels of the work force. They come with different levels of education, motivation, and desire to learn and to do a good job. They have a variety of needs and values that can ultimately produce changes in the organizations for which they work. We noted that this occurred when the generation labeled the "new breed" entered the work force. Their presence forced many organizations to change to adapt to their needs. It has also been suggested that managers and employees who teach and coach new workers may, as a result of those experiences, enhance their organizational commitment and performance (Sutton & Louis, 1987).

Our concern in this section, however, is not with the effect of the new employee on the organization but rather with the effect of the organization on the new employee. New employees have much to learn, more than just a set of work skills for their particular job. They must also learn to adapt to the organization, the appropriate roles to play, the organization's values, and the norms of their work group—its acceptable and unacceptable behaviors. This learning and adjustment process has been called *socialization* to the organization and has been compared with what anthropologists call "rites of passage," in which members of a culture enter into a new stage, such as adulthood (Beyer & Trice, 1987).

Socialization is part of the process of organizational entry, which we discussed in Chapter 3. There we were concerned with potential employees

Interaction between older and new employees should be part of an organization's socialization or orientation program.

before they are hired, with aspects of recruitment and the initial contacts with a company through the personnel office. Our discussion of organizational entry also covered specific selection techniques as well as procedures such as realistic job previews. That can be designated as the prehiring phase of organizational entry, whereas socialization is the posthiring phase that deals with the new employee's first days and weeks on the job.

Both phases of organizational entry, selection and socialization, are vital to the future success of the individual and the organization. Poor socialization to the organization, however—a slipshod, haphazard introduction to the company's policies and practices—can undermine the work of the most sophisticated selection program. An organization may select and hire the most qualified people for its jobs, only to lose them in the early stages of employment because of an inadequate reception to the new company. Poor socialization may foster frustration, uncertainty, anxiety, and dissatisfaction for the new employee from the beginning. And these, in turn, can lead to low job involvement and organizational commitment, low motivation and satisfaction, low productivity, and a desire to quit.

Proper socialization involves several organizational strategies. The company should provide the new employee with a challenging job that offers opportunity for growth, development, competence and confidence, success experiences, positive interactions with senior managers, the necessary training to succeed on the job, consistent feedback on progress, a caring and competent supervisor, and co-workers who have high morale and a high regard for the company (Nicholson & Glynn-Jones, 1987). In addition, the organization should offer a relaxed orientation program.

Research has suggested sex differences in reactions to socialization programs. In one study, 134 men and 84 women were followed for nearly a year after beginning their first job after graduation from college. No evidence was found to indicate that men and women employees were treated differently. The activities and events of the orientation and socialization period were the same for both groups. The men, however, perceived the socialization experiences as being significantly more helpful than did the women (Posner & Powell, 1985).

Another study demonstrated the importance of the relationship between new employees and their immediate supervisors as part of the socialization experience. The new employees—college graduates in their first year with an insurance company—were paired with supervisors who served as mentors. Questionnaires given to the employees and their supervisors showed that the perceived quality of the relationship significantly affected the organizational commitment and performance of the new employees (Blau, 1988).

It has also been suggested that the socialization process will occur more rapidly if there is a greater interaction between newer and older employees. These interactions include asking questions, holding informal conversations, and taking breaks together, as well as formal activities such as performance appraisals and mentoring programs (Reichers, 1987).

It is the orientation program that the new employee encounters before any of the other factors—the training, supervision, or co-workers, for example—come into operation. The program can set either a positive or a negative tone and will determine how the employee reacts to the other features of the work environment. It is also perhaps the simplest of the socialization strategies, the one requiring the least effort and money to implement. Yet, organizational psychologists have found that comprehensive programs for assimilating new employees into the organization are relatively rare (Meier & Hough, 1982).

Consider the experience of Corning Glass Works, which did not have an orientation program. The company's selection procedures were excellent; highly talented people were being hired. But Corning was doing a poor job of managing the socialization of the new employees once they were hired. A training director at Corning said, "Our new people were getting the red-carpet treatment while being recruited, but once they started work, it was often a different story—a letdown. Many times we threw them right into the fray, before they learned the ropes. Often their first day was disorganized and confusing, and sometimes this continued for weeks. One new person told us: 'You're planting the seeds of turnover right at the beginning' " (McGarrell, 1983, p. 33).

Corning was losing up to half of its new professional employees. To try to reduce such costly turnover, the management consulted with 50 newly hired persons and with supervisors and middle managers and instituted a comprehensive socialization program. Both the new employee and his or her supervisor received detailed orientation guides before the employee reported to work. The timetable of events in the Corning socialization program is shown in Table 9-2.

In its first 2 years of operation, turnover at Corning was reduced by 69%, attesting to the importance of the proper socialization of new employees in their early days and weeks with the organization (McGarrell, 1983).

Labor Unions

In addition to the company or agency for which a person works, he or she may belong to another formal organization: a *labor union*. That membership may contribute to job satisfaction and productivity in concert or in competition with the practices of the employing organization. Membership in a labor union can be a powerful force in shaping employee attitudes toward both their jobs and their employers. Nearly 20% of the American labor force belongs to unions. Unionized employees include, among others, blue-collar factory workers, teachers, and state and local government workers.

Belonging to a union can satisfy a number of motives. It can lead to higher pay, greater job security, and increased fringe benefits, all of which contribute to the satisfaction of what Maslow called the lower order needs (the physiological and safety needs). In Chapter 8, we saw that pay is an important motivator and satisfier, particularly for blue-collar workers, who constitute a significant portion of union members.

TABLE 9-2   The Employee Orientation System at Corning Glass Works

---

Pre-Arrival Period

Supervisor maintains contact with new employees, helps with housing problems, prepares the office, and arranges the interview schedule. Supervisor and employee discuss the design of the job and make a preliminary management-by-objectives (MBO) list.

Day 1

New employees have breakfast with the supervisor, have their records processed by the personnel department, attend a "Corning and You" seminar, have lunch with the seminar leader, read the workbook for new employees, take a tour of the building, and are introduced to co-workers.

Week 1

New employees have individual interviews with the supervisor, with co-workers, and with specialists. Employees learn the "how-tos, wheres, and whys" connected with the job, answer questions in the workbook, and discuss the MBO plan with the supervisor. Employees also get settled into the community.

Week 2

New employees begin regular assignments.

Weeks 3 and 4

New employees attend a community seminar and an employee benefits seminar (a spouse or guest may be invited).

Months 2 through 5

Assignments are intensified. New employees hold biweekly progress reviews with the supervisor. New employees attend six 2-hour seminars (on quality and productivity, technology, performance management and salaried compensation plans, financial and strategic management, employee relations, and equal employment opportunity and social change), answer workbook questions about each seminar, and review their answers with the supervisor.

Month 6

New employees complete their workbook questions, review their MBO plan with the supervisor, and participate in a performance review. They receive a certificate of completion for Phase I orientation and make plans for Phase II orientation.

Months 7 through 15

During Phase II orientation employees participate in division orientation, function orientation, education programs, MBO reviews, performance reviews, and salary reviews.

Adapted from "An orientation system that builds productivity" by E. J. McGarrell, Jr., 1983 *Personnel, 60*(6), p. 34.

Union membership can also satisfy the need for status as well as for Maslow's higher order needs of belonging and esteem. Some union members report a greater sense of loyalty to their union than to their company. Membership may provide a sense of power through the union's opposition to management and the knowledge that the employees possess a powerful weapon, the threat of a strike.

The fact that union membership is able to satisfy certain motives, however, does not mean that it automatically leads to job satisfaction. Quite the opposite may be true, at least for some facets of job satisfaction. For example, union membership tends to decrease satisfaction not only with the task itself but also with supervision and with promotion policies. Not surprisingly, membership in a union increases satisfaction with wages and fringe benefits. In terms of global or overall job satisfaction, researchers have found a negative relationship between it and union membership (Berger, Olson, & Boudreau, 1983).

The influence of union membership on productivity is less clear. Unions often oppose measures designed to increase the level of production. In Chapter 5, we mentioned the frequent opposition of labor unions to performance appraisal systems, believing instead that seniority should be the basis for promotion and pay increases. In addition, some unions oppose QWL programs, viewing them as a management tool to force employees to work harder without any increase in pay. Union officials are also concerned that such programs will erode loyalty to the union as well as the union's power by opening direct lines of communication between workers and management.

A study of more than 600 union members of a large utility company showed that more than 85% wanted their union to be involved in such programs. Thus, union leadership may be out of step with the membership on this issue. The study also found that after participation in a QWL program designed jointly by union and management, union members perceived a higher level of union influence in areas of work with which they had not been previously involved, such as implementing technological change and improving customer service. Finally, those union members who believed that the QWL program was successful credited that success equally to the union and to management. Those few who considered the program unsuccessful blamed management for the failure (Thacker & Fields, 1987).

I/O psychologists do not suggest that all union leaders are opposed to techniques such as participatory democracy, job enrichment, and other programs for improving the quality of work life for their members. Recall, for example, the cooperation between the United Auto Workers and General Motors in establishing GM's QWL program. In general, it is union leaders who have had no direct experience with these programs who continue to argue against them. Those who are familiar with these interventions for change tend to be more supportive. It is a challenge for psychologists and management to communicate the benefits of such programs to all union officials and to enlist their participation in establishing them.

Another aspect of union activity that can influence employee attitudes and behavior is the formal grievance process, provided for in nearly all union contracts. Through these procedures, workers can air their complaints and have them handled through a formal mechanism involving union and management personnel. The number and focus of grievances can serve as an indication of job dissatisfaction and can help to pinpoint the causes of problems in the workplace. Grievance procedures also provide employees with a means of upward communication to management. They serve as a kind of pressure valve, an approved means of venting frustrations that might otherwise be expressed indirectly through work slowdowns, stoppages, or sabotage. Grievances, then, serve useful purposes for both workers and management.

Research shows that the rate of grievances within an organization varies with the nature of the job and with certain social factors. For example, jobs involving monotonous and repetitive work performed under uncomfortable conditions by unskilled workers, such as many assembly lines, are associated with a very high grievance rate. Work groups that are highly cohesive tend to file more grievances than groups that lack an internal unity and closeness. Also, first-line supervisors who are low in consideration behaviors are the targets of many more grievances than supervisors who are high in consideration (Gordon & Miller, 1984). An analysis of 324 union members who filed grievances found that winning a grievance contributed to job satisfaction. Worker relations with managers deteriorated when the grievance was settled in favor of management. Workers who won a grievance procedure were more likely to perceive the system as fair than were those who lost (Gordon & Bowlby, 1988). Much remains to be learned about the effect of union membership on attitudes and behavior at work, and it is a highly promising and fertile field for I/O psychologists.

The Organization Within the Organization: Informal Groups

Within every organization—whatever its style or form—cohesive informal groups develop. Extensive research in social and organizational psychology has shown that these informal work groups have tremendous power in shaping attitudes, behavior, and, consequently, production.

Every group of people that meets regularly, no matter how informal or loosely structured it may be, develops communal norms—a shared set of beliefs, values, and socially acceptable behaviors. In other words, group members come to think and act in similar ways, and this encourages feelings of closeness among them.

In industry, workers band together in informal groups and develop a common set of norms. It is important to remember that these groups are not established by management. They are generally beyond the control of management, and they do not appear on organization charts.

What happens when new workers are hired and placed to work in the midst of an existing informal group? In time, usually a short time, the new workers adopt the characteristics of the group. The group teaches them (in ways sometimes subtle and sometimes direct) their way of thinking and behaving and demands conformity.

The importance of this for organizational psychology is that the informal group determines for new employees how they will feel about management and about all other aspects of organizational life. The influence of informal work groups is pervasive, and they are a vital part of the total organizational environment. They can work for or against management by encouraging cooperation and increasing production or by sabotaging management and slowing production.

Informal work groups exist in virtually every organization. These designers working in the drafting room of a large architectural firm have similar backgrounds, interests, and lifestyles.

An Informal Group in Action

For an example of an informal work group, recall the Hawthorne studies (Roethlisberger & Dickson, 1939). A major finding of this research program was the revelation of the ways in which these groups operate. The existence of informal groups was known 30 years before the Hawthorne studies, but this classic research provided the first empirical evidence on their nature.

The study involved 14 men working in the bank wiring room of the Western Electric plant who were observed for 6 months. The observer was present every day and succeeded in gaining acceptance. He was known not to be working for the company and tried to become as much like the workers as possible in speech and behavior. After about 3 weeks, the workers felt comfortable with the observer and behaved as they had before the observation began.

It was soon noticed that the group had its own standards of behavior and production. The men shared many interests in their conversations; engaged in rough, but friendly, play or pranks; and they were always ready to help one another in their work. They formed a close-knit group and displayed many of the characteristics of a family. They valued the friendship and acceptance of the others and avoided doing anything that might bring disapproval from the group.

The most dramatic impact of the group was its determination of a fair and safe day's level of production. Management had set a standard daily output with an incentive to be paid for meeting and exceeding that level. Thus, a worker could make more money by working faster; management thought this would guarantee maximum production. However, the workers as a group had a different idea about production and had set its own standard that never exceeded the company's level. Believing that if they consistently met or exceeded management's standard, the company would reduce the rate and force them to work harder, the group set a leisurely, easily attainable production rate, willing to forgo the temptation of extra money. (And this study was conducted during the Great Depression of the 1930s.)

Some men worked fast in the morning hours, then slowed down during the afternoon; others worked at a slower pace all day. On some days, the group completed extra work but saved it for a day when production might be lower. If a worker did not feel well, the others would work harder to take up the slack. Sometimes they reported more production than they had actually accomplished, but, over the course of a week, they would plan to achieve their standard.

The men readily admitted to the observer that they could produce more (and, thus, make more money), but to do so would have defied the group's norms, and the group had effective (and accepted) ways of enforcing the norms. Anyone who worked too slow (unless he was ill) or too fast was subjected to name-calling (rate buster, speed king, slave). Deviants were also binged (hit hard on the muscles of the upper arm). A new worker quickly learned what was expected—what behaviors would be tolerated and what would not. The group assumed such stature in the workers' daily lives that they considered group acceptance more important than the extra money that could have been earned. Frederick Taylor, the father of scientific management, had observed this tendency of groups of workers to restrict their output several decades before the Hawthorne experiments. He called the phenomenon "systematic soldiering" (Locke, 1982).

It is interesting that the management of the company was ignorant of the existence of these informal work groups until informed by the researchers.

Another effect of informal group membership is a phenomenon known as "social loafing," the idea that individuals do not work as hard in a group as they do when working by themselves. This tendency for people to goof off more when working in a group was recognized in the early years of the 20th century but did not become the focus of research attention in social psychology or I/O psychology until the 1980s (Kravitz & Martin, 1986).

One explanation for social loafing is that people believe they can be lost in a crowd and that, therefore, their slower work will not be detected. Another explanation is that people expect (based on past experiences in groups) that the others will goof off, so they might as well, too.

Research supports both explanations. For example, studies show that subjects did not evidence social loafing when they were told that their individual output would be identified, or when they were told what others in the group were expected to produce. Social loafing was also reduced in situations in which subjects believed that they would be personally affected by the outcomes of their efforts (Brickner, Harkins, & Ostrom, 1986; Jackson & Harkins, 1985; Williams, Harkins, & Latané, 1981).

It is important to note that this research on social loafing was conducted in laboratory settings using college students as subjects. How generalizable the results might be to the workplace has yet to be established.

Nature of Informal Groups

Informal groups exist in virtually every type of organization, setting and enforcing their own standards of behavior and production. They are characterized by intimate face-to-face interactions occurring over an extended period of time. The members must meet frequently for the closeness and communality to develop. They have a common identity (such as workers in the same department of the plant), a central focus, and the same physical work space. Such groups are not too large because they require direct and frequent personal contact. (Usually, the larger the group, the less personal and direct is the contact among members.)

Most people have a need for affiliation and companionship, and this can be satisfied by the informal group. But the informal work group does more than provide a sense of identity and belonging; it can help workers perform their jobs by defining how to work and how much to work.

The group also protects workers; the strength of numbers can help them resist management demands better than can an individual alone. Thus, there are many reasons why workers may seem loyal to the point of subservience to their informal work group.

The group norms and standards pervade other aspects of life, not just how fast the members work. The group can influence political and racial attitudes, voting decisions, consumer behavior, style of dress, what to eat for lunch, and even where to go on vacation.

Because group membership is so pervasive and satisfies so many needs, individuals place a high premium on being accepted and liked by the other members of the group. As a result, deviant behavior is rarely encountered except with new workers who need a little time to learn the group's ways.

Teaching and enforcing these expectations proceed in three stages. First, new workers are told what the situation is, what the group does and likes, and, most important, what it will not tolerate. Second, new workers are observed to see how well they are conforming. As with any learning process, people are apt to make mistakes; when this happens, the group is ready with a warning and perhaps additional instruction. Third, after an appropriate period of time (the length of which is another group standard), new workers have either conformed or have not and appropriate rewards or punishments are accorded (Shipper, 1983). It has happened that nonconforming workers were made so uncomfortable that they transferred to other departments or quit. Social ostracism—being the lone outcast in a group with which one must spend 40 hours a week—is a painful experience that few can tolerate.

The degree of closeness of a group is known as *group cohesiveness*. The greater the cohesiveness, the greater is the power of the group over its members and the pressure exerted on them to conform. Several factors influence cohesiveness. In general, cohesiveness declines as the group gets larger because there is less opportunity for frequent direct contact and more opportunity for the formation of subgroups or competing groups. Diversity of background, interests, and lifestyles can greatly reduce cohesiveness. A work team composed of employees of similar ethnic and religious backgrounds who live in the same neighborhood will be more cohesive than a team composed of diverse ethnic groups, races, or lifestyles.

The nature of the work can also influence group cohesiveness. For example, a wage-incentive system that rewards on an individual rather than on a team basis can reduce feelings of closeness among group members. Individual reward systems induce competition among workers; team rewards bring about cooperation because everyone is working together for a common goal.

Outside pressure or threat affects group cohesiveness. Just as a nation under attack will usually pull together and submerge individual or regional differences, so will a small work group faced with a situation such as an unfair supervisor. Indeed, few things can unite a group faster than shared hatred of a superior.

Another characteristic of informal work groups is *emergent leadership*. Inevitably, one person emerges as a leader, usually someone who conforms closely to the group's norms. If the leader is effective, however, he or she is capable of changing those norms. Thus, although the organization chart may show that employees work for the company supervisor, their own group leader may well have more influence over them.

Informal Groups and Management

There are many opportunities for conflict between the needs and goals of the informal work group and the needs and goals of the organization. In the Hawthorne study, the workers met their own production standard rather than the one set by the company. And, in that example, there was no evidence of hostility toward the company. Had hostility existed, production would probably have been lower or of poorer quality.

If management is to deal effectively with informal groups, it must recognize their existence and try to understand them. Also, supervisors, the representatives of management closest to these groups, must recognize, respect, and, to some degree, accept the group's standards; and they must, in turn, be accepted by these informal groups. Supervisors should be both the formal leaders of the departments or sections and informal leaders as well. This is part of the thin line of leadership the first-line supervisors must walk, balancing the needs of the organization with the needs of the workers. If supervisors lose the balance in either direction, they have failed.

A proper rapport between first-line supervisors and informal group leaders is essential because the latter influence the group to either cooperate with or obstruct management goals. When cooperation between formal and informal groups can be accomplished, it is usually followed by increases in morale and production and decreases in absenteeism and turnover.

A pervasive and powerful condition of work, the informal group serves many needs of the workers. It can serve the needs of the organization as well, or it can defeat them.

Computers and the Structure of Organizations

The widespread and rapidly growing use of computer-aided manufacturing and office equipment is drastically changing the ways in which work is performed. This type of equipment is also changing the formal and informal structure of organizations. With regard to the formal structure of organizations, computer technology influences the integration of various organizational units, the formalization of rules and procedures, and the locus of decision-making authority.

Computer technology creates the need for greater coordination and integration of different units within an organization, something that can only be achieved by developing new reporting hierarchies. At one plant, for example, whose operations were completely computerized, the engineering staff in all sections was reorganized so that it would report to the marketing department, a unit with which it had no previous direct contact. This was done to bring about closer coordination of the needs of the customers (marketing) with the development of the company's products (engineering).

Often, in such situations, task forces, committees, and work teams are established to achieve this revised level of integration. Thus, technology often renders old reporting hierarchies obsolete, useless, and even detrimental. Organization charts must be redrawn as work units, levels, and departments are forced to establish more direct lines of communication.

Computers also require greater formalization of rules and procedures. For example, precise rules that allow no worker discretion or flexibility need to be established to dictate the ways in which data are entered into the computer files. Fixed procedures, rigidity, and regimentation are called for both for operators of the equipment and those who manage them. This necessarily permits less individuality in the structuring or organization of work.

Computer technology also changes the locus of decision-making authority—the level within the organization at which decisions are made—but the direction of this change is not always clear. In practice, automating an office or a manufacturing plant has sometimes resulted in greater centralization of decision making, restricting it to fewer levels on the organization chart. In other cases it has resulted in decentralization, giving greater decision-making authority to the worker at the video display terminal (VDT).

Computers introduce changes in the organization's informal structure by causing dislocations in the traditional communication and power arrangements. Computerization may alter informal communication networks among employees; indeed, it can virtually eliminate them. In companies where clerical workers have their desks side by side and in open view of one another, they can easily communicate about work-related or personal matters. Where such jobs have been automated, the workers are usually physically separated from one another, in walled cubicles that prohibit talking and socializing.

We noted that the development of group cohesion requires frequent and direct personal contact. This is often no longer possible in computerized offices. Group cohesion can be inhibited or destroyed by this lack of personal contact. Of course, both formal and informal communications are possible via computer terminals, but this lacks the spontaneity and intimacy afforded by face-to-face interaction. Communicating with another person through a VDT is not like chatting with someone at the next desk. Automated offices can become rooms full of strangers, even though they are working at the same tasks.

Power relationships within an organization are altered by the widespread use of computers. In general, it is the operators of the equipment, rather than their supervisors, who are more knowledgeable about the equipment and its capacities. Thus, power may shift from managers to workers, and, as a result, managers may have less understanding and contact with the work they are supposed to supervise. This change can disrupt the worker/manager relationship or at least put additional strain on it.

Organizations today are adapting to computer technology by trying to evolve the best ways of restructuring the nature of the work and the organization as a whole.

Summary

All work occurs within some sort of social/psychological organization. Whether the organization is **formal** or **informal**, it dictates ways of behaving, thinking, and feeling to its members. As such, the organization is a powerful influence in the world of work. The field of **organizational psychology** is concerned with the study of various organizational climates and styles and the ways in which these affect the worker on the job.

The two basic organizational styles, **classic** and **modern**, differ in terms of degree of control, rigidity, permanence of structure, and amount of worker participation.

The clearest example of the classic style of organization is the **bureaucracy**, once a humanistic social protest movement against the dictatorial management systems at the beginning of the industrial revolution. Formalized by Max Weber, bureaucracy was intended to be a rational structure in which rules of conduct and lines of authority were rigidly drawn and in which personal bias and prejudice had no place.

Bureaucracy has four major dimensions: (1) **division of labor** (making jobs simpler and more highly specialized), (2) **delegation of authority** (decentralizing management into small units), (3) **span of control** (number of workers for whom each manager is responsible), and (4) **structure** (height and width of the organization as depicted by an organization chart).

Criticisms of bureaucracies include the charge that they ignore the human element—the worker's values, needs, and motivations. Employees are seen as interchangeable units, passive and dependent on the organization with neither the ability nor the desire to have any say over the conditions of their working lives. Bureaucracies are also criticized for their insistence on rigidity and permanence, making them generally impervious to change. They do not adapt well to changing social or technological innovations. The more heavily bureaucratic employees perceive their organization to be, the lower is their job satisfaction.

The modern organizational style, by contrast, focuses on the individual human beings who make up an organization. It is concerned with the intellectual, emotional, and motivational characteristics of employees. Based on McGregor's Theory Y assumptions about human nature, modern organization theory argues that an organization must enrich and enlarge jobs and workers' opportunities to express their full human potential. To accomplish this, less autocratic leadership, and participation by workers in decision making at all levels of the organization are favored. This participative style of organization has been called high-involvement management.

Quality-of-work-life (QWL) programs have become popular in the United States and Western Europe. These programs involve a restructuring of jobs and management. QWL movements are time consuming and require flexibility, experimentation, and increased worker participation in decision making, but can result in increased satisfaction and performance.

Several conditions must be satisfied if **worker participation** in decision making is to be effective: (1) employees must be psychologically involved, (2) employees must agree with the idea of participation, (3) decisions must be viewed as personally relevant to employees, (4) employees must have the ability and experience to express themselves, (5) sufficient time for decision making must be allowed, (6) the cost must not be prohibitive, (7) employees must be protected from retribution, (8) efficient communication channels must be provided, and (9) employees must be trained in the participative process. Worker participation is most likely to lead to increases in production when it is combined with financial incentives.

Another approach based on worker participation is the **quality-control circle** movement from Japan. Small groups of workers meet periodically to solve problems relating to the quality and quantity of production. A useful by-product is employee growth and development, as well as decreased absenteeism and turnover. Quality circles are popular but more research is needed to determine their level of success. A new form of worker participation is the **self-managing work group**, in which a work team controls all aspects of the job.

A problem faced by many organizations is employee resistance when a new work method, piece of equipment, or other change is introduced. However, it has been demonstrated that when workers are allowed to participate fully in decisions concerning the change, they will enthusiastically support it. This positive effect of worker participation has been shown to last more than 4 years after the introduction of a major change.

A series of techniques for successfully introducing large-scale organizational changes is **organizational development (OD)**. The process is carried out by consultants (change agents) who diagnose the organization's problems and devise appropriate strategies to eliminate them. The implementation of those strategies is called **intervention**, which operates throughout the organization, usually beginning with top management. Most OD programs, although differing in their particulars, are oriented toward making the organization less rigid in structure and more openly participative.

New employees in an organization must undergo a period of adjustment known as **socialization**. This is the posthiring phase of organizational entry; selection is the prehiring phase. A poor socialization program can lead to frustration and dissatisfaction. Proper socialization involves providing new employees with a challenging job, proper training, feedback, a caring supervisor, co-workers high in morale and in regard for the company, and a relaxed orientation program.

Membership in a **labor union** can affect job satisfaction and productivity. Belonging to a union can satisfy the physiological and safety needs through better pay, job security, and fringe benefits. It can also satisfy belonging, esteem, status, and power needs. Union membership decreases satisfaction with the task itself, with supervision, and with promotion policies. It increases satisfaction with wages and fringe benefits. Union grievance procedures can serve as an indication of job dissatisfaction, provide employees with a means of upward communication, and serve as a safety valve for discontent.

In every organization, **informal work groups** develop that exert considerable influence on employee attitudes and behavior on the job. Beyond the control of management, these informal groups have their own standards of conduct in regard to production levels and relations with management. Often, the ideals and standards of these groups conflict with those of the formal organization. New employees who do not conform to the group norms may be ostracized. **Social loafing** refers to the idea that people do not work as hard in a group as they do when working by themselves.

Computer technology in offices and plants is changing the structure of organizations. With regard to formal organizational structure, computer technology influences integration of work units, formalization of procedures, and the locus of decision making. It also affects informal communication and worker power.

Key Terms

bureaucracy	organizational development (OD)	quality-of-work-life (QWL) programs
change agents		
emergent leadership	organizational psychology	self-managing work groups
group cohesiveness		
informal work groups	participatory democracy	socialization
labor unions		worker participation programs
organization chart	quality-control circles	

CASE STUDIES

Quality Circles and Self-Esteem

Nine quality circles in operation at a computer manufacturing plant were studied to determine if the self-esteem of the members was related to group success. The quality circles consisted of 3 to 12 members and had been meeting regularly for up to 12 months. Four of the circles were designated as "successful," and 5 as "unsuccessful." The criterion for success was the generation of at least 3 solutions to company problems that management had actually implemented. The self-esteem of the individual quality circle members was assessed by an 18-item questionnaire, which previous research had identified as a valid measure of self-esteem.

The results were clear. The mean level of self-esteem for the successful groups was significantly higher than that for the unsuccessful groups. Thus, self-esteem of the participants in the quality circles correlated positively with group performance. Successful and unsuccessful groups did not differ on any other variable studied (size, longevity, or type of function).

QUESTIONS

1. What limitations or weaknesses do you find in this research?
2. What do you conclude about the relationship between self-esteem and the level of success of these groups? Which one caused the other?
3. How might employees high in self-esteem behave differently in a quality circle from employees low in self-esteem?
4. What other variables can influence the productivity and success of quality circles?

Reference: J. Brockner & T. Hess. (1986). Self-esteem and task performance in quality circles. *Academy of Management Journal, 29,* 617–623.

Delegation Versus Participation in Management

The conditions under which managers chose participation or delegation in reaching decisions were examined. Subjects were 98 managers from various business and government organizations and 26 insurance claims supervisors. In the participative approach, power was shared with subordinates and decision making was a collaborative process. In the delegating approach, managers relinquished authority to their subordinates, who were given autonomy in making decisions. Some of the subjects provided responses to approximately 20 standardized cases in which they assumed the role of leader and selected 1 of 5 decision-making options. The remaining subjects reported on their actual on-the-job use of either delegation or participation in making decisions.

The results showed that the managers used delegation when they viewed their subordinates as being capable of making good decisions and when those decisions involved only minor organizational matters. In addition, these managers chose to delegate when they were under the pressure of a heavy work load. Managers preferred the participative approach when dealing with matters of greater importance to the organization, when they viewed their subordinates as less capable of making appropriate decisions, and when they felt less work pressure.

QUESTIONS

1. This investigation relied on the managers' reported use of each decision-making process. How might this have affected the findings?

2. What do these results suggest about the role of participatory democracy in organizations that are characterized by heavy work loads and high stress?

3. What other factors have been found to influence managers' interest in worker participation programs?

4. What social/psychological conditions must be satisfied in order for worker participation to be maximally effective?

Reference: C. R. Leana. (1987). Power relinquishment versus power sharing: Theoretical clarification and empirical comparison of delegation and participation. *Journal of Applied Psychology, 72*, 228–233.

Additional Reading

Beyer, J. M., & Trice, H. M. (1987). How an organization's rites reveal its culture. *Organizational Dynamics, 15*, 5–24. Examines the concept of organizational or corporate culture (shared norms and values) and the communication of this culture to new employees and managers through rites of initiation or socialization.

Connor, P. E., & Lake, L. K. (1988). *Managing Organizational Change*. New York: Praeger. Summarizes the major issues involved in managing various types of organizational change from minor changes in methods of individual job performance to major changes in supervisory, communication, appraisal, and decision making processes.

Hackman, J. R. (1986). The psychology of self-management in organizations. In M. S. Pallak & R. O. Perloff (Eds.), *Psychology and Work: Productivity, Change, and Employment* (pp. 85–136). Washington, DC: American Psychological Association. Discusses the advantages of self-managing work groups as a way of fostering organizational commitment. Cites the difficulties of implementing self-management programs in traditional organizations.

Heckscher, C. C. (1988). *The New Unionism: Employee Involvement in the Changing Corporation*. New York: Basic Books. Notes the present status of labor unions and proposes a new system of worker representation that would be more responsive to economic changes, current management practices, and employee rights.

Lawler, E. E., III, & Mohrman, S. A. (1987). Quality circles: After the honeymoon. *Organizational Dynamics, 15*, 42–54. Describes the benefits of quality circles as well as the problems that develop in trying to sustain their use over the long term.

PART IV

The Workplace

We discussed in the last section the effects of the social/psychological climate in which work takes place. The form of the organization—its formal and informal structures—the style of leadership, and the motivations of the employees, all influence productivity and job satisfaction.

We turn now to a consideration of more tangible factors that form a part of the immediate workplace. Work is influenced by physical factors such as the design and layout of a work station; the levels of light, heat, and noise; and the number of hours spent working. In addition, the workplace can be affected by accidents and by the physical and mental health of the workers—whether they are under the influence of alcohol, drugs, or stress. These factors can lead to poor quality work, irritability, fatigue, boredom, and a host of other effects that are harmful to the quality of working life.

Psychologists have long been interested in physical aspects of the workplace. Their research efforts have helped to alleviate many detrimental conditions. Psychologists have been influential in designing more comfortable, safe, and efficient places and tools of work. From high-rise office buildings to assembly lines, psychologists are involved in all facets of the workplace, an involvement that will make your own work in the future easier and more productive.

Chapter 10 deals with conditions of work including light, noise, temperature, color, and music. The temporal conditions of work—the number of hours worked and how these hours are arranged—are discussed, along with the boredom and monotony produced by some jobs.

Chapter 11 is concerned with the tools, equipment, and layout of work stations. The field of engineering pyschology involves the design of machinery used by today's workers—everything from a simple hammer to a sophisticated industrial robot. The goal of engineering psychology is to provide the best possible coordination and integration of the capabilities and limitations of humans and machines.

Three serious problems that affect the workplace—accidents, alcoholism, and drug abuse—are discussed in Chapter 12. Accidents are a major problem in some industries, and psychologists help in determining causes of accidents and ways to prevent them. The dependence on alcohol and illicit drugs represents personal tragedies as well as personnel problems. Many organizations try to help troubled employees, a responsibility in which psychologists are involved. Chapter 13 considers stress that results from physical and psychological conditions of work. Stress can impair employees' health and productivity. Psychologists and management are working to develop methods of preventing stress and treating its effects.

Chapter 10

Conditions of Work

Introduction

We are all aware of the fact that the conditions under which we attempt to accomplish something can greatly influence the efficiency and rapidity of our efforts. Whether we are trying to study, read, change a tire, or process electronic mail, the immediate environment affects our motivation to perform the task as well as our actual ability. Is it too hot or too cold? Too noisy or too quiet? Too lonely or too distracting? Is the room or plant depressing in its appearance and inconvenient in its physical arrangement? Is the task boring and repetitive or demanding and exciting? Can you work in your own way or must you follow the procedures dictated by your supervisor?

These are just some of the conditions that facilitate or hinder workers in the performance of their jobs. A company can select the best employees, train them thoroughly for the job, provide them with top supervisors and an optimal organizational climate—all necessary factors for maximizing production—but, if the physical working conditions are inadequate, production may suffer.

Beginning with the classic Hawthorne studies, I/O psychologists have conducted extensive research programs on all aspects of the physical work environment. Factors such as temperature, humidity, lighting, and noise level have been examined in a variety of work settings. Guidelines for the optimal level or range of each of these factors have been established. Much is now known about the work-facilitating characteristics of the physical work environment. There seems little doubt that an uncomfortable work setting can have harmful effects: decreased productivity and satisfaction, increased errors, higher accident rates, and greater turnover.

When a work setting is made more pleasant and comfortable, production usually increases, at least temporarily. But a serious problem exists for the psychologist and the organization in interpreting any such changes in production. It is difficult to determine precisely what caused the higher production rate. Is it attributable to the new air-conditioning system or brighter lighting or the improved soundproofing (the actual physical changes)? Or is it because of more subtle psychological factors such as a more positive attitude of the workers toward management for instituting the changes? Perhaps the workers' perceptions of, or psychological reactions to, the physical changes, and not the changes themselves, cause production to increase and performance to become more efficient. Either way the company is getting what it wants and the workers are happier and more comfortable in the process.

Although it is true that the results might be the same whatever the cause, it is vital that the psychologist and the organization be able to determine precisely the reason for the increased production. For example, suppose it was because of a better attitude on the part of the workers who felt that the company was now interested in them as human beings, not as mere cogs in a machine. If this were the case, it might be possible to influence worker attitudes positively and thus improve production through some means other than expensive physical changes in the work environment.

In many industries, there are examples of people working at peak efficiency under seemingly intolerable or, at least, uncomfortable conditions. And there are many examples of poor production and morale in the most modern, elaborate, and comfortable surroundings. The point is that although the physical conditions of the working environment are important, they are not the whole story. The effects of any physical changes introduced in a plant may be modified or influenced by how the workers perceive and adapt to these changes.

One's perception of reality determines behavior. However, that perception does not always reflect accurately the objective reality of a situation. For example, one Texas factory provided perfect control of temperature, humidity, and air circulation in its plant. From the day the plant opened, however, the employees complained bitterly about the heat, humidity, and lack of air circulation. A thorough check of the system showed it to be working properly, providing correct temperature and humidity levels for the building.

What was wrong? Why were the employees convinced they felt too hot and sticky when they could not, in fact, have been? The answer is a function of the workers' perception of the reality of the situation. Most of the employees had been farmers who were not used to spending their days inside a windowless building; they were accustomed to the outdoors and to feeling a breeze. In the factory, the air-conditioning vents were near the 50-foot ceiling so that no one could feel the air circulating. A clever and simple solution was to attach long tissue streamers to the vents. Although the workers still could not feel the air circulating, at least they could see that it was doing so, and their complaints stopped.

We shall discuss several physical aspects of the work environment, from the location of the plant to piped-in music, and we shall see that such physical changes can affect production, partly because of what these changes mean to the workers. This does not diminish the importance of the physical side of the working environment, but it does suggest that it must always be considered in the light of more subtle and complex psychological forces. Conditions of work also include temporal factors (hours of work, how the hours are arranged, and the number of workdays per week); individual psychological factors (boredom, monotony, and fatigue); and the manner in which the job itself is performed. All of these factors interact to form the immediate physical environment of a job, and this environment helps determine how well or how poorly the work is done.

Physical Conditions of Work

The physical work environment includes everything from the parking facilities outside the plant and the location and design of the building to the amount of light and noise impinging on an individual's desk or work space. Inadequate parking spaces or a parking lot too far from the building may so irritate employees that their attitudes toward their jobs and employer are negative before they even arrive at their work stations. A foundry in New Jersey surveyed its employees and learned that nearly all of them were extremely dissatisfied with the poor conditions of the parking lot. They had to arrive at work unusually early in the morning if they wanted to find a place to park. As a result, many workers frequently became angry and were late to work. After the company paved the lot and assigned each employee a parking space based on seniority, the workers reported that they were much happier with their jobs, and they were seldom late for work (Wright, 1986).

Many manufacturing and business concerns are transferring the plant or office from the downtown section of a city to a suburban location. Corporations can obtain larger quarters with ample room for expansion at a much lower cost than in the city. In 1988, two thirds of all new office space under construction was in the suburbs.

Although there are economic benefits from such moves, there are also personnel problems, particularly with clerical and secretarial employees. Most of these are young single women who prefer to work and live in the more dynamic city than in the quieter and more remote suburbs. Suburban locations appeal primarily to married people who already live there. Those remaining in the city find they must commute great distances to get to the new plants. One company, in the process of relocating its offices 20 miles from New York City in a suburban office park, surveyed its employees to determine what concerned them about the move. Management learned, to its surprise, that 85% of the employees commuted less than 30 minutes to the office in the city, and that 69% of them were very concerned about how long it would take them to reach the new location (Krigsman & Krigsman, 1988).

Many employees are dissatisfied with suburban locations because they are isolated from the variety of shops, services, and restaurants so readily available in a city. They want to have these services convenient to their work. The suburban office is often isolated from everything except other offices, so employees cannot combine work with access to necessary services.

Suburban office parks can be dull and sterile places. Often the only place to take a walk is through the parking lot. Some companies are trying to overcome the isolation and barrenness by providing the kinds of sights, sounds, and activities that are the essence of a vital urban area. By adding walkways, jogging paths, waterfalls, shops, and cafés, a number of suburban plants and offices have recaptured some of the diversity that was so readily available in their previous city locations.

Many organizations, particularly those in more isolated suburban locations, have established day-care facilities for the young children of their employees. Indeed, this has become a significant issue for corporations today and may become a vital fringe benefit in the workplace of the 1990s (Machlowitz, 1987b). Because of a decline in the birthrate in the 1970s, there will be a shortage of new workers in the late 1990s, and more than half those available for employment will be women of childbearing age. If companies expect to hire these workers, they should be prepared to provide day-care facilities for their children.

Such facilities are already found in many companies. In 1970, fewer than 50 organizations in the United States had established day-care programs for the children of their employees. By 1986, the number had increased to more than 2,000, and companies were reporting benefits from such programs in terms of reduced absenteeism, reduced turnover, increased job satisfaction, and greater productivity. At Hoffmann-LaRoche, for example, a survey of employees with young children found that 78% of them believed that their work had improved since the company opened a day-care center (Petersen & Massengill, 1988).

Other research is less supportive of the claims of positive effects of providing day-care services, but few corporate executives today dispute the need for doing so. A survey of companies in California reported that 81% of their executives believed that problems of child care influenced the productivity of their workers and that 71% believed that providing child care benefits would reduce turnover and aid in recruitment. Despite these beliefs, however, 71% of the companies reported that they did not want to establish such facilities themselves (Campbell & Campbell, 1988).

Another problem, this one facing mostly older employees, involves caring for elderly parents. A survey at the Travelers insurance company found that 1 out of every 5 of their employees over the age of 30 provided some sort of care for an aging parent. Other surveys have put this figure as high as 40%. Such employees frequently find themselves under financial and emotional stress and spend from 10 to 35 hours a week tending to family concerns. This cannot help but have some impact on their productivity at work. The problem will affect growing numbers of employees as the population ages. Some employers are already offering in-house counseling support and paid leave, and a few have established on-site centers for the daily care of these dependents (Fritz, 1988b; H. E. Johnson, 1988; Stautberg, 1987).

Once inside the place of employment, other physical features can create dissatisfaction and frustration, such as the ventilating, heating, and air-conditioning systems. In glass-wall buildings, for example, temperatures get uncomfortably hot on the sunny side and far too cool on the shady side. A frequent complaint is having to wait too long for elevators in high-rise office buildings.

Other studies have noted numerous complaints about the food in a company facility. Many company cafeterias, intended as a fringe benefit, actually become sources of dissatisfaction. Another frequent irritant is the number, location, and condition of rest rooms.

The design and size of offices affects employee satisfaction and, to some extent, productivity. For example, the layout of a set of offices can affect the behavior of managers who rely on spontaneous meetings with other managers as a way of obtaining information. The closer their offices are, the more likely are the managers to meet one another throughout the workday. Physical separation—for example, management offices on different floors—will decrease the amount of unplanned contact. For this reason, the typical practice of isolating high-level executives on the top floor of a building, where they rarely have informal contact with others, may not be the best policy from the standpoint of organizational efficiency (Steele, 1983).

The size of an office building may also influence working relationships. The smaller the building, the more intimate those relationships tend to be. As we noted, the more distant employees are from one another, the fewer interactions they will have. Relationships tend to be more formal and impersonal. Recognizing this, Levi Strauss & Co., when it moved from its 34-story office headquarters in San Francisco, designed a smaller campuslike building to bring managers into more frequent personal contact (T. R. V. Davis, 1984).

All of these factors, none of which involves the actual work itself, can impair productive efficiency on the job. Through poor building location, size, or design, an employee's morale and attitude may be low even before the workday begins.

As with most decisions affecting their working lives, employees appear to be much more satisfied with their place of work when they have been given the opportunity to participate in its design. Unfortunately, employees are rarely called upon to do so when companies build new facilities.

The location and design of the building are critical for handicapped persons who often are barred from work, not because of lack of ability, but simply because they cannot get to the work station. Steep flights of stairs, aisles and doorways that are too narrow to accommodate a wheelchair, and inadequate rest room facilities have prevented handicapped workers from being employed.

This unfortunate situation has changed greatly under the impact of the 1973 Rehabilitation Act, which requires affirmative action in employment for the handicapped. In addition to its impact on selection and training programs, this legislation affects building design by requiring the removal of all architectural barriers to the handicapped. All parts of a building must be accessible to those in wheelchairs. This has led to the installation of automatic doors, ramps and elevators, hand holds, wider doorways, and lower wall telephones.

A survey of 300 personnel directors found that 91% of their companies had designed workplaces to be wheelchair-accessible (Feldman, 1988a). IBM, which has been employing handicapped workers for more than 30 years and which is in the vanguard in redesigning workplaces, has built ramps, widened doorways, installed a foot-operated door for an employee who could not use his hands, and installed speaker phones for persons who cannot hold a regular phone.

Redesigning the building for the handicapped worker shows how the physical workplace can influence not only production but also employment opportunities.

Beginning in the mid-1960s, the discipline called *environmental psychology* has sparked a revolution in the design and appearance of work facilities. Combining the talents of architects and psychologists, this field is concerned with all aspects of natural and built environments and their impact on human beings.

Consider, for example, research conducted on office design. Only in recent years have the relationships been recognized between the physical aspects of offices and work behavior. The layout of an office can affect communication between and within departments, the flow of work to and from various groups, leader/follower relationships, and group cohesiveness.

A different concept in office design is the *landscaped office*, which originated in Germany and has become popular in the United States. In contrast to private, separate offices, the landscaped office consists of a huge open area (sometimes larger than a football field); there are no floor-to-ceiling walls to divide the area into separate rooms. Instead, all employees, from clerks to corporate officers, are grouped in functional work units, each of which is set off

The landscaped office, such as this one for reporters at a major metropolitan newspaper, has no floor-to-ceiling dividers. It may enhance communication and social relations but may also be noisy and distracting.

from other units by landscaping such as trees and plants, low screens, cabinets, and bookcases.

In addition to being cheaper to construct and easier to maintain, landscaped offices are said to facilitate communication and work flow. Moreover, the openness enhances group cohesiveness and cooperation and reduces psychological barriers between management and employees. Studies of employee reactions to landscaped office design reveal that it has both advantages and disadvantages. Employees find landscaped offices to be more aesthetically pleasing and more conducive to friendships and social relations. Managers find that communication is improved. The major complaints about landscaped offices relate to lack of privacy, noise, and difficulty in concentrating.

However, research on landscaped offices suggests that the approach has not led to the increases in productivity or job satisfaction that had been expected (Sundstrom, 1986). A study of 109 clerical workers in a large university found that they were dissatisfied with working in offices where there were few enclosures surrounding their work areas, where their desks were close to one another, and where many employees worked in a large open office (Oldham & Fried, 1987). Another study of 247 employees in a government agency found that changing to an open style of office led to decreased job satisfaction and lower trust in management. These effects were greater for clerks and managers than for professionals, however (Zalesny & Farace, 1987). Additional research on university clerical workers found that intrusions and noise from other workers were significantly related to dissatisfaction with the work station. "Employees who cannot shut off their work stations from others [by closing a door, for example], do not have the opportunity to regulate unwanted and unpredictable interruptions" (Sutton & Rafaeli, 1987, p. 270).

Thus, there are obvious problems with the open, landscaped office, but many organizations have switched to it and most are reluctant to bear the expense of reconverting to the old style. In addition, computerized work stations are generally of the open style. Since more jobs are expected to rely on computers in the future, the landscaped office will probably become standard.

In large landscaped offices with computerized work stations, great numbers of workers are crowded in what is inevitably a noisy, high-density area. Their high-tech cubicles, typically separated only by low dividers, tend to lack the signs of personalization—such as photographs, plants, posters or knick-knacks—found in more traditional offices, which may contribute to feelings of individuality and satisfaction. Offices may be becoming more functional but less friendly places in which to work (Pearce, 1987; Sundstrom, 1986).

In addition to studying large-scale questions of work-space design, psychologists have conducted extensive research on specific environmental factors, including illumination, noise, color, music, and temperature and humidity.

Illumination

It seems like common sense to suggest that the quality of work suffers in the absence of sufficient light. In addition, it is known that continued exposure to inadequate illumination, particularly while reading or performing detailed operations, can be harmful to one's eyesight. Despite this awareness, people still try to read by the light of a 25-watt bulb, and industrial employees sometimes operate under not much better conditions. Research shows that inadequate lighting is a source of distress and that high levels of glare, dim illumination, and a lack of natural light, all can have negative effects on job performance (Knave, 1984; Sutton & Rafaeli, 1987).

Intensity, or level of brightness, is the most common factor associated with illumination. Obviously, the optimal level of intensity varies with the nature of the task to be performed and with the age of the worker. Older workers generally need brighter light than younger workers for satisfactory performance of the same tasks. A job involving the precise manipulation of small component parts—for example, watchmaking or electronics assembly—requires brighter lighting than many other kinds of jobs. Although there is no agreement about ideal levels of intensity, the Illuminating Engineering Society has recommended minimum intensity levels for a variety of work areas, as indicated in Table 10-1.

Another factor in illumination is distribution of light in the room or work area. The ideal arrangement is for the light to be uniformly distributed throughout the entire visual field. Illuminating a work area at a much higher intensity than the surroundings causes considerable eyestrain over a period of time. The reason for this is the somewhat natural tendency for the eyes to shift

TABLE 10-1   Recommended Lighting Levels for Selected Industrial and Business Situations

Job	Minimum footcandles[a]
Aircraft manufacturing, supplementary illumination for welding	2,000
Assembly, extra fine	1,000
Cleaning and pressing industry, inspection and spotting	500
Cloth products, cutting	300
Dairy products, bottle washers	200
Tobacco products, grading and sorting	200
Banks, tellers' stations	150
Candy making, hand decorating	100
Barber and beauty shops	100
Photo engraving, etching	50
Hotels, front office	50
Store interiors, stockrooms	30
Laundries, washing	30
Iron and steel manufacturing, stripping yard	20
Offices, corridors and stairways	20
Airplanes, passenger compartment	5

[a] A footcandle of light (or standard candle at a distance of 1 foot) is approximately the brightness produced if a 100-watt bulb were held 10 feet over your head on a completely dark night.

From *Foot-candles in modern lighting*. (1971). Technical Publication TP-128. Nela Park, Cleveland, Ohio: General Electric Company.

around a room. When a person looks up from a brightly lit area to one more dimly lit, the pupil of the eye dilates. Looking back to the brightly lit area causes the pupil to contract. This constant pupillary activity can cause eyestrain.

That is why, when studying or working at a desk, you should have a ceiling light on as well as the desk lamp focusing on your work. This will give a uniform distribution of light throughout the room. Similarly, it is less fatiguing to the eyes to have some illumination in the room while watching television instead of watching in a totally dark room.

Another factor that reduces visual efficiency and promotes eyestrain is glare, which is caused by light of a brighter intensity than that to which the eye is accustomed. The brightness comes from the light source itself or from highly reflective surfaces. Studies in laboratory settings have shown that glare produces increased errors in detailed work in as short a time as 20 minutes. Not only does glare cause eyestrain but it can also obscure vision; you may have experienced this when driving at night and confronted with an oncoming car using its high-beam headlights.

Glare can be eliminated in several ways. Extremely bright light sources can be shielded or kept out of the worker's field of vision. Workers can be supplied with visors or eyeshades such as the type professional gamblers use. Highly reflective surfaces can be eliminated, for example, by painting a high-gloss surface with a dull matte finish. Glare is also a problem with video display terminals, as we shall see in Chapter 11.

The best way to prevent glare is to provide uniform illumination in the work area in the first place. This is best accomplished through the use of indirect lighting. With direct lighting—bulbs located at various points in the ceiling—.the light is concentrated or focused on specific areas, causing bright spots and glare. With indirect lighting, however, no light strikes the eye directly; all light is reflected. Laboratory studies involving a 3-hour reading test under indirect and direct lighting show the clear superiority of indirect-lighting sources (IES Lighting Handbook, 1972).

Illumination is also affected by the nature of the light source. There are three types most commonly used in homes, offices, and factories: the standard incandescent light bulb, fluorescent lighting, and mercury lighting. Each source offers advantages and disadvantages in terms of cost, brightness, and color. Ordinary fluorescent bulbs create slightly colored light that can give people and some colored objects an unusual appearance. Mercury lamps (often used to illuminate streets and parking lots) create a blue-green color. In jobs where color is important, such as visually inspecting for product defects, the choice of light source is particularly crucial. In sum, the choice of light source must depend on the specific job involved.

In addition to the physical aspects of lighting, there is a psychological component with regard to natural versus artificial lighting. Because so many buildings are being designed without windows, the importance of this consideration is increasing. People who work in windowless offices express a strong desire for windows, regardless of the adequacy of the artificial illumination. Not only do most workers like to be able to see outdoors but they also believe that natural light is better for their eyes than artificial light. In one study, clerical workers whose desks were far from windows significantly overestimated the amount of natural light they were receiving. This suggests the psychological importance to these workers of having natural light (Wells, 1965.)

There may also be a physiological need for a certain amount of full-spectrum or natural light. Spending 8 hours a day in artificial light may be harmful to certain chemical functions within the body.

Another potential health problem is caused by fluorescent lighting. Studies have shown that such narrow-band lighting can lead to physical and mental stress and a decline in strength and motor performance. Fluorescent lighting has also been linked to hyperactivity in children, and it may even be unhealthy for plants. In hothouses illuminated by fluorescent lights, plants have developed mutations never seen in plants grown under natural light.

Noise

Noise is a common cause for complaint in modern life. At home, on busy streets, and in the office and factory, we suffer what has been called noise pollution. Noise in these environments makes us irritable and nervous, interferes with sleep, and produces physiological effects such as deafness. Whether noise is also capable of interfering with productive efficiency on the job, however, is questionable—the evidence is contradictory (Glass & Singer, 1972).

The basic unit for measuring noise is the *decibel* (db), which technically measures sound-pressure levels. Psychologically, the decibel is a measure of the subjective or perceived intensity of a sound. Zero db is the threshold of hearing, the faintest sound that most of us can hear. Table 10-2 contains sample decibel levels for various familiar situations. As you can see, we are often assaulted by noises in our own kitchens and backyards as loud as those produced by factories.

Certain loudness levels are known to be threats to hearing. For example, a worker who is exposed daily to decibel levels above 85 for a long period of time will undoubtedly suffer some hearing loss. Exposure to levels over 120 db can cause temporary deafness. Brief exposure to decibel levels in excess of 130 can cause permanent deafness (Trahiotis & Robinson, 1979).

In 1971, the federal government established maximum sound levels to which workers may be exposed: 90 db for an 8-hour day, 100 db for only 2 hours a day, and 110 db for only 30 minutes a day.

Examining the noise levels for work situations shown in Table 10-2, we find that many factory workers are exposed routinely to dangerous loudness levels. Indeed, this is a source of concern to industry; organizations are faced with hearing-damage claims from workers that total millions of dollars each year.

TABLE 10-2   Decibel Levels for Familiar Sounds

Source of noise	Decibel level
Breathing	10
Whisper, 5 feet away	30
Quiet office	40
Average home	50
Normal conversation, 3 feet away	70
Average automobile, 30 feet away	75
City traffic	80
City bus or truck	90
Kitchen appliance such as food blender	95
Average factory	100
Automobile horn, 15 feet away	100
Loud power lawnmower	110
Crying baby	110
Snowmobile	115
Thunderstorm	120
Pneumatic hammer; 3 feet away	120
Siren, 50 feet away	130
Electronically amplified rock band	140
Jet airplane at takeoff	150
Rocket launching pad	180

Hearing loss is a recognized occupational hazard for jobs such as riveters, boiler makers, aircraft mechanics, and foundry and textile workers.

The Committee on Environmental Quality of the Federal Council for Science and Technology estimates that the number of workers exposed to unsafe noise levels is at least 6 million and may be as high as 16 million. The individual hearing-loss claims against industry average about $2,000, and more and more workers are becoming aware of their right to compensation for job-induced hearing loss. The potential cost to American industry is staggering. For economic reasons, then, and to comply with federal legislation on noise levels, industry has become noise conscious.

There may be other physiological costs of high noise levels. Research has shown that when subjects are exposed to noises in the 95–110 db range, blood vessels constrict, heart rate changes, and the pupils of the eyes dilate. The constriction of the blood vessels continues for some time after the noise stops and alters the blood supply throughout the body. It has been suggested that continuous exposure to loud noise can raise blood pressure and perhaps contribute to heart disease. Loud noises also increase muscle tension (W. Burns, 1979; Kryter, 1970).

As if these physiological effects were not serious enough, some psychologists have suggested that noise can impair emotional well-being and serve as a source of stress. Those who work in extremely noisy environments are more aggressive, distrustful, and irritable than those who work in quieter surroundings (Donnerstein & Wilson, 1976).

Not all kinds of noise are equally annoying or distracting. An important characteristic of noise is whether it is constant or intermittent. The intermittent or irregular noise is much more disturbing than the steady or constant noise. Humans are able to adapt to continuous noises. When a noise is first introduced into our environment, it is disturbing because of its contrast with the relative quiet that preceded it. After a while, however, we may no longer notice the continuous sound. It becomes part of the background because we have adapted to it. For example, when a fan or air conditioner is turned on, we are aware of the sound, but this conscious awareness fades with continued exposure. For the same reason, we no longer hear the noise of the engines on a flight in a jet airliner after a short period of time. We are also able to adapt to intermittent sounds that appear regularly, but we find it difficult, if not impossible, to adapt to noises occurring on a random basis.

It is important to note that this adaptation may be occurring only at the conscious level. That is, workers may not hear the loud noise or production machinery after a period of time, but the physiological effects may still be taking place. Hearing suffers, blood vessels constrict, and more energy is required to continue work at the same pace. Although workers are not consciously aware of the noise, these physiological effects plus the additional energy needed for work may cause them to feel tired and irritable. Thus, loud noise may exact its toll on the human body, even if we consciously adapt to it.

Noise can also interfere with communication in the workplace. If the background level of noise is low—between 50 and 60 db—then two people can conduct a conversation without raising their voices at a distance of up to 5 feet. As the background noise level rises, people must either talk louder or stand closer together. The decibel level of an average factory, about 100 db, forces workers to shout at one another in order to be heard. Under these conditions, it is likely that key words will be lost.

Landscaped offices, although usually not as noisy as factories, are nevertheless noisier than traditional offices. Many people are talking, without the barriers or buffers of walls, and office equipment is usually clacking or humming. Surveys show that between 20% and 50% of all office workers, particularly those who work in landscaped offices, are annoyed by unwanted sounds ranging from ringing telephones to co-workers' conversations (Sundstrom, 1986).

Computer technology has introduced additional annoying noises from high-speed printers and terminals that whine and beep. Many office workers, usually younger ones, complain about these sounds. Managers and supervisors, who are typically older, do not report being so bothered by high-tech sounds. It is likely, however, that as a normal consequence of aging, they have lost their ability to hear the higher frequencies (Pearce, 1987). Also, they are more likely to have private offices and thus would be protected from most routine office noise.

All sounds are not equal. Some noise is greatly disturbing, some barely noticed, and some peaceful and soothing such as the sound of the ocean. Also, as with virtually everything, there are individual differences in noise tolerance. One person may not notice the noise that is driving the neighbors berserk. There are people for whom too much quiet is disturbing, for example, those who live in the city and find themselves unable to sleep when visiting in the countryside. "The silence," they say "is deafening."

What are the effects of noise on productive efficiency? We have noted that noise can distract, disturb, deafen, impair physiological functioning, and lead to fatigue. Can it also affect working ability? Because of all the harmful effects of noise, it is usually assumed that noise lowers efficiency on the job. The empirical evidence, however, is contradictory; research has failed to resolve the issue. The question is complicated by factors such as the type of work (a telephone operator may be more distracted by noise than a pneumatic drill operator), the kind of noise involved, and the personal characteristics of the employee.

Studies conducted on the job have shown that noise reduction did not lead to improvement in production levels, but it did lead to a reduction in errors (Broadbent & Little, 1960). Research on jobs requiring long periods of sustained attention, such as watching a radar screen, also show a lack of consistency of the effects of noise (Koelega & Brinkman, 1986).

Thus, we cannot be certain of the effects of high noise levels on production. However, even if it were shown that noise has no effect on working efficiency, industry still must reduce noise to protect the health of employees. Preventing industrial noise is an engineering and design problem, but, with some items of equipment, it is a tremendous challenge. Building quieter machines, particularly for the construction industry, can be very expensive. Also, it has happened that noise reduction was obtained at the cost of reduced efficiency of the equipment. For other types of machinery, mufflers and sound baffles are effective.

One way to prevent noise in adjacent areas of a plant is to move the noisy equipment or to enclose the area with sound-absorbing materials. This does not reduce the noise level for workers who must operate the equipment, but it does prevent others (such as office personnel) from being disturbed by it.

If the noise cannot be reduced at its source, the next step is to safeguard the workers through some sort of ear protection such as earplugs, muffs, or helmets worn over the head and ears. Earplugs are the cheapest and easiest means of protection but have not gained wide acceptance in industry, partly because they can be uncomfortable. Properly fit and continuously used, however, earplugs can prevent the hearing loss that results from constant exposure to high noise levels. Heavily padded earmuffs are used by persons who work around jet engines, rocket test and launching stations, and other areas of intense noise.

Color

Exaggerated claims have often been made about the benefits of the proper color or combination of colors for homes, offices, and plants. Color, it has been alleged, can increase production, lower accidents and errors, and raise morale. Articles in popular magazines tell us that colors can reflect our personalities or change our lifestyles. These claims are not supported by empirical evidence, and there is no validity to the purported relationship between the use of a specific color and resulting production, fatigue, or job satisfaction.

This does not mean, however, that the proper use of color has no place in industry. Color can provide a more pleasant working environment and can aid in safety. For example, color is used in many plants as a coding device. Fire equipment is red, danger areas are yellow, and first-aid equipment is green. This allows such equipment and areas to be quickly and positively identified.

Color can also be used to prevent eyestrain because colors differ in their reflective properties. A white wall reflects more light than a dark one. Thus, the appropriate use of color can make a room seem lighter or darker.

Colors can create differing illusions of size and temperature. A room painted a dark color will seem smaller and more closed in than it actually is. Light-colored walls give the feeling of greater space and openness.

Interior decorators tell us that blues and greens are cool colors and reds and oranges are warm colors. Anecdotal evidence suggests that these colors may influence our perception of how warm or cool the workplace is. One psychologist reported the case of an office that was repainted from a drab color scheme to one that featured blue (Sundstrom, 1986). When winter approached, the employees complained that they were cold, yet the indoor office temperature was just what it had been every winter.

The temperature was raised 5 degrees, but the complaints persisted. The office was repainted in so-called warm colors and soon the employees complained of feeling too hot. The temperature was lowered 5 degrees, to where it had been previously, and the complaints ceased.

TABLE 10-3 Preferences for Color Schemes Among 1,097
Office Workers

Color scheme	Preference (percentage)
Cool colors (blues and greens)	72
Pastels (light blue, pale yellow)	67
Warm colors (yellows and reds)	59
Subdued colors, intense accent colors	53
Neutral colors (beige, putty, tan)	50
White	26
Intense colors (bright reds and greens)	20
Grays	10

Adapted from *Work Places: The Psychology of the Physical Environment in
Offices and Factories* (p. 182) by E. Sundstrom, 1986, Cambridge, England:
Cambridge University Press.

When office workers were asked for their color preferences for their
workplace, the majority expressed a preference for cool colors, as shown in
Table 10-3. Decorators claim that people are more excitable and animated in a
warm room, more relaxed and calm in a cool one. Again, there is little empirical
support for this notion.

If a work area is dingy and dreary, repainting it may improve employee
morale. A fresh paint job under these circumstances—in any color—may,
indeed, make people happier with their work environment. However, there is
little to be said with assurance about the effects of color on behavior at work.

Music

The use of music at work may be as old as work itself. Workers traditionally sang
at their jobs, even when the factories of the Industrial Revolution brought heavy,
noisy machinery. During the late 1800s and early 1900s, quieter factories, such as
those in the tobacco industry, encouraged singing on the job. Some companies
hired orchestras to play for the workers, and by the 1930s, many also had bands
and glee clubs (Sundstrom, 1986).

As with color, extravagant claims have been made about the effects of music
on production and morale. Employees are allegedly happier, work harder, have
fewer absences, and are less tired at the end of the workday as a result of
listening to music while they work. A few studies, undertaken by the firms that
supply the music, support these claims, but their research leaves much to be
desired in terms of thoroughness and competence of design.

Most of the early research on music indicated that the majority of people
liked the idea of music during work and thought it would make them happier
and more productive. However, there seems to be no valid support for the idea
that music will increase production levels for all kinds of work. The effect of

music depends, in part, on the nature of the work involved. Research suggests that music may increase productivity slightly on jobs that are reasonably simple, repetitive, and involve units of very short duration such as assembly-line work (Fox, 1971; Wokoun, 1963). This type of job is regarded by most people as monotonous and not sufficiently demanding to engage the workers' attention fully. Thus, the music might provide a focus—something to occupy the mind—and cause the workday to pass more quickly and enjoyably.

The situation is different with complex and demanding work. There is no evidence that music will increase production on a difficult job for one very good reason: The complexity of the work demands full and concentrated attention. At the very least, workers would be unable to attend to the music and, if the work were extremely demanding, the music could become distracting and interfering.

Think of the jobs of air traffic controller and assembly-line worker at an automobile plant in terms of complexity and demands on the individual. We can understand how music could be soothing and enjoyable to the latter person and annoying or simply unheard by the former.

The effectiveness of music, if any, also depends on the kind of music played. There are individual and group differences in the type of music appreciated. A younger group of workers would probably choose different music than a group of employees over age 45. Some studies have reported differences in productive output as a function of various kinds of music (although other studies have failed to confirm this finding). But, whatever the effect on production, there is no doubt of the existence of musical preferences. The development of personal stereo equipment with headphones allows employees to select their own music and listen to it without disturbing others.

Most industrial music is now of the piped-in or Muzak type. Muzak, in business since 1934, is now played to some 80 million people every day in more than 110,000 American businesses. Company officials at Muzak contend that its purpose is to "humanize the work area" by giving workers "a lift." A new musical program of 486 songs is created for each day, and the tempo of the music corresponds to changes in workers' moods and energy levels. It is supposed to be more stimulating at midmorning and midafternoon.

The effect of music on production is another area in which competent research is needed. Most employees say they like music at work. It may improve production for simple jobs and make some work more pleasant (or less unpleasant), but there are still many unresolved questions.

Temperature and Humidity

We have all experienced the effects of temperature and humidity on our morale, our ability to work well, and even our physical and emotional well-being. The weather and climate affect people in diverse ways. Some of us are happier and have more vitality in cold weather, whereas others prefer hot weather. Some are severely depressed by several days of rain, whereas others barely notice it.

Our bodies maintain a constant temperature of about 98.6°F through an elaborate and precise regulatory system. To a great extent, the body is able to maintain this temperature stability despite drastic changes in external temperatures. We help by wearing more clothes in winter and fewer in summer and by adjusting heating or air-conditioning systems accordingly.

For work that takes place indoors, the temperature and humidity can be precisely controlled, assuming the company is willing to spend the necessary money and that the facilities are amenable. A huge steel mill, for example, would be prohibitively expensive to air condition.

Research has established optimal temperature and humidity ranges within which most people feel comfortable. According to heating and ventilation engineers, the most comfortable temperature range is 73°F to 77°F, and the ideal humidity range is 25% to 50%. These levels apply regardless of the outside temperature and humidity. The expressed temperature preferences of most of us, however, do not agree with these estimates. People seem to prefer somewhat warmer indoor temperatures in winter (69°F to 73°F) than in summer (65°F to 70°F).

Although most of us work in facilities where temperatures and humidity are controlled and where we are not bothered by extremes in weather, there are still many whose places of work are affected by outside temperatures, particularly in summer. How does this affect worker productivity?

The human body can adapt to many conditions: combat, concentration camps, submarines, or space capsules. This adaptability also applies to extremes of weather. Most of us can accept extremely high temperatures and (although it may take up to a week to adapt) can maintain the ability to work in hot and humid weather for long periods of time. For example, shipyard workers in summer can feel the intense heat of the steel decks through heavy shoes. Such people successfully spend their careers under nearly intolerable working conditions (given enough salt tablets and water).

Although we can physically adapt to temperature extremes, can we work as efficiently as under more comfortable conditions? Research in this area is complicated by two additional conditions that interact with temperature to form *effective* temperature (the thermometer reading is called *absolute* temperature). These variables—humidity and air movement—are each capable of influencing the other, and all three factors must be considered in combination.

For example, the same temperature can be perceived as both tolerable or intolerable, depending on the humidity. In one research study, subjects judged a temperature of 140°F to be tolerable when the humidity was low (10%), but intolerable when the humidity was high (80%). Similarly, the rate of air circulation over the skin can affect the tolerability of a particular temperature and humidity level. Air flow facilitates the evaporation of perspiration and, thus, makes a person feel cooler. A room at 80°F with 60% humidity but no circulating air is felt to be much less comfortable than the same temperature and humidity levels with moving air.

Research dealing with physical labor has shown that uncomfortable climate conditions can influence the quality and quantity of work performed. Production can fall under extremely hot and humid conditions but, even in the few cases where production remains the same, workers are forced to expend more energy to maintain the same output. Other studies have shown that manual laborers must take more frequent rest pauses under hot and humid conditions (Osborne, 1982). These conditions can be better tolerated if there is sufficient air movement. The installation of forced ventilation systems in factories has resulted in higher production levels even though the temperature and humidity have remained the same.

Motivation plays a great part in worker efficiency under extremes of climate. Research conducted by the military has demonstrated that highly motivated persons are able to maintain constant work rates under extremes of both heat and cold.

Mental work seems to be less affected by heat and humidity than physical labor, at least under laboratory conditions, although some slight effect has been demonstrated outside the laboratory (Wing, 1965).

It is unfortunate that factory and manual laborers (those most affected by temperature-humidity extremes) are usually the least protected, whereas those working in offices (whose work is less affected) usually are provided with efficient climate-control systems.

Where practical, a company's investment in climate-control systems for factories and offices would reap the benefits of more comfortable and productive employees. Where it is not feasible to install air conditioning, fans to circulate the air will accrue some benefits. At the very least, a company should provide salt tablets to its workers so that they can replace the salt lost through perspiration.

Finally, computerized office equipment has been found to be capable of changing temperature and humidity levels. A single computer terminal may not generate much heat by itself, but when dozens of terminals, disk drives, printers, and word processors are operated in the same office, employee complaints about the heat generally increase, as do problems with static electricity. Humidity levels usually drop, which irritates employees who wear contact lenses (Pearce, 1987).

Indoor Pollution: Effects of the Work Environment on Health

Most people work indoors, and more than 25% of the American work force spends its days in offices. Many office buildings are sealed environments, designed to be tightly closed against the intrusion of outside air. Windows cannot be opened and employees breathe only filtered cooled or heated air that is constantly recirculated. Such buildings may be cost efficient, but a growing body of research suggests that such artificial environments are hazardous to employee health. According to the World Health Organization, the physical complaints brought on by such work environments can include eye, ear, and throat irritations; dry nasal membranes; reddened skin due to inflammation of the capillaries; fatigue; headaches; nausea; and dizziness (Edmunds, 1987).

Consider a few examples. In a sealed office building in San Francisco, most of the 250 employees complained of headaches, sinus problems, allergic skin reactions, and general discomfort shortly after they started working in the building. Four people suffered reactions so severe that they had to leave their jobs. When the air-filtering system was changed to allow more fresh air to circulate, the symptoms disappeared. In another new building, the workers found themselves in a dazed, stuporous condition every afternoon. This was particularly evident on hot days, even though the air conditioning maintained a comfortable temperature in the offices. The problem was traced to the roof, where, on hot days, the tar was releasing fumes that were drawn into the air-conditioning system and distributed throughout the building. In Stockholm, Sweden, several new schools were closed because of the bad quality of the air, and in West Germany some new office buildings were shut down for the same reason.

New buildings contain a frightening number of harmful chemicals. Because these environments are so tightly sealed, the chemicals are not dissipated or diluted by fresh air. Solvents, adhesives, cleaning fluids, fire-retardant chemicals, additives to prevent the aging of paint, asbestos and formaldehyde in insulation, and other harmful substances abound in carpeting, walls, wall coverings, draperies, and office furniture.

Copying machines produce ozone, which can cause headaches and upper respiratory tract infections. Toxic solvents are found in printing and typing materials such as carbonless paper. Electronic equipment—computers, video monitors, and word-processing apparatus—may be producing their own form of electronic pollution. Long-term exposure to cathode ray tubes and other video display devices, now so common in offices, may be related to eyestrain, headaches, cataracts, and neurological disorders. Invisible microwaves, of the sort commonly used in communications gear, and other sources of radiation have reached high levels in many office buildings. Research has linked radiation to such effects as eye damage, emotional instability, memory loss, reduced intellectual capacity, loss of appetite, heart and thyroid disturbances, leukemia, and birth defects.

These problems resulting from electronic and indoor air pollution have long-term health effects. Also, although no one has died after a week in a new office building because of chemical or radiation pollution, another form of indoor pollution has been fatal—legionnaires' disease. This mysterious pneumonia-like ailment strikes people in a particular high-rise building; the cause seems to be a bacterial infection nurtured and transmitted by the ventilation and heating-and-air-conditioning system. Perhaps some modern office buildings should be labeled: "Caution: Working Here May Be Hazardous to Your Health."

Temporal Conditions of Work

A vital part of the overall work environment is the amount of time spent on the job. The number of hours worked (daily or weekly), and the amount of rest allowed during working hours are capable of influencing satisfaction and productivity. A number of alternative work schedules have replaced the once standard 5-day, 40-hour week in which all employees of an organization arrived at and left work at the same time. One example of an innovative work schedule is offered by the New York state government. Its 64,000 managerial and professional employees have the opportunity to reduce their work schedules by as much as 30%, while taking a corresponding cut in salary. More than 1,000 employees have taken advantage of the program, most of them to devote more time to their families, but some to use the time to pursue new interests or academic studies. Typically, the employees have chosen to reduce their working hours by 10% to 20%. For lower level employees, the state offers a summer vacation program in which they can exchange a portion of their salary and fringe benefits for an extended vacation period. Between 1980 and 1984, participation in this program grew 400% (B.A. Solomon, 1986). The standard workweek and work year in which everyone keeps to the same schedule is now a thing of the past.

After we discuss the number of hours traditionally worked each week, we shall describe three alternative work schedules now in regular use: permanent part-time employment, the 4-day workweek, and flexible working hours. We shall also discuss rest pauses and shift work.

Hours of Work

How long should a person be expected to work each week? Our expectations have changed greatly over the years. At one time in the United States, 6-day weeks of 10 and more hours a day were standard. The reduction to a 5-day, 40-hour week became the norm in the United States in 1938, with the passage of the Fair Labor Standards Act. The United States became the first country to formally establish a 5-day, 40-hour workweek. Overall, there has been a steady decline in the amount of time employees must devote to a job. There is nothing sacred about a 40-hour week; it is not necessarily the most efficient working schedule. For social reasons and for increased efficiency of production equipment, workers accept the 40-hour week as the normal condition. In other times, they accepted 48 hours or 60 hours as the standard. Perhaps some day a 20-hour week will be standard, and we shall wonder how people could have devoted 40 hours each week to a job.

There is another consideration: the tendency to spend as much time as is allowed to complete a task. C.Northcote Parkinson, the British author and historian, wrote that work will expand to fill the time that is available for it. If workers are expected to complete six units of a product each workday, they will tend to finish six units whether the workday is 12, 8, or 6 hours long (Parkinson, 1957).

There is a great difference between *nominal* working hours (the prescribed number of hours workers must spend at their desks or machines) and *actual* working hours; the two rarely coincide. Indeed, surveys show that workers may spend no more than half of the workweek in actual work.

Some of the lost time is scheduled by the company as official rest pauses, but most of it seems to be unauthorized and beyond company control. When

In some jobs, such as supermarket checkout clerk, employees must punch a time clock at the beginning and end of their work shift. Other jobs have more flexible work schedules.

workers arrive each morning, it may take a long time for them actually to begin work. They may shuffle papers, sharpen pencils, oil machines (whether or not they need it). During the workday, employees talk socially with co-workers, exceed the length of the lunch break, and take unofficial rest pauses at the water cooler, in the rest room, or by daydreaming.

A research study dealing with managers revealed that 25% of each workday was wasted, that is, it was considered to be nonproductive (Goleman, 1983). Some of that time was lost in waiting for meetings to begin, but much of it was spent on the activities already mentioned: daydreaming, taking excessively long lunch periods, shuffling papers, and engaging in social conversation. A survey of more than 1,000 personnel managers revealed that they believe that 18% of their employees spend an hour or more each day in socializing, and that another 46% spend up to an hour each day engaging in this nonwork activity ("Work Gossip," 1987).

There is an interesting relationship between nominal and actual working hours: When nominal hours of work are increased, there is a *decrease* in actual hours of work. The longer the workday or workweek, the lower the actual production per hour. This relationship has been demonstrated by considerable research; its validity seems beyond question (Bartley & Chute, 1947).

This finding holds even for highly motivated workers. In the early days of World War II in England, that country was trying desperately to hold out against Nazi Germany; patriotic fervor was at a peak. Dangerously low on supplies and equipment, the government increased the workweek in war plants from 56 to $69\frac{1}{2}$ hours. At first production increased 10% but, very shortly, it fell 12% below the earlier level.

Additional consequences of increasing nominal working hours include marked increases in accidents, illness, and absenteeism. The actual work hours were only 51 out of the $69\frac{1}{2}$-hour week; with the previous 56-hour week, actual work hours were 53. Thus, the workers were less productive with the longer workweek, and these employees were working for their own survival as a nation, which was very much in doubt at the time.

A study conducted in the United States during World War II showed that the 7-day workweek (adopted by many companies during the war) resulted in no more production than a 6-day week. One day of the 7 was lost time. The same results apply to peacetime conditions as well (Kossoris & Kohler, 1947).

The relationship between nominal and actual working hours also holds with overtime (when employees are asked to work several hours beyond their normal day for markedly higher rates of pay). Much of this extra time is not productive. Unless there is no alternative, the provision for overtime work is not worth the investment. People adjust to longer hours by working at a slower rate.

If we increase working time and production goes down, will production rise if we shorten the workday or workweek? Some research indicates that the answer is yes. Other studies show that a decrease in nominal working hours has no effect on actual work time, that is, actual working hours remain the same, even though the worker spends less total time on the job (Alluisi & Fleishman, 1982).

In one case of historical interest (during the 1930s Great Depression), a plant reduced its nominal working time by $9\frac{1}{4}$ hours per week, yet actual work time fell only 5 hours. Another plant reduced its nominal workweek by $18\frac{1}{2}$ hours and hourly production increased 21%. Hourly production increases of about 20% have been reported by a number of plants that, in the days before the 40-hour week, cut nominal work time. As to how much the nominal workweek could be reduced, there is no answer yet, but the trend is undoubtedly toward shorter workweeks.

What, then, is the optimal period of time to work? The answer keeps changing. What is normal and most productive at one time may appear excessively long and unproductive 5 or 10 years later. Research studies show the 5-day, 40-hour week to be the most efficient, for now. A typical study compared hourly productivity among groups performing the same job, some for 44-hour weeks and others for 36- and 40-hour weeks; the results favored the 40-hour week. We must, however, examine the context within which these studies were conducted. Virtually all of them were undertaken at the end of the Great Depression or during World War II, times when the normal workweek ranged from 48 to 60 or more hours. The same studies conducted today would be in a totally different context. The 40-hour week is now expected—not 50 or 60 hours—and it seems likely that current research would show a workweek shorter than 40 (nominal) hours to be most effective.

Permanent Part-Time Employment

One trend in working hours is the provision of permanent job opportunities for those who want to work less than the standard 40-hour week. Part-time employment (usually halftime or 20 hours a week) is growing in popularity among both employees and managers and is the most popular form of alternative work schedule (H. Z. Levine, 1987a). In 1963, 10% of the work force in the United States was employed part time. Today, more than 20% hold part-time jobs. In Britain, the figure is 24% and is expected to reach 30% by the year 2000 ("Must Part-timers Be," 1988). Part-time employment has grown twice as fast as full-time employment. Much of the increase is in retail businesses where more than one third of all employees work part time (Gable & Hollon, 1982). The largest employer of part-time workers is the federal government. Since 1978, the number of part-time executives and managers has increased 150%.

As noted, full-time employment does not mean that the organization is getting 40 hours of work per week from each employee. And, it is being recognized that some jobs can be accomplished just as well in 20 hours as in 40, particularly writing and research jobs in which there is a great deal of independent work. Also, many lower level assembly-line and clerical jobs can be performed by two persons, each working halftime, as well as by one person working full time.

Part-time employment is especially attractive to persons who have family responsibilities. By working only halftime, they are able to combine family and career. Physically handicapped persons often find part-time employment appealing because of their mobility problems. Many managers and professionals welcome part-time employment because it gives them the chance to return to school or to explore other growth opportunities with the extra time provided them. And, some employees prefer part-time jobs simply because they do not want to spend 40 hours a week working in an office or plant.

The U.S. Department of Health and Human Services found that supervisors of part-time employees were strongly in favor of the concept. A study of part-time caseworkers in Massachusetts showed that those who worked 20 hours a week had a lower turnover and a higher caseload contact than full-time employees. The Wisconsin civil service also found that permanent part-time employees (social workers, attorneys, and research analysts) accomplished as much, or more, work as their full-time colleagues. Perhaps part-time employees do not take as many unauthorized breaks as those who work 40 hours a week.

Opportunities for part-time employment are growing rapidly. The federal civil service and several states (California, Colorado, Georgia, Maryland,

Massachusetts, Minnesota, Oregon, and Wisconsin) have permanent part-time employment programs. Although private industry has been slower to accept part-time employment, the number of companies instituting such programs is increasing.

Part-time employees differ from full-time employees in several ways, and they are treated differently by their organizations. Part-time workers are primarily women and include the younger and older segments of the work force. They tend to be concentrated in lower level jobs and receive lower pay than full-time workers. With the notable exception of those who work for the federal government, most part-time workers receive fewer fringe benefits (minimal or no paid vacations, sick leave, or medical insurance) and this seems to be their major source of job dissatisfaction. They also get considerably less training than full-time employees and have fewer opportunities for promotion.

Labor unions, in general, are not in favor of part-time employment. They fear that it could lead to an increase in job competition, impair pay and fringe benefits for their full-time members, and disrupt established rules for overtime. For example, companies might elect to hire part-time workers for overtime, thus reducing the income of full-time workers. Scheduling of part-time employment, as with other changes in work schedules, usually proceeds more smoothly when management actively enlists the participation of local union representatives in designing and implementing the changes.

The Four-Day Workweek

Another way to alter the workweek significantly is to reduce it to only 4 days. By the mid-1970s, many factories, offices, and government agencies had changed to a 4-day workweek schedule. This usually involves either 4 days at 10 hours a day (thus maintaining the 40-hour week), or 4 days at 9 hours a day (a 36-hour week with no reduction in pay). Union leaders, management consultants, and most of the firms that have tried it are highly enthusiastic.

In most cases, the initiative to shorten the workweek has come not from the union or the employees (as one might expect), but from management. This is for several reasons: the possibility of increased productivity and worker efficiency, an incentive for recruiting and retaining employees, and the hope of reducing absenteeism, which, in many companies, has reached epidemic proportions, particularly on Mondays and Fridays.

Converting from a 5- to a 4-day week is difficult and requires flexibility on the part of management. Perhaps this is why smaller firms took the lead in implementing this work schedule. The change requires careful planning and the wholehearted cooperation of the employees. A change of this magnitude cannot be dictated to a company's workers, not if the company expects it to be successful. Management must explain the entire procedure to the workers and allow them time to examine and comment on the new schedule.

Reports from companies that have adopted the 4-day workweek are generally full of praise for it, citing improved job satisfaction and productivity, reduced absenteeism, and easier scheduling of work. The major complaint is greater fatigue, but the employees themselves are almost unanimous in approving this type of work schedule (H. Z. Levine, 1987b). Empirical research conducted on the job shows that changing to a 4-day workweek has little effect on production, but the studies do confirm the popularity of the schedule with the majority of employees who have tried it (Dunham, Pierce, & Castañeda, 1987).

The appeal of the 4-day week was demonstrated by a Gallup poll that indicated that 45% of men of all ages would like to work on that basis. Wives, however, opposed the new workweek by a ratio of 2:1. Some said that 9 to 10 hours of work each day would be too hard on their husbands. A few said they did not want their husbands home an extra day each week. Women who work, however, are more favorable to the idea. Finally, a survey taken at 13 companies already on a 4-day week revealed that 92% of the workers liked the new schedule and wanted to stick to it.

Some problems with the 4-day workweek are giving some organizations second thoughts. Some companies have found that the benefits of the schedule decline after a while. Also, older workers have complained that the longer workday is too physically taxing. Younger workers say that it interferes with social life. Employees with young children also find the schedule difficult (Goodale & Aagaard, 1975).

Overall, the 4-day workweek has been successful in most cases, but it is not without its critics. There are signs that its use is declining slightly, relative to another arrangement of work time—flexible working hours.

Flexible Working Hours

A more radical change in work scheduling is to let employees decide for themselves when they will begin and end the workday. Traditionally, all employees of a firm begin and end the workday at fixed times. This practice was rarely questioned until the late 1960s when several business firms in West Germany, after much study and planning, tried *Gleitzeit* (gliding or flexible hours of work)—called in the United States flexitime—to deal with traffic congestion during rush hours. Under this plan, the workday is divided into four parts, two of which are optional and two mandatory (see Figure 10-1).

Figure 10-1 A typical flexitime work schedule.

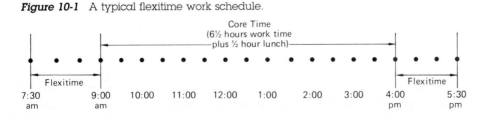

Employees can report to work any time between 7:30 and 9:00 in the morning and leave any time from 4:00 to 5:30 in the afternoon. The two mandatory periods during which everyone must be on the job are the morning hours from 9:00 until the half-hour lunch break and the afternoon hours from lunch to 4:00. Thus, everyone must work a minimum $6\frac{1}{2}$-hour workday; the optional maximum is $9\frac{1}{2}$ hours per day.

What determines how long each employee will work each day? This is set up on an individual basis within each department or section as a function of the company's needs. Thus far, flexitime has been most successful and offers several advantages. Rush-hour traffic congestion into and out of plants and offices has been considerably reduced; indeed, in some cases it is no longer a problem. Because employees spend less time and energy commuting, they arrive at their jobs more relaxed and ready to begin work promptly.

I/O psychologists have found that workers may not change their habits very much under flexitime. In a study of government workers in the United States and in Israel under a flexitime program, it was found that the average employee began work only 8 minutes later than before and stayed at work 22 minutes longer (Bridgwater, 1982). Apparently, the inflexible demands of commuting, car pooling, and family responsibilities held them to work schedules not so dissimilar to those before flexitime was introduced. However, the employees felt that having the choice of when to arrive and leave work enhanced their sense of personal freedom. It is also important to remember that the times given in this study are averages; some employees did change their starting and quitting times much more radically.

Surveys of organizations that use flexitime have revealed the following advantages. These results are similar to those obtained in a survey conducted 3 years earlier, which also showed that the benefits of flexitime appeared to be stable over time (Petersen, 1980).

1. Productivity was increased in almost half of the organizations.
2. Absenteeism was reduced in more than 75% of the organizations.
3. Lateness was reduced in 84% of the organizations.
4. Turnover was reduced in more than 50% of the organizations.
5. Employee morale increased in almost all of the organizations.

Some comprehensive research studies confirm the reduction in absenteeism and the increase in morale but fail to support the reported increases in productivity (Dunham & Pierce, 1983; Narayanan & Nath, 1982). Other research produced less optimistic results, reporting no significant differences in productivity, satisfaction, or absenteeism as a result of a change to flexitime. However, as with the 4-day workweek, this research shows that employees who have tried flexible working hours are highly supportive and believe that the schedule has improved their family and social lives (Buckley, Kicza, & Crane, 1987; Dunham, Pierce, & Castaneda, 1987; McGuire & Liro, 1986). Employee surveys report that between 75% and 97% of the employees questioned wanted to keep their flexitime schedule and did not want to return to a fixed-hour system ("Flex-itime," 1984; "Flex Hours," 1988).

The scheduling of flexible working hours has spread rapidly throughout Western Europe. More than half of the West German white-collar work force is now on flexitime, as are 30% of the French work force and 40% of the Swiss work force. In Britain, 500,000 civil servants and more than 80 private firms have adopted flexible hours of work. The popularity of flexible working hours has been growing in the United States since the early 1970s. Flexitime is being used successfully by the Baltimore, Maryland, and Washington, D.C., city governments, Sun Oil, Hewlett-Packard, Samsonite, Scott Paper, Occidental Insurance, Montgomery Ward's Chicago headquarters and New York buying office, and Westinghouse's Pittsburgh nuclear center.

Flexitime programs are also growing in popularity among federal government agencies such as the Library of Congress, the Environmental Protection Agency, the Treasury and Agriculture Departments, and the Civil Service Commission. The widespread use of flexible hours will allow government agencies to provide services to the public for a greater number of hours each day.

Flexible working hours seem to be appropriate for a variety of jobs such as research and development, clerical, and light and heavy manufacturing. In assembly-line and shift-work operations, however, flexitime is difficult to implement because of the high degree of interdependence among the workers. Overall, however, the flexible approach to work scheduling appears to be a fair, sensible, and low-cost arrangement that offers considerable advantages for both employers and employees.

Rest Pauses

Ever since the Hawthorne studies, the importance of company-provided rest breaks has been widely recognized. Not only have their beneficial effects been amply demonstrated, but a more urgent reason also exists for giving employees rest pauses: The employees will take breaks whether or not they are offered. If the time will be lost anyway, the company may as well appear beneficent and supply the rest pauses as fringe benefits.

When authorized rest pauses are introduced, unauthorized breaks decline, although they do not disappear altogether and probably never will (Janaro, Bechtold, & Klippel, 1988). Other potential benefits of formal rest periods are increased morale and production as well as reduced fatigue and boredom. This is another example of how a decrease in working time can result in an increase in efficiency.

Workers engaged in heavy physical labor obviously benefit from rest pauses. Muscles in continuous use tire and become less effective. Periodically resting the muscles is necessary to maintain performance levels. Even for more sedentary or intellectual work, however, the change of stimulation provided by a rest break is helpful; it allows boredom to dissipate and the opportunity to think about something else or to talk with other employees.

Another possible reason for the effectiveness of authorized rest pauses is the improved attitudes of workers toward their employer. When a rest program is introduced, workers may feel that it is an expression of management's concern for them as individuals.

Several factors influence the effectiveness of rest pauses. It must be determined at what time or times of day rest breaks will be most effective, how long they should last, how often they should be provided, whether the company should offer coffee or snacks in an employee lounge or at the work station during rest breaks or give nothing beyond the break itself. In part, these questions must be answered by a company in terms of each type of job. Workers conducting physical labor outdoors during summer months may need frequent breaks, iced water, or salt tablets. Workers in air-conditioned offices may need fewer actual breaks but may need the opportunity to leave their desks for a change of scene.

The details of a rest-pause program can usually be worked out on the basis of research on the nature of the job, polling employee preferences, or common sense. The rest pause has come to be an institution. It is expected by new employees and not given up by present employees without a comparable gain in some other area (such as the shorter workweek). In sum, rest pauses are effective, expected, and will be taken anyway, regardless of company rules.

Shift Work

Another temporal condition of work that affects a great many employees is the time of day or night the work takes place. Not everyone works from 9 to 5. Many companies are in operation more than 8 hours each day. Indeed, some operate around the clock and employees must work one of three shifts, usually 7:00 a.m.–3:00 p.m., 3:00 p.m.–11:00 p.m., and 11:00 p.m.–7:00 a.m. Some firms assign individuals to one shift on a permanent basis, whereas others rotate workers, switching them each week or so to a different shift. In most cases, those who work evening or all-night shifts receive extra pay to compensate them for the inconvenience of their working hours.

The number of employees on shift work is growing as a result of increased automation, round-the-clock manufacturing processes (such as steel mills and chemical plants), and computer operations. The provision of 24-hour services in medical care and transportation also requires shift work. Some 25% of the work force in the United States and England is on shift work, and many of these jobs are more mental than physical in nature. Thus, shift work involves both blue-collar and white-collar employees.

How do the conditions imposed by shift work affect people? Research conducted in the United States and in Europe has shown that the same workers are less productive on the night shift than the day shift (Vidaček, Kaliterna, & Radošević-Vidaček, 1986). In addition, they are prone to make more errors and have more serious accidents. The accidents at the Three Mile Island nuclear facility in the United States and at the Chernobyl nuclear plant in the Soviet

Union occurred during the night shift. In addition, the Peach Bottom nuclear plant in Pennsylvania was closed by the Nuclear Regulatory Commission in 1987 when it found control room personnel asleep on the job. Further, an analysis of bus accidents in Holland found that the accident rate was much higher on shifts that began early in the morning than on shifts that began in late afternoon (Pokorny, Blom, Van Leeuwen, & Van Nooten, 1987). Absenteeism, however, does not seem to differ from one shift to another (Gannon, Norland, & Robeson, 1983).

Not only is production lower during the night shift, but the disruption of the normal sleep-wake cycle can also produce physical and psychological effects. Humans develop a *diurnal rhythm*, a regular cyclic patterning of the activities of various bodily organs and glands and the chemical composition of the blood. This rhythm is consistent from one 24-hour period to the next, and it means that most of us are more alert and productive during the normal waking hours of the day. When the diurnal rhythm is disrupted, the body undergoes dramatic physical changes. At the very least, it is hard to sleep on the new schedule. The main objection of people who must work at night is this inability to sleep during the day, a difficulty abetted by daylight, noise, and the activities of others in the house. A study of 29 shift workers found that those who slept 10 or more hours on their days off were significantly sleepier when they returned to work than those who slept fewer than 10 hours (Anderson & Bremer, 1987).

There are also social and emotional effects. The family must try to keep the house quiet, and normal household routines are disrupted. Employees are forced to spend less time with the family, normal social life is difficult, and routine activities such as shopping become difficult to fit into the available waking hours. Also, those who work at night or on rotating shifts have reported a higher incidence of stomach disorders, sleep disorders, cardiovascular disease, marital problems, and feelings of isolation and irritability (Wolinsky, 1982). A study of 3,446 workers in the West German chemical industry showed that those on shift work reported a significantly higher incidence of psychosomatic complaints and of stress than did those not on shift work (Frese & Semmer, 1986).

However, research suggests that not all workers on rotating shifts suffer from physical or adjustment problems. In a study of 732 workers at a power-and-gas utility company, 32% indicated no desire to change from their rotating shift arrangement. These employees were satisfied with their work schedule and reported fewer health, social, and marital problems than employees who were dissatisfied with the rotating shift work schedule. The satisfied workers had been able to adapt successfully, although the majority of the workers had not. Thus, some people can adjust better than others to shift work (Zedeck, Jackson, & Summers, 1983).

There is general agreement among psychologists in industry that if there must be shift work in a plant, fewer problems are encountered with the fixed-shift system than the rotating-shift system. Persons working permanently on one shift are often able to adjust to a new body rhythm (although it is difficult and the social problems remain). With the rotating system, however, workers must make a new adjustment every week or so, whenever the shift is changed. Thus, they may not be fully adjusted to one schedule before beginning another; before they can adjust to the second schedule, they begin a third. This is a difficult way to live.

There are ways of alleviating the problems caused by shift work. The most obvious is to employ the fixed-shift arrangement; there will still be production and personal problems, but they will be less severe. When the rotating-shift system must be used, the changes from one shift to another should be made as seldom as possible (for example, every few weeks instead of every week, as is now often the case).

When the police department in Philadelphia, Pennsylvania, altered its shift work schedule so that officers changed shifts every 18 instead of every 8 days, and worked only 4 consecutive days instead of 6, a number of behavioral changes were observed. After almost a year on the new schedule, there were significant decreases in sleep problems, in sleepiness on the job, and in fatigue, and an increase in alertness. Automobile accidents on the job dropped by 40%, the use of sleeping pills and alcohol by 50%, and the taking of sick leave by 23%. The officers reported that they felt more energetic and less irritable and got along better with their families ("Night Beat," 1988).

Better personnel selection can also be an aid to successful shift work. As we said, some people are much better able than others to adjust to new rhythms. Those whose bodies are particularly resistant to diurnal pattern changes should be allowed to work only during the day, for their own good as well as the organization's. Such employee selection is routinely practiced in many European companies (Haider, Koller, & Cervinka, 1986).

One way to facilitate the change from one shift to another is to lengthen the time off between shift changes. A longer interim period makes the change less abrupt and allows employees to catch up on their rest before starting a new schedule. Also, because the night shift is the most trying for the worker (and the least productive for the company), it could be shortened to make it less stressful and objectionable.

An unusual and potentially harmful form of shift work, one that affects the lives of thousands of people every day, is the erratic pattern of work followed by commercial airline pilots. They often change from night flights to day flights and back again, sleeping at irregular intervals and totally disrupting their diurnal rhythms. Consider a typical workweek for one pilot:

Day 1. Up at 4:15 a.m. for five flights.
Day 2. Up at 4:45 p.m. for three flights.
Day 3. Up at 3:30 p.m. for four flights.
Day 4. Up at 6:45 a.m. for four flights.
Day 5. No flights scheduled.
Day 6. Up at 7:00 a.m. for four flights.
Day 7. Up at 3:30 a.m.

On Day 7, this pilot crashed, killing everyone aboard his aircraft. He was so tired because of his erratic sleep-wake cycle that he misread the plane's altitude.

Many air crashes and near misses have been linked to fatigue from poor sleep patterns. One involved a 747 that was lifting off the runway at Honolulu. The co-pilot glanced at the pilot and saw that he had fallen asleep. On another occasion, a 707, due to land in Los Angeles, passed the airport, continued over the city, and headed out over the Pacific Ocean. The entire crew had fallen asleep and had to be awakened by the control tower.

Some pilots spend a week or longer on international flight schedules, trying to stay awake for many hours at a time as they cross several time zones. Their diurnal rhythms are so disrupted that they report great difficulty falling asleep during layover periods. The new, longer-range aircraft will only aggravate the problem. They are capable of making longer nonstop flights, which means that crews will have to be on duty for greater periods of time.

Further, computerized navigational equipment and sophisticated automatic pilots are decreasing the work demands on air crews, leaving them little to do except monitor the equipment during the periods between takeoff and landing. It is not surprising, then, that studies of air crew performance find that nodding off to sleep in the cockpit is a common occurrence. One group of 30 pilots averaged 32 instances of falling asleep on duty per month. A highly experienced pilot noted, "In many Pacific flights, pilots are sleeping in the cockpit, and when they arrive they are fatigued and impaired for a critical approach and landing" (Stockton, 1988, p. 1).

Unfortunately, despite the great amount of information available on the diurnal rhythm and its relationship to productive efficiency, well-being, and errors and accidents, government and industry have been slow to recognize it and to design work conditions accordingly.

Psychological Conditions of Work

Other factors that make up the work environment are concerned with the nature of the job itself and its impact on the workers—what may be called the internal environment of the job. Do the jobs provide a sense of satisfaction or achievement, or do they make workers tired, bored, or even ill?

As discussed in Chapter 8, the design of the job can influence satisfaction and motivation. The quality-of-work-life movement has been somewhat successful in improving morale and motivation. At the other extreme, jobs designed to be so simple that they make no demands on the worker's intelligence, need for achievement, or even attention result in boredom, monotony, fatigue, and, of course, less efficient production.

Simplified, fragmented, and repetitive jobs can also affect the workers' mental and physical health. Those who hold such jobs on a rigid work schedule report a higher level of anxiety, depression, and irritability than workers doing the same kinds of jobs under a more flexible schedule (Stagner, 1975).

Other research has shown that simplified, repetitive work can lead to the kind of deterioration in cognitive or mental functioning usually associated with old age. For example, these workers are prone to absentmindedness, forgetfulness, and disorientation. Assembly-line workers also complain more about their physical health and visit the company medical facility much more frequently than those doing less highly simplified work (Broadbent, 1978; Caplan, Cobb, French, Van Harrison, & Pinneau, 1975).

The history of job simplification dates from the beginnings of mass production in the early part of the 20th century. If relatively expensive consumer goods such as automobiles were to be produced in sufficient quantities and at lower costs, old-style production methods—building each unit by hand—would have to be changed. Mass production called for product consistency and standardization so that parts could be interchangeable. It also called for fractionation of the work itself. It was no longer economically or technically feasible for one person to make an entire product; the work had to be divided so that each worker made only a small part of the finished product.

Under the impact of scientific management and time-and-motion studies of work, jobs were fractionated into their smallest possible components. The ideal was to reduce every manufacturing process to the simplest elements that could be performed by a single employee.

Job fractionation and simplification offered advantages to industry and to consumers. It allowed the lowest possible cost per unit produced. When Henry Ford established his assembly line, he was able to sell cars at a price within reach of many people who previously could not have afforded them. The same thing soon occurred with other consumer goods. The factory-produced chair in which you are sitting costs considerably less than one handmade by a skilled furniture craftsperson. That points to another advantage of job simplification: Industry no longer had to rely on skilled craftspersons, the workers who required years of apprenticeship, expected high wages, and were apt to be independent. The assembly line employed workers with little skill or training; these people could learn an assembly-line job quickly. The process also made workers more docile and easier to manage (before the advent of unions). Because they possessed no real usable skills, employees knew they could easily be replaced. They were as interchangeable as the parts they produced.

There is no denying that job simplification had a tremendously stimulating effect on the nation's economy. More jobs were available and people had more money to buy the plentiful automobiles and consumer goods. The more people bought, the more factories had to be expanded and that, of course, meant more jobs. Also, new products on the market required additional businesses to sell and service them. Such economic growth could never have taken place if production methods had remained limited to the handcraft approach. We are learning, however, that there is a price to be paid for affluence and industrial growth. As we breathe polluted air, search in vain for clean beaches, and get stuck in traffic jams, we may suspect that the price of growth is quite high.

Assembly-line workers paid, and are still paying, a high cost for their role in this widespread attainment of affluence. Personal value and meaning of work are destroyed the farther removed workers are from the finished product. The craftspersons who shaped a finished piece of furniture from the raw materials knew the pride and fulfillment of achievement and the challenge of properly using skill, imagination, and intelligence.

Where is the challenge and the satisfaction in making television tuning knobs by machine over and over again, day in, day out? In most cases, the machine makes the part; the worker is simply an adjunct, pressing a button or pushing a lever, or simply watching in case something goes wrong. Anyone could do it; it has been shown that even chimpanzees can perform many of the production jobs in industry today. All too often, assembly-line workers do not even know what happens to the part they make or what it has to do with the finished product. Such work has little meaning, provides less satisfaction, and is soon frustrating, boring, and monotonous. Workers become understandably apathetic and uninterested, morale declines along with the quantity and quality of production. It is easy to understand why we find such poor quality construction in our cars and appliances.

This problem, once restricted to blue-collar workers, now affects white-collar and managerial employees because computerized equipment has turned many offices into electronic assembly lines. Increasingly in white-collar jobs work is fragmented, simplified, and made repetitive. As a result, office workers are becoming cheaper to train and easier to replace. This trend is neatly captured in the title of a recent book, *The Electronic Sweatshop: How Computers Are Transforming the Office of the Future into the Factory of the Past* (Garson, 1988).

Boredom and Monotony

Two major consequences of job fractionation, boredom and monotony, are important components of the psychological work environment. Boredom, sometimes called mental fatigue, usually results from the performance of a repetitive, monotonous, and uninteresting activity. Boredom can cause a feeling of general malaise, a restless, unhappy, and tired feeling that drains us of all interest and energy. Further, boredom can be caused by many things that once seemed exciting such as reading, watching television, or listening to music.

What is dull and boring for one person may be exciting and challenging for another; this applies even to the assembly-line type of fractionated work whether performed in a factory or an office. Although most people find it boring and monotonous, some do not. And some workers engaged in seemingly challenging work also report boredom and monotony. Motivation is a relevant factor here. The person who is highly motivated to turn out as many units as possible per day will be less bored than a worker who lacks this motivation.

In general, research on boredom shows a resulting decrease in production and greater variability in the work rate. These effects seem to be most severe in the middle of the workday and decrease greatly as the end of the work period approaches (R. P. Smith, 1981).

One kind of work that is particularly prone to boredom and monotony is that which requires sustained attention, the type of task psychologists refer to as vigilance. Consider a radar operator, whose job requires constant alertness in order to detect small pips on the radar screen. Research has consistently shown that performance on the job deteriorates after no more than 30 minutes, and even as early as 5 minutes if the signals are difficult to see (Warm & Dember, 1986). One way to prevent this loss of performance is to make the task more complex and stimulating, but not so complex that it becomes distracting. The simpler the task is, the more boring it becomes, and the harder it is to do well for long periods of time.

The observation of individual differences in boredom level led psychologists to investigate personal characteristics to try to identify and predict the boredom-prone individual. Such people, then, should not be hired for monotonous, repetitive jobs. The research in this area has focused on intelligence and personality. It seems plausible to suggest that the higher a person's level of intelligence, the more likely it is that he or she will be bored by repetitive, nondemanding work. Some research confirms this suggestion; very intelligent people manifest a higher than usual turnover rate in dull, routine jobs—certainly an indication of boredom and dissatisfaction. Persons of lower intelligence may be considerably less bored by the same task. In a study of age and sex differences, younger men were shown to be highly susceptible to boredom (Stagner, 1975).

The bored and the not bored also tend to show differences in personality characteristics. In a study of women workers, those who reported the greatest boredom also evidenced a dislike for routine in any aspect of life, preferred active recreational and leisure pursuits, and were somewhat dissatisfied with their home and personal lives. Those workers who reported much less boredom had a more placid outlook and were generally more satisfied with their lives. Other research has suggested that extraverts were more easily bored than introverts (Hill, 1975). These findings on personality characteristics are of interest, but the evidence is not overwhelming. More research is needed before the relationship between boredom and personality can be fully explained.

The obvious problem for industry is how to counteract, prevent, or reduce boredom. Proper personnel selection and placement could help to prevent boredom. For example, a person with an IQ of 150 should not be placed on an assembly line. But this will not completely eliminate the problem of bored employees because selection and placement techniques are imperfect, and the relationship between personal characteristics and boredom has not been fully established.

A second way of reducing boredom is to enlarge the scope and demands of the job, to make it more complex, stimulating, and challenging. For jobs to which this technique can be applied, it has been most successful as an effective motivator and preventer of boredom.

A third method of preventing boredom is to alter the physical, temporal, or social conditions of work. Proper attention to noise reduction, illumination, pleasant colors, and music might counteract the effects of repetitive work. A congenial informal work group can also help. Appropriately scheduled rest pauses have proven effective in helping to alleviate boredom, not because workers on repetitive jobs necessarily need the physical rest, but because they need a change of activity. The greater the change during the rest breaks or lunch hour, the less disruptive will be the effects of boredom.

Other techniques have been used to fight boredom with varying degrees of success. Some companies have tried job rotation—letting workers periodically change to a different activity, sometimes as often as every 2 hours. Such a practice can only be successful if the alternate activity is not very similar to the original one. If the two jobs are much alike, switching from one to the other will provide little change for the workers. Of course, if the jobs are too dissimilar, extensive training may be required before the worker can make the switch. Some research indicates that job-rotation programs lead to a reduction in boredom and to increased job satisfaction, but other studies have failed to confirm this. One interesting finding concerns the attitudes of workers toward job rotation. When asked how they would feel about a rotation system, only 37% of a group of workers thought they would like it. However, 70% of those already involved in a job-rotation system reported that they liked it very much (Mann & Hoffman, 1960).

Another method of counteracting boredom is to teach the workers the value and meaning of their jobs. Greater interest has been engendered among workers who are told how their work (or the part they are producing) fits into the overall plant operation and the finished product. Sometimes, workers of 20 years' experience have had no idea how their work related to the production process as a whole. This kind of awareness can be easily and quickly taught in a few lectures and a tour of the entire plant. When carefully planned and presented, such programs have helped workers develop a new pride in their jobs and a feeling, often for the first time, that their work is important. The programs have also led to increased motivation and, correspondingly, a greater tolerance for repetitive work.

The QWL programs discussed in Chapter 9 make use of some of these techniques for reducing boredom. Just because a job is repetitive, it does not follow that it must be boring. An alert, imaginative, and understanding management can prevent boredom and monotony and create interest and motivation instead.

Fatigue

Fatigue is closely related to boredom in its effect on behavior although the causes of the two conditions can differ greatly. Also, there are really two kinds of

Employees in physically demanding and repetitive jobs that require them to be on their feet throughout the workday should be given formal rest periods to alleviate fatigue and boredom.

fatigue: psychological fatigue (which is similar to boredom) and physiological fatigue, caused by excessive use of the muscles of the body. Although the latter is not a psychological condition of work, it still constitutes part of the internal work environment. Both types of fatigue can cause performance decrements as well as increased errors, absenteeism, turnover, and accidents. Because of its obvious influence on work behavior, fatigue has been the subject of intensive research by industrial psychologists since the scientific-management work of Frederick Taylor in the first decade of this century.

Whereas boredom and monotony are basically psychological, fatigue, as noted, has both psychological and physiological components. Prolonged or heavy physical work produces definite and measurable physiological changes in the body. Processes such as heart rate, oxygen consumption, and muscle tension operate at different levels under fatigue. Thus, physiological fatigue can be defined with precision.

The psychological or subjective aspects of fatigue are more elusive in terms of measurement, but no less disturbing to individuals or impairing of their output. We know that we experience feelings of strain, irritability, and weakness when we are excessively tired, and we find it difficult to concentrate clearly, think coherently, or work effectively.

On-the-job research shows that the level of production closely parallels reported feelings of fatigue, that is, high reported fatigue is a reliable indicator that production will shortly decline. With most physical work, employees report that they are most tired at the beginning of work in the morning, again just before the lunch break, and finally at the end of the work period. Thus, fatigue does not build up over the course of a work period; it appears and disappears at least three times during the day. This strongly suggests that factors other than the actual work—motivation, for example—play a part in this type of fatigue. It often happens that a person who leaves work at the end of the day feeling exhausted finds that the fatigue suddenly disappears on arriving home and anticipating a date for the evening. However, regardless of its psychological or motivational components, this fatigue is real to the worker and is still capable of causing a decline in productivity.

Research on physiological fatigue has indicated that greater amounts of physical work can be accomplished when the daily work pace is more gradual. Too rapid a rate of heavy work dissipates the body's energy too quickly so that the worker must then proceed at a slower pace for the rest of the work period. The analogy is made to long-distance runners who must pace themselves so as not to use up all their energy before the distance is covered.

Rest periods are necessary for jobs involving heavy physical labor. Experience has shown that rest pauses should be taken before fatigue has a chance to become complete. The greater the amount of fatigue before the break, the longer the rest period must be. The solution seems to be more frequent rest periods. Also, for rest periods to be maximally effective, they must provide total relaxation, not merely a work stoppage. It is the manual laborer much more than the office worker, who can benefit from comfortable lounges and canteens. Unfortunately, it is usually the case that those who work the hardest physically have the least desirable rest facilities.

There exists a wide range of individual differences in ability to perform physical labor. People differ in physical fitness and general health, and these factors influence how well and how fast they can work. Age is also important; the younger worker is usually better able to maintain a high level of physical labor.

Diet is an influencing variable. Studies of American eating habits show that youngsters and others of lower socioeconomic levels do not have a proper diet because of ignorance of nutritional matters, lack of money, or lack of concern. Most of us eat enough food, but often it is not the right kind of food.

Management can take several steps to alleviate physiological and psychological fatigue. Because psychological fatigue is similar to boredom and monotony, the steps suggested in the last section can also be effective in counteracting subjective fatigue. To alleviate physiological fatigue, proper selection of workers for heavy labor, in terms of general health and physical condition, can prevent those for whom the work would be too taxing from entering such occupations. Attempting to get the workers to maintain a steady and somewhat gradual work pace, instead of working at full capacity for short periods, would also be effective. Adequately spaced rest periods are particularly necessary. Providing facilities where workers can relax in comfort and offering proper nourishment through a company cafeteria can also reduce the effects of physical fatigue.

Fatigue seriously interferes with the quantity and quality of all kinds of work. It probably cannot be eliminated entirely, but an enlightened management can keep its effects to a minimum.

Telecommuting: The Workplace at Home

We have seen that the hours people work have become quite flexible in recent years. That flexibility has also come to characterize the workplace. Not everyone works at the factory or office of the organization that employs them. Some employees work at home, thanks to advances in computer technology. This move toward decentralized work, or *telecommuting*, is already in effect at more than 600 companies, including Aetna Life and Casualty, Control Data Corporation, and JCPenny. Although no more than about 10,000 employees are involved now, industry leaders estimate that, by the mid-1990s, as many as 15 million people may be performing their jobs at home ("Offices of the Future," 1984).

The head of a small advertising agency in Rhode Island operates the business from his home.

Essentially, any task that can be done by computer or word/ undertaken at home, as long as the company provides the nec (something it does for its office-based employees). Jobs such as programmer, financial analyst, writer, airline reservations agent, and catalog sales agent can all be performed at home. The opportunity to work at home has become so popular in California that some home builders are installing computer connections in their new houses and advertising the benefits of not commuting to San Francisco. I/O psychologists suggest that telecommuting is a particular advantage for persons with preschool children at home and for some physically handicapped workers.

Initial research findings on the benefits of telecommuting are positive. Companies providing for work at home cite impressive gains in productivity, and, of course, sharp declines in absenteeism. People working at home usually have fewer interruptions than those working in offices, and they are able to concentrate more effectively. They are not prevented from getting to work by bad weather or minor illnesses. A catalog sales agent for JCPenney said, "When I have a cold in the winter I'm not going to put on my boots and trudge to the office. But if I'm at home, I put on my bathrobe and get a hot cup of tea and go to work" (M. M. Kelly, 1984, p. 50). There are also advantages for the organization in terms of lower costs for salaries, fringe benefits, and office overhead.

Not everyone likes the idea of working at home. Some people miss the camaraderie and social stimulation of co-workers. Others are not sufficiently disciplined or motivated to work steadily without supervision. In addition, some supervisors fear that they will lose their authority over subordinates who are not physically present. Unions have been cool to the idea of telecommuting, concerned about the declining loyalty of members who do not work together on the job.

Despite these problems, there are indications that for many workers, home may be the workplace of the future.

Summary

Many aspects of the physical work environment influence job satisfaction and productivity. The focus in this chapter is on three such aspects: physical, temporal, and psychological conditions of work.

Physical conditions of work include a wide range of factors. The location of the place of employment influences employees through proximity to shops, restaurants, banks, and other urban amenities. Inadequate heating and air-conditioning systems, elevators, company cafeterias, and rest rooms can also impair efficiency on the job, even though they have no direct bearing on the actual job. Many companies provide day-care facilities for the children of their employees. Handicapped workers are often prevented from accepting certain jobs by design features of buildings that inhibit easy access. Federal legislation now requires the removal of architectural barriers to the handicapped.

Environmental psychology is concerned with the impact of the environment on human behavior. Research has been conducted on the design of offices, including the landscaped office in which people are grouped in functional units with no floor-to-ceiling barriers between them, an arrangement that may contribute to job dissatisfaction.

In addition to large-scale design problems, psychologists are concerned with no floor-to-ceiling barriers between them, an arrangement that may color, music, and temperature and humidity.

With respect to **illumination**, standards exist for determining the desirable intensity levels for different kinds of workplaces. The distribution of light and glare are also problems that must be considered in the design of proper lighting for work.

Noise is a common problem in many work areas and can lead to temporary or permanent deafness. In an effort to reduce this health hazard, federal legislation has established maximum noise levels to which workers may be exposed. Noise can also produce other physiological effects, including increased muscle tension and blood pressure and constriction of blood vessels. Although noise can be a physical and psychological health hazard and interfere with communication in the workplace, its effects on productive efficiency are not clear.

Color in industry is useful as a coding device, to prevent eyestrain, to create differing illusions of size and temperature, and to improve the aesthetic quality of a workplace. Color, however, does not seem to have any bearing on production. The use of **music** at work also seems not to affect productivity for all kinds of work, although some employees say they like it. Music can make some work environments seem more pleasant.

Optimum **temperature and humidity** ranges have been established for workplaces. How comfortable a certain temperature feels depends on the humidity and the amount of air movement. Uncomfortable climate conditions can lower production, particularly on jobs involving physical labor.

Indoor pollution from chemical or radiation sources is a serious health threat in modern sealed office buildings. Noxious substances are also found in carpeting, furniture, paint, copying machines, and electronic office equipment.

Temporal conditions of work include the number of hours worked and the way in which those hours are arranged. Much scheduled work time is lost to unauthorized breaks. In general, when the required number of working hours is reduced, less time is lost and production tends to increase.

Several ways of scheduling work are part-time employment, the 4-day workweek, and flexible working hours. **Part-time employment** offers opportunities for those who want to combine a career with family, educational, leisure, or other pursuits and may result in a higher level of productivity. Part-time employees tend to work at low-level jobs and receive fewer fringe benefits and less training than full-time workers. The **4-day workweek** has become popular and apparently results in lower absenteeism and higher morale, but has little effect on productivity. There are signs, however, that it may be declining in popularity. **Flexible working hours,** in which employees can begin and end the workday when they wish (within a specified time period), are popular with employees but may have no effect on production or satisfaction. This schedule gives an added sense of responsibility to workers and also eases traffic congestion at rush hours.

Rest pauses are taken by employees whether or not officially sanctioned. They are necessary with manual labor to rest the muscles and with more sedentary work to provide a change of pace and prevent boredom.

Shift work can be very disruptive to the workers' diurnal rhythm and can cause social and psychological problems, especially by forcing workers to sleep when everyone else is awake. Production is lower on the night shift; serious accidents and errors are higher. Disruption of the diurnal rhythm is also a severe problem with airline pilots. Shift work is less disruptive when the change from one shift to another is made less frequently.

Psychological conditions of work deal with the design of the job and its effects on the workers. As a result of scientific management, time-and-motion study, and assembly-line manufacturing, many jobs have been simplified or fractionated to the point where they produce boredom and fatigue as well as harmful effects on mental and physical health.

Boredom results from repetitive and monotonous work and can lead to restlessness, tiredness, and lower productivity. **Vigilance tasks,** which require sustained attention, are prone to boredom. Boredom can be relieved by making the work more complex and stimulating, job rotation, improving the conditions under which the work is performed, scheduling rest pauses, and teaching workers the value and importance of their jobs. **Fatigue** can be psychological or physiological and can impair production. Proper selection of workers as well as attention to diet, rest periods, and proper work pacing can help to alleviate fatigue.

Telecommuting, performing jobs at home, is becoming increasingly popular as a result of the use of computers. Initial reports indicate gains in productivity and reductions in absenteeism among employees working at home. However, many managers, unions, and some employees are not in favor of the idea.

Key Terms

boredom	fatigue	rest pauses
decibel (db)	flexible working hours	shift work
diurnal rhythm	(flexitime)	telecommuting
environmental	landscaped offices	vigilance tasks
psychology		

CASE STUDIES

Employee Reactions to Conditions of Work

More than 100 employees of a large university served as subjects in an investigation of the effects of four work space characteristics: social density, room darkness, number of enclosures such as walls or partitions surrounding an employee's desk, and interpersonal distance (amount of separation between co-workers). The dependent variables were turnover, job satisfaction, and leaving the work space during discretionary periods such as coffee breaks.

Data on turnover were collected from personnel records. Discretionary absence was determined by questionnaires. Job satisfaction was assessed by the Job Diagnostic Survey (see Chapter 8).

The results showed that the physical characteristics of the work space affected employee attitudes and behavior. Employees were most likely to leave their offices during discretionary periods and to report low job satisfaction when their work spaces were dark,

when their desks had little privacy, when they were seated close together, and when many employees occupied the same work area. Employees reacted much less negatively to their work space in the absence of any of these conditions.

QUESTIONS

1. What other aspects of a work space might produce similar effects?
2. What implications would you draw from this study about the effectiveness of landscaped offices?
3. Which of the four work space characteristics might be the most harmful? Why?
4. What have I/O psychologists learned about the effects on employees of high levels of office noise?

Reference: G. R. Oldham & Y. Fried. (1987). Employee reactions to workspace characteristics. *Journal of Applied Psychology, 72,* 75–80.

Effects of Shift Work

Questionnaires to measure environmental and psychological job stress, as well as psychosomatic and other health complaints, were administered to more than 3,000 blue-collar workers at chemical plants in West Germany. Employees on shift work schedules and employees on normal daytime work schedules were investigated. Three groups of the latter nonshift workers included (1) those who left shift work for health reasons, (2) those who left for reasons other than health, and (3) those who had never been employed on a shift work basis. Responses to the questionnaires were voluntary; the response rate was 61.5%.

The results showed that the subjects fit into two major groups in terms of the similarity of their questionnaire responses. Those groups

were (1) shift workers and those who left shift work for health reasons, and (2) workers who had never been on shift work or who had left shift work for reasons other than health.

Shift workers reported $2\frac{1}{2}$ times the number of serious psychosomatic complaints as did those who had never been on shift work. Shift workers also reported a considerably higher degree of irritability and strain. It was concluded that shift work was harmful to employee health.

QUESTIONS

1. What other factors might have contributed to the greater number of health complaints among the shift workers?

2. What criticism would you make of the data gathering technique used in this study?
3. How is productivity affected by shift work?
4. In what ways can the problems caused by shift work be alleviated?

Reference: M. Frese & N. Semmer. (1986). Shiftwork, stress, and psychosomatic complaints: A comparison between workers in different shiftwork schedules, and non-shiftworkers, and former shiftworkers. *Ergonomics, 29*, 99–114.

Additional Reading

Long, R. J. (1987). *New Office Information Technology: Human and Managerial Implications*. New York: Croom Helm/Methuen. Describes the impact of computer technology on employees, organizations, and society at large. Includes a chapter on the advantages and disadvantages of home-based telecommuting.

Stautberg, S. S. (1987). Status report: The corporation and trends in family issues. *Human Resource Management, 26*, 277–290. Reviews corporate policies affecting the two-career family, including parental leave, child care, part-time employment, flexitime, and job sharing.

Sundstrom, E. (1986). *Work Places: The Psychology of the Physical Environment in Offices and Factories*. New York: Cambridge University Press. Discusses the history, research, and theory of the effects of the physical work environment on job satisfaction and performance, interpersonal relations, and organizational effectiveness. Covers temperature, air quality, lighting, windows, noise, music, color, work space design, and landscaped offices.

Chapter 11

Engineering Psychology

Introduction

We have discussed several ways in which I/O psychologists contribute to the goals of increasing employee efficiency, productivity, and job satisfaction. We have seen how the workers with the best abilities can be recruited and selected, how they can be trained for the job in question and supervised and motivated in the most effective way, and how certain techniques can be used to optimize the quality of work life and the conditions of work. All of these methods and procedures are time- and research-tested means of aiding the worker in the proper performance of the job.

But there is one aspect of work that has been mentioned only briefly, a factor clearly as influential as any of those discussed: the design of the machinery and equipment workers use to perform their jobs. The importance of using the right kind of tool in the proper way is evident from your own experience. To hang a picture you could use a doorknob or a rock to hammer the nail into the wall. Both of these would probably work, but you would get the job done in less time and with less aggravation if you used a hammer, the tool specifically designed for your purpose.

Of course, there are many different hammers. You could use one from a child's toy toolbox or a 20-pound sledgehammer or the standard homeowner's hammer. Again, you could probably accomplish the job with any of those tools, but the standard hammer will be the most efficient. Having chosen your tool, you could hold the hammer either near the striking surface or back at the end for better leverage, but one way is more effective than the other.

The point is that the job can be performed in a variety of ways and with more than one tool or object, but, as a rule, there is one best tool and one best way of using it. For the occasional picture hanger this is not too great a problem, but for carpenters who must hammer nails all day, it can be. Providing carpenters with properly shaped hammers of a specific weight and ensuring that they use them in a certain way not only allows them to hammer more nails during the work period but also makes the job safer, easier, and less fatiguing.

The same may be said of virtually every industrial job. No matter how well selected, trained, and motivated are the workers, the finished product (and the efficiency with which it is produced) is only as good as the tools or equipment supplied them. This principle applies to everything from a pair of pliers to the video display unit of a computer.

Equipment must be designed to be compatible with the workers who use it. In a sense, we can think of this as a team operation, a worker and a machine functioning together to perform a specific task that could not be accomplished by either working alone. It is a system—a *man-machine system*—and, if the person and the machine are to work in concert, they must be matched to one another, each making the best use of the strengths of the other and, where necessary, compensating for the weaknesses of the other. (The word *man* in man-machine system refers to both men and women workers. Some I/O psychologists have suggested the terms *person-machine system* and *human-machine system*, but their use is not widespread.)

This matching of operator and machine is the province of engineering psychology, also called human factors or human engineering. British psychologists refer to the field as ergonomics, a word derived from the Greek *ergon*, meaning work, and *nomos* meaning natural laws. This is a highly appropriate term because the goal of engineering psychologists is to formulate the natural laws of work. The field is a hybrid of engineering and psychological knowledge. We may formally define it as *the science of engineering machinery or equipment for human use and the science of engineering human behavior for proper operation of the machines.*

Until the 1940s, the design of machinery, equipment, and industrial plants was solely the responsibility of engineers. They made design decisions on the basis of mechanical, electrical, space and size considerations, giving little, if any, thought to the workers who would have to use the machines.

In this situation, the machine was a constant factor, incapable of being changed to meet human needs. Workers, therefore, had to adapt to the machine. No matter how uncomfortable, tiring, or unsafe the equipment, the operators, as the only flexible part of the man-machine system at that time, had to make the best of it and fit themselves to the machine's requirements.

Adapting the worker to the machine was accomplished by means of time-and-motion study, a precursor to engineering psychology, which analyzed the worker's job to determine how it could best be simplified. (As we shall see, the early time-and-motion study engineers also made rudimentary efforts at reshaping tools.)

The design of machines by engineers with no consideration for the needs of the people who operated them could not continue indefinitely. The machines were becoming too complex and requiring increasing levels of speed and precision for their proper operation. They were exceeding human capabilities to control them.

What could be done? Selection and training could help, of course, by finding and training people possessing the necessary skills, but that approach was limited by the relatively small numbers of qualified workers. By the time of World War II, the situation had become critical.

Sophisticated war machinery placed great demands on human capacities, not only on muscular strength but also higher level abilities of sensing, perceiving, judging, and rapid decision making. Pilots flying new and faster planes were allowed less time to react, make a decision, and initiate proper action. Equipment such as radar and sonar required new high-level human skills.

For the most part, the equipment worked well, but mistakes were being made: The most precise bombsight ever developed was not bringing about accurate bombing; friendly ships and airplanes were identified incorrectly and fired on; whales were mistaken for submarines. In short, although the machinery and equipment seemed to function properly, the system—the interaction of the worker and the equipment—did not.

So, it was this urgent wartime need that gave rise to engineering psychology (reminiscent of World War I and the need for widespread psychological testing). It was recognized that the capabilities and limitations of human operators would have to be considered in the design of machines in order for the system to function well. Psychologists, physiologists, and physicians found themselves in unusual environments working with engineers in designing aircraft cockpits, submarine and tank-crew stations, and even components of uniforms.

An example of this early work involved providing assistance to airplane pilots during World War II. In those years, there was no consistent or standard arrangement of displays and controls in the cockpits of the different aircraft. A pilot used to one type of plane who was suddenly assigned to another was confronted by a different cockpit layout. The lever to raise the wheels in the new plane might be in the same place as the lever to operate the flaps was in the old one.

Imagine trying to drive a car in which accelerator and brake pedals are reversed. In an emergency, you would probably step on the brake—at least, where you expect the brake to be—only to find yourself stepping on the gas. This was the situation facing the pilots in World War II. And there were other problems. There was no consistency in the operating characteristics of the aircraft controls. In the same airplane, one control would be switched upward to turn something on, another switched downward to turn something on. A number of different controls, all with identically shaped knobs, were placed close together so that a pilot who had to look elsewhere for a moment would not be able to discriminate among these controls on the basis of touch alone. Once such problems were recognized, they were corrected in aircraft design, but many pilots were killed because their machines were poorly designed, not from an aerodynamic standpoint, but from the standpoint of the frail human being whose job it was to direct, control, and tame so much power.

Since World War II, military equipment has become even more demanding on the people who must operate it. Aircraft fly at supersonic speeds and fire at planes or missiles they cannot see. How much time does a person have in which to decide to initiate some action and, then, to implement the decision? As a rule, not enough, and so the person must be given help. Computers and other electronic aids provide information to help make such rapid decisions or, in the case where the alternatives are limited and known, to make them for the human operator.

The growth of engineering psychology has been dynamic, and its practitioners are employed by every area of the military, by defense contractors, by manufacturers of dental and surgical instruments, and by consumer industries. They are also consulted by companies involved in the design of machines used in manufacturing.

Often, poor design has led to accidents. A particularly disastrous occurrence involved the nuclear power plant at Three Mile Island, Pennsylvania, in 1979. We noted in Chapter 10 that the accident occurred on the night shift, when the operators were less alert. However, part of the problem also involved the lack of attention to human engineering concerns. In the power plant's control room, instrument dials and controls were not sufficiently close to each other. When operators detected a dangerous reading on one of the dials, precious seconds were lost because they had to run to another part of the room to operate the controls that would correct the malfunction. To prevent a recurrence of this kind of situation, the Nuclear Regulatory Commission in 1983 mandated the modification of all nuclear control rooms from the standpoint of human factors.

To deal with the human factor in aircraft accidents, 66% of which result from human error, the National Transportation Safety Board, the federal agency that investigates airplane crashes, recently added engineering psychologists to its staff. Their function is to investigate pre-accident factors such as pilot and crew fatigue, shift work schedules, medical problems, stress, and human factors design considerations that might have contributed to the accident.

A great deal of human factors research has been conducted on passenger vehicles in an effort to make them safer. This research, much of it carried out at the Human Factors Division of the University of Michigan Transportation Research Institute (formerly the Highway Safety Research Institute), covers a wide range of topics. These include the brightness level of automobile and motorcycle headlights; the position, color, and brightness of brake lights; and dashboard controls and displays. In addition, engineering psychologists are investigating ways in which license plates and traffic signs can be made more legible and noticeable at night. Much research is also being conducted on driver reaction time, driver perception of risky situations, and alcohol-impaired drivers (Sivak, 1987).

Engineering psychologists are also working on consumer products, ranging from telephones to automobiles (see Figure 11-1). The phenomenal growth of space exploration has placed demands on the skills of engineering psychologists as has the use of word-processing equipment. Computers in the workplace are presenting problems of comfort, health, and productivity for engineering psychologists to solve. The organization Nine to Five, the National Association of Working Women, has engaged in a campaign to alert managers and employees to the potential health dangers of poorly designed computers and work stations. They claim that unnecessary eyestrain and lower back pain are caused by improperly designed machines, desks, and chairs. In San Francisco, 1,000 workers at Blue Cross of California walked off their jobs to protest poor human factors design in the workplace. Their grievances included chairs that could not be adjusted and overhead lights that caused excessive glare on computer screens. As we shall see, the design and use of computers presents an important challenge for engineering psychologists.

Because the field of human engineering is a hybrid, it is not surprising that its practitioners have diverse backgrounds. The membership of the Human Factors Society includes physicians, sociologists, engineers, anthropologists, and other behavioral and physical scientists. More than 50% of the members, however, are psychologists. A number of universities offer graduate and under-graduate degrees in engineering psychology.

Time-and-Motion Analysis

Time-and-motion study was an early attempt to reshape the way workers performed their jobs and to redesign work tools. This field, also called industrial engineering, can be traced to the beginnings of industrial psychology, and its growth has paralled psychology's attempts to increase the productive efficiency of work. Time-and-motion study and engineering psychology are not synonymous terms or procedures, but they are closely linked, historically and procedurally, and their goals are identical.

The first systematic attempt to study the way in which work was performed occurred in 1898 when Frederick W. Taylor, the developer of scientific

We don't buy just any seats. We design them.

GM begins with detailed studies of the human body. Biomedical research. The kind of comprehensive investigation of anatomy da Vinci undertook in the 1500s.

As a leader in the field of Human Factors Engineering, we design interiors scientifically to minimize the possible distractions from your driving.

It may take us two years and countless clay models to arrive at a more comfortable, durable seat for new GM cars and trucks. But we think it's worth it.

And we believe old Leonardo would have thought so, too.

We believe in taking the extra time, giving the extra effort and paying attention to every detail. That's what it takes to provide the quality that leads more people to buy GM cars and trucks than any other kind. And why GM owners are the most loyal on the road.

That's the GM commitment to excellence.

Figure 11-1 Engineering psychologists help design consumer products. (Reproduced by permission of GM.)

management, undertook an investigation of the job of shoveling at the Bethlehem Steel Company. He learned that the workers were using shovels of many sizes and shapes and, as a result, the loads lifted by each man ranged from $3\frac{1}{2}$ pounds to 38 pounds. By experimenting with different shovel loads, Taylor determined that the optimum shovel size held $21\frac{1}{2}$ pounds; using this size shovel, the workers were the most efficient. Heavier or lighter loads resulted in a decrease in total daily output. Taylor also introduced shovels of different size for handling different materials—a small one for heavy iron ore and a larger one for ashes. Such changes may sound trivial, but Taylor's work resulted in savings to the company of $78,000 a year. With the new shovels, 140 men could accomplish the same amount of work that had formerly required 500 men. Also, by offering an incentive of higher pay for higher production, the workers' wages increased by 60% (F. W. Taylor, 1911).

This was the first empirical demonstration of the relationship between the tools of work and the efficiency with which a job could be performed. When companies realized how much money could be saved through proper investigation of work habits and tools, the field of time-and-motion analysis received a hearty welcome.

The next pioneers in this area were Frank B. Gilbreth, an engineer, and his wife Lillian, a psychologist, who did more to promote the growth of time-and-motion study than anyone else. Where Taylor had been concerned primarily with tool design and incentive wage systems, the Gilbreths were concerned with the way in which workers performed their jobs. Their overall goal was to eliminate all unnecessary motion (Gilbreth, 1911).

It all began when Frank Gilbreth, at age 17, was an apprentice bricklayer. On his first day at work, he noticed that the bricklayers were engaged in many unnecessary motions in their work. He thought he could redesign the job to make it faster and easier, and, within a year, he was the fastest bricklayer on the job. Once Gilbreth convinced his co-workers to try his methods, the whole crew was accomplishing more work than they had ever done before without being exhausted at the end of the workday.

First, Gilbreth designed a scaffold that could be raised or lowered so that the worker would always be at a level convenient to the work. By analyzing the individual hand and arm motions involved in bricklaying and making the necessary changes in the way the job was performed, the bricklayers could lay 350 bricks per hour instead of the usual 120. This increase in productivity was brought about not by forcing the men to work faster, but by reducing the number of motions involved in the laying of each brick from 18 to $4\frac{1}{2}$.

The Gilbreths, incidentally, organized their daily lives around the principles of time-and-motion economy and tolerated no wasted motions. Every activity of each member of the family was scrutinized for unnecessary motions. Gilbreth, for example, always buttoned his vest from the bottom up because it took 4 seconds less than buttoning it from the top down. He used two brushes, one in each hand, to lather his face for shaving, a saving of 17 seconds. He also tried shaving with two razors, but found that he lost more time bandaging his face than he saved in shaving. The activities of the children were noted on charts so that every minute of the day was as gainfully employed as possible. In spite of this (or perhaps as evidence of increased productivity), the Gilbreths had 12 children, the subject of the book and movie *Cheaper by the Dozen*.

As a result of the efforts of Taylor and the Gilbreths, time-and-motion engineers (or efficiency experts, as they came to be called) studied all types of jobs with the overall goal of reducing to the absolute minimum the number of motions in the performance of a job. Their work revolutionized many jobs, even those in hospital operating rooms. Before Gilbreth analyzed the motions involved in surgery, surgeons had to seek out each tool they wanted to use. Gilbreth urged that a nurse place the required tool in the surgeon's hand, a saving of motion that reduced operating times by as much as two thirds.

The investigations of the efficiency experts provided the most significant results with routine and repetitive work. In a motion study, a worker's individual movements are studied in detail with a view toward modifying or eliminating as many movements as possible. To accomplish this with the greatest precision, motion pictures are taken of job performance and analyzed on a frame-by-frame basis to discover inefficient or wasteful motion.

Through these studies, rules or guidelines for efficient work have been developed. The following is a list of some rules designed to increase the ease, speed, and accuracy of jobs involving manual operations (Barnes, 1980; Niebel, 1972):

1. Minimize the distance workers must reach to get tools, supplies, or operate machines. Reaching motions should be as short as possible.
2. Both hands should begin and end their movement at the same time. Movements should be as nearly symmetrical as possible; for example, the right hand should reach to the right for one item as the left hand simultaneously reaches to the left for another. Such simultaneous movements feel natural and do not disturb balance.
3. The hands should always be in motion, never idle, except during official rest periods.
4. The hands should never be given tasks that could be performed more appropriately by other parts of the body, particularly by the legs and feet. Leg muscles are strong and a foot control can often be used, thus relieving the hands of one more operation.
5. Wherever possible, work materials should be held by a mechanical device such as a vise instead of being held by the hand. Once again, this releases the hands for another operation.
6. Circular movements of the hands between two points are more efficient than straight-line movements, particularly if the movement is made repeatedly and quickly.
7. The workplace should be so arranged to permit workers to sit or stand alternately to perform the job. Thus, the workbench or table should be of sufficient height that the job can be performed when sitting on a high stool or when standing. Alternating positions relieves fatigue.

8. Wherever possible, tools should be combined to eliminate the wasteful motions of putting one tool down and picking another up. If the two tools can be combined into one, these motions are dispensed with.

9. Movements should always occur in the direction in which gravity will aid the movement; for example, pulling a heavy weight down instead of pushing it up.

10. Picking up and handling objects should be accomplished in such a way as to require the least amount of precision. Large gross movements are easier, less subject to error, and less fatiguing.

Criticisms of Time-and-Motion Analysis

At first glance, it might seem that these methods of work simplification should have met with enthusiastic acceptance both from management, which receives a greater output, and from labor, whose work is made easier. Although management has indeed been delighted with time-and-motion study, the workers have definitely not been pleased. Their reaction has been characterized by suspicion and hostility.

Individual workers and organized labor have argued, throughout the years, that time-and-motion studies benefit only the company and adversely affect the workers. Employees suspect that the only reason for such studies is to force them to work faster. They believe that this will lead to lower rates of pay and to dismissals because fewer workers will be required to maintain the same production level. And it must be noted that this has occasionally been a consequence of time-and-motion studies.

Other worker complaints are that job simplification can lead to monotony, boredom, lack of challenge and responsibility, and an ultimate decline in productivity. As noted in the discussion of motivation, many human needs are not being satisfied (in fact, are being thwarted) by the reduction of work to its simplest components.

It is well known in industry that when workers are observed by an efficiency expert, they commonly react by slowing their normal work pace. Too many organizations send industrial engineers to observe a job, often for several days, without informing the workers about the purpose of the time-and-motion analysis and the possible effects the results may have on their jobs. It has been demonstrated (initially by Gilbreth) that employees are much more accepting of time-and-motion studies when management fully informs them of the nature and purpose of the observations. This simple and honest technique usually increases cooperation and the value of the study.

Criticisms from industrial psychologists and engineers have been directed against certain basic premises of time-and-motion study. They argue that the wide range of individual differences that exists in job abilities and skills negates the idea that there is only one best way of performing a job that is effective for all employees. Because of individual differences in physical characteristics and attitudes, the work methods suitable for one employee might not be suitable for another. People are not standardized or interchangeable parts; to assume that they can and must follow identical work routines is to look on them as nothing more than machines or robots.

A second professional criticism of time-and-motion study has to do with inadequate sampling. The optimum movement pattern and time for a job are often established on the basis of a limited number of observations, usually involving only a small number of the total work force in a specific job category. Of course, if a small number is a representative sample of the work force there would be no problem, but, invariably, it seems that only the best workers already performing the job are studied. The resulting work methods, then, are based on behavior that was desirable for a few superior workers, a sample clearly not representative of the full range of skills and abilities found in the work force.

Also, the sample of the workday or workweek studied is often inadequate. For example, a time study might be taken only on Thursday and Friday of a particularly hectic week when workers are more tired and less efficient than normally.

Critics of time-and-motion study also question some of the basic rules of motion listed previously. For example, research suggests that it may not be as efficient to use both hands simultaneously as had previously been thought. Additional research is needed to verify these principles and guidelines.

These criticisms have not been directed against the concept of developing more efficient work methods, but rather against certain weaknesses in the techniques by which work methods have been developed. When these criticisms are taken into account, time-and-motion analysis still can serve to make the worker's job easier and safer and the company's profits larger.

Many satires and parodies have been written about the notion of judging everything by the criterion of greater efficiency. Suppose, one author noted, we were to undertake a time-and-motion study of a symphony orchestra performance.

> For considerable periods the four oboe players had nothing to do. The number should be reduced and the work spread more evenly over the whole of the concert. . . .
>
> All the twelve violins were playing identical notes; this seems unnecessary duplication. The staff of this section should be drastically cut. . . .
>
> There seems to be too much repetition of some musical passages. Scores should be drastically pruned. No useful purpose is served by repeating on the horns a passage which has already been handled by the strings. It is estimated that if all redundant passages were eliminated the whole concert time of 2 hours could be reduced to 20 minutes. . . . In many cases the operators were using one hand for holding the instrument, whereas the use of a fixture would have rendered the idle hand available for other work ("How to be Efficient," 1955, pp. 454–455).

Time-and-motion study is alive and well today, but its use is largely limited to relatively simple and routine tasks such as assembly-line jobs. When job operations, equipment, and functions become more complex, a more sophisticated procedure for optimizing work methods and procedures is needed; this is the task of engineering psychology.

Man-Machine Systems

As we have noted, the early World War II efforts of engineering psychologists were concerned with specific problems of equipment design. Indeed, the field was sometimes referred to as knob and dial work because so much of the initial effort was concerned with the proper location and design of individual controls and displays.

As engineering psychology expanded in numbers and expertise, its interests grew to embrace the total relationship between the human operator and the machine. Though still concerned with the design of knobs and dials, engineering psychologists now begin work with an analysis of the task to be performed and a determination of the most effective combination of worker and machine skills to accomplish that task. In other words, engineering psychologists make their input from the earliest stages of a design problem. Instead of being called in, for example, to design and place the pilot's instrument panel components after the airplane has been designed, human engineers now participate in the design of the total airplane as a man-machine system. Problems include the best allocation of functions between the operator and the machine, the kinds of information the operator will need, the kinds of judgments and decisions that

An airplane cockpit is a man-machine system. Displays and controls must be designed so that the pilots receive information from the machine and can initiate the appropriate actions.

will be required, and the quickest and safest way of communicating these decisions to the machine. These are studied in advance and the answers to these questions are used to shape the final design of the machine.

A man-machine system is one in which both components must work together to accomplish the job; neither part of the system is of value without the other. Using this definition, many routine tasks are examples of man-machine systems.

A person pushing a lawnmower is such a system. A person driving a car or operating a word processor is a man-machine system, albeit a bit more complicated. At a still more sophisticated level, the Concorde supersonic airliner and its required crew of specialists (each responsible for a different part of the operation) constitute a man-machine system.

Even more complex is an air traffic control system at a busy airport. Here the total system includes a number of separate man-machine systems, each an integral part of the whole. If one small part (mechanical or human) fails, all the other parts of the system are affected.

Man-machine systems vary greatly in the extent to which human operators are actively and continuously involved in their operation. In flying an airplane or controlling traffic at a busy airport, operators are an integral part of the total system; their presence is necessary most of the time. Even when an airplane is on automatic pilot, the flight crew must be available to resume control immediately in the event of an emergency.

There are other man-machine systems in which humans interact less continuously. Large-scale production processes such as those used by oil refineries operate with highly automated equipment. Some products are built entirely by robots. No human being is needed to run the machines. But, whereas it can be said that automated equipment runs itself, it cannot design, build, or maintain itself. It cannot even replace its own light bulb. Human beings are still important components of the system even when they are not directly or continuously operating the equipment.

Thus, automation has not diminished the need for engineering psychology. If anything, it has complicated the task of engineering psychologists because they now must deal with new kinds of jobs. Workers required to monitor automated equipment can find the task more fatiguing and boring than actually operating a machine, as we noted in our discussion of vigilance. Monitoring equipment must be designed to keep observers alert so that they can immediately determine when something goes wrong. Also, humans must maintain mechanical systems, so the machines must be designed to facilitate troubleshooting, locating, and replacing defective parts.

The definition and the requirements of man-machine systems remain the same, in principle, regardless of the degree of involvement of the worker with the machine. We are still vital to the system, whatever the degree of automation. (If we should ever develop machines that are able to design, build, and maintain other machines, then we have a problem of a different sort. Perhaps, the machines then will produce books about how to engineer human beings to fit the machines' needs.)

Open-Loop and Closed-Loop Systems

There are two varieties of man-machine systems: open loop and closed loop. The basic difference between them is their self-correction, that is, whether or not the operation of the machine provides feedback to itself that can then cause a change in its operation.

In the open-loop system, an input enters at a particular point, activates a controlling mechanism, and some sort of activity occurs. This is what happens, for example, with overhead sprinkler systems installed in many buildings in case of fire. The input is a certain level of heat in the room. When the temperature exceeds this predetermined level, the heat melts a metal plug in the water line, thereby releasing the flow of water (the output).

The system is simple and is not self-regulating. If the room temperature then decreased to below the critical level, the system would not shut itself off. The water would continue to flow until stopped by some external agent such as the owner of the building or the fire department.

A closed-loop system is self-regulating, for example, a building's central heating system. Once the controlling agent—the thermostat—is set at the desired temperature, the furnace turns itself on and off to adjust to temperature fluctuations. The input (the desired temperature) controls the operation of the furnace. When the furnace has run long enough to raise the temperature to the thermostat setting, this new input causes the controlling thermostat to shut the furnace off.

Human beings are self-regulating closed-loop systems. We receive information (inputs) from the environment through the senses. We process the information in some way, storing it for future use, forgetting it because it is trivial, or taking some immediate action (output) on the basis of it.

A closed-loop man-machine system is more efficient than an open-loop system; therefore, the latter is seldom used. Figure 11-2 depicts a closed-loop man-machine system. The human operator (the regulator or thermostat) receives input on the status of the machine from the displays. On the basis of that information, he or she regulates the machine by initiating some controlling action.

Suppose you are driving your car on a highway at a constant speed. You receive input from the speedometer, process this information, and decide that you are driving too fast. Through the control action of easing your foot off the accelerator, you cause the car to slow down. This decrease in speed is displayed on the speedometer for your information and the process continues.

A driver also receives information from the environment, such as a sign noting a change in the speed limit or a slow car ahead. This information is processed, and a change in speed is dictated to the machine. Verification of the changed status of the machine (the new speed) is seen on the speedometer.

Although more complicated, the principle is the same for the most sophisticated man-machine systems, and it is the system as a whole that is the starting point for the engineering psychologist's job.

In designing a man-machine system, there are two broad categories of human engineering considerations, that is, two methods of matching the often

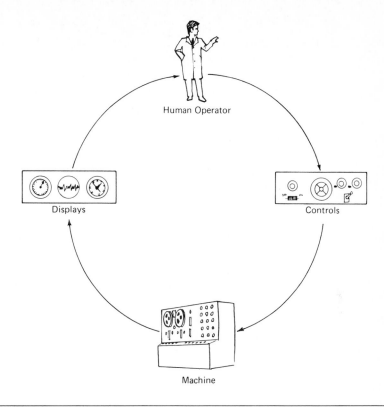

Figure 11-2 Closed-loop man-machine system.

conflicting requirements of the worker and the machine. First, there are techniques for designing the physical equipment with which the operator will work. This is properly the province of engineering psychologists. Second, once the system is designed, there are methods of selecting and training persons who possess the abilities to perform the job. This is the province of personnel or industrial psychologists. Both considerations are necessary for efficient perform-ance, but, in a complex man-machine system, the problems of equipment design (the so-called hardware problems) are more important.

Allocation of Functions in Man-Machine Systems

An initial step in the design of any man-machine system involves making decisions (as many as the complexity of the system requires) about the division of labor between the human operator and the machine. The system require-ments (its goals) are nearly always known from the outset. The problem is how to combine the capabilities and the limitations of the two major system components to best fulfill these requirements.

Each step or process in the functioning of the total system must be examined to determine its characteristics; the speed, accuracy, and frequency with which it must be performed; the stress under which it occurs; and the like. When this information is analyzed, it becomes possible to match the system requirements with the characteristics of the person and the machine. These matching decisions must also consider information about the number of persons necessary to function as the human part of the system, their background characteristics (such as intelligence), and the training needed to transform general abilities into specific skills.

These highly complex decisions must be made early in the design process. Their results will help determine the shape and nature of the total system.

Consider the following example from the Japanese steel industry, where the speed of operation had to be matched along with the capacities of the employees who were to work with the machinery (Oshima, Hayashi, & Noro, 1980). Decisions had to be made as to which functions should be allocated to human operators and which to machines.

Because of technological innovations, Japanese steel mills were processing steel at an ever-increasing rate. It became apparent that inspectors were having difficulty performing their job because the steel passing in front of them on a conveyor belt was moving too rapidly. The accuracy of the inspectors in checking for defects was declining. As a result, some substandard steel was being sent to customers.

Human factors engineers studied the physiological limitations of the human eye by using a camera that measured the eye movements of the inspectors on the job. The psychologists concluded that when the speed of the conveyor belt exceeded a certain level, the human eye could not move quickly enough to keep pace. As a result of this research, Japanese engineers developed an automatic flow-detection device for use when the speed of the mill exceeds the human capacity. The employees could perform the job well up to a point, but, beyond that, a machine was needed to compensate for the physiological limitations of the human inspectors.

Many industrial inspection functions have now been allocated to machines. Many kinds of metal products, textiles, nuclear power fuel elements as well as coal particles moving on a conveyor belt can be inspected faster and more accurately by machines than by humans. Lest we begin to feel inferior, it is reassuring to report that there is at least one inspection process, that involving metal cylinders, in which experienced and highly motivated human inspectors were shown to be superior to a machine. The machine was able to detect most of the flaws, but it was unable to classify them as acceptable or unacceptable as consistently as humans could. In this case, humans were better because of their more sophisticated decision-making capabilities (Drury & Sinclair, 1983).

There are a number of criteria or guidelines available to facilitate decisions about the allocation of functions. Research by psychologists, physiologists, and physicians has revealed much information about human strengths and weaknesses, so we are aware of those functions for which humans are superior to machines as well as those for which humans are inferior. Similarly, engineers (in conjunction with engineering psychologists) are aware of the relative effectiveness of the machines (Chapanis, 1965b).

In general, humans are superior to machines in performing the following kinds of functions:

1. Detecting a wide range of stimuli through the senses of sight, hearing, touch, taste, and smell.
2. Picking out infrequently appearing or low-level stimuli against a confusing background such as detecting words in radio transmissions containing a lot of static or detecting blips on a radar screen having poor reception.
3. Sensing, detecting, and recognizing highly unusual or unexpected stimuli in the environment.
4. Using a wide range of past experiences in making decisions.
5. Responding and adapting quickly to diverse situations and emergencies—we do not require prior programming to meet all situations.
6. Drawing generalizations on the basis of a number of specific observations (inductive reasoning).
7. Exhibiting flexibility in problem solving, including the development of new solutions never before applied to a problem.

Thus, human operators bring to the man-machine system a host of remarkable abilities and skills, the more sophisticated of which have not been duplicated in the most expensive, complex, and cumbersome of machines. However, humans also have weaknesses that must sometimes be compensated for in the man-machine system.

In general, humans are inferior to machines in performing the following kinds of functions:

1. In the range of detection of sensory stimuli—for example, we cannot detect auditory stimuli beyond frequencies of 20,000 cycles per second.
2. Long-term monitoring activities such as watchkeeping or radar observation; human performance is not very reliable over long periods of time in these vigilance tasks.
3. The number of mathematical calculations that can be carried out rapidly without mechanical aids.
4. Retrieving large amounts of data reliably and quickly.
5. Applying physical force, particularly where precision and continuous application are necessary.
6. Routine repetitive performance over long periods of time—human performance is subject to deterioration under conditions of stress or fatigue.

We can readily see which functions are performed better by machines.

1. Machines can detect stimuli such as radar wave lengths and ultraviolet light, which are beyond human sensory powers.
2. Machines can monitor reliably for extremely long periods of time. (The stimulus in question must be programmed or specified for the machine in advance.)

3. Machines can make large numbers of rapid and accurate calculations.
4. Machines can store and retrieve huge amounts of information with a high level of accuracy.
5. Machines can apply greater physical force continuously and rapidly.
6. Machines can engage in highly repetitive activities with no performance deterioration as long as proper maintenance is applied.
7. Machines do not get tired.

Machines are not perfect, of course. They also have the following weaknesses and limitations:

1. Machines are not very flexible. Even the most sophisticated computer can only do what it is programmed to do. Where adaptability to meet new, rapidly changing circumstances is important, machines are at a disadvantage. They can perform their prescribed functions well, but they can only do what a human operator tells them to do.
2. Machines cannot benefit from past experiences or mistakes. They cannot learn and modify their performance on the basis of experience. Any change in operation must be built into the system by a human programmer.
3. Machines are unable to reason or examine various unprogrammed alternatives. In other words, machines cannot improvise.

As these lists seem to indicate, it is perhaps naïve to talk, as some futurists do, about redesigning humans out of the system altogether. We can perform certain vital functions that machines cannot. In other cases, we can perform functions at least as well as, and often cheaper than, machines. And, as long as machines lack flexibility and responsiveness, human operators are a necessary component of properly functioning systems.

The problem of function allocation in the design of a man-machine system is not resolved by a designer referring to lists such as these and checking whether a person or a machine can perform the task better. These are guidelines only. There are several considerations beyond the simple superiority of one component over the other. The designer may take note of these guidelines, but they frequently must be modified in the light of other factors.

Some man-machine comparisons are modified by cost. Although it is true that some electronic inspection devices are more efficient than a human at inspecting items on a fast-moving assembly line, they may cost a great deal more. If cost is an important consideration or if the project budget requires a cutback in expenses, then speed of inspection may have to be sacrificed if a person can do the job almost as well (assuming "almost as well" allows the total system to function satisfactorily).

There may also be social and political considerations, particularly in assigning priority to machines in production facilities. In times of massive unemployment, it would be unwise to automate a process that formerly required the skills of a large number of workers. Even though the job may be performed faster and more accurately by machines, is this worth the cost of creating additional unemployment?

The opposite situation of not having enough workers can also influence allocation decisions. Jobs that could be performed quite well by humans must be automated, even though it may cost more to make the finished product. In short, allocation decisions often cannot be based solely on the issue of the superiority of humans or machines for the task.

Their relative superiority must be constantly reevaluated under the impact of technological innovations and developments. A new machine or process can influence a system already in operation. For many years, for example, the banking system in the United States required numerous employees to read and sort checks into their proper accounts. This was a constant in the design of such systems; a human operator was vital to the performance of this task. Today, machines perform these operations by scanning computerized check numbers, thus altering the whole procedure and making it faster and more efficient. The system has been redesigned and improved because of technological advances.

The entire allocation question represents a bumpy road full of compromises that must be resolved to the satisfaction of system performance as well as economic, social, and cost considerations. The advantages of selecting one component over the other must constantly be compared with the disadvantages.

This was particularly apparent in the design of vehicles for space exploration. For several reasons (technical, social, and political), the U.S. space program insisted on using humans in the vehicles. There are obvious advantages to their use (although many argue that just as much information could be collected without a human component in the system). Whereas humans offer certain advantages, the difficulties of keeping them alive in the spacecraft required costly, heavy, and extensive life-support systems, that is, crews had to be provided with an artificial environment to survive. Thus, much weight and space had to be added to the total system. This was a great disadvantage, but it was necessary to realize the advantages of accommodating humans in the system.

This initial stage of system design, the allocation of functions, is difficult and demanding, but, unless all functions have been properly allocated, it is unwise to proceed to the design of the machine itself.

Work-Space Design

The harmful effects of poor work-space design were readily apparent in the U.S. Army's highly touted M-1 Abrams tank, built in the mid-1980s (Cordes, 1985). The interior of a tank is the crew's work space, and the nature of its design can strongly influence job performance, in this case, the crew's fighting efficiency. The tank was designed without the contributions of human factors research, and when it was tested, 27 of the 29 test drivers developed neck and back pains so severe that they required medical attention. Further, the drivers were unable to see the ground in front of the tank for a distance of 9 yards, making it difficult to avoid obstacles and cross trenches.

More than half of the tank's gunners, loaders, and drivers could not hear one another well enough to communicate when the tank's engine and turret blowers were operating because the machinery was simply too loud. All crew members reported visibility problems at their various work stations. When the drivers and tank commanders traveled with an open hatch, they found that the front fenders had been so poorly designed that they did not protect the crew from rocks, dirt, and mud churned up by the tank's treads. You can see that the M-1 tank was not an effective work space and had not been designed well from a human engineering standpoint.

In contrast, consider the human factors research that was part of the design of another work space, the cab of a new locomotive built by a manufacturing plant in Sweden (Hedberg, 1987). Based on extensive studies carried out on 150 railroad engine drivers, psychologists collected data on the drivers' complaints about the back, neck, and shoulder pain they experienced while working in the present locomotives. It was found that only drivers below a certain height were subject to such physical discomfort. The cab—the seats and the location of the controls, in particular—had been designed only for taller drivers. Based on this information, the new locomotive cab was designed to be more comfortable and efficient for both men and women drivers of a wide range of heights.

Human factors engineers devised a seat and footrest that were fully adjustable so that drivers could operate the locomotive from standing and sitting positions and could also alter the height of the seat. Other changes were made in the control panel, placing the most frequently used controls within easier reach and making the speedometer display more clearly visible.

After the prototype locomotive was built, a sample of 50 drivers were asked to test it and to complete a questionnaire comparing the old and new work spaces. The majority of the drivers thought that the changes would make their work easier, safer, and less fatiguing, and they suggested a few additional refinements in the design. Long-term research is now underway to determine if the new design will reduce the physical complaints associated with the old seats and control panels.

The effective design of the human operator's work space—whether it is a workbench for electronic parts assembly, an air traffic control center, a tank, or the cab of a locomotive—involves certain established principles of design and work economy from the fields of human engineering and time-and-motion study. System analysis of the job and allocation-of-function decisions help determine the kinds of tools and equipment needed by human operators to perform their missions in the system. Once the specific items of equipment are determined, the task is to position or arrange them in such a way to facilitate job performance.

Some of the principles of motion economy discussed earlier serve as guidelines in work-space design, and common sense and empirically tested principles are also available.

The first principle of work-space design is that all materials, tools, and supplies needed by workers should be placed in the order in which they are to be used so that the paths of the workers' movements are continuous. Also, the knowledge that each part or tool is always in the same place saves the time and annoyance of searching for it.

The second principle is that tools should be pre-positioned so that they can be picked up ready for use. For a job requiring repeated use of a screwdriver, for example, that tool can be suspended just above the work area on a coil spring. When it is needed, workers do not even have to raise their heads to see it. They merely reach up and pull it down in a position ready for immediate use.

The third principle of work-space design is that all parts and tools—such as the controls in the locomotive cab—be placed within an easy and comfortable reaching distance. It becomes fatiguing if workers must constantly change positions (either sitting or standing) to reach beyond the normal working area. All work should be able to be accomplished within the maximum reach, as shown in the work assembly station pictured in Figure 11-3. The work activities depicted here can all occur within the confines of the normal arm reach. No movement beyond the maximum reaching distance is ever required. Obviously, the greater the distance the arms are forced to reach, the longer the operation will require. Note, too, that the bins containing the components for the assembly task are arranged in a semicircle in front of the worker rather than a straight line. This eliminates excessive reaching that might otherwise have been required; in a straight-line arrangement, the end bins are farther away.

This semicircular work-space arrangement is ideal for any situation involving repeated reaching for several items in a fixed sequence.

In Figure 11-4, the top drawing shows the old locomotive cab we described earlier. The bottom drawing shows the new work-space design with the displays

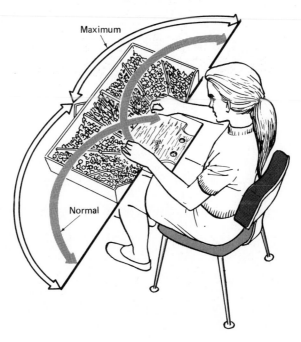

Figure 11-3 Work assembly station. (From *Motion and Time Study*, (5th ed., p. 259) by R. Barnes, 1963, New York: Wiley. Reprinted by permission.)

Maximum

Normal

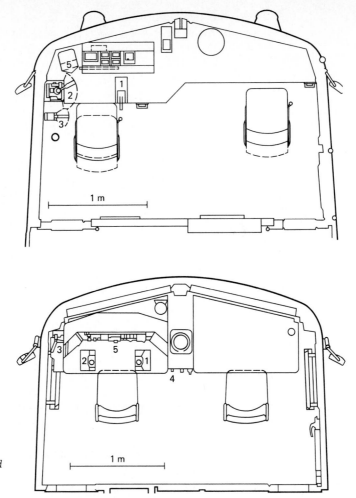

Figure 11-4 Locomotive cab designs. (From "The evaluation of the driver's cab in the Rc5 engine" by G. Hedberg, 1987, *Applied Ergonomics*, *18*(1), pp. 36, 37.)

in a semicircular arrangement and the controls within the span of a normal arm reach. The number 5 indicates the position of the speedometer. In the old arrangement it was in the left corner of the cab and difficult to see. In the new arrangement it is in the center of the display panel.

Similar design principles apply to the work space required by a radar operator or a person seated before a panel or console of lights, dials, and switches who is monitoring and controlling the operation of complex machinery. Such an operator's console is shown in Figure 11-5. As with the work-assembly station and the locomotive cab, the monitoring console is designed so that operators can see and reach everything necessary to the successful performance of the task without leaving the chair or even reaching excessively

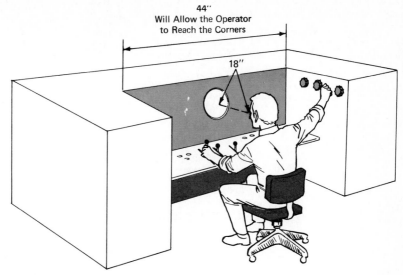

44"
Will Allow the Operator
to Reach the Corners

18"

Figure 11-5 Monitoring console work arrangement. (From W. Woodson, *Human engineering guide for equipment designers.* Berkeley, Calif.: University of California Press, 1954, p. 1–37. Copyright © 1954 & 1964 by The Regents of the University of California; reprinted by permission of the University of California Press.)

beyond normal seated posture. Studies have shown that average reaching distance is 28 inches. Therefore, all controls, particularly those used most frequently, should be within that distance. Details of shape and arrangement of controls and displays are discussed in the next section.

Another important consideration in work-space design is the size and shape of individual hand tools that employees must use repeatedly. Applying the principles of human engineering can improve even such a basic tool as a pair of pliers to make them easier and less tiring to use, and less prone to cause injury. Hand tools should be designed so that workers can use them without bending their wrists. Research has shown that hands are stronger and less vulnerable to injury when the wrists are kept straight. Human engineering principles applied to the design of pliers are shown in Figure 11-6.

The proper design of hand tools affects productivity, satisfaction, and, as noted, physical health. Studies have shown that the repeated use of hand tools that require the wrist to be bent while the worker applies a strong grip can lead to the development of *carpal tunnel syndrome*, a nerve injury inside the wrist. This condition, suffered by more than 23,000 workers every year, is painful, debilitating, and expensive, often requiring surgery to remedy. (Carpal tunnel syndrome is also prevalent among people who spend a great deal of time playing the piano, knitting, or playing video games, a finding that may influence your choice of hobbies.)

Research on the effects of changing the diameter of the grip of the powered screwdriver, a standard factory tool, found that the smallest diameter of the six tested (2.86 centimeters) required significantly greater effort to use than a grip almost twice as large. The simple redesign that resulted from this research not only made the screwdriver easier to use, but it also reduced the potential

Avoid short tool handles that press into the palm of the hand. The palm is very soft and easily damaged.

Avoid narrow tool handles that concentrate large forces onto small areas of the hand.

Tools and jobs should be designed so that they can be performed with straight wrists. Hands are stronger and less vulnerable to injury when the wrists are kept straight.

Figure 11-6 Application of human factors principles to the design of pliers. (From "Ergonomics," 1986, *Personnel Journal*, 65(6), p. 99.)

injurious effects (S. L. Johnson, 1988). The study provides an excellent example of how human factors research can improve the match between the worker and the machine.

Other important research on work-space arrangement has been conducted by a branch of engineering psychology—known as *human anthropometry*—which is concerned with the measurement of the physical structure of the human body. Complete sets of body measurements have been taken from large populations when at rest and in the performance of various activities: height (standing and sitting), shoulder breadth, back height, seat height, foot and hand length and breadth, chest depth, and so on (see Figure 11-7). These measurements are useful for many aspects of work-space design such as normal and maximum reaching distances, heights of proper tool and desk arrangement, and the size and shape of aircraft and automobile seats.

For the millions of us who work or study seated at a desk or worktable, the chairs we sit in, if improperly designed, can cause back and neck pain and lead to fatigue. This, in turn, can reduce our productive efficiency. Research has been conducted on every conceivable aspect of the design of workplace seating, and guidelines are readily available for the best type of seating for various kinds of jobs (Bendix & Bloch, 1986; Tougas & Nordin, 1987).

Display Functions: The Presentation of Information

In man-machine systems, operators receive inputs from the machine through one or more physical senses. In driving a car, for example, we receive some information on the operating status of the machine from visual displays (speedometer, temperature indicator, gas gauge) and some from auditory displays (the buzzer that indicates that the key is still in the ignition when the

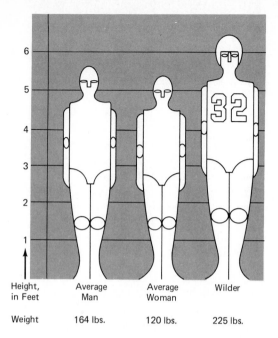

	Average Man	Average Woman	Wilder
Height, in Feet			
Weight	164 lbs.	120 lbs.	225 lbs.

Figure 11-7 Height and weight of the "average" man and woman compared to running back James Wilder of the Tampa Bay Buccaneers football team. (Reproduced by permission of the *St. Petersburg Times*.)

door is open). On an informal basis, we even receive inputs tactually such as when a poor performing engine causes the car to vibrate.

All three of these senses have been used to present inputs to a human operator although the visual mode is the most frequently used. One of the earliest decisions, then, concerning the presentation of information is to select the most effective means of communication for various kinds of information. The choice depends on the nature of the information and how it is to be used, the location of the operator relative to the machine, and the characteristics of the specific sense organ.

The visual presentation of information is more appropriate when

1. The message is difficult, abstract, and lengthy.
2. The information will be referred to at a later time or a permanent record is desired (a permanent record of an aural message must be made at the moment of transmission).
3. The environment is too noisy for aural messages.
4. There is no urgency or the aural channels of communication are overloaded.
5. The message consists of many different kinds of information that must be presented simultaneously.

Aural communication of information is more effective when

1. The information is simple, short, and straightforward.
2. The message is urgent (auditory signals will usually attract attention more readily than visual ones).

3. The environment does not allow for visual communication, for example, dark conditions.
4. The operator's job requires movement to a number of locations (ears can receive messages from all directions).
5. The message deals with a precise moment such as telling someone when to fire artillery (aural presentation allows for more precise pinpointing of time).

Other conditions can determine the relative effectiveness of these two communication channels, but the previous lists amply demonstrate that situational requirements dictate the choice. We deal mainly with the visual presentation of information because that is the most frequently used mode in man-machine systems.

Visual Displays

One common error made in the visual presentation of input is to provide more information than the operator needs to run the machine. Particularly in the days before the application of human engineering knowledge, instrument panels and display consoles were cluttered with information that served no useful purpose.

For example, most automobile drivers do not need a tachometer to indicate engine rpm; this information will be of little value. It may not be a problem in an automobile, but, in an airplane, where large amounts of vital information must be displayed, any useless input only adds to the display problem.

The first question, then, in visual display design is, Is this information necessary to the operation of the system? If the system can function without it, there will be one less item with which to confront or confuse the already busy human operator. If the information is vital to the operation of the system, the most effective method of displaying it, so that it can be perceived quickly and accurately, must be determined.

Three types of visual displays are commonly used in man-machine systems: quantitative, qualitative, and check reading.

Quantitative displays present quantitative information, that is, a precise numerical value. In situations dealing with speed, altitude, or temperature, for example, the human operator must know the precise numerical value of a condition of the system. A pilot must know if the altitude is 10,500 feet as dictated by the flight plan. An approximate indication of altitude instead of a precise one could lead the plane into the flight path of another aircraft or into a mountain in a fog. Five ways of presenting quantitative information along with their relative reading accuracy are shown in Figure 11-8.

The study showed that the open-window type of display is read with the fewest errors. The vertical display is misread more than one third of the time. One variable that may tend to influence reading accuracy is the relative size of the area the observer must view to get a reading. In Figure 11-8, the larger the area to be scanned, the greater the errors. However, these results are from an experimental situation in which the subjects were required to read the displays

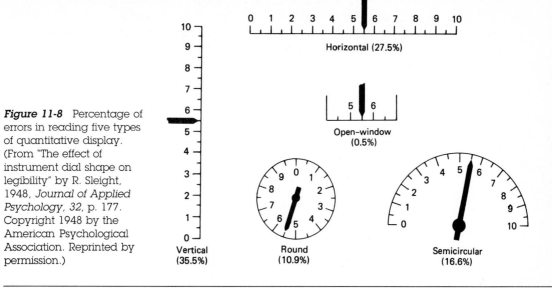

Figure 11-8 Percentage of errors in reading five types of quantitative display. (From "The effect of instrument dial shape on legibility" by R. Sleight, 1948, *Journal of Applied Psychology, 32,* p. 177. Copyright 1948 by the American Psychological Association. Reprinted by permission.)

in a fixed short period of time. In some situations, the human operator may be able to take more time to read quantitative displays.

Other research has not consistently supported the order of reading accuracy shown in Figure 11-8. In general, however, research indicates that the open-window design does allow for the most accurate readings, particularly when the reading must be made quickly. As to the relative order of accuracy of the other types of quantitative display, the time available in which to read the display appears to be the critical factor.

A quantitative visual display that is even easier to read than the open-window type of display is the digital display or counter, in which the actual numbers are shown. The familiar digital clock or wristwatch is an example of this type of display. Digital displays are also used in most modern electronic equipment such as compact disc players and videocassette recorders. Research consistently reports that digital displays are read in the fastest time with the smallest number of errors (Sinclair, 1971).

Despite the ease and accuracy with which digital displays can be read, they cannot be used in all situations. For example, if the information being presented changes rapidly or continuously, each set of numbers might not remain in place long enough to be read and assimilated before it changes. Also, digital displays are unsuitable when it is important to know the direction of change (Is the temperature rising or falling?) or the rate of change (Is the temperature rising rapidly or slowly?). These are not as readily obtained from a digital display as from other types of displays.

Many specific design questions must be answered once the type of quantitative display has been chosen. These include the effect on accuracy of the design of the pointer, the size and number of scale markers, the design and location of the numerals, and the separation between the scale markers.

The second type of visual indicators, the *qualitative displays*, are used when a precise numerical reading is not necessary. Again, no more information than is necessary for the operation of the system should be presented. If the operator does not need a precise numerical indication of the status of a portion of the system, no useful purpose is served by presenting it.

Most automobile drivers, for example, do not need to know the precise engine temperature. All most of us want to be sure of is that the temperature is within the safe operating range. This is the case with many components of man-machine systems; it is necessary to know only within what range the system is functioning and whether the values are increasing or decreasing over time. If drivers see that the engine temperature is rising, they may want to take some corrective action. They do not have to know the precise temperature, but they do need an indication of normal and abnormal operating ranges and whether the temperature is changing over time.

A typical qualitative display is shown in Figure 11-9. Often, the operating ranges are color-coded with the dangerous operating range (the Hot portion of Figure 11-9) shown in red and the safe operating range in green. Such a display not only allows quick and accurate verification of the status of the system, but it also reduces the amount of technical information of which the operator must be aware.

When several qualitative displays must be frequently checked, consistent patterning greatly facilitates quick and accurate reading, as shown in Figure 11-10. The placing of the dials so that they always face the same way in the normal functioning range makes it easier to detect an unsafe reading than in the helter-skelter arrangement (the unpatterned display). The latter forces the operator to look at each dial separately. A quick scanning of the patterned arrangement can usually detect a deviation.

Patterned displays are found frequently in aircraft cockpits, power plant control rooms, and automated industries of all kinds. One study of patterned displays found that the more time the subjects (50 men and women engineering students) had to view a cluster of 16 qualitative displays, the fewer errors they

Figure 11-9 A qualitative visual display.

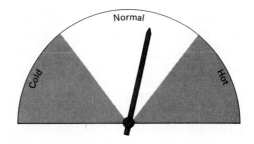

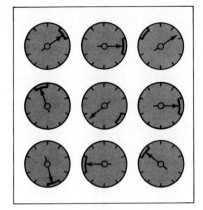
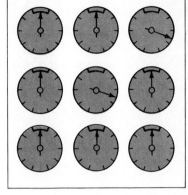

Figure 11-10 Patterned and unpatterned dial displays. (From *Applied Experimental Psychology* (p. 151) by A. Chapanis, W. Garner, & C. Morgan, 1949, New York: Wiley. Reprinted by permission.)

Unpatterned Dial Display   Patterned Dial Display

made. Thus, their accuracy was a function of viewing time. Significantly fewer errors were made, for example, when the displays were seen for a half second than when seen for only a quarter of a second.

Another variable studied was the background color of the dial displays. There were significantly fewer errors made with black pointers on a white background than with white pointers on a black background. The position of the pointer was also investigated. In some cases, the normal pointer position was at 12:00 (on a clock face), as in the patterned display in Figure 11-10, while in other cases, the pointer was at the 9:00 position. There were no differences in errors between the two positions, but when questioned, the subjects said they preferred the 12:00 position (Mital & Ramanan, 1986).

Check reading visual displays tell the operator whether the system is on or off or whether it is operating normally or abnormally. With an automobile engine temperature gauge, for example, designers have concluded that it is not important to know where in the safe range the temperature is. It is only necessary to know if the engine temperature is safe or unsafe. Can we continue driving the car, or must we stop because the engine is too hot?

Oil pressure is another case in which we only need to know if the system is satisfactory or unsatisfactory. This kind of display is sometimes referred to as a go/no go display—either the system is in condition to operate (to go) or it is not.

This is the simplest kind of visual display and can be represented by a warning light. When the light is not illuminated, the system is functioning satisfactorily; when the light comes on, it indicates a system malfunction serious enough to require immediate corrective action.

There are several considerations in the design of warning lights, especially level of brightness. On a display panel containing several sources of illumination, for example, it is vital that warning lights be at least twice as bright as the background illumination. Location of warning lights is also important. They

The visual displays in the radar room at Chicago's O'Hare airport present flight information in words, symbols, and graphics.

should be as centrally located as possible within the operator's field of vision. Warning lights placed too far to one side of a console may not attract attention when the operator is attending to other more centrally located displays and controls. Finally, flashing lights have been shown to attract attention much more quickly than continuous warning lights (Huchingson, 1981).

In automated factories such as automobile assembly plants it is not unusual for workers to be confronted by display panels containing 200 to 300 check reading displays and their associated switches. The workers must constantly monitor the panels, and when a warning light flashes, they must quickly determine the nature and location of the problem (as indicated by the legend beneath each light), and take the necessary corrective action.

In modern equipment, visual displays include more than lights, dials, and gauges. Much information is displayed on video screens and in words, symbols, and graphics. For example, the electronic flight information system used in military and civilian aircraft combines lines, numbers, and pictorial symbols to present precise information about an aircraft's location. Research has shown that adding color to the display of information reduces errors and response times in reading such displays (Macdonald & Cole, 1988).

A different type of visual display is being tested by the U.S. Air Force and the U.S. Navy for use in jet fighter planes. These aircraft travel at speeds in excess of 800 miles per hour, and the saving of even a fraction of a second in the movement of a pilot's eyes can be crucial to the success of a mission. At these speeds, it is difficult for a pilot to look through the windscreen at a target and simultaneously scan the instrument panel for information. The new approach enables the pilot to project the required information—such as the fuel level or a target display—directly and instantaneously onto the windscreen. Thus, the pilot does not have to keep shifting his or her eyes from place to place.

Auditory Displays

A less frequently used, but still important, means of presenting information to human operators in man-machine systems is auditory signaling. Properly designed, an auditory device can be more compelling than visual presentation for three reasons: The ears are always open, but the eyes are not; we can receive auditory information from all directions (we do not have to face a sound to hear it, but we must face a visual display to see it); because so much information must be presented visually, that sense is often taxed to capacity in complex systems.

Most auditory signals are used to transmit warning messages and involve buzzers, bells, horns, chimes, or sirens (the latter being the most far-reaching, especially out of doors). Military and commercial aviation make widespread use of auditory warning devices to signal crew members of emergency situations or changes in system performance that require immediate action on their part.

Aside from the obvious necessity of being heard, warning signals should compel instantaneous reaction, be informative, and be easy to discriminate from other signals. Although auditory displays must be loud and compelling, they must not be so loud as to startle the operator or cause pain or hearing damage. Table 11-1 presents the major kinds of auditory alarms.

TABLE 11-1 Characteristics of Auditory Warning Signals

Type of alarm	Intensity or loudness	Attention-getting ability
Foghorn	Very high	Good
Horn	High	Good
Whistle	High	Good if intermittent
Siren	High	Very good if pitch is modulated
Bell	Medium	Good
Buzzer, chimes, or gong	Low to medium	Good to fair
Music	Low to medium	Fair
Human voice	Low to medium	Fair

Adapted from "Auditory and other sensory forms of information presentation" by B. H. Deatherage, 1972, *Human Engineering Guide to Equipment Design*, Washington, DC: Government Printing Office.

A human factors evaluation of the auditory warning signals used in U.S. Air Force planes revealed some potentially harmful problems (Doll & Folds, 1986). First, auditory signals are not well standardized among aircraft, not even among those with similar combat roles. This violates a basic human factors consideration—the consistency of displays and controls among similar types of machines. Second, large numbers of nonverbal auditory warning signals are used. The F-15 fighter plane, for example, has 11 auditory signals (tones at different frequencies and different numbers of repetitions), each one signifying a different condition, such as external threat, low altitude, or position of landing gear. In times of stress, these signals can easily be confused and cause a pilot to initiate the wrong action. Further, many of these auditory signals are so similar that they may lead to confusion even under ordinary conditions.

Third, the signals do not provide any indication of the urgency of the problem. If two signals are activated close in time, the pilot may not know quickly enough which problem is the more urgent and requires immediate attention. It appears that not enough consideration has been given to the design of the auditory signals from the standpoint of the human operator.

It must also be noted, however, that even the most exquisitely designed system will not work as intended if the human operator violates the conditions under which the system is supposed to function. That occurred on the night of May 17, 1987, aboard a navy frigate, the USS *Stark*, on duty in the Persian Gulf. A radar operator was monitoring a highly sophisticated radar system that tracked all nearby radar signals. The system had both auditory and visual warning devices to alert the operator if hostile radar was detected. Thus, it was thought that there was no way the operator could miss the warning. If he was looking away from the screen for a few seconds, the auditory signal—a rapid beeping—would get his attention.

On the night in question, hostile radar was detected and the visual warning signal flashed on the screen. The operator was looking elsewhere, and the auditory signal failed to sound. The radar operator (or some other operator on an earlier shift) had disconnected the auditory alarm because he thought it was bothersome and annoying, sounding frequently because the ship was in enemy territory. And so the auditory alarm was disabled and could not provide a warning when an enemy jet fighter from Iraq fired an Exocet missile at the *Stark*. The equipment worked fine, but the human operator did not, and 37 sailors died as a result.

Auditory signals may also be used to transmit more complex information. One example is the shipboard operation of sonar for detection of underwater objects. A high-frequency sound is transmitted from beneath the ship through the water. When it strikes a large enough object, it is reflected back to the ship and reproduced as the familiar ping sound heard in old war movies.

The job of interpreting the sound (the message or information the sound conveys) is difficult. Intensive training is required to be able to discriminate among the various qualities of a sound. For example, with sonar, if the detected object is moving away from the ship, the reflected sound is of a lower frequency than the transmitted sound. An object moving toward the ship provides a higher frequency of returning sound.

The radio-range signals used in air navigation are another example of information transmission by auditory signal. Two directional radio beams at right angles produce the sound. One beam transmits by Morse Code the letter *A* (dot-dash) and the other the letter *N* (dash-dot). When the receiving airplane is flying just between the two crossed beams (on the beam), the pilot hears one continuous signal. If the plane is too far to the right or left, the pilot will hear the *A* or *N* signal.

Another form of auditory display involves the use of computer-generated speech. Research comparing the presentation of the same information by means of this synthesized speech and by a computer-generated pictorial display has produced contradictory results. In some experiments, subjects responded faster to pictorial displays. In other experiments, they responded faster to speech displays (Robinson & Eberts, 1987). Still, the technique is thought to hold promise as a means of presenting information.

Our auditory sense provides a sensitive indicator of the condition of the machine portion of the system. Through formal signaling procedures such as those described and through informal signals such as detecting a misfire in an engine, we receive and interpret a variety of information.

Tactual Displays

The communication of information tactually (through the skin senses) is seldom used in man-machine systems. In one form, however, tactual communication is used daily by people throughout the world. Blind persons read through the braille system of tactual displays by passing their fingers over raised dots or points on a flat surface. This is a highly efficient and rapid way for them to receive information. Persons skilled in braille can read up to 200 words per minute.

Research has been conducted on the use of dynamic or changing tactual displays to present information to the human operator. One effective technique involves the use of vibrations on the surface of the skin. It has been found that subjects can learn to perceive many distinct tactual sensations through application of the vibrating stimulus to five different areas of the chest, at three different durations, and at five levels of intensity. Subjects learned to receive messages in a language of 26 letters, 10 digits, and 4 frequently used words; indeed, this language could be learned as quickly as Morse Code. Trained subjects were able to receive and understand the tactual messages much faster than subjects trained in Morse Code (Geldard, 1957).

Another example of tactual communication involves the ability of airplane pilots to learn quickly to identify control knobs of different shapes by touch or feel alone. As we shall see in the next section, the pilots can then operate these controls without looking at them.

Large-scale tactual communication is not yet in use, but its potential for information transmission seems great.

Control Functions

In man-machine systems, once human operators have received inputs through the displays and processed the information received, they communicate with the machine through the initiation of some control action. Human operators can transmit control decisions by using switches, push buttons, levers, cranks, steering wheels, foot pedals, and the like.

As is the case with the design and arrangement of displays, decisions must be made with respect to the choice of the controls, their location, and their shape. These decisions will be based in large part on the requirements of the specific task, by what the operator is trying to accomplish or perform. Different kinds of tasks dictate different types of controls.

Thus, engineering psychologists must know in precise terms the nature of the task. Does it involve simply turning on a light or a radio or some other system component? Or does it involve a fine adjustment such as selecting one radio frequency from the entire spectrum of frequencies? Does the task require frequent and rapid readjustment of a control? Or is one setting sufficient for the completion of the operation? Questions about the amount of force the operator must exert on the control and about the environmental conditions must also be resolved. For example, if the control is to be operated outdoors in any kind of weather, will the necessity of wearing gloves interfere with the proper operation of the control? Also, if the control must be operated in the dark, it may require shape coding to be easily identified.

Once system designers have answered these questions, they can proceed to select the best control for the particular job. Some general guidelines are available about what type of control is most appropriate for a particular control action. For example, for a task requiring two discrete settings of a control such as "on" and "off," a hand or foot push button is appropriate to use as an on/off switch. For four or more discrete settings, a group of finger push buttons or a rotary selector switch should be used. For continuous settings, knobs or cranks are preferred. Examples of controls and the control actions they are used for are shown in Figure 11-11.

These are recommendations only; the control choice may have to be modified in the light of other conditions or requirements of the total system.

For proper use, controls must satisfy the following two additional criteria:

1. *Proper control and body matching.* Although some controls could be activated with the head or the elbow, most of us use only our hands and feet. It is important that no one limb be given too many tasks to perform. Wherever possible, control activation should be distributed among the limbs. The hands are capable of greater precision in control operation, and the feet are capable of exerting greater pressure or force. More control functions should be designed for right-hand operation because the majority of the population is right-handed.

For transmitting discrete information

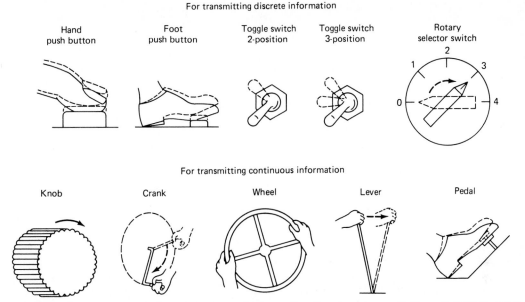

Hand push button   Foot push button   Toggle switch 2-position   Toggle switch 3-position   Rotary selector switch

For transmitting continuous information

Knob   Crank   Wheel   Lever   Pedal

Figure 11-11 Control devices and the type of information they best transmit. (From E.J. McCormick and M. S. Sanders, *Human factors in engineering and design*, 5th ed. (Copyright 1982, McGraw-Hill Book Co. Used with permission.)

2. *Control-task compatibility.* Where possible, a control action should imitate the movements it produces. Pulling the control column in an airplane to the right pulls the plane to the right; the control movement and the machine movement are parallel. To lower the flaps or landing gear of an airplane, the appropriate controls should move downward. As another example, we usually turn a knob to the right (clockwise) to turn something on. A control that turns to the left to turn something on (to perform the same function) will take a long time for one to adjust to it. Parallel control movements seem the most natural to associate with the resulting machine movements and make the task easier for the operator.

Combining Related Controls. It is simpler and more efficient, in general, to combine controls that perform similar or related operations. For example, there are three control functions on a radio: on/off, volume, and station selection. Yet, there are only two controls. The on/off and volume controls, performing highly related functions, are combined. Not only does control combination reduce the number of separate actions required of the human operator, but it also saves space on the control panel (which, in a complex system, is usually crowded).

Identification of Controls. Controls must be clearly marked or coded to assure their correct and rapid identification. Automobile manufacturers code instrument panels by using pictorial symbols to represent the function of each control (a miniature wiper identifies the windshield wiper switch, for example). On a crowded instrument panel, easily identified controls help minimize potential errors caused by activating the wrong control.

Another useful method of control identification is shape coding. Each knob on a console is of a recognizably different shape. This provides for rapid visual identification of the correct control and allows tactual identification in the dark or when the eyes must focus elsewhere. An efficient means of facilitating identification by shape is to design the control so that its shape represents or symbolizes its function.

The U.S. Air Force, through the results of psychological research, developed a series of shape-coded knobs for use in aircraft. Some of the controls are more symbolic of their function than others. The landing flap control looks like a landing flap, but, admittedly, it is difficult to design something to symbolize carburetor air. However, the important point is that each control is unique in touch and appearance, and the control functions can be learned quickly. Standardizing these controls on all aircraft greatly reduces the opportunity for pilot error. Also, it has been demonstrated that these controls can be properly identified even when the pilot is wearing gloves ("Design of Controls," 1977).

A study conducted for AT&T investigated various control shapes and sizes to determine which knobs could be most easily turned by employees working on telephone poles and transmission towers. Four sizes and five shapes were tried. The results showed that the triangular shape $3\frac{1}{2}$ inches in diameter offered the greatest comfort and ease of turning. In situations where greater force was needed to turn the knobs, larger triangular or square shapes were more effective (Kohl, 1983). The superiority of the triangular shape was confirmed in later research on handles for hand tools such as knives and screwdrivers (Cochran & Riley, 1986).

Once the kind and shape of the control have been selected, the engineering psychologist determines the placement of the control on the control panel, and, where appropriate, its relationship to an information display. The location of the control on the operator's console depends primarily on the characteristics of the specific system, but some general design considerations are applicable to most man-machine systems.

A primary requisite for control location is consistency or uniformity of placement. As noted earlier, havoc would be created if the gas pedal were not consistently located to the right of the brake pedal on all types of automobile. The greater the standardization of control arrangement, the easier and safer it is for an operator to work with different models of the same system.

This principle seems to be common sense, yet it took many years of high-level systems analysis before control arrangements achieved some standardization on aircraft instrument panels. There have been fatal accidents as a result of ignoring this vital and simple rule, and, in many consumer products, it is still not being followed.

Consider an item that is found in every home and used every day by millions of people—the kitchen range. Usually, there are four burners on top and four knobs on the front panel to control the burners. There is little consistency in the relationship between knobs and burners as to which control operates which burner. A survey of 49 different ranges revealed six different knob-burner linkages.

Although this is not as serious a problem as a lack of standardization in the controls of an aircraft cockpit, this inconsistency can be a nuisance and a danger. The problem is less acute with gas ranges because we receive immediate feedback when we turn a knob; we see instantly which burner is on. With electric ranges, however, we could place a pan on a burner only to find out later that it was not the one we activated. Or, we could touch a burner, thinking it was cold, to find it was the one we had turned on.

Human factors engineers surveyed 222 adults to determine popular conceptions of this kind of control situation. They were shown a drawing of a typical kitchen range and asked which knob they would use to turn on each of the four burners (Shinar & Acton, 1978).

The results showed a strong bias that characterized 98% of the adults questioned. They expected that the two burners on the right would be controlled by either of the two right-hand control knobs and the two burners on the left would be controlled by either of the two left-hand knobs. Within each pair of knobs (right versus left), there was no general agreement about which knob controlled the front burner and which controlled the rear burner. Another study showed that 36% of the subjects expected that for each pair of knobs, the one on the left would control the rear burner. However, 64% believed it would control the front burner (Rice, 1984b).

The stereotypes chosen by the majority of the subjects were found to be common on many kitchen ranges currently in use. However, 27% of the ranges now in use have a control-burner linkage that violates the common view. In these appliances, burners on the right are linked to controls on the left and burners on the left are linked to controls on the right. Thus, 1 out of every 4 ranges operates in reverse fashion to what most people expect, a potentially hazardous situation.

Other aspects of the placement of controls must be considered. When system requirements call for the sequential operation of several controls, they should be arranged so that they can be activated in a smooth and continuous manner. If five push buttons must be operated always in the same order, they should be placed in a straight line so that the hand can move quickly and easily from one to another, affording no possibility of their being operated in the wrong sequence.

Controls that are associated with emergency functions should be placed in the normal line of sight where they can be clearly distinguished from other controls, reached quickly, and protected so that they cannot be accidentally activated. The latter is usually accomplished by using a cover or shield that must be raised before the emergency control can be operated.

When displays are associated functionally with controls (such as a dial that must be set by turning a knob), they should be placed as close together as possible. It is often desirable to group related displays and controls according to their function. In an aircraft cockpit, for example, all displays and controls involved with the performance of the engines are grouped together. Displays and controls can also be grouped sequentially and in order of use when that order is consistent.

Another way of grouping controls—frequently found in power plant control rooms and on some complicated machinery for which there are separate but functionally equivalent panels—is mirror-imaged control panels. This involves reversing the arrangement of identical controls on the separate panels, as shown in Figure 11-12.

With the operator seated in front of the display, the controls on the operator's left (Panel A) would be reversed on the operator's right (Panel B). With a non-mirrored arrangement, the controls on the left of the panel would always be on the left, regardless of whether the panel itself was on the operator's left or right side.

Research comparing the two control arrangements showed that college student subjects were slower to respond and made more errors on the mirror-

Figure 11-12 Mirror-imaged and non-mirror-imaged control panels. (Adapted from "The effects of panel arrangement and locus of attention on performance" by J. V. Downing & M. S. Sanders, 1987, *Human Factors, 29,* p. 552.)

Mirror-imaged panels

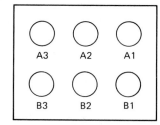

Non-mirror-imaged panels

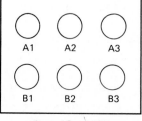
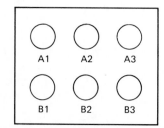

imaged panel, particularly during simulated emergency situations. Even in routine operations, the mirror-imaged panel required greater concentration and induced higher levels of strain and fatigue than the non-mirror-imaged panel (Downing & Sanders, 1987).

Computers

A person operating a computer is a man-machine system. Thus, computers come within the province of engineering psychology. We mentioned earlier that computers in the workplace have been linked with health, comfort, and productivity problems. We shall examine some of these problems and describe what engineering psychologists are doing to solve them.

The introduction of computers at work has had an immense impact on many jobs, changing some, eliminating others, and creating new ones. In the process, the daily lives and the livelihoods of millions of employees have been affected. This number will increase over the next decade as computer technology is applied to more and more jobs.

Many employees are delighted with computers in their workplace. Computers can eliminate the tedious and time-consuming aspects of some jobs, enriching them by offering employees greater responsibility and challenge. However, many others who work with computers experience psychological and physical difficulties. Indeed, some employees become computer phobics, manifesting an intense fear and even hatred of computers. One psychologist studied several hundred managers and college students who worked with computers. Galvanic skin response (GSR) measures were taken while they operated their machines. Recall from our discussion of lie detectors in Chapter 3 that the GSR detects changes in emotion. The results of the computer study showed that almost one third of the users were highly anxious while working with the computer and that 5% showed symptoms of phobia, that is, nausea, dizziness, cold sweats, and high blood pressure (Rice, 1983a).

On the job, many clerical workers with automated word-processing equipment have found that a workday spent at a VDT is boring and monotonous and that the pace at which they must work has been greatly speeded up. In some cases, jobs have been fractionated, made simpler, and broken up into less skilled, less challenging, and sometimes lower paid work, producing what was referred to earlier as an electronic assembly line. The introduction of computers in office work has also had a disproportionate effect on women employees who constitute 80% to 95% of typists, secretaries, bank tellers, and keypunchers.

Of course, it is not only white-collar and clerical workers in offices who are affected by computers. Many blue-collar skilled and semiskilled workers have also seen their jobs change as a result of microprocessor technology. Consider the highly skilled jobs of typesetter and compositor in the newspaper industry. The work is physically demanding, crucial to the publishing process, and takes considerable time to master. The workers are true craftsmen and the jobs are held to be high in status.

The introduction of computer technology changed all that. Typesetting is now done routinely on VDTs, and the only skill required is keystroking. The jobs have become simpler, much easier to learn and perform, and downgraded in terms of the knowledge and experience required to perform them.

A group of typesetters and compositors in Australia were interviewed in person and by questionnaire 3 years after their jobs were computerized to ascertain their views on the change (Patrickson, 1986). Approximately one fourth of them said they welcomed the change, but the majority expressed dissatisfaction and the feeling that their jobs had become less skilled. They reported that they were unhappier at work, experienced greater job dissatisfaction, and believed they had fewer opportunities for promotion and pay increases. The older the worker, the greater the dissatisfaction. Overall, however, most of the workers had come to terms with the change and had accepted the new situation.

Computer processing on the job affects managers and executives as well. Some, particularly older ones, still resist the widespread application of computers. One reason for this opposition is that operating a keyboard is like typing, a skill traditionally viewed by managers as being low in status. Studies of managers have shown that some are unwilling to take the time to learn to use the computer efficiently or to participate in group training programs. Companies have reported greater success when they train their managers individually and privately (Paxton & Turner, 1984).

Lower level managers sometimes resent the use of computers because they fear the loss of power that comes with the increase in information a computer network provides to their subordinates. There is some justification for this fear. In many automated plants, workers operating the terminals now have access to the information previously available only to managers, such as the precise costs of various manufacturing processes or the specifications for new equipment. This has often put decision-making capability in the hands of workers, power previously held by managers. Also, computer technology has resulted in the redefinition and elimination of many lower and middle level managerial jobs (Sinclair, 1986).

It may be more difficult for managers to adjust to computer use than it is for their subordinates. Some managers have even tried to sabotage the introduction of computer technology. When Procter and Gamble built a new plant, computerization was so extensive that executives at the company's headquarters, 500 miles away from the plant, were given the ability to monitor the plant's output at any time. This continuous check on performance made the managers feel that someone was always watching them. To counter this, the managers made sure that the electronic connection to headquarters was only partially activated so that corporate executives had only limited access to production information. In that way, the plant managers could continue to control and manipulate the availability of that information, as they had previously done with paper memos and reports (Goleman, 1988).

Higher level executives seem more receptive to the role of computers in their companies, largely because of the immediate and complete access it gives them to information not so readily available previously, and because they can continuously monitor all aspects of organizational and employee performance. Some 15% of chief executive officers (CEOs) routinely use computers today. By the mid-1990s, more than half of them are expected to do so. A survey of CEOs at major U.S. corporations found that only 2% seriously doubted the usefulness of computers and 79% foresaw large potential benefits from their use (DeLong, 1988).

For all corporate levels, from clerk to executive, proper training is vital if employees are to adapt successfully to the demands of computer use. Employee hesitation or difficulty with regard to computers can be largely overcome with sufficient training. This assumes that, when these employees begin to work with their machines on the job, the human factors aspects of their work stations are adequately considered.

Physical strain and discomfort are the likely result when the human factors aspects of computer usage have been neglected. The concern about health effects of computers stems from about 1977 when two employees of the New York Times Company reportedly developed cataracts after working at VDTs. Since then, many computer users have complained of eye problems such as blurred vision, eyestrain, and changes in color perception. A study conducted in Switzerland found that computer operators had $5\frac{1}{2}$ times as many visual complaints as office workers who were not using computers (Mason, 1984).

The organization Nine to Five, the National Association of Working Women, established a telephone hot line to take complaints from computer users. In a 2-month period, it received more than 3,000 calls, 17% of which concerned eye problems. In 1983, the National Academy of Sciences studied the problem and concluded that there was no scientific evidence that computers themselves caused damage to the human eye ("Relieving the Stress," 1984). A study of telephone operators in The Netherlands also showed no deterioration in vision after 2 years of using VDTs (DeGroot & Kamphuis, 1983). And a study of VDT users and nonusers performing similar tasks found no differences between the groups in complaints of vision problems (Howarth & Istance, 1986).

It appears that complaints about visual disturbances result not from the VDTs themselves, but from the quality of the equipment used with them and the design of the work station. Equipment factors studied by engineering psychologists include the color of the phosphor used in the cathode ray tube (CRT) that makes up the screen, the size of the screen, the degree of flicker of the characters on the screen, and the rate at which individual characters are generated on the screen (Harwood & Foley, 1987). The most important design factor is the lighting of the workplace, which is related to glare, a major source of eyestrain. Antiglare coatings can be applied to screens and shields can be built around them to reduce glare. The overall illumination of the work station can be reduced, walls can be painted in darker colors, and the fluorescent lights used in most offices can be replaced by indirect lighting. All of these changes have been found to enhance visual comfort for computer users (Marriott & Stuchly, 1986).

Also, there is ample evidence that people read more slowly from VDTs than from paper, a finding that may have little to do with visual complaints about VDTs, however. Research has not yet identified any specific factor, either in the display itself or in the user (such as length of time spent at the terminal), but psychologists have suggested that the slower reading speed may be related to the image quality of the characters on the screen, that is, their size, type style, clarity, and contrast with the background (Gould, Alfaro, Barnes, Finn, Grischkowsky, & Minuto, 1987; Gould, Alfaro, Finn, Haupt, & Minuto, 1987).

Other complaints received from computer users are fatigue and lower back pain, both of which can be traced, in part, to a lack of attention to human engineering concerns (Grieco, 1986). The desks and chairs used with computer equipment are often poorly designed for jobs that involve sitting for long periods of time. Research by engineering psychologists has found that the best chair is an adjustable one, enabling each operator to adapt it to his or her height and weight. Also, periodically changing position in one's chair can reduce fatigue, and this is easier to do with an adjustable chair. In addition, chairs designed for American and European workers were found to be unsuitable for Oriental workers, as a study of VDT operators in Singapore showed. The Oriental workers were not only generally shorter, but they also had shorter elbow-to-fingertip measurements and preferred a different seating posture (Ong, Koh, Phoon, & Low, 1988).

Separating the computer keyboard from the display screen can increase user comfort. Desks with split and adjustable tops will hold these components at separate levels. Also, if the angle of the keyboard can be tilted to individual needs, fatigue and back pain can be minimized. Human engineering research has determined that the acceptable range for comfort is a keyboard angle of 7 to 20 degrees to minimize the bending of the wrists (Miller & Suther, 1983; Tougas & Nordin, 1987).

Extensive human factors guidelines are available on the design of computer work stations to minimize the incidence of fatigue and lower back pain.

Industrial Robots

Another innovation in the workplace that is causing drastic changes in the nature of some types of work is the use of industrial robots to perform jobs formerly done by humans. Whereas computers are affecting jobs at all levels, from the assembly line to the executive office, robots are changing the nature of blue-collar jobs. Those most affected, so far, are mechanics, assemblers, welders, painters, assembly-line workers, and other semiskilled and unskilled industrial employees. Psychologists estimate that by the year 2000, as many as 4 million factory jobs will be performed by robots. In 1987, the International Federation of Robotics was established. A massive effort on the part of workers, managers, and engineering psychologists will be required to make the most effective use of this new form of man-machine system.

In a plant manufacturing booster rockets for NASA's space shuttle, an industrial robot sprays an epoxy coating on a nose cone to a specified width and thickness more precisely than a human worker could. The operator of the robot wears protective clothing because exposure to the epoxy could cause cancer.

The Robot Institute of America defines a robot as "a reprogrammable, multifunctional manipulator designed to move material, parts, tools or specialized devices through variable programmed motions for the performance of a variety of tasks" (Condon, 1983, p. 16). Essentially, a robot is a mechanical manipulator that receives its instructions from a computer. It can be programmed to carry out a number of motions and routines simultaneously.

Japan leads the world in the use of industrial robots. More than 66% of all industrial robots are in use in Japanese industry. A survey of 1,200 Japanese workers revealed that the use of robots brought about increases in productivity and product quality but eliminated many jobs (Nagamachi, 1986). A survey of 461 American workers in a company that expected to introduce robots found that low-level unskilled workers perceived robots as threats to their jobs. Skilled workers reacted more positively, considering robots as presenting an opportunity to expand their skills (Chao & Kozlowski, 1986).

To date, one fourth of the robots in the United States are in use in the automobile industry where they are engaged primarily in the welding and painting of car bodies (Feulner & Kleiner, 1986). The second largest users of robots are manufacturers of such appliances as dishwashers and refrigerators. Robots are particularly valuable in jobs that are dangerous such as spray painting, which involves exposure to hazardous solvents (Lambrinos & Johnson, 1984).

Robots have many positive features. They consistently perform better than humans in routine, repetitive work, producing more products of higher quality. For example, in one locomotive plant, 8 unskilled workers plus robots can produce a locomotive frame in 1 day. Before the robots arrived it took 68 skilled machine operators 16 days to produce a locomotive frame (Foulkes & Hirsch, 1984).

Robots will work under all sorts of conditions including extremes of noise and heat without any deterioration in performance. They are cheaper than human labor at an average cost of less than $5 per hour, compared to an average cost of $15 per hour for a human worker. In addition, robots can operate around the clock without experiencing fatigue or making mistakes. They require no vacations, sick leave, medical insurance, or pensions, and they have never been known to file a grievance.

Aside from freeing some workers from dangerous or uncomfortable working environments, most of the advantages of robots appear to accrue to management. Workers fear losing their jobs and being replaced by robots or having to match their work habits to the robot's pace. Also, there may be safety problems with robots. Two workers have been reported killed by robots. In both cases, the accidents were attributed to human error.

When robots are introduced into the workplace, the content or nature of the jobs for the human employees necessarily changes. Also, in a robotized plant, greater physical distances separate the employees. Because they are farther apart, there is less opportunity for social contact or for developing and maintaining a sense of group cohesiveness. More of the workday is spent in isolation. Some workers feel so threatened by robots that they have engaged in sabotage against the machines. The number of such incidents is likely to increase as the use of industrial robots spreads. Reports from the Soviet Union indicate that worker sabotage of robots is also occurring in that country. In one Russian plant, heavy metal barricades had to be erected around the robotized equipment to protect it from the workers. When a metal slab somehow fell on a group of robots and damaged them, the barriers were raised to the ceiling.

A number of human engineering considerations have become evident since the introduction of robots. Robots are, as we noted, man-machine systems, although at first glance they would seem to be machines only. It is true that robots, once designed, built, programmed, and properly maintained can perform their work with little human contact or intervention. But those functions of design, manufacture, programming, and maintenance must, of course, be performed by humans.

Human engineering is applied to the design of both the hardware and the software for robots. The hardware includes control panels with their knobs and dials, warning signals, work-space features, seating, level and kind of illumination, and all the other physical attributes that pertain to a man-machine system. Among the software aspects are the programming of the robot's computers, the computer language, and the means of presenting information on the display screen.

Perhaps the most crucial issue for engineering psychologists is the division of labor or the allocation of functions between robots and humans. A number of factors enter into this decision, including the cost of developing a new robot, the complexity of the task, safety considerations, space limitations, and the degree of accuracy required.

One human engineering analysis proposes a set of nine activities in which humans operate in conjunction with robots to perform a job. These tasks can easily be remembered by the word SIMBIOSIS, each letter standing for the first letter of each activity (Parsons & Kearsley, 1982).

1. Surveillance. Humans must monitor all kinds of automation to make sure the system is functioning properly.
2. Intervention. Humans must take care of the robot, starting it, shutting it down, programming it, and correcting it in case of malfunction.
3. Maintenance. Humans must periodically, and on demand when emergencies occur, engage in repair, calibration, inspection, and troubleshooting activities.
4. Backup. Humans must be ready to substitute another robot or a manual operation in case of breakdown so that production can continue.
5. Input. Raw material and parts of the finished product have to be fed to the robot, either manually or mechanically. Either way, a human has to set up the procedure and ensure its continued functioning.
6. Output. When a robot has performed its task, a human has to arrange for the finished product to be transferred, either manually or mechanically, to the customer or to the next step in the manufacturing process.
7. Supervision. Humans must manage the overall system, consisting of humans and robots; plan the operation; and deal with emergencies.
8. Inspection. Humans may interact with computers to inspect the quality of the finished product.
9. Synergy. Both human and robot must combine and interact so that the process is performed more efficiently and effectively than if either one did it alone.

The challenges presented by industrial robots to engineering psychologists will grow as the number of robots on the job increases and as the number of jobs they can perform expands. Today, robots do detailed and skilled factory jobs such as assembling computer components and undertaking maintenance operations in nuclear power plants. In addition, they are moving out of the factory and into the service industries (Rogers, 1988). In some plants, robots now function as tireless, ever-vigilant security guards, making the rounds of buildings at night and summoning human guards when they sense an intruder.

Soon to be marketed are robot janitors that will clean office buildings at night, programmed, no doubt, to avoid bumping into the robot security guards. Several fast-food chains, concerned about the declining number of teenagers available for minimum-wage jobs, are experimenting with robot-operated restaurants. One research laboratory has developed a robot that can flip hamburgers. Yes, it is called McRobot!

In the years to come, I/O psychologists will have to deal with problems of morale, satisfaction, and retraining for the many employees who will need to adapt to the presence of robots in the workplace.

Summary

Engineering psychology is concerned with the design of the tools and equipment that are used in the performance of work to make them compatible with the characteristics of the workers who use them. The field endeavors to blend the limitations and capabilities of operator and machine into a smoothly functioning **man-machine system**. Engineering psychology has grown rapidly since World War II as the machinery of daily life and work have become more complex and difficult to operate.

A precursor to engineering psychology was **time-and-motion study**, which attempted to shape the way in which workers performed their jobs and, to some extent, to redesign the tools of work. Pioneered by Frederick W. Taylor and Frank and Lillian Gilbreth, time-and-motion study focused on tool design, wage-incentive systems, and the elimination of all unnecessary and wasted motions. Practitioners of time-and-motion study developed rules for efficient work.

Time-and-motion study is not popular with many workers who fear that it will require them to work faster. Other criticisms of time-and-motion study are that people are not alike, so there may not be only one best way to perform a job, and that time-and-motion studies are based on inadequate sampling of workers and of time of work.

Whereas time-and-motion study is still applied to routine and simple jobs, engineering psychology is used for more sophisticated jobs involving complex man-machine systems.

There are two types of man-machine systems: open loop and closed loop. **Open-loop systems** are not self-regulating, **closed-loop systems** are.

The initial step in the design of a man-machine system is the **allocation of functions** between the human operator and the machine. Each stage and process of the task must be analyzed to determine if it should be performed by a human or by a machine. Humans are superior to machines in detecting a wide range of stimuli, detecting seldom-appearing or low-level stimuli from a confusing background, sensing and recognizing unusual or unexpected stimuli, remembering a large amount of information for a long time, recalling relevant information, using a wide range of past experiences in making decisions, responding and adapting quickly to diverse situations, using inductive reasoning, and exhibiting great flexibility in problem solving.

Machines are superior to humans in detecting stimuli beyond human powers of sensing, monitoring for long periods of time, calculating rapidly and accurately, storing and retrieving large amounts of information, applying physical force, engaging in repetitive tasks with no performance deterioration, and not tiring easily.

Social, political, and financial questions are also involved in the allocation of functions decisions.

Work-space design involves some of the principles of motion economy as well as data from human anthropometry (measurements of the physical structure of the human body). There are three general principles of work-space design: (1) all materials, tools, and supplies should be located in the order in which they are to be used; (2) tools should be pre-positioned so they can be picked up ready for use; and (3) all parts and tools should be within easy and comfortable reaching distance.

Another task in man-machine system design is deciding the most effective way to **present information** to the human operator. Visual and auditory senses are most frequently involved although the tactual sense is occasionally used.

There are three types of **visual display:** quantitative, qualitative, and check reading. A **quantitative display** provides a precise numerical value; a **qualitative display** provides an indication of relative operating conditions; a **check reading display** tells whether a system is operating normally or abnormally, is on or off.

Auditory displays are used as warning signals and to transmit complex information. They can attract attention more readily than visual displays because the ears are always open and sound can be received from all directions. Problems can occur with auditory warning signals when they are not standardized on similar equipment, when too many are used in the same system, when they are so similar in sound as to be confusing, and when they fail to indicate the urgency of the problem.

Tactual displays (receiving information through the skin senses) are occasionally used. Research has demonstrated that people can be trained to receive a good deal of information tactually.

Controls must be designed to be compatible with the task and with the limitations and capabilities of the operator. They should be combined when they are used to perform similar or related operations and must be capable of being rapidly and readily identified.

Control identification can be accomplished through the use of pictorial symbols or shape coding.

Computers are man-machine systems that can cause problems that range from the downgrading of skills and job dissatisfaction to fear, boredom, and monotony. Physical complaints include eye problems, fatigue, and back pain. Eyestrain may be caused by the quality of the computer equipment and the design of the work station. Poor lighting can produce glare on the display screen. Fatigue and back pain have been related to the design of the desks and chairs used with the computer components. The operator's chair and the angle at which the keyboard rests should be adjustable to individual preferences and comfort.

Industrial **robots** have altered the jobs of large numbers of blue-collar workers, many of whom view robots as threats to their jobs. Robots can consistently perform better than humans in routine, repetitive work, producing more products of higher quality. They can work under all sorts of conditions and for long periods of time without any deterioration in performance. The use of robots usually causes greater physical separation between employees, providing less opportunity for social contact.

Engineering psychology has been applied to the design of both hardware and software for robots. The most crucial issue is the allocation of functions between robots and humans. One analysis, called SIMBIOSIS, proposes nine activities in which humans and robots interact to perform a job: Surveillance, Intervention, Maintenance, Backup, Input, Output, Supervision, Inspection, and Synergy.

Key Terms

auditory signals	human factors	robots
check reading visual	engineering	shape coding
displays	man-machine systems	time-and-motion
closed-loop systems	open-loop systems	analysis
engineering	quantitative and	video display
psychology	qualitative visual	terminals (VDTs)
human anthropometry	displays	

CASE STUDIES

Vision Problems of Video Display Terminal (VDT) Operators

To investigate the vision problems of employees working at VDTs, 192 British office workers were given a questionnaire about their various visual complaints. Some of the subjects were VDT operators. Others were typists and clerical workers whose jobs did not involve the use of VDTs. The questionnaire asked how frequently the following symptoms were reported: sore or tender eyes, watery or runny eyes, dry eyes, hot or burning eyes, the feeling of "sand in the eyes," tired eyes, and overall visual discomfort. These complaints were recorded before the study and at the beginning and end of each workday for a period of 1 week.

The first five symptoms on the list were seldom reported, either before or during the survey period. There were some inconsistencies in the workers' reports, however. Half of those who said before the investigation that they never experienced sore eyes, reported the presence of this symptom at least once during the survey week.

The overall results revealed no significant differences between VDT users and nonusers, a finding that contradicts some of the earlier research on visual discomfort of VDT operators.

QUESTIONS

1. How would you design a laboratory experiment to investigate the vision problems of VDT operators?
2. How might the Hawthorne effect have influenced the results of this study?
3. What factors other than the VDT equipment can lead to visual discomfort?
4. In what other ways do computers on the job affect employees?

Reference: P. A. Howarth & H. O. Istance. (1986). The validity of subjective reports of visual discomfort. *Human Factors, 28,* 347–351.

Employee Reactions to Robots

A large U.S. manufacturing company planned to introduce robots on its assembly line to perform some of the operations presently done by unskilled workers. All of the plant's employees were informed of the anticipated change. To determine how the change would be perceived by the employees, management asked two psychologists to study the problem. A 58-item questionnaire was developed to assess four components of employee attitudes toward robots: general robotics orientation (beliefs about the advantages and disadvantages of robots), job security, management concern during robot implementation, and expected changes after the introduction of the robots.

Three groups of workers were studied: unskilled assembly-line workers, semiskilled workers in routine maintenance jobs, and highly trained technicians in skilled maintenance and repair jobs.

The unskilled and semiskilled workers saw the use of robots on the assembly line as a much greater threat to job security than did the more highly skilled workers. The latter group reacted more positively to the robots and viewed the change as an opportunity to enlarge their skills by learning to repair these more complex machines.

QUESTIONS

1. How could this company minimize the concerns of its unskilled workers about the introduction of robot technology?

2. What human factors considerations are involved in the design of robots?
3. How will the robots change the social conditions of a job?
4. What kinds of activities can human operators perform effectively in conjunction with robots?

Reference: G. T. Chao & S. W. J. Kozlowski. (1986). Employee perceptions on the implementation of robotic manufacturing technology. *Journal of Applied Psychology, 71,* 70–76.

Additional Reading

Gopher, D., & Kimchi, R. (1989). Engineering psychology. *Annual Review of Psychology, 40,* 431–455. Discusses the visual presentation of information, especially by means of computer graphics, and reviews the problems of man-machine interaction and information processing.

Mark, L. S., Warm, J. S., & Huston, R. L. (Eds.). (1987). *Ergonomics and Human Factors.* New York: Springer-Verlag. A well organized and edited collection of papers on 3 major topics: (1) human information processing and cognitive processes, (2) the design of safe working environments, and (3) the person-computer interaction.

Sanders, M. S., & McCormick, E. J. (1987). *Human Factors in Engineering and Design* (6th ed.). New York: McGraw-Hill. The latest edition of a classic textbook on human factors research emphasizing the application of psychological knowledge about human capacities to the design of equipment, work environments, and transportation systems.

Sivak, M. (1987). Human factors and road safety. *Applied Ergonomics, 18,* 289–296. Reviews human factors research on highway safety, considering both the design of the vehicle and the behavior of the driver.

Chapter 12

Employee Safety and Health

Introduction

One aspect of modern industrial life that receives limited publicity is its high level of danger. Accidents occur daily, some involving no more than a bruise or a scrape, others resulting in permanent disability or death. Industrial safety is a very serious problem. A former assistant secretary of the Department of Health and Human Services described it in these terms: "We are experiencing a national tragedy of occupational injury, disease, and death. The scope of this tragedy, the number of its victims, we can only guess at, and acknowledge that our guess is probably low.... Maimed and broken bodies, poisoned lungs and eroded kidneys, workers burned, blinded, or gravely injured in some other way—these are among the regular daily fare of hospitals in every part of the country." The director of health and safety for the AFL-CIO has spoken of the "thousands of workers being killed every year from occupational injuries and scores of thousands suffering from occupational diseases" (Noble, 1988).

More than 14,000 people are killed annually in industrial accidents. And the number of disabling injuries, though not fully known, is staggering; an estimated 2.2 million people are disabled each year because of work-related accidents. However, a study by the Bureau of Labor Statistics shows that for each reported disabling injury, 10 are not reported. The inevitable conclusion is that as many as 25 million workers sustain injuries each year.

The economic cost is also staggering, both to the companies involved and the country as a whole. Billions of dollars are forfeited through lost wages and millions are paid out in workers' compensation and medical benefits. The lost working time because of injuries is now five times greater than the lost working time because of strikes. Yet strikes achieve national publicity; the worker who loses a leg on the job does not.

The death and disablement toll from work-related disease may be even higher than the industrial accident toll. Such illnesses and deaths are more insidious than the sudden traumatic accident because they develop slowly over many years before the worker manifests obvious physical symptoms. As many as 390,000 employees develop work-related diseases every year and more than 100,000 people annually are expected to die from them.

Coal miners, for example, develop a unique respiratory disease called pneumoconiosis, or black lung, a progressively crippling disorder that reduces life expectancy. Respiratory disease kills five times as many coal miners as it does workers in other occupations. A U.S. senator noted: "Coal miners have been coughing their lives away for 200 years. Any literature you read ... about coal miners, all through the literature runs the description of a man coughing out his life—a coal miner."

Many chemical industries are fraught with health perils to workers, dangers that are not fully known. As many as 10 million workers are exposed daily to chemicals for which safe thresholds have not yet been established. The Environmental Protection Agency (EPA) lists 16,500 chemical substances regularly used in the workplace that are known to be toxic. Over 150 of these chemicals have been classified as neurotoxins, that is, they can damage the human nervous system. More than 50,000 other chemical substances, the toxicity of which has not been determined, are being used in American industry.

Nearly 1.6 million people are exposed to asbestos in their jobs, where they face the danger of lung cancer at seven times the national average as well as a form of pneumoconiosis known as asbestosis. As many as 10% of the country's textile workers are known to have byssinosis, or brown lung, a disease from inhaling cotton dust. Of the 6,000 persons who have worked in uranium mines, up to 1,000 will die of lung cancer because of high levels of radiation exposure. Further, we have already described the harmful effects of chemical and radiation pollution in modern office environments (see Chapter 10). Table 12-1 shows some of the most frequently used dangerous chemicals along with the diseases they can cause and the kinds of workers who are endangered.

TABLE 12-1 Hazardous Substances and On-the-Job Diseases

Potential dangers	Diseases that may result	Workers exposed
Arsenic	Lung cancer, lymphoma	Smelter, chemical, oil-refinery workers; insecticide makers and sprayers—estimated 660,000 exposed
Asbestos	White-lung disease (asbestosis); cancer of lungs and lining of lungs; cancer of other organs	Miners; millers; textile, insulation and shipyard workers—estimated 1.6 million exposed
Benzene	Leukemia; aplastic anemia	Petrochemical and oil-refinery workers; dye users; distillers; painters; shoemakers—estimated 600,000 exposed
Bischloro-methylether (BCME)	Lung cancer	Industrial chemical workers
Coal dust	Black-lung disease	Coal miners—estimated 208,000 exposed
Coke-oven emissions	Cancer of lungs, kidneys	Coke-oven workers—estimated 30,000 exposed
Cotton dust	Brown-lung disease (byssinosis); chronic bronchitis; emphysema	Textile workers—estimated 600,000 exposed
Lead	Kidney disease; anemia; central-nervous-system damage; sterility; birth defects	Metal grinders; lead-smelter workers; lead storage-battery workers—estimated 835,000 exposed
Radiation	Cancer of thyroid, lungs and bone; leukemia; reproductive effects (spontaneous abortion, genetic damage)	Medical technicians; uranium miners; nuclear-power and atomic workers
Vinyl chloride	Cancer of liver, brain	Plastic-industry workers—estimated 10,000 directly exposed

From *Healthy People in Unhealthy Places: Stress and Fitness at Work* (p. 90) by K. R. Pelletier, 1984, New York: Delacorte.

Why has so little been done? Who is to blame for these deplorable figures? Employers, politicians, unions, and workers themselves all share the blame for this widespread crippling and death. Unions often downgrade safety considerations to focus on economic matters. Companies try to cut costs by not enlarging their safety staffs and by continuing to use obsolete or unsafe materials and equipment. State and federal government safety standards are often ineffective and poorly enforced.

On December 29, 1970, the U.S. Congress passed the Occupational Safety and Health Act establishing the Occupational Safety and Health Administration (OSHA) in the Department of Labor, the purpose of which is to assure safe and healthful working conditions by combating industrial accidents and disease. By developing and enforcing federal industrial safety standards and by sponsoring research into the causes and prevention of accidents and disease, it is hoped that working conditions can be made less dangerous.

Let us consider the general accident picture in the United States. If we include accidents that occur on the highways and in the home, the fatalities dwarf the figures from cancer, heart disease, and other killers. More Americans were accidentally killed and injured at home in the United States during the years of World War II (1941–1945) than suffered death in combat abroad. Each year, more than 100,000 people are killed in accidents and about 10 million are reported injured. Almost half of the deaths result from automobile accidents. The problem of accidents has reached serious proportions and is not receiving the attention that it deserves.

The discussion here is limited to industrial accidents. Psychologists have conducted many research studies on accidents, focusing on the conditions giving rise to them, the personality patterns of those who seem to have an unusually high number of accidents, and the design of the equipment or machinery involved in accidents.

We cannot accuse industry of ignoring the problems of accidents and safety; this is not the case. Although some companies have not done as much as they could, many have invested considerable time and money for accident prevention programs, as we shall see. Accidents are expensive to employers; they reduce output. Trained workers who have been injured must be replaced, damaged equipment must be repaired, and the morale of a work crew that has suffered the loss of a co-worker must be improved. This all costs money, therefore companies are understandably concerned with reducing the accident toll. And, it is reasonable to suppose that without industry's present accident-prevention programs (however imperfect they may be), the accident toll would be even higher.

Also, safety is not the exclusive responsibility of management. Workers must do their part as well. It has been found that most accidents are caused by the human element, not the machine, and this suggests that workers must take their roles more seriously. For example, the company can provide the best available protective goggles, but, if workers will not wear them, the goggles are worthless. Inspectors for OSHA report that workers are often hostile toward protective equipment that is uncomfortable to wear such as hard hats. Also, workers sometimes oppose safety legislation because of fear that the additional cost of safety measures will jeopardize their jobs. As the National Safety Council notes: "Safety is everybody's business." As an employee, a manager, or a driver, safety is your business.

Accident Statistics

We noted in Chapter 2 that statistics do not lie but that sometimes people who use statistics distort facts in their own favor, backing up their distortions with figures. This is the situation with accident research. The problem is to define an accident precisely, which is not as ridiculous as it may sound.

How severe must an accident be for it to be included in a company's accident statistics? It seems that different people define accidents in different ways. Suppose a worker drops a heavy barrel. Is this an accident? Technically, yes. Whether it is listed as an accident depends on the consequences of the act, not on the act itself. If the dropped barrel is not damaged and no one is hurt, the episode will not be recorded as an accident. But suppose the barrel falls on the worker's foot and breaks a few bones. Is this an accident? Not necessarily. Many companies will not list this as an accident, even though the worker is hurt and requires medical treatment. The injured worker may not be able to walk for a while, but, if the company provides a desk job until the worker is better, he or she will not have lost any time from the factory. Here we have an accident resulting in an injury, yet it may not be included in the accident statistics, and the company's safety record remains intact. The definition of an accident in this case depends on whether the injured worker actually loses time from work. According to the Bureau of Labor Statistics, this distinction keeps many serious accidents from ever being reported.

The nation's largest meat packer, IBP, Inc., was fined $2.59 million in 1987 for failing to report 1,038 job-related injuries and illnesses among its workers over a 1-year period. Statistics on railroad accidents are also unreliable. An independent investigation of 25 Amtrak accidents found that although 1,338 people had been injured, the official government report stated that only 494 injuries had occurred (Kaye, 1987).

It is this failure to record all injuries on the job, not just those injuries that keep workers at home, that led the Bureau of Labor Statistics to conclude, as we noted, that for each reported disabling injury there are 10 serious injuries not reported. Unreported accidents include eye injuries, broken toes and fingers, and loss of consciousness, but these events are defined as accidents only if they result in lost work time.

Incomplete reporting of industrial accidents makes research into the causes and prevention of accidents more difficult. The available statistics show the results of only a small portion of the accidents and provide little information on the causes. Further, by concentrating on lost-time accidents, the figures provide an inaccurate picture of what has occurred in a particular department or plant.

Organizations like to claim good safety records. A good record shows that a company is doing all it can to promote a safe working environment for its employees. Workers might avoid a company that had acquired the negative public image that follows a high reported accident rate. Higher insurance costs to the company may also be a consequence of a higher number of reported accidents. To achieve a good safety record and, consequently, a good public image, some companies resort to extreme measures such as closed-door accident investigations, inaccurate reporting, and outright distortion of the facts.

The solution is obvious: All accidents, whatever their severity, must be reported. Also, all accidents must be reported in detail. Only through thorough analyses of past accidents can the same mistakes be prevented in the future and unsafe conditions be eliminated. Lost-time accidents are undoubtedly the most severe to the worker and the company and deserve a major share of attention, but less severe accidents must be studied just as comprehensively. The conditions that lead to an accident today in which a worker merely scrapes a leg could lead to an accident tomorrow in which the leg is lost.

Further, it is important that accidents resulting in no injuries be reported and investigated. The conditions under which a worker drops a heavy barrel are the same whether no harm is done, the worker breaks a foot, or the barrel rolls down an incline and kills a co-worker. To prevent a recurrence, the worker's behavior and the circumstances of the accident—not just the result—must be studied.

Not all the blame for inaccurate accident reporting can be placed on the company. Sometimes the workers themselves distort the facts. Some employees fail to report minor accidents for fear of acquiring a reputation as careless or accident prone. Others fear possible punishment because an accident was their fault, if, for example, they did not follow accepted operating procedures or neglected to use a safety device.

Causes of Accidents

The human element—the worker, the driver, the homemaker—seems to be responsible for most accidents whether they occur at the factory, on the highway, or in the home. Thus, factors such as emotional state, attitude, and general behavior characteristics play an important role in determining the causes of accidents. However, conditions of the work environment and the nature of the job itself can also contribute to accidents. These include physical aspects of the workplace, type of industry, hours of work, lighting, temperature, and equipment design.

Conditions of the Workplace

The Physical Environment. Modern technology has created new work environments and machinery that bring new hazards to the workers. For example, high energy sources such as laser beams, once found solely in laboratories for research purposes, are now commonplace for such uses as cutting cloth for the garment industry. Innovative production processes, sophisticated high-speed machinery, and industrial robots add considerably to the complexities and dangers of work. We are creating work environments that make fresh demands and require new responsibilities of workers, without, of course, being able to change the workers very much. The evolution in technology proceeds at a faster pace than the evolution of human employees who must understand, operate, and control these advanced machines.

The difficulties in designing a safe working environment grow each year. Workers can and must be trained in safety practices and principles, but training alone does not solve the problem. We must ensure that if workers are doing all they can to protect themselves, they are further protected by properly designed machinery and equipment.

Type of Industry. The frequency and severity of accidents vary as a function of the type of industry and the kind of work being performed. A steel mill provides more opportunities for accidents than does a bank. The more demanding the physical requirements made on the worker, the higher the accident rate. Stressful and tiring work results in more accidents. In general, industries such as construction, forestry, and mining are high in frequency and severity of accidents; industries such as warehousing, aircraft and automobile manufacturing, and communications are usually low in frequency and severity of accidents. Additional types of factories that are prone to high rates of accidents and illnesses are shown in Table 12-2.

There are exceptions to these data. Cement and steel industries report a low frequency of accidents, but when they do occur, they are usually quite severe. Electric utility companies report few accidents, but these tend to be severe because of the high voltages involved. Wholesale and retail businesses report high accident rates, but injuries that cause employees to miss work are relatively rare.

TABLE 12-2   High-risk Industries for 1986 (Bureau of Labor Statistics data)

Industry	Illness/injury rate per 100 full-time workers
Meat packing plants	33.4
Mobile home manufacturing plants	29.8
Vending machine manufacturing plants	28.1
Wooden roof supports manufacturing plants	27.1
Sugarcane processing plants	26.2
Wood buildings prefabricators	26.0
Scrap rubber reclamation plants	25.7
Sawmills	25.4
Boat builders and repairers	24.2
Plumbing fixture manufacturers	23.5

Hours of Work. We might suspect that the greater the number of hours worked, the higher the accident rate, but the evidence does not clearly support this idea. Of course, the longer workers are on the job during a workday, the more opportunity they have for accidents, but no evidence indicates that shortening the work period leads to a decrease in accidents. Similarly, there is no support for the notion that lengthening the workday increases accidents. As we noted in Chapter 10, work tends to expand to fill the time available for it, so a lengthened work period usually results in a slower work pace. Thus, the number of accidents per unit of time actually declines, creating the illusion that longer periods of work are safer.

What does seem to make a difference in accident rate is whether the work is performed on day or night shifts. Fewer accidents occur during the night shift (although those that do occur are usually more serious), apparently because the artificial illumination provided at night is more effective than the natural illumination conditions during the day. This relationship has been borne out by research comparing the effects of different levels of artificial illumination on accidents during the night shift. The research has shown that accidents tend to increase as lighting becomes less satisfactory.

An investigation of the injuries occurring in a steel mill confirmed the difference in accident rate and severity between day and night shifts (Ong, Phoon, Iskandar, & Chia, 1987). More than 41% of all accidents took place during the morning shift (7:00 a.m. to 3:00 p.m.); 23% during the afternoon shift (3:00 p.m. to 11:00 p.m.); and 16% during the night shift (11:00 p.m. to 7:00 a.m.). However, for the accidents that occurred on the night shift, the injured workers required a significantly longer period of sick leave, indicating that those injuries were more serious than those that occurred on the other shifts. In addition, the psychologists documented two peak accident periods during the day: between 9 and 10 o'clock in the morning and between 2 and 3 o'clock in the afternoon.

Lighting. As noted, good lighting can lead to a reduction in the accident rate. One insurance company estimated that 25% of all industrial accidents are caused by poor lighting. Accidents are higher in plants that continue production through dusk before the lights are turned on. (Dusk is also a time of frequent automobile accidents.) The relationship between level of illumination and accident rate seems firmly established, and a poorly lit work area can be easily corrected by an alert management.

Temperature. The temperature at which work is performed also affects the accident rate. Studies of factory workers show that the accident rate is lowest when the temperature is around 68°F to 70°F. Accidents increase when the temperature varies in either direction and are particularly frequent under extreme temperatures. Studies carried out in coal mines show that at temperatures approaching 85°F minor accidents are three times more frequent than at lower temperatures (to 62°F). It seems likely that workers become careless in their work habits under the discomfort produced by high temperatures.

A work environment such as this natural gas drilling plant must be designed so that emergency controls are easy to reach.

Evidence also suggests that older workers are more affected by temperature extremes than younger workers. Research has shown, for example, that in hot work environments, older employees are much more likely to have accidents.

Equipment Design. Another aspect of the physical work environment related to accidents is the design of the equipment or machinery used on the job. Too often, equipment is planned for the convenience of the design engineer or along aesthetic lines without due consideration of the limitations and capabilities of the worker who has to use it. Locating a stop button where it is difficult to reach, for example, can have deadly consequences if the machine must be shut down immediately. Poor placement of switches and other controls, inadequate warning lights for system malfunction, and dials that are difficult to read can all lead to accidents. The proper matching of the machine with the capabilities of the operator is, as we saw in Chapter 11, the province of engineering psychologists. Their work on equipment design has been effective in accident prevention.

Also important in the design of safe machinery is the development of built-in safety devices and other aids to prevent accidents. Safety devices must not interfere with the actual operation of the machine but function, for example, to keep a worker's hand away from sharp moving parts or to cut off automatically the power supply and stop the machine in an emergency.

Proper attention to equipment design and to the work environment can help reduce the frequency and severity of accidents. Overall, however, the human element is the more important causal factor in accidents.

Personal Factors

Psychologists have conducted much research on the relationship between personal characteristics or abilities and accidents. Success has been mixed, partly because the complex interrelationships of some variables make it difficult to interpret the results clearly. There are also confounding variables such as *self-selection* in taking a job initially and remaining on the job for any length of time. If a job is known to be dangerous, certain people will not even apply for it. When, for example, psychologists wish to study the personality characteristics of construction workers who have had several accidents versus those who have not, the task is made more difficult by the factor of self-selection; only workers who possess specific personality traits may be working in that job.

Self-selection also applies to the length of time employees remain on a job. If there is danger involved in the task, many workers (those who are afraid, have had too many accidents, or have been disabled on the job) will not stay very long. If psychologists wish to compare more experienced with less experienced workers in terms of accident rate, they may find themselves dealing with workers who differ in more ways than just length of work experience; those workers who have remained on the job have been self-selected in terms of lower levels of fear or susceptibility to accidents.

These difficulties do not mean that research on personal causes of accidents is impossible, only that great care is necessary in the design and interpretation of such studies. Some of the personal factors in accidents studied by psychologists are alcohol and drug use, cognitive ability, health, fatigue, work experience, age, and personality.

Alcohol and Drug Use.   We shall see later in this chapter that large numbers of employees use alcohol or illicit drugs on the job. Not surprisingly, this abuse has been related to accidents. According to one estimate, an employee with a drinking or drug problem is 3.6 times more likely to be involved in an accident than an employee without such a problem. Approximately half of all on-the-job accidents, as well as automobile accidents, may be linked to excessive drinking (Cowan, 1987).

Cognitive Ability. It seems reasonable to expect intelligence to correlate negatively with accident rate; we would expect less intelligent workers to have more accidents than more intelligent workers. However, the evidence does not clearly support this idea. Some studies suggest that intelligence is related to accident-free behavior only in certain kinds of jobs, for example, those requiring a high degree of judgment (as opposed to those involving repetitive manual labor).

Cognitive activities such as perception, information processing, and judgment are involved in the performance of many types of work from office jobs to the operation of complex machinery such as airplanes. A study of 1,448 fighter–bomber, helicopter, and cargo pilots in West Germany's air force linked pilot errors to lapses in cognitive functioning that led to hazardous situations (Gerbert & Kemmler, 1986). The pilots completed a 315-item questionnaire covering personal factors, the hazardous incident in question, and information about their physical and psychological states. The most frequent pilot errors are listed in Table 12-3.

The study also identified a number of internal cognitive states associated with the pilot errors (Table 12-4).

Health. It is well documented that health is related to accidents. The evidence shows that employees who are in poor health or have had frequent illnesses tend to be highly susceptible to accidents.

Physical disabilities, assuming that the workers' general health is good and that they are assigned jobs commensurate with their abilities, do not necessarily predispose workers to accidents. Indeed, physically handicapped workers are usually highly motivated to work well and safely, often more so than nonhandicapped employees. Assuming proper placement, accident rates among the handicapped are lower than accident rates for able-bodied workers.

TABLE 12-3   Pilot Errors

Errors	*Percentage*
Delay in taking necessary action	43.2
Misjudgment of weather conditions	30.2
Misjudgment of distance	21.3
Misjudgment of altitude and clearance	20.9
Misjudgment of airspeed	20.6
Spatial disorientation	20.2
Poor instrument scan	19.8
Failure to see obstacles	19.7
Misjudgment of aircraft attitude	19.7
Failure to check and maintain aircraft attitude	17.2

From "The causes of causes: Determinants and background variables of human factor incidents and accidents" by K. Gerbert & R. Kemmler, 1986, *Ergonomics, 29,* p. 1442.

**TABLE 12-4 Cognitive States Associated
with Pilot Errors**

Cognitive states	Percentage
Information deficit and time pressure	49.9
High tension and activation level during flight	43.0
Diverted attention	29.9
Lack of awareness of risk	26.6
Task overload	26.3
Excessive motivation to succeed	23.4
Overconfidence	17.9
Distraction of attention	14.6
Low overall flying experience	11.7
Lack of motivation	10.6

From "The causes of causes: Determinants and background variables of
human factor incidents and accidents" by K. Gerbert & R. Kemmler, 1986,
Ergonomics, 29, p. 1442.

One physical defect that is related to accidents is poor vision. On the
highway as well as in the factory, tests have shown that people who have fewer
accidents generally have better vision.

Except in extreme cases, a company's medical department can identify
and correct vision problems, and, in terms of accident rate (and probably productivity as well), it would be worthwhile to do so. A few companies provide free periodic vision examinations for their employees and recommend
corrective action where necessary. In cases incapable of correction, workers
with poor vision could be placed in less hazardous jobs to reduce their accident potential.

Fatigue.   Fatigue causes a decline in production and an increase in accidents.
Indeed, there is a close relationship between accident frequency and production level. During a typical 8-hour workday, periods of production increase are
accompanied by decreases in accidents. In a 10-hour workday, a sharp rise in
the accident rate during the last 2 hours has been reported in some heavy
industries, presumably because of fatigue.

Work Experience.   A lower level of on-the-job work experience tends to result
in a higher accident rate. Studies have shown a decrease in accidents over the
period from the beginning of a new job to $1\frac{1}{2}$ years later. A 7-year study of more
than 35,000 accidents among U.S. Navy shore-based enlisted personnel found
that 35% of them occurred during the first month in a new job assignment
(Helmkamp & Bone, 1987). After that initial month, the accident rate dropped
rapidly and continued to decline as time on the job increased (see Figure 12-1).
Thus, there is a need for comprehensive safety training before the worker
actually begins the job. It is not enough to train new workers in the specific skills
and abilities required for successful performance of their jobs. They must also

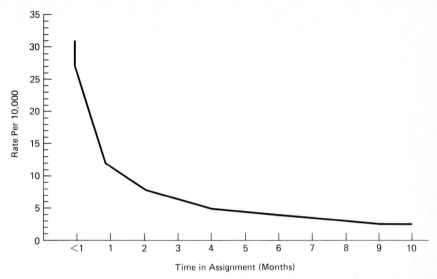

Figure 12-1 Accident and injury rate among navy personnel. (Data from "The effect of time in a new job on hospitalization rates for accidents and injuries in the U.S. Navy, 1977–1983" by J. C. Helmkamp & C. M. Bone, 1987, *Journal of Occupational Medicine, 29,* p. 654.)

learn safe work rules and proper attitudes toward safety. In comparing groups of workers that had received safety training with those given no such training, the first group experienced many fewer accidents in their early days on the job.

The relationship between accidents and long-term work experience is not as clear. Although studies report fewer accidents among workers who have greater experience, these findings may be biased by the self-selection factor discussed previously. Workers who have had numerous accidents may have been fired, transferred to other jobs, or quit to search for safer work. Therefore, we cannot conclude that longer work experience by itself leads to a reduction in accidents. The decrease in accidents for experienced workers may be caused by the fact that those who had more accidents may have dropped out. It also could be because of age.

Proper research on accidents as a function of job experience does not involve simply the comparison of a low-experience group with a high-experience group. The psychologist must study the accident records of a group of workers over a period of time, beginning with their early employment. When this is done for 1 or 2 years, the results support the suggestion that more experienced workers have fewer accidents. Studying the same group of workers over 10 to 20 years, however, is extremely difficult because of the changes in work methods, equipment, and conditions that can take place during so long a period. In the face of marked differences in conditions of work, it is not meaningful to compare accident rates in one time period with accident rates many years later.

Age.   The relationship between age and accidents is similar to the relationship between experience and accidents because of the high correlation between age and experience. Older workers have spent more time on the job and so are more experienced than younger workers. Because of this interaction of age and experience, studies comparing the accident rates of different age groups are complicated by the self-selection problem.

Other factors that may interact with age are health and attitude. As a rule, the state of health as well as specific abilities such as vision and hearing deteriorate with advancing age. Perhaps counteracting this factor are the greater job knowledge and more highly developed job skills evidenced by older workers. Older persons' reaction time or eye-hand coordination may no longer be as good, but, by virtue of their greater experience, they may have a fuller command of the nuances and demands of the job. Younger workers' attitudes toward safety as well as toward other aspects of the job may tend to be less serious than those of older employees.

With these considerations in mind and noting the influence of job experience, it is possible to conclude that older workers have fewer accidents than younger ones. Again, it must be stated that age alone may not be the single determining factor in accident rates but rather one that represents a constellation of variables.

Although the frequency of accidents declines with age, the severity of accidents increases. When older workers do have accidents, they are likely to be more severe in terms of their physical consequences and time lost from the job (Rhodes, 1983).

Personality Characteristics.   One popular belief in the field of accidents and safety is that persons who tend to have a great many accidents possess a unique set of personality characteristics that clearly distinguish them from those persons who have few accidents. Research has not consistently supported this contention, but there is some evidence to suggest that people who have a high number of accidents have some similar personal characteristics.

One study revealed that a group of drivers with high accident rates were excessively ambitious and revengeful and, at the same time, afraid and fatalistic. The low-accident group did not display these characteristics to the same degree (McGuire, 1976). Other research has suggested that accident repeaters are less emotionally stable, are hostile toward authority, are high in anxiety, do not get along well with others, and have erratic work histories (Shaw & Sichel, 1971). A study of 416 air traffic controllers found that those high in Type A behavior had more than 3.5 times the injuries of those low in Type A behavior (Niemcryk, Jenkins, Rose, & Hurst, 1987).

It must be emphasized that the relationships between personality characteristics and accident frequency are not very strong. There is no basis for concluding that the high-accident repeater has a personality clearly different from that of the accident-free individual.

However, emotional factors are of some consequence in accidents; accidents seem to vary as a function of a person's temporary mood. For example, the person who is angry with a spouse or boss, or angry with the anonymous driver who cuts ahead on the highway in the morning, or the person who is anxious about money matters or family affairs is likely to be less attentive on the job and, therefore, more susceptible to accidents. In the study of air traffic controllers, those highly dissatisfied with management had 2.5 times the rate of injuries as did those who were satisfied with management.

In studies comparing emotional state and accident frequency, results show many fewer accidents when workers are happy and content than when they are angry, frustrated, or worried. One group of factory workers studied were reported to be depressed nearly 20% of their time at work. Regardless of the reasons for the depression, the findings clearly revealed that more than 50% of the accidents that occurred during the time of the study took place during this negative emotional period (Hersey, 1932; Wrogg, 1961). (Production is also affected by transitory emotional states, decreasing during emotional lows.)

Thus, temporary emotional states, more than general personality patterns, seem to be causal factors in accidents. Workers subjected to the stress of an unhappy home life or other personal or job-related problems are more susceptible to accidents on the job (and, of course, on the highway). Identification of employees undergoing such strains, followed by effective counseling, could help to reduce accidents.

The theory of *accident proneness*, that certain people are more likely than others to have accidents, has been popular for many years. Its simplicity and apparent potential for reducing accidents have made it attractive. According to proponents, it is only necessary to measure the characteristics of those who have large numbers of accidents and then use these measurements as predictive devices. That is, those who scored high on these factors could be placed in jobs where there are few opportunities for accidents to occur; high-risk jobs would be given to those scoring low on accident-proneness tests.

The theory rests on the assumption that most accidents are caused by, or involve, the same few people. It is also assumed that accident-prone individuals are likely to have accidents, regardless of the situation. Whatever they are doing, the theory states, accident-prone individuals are likely to have an accident when doing it. Suppose that 10% of a work group had 50% of the accidents. Some people in the group had no accidents, whereas others had a number of accidents; therefore, according to the theory, the latter are accident prone.

Is it reasonable to assume, however, that all people in a group are expected to have the same number of accidents, and, further, that any deviation from this expectation (those few people who have more accidents than others) is the result of accident proneness? Critics of the theory believe that these assumptions are false (Kirchner, 1961).

One frequently overlooked factor is that the number of accidents in a group for a given period of time is likely to be smaller than the number of people in the group. If 100 workers in a department had 50 accidents in one year, it is possible that no more than 50 workers had accidents, in which case 50% of the group caused 100% of the accidents. This assumes that each person had one accident. This is hardly accident proneness. Yet it is possible for an investigator to conclude that because these 50 persons had all the accidents and the other 50 had none, the former group must be accident prone.

Similar reasoning could be applied if 25 workers in the group each had two accidents during the year. Random factors or equipment failures could have caused the accidents to happen to these particular workers and not to the others. In the following year, these 25 people may have no accidents. Interpretation of such statistics is fraught with potential error.

An effective way to test the accident-proneness theory is to compare accident records of the same individuals for two different time periods, thus determining if the same people had repeated accidents. Psychologists have made such comparisons, and the resulting correlations have not been high. This suggests that a person's past accident record is not a valid predictor of the future record.

A noteworthy finding involves a second look at a set of accident statistics that had originally been interpreted as supporting the accident-proneness theory. In analyzing driving records of nearly 30,000 persons, it was found that less than 4% of them accounted for more than 36% of the accidents in a 6-year period. This seemed to suggest that a small group was involved in a large number of accidents; if they could be prevented from driving, the accident rate would be cut by more than one third.

The same statistics were reanalyzed by comparing the accident records for the first 3-year period with those for the second 3-year period. This time it became clear that the accidents did not involve the same drivers during the two time periods. Those identified as safe drivers during the first 3-year period (having had no more than one accident), accounted for more than 96% of all the accidents in the second 3-year period. This is highly damaging to the theory of accident proneness: If those who had most of the accidents during the first period had been predisposed to accidents by some unique set of personal characteristics, then they should have had the majority of the accidents during the second period. They did not. Other research confirms the notion that the apparent accident proneness of some employees is the result of chance (DeReamer, 1980).

Although the accident-proneness theory still has ardent supporters, it no longer enjoys the credibility it once did. Evidence does suggest, however, that some people might be predisposed to have more accidents in certain situations; some workers will have a high number of accidents in one type of work but not in another. Accident proneness may be specific to the situation and not a general tendency in all situations. This specificity limits the predictive value of the theory (Arbous & Kerrich, 1951; Kerr, 1957).

A final argument against accident proneness involves the assumption that the characteristics of high-accident repeaters are distinct from those who have few accidents. As noted in our discussion of personality and accidents, the research does not strongly support this contention.

Accident Prevention

There are several procedures an organization can use in a campaign designed to prevent or reduce accidents.

Reporting and Analyzing Accidents

First, detailed and accurate data on past accidents in the organization must be accumulated. Surely the best way to develop protective and preventive measures against future accidents is to find out what went wrong in the past. Accident data from different firms and from various departments and activities within the same firm can be analyzed to determine particularly dangerous industries and operations so that greater attention can be focused on them. It is probably true that an accident program is no better than the quality and thoroughness of its accident reports. All accidents, no matter how minor any personal injury, should be reported.

An accident report should contain the following information:

1. *Precise time and location of the accident.* Many aspects of a job as well as overall working conditions can change during a workday, especially from one shift to another. These background factors must be thoroughly understood because they may have contributed to the accident.
2. *Type of job and the number of employees performing it.* Specifics of the job classification and required operating procedures should be known as well as the number of people performing that job. It is important to determine how many employees in the same job have had accidents in a given period of time.
3. *Personal characteristics of the accident victim.* Age, health, and job experience are influential factors in accident behavior. This information plus psychological test and background data, available from selection procedures and supervisors' ratings of performance efficiency, should all be reported in as much detail as possible.
4. *Nature and cause of the accident.* The accident report should describe exactly what led up to the accident, what happened to the worker(s), and, if applicable, damage to equipment. The cause, if known or suspected—such as equipment failure, careless operating procedures, or failure to use safety devices—should be noted.
5. *Results of the accident.* Specific damage to equipment, raw materials, and the manufacturing process should be described. If a personal injury resulted, a detailed medical report of the extent of the injuries, treatment, and prognosis for recovery should be included.

Design of the Work Environment

Although most accidents are caused by the human element, the physical work environment can, as we have seen, include hazards that are potential sources of accidents. For example, a poorly designed machine or work area often leads to what is defined in an accident report as a human error, but it is an error that could have been prevented through proper equipment design. Thus, we see that the work of engineering psychologists can contribute directly to accident prevention.

This aspect of accident prevention, the engineering phase, is probably the single most important aspect of a safety program. No matter how much is known about past accidents or how well trained and motivated the workers are in safety procedures, if the equipment is unnecessarily dangerous, accidents are likely to occur. Machinery and work areas designed for safety may also serve to increase workers' confidence and allay apprehensions about accidents.

As far as the work environment is concerned, the illumination must be adequate for the job tasks and the temperature maintained at a comfortable level. The work area should be kept clean and orderly; accidents have been traced directly to poor housekeeping. Oil or grease spots on the floor and equipment cluttering stairways have directly caused expensive and injurious accidents that could easily have been prevented.

Proper maintenance of all operating machinery is also a safety aid. A machine allowed to function improperly or one that has been repaired incorrectly often causes accidents.

First-aid equipment, fire extinguishers, and other safety accessories should be conveniently placed throughout a work area and painted in easily identified colors. Time lost in searching for a fire extinguisher, for example, greatly increases the seriousness of the accident.

We discussed the importance of properly designed production machinery and noted that it must be compatible with the capabilities and limitations of the operators. Controls that are hard to reach or require unusual force to operate or dials and displays that are excessively complicated and, therefore, easily misread are obvious design mistakes that are ready sources of accidents.

Emergency controls must be easily accessible and quickly operated. A machine designed so that the shut-off control is difficult to reach if a worker gets a hand caught, is an open invitation to a serious accident. Safety engineers and engineering psychologists are now aware of these design dangers.

The design of safety aids and devices is a crucial part of the engineering phase of accident prevention. Perhaps no machine safety device can be made totally foolproof, but it is possible to come close. Two general principles apply to the design of safety devices. First, the machine should not function unless the safety device is in place or in operation. A punch press that will not work unless the handguard is in place is as safe as possible. In this case, the worker is forced to manually engage the handguard to operate the machine. If the press were designed to operate whether or not the handguard was in place, a lazy or careless worker might decide it was not worth the effort to swing the guard into place each time, and lose a hand as the result.

Second, the safety device must not interfere with production. If the installation of a safety guard on the punch press means that 15 fewer units will be produced each day, management and the incentive-paid worker will be dissatisfied. Also, the safety device should not cause the employee to work harder or to engage in additional operations to maintain the same production

Safety devices such as face shields should be easy to use and should not interfere with productivity.

level. The frustration and possible fatigue induced by such extra effort may in themselves lead to accidents.

There are, then, several steps a company can take in the proper design of the equipment and the work environment to reduce the possibility of accidents. Although the engineering phase is vital to the success of an accident-prevention program, the program may not be totally effective unless the organizational climate is highly supportive of safety and the workers are carefully trained and sufficiently motivated to work safely.

Organizational Climate

No matter how sophisticated a company's safety program, it will not be maximally effective unless the employees perceive that the organizational climate is highly supportive of safety on the job. This was demonstrated in a study of 20 industrial organizations in Israel (Zohar, 1980).

A safety-climate questionnaire was developed to measure the following dimensions of organizational climate:

1. Degree of management commitment to safety.
2. Effects of safe job performance on promotion.
3. Effects of safe job performance on social status.

4. Status of safety personnel in the organization.
5. Perceived importance and effectiveness of safety training.
6. Risk level of the workplace.
7. Relative effectiveness of enforcement versus guidance in promoting safety.

These dimensions had been found to correlate with safety on the job in earlier research, and they constitute the perceived climate of the organization with respect to safety.

The questionnaire was given to employees at 20 factories and the results compared with ratings of the safety practices of these companies made by experienced safety inspectors. The results showed that the higher the perceived safety climate of an organization, the higher it had been rated on its safety practices. The two most important dimensions in determining the organizational climate with regard to safety were management attitudes toward safety and the relevance of safety to job behavior (the perceived importance and effectiveness of safety training).

Training for Accident Prevention

Some safety experts believe that training is the single most important technique in bringing about safe worker behavior, particularly when dealing with high-tech automated equipment (Spettell & Liebert, 1986). Training is considered to be so vital that 83% of the companies questioned in one survey said that they had established formal safety training programs (Levine, 1983).

The training phase of an accident-prevention program focuses on safe job skills and attitudes toward safety. Neither aspect is fully effective alone: Both on-the-job behavior and attitudes must be oriented toward reducing accidents. Workers may be well aware of the safest way to operate the equipment, but if their attitude toward safety is negative, this job knowledge alone may not protect them from harm. Similarly, a positive attitude will not prevent accidents if employees do not know the rules for safe operation of their equipment.

With respect to job skills, inexperienced workers are highly susceptible to accidents during the initial period on the job. Training in the safe way of performing a work task can lead to a reduction in accidents for new employees.

Most company training programs devote some time to safety matters. Special dangers and potential hazards of the job are pointed out and information presented on the nature, causes, and results of past accidents. The company's rules for safety on the job are taught, as are the location of emergency first-aid equipment and the medical facility. For particularly dangerous jobs, it is not unusual to teach employees the principles of first aid. Safety training, however, does not stop when employees begin work. Most companies continue some form of safety training throughout an employee's career. Systematic safety inspections are frequently made and safe working habits continually checked. Publicity campaigns designed to maintain safety awareness are periodically launched.

Further, when accident rates are observed to increase, retraining is often put into effect. Sometimes experienced employees become careless or forgetful of safety procedures so that a refresher course is required. Some firms periodically offer safety retraining programs to all employees, regardless of the accident rate. The goal is to maintain in employees a constant awareness of safety and a continuing interest in safe working habits. Generally, firms that continue safety efforts in systematic and thorough fashion have been rewarded with substantial reductions in lost hours of work. The money thus saved usually more than pays the cost of the safety training programs.

A particularly effective approach to safety training is behavior modification. This technique has been used extensively in training programs to change a number of job-related behaviors (see Chapter 6). It also works well with safety behaviors.

One attempt to apply behavior modification to safety took place in a large food manufacturing plant. Psychologists observed specific job behaviors and the safe versus unsafe ways of performing them. Employees were given training in the safe ways of performing those behaviors through slide presentations, discussion sessions, and a list of reminders of safe practices.

They were also shown a graph depicting their current percentage of safe behaviors. This information indicated that they were working safely about 70% of the time. They were then exhorted to increase that level; a goal of 90% was suggested by the employees. They were told that observers would be assessing their performance and that the results would be made public.

The periodic posting of the employees' safety performance provided feedback. Positive reinforcement was given by supervisors who praised workers whenever they engaged in safe job behaviors. Employees were enthusiastic about the program and even applauded when the initial results were marked on the graph. The incidence of safe job behaviors increased rapidly from 70% to the goal of 90%, and the group often achieved the 100% level (Komaki, Barwick, & Scott, 1978).

Another training program involved mechanics employed by the public works department of a large city. The results confirmed the effectiveness of feedback and the behavior modification approach. Safe and unsafe behaviors were identified, slides were made to illustrate the behaviors, and employees were asked to set goals for improving their safety records. Graphs were kept of the workers' behaviors for a period of 10 weeks. Safety performance improved slightly during the training period when the slides were being shown and discussed. However, safety performance improved significantly when feedback, in the form of the graphs, was given to the workers (Komaki, Heinzmann, & Lawson, 1980).

A key role in any successful safety training and awareness program is played by the first-line supervisor. More than any other level of management, supervisors, because of their close daily association with workers, must be alert to unsafe working conditions and practices. They are in the best position to remind employees of safe working habits and to arrange for proper maintenance of machinery and the work environment.

Supervisors are also in the best position to advise the safety engineer on weaknesses in the safety program and to suggest to the training department when retraining might be advisable. The best safety training program will be less than maximally effective if supervisors do not follow it up by insisting on adherence to safe working procedures. Further, supervisors, by example and instruction, can maintain proper motivation toward safety. If they display a lack of concern for safe procedures, certainly the workers will not be concerned about them.

However, supervisors cannot be expected to continue to display proper awareness of safety problems unless their superiors reinforce that awareness. Tolerance of sloppy accident reporting and a negative or even neutral attitude toward safety on the part of higher management neither encourages nor reinforces attention to the problem. As we noted earlier, active management support of safety is a key dimension of a proper organizational climate. All levels of supervision must demonstrate to subordinates that safety is everybody's responsibility. Only with such broad support will training programs be most effective.

One way of assuring continuing supervisor awareness of safety needs is to periodically and formally evaluate their safety records. A survey of human resource directors at 64 companies of varying sizes found that 48% of them evaluated supervisors on the safety records of their work units and that 34% made such evaluations a formal part of their performance appraisal program (Lo Bosco, 1986b).

Safety Publicity Campaigns

To motivate employees to follow the safe working practices they have been taught, many organizations engage in publicity and promotional campaigns. Bright, attractive posters are located throughout the plant, booklets on safety are distributed, charts noting accident-free days are displayed, and safety contests (companywide or nationwide) are conducted.

Posters are the most frequently used technique; 93% of companies surveyed use them (Levine, 1983). Their effectiveness, however, depends on the kind of message displayed. Negative themes ("Don't Do This") coupled with gruesome scenes of mangled bodies ("or This Is What Will Happen") are particularly ineffective. These fear-oriented appeals create resentment and even anger toward the company as well as toward the message itself. The most effective safety posters stress positive themes such as "Wear Hard Hat in This Area" or "Hold On to Railing." They should be attention-getting through the use of bright colors, sharply defined lettering, and visible placement. The use of safety posters has resulted in increases in safety practices within 6 weeks after the introduction of posters in the plant (Sell, 1977).

Posters and signs displaying warnings should meet four criteria (Wogalter, Godfrey, Fontenelle, Desaulniers, Rothstein, & Laughery, 1987):

1. *Signal word.* Warnings should have signal or key words that are appropriate to the level of danger, for example, "Danger," "Warning," or "Caution."

2. *Hazard statement*. Warnings should tell clearly what the dangers are.
3. *Consequences*. Warnings should tell clearly the results of failing to comply with the warning.
4. *Instructions*. Warnings should tell workers what to do, or not do, to avoid the danger.

The following example makes use of these four criteria.

WARNING	(Signal word)
UNDERGROUND GAS LINE	(Hazard statement)
EXPLOSION AND FIRE POSSIBLE	(Consequences)
NO DIGGING	(Instructions)

Employees at a North Carolina plant earn safety stickers for each month without a serious accident. The stickers on the supervisor's hard hat read "I have worked 2 years without injury" and "I have worked 1 month without injury."

Booklets of instructions and safety rules do not seem to be very effective, no matter how widely they are distributed. It is relatively simple to make sure that all workers in a factory receive a booklet. It is far more difficult to make them read it. In truth, such booklets are rarely read.

Safety contests can be an effective device for maintaining an interest in safety. Some contests reward workers on an individual basis for accident-free work over a given period of time. Other contests operate on a group basis; the work crew or department receives an award if it remains accident free for a period of time. Another approach pits one department against another to see which has fewer accidents per unit of time. Nationwide contests are sponsored by organizations such as the National Safety Council.

A large bus company used this safety contest approach to try to reduce the high accident rate among its drivers. Four teams of drivers were designated to compete with one another for safe driving prizes that averaged $5 in value for each member of the winning team. Feedback was provided on a daily basis through charts showing each accident for every driver and for every team of drivers. This program, combining team competition, incentives, and feedback, reduced accident rates by 24.9% (Haynes, Pine, & Fitch, 1982).

Contests serve to make workers more conscious of safe operating procedures and, thus, result in a reduction in accident rates. Unfortunately, this awareness may not last much longer than the life of the contest. One possible solution is to have continuous contests, changing the awards frequently enough to maintain interest.

A disadvantage of safety contests is that they may pressure workers, supervisors, or executives to suppress the number of reported accidents. However, incomplete accident records will be self-defeating in the long run because successful accident-prevention programs depend on accurate and complete statistics.

If any one of these steps to accident prevention—analyzing past accidents, optimizing work conditions and equipment, maintaining a proper organizational climate, training employees in safe working procedures and attitudes, and continually promoting safety awareness—is ignored, the safety program as a whole will suffer.

Alcoholism in the Workplace

More than 10 million people in the United States are known to be alcoholics; the actual figure may be higher. The U.S. Public Health Service considers alcoholism one of the four major health threats along with heart disease, cancer, and mental illness. Although the country as a whole has begrudgingly admitted its alcoholic problem, it has been slow to react in terms of treating alcoholism as a disease rather than as a symptom of low will power or degeneracy.

The American Medical Association has published a *Manual on Alcoholism*, incorporating the medical community's current thinking about the problem and its treatment. Alcoholism is defined as an illness characterized by an inability to control the consumption of alcohol to the extent that intoxication is the inevitable result once drinking has begun. Medically, then, alcoholism is an addiction, a pathological drug dependence that is harmful to health and that interferes with normal functioning. Many alcoholics can be successfully treated through a variety of methods. Research at the Bell Telephone Company has found that 72% of its identified alcohol-impaired employees could be rehabilitated (Lewis & Lewis, 1986).

With so many chronic alcoholics among the population, it follows that many of them are working in business, industry, and government where their drinking can interfere with productivity and performance on the job.

Up to 10% of the American work force is estimated to be alcoholic. The cost to the nation's economy and to employers is put in excess of $117 billion a year. Employers of alcoholic workers are plagued by tardiness, absenteeism, errors and accidents, low productivity, inefficiency, and, often, the eventual loss of an employee in whom much money and training may have been invested.

It should be noted that not everyone agrees on the extent of alcoholism in the work force or on its harmful effects. One psychologist suggested that the problem was overstated by therapists, consultants, and directors of rehabilitation programs whose livelihoods depend on the idea that alcoholism is rampant in industry and that their programs can cure it (Weiss, 1987). Such critics do not deny, however, that alcoholism in the workplace does exist.

The problem of the alcoholic employee can be found at all levels of corporate life. Most alcoholics in our society are not skid-row derelicts. According to the National Institute on Alcohol Abuse and Alcoholism, more than 70% of the known alcoholics live in good neighborhoods and are professional, semiprofessional, or managerial employees earning between $35,000 and $50,000 a year. More than 50% of all alcoholics are college graduates or have attended college. The greatest incidence of alcoholism occurs among employees between the ages of 35 and 55 (Harris, 1988).

As noted, there is a growing recognition of this problem on the part of employing organizations. The Department of Labor advises its offices throughout the country to consider alcoholism as a handicap and to treat these workers as disadvantaged in helping them find employment. Labor unions have undertaken extensive campaigns to warn members of the dangers of the excessive use of alcohol and have organized and supported rehabilitation programs. Many large corporations try to help alcoholic employees through company-sponsored employee assistance programs (EAPs).

Effects of Alcoholism on the Job

Alcoholics tend to believe that drinking will not affect their behavior at work and that no one will notice any difference in the way they perform their jobs. This is decidedly untrue. The deteriorating effects of excessive drinking are evident almost immediately. However, at the beginning stages of alcoholism, it requires a trained observer to notice the changes.

Behavioral changes occur gradually, but, after 3 to 5 years of steady drinking, performance and efficiency have deteriorated so greatly that the changes become obvious to any alert supervisor. The general downward path of an alcoholic's behavior is portrayed graphically in Figure 12-2. The right-hand column lists the definite visible signs of altered job performance during the first few years of drinking: excessive absenteeism, long lunch breaks, lies, mistakes,

Figure 12-2   Deterioration in behavior and job performance of an alcoholic as a function of time (© 1967 Doyle Lindley, Bechtel Corporation, and reproduced by permission. Reprinted in "Booze and business" by A. Carding, 1969, *Administrative Management, 30*, p. 21.)

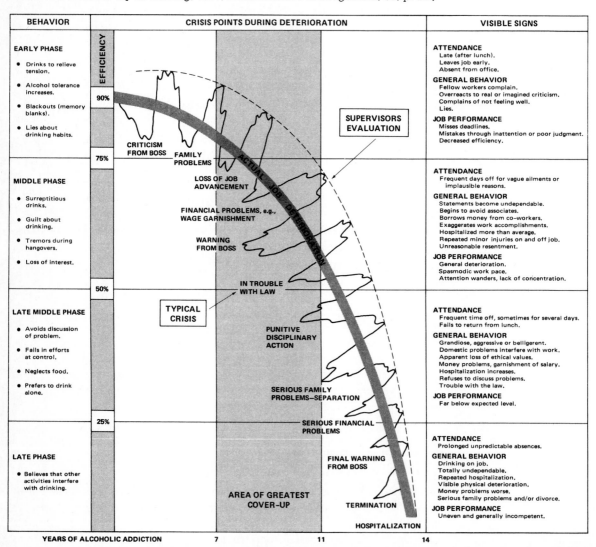

reduced efficiency, and so on. In the middle phase of the drinking problem, we see gross changes in behavior that can no longer be overlooked. By this time, the alcoholic has usually been given at least one warning from superiors and is no longer considered for promotion.

Finally, as the job deterioration curve shows, everything goes downhill for the alcoholic: family life, reputation, financial stability, and, of course, the job. Ironically, yet understandably, each crisis precipitated by drinking is yet another reason to continue drinking, so a vicious cycle is established that, unless help is offered and accepted, leads to failure in every sphere of life and to jail, hospitalization, or an early death.

Because of the effects of alcoholism on job performance and efficiency, the problem must be faced. When a worker's superiors continue to ignore excessive drinking, thinking they are helping the worker, they are actually only prolonging the difficulty. Help at an early stage is vital to an alcoholic's recovery.

The Alcoholic Executive

The plight of any alcoholic employee is tragic and costly, but, when the alcoholic is an executive, the cost to the company is greater. There are no exact figures on the number of alcoholic executives, but it is clear that they constitute their proportionate share of all alcoholics in the world of work. When a company loses an executive because of a drinking problem, it has lost someone in whom it had invested a great amount of money to train, whose salary was high, and whose responsibilities, judgment, and decision-making ability were important to the success of the organization. Business and management publications speak in circumspect tones about one of the most disastrous business mergers of all time, a merger that had been arranged by a high-level executive while intoxicated.

Executives at all levels are called on daily to make important decisions, and those persons who are under the influence of alcohol are no longer equipped to exercise decision-making skills. Usually, it is not the younger executive (whose responsibilities are not as great) who is prone to alcoholism. Rather, the National Council on Alcoholism has reported that the problem is greatest among executives between ages 35 and 50, their years of primary value to the company.

Alcoholic executives, more than factory workers, are adept at concealing their problem for a longer period of time. They work in an environment in which drinking is an accepted and sometimes necessary part of the workday. Many private offices have their own bars, and it is not unusual for executives to have a drink or two with lunch.

Another aid to drinking executives are secretaries, who are often willing and able to cover up for executives' indispositions. Thus, with no one observing executives (in the way in which production workers are always visible to superiors) and with secretaries to make excuses for them, alcoholic executives are able to escape detection longer than their counterparts on the assembly line.

There is one final comfort for executives who drink: They are not as likely to be fired as are factory workers. The alcoholic executives' chances of being ignored or given a make-work job are much greater; although management has finally recognized the problem of alcoholism on the factory floor, it is somewhat reluctant to admit that it exists in the neighboring executive office.

Rehabilitation of Alcoholics in Industry

Alcoholics can be rehabilitated and, fortunately, industry's interest in helping its drinking employees has increased in recent years. More than 3,000 American corporations and federal government agencies sponsor formal alcoholic rehabilitation programs; more companies join this list every year. Concerned firms include Allis-Chalmers, DuPont, Eastman Kodak, Consolidated Edison, Stroh Brewing Company, New York Times Company, and the Kemper Insurance Group. About half of the largest companies in the United States have such programs.

Commonly referred to as employee assistance programs (EAPs), these rehabilitation efforts have been shown to return as much as $20 for every dollar invested in them. The return is in terms of higher productivity, reduced absenteeism, and less frequent use of company-provided health care services. One company reported a 48% drop in its hospital, medical, and surgical costs after establishing an EAP. General Motors found that over a 2-year period, two alcoholic employees had cost the organization in excess of a quarter of a million dollars in medical expenses. Recovery rates for alcoholic employees under EAPs average 50% (Quayle, 1983).

There are other benefits from EAPs. Kimberly-Clark found that after one year, its alcohol program had reduced absenteeism by 43% and cut accidents by 70%. Kennecott Copper was able to reduce absenteeism by 53% and cut sickness and accident costs by 75% as a result of its alcohol treatment program ("Wellness," 1982).

There is some feeling of corporate humanitarian responsibility to help alcoholic employees, but the major reason for the interest in rehabilitation is pragmatic: By rehabilitating rather than firing alcoholic employees, a company saves money in the long run. The president of one major corporation said: "The most expensive way to handle alcoholic employees is to fire or ignore them, and the most profitable and effective way to handle them is to help them to recover."

It is interesting that employers may be able to offer a much greater motivation for alcoholics to seek help than can families or friends—that is, their job (see Figure 12-3). Many psychologists and physicians who work with alcoholics agree that the fear of losing their jobs may carry more weight with alcoholic workers than any cajoling or threatening from spouses or even the danger of an early death. To alcoholics, keeping the job may be the last defense against admitting that they have a problem. When that defense is jeopardized, the motivation to seek or accept help is usually great.

How do rehabilitation programs in industry work? Most of them seem to follow the three-step process suggested by the National Council on Alcoholism.

Helping an employee
kick an alcohol or drug habit.

That's a Bethlehem commitment.
And we're succeeding.

What do you do with employees who have a drinking or drug problem? Fire them?

Here at Bethlehem we have a better solution. Better for them, better for us. Sixteen years ago our medical people developed an alcoholism program built on rehabilitation. Eleven years ago a similar program for drug abuse was begun. Each employee with a drinking or drug problem is urged to seek help through one of these programs.

Some cases are, of course, difficult. Some people simply cannot hold a job. But thanks to the understanding, care and professional assistance made available to them, several thousand of our employees have made dramatic progress toward recovery.

A self-serving corporate program? Yes. But every employee returned to a more productive life at work also returns to a more productive life at home and in his or her community. And that serves society.

Bethlehem
Bethlehem Steel Corp., Bethlehem, PA 18016

Figure 12-3 One company's commitment to employee rehabilitation. (Reproduced by permission of Bethlehem Steel Corp.)

1. *Education of managers and supervisors.* The purpose is to convince these leaders that alcoholism is not a moral or ethical issue but rather a medical problem—an illness or disease that can be cured.
2. *Early detection of alcoholic workers.* Supervisors should be instructed about what symptoms and behavioral and performance changes to look for. Early detection improves the chances of recovery.
3. *Referral of alcoholic employees for help.* Some companies use their own medical and psychological staff to treat alcoholics. Others send workers to outside, often live-in, clinics. Most organizations provide for treatment on company time and continue the workers' salaries while they are undergoing treatment.

A very useful method of treatment involves other employees who are members of Alcoholics Anonymous. This organization is extremely effective in dealing with the problems of alcoholism because its members have all experienced the illness and know all too well what it is like.

There is some evidence (although it is not very strong at present) to suggest that reformed alcoholics are better workers. Their performance no longer suffers from their drinking, they may realize that this is their last chance, and, thus, they put forth extra effort. However, even if their job performance were not better than it was before rehabilitation, the company still has reclaimed trained and experienced workers who otherwise would have been lost to themselves and to the organization.

When 10% of a company's employees suffer from a disabling illness, someone must help. Whatever their motivation, it is refreshing to see industry assume this responsibility.

Drug Use in the Workplace

In the late 1960s, illicit drug use became a serious and visible problem, particularly among the nation's youth. In high schools and colleges as well as among the military, drug taking approached epidemic proportions. Estimates of high school and college students taking some drug ranged from 30% to 60%. It was inevitable that drug use would also become a problem at work. There was no reason to suspect that people who used drugs would suddenly stop when they graduated from school or got out of the army and found jobs. Therefore, seemingly overnight, industry found itself with a serious drug problem.

By 1971, the problem had become severe enough for the American Management Association to hold its first seminar on drug abuse and for management and labor to become alarmed. Although the number of drug addicts in the work force does not approach the number of alcoholics in industry, drug use on the job remains a serious problem that is likely to grow.

Marijuana is the principal drug used and may account for up to 90% of drug problems in the workplace. Amphetamines, barbiturates, heroin, and PCP are also used on the job as well as Quaaludes and prescription drugs such as tranquilizers. The National Institute on Drug Abuse reports that about a half million people use heroin, 5 million use cocaine regularly (and 24 million may have tried it once), and some 18-20 million use marijuana. The institute also estimates that about 30% of all college students will have tried cocaine by the time they graduate, and 42% will have smoked marijuana. The total number of regular drug users in the United States is estimated at 50 million. Some 20% of the work force is thought to abuse drugs at some time, though only a small number of these are addicts (Holman, Abbasi, & Murrey, 1987).

Drug use has been documented at all levels of business and industry from the assembly line to the highest corporate office. A survey of 1,090 human resource directors conducted by the American Management Association found that 93.5% of the companies reported dealing with some kind of drug abuse problem (Masi, 1987b). Users include the young and disadvantaged as well as the older, better educated, and affluent. People who use drugs at work can be found in conference rooms, hospitals, newsrooms, factories, and military bases. A nuclear power facility in California had employed security guards who were caught using drugs. The U.S. Navy discovered that two thirds of the crew of an aircraft carrier regularly used marijuana and amphetamines. An oil company found that workers on its offshore drilling platforms in the Gulf of Mexico were often under the influence of marijuana.

The cost of drug use to employers is approximately $26 billion a year, $16 billion of this in lost productivity. Drug users are one third less productive than nonusers, and they are three times more likely to be absent and to have accidents on the job. In addition, they use three times the normal level of sick benefits (Bensinger, 1982; Cowan, 1987).

In one sense, drug abuse may be a greater problem in industry than alcohol in terms of the disruptive effects on production and efficiency. Aside from the legal question, drug users are potentially more dangerous to an organization because they frequently attempt to hook others in the hope of selling them drugs to finance their own habit.

Effects of Drug Use on the Job

Behavioral effects vary with the kind of drug taken. Generally, the new user exhibits marked changes in behavior such as deterioration in attendance habits, work quality, personal hygiene, and manner of dress as well as flareups in temper, a tendency to borrow money, and the wearing of dark glasses. There is also likely to be impairment in judgment and reflexes, sluggishness of movement, dilation or contraction of the pupils of the eyes, bloodshot eyes, and, in extreme cases, needle marks on the arms or elsewhere.

Obviously, these behavioral changes influence on-the-job performance and efficiency. Also, depending on what there is to steal in the company, drug use can lead to an increase in thefts by workers who are trying to support an expensive drug habit. In short, drug users become marginal employees who are an administrative and economic burden to management and potentially harmful to the morale and safety of other employees. Particularly in hazardous occupations, drug users, like alcoholics, can be a menace to themselves, their co-workers, and the general public.

Thus, even those who have never used drugs may be put at risk. Workers on a construction site have the right to know that the crane operator who is dangling a load of steel over their heads is not smoking marijuana on the job. When we board a bus, train, or plane, we have the right to expect that our lives are not in danger because the operator's or pilot's judgment is impaired by drugs. Proponents of on-the-job drug screening suggest that this issue of public safety is the strongest argument in favor of mandatory drug testing (Finney, 1988).

Drug Testing and Organizational Policies

The chances that you will be tested for drug use when you next apply for a job are rapidly increasing. Some 28% of the largest corporations in the United States—including AT&T and General Motors—routinely screen job applicants for drug use, and that number is expected to climb sharply. Approximately 50% of the companies that recruit on college campuses now test for drug use as a condition of hiring, a figure 33% higher than the previous year (Isikoff, 1988; Reed, 1988).

Urine or blood testing for drug use is controversial, and a number of guidelines have been suggested to make it as fair as possible (Cowan, 1987; Murphy, Barlow, & Hatch, 1988b).

1. The organization should issue a statement to all employees describing its drug abuse policy and its procedures for testing.
2. If the employees belong to a union, the company's drug policies and procedures must be submitted to collective bargaining before being put into effect. Employers who refuse to bargain with the union about such matters are subject to charges of unfair labor practices.
3. The drug testing procedures should apply equally to all employees. No specific group should be singled out for testing.
4. No random or across-the-board testing of all current employees should be introduced. Current employees should be tested only in documented cases of job impairment or because there are other indications of probable cause. There must be a valid reason for suspecting drug use.
5. All employees should be informed in advance of drug testing procedures, including the drugs being screened for, the types of tests to be used, and the consequences of refusing to be tested.
6. All positive test results should be confirmed by a second, more accurate test. Drug tests may yield false positive results.
7. Drug test results should be kept strictly confidential.

A survey of 190 human resource directors found that employers are generally in favor of these guidelines. Also, they believe that drug abuse should be treated in the same way as alcoholism. Drug users should be given the opportunity for rehabilitation in a drug treatment program (Gomez-Mejia & Balkin, 1987).

As mentioned, drug testing is controversial for several reasons. First, it can be argued that such testing infringes on employees' rights of privacy and confidentiality, and security from unreasonable search and seizure, to the point where it may negatively affect morale. It can also damage employee trust and create a repressive work climate that dampens productivity (Vodanovich & Reyna, 1988).

Second, the validity of drug testing is an issue. The Centers for Disease Control report that gross drug screening can incorrectly indicate the presence of drugs in up to two thirds of the tests, particularly when inexpensive and relatively unsophisticated procedures are used. This means that a disturbingly large number of employees can falsely be labeled as drug users. You can see the importance of requiring a second, confirming test (Rosen, 1987).

The lack of accuracy can occur because of false readings, laboratory errors, and cheating on the part of employees. Other substances in the urine or blood sample can mistakenly indicate the presence of drugs. Poppy seeds, for example, can indicate the use of opiates. Marijuana can be falsely indicated by such popular medications as cough and cold products (Contac, for example), and painkillers (such as Advil and Nuprin).

Further, laboratory technicians can inadvertently mix up samples or make other careless errors. In 1984, the U.S. Army found that half the urine samples of a group of 60,000 soldiers had been so mishandled in the laboratory that none of the test results could be relied upon.

Employers and job applicants being tested for drug use may try to cheat the system by bringing in someone else's drug-free urine or by adding some adulterant such as laundry bleach to mask any trace of drugs. For this reason, most employers insist that employees urinate in the presence of an observer, a practice many find personally offensive.

For all of its problems, drug testing on the job is unlikely to be discontinued, but it is not the only method used by employers to manage drug use in the workplace. Organizations are reacting to drug problems in several ways in addition to testing.

Some companies have enlarged their security departments and use undercover agents to detect employee drug use. They are taking more care to screen job applicants for any indication of past drug use and are firing users immediately on detection. Many companies also engage in educational and rehabilitation programs.

The first step taken by many organizations is a simple and direct statement to employees and job applicants about their policy concerning drug use, drug testing, and the consequences of violating that policy. Table 12-5 contains the rules on drug use at the Duke Power Company in North Carolina (Wagel, 1986d). Employees know exactly what to expect from the company and what is expected of them in return. They know that the company stands ready to support and assist those who want to be treated for their drug problem, and they also know that their jobs are in jeopardy if they continue to use drugs.

The second step is careful screening of all job applicants. Personnel departments look attentively for gaps in employment history, less than honorable military discharges, and physical signs of drug addiction.

TABLE 12-5 Drug Policy Rules of Duke Power Company

When a drug screen is positive for the first time but no evidence of drug use on the job exists, an employee will be suspended without pay.

The employee must visit the employee assistance program [EAP] at least once to learn what drug counseling resources are available.

The employee will be required to seek treatment for drug abuse from a recognized professional and/or institution. Refusal to do so will be viewed as insubordination, and the employee will be subject to discharge.

The employee must have a negative test result in a screen administered by the company within a period of six weeks from the date of suspension; otherwise, the employee will be discharged. If the employee has a negative result within the six-week period but cannot return to work for good reason (such as participation in a treatment program), the suspension period will be extended. After the employee returns to work, random drug screening will be conducted for an indefinite period of time.

If a physical examination is not required for a job and/or public and employee safety is not a factor, an employee will be allowed to return to work upon receipt by the company of a negative test result.

If a physical examination is required for a job and/or public and employee safety is a factor, an employee will be allowed to return to work only upon providing to the EAP certified documentation from a recognized professional indicating that the professional has a reasonable degree of confidence that the employee is capable of performing his or her assigned job duties without impairment.

Employees who have been suspended for a positive drug test and allowed to return to work will be discharged for a positive result on any subsequent drug screen.

From "A positive approach to alcohol and drug abuse" by W. H. Wagel, 1986, *Personnel*, 63(12), p. 9.

The third and most difficult step is to detect current employees who are using and selling drugs. One large firm hired an ex-addict to work in various parts of the plant, where he spotted drug users and eventually broke the drug ring. A telephone company hired private detectives who posed as employees and uncovered a drug ring operating out of a rest room. Some companies such as Shell Oil, Exxon, and Rockwell International have used drug-sniffing dogs in factories and offices. The dogs can also detect the presence of drugs in employees' cars in the company parking lot ("Dogging Drugs," 1988).

Most companies differentiate between occasional users of soft drugs or addicts and pushers of hard drugs. If occasional users have a good performance record and if they agree to undergo treatment, many companies will arrange for medical help and even pay for it. If users refuse help, they are usually fired. Some companies have established their own treatment facilities, but most rely on outside rehabilitation centers. Many firms, however, still fire even the occasional drug user and would not knowingly hire such a person. Drug pushers are arrested as quickly as plant security personnel can identify them and call the local police.

Organizations are also making efforts to rehabilitate employees through EAPs. General Motors established a substance-abuse program at 130 of its plants.

Every year, some 10,000 GM employees are treated for drug problems and the results have been encouraging. Employees who were treated showed a 40% reduction in lost time, a 50% reduction in accidents on the job, and a 60% reduction in sickness and accident benefits. Other companies report equally dramatic results. Phillips Petroleum claims that its EAP saved over $8 million a year owing to fewer accidents, less sick leave, and greater productivity. EAPs claim a success rate of 60% to 80% among drug users, with success defined as remaining drug free with satisfactory job performance for 1 year after treatment. After a person has lost his or her job, the recovery rate for drug abuse drops to only 5%, a clear indication of the importance of detecting and treating a drug problem while the person is still employed (Cowan, 1987).

Computers and Employee Health

We saw in Chapter 11 that employees who work with computers report a high incidence of low back pain, fatigue, and visual complaints. Further, we noted that these problems could be ameliorated by changing certain design and illumination features of the workplace. There may be additional health problems associated with working at VDTs and with manufacturing computer chips that may not be capable of being corrected by human engineering or other design modifications.

Some psychologists suggest that working where computer chips are manufactured causes health problems ranging from headaches to miscarriages. One study showed that women working in computer chip assembly rooms had twice as many miscarriages as expected on the basis of chance. The sample was small, however, and the evidence must be considered inconclusive (Pollack, 1988).

Such work is potentially dangerous because it involves a variety of chemicals including arsenic, cyanide, acids, and noxious solvents. Some workers claim that exposure to these chemicals causes painful headaches and loss of concentration, and many experts are concerned about the long-term health effects. Research to date neither confirms nor refutes these charges. Nevertheless, companies such as AT&T have transferred pregnant women employees out of computer chip work areas to other jobs. Other organizations have informed their workers of the potential hazards of such work and have offered them the option of undertaking other kinds of jobs.

Potential health problems associated with VDT work include angina pain, miscarriages, and birth defects. One study of 278 telephone operators working at video screens found that nearly 15% of them suffered symptoms of angina. This was twice the rate of employees who did not work with VDTs (Brooks, 1986).

Also of concern are studies showing a higher rate of miscarriages among women who work more than 20 hours per week with VDTs, compared to women doing other kinds of office work. Animal research has demonstrated that the low frequency, pulsed, electromagnetic radiation emitted by VDTs causes miscarriages and birth defects. The evidence with humans, however, is sketchy. In one study of 1,538 pregnant women, those who worked with VDTs had almost twice as many miscarriages as other office workers (Altman, 1988; Rieland, 1988).

Some health experts suggest that the source of the problem is the stressful assembly-line type of atmosphere in which VDT operators function, rather than the radiation emitted by the screens. In the study of pregnant women previously cited, the clerical workers had a much higher miscarriage rate than the managerial and professional women who spent the same amount of time at computers. The researcher suggested that the work of the managerial and professional women was less stressful and more satisfying (Lewin, 1988). Other research involving pregnant VDT operators in Finland and in Canada found no evidence of increased risk of either miscarriages or birth defects from working with computers (Marriott & Stuchly, 1986; McDonald, Cherry, Delorme, & McDonald, 1986).

Until the issue is resolved, it has raised the problem of potential discrimination that we alluded to earlier with computer chip work. Some companies are following a practice called protective exclusion, that is, they are excluding women of childbearing age from working with computers out of fear of lawsuits should it be shown that working with VDTs does, indeed, cause miscarriages. In some companies, women job applicants are asked to give urine samples and are not being informed that the urine is being tested not for drug use but for pregnancy. When pregnant women are then not hired on this basis, the policy is a form of sex discrimination.

VDTs emit other forms of radiation including X rays and infrared, magnetic, and electrostatic fields, the long-term effects of which have not been determined. We have seen throughout this book that computers have redefined the nature and conditions of work for millions of employees. Research is necessary now to learn whether computer use is also adversely affecting employee health.

AIDS in the Workplace

AIDS (acquired immunodeficiency syndrome) has reached epidemic proportions in the United States and other countries. This fatal disease is spread through intimate sexual contact, direct contamination with infected body fluids, and infected hypodermic needles used for drug injections. The Centers for Disease Control estimate that between 1 and 1.5 million Americans already carry the AIDS virus and that some 250,000 more cases will be diagnosed by the early 1990s. With the number of AIDS patients doubling every 12 to 15 months, more and more employees with AIDS are to be found in the workplace (Franklin & Robinson, 1988; Levine, 1986a; Puckett, 1988).

You may wonder why AIDS should be considered an employee problem. It is not an illness caused by the conditions of work, yet it can have a profound effect on job performance, not only on the productivity of the person afflicted by the disease, but also on the morale of his or her co-workers. The presence, or even the suspicion, of AIDS on the job has engendered a high level of panic and fear, usually based on ignorance, within an organization (Rowe, Russell-Einhorn, & Baker, 1986).

At New England Bell, a group of 30 terrified employees walked off their jobs when they learned that one of their co-workers had AIDS. This type of reaction has also occurred in other organizations, and it has been known to turn to anger. Employees have branded people with AIDS as homosexuals or drug users and have physically harassed them. A survey of employees in 72 companies found that fear was named by 40% of the respondents as the biggest problem caused by AIDS in the workplace (Magnus, 1988a).

Another problem confronting both organizations and employees is the greatly increased cost of health insurance. AIDS is the first epidemic to occur since employer-paid health insurance became a standard fringe benefit of most jobs. Such insurance, already expensive, will become even more so because the cost of treating AIDS patients runs into billions of dollars. At present, insurers are prohibited by law from excluding AIDS coverage in their policies.

Employers, like insurance companies, cannot discriminate against people with AIDS, either in hiring or in retaining them. The U.S. Supreme Court ruled that AIDS patients cannot be fired because of fear of contagion. The Centers for Disease Control have concluded that AIDS cannot be spread through casual contact in the workplace and that people with AIDS do not present a danger to their co-workers.

Industry leaders are slowly becoming aware of the impact of AIDS on the job. A survey of 600 senior human resource directors conducted in 1987 showed that 64% of them were concerned about the problem, but that 89% had not formulated policies for dealing with employees who have AIDS (Masi, 1987a). A poll of 332 industrial relations executives revealed that only 10% of them had specific policies concerning AIDS but that 27% had already been forced to deal with employees who either had AIDS or were suspected of having the disease ("AIDS #1 Workplace Issue," 1988). Industries expected to be most affected by AIDS include health care, pharmaceuticals, broadcasting and communications, and food services (Backer, 1988).

Companies are tackling the problem in different ways. First, they are beginning to educate their employees to reduce potential fear and panic, something that should be done before the first case of AIDS appears in their plant or office. Bank of America provides AIDS information in its regular employee newsletter. Pacific Bell Telephone provides educational videotapes to workers. Wells Fargo Bank sponsors informal brown-bag lunches with medical experts (Puckett, 1988). Such company-sponsored educational programs might have the additional benefit of inducing employees to modify their behavior in ways that will reduce their risk of contracting AIDS.

Managers should be taught about the disease and how it is—and is not—transmitted so that they will be prepared if an AIDS-related crisis develops on the job.

A few organizations are screening job applicants for AIDS through blood testing to detect the presence of antibodies to the AIDS virus. In one survey of 995 human resources managers, 6% indicated that their organizations offer the test to job applicants and to current employees on a voluntary basis. Only one fifth of these organizations have made the test mandatory, and even fewer refuse to hire applicants whose test results are positive (Lutgen, 1987).

Most of the organizations that offer testing are health care providers such as hospitals, clinics, and laboratories. To date, few American companies require AIDS testing as a condition of employment, but a number of British companies, including British Airways and Texaco, use the test for screening even though it is subject to inaccuracies (Aikin, 1988).

With neither a vaccine nor a cure yet available for AIDS, it is likely to become increasingly prevalent throughout all levels of employment, making it a major health, social, and economic issue of the 1990s.

Summary

Accidents on the job result in approximately 14,000 deaths and as many as 25 million injuries every year. In addition, workers may be subject to disease contracted on the job such as pneumoconiosis or black lung disease, byssinosis or brown lung disease, and many forms of cancer. To try to counteract industrial accidents and disease, the U.S. Congress passed the Occupational Safety and Health Act, which has established, and tries to enforce, industrial safety standards. If we add those killed in household and automobile accidents to those killed on the job, the accident toll rises to over 100,000 victims a year.

One problem with accident research is that many employing organizations distort their **accident data** through incomplete recording in an effort to keep safety records intact.

There are several causes of accidents; some relate to the physical environment in which work takes place and others to workers' personal characteristics.

Aspects of the **work environment** that affect accident rates include type of industry (industries such as mining, construction, and lumber are more dangerous than others); temporal working conditions (although the total number of hours worked is not related to accidents, when the work is performed is important); lighting (poor lighting seems to be associated with a higher accident rate); temperature (accidents increase when temperatures rise above 70°F or fall below 68°F); and equipment design (the absence of built-in safety devices and poor design of machinery can increase accidents).

The **personal factors** in accidents that have been studied include alcohol and drug use; cognitive abilities (there seems to be no relationship between intelligence and accident rate); physical condition and health (both factors, particularly poor vision, contribute to accidents); fatigue (fatigue is closely related to accident rate); work experience and age (although there are complicating variables, older workers with more job experience generally have fewer accidents than younger workers who are new to the job); personality characteristics (although accidents seem to vary as a function of a person's temporary emotional state, they do not seem to be strongly related to general personality patterns). The concept of **accident proneness**—that some people are more likely to have accidents than others—is a popular notion, but one that enjoys little experimental support.

An organization can take a number of steps to try to **prevent accidents** from occurring: (1) complete reporting and analysis of all accidents—each accident must be investigated thoroughly and reported in detail so that comparative accident data can be studied; (2) proper design of the work and its environment —work areas must be well lighted, clean, and orderly; machinery must be well maintained and designed to be compatible with the capabilities of the workers; safety devices must not interfere with production and must be designed so that machinery will not operate unless they are in place; (3) provision of the proper organizational climate, particularly strong management support of safety and the employees' perception of the importance and effectiveness of safety training; (4) training for accident prevention—workers and supervisors must be trained not only in specific job skills but also in attitudes toward safety; (5) safety publicity campaigns and safety contests, particularly if they are based on competition, incentives, and feedback.

Alcoholism in industry affects more than 10% of the work force and is responsible for tardiness, absenteeism, increased errors, inefficiency, and much human misery. Although alcoholism is a problem among all levels of employee, it is particularly costly to organizations when it occurs among executives. Industrial and government employers try to help alcoholic workers through **employee assistance programs** (EAPS), education of managers, and early detection of alcoholics.

Drug use in industry, although not as serious a problem as alcoholism, is increasing. Drug use occurs in all segments and levels of the work force and may affect 3% to 7% of all employees. Employing organizations are beginning to institute rehabilitation programs, but many drug users are fired and drug pushers are arrested. In general, industry treats drug users more severely than it treats alcoholics. Employee **drug testing** is growing, though the tests may not always be accurate and may violate employees' rights to privacy.

Effects on employee health of prolonged computer use include possible risks of miscarriage among pregnant workers in computer chip assembly and VDT operations. Evidence is inconclusive but some organizations have banned women from these jobs, an action that may be considered discriminatory.

AIDS in the workplace can affect productivity and morale; co-workers may react to an employee with AIDS with fear and panic due to ignorance. Employers are beginning to educate workers about AIDS and how it can and cannot be spread. A few companies are screening job applicants for the AIDS virus.

Key Terms	accident proneness AIDS	alcoholism drug testing	employee assistance programs (EAPs) self-selection

CASE STUDIES

Paying for Safe Performance

In 1985, the James River Graphics Company of Massachusetts established a safety program to try to reduce the high incidence of on-the-job accidents. Most of the employees became involved in the effort, which was named STOP (Safety Training Observation Program). A company-wide safety committee was organized to train employees to be aware of unsafe acts and to report all safety violations. The incentive for developing and maintaining safe working practices was a financial one; the fewer the accidents, the higher the workers' wages.

The present profit-sharing plan distributed 3% of the company's annual pretax profits to the workers. Under the new STOP program, when the company met its annual safety goal, an additional percentage of the profits would be distributed to the workers. In addition, monthly safety contests were held in each department. After each month without a lost-time accident, employees in that department became eligible for a drawing. The prize was dinner for two at a local restaurant. The contests generated considerable employee enthu-

siasm, and management reported a positive impact on morale.

Safety committee meetings are held regularly, along with periodic audits of safe and unsafe work practices. Attendance at the safety committee meetings is voluntary, but interest in the STOP program is so strong that 90% of all employees attend. The accident rate fell 30% during the program's first year.

QUESTIONS

1. What other behavior modification techniques can be used to lower the company's accident rate?
2. Do you think this program will be as effective five years from now? Why or why not?
3. How do the design of a working environment and the organizational climate affect accident rates?
4. How do the personal factors of intelligence, age, fatigue, and personality influence accident rates?

Reference: W. H. Wagel. (1986). The safe way to quality. *Personnel, 63*(8), 4-6.

Effects on Accidents of Time on the Job

Data were collected on more than 35,000 accidents that led to hospitalization among U.S. Navy shore-based enlisted personnel over a 7-year period. No injuries that were self-inflicted or the result of combat or assault were included. Up to 35% of the accidents occurred during a sailor's first month in a new job assignment. After the initial month, the accident rate dropped sharply and continued to decline as time on the job increased.

Off-duty accident rates among shore-based personnel followed the same pattern, with most accidents occurring during the first month in a new duty station. Accidents attributable to athletics, falls, motorcycles, auto-

mobiles, and other machinery occurred far more frequently among off-duty shore-based personnel than among off-duty sea-based personnel (presumably because the latter had fewer opportunities at sea to ride motorcycles or drive cars).

In general, accident rates for sailors serving aboard ship did not parallel the accident rates for shore-based personnel in a new assignment but remained low even during the first month in a new job. Accident rates were lowest for higher ranking personnel, supporting other research findings that accidents decrease with job seniority.

QUESTIONS

1. What steps can the U.S. Navy take to reduce the high number of accidents that occur during the first month in a new duty assignment?
2. Describe the relationship between personality and accidents.
3. What kinds of lapses in cognitive functioning have been shown to be related to pilot errors?

4. Why do so many accidents in the workplace go unreported?

Reference: J. C. Helmkamp & C. M. Bone. (1987). The effect of time in a new job on hospitalization rates for accidents and injuries in the U.S. Navy, 1977–1983. *Journal of Occupational Medicine, 29*, 653–659.

Additional Reading

Pelletier, K. R. (1984). *Healthy People in Unhealthy Places*. New York: Delacorte. Discusses environmental health threats to people who work in offices, factories, shipyards, oil refineries, and mines, and in jobs that require exposure to engine exhaust such as taxi, bus, and truck drivers as well as auto mechanics.

Psychology and AIDS. (1988). *American Psychologist* [special issue], *43*(11). Deals with public health, scientific, counseling, and educational considerations of AIDS. Includes an article on managing AIDS at work.

Rosen, T. H. (1987). Identification of substance abusers in the workplace. *Public Personnel Management, 16*(3), 197–207. Reviews the impact of substance abuse on on-the-job injuries and productivity. Describes the issues involved in implementing a urinalysis drug testing program.

Scanlon, W. E. (1986). *Alcoholism and Drug Abuse in the Workplace: Employee Assistance Programs*. New York: Praeger. Describes and evaluates the role of employee assistance programs (EAPS) in industry and the corporate responsibility for providing appropriate treatment opportunities.

Chapter 13

Stress in the Workplace

Introduction

We have mentioned several ways in which work can be harmful to your health. Accidents on the job and exposure to noxious chemicals in factories and sealed office buildings account for thousands of injuries and deaths every year. There is a more subtle and serious danger to be found in most workplaces. It affects workers by the millions, but it does so in silent, invisible ways. Whereas accidents and hazardous chemicals are physical agents that affect health and productivity, stress is a psychological agent that affects our well-being and our ability to perform on the job.

I/O psychologists have focused their attention on the causes and effects of stress in the workplace for two reasons. First, there is a general awareness that stress-related diseases are widespread among the American population. More people are disabled today as a result of stress than at any other time in our history. It is estimated that some 25% of all Americans are experiencing severe stress. As many as half of all visits to physicians are the result of stress and a major portion of all physical disease may be *psychosomatic*, that is, actual physical disorders caused by or related to emotional factors such as stress.

A nationwide survey conducted by Blue Cross/Blue Shield indicated that 5 out of every 6 workers questioned said that stress was a major factor in their work. They related stress to job dissatisfaction and low self-esteem. A survey conducted by Nine to Five, the National Association of Working Women, revealed that 33% of women employed outside the home described their jobs as very stressful, and 62% said their jobs were somewhat stressful. Only 5% of those questioned said that their jobs were not stressful (Pelletier, 1984).

Equally alarming is the number and variety of physical problems associated with stress: gastrointestinal disorders such as ulcers and colitis, coronary heart disease, arthritis, skin diseases, allergies, headaches, neck and lower back pain, and even some cancers.

A second reason why psychologists are concerned about stress in the workplace is a practical one. Stress on the job is costly and is reflected in a lower productive efficiency in the organization. Stress has been shown to reduce employee motivation and the physical ability to perform a task well. This may result in lower production levels and increased errors and accidents.

In addition, stress contributes to increased health care costs. The estimated health care expenditures for two stress-related diseases—coronary heart disease and ulcers—approximate $45 billion a year. Stress may be more costly for companies than accidents. For every worker killed in a job-related accident, at least 50 suffer some form of heart disease. A study of more than 960,000 workers in the United States and Sweden found that those in high-stress jobs had a rate of heart disease four times higher than those in low-stress jobs (Tierney, 1988).

The cost of all stress-related disorders is now about $150 billion a year, including medical costs, absenteeism, and lost productivity (Landers, 1987). Also, stress-related workers' compensation claims accounted for 14% of all occupational disease claims in 1987, up from less than 5% in 1986 ("Stress on the Job," 1988).

In addition, we cannot estimate the effects on co-workers and subordinates of an employee or supervisor whose behavior has changed because of stress. One person under stress can be a cause of stress in others.

At one time, it was thought that such disorders were medical problems, physical in origin, and that there was little psychologists could do about them. Now, however, they are seen as psychological problems, arising from the physical, social, and psychological conditions of work. They are legitimate concerns for psychologists involved in the world of work. Dealing with stress on the job is yet another way in which psychologists assist both employees and employers by improving the quality of life and work for both sides.

The federal government has provided an added impetus for I/O psychologists to concern themselves with problems of stress. The Occupational Safety and Health Act of 1970, which created the Occupational Safety and Health Administration (OSHA) and the National Institute for Occupational Safety and Health (NIOSH), contains a mandate for psychologists. It directs that research be conducted on those factors in the work environment that can cause stress.

In Chapter 10, we mentioned standards for the physical conditions of work, for example, optimum light, noise, and temperature levels. Perhaps, in the not-too-distant future, we shall also be able to develop standards for optimum psychological conditions of work to reduce stress on the job. Indeed, Norway and Sweden already have standards for tolerable levels of stress at work.

It should be noted that the effects of stress on the individual are difficult to measure objectively, which makes the setting of such standards imprecise. Despite the obvious physiological changes that accompany stress (described later), the relationship between self-reported stress and biochemical measurements is weak (Steffy & Jones, 1988). The usual way to measure job stress is through self-report inventories. Two widely used questionnaires are the Human Factors Inventory, a 162-item scale surveying organizational climate, and the Work Environment Scale, a 90-item instrument assessing organizational stressors (Jones & DuBois, 1987; Moos, 1981). Both scales have shown moderate to high levels of validity and reliability.

It is unlikely that in the course of your career you will be able to avoid the consequences of stress. No matter what you do, where you work, or at what level you function, stress may be an ever-present accompaniment of your work life. Obviously, it is in your best interests—and your organization's—to understand the nature of stress and the ways of minimizing its effects.

The Nature of Stress

You have, of course, experienced stress many times in your life. Some students have stress every time they take an examination. We experience stress when an automobile runs through a stop sign and almost hits us or when a sinister figure runs after us down a dark street. We well know the feeling when something like that happens; we feel anxious, tense, and fearful.

Inside the body, dramatic physiological changes take place under stress. Adrenalin, released from the adrenal glands, speeds up all bodily functions. Blood pressure rises, heart rate increases, and extra sugar is released into the bloodstream. The increased circulation of the blood brings additional energy to the brain and muscles, making us more alert and stronger so that we can cope with the sudden emergency—such as fleeing the speeding car or the attacker.

A stressful situation, then, mobilizes and directs our energy, boosting it far beyond its normal level. If we remain in such a state of supercharged energy for too long, we shall reduce the body's reservoir of energy. We need to rest so that the energy supply can be replenished.

Thus, as we get older, the amount of energy we can draw on steadily diminishes. The more stresses we face in life, the more quickly our energy supply diminishes.

Most of us rarely encounter extreme emergency situations such as being attacked by a mugger; few jobs expose people to physical threats such as those faced by police or fire-fighting personnel. For the majority of employees, the stresses we face on the job are psychological in nature—an argument with the boss or a colleague, the feeling that we have been treated unfairly, worry about the next promotion or pay raise, or simply not finding a parking place in the morning. These constitute what we commonly call the minor hassles or little insults of everyday life on the job (Lazarus, 1981).

These are low-level sources of strain and tension individually, but they, nonetheless, produce wear and tear on the body because they accumulate. Each stress adds to the previous one and may serve to tax the body's reserves of energy because each low-level stress produces the physiological changes mentioned earlier. If sources of tension are present frequently in a person's workplace, his or her heart and circulatory rates will remain at high levels and extra adrenalin will constantly be coursing through the bloodstream. In time, the body may suffer physiological damage and the person may become ill.

This is how prolonged stress leads to the psychosomatic disorders listed earlier. Remember that psychosomatic diseases are not imaginary. They are real and involve specific tissue and organ damage. Although their cause is psychological, they themselves cause actual damage to the body. In addition to organic damage, the demands on the body's energy reserves may make the person more vulnerable to infection. Further, the illness brought about by prolonged stress can itself serve as a new source of stress, establishing a vicious circle. And, when physical health is affected, resistance lowered, and bodily energy reduced, it is obvious that motivation and job performance will suffer as well.

It is important to note that not all employees are affected by stress in the same way. Consider the work of air traffic controllers who are generally considered to have one of the most stressful jobs. Hour after hour they must exercise constant vigilance, keeping track of scores of aircraft at various speeds and altitudes, all converging on or leaving from the same place. This is hectic, frantic work, difficult and demanding, and with the additional burden of the responsibility for hundreds of lives every minute of the workday.

The bodies of these employees reflect the pressures of their job. As the air corridors in their sector become more crowded, arteries constrict and blood pressure jumps as much as 50%. The incidence of hypertension among air traffic controllers is as much as three times higher than normal for people of that age.

Here we seem to have a classic case of the deadly effects of stress. The rate of heart attacks, strokes, and other stress-related diseases surely must be many times higher than that for the rest of the population. But research indicates that this is not the case. On some measures, air traffic controllers are healthier, on the average, than the general population. Although some show the pattern of disease and the early death we would expect in such a high-stress occupation, others are quite healthy.

What makes the difference? Why do some remain well and others die young? Why does not the stress of the job affect them all in the same way? The difference lies in the degree of job satisfaction the controllers get from their work. Those who are very satisfied with their job do not suffer the harmful effects of stress; those who are dissatisfied with their job do show the effects.

Consider another high-stress position, that of the corporation executive. It is generally believed that executives have a great deal of stress at work and, consequently, have a much higher rate of heart attacks than the general population. This, too, is not true. High-level executives have 40% fewer heart attacks than middle-level managers, people who are assumed to work under less stressful conditions (Pelletier, 1984).

The reason why top executives are relatively less affected by the stresses of their job apparently has to do with the degree of autonomy and power that they have over their work. Middle managers, in contrast, have less autonomy and power. Thus, although they may be subject to less stress than top managers, they suffer more harmful stress effects. Other research has shown that being able to control events in the work environment reduces the amount of job stress reported (Hall & Savery, 1986; Tetrick & LaRocco, 1987).

What these findings mean is that if we are properly to examine the causes of stress on the job, we must include certain individual factors that can render an employee more or less vulnerable to stress. Not all stresses at work affect people in the same way. A type of stress that ruins the health of one worker may exert no noticeable effect on a co-worker at the next desk or the next machine.

Individual Differences in Vulnerability to Stress

We have already mentioned two factors that can reduce the effects of stress on the job: high *job satisfaction* and high *autonomy* and power. With regard to job satisfaction, we noted in Chapter 1 that the single greatest predictor of longevity was job satisfaction. Someone who is dissatisfied with his or her job may become ill from the stress, whereas someone else in the same job whose job satisfaction is high may show no effects of stress.

Another factor that affects vulnerability to stress on the job is *social support*, one's network of social and family ties. The person who is alone physically or psychologically (for example, emotionally alienated from others) is more vulnerable to stress than someone who has strong social relationships. Social support comes from two sources: the job and the family. Support from the family can reduce the effects of job dissatisfaction by providing other satisfactions and accomplishments outside the work situation. These can compensate for negative feelings about one's work and provide self-esteem, acceptance, and worthiness. Social support on the job also ameliorates the effects of stress. Studies have shown that the cohesion of the work group and the degree of liking for one's supervisor correlate highly with reduced stress and better health (Seers, McGee, Serey, & Graen, 1983).

One's *physical condition* also relates to one's vulnerability to stress effects. Persons in better physical condition suffer fewer effects of stress than those in poor physical condition. One effective way to combat stress is through exercise to improve physical condition.

Level of *ability* to perform a job can make people more or less resistant to the stresses of that job. Employees with a high level of the skills needed for the job usually find the work easier and less stressful than employees with a lower level of ability. You have no doubt noticed this with your classmates. Students who are barely able to keep up in a course are, as a rule, much more anxious and tense about a forthcoming examination than are those who are brighter and have less difficulty learning the material.

Personality seems to be related to one's ability to tolerate stress. This is particularly apparent with the so-called *Type A* and *Type B* personalities and what was thought to be their differential susceptibility to heart disease, one of the major effects of stress (Friedman & Rosenman, 1974). Although certain physical factors may cause heart disease (smoking, obesity, and lack of exercise, among others), these may account for no more than 25% of the cases. The rest are thought to be caused by stress related to a specific personality pattern. Persons with one type of personality almost never have heart attacks before the age of 70, regardless of their job or their eating and smoking habits. This is the Type B personality.

Early research suggested that the Type A personality is highly prone to heart disease by middle age, independent of physical factors and their type of work. The two primary characteristics of the Type A personality are a very high *competitive drive* and a constant sense of *urgency about time*. These persons are intensely ambitious and aggressive, always working to achieve something, racing against the clock, rushing from one self-imposed deadline to the next, always in a hurry. When they set out to accomplish something, it must be done immediately; tomorrow is too late. Type A personalities are hostile people, although they successfully hide it from others. They express their hostility and aggressiveness primarily by competing with others, particularly on the job, and also in other spheres of life. They are impatient with other people and quick to anger if they think others are working too slowly.

As a result of these characteristics, Type A people are always in a state of tension and stress. Even when their work is relatively free of sources of stress, they bring their own stress with them as a fundamental part of their personality. Stress, therefore, is always present at work or at leisure. It is no surprise that they may be so prone to heart attacks.

Type B people may be just as ambitious as Type A people, but they have none of their other characteristics. They function under far less stress in all aspects of life including work. Thus, these people can work just as hard as Type A people, in equally stressful environments, and seem to suffer fewer (or none) of the harmful effects of stress. Some typical Type A behaviors are shown in Table 13-1.

These two distinct personality types react in different ways to prolonged stress over which they have no control. At first, Type A's will struggle to try to master the situation; if they are not successful, they give up in frustration. Type B's in a similar situation will try to function as effectively as possible given the circumstances, but they do not give up as Type A's do (Matthews, 1982).

The research we have described showing a clear link between Type A behavior and heart disease was conducted primarily in the 1960s and 1970s. Some later research has failed to confirm that relationship. One extensive study,

---

TABLE 13-1   Are You a Type A Person?

Do you

_____   always do everything very rapidly? *Type A people eat, move, walk, and talk at a brisk pace. They speak with emphasis on certain words, and the ends of their sentences are spoken much faster than the beginnings.*

_____   become extremely impatient with the speed at which things are accomplished? *Type A people continually say "yes, yes" or "uh-huh" to whoever is talking to them, and even finish other persons' sentences for them. They become outraged by a slow car ahead of them or a slow-moving line in a restaurant or theater. When they read, they skim the material quickly and prefer summaries or condensations of books.*

_____   always think about or try to do two or more things at the same time? *For example, Type A people may think about one thing while talking to someone about something else, or they may try to eat and drive at the same time, in an effort to get more accomplished in a given period of time.*

_____   feel guilty when you are on vacation or trying to relax for a few hours?

_____   fail to be aware of interesting or beautiful things? *Type A people do not notice a lovely sunset or the new flowers of spring. If asked, they cannot recall the furnishings or details of an office or home they just visited.*

_____   always try to schedule more events and activities than you can properly attend to? *This is another manifestation of the sense of time urgency Type A people feel.*

_____   have nervous gestures or tics such as clenching your fists or banging on a desk to emphasize a point you are making? *These gestures point to the continuing tension at the root of the Type A personality.*

_____   consistently evaluate your worth in quantitative terms? *For Type A persons, numbers alone define their sense of accomplishment and importance. Type A executives boast about their salary or their company's profits, Type A surgeons tell how many operations they have performed, and Type A students report how many A's they have received in school. These people focus on the quantitative rather than the qualitative aspects of life.*

From *Psychology in Use* (p. 148) by D. P. Schultz, 1979, New York: Macmillan.

---

a 9-year investigation of 12,000 middle-aged men, found that Type A behavior was not significantly associated with the risk of heart disease. However, there have been substantial criticisms of the method of interviewing subjects in that study and the subsequent classification of the subjects into Type A and Type B personalities (Fischman, 1987c; Machlowitz, 1987a).

The relationship between Type A behavior and coronary heart disease, once thought to be so clear, is now not so straightforward, although few psychologists have gone so far as to claim that there is absolutely no relationship between the two variables. Research is continuing in an effort to determine what aspects of the Type A personality (and of personality in general) may be related to heart disease.

A meta-analysis of 87 studies found a modest relationship between Type A behavior and heart disease, and a stronger relationship between heart disease and anger, hostility, and depression. The authors of the study concluded that the coronary-prone personality "does not appear to be that of the workaholic, harried, impatient individual," but rather "a person with one or more negative emotions: perhaps someone who is depressed, aggressively competitive, easily frustrated, anxious, angry, or some combination" (Booth-Kewley & Friedman, 1987, p. 358).

Thus, the relationship between heart disease and personality factors remains intact, but it may include psychological attributes in addition to those originally associated with Type A behavior. Other analyses have linked a sense of time urgency, and anger and hostility (two major components of Type A behavior), with coronary heart disease (Wright, 1988).

Another personality variable that may account for individual differences in vulnerability to stress is *hardiness*. People characterized as high in hardiness believe that they can control or influence events in their lives. They are deeply committed to their work and to other activities they find of interest, and they look on change as being exciting and challenging rather than threatening or frightening (Fischman, 1987a; Kobasa, 1979).

Measures of stress, physical health, and personality were taken from a large number of male middle- and high-level executives of a large public utility company. On the basis of these measures, the executives were divided into two groups, those under high stress who were low in illness and those under high stress who were high in illness. The first group—those who were in good health, despite the high stress of their jobs—was found to be higher in hardiness. Those who were in poor health felt powerless to cope with stress, were low in the need to achieve, had little commitment to their work or to anything else in their lives, and viewed the prospect of change as a threat. This group was lower in hardiness (Kobasa, Maddi, & Kahn, 1982). Another study of male executives confirmed the relationship between hardiness and less illness in the face of stress (Kobasa, Maddi, Puccetti, & Zola, 1985). A study of female secretaries failed to confirm the relationship (Schmied & Lawler, 1986).

The personality variable of internal/external control also influences an individual's reaction to stress. Persons rated high on internal control believe that they can control the forces and events that shape their lives. Those scoring high on external control believe that life is determined by events and forces beyond their control (Rotter, 1975). Managers high in internal control experience much lower levels of stress than managers in the same kinds of jobs who are high in external control (Gemmill & Heisler, 1972). Apparently, the belief that one is in control of one's life (a component of hardiness) significantly reduces the effects of stress.

The breakup of the Bell telephone system, the largest corporate reorganization in history, gave I/O psychologists an excellent opportunity to study how managers coped with the highly stressful changes brought about by that reorganization. The researchers found that some managers were able to cope much more effectively with the stress than others.

Those who coped well looked on the organizational changes as challenges rather than threats. These managers were highly flexible and adaptable, willing

Construction work can be a highly stressful job not only because of the physical hazards but also because of external pressures beyond the worker's control, such as completion deadlines and problems with delivery of supplies.

to try new ways of dealing with obstacles and frustrations. They were also action oriented, able to confront stressful situations directly, and were high in problem-solving skills. Those who did not cope well feared the organizational changes, were inflexible and not very adaptable, were not action oriented, and were lower in problem-solving skills (Summers, 1983).

Type of Occupation and Stress

We have seen that people react to stress in different ways, some coping much better than others and suffering fewer of the harmful effects of stress. Just as stress differs as a function of the individual, it also differs as a function of one's type of occupation. Some jobs are more stressful than others.

The National Institute for Occupational Safety and Health (NIOSH) has ranked 130 occupations in terms of the level of stress they engender. The 12 jobs with the highest levels of stress follow:

1. Laborer.
2. Secretary.
3. Inspector.
4. Clinical lab technician.
5. Office manager.

6. First-line supervisor.
7. Manager or administrator.
8. Waitress or waiter.
9. Machine operator.
10. Farm worker.
11. Miner.
12. Painter.

Other occupations considered to be high in stress are police officer, fire fighter, computer programmer, dental assistant, electrician, plumber, social worker, telephone operator, and hairdresser. In general, clerical and blue-collar workers suffer more stress than managerial and professional workers, perhaps in part because they have little control over their work and working conditions (Cooper & Smith, 1986).

The nationwide survey conducted by Nine to Five, the National Association of Working Women, uncovered differences in stress reactions between women managers and women workers in lower level jobs. The managers were much more likely to describe their jobs as stressful, yet they did not experience poorer health than the average respondent. Lower level workers, on the other hand, were less likely to describe their jobs as stressful, yet they experienced a higher incidence of health problems ("Stress on Your Job," 1984).

The survey also found that among women who work outside the home, some of the most stressful jobs are in the health care industry. Nurses in particular are subject to stress. A study of 104 nurses in four hospitals found that the causes of stress included work overload, uncooperative patients, criticism, negligent co-workers, lack of support from supervisors, and difficulties with physicians (Motowidlo, Packard, & Manning, 1986). In addition, medical and dental technicians, lab workers, and social workers report extremely high levels of stress on their jobs. (One of the least stressful jobs for both men and women is that of college professor.)

Women managers have to cope with more stressors than men do in both their work and home lives. We noted some of the problems of women in management in Chapter 7. In addition to the pressures of the job, which are generally similar to those experienced by men, women must cope with such stress factors as sexual harassment, prejudice, discrimination and stereotyping, lack of role models, and feelings of isolation (Chusmir & Durand, 1987).

Studies of women managers in the United States and in Britain show that they report significantly higher levels of stress in relation to conflicts between career and family than do men managers. Perhaps because of all these sources of stress, women managers report a higher number of psychosomatic complaints and feelings of nervousness, tension, and tiredness. Also, when men managers develop stress-related illnesses they tend to be physical in nature, whereas with women managers the stress is more likely to be manifested in emotional ill health (Davidson & Cooper, 1987; Lam, Lee, Ong, Wong, Chow, & Kleevens, 1987).

Women who are not employed outside the home are also subject to high levels of stress. Research suggests that a woman's work as wife and mother brings considerable role conflict, role overload, and role disenchantment. Many women homemakers report higher levels of depression, and believe that more demands are placed on them than on women who work outside the home. The homemaker role combines psychological demands with a low level of control (Baruch, Biener, & Barnett, 1987).

Another type of occupation deserves mention because it is extremely high in stress, that of being an entrepreneur (in business for oneself). A study of 450 persons who head their own small companies found that as many as two thirds suffered from such stress-related disorders as back problems, indigestion, insomnia, and headaches at least once a week. It should be noted that entrepreneurs also rate high in job satisfaction. Although their jobs are stressful, the satisfactions of being in business for oneself are likely to outweigh the effects of stress (Boyd & Gumpert, 1983).

Causes of Stress at Work

Several aspects of work, the so-called *stressors*, can cause stress. No doubt you can think of some from your own experience, including a condition that may be affecting you now—overwork. Psychologists use the term *overload* and have identified two types: quantitative overload and qualitative overload (Margolis, Kroes, & Quinn, 1974).

Quantitative overload is the condition of having too much work to do in the time available. A study of white- and blue-collar workers at a Volvo auto manufacturing plant in Sweden found that the most prominent stress factor was the feeling of work overload (Wallin & Wright, 1986). Research on veterinary medicine students also found that work overload was a significant source of stress (Osipow & Davis, 1988). It is an obvious source of stress and clearly linked to stress-related diseases. For example, a study of young heart-attack patients found that 70% of them were working more than 60 hours per week. They reported feeling under an emotional strain just before their heart attack. Other research supports this correlation between work overload and heart disease as well as a relationship to excessive drinking and low self-esteem (Sales, 1969). More recent research suggests that the source of stress may have less to do with the amount of work than with the degree of control the workers have over the rate at which they must perform their work. The less control they have over the pace of work, the greater the stress they experience (Hurrell, 1987).

Qualitative overload involves not too much work to do but work that is too difficult. We have already suggested that having insufficient ability to perform a job is stressful. Even those employees with the highest ability levels can sometimes find themselves in a situation in which they cannot cope with the demands made by their work.

If having too much work or work that is too difficult is so stressful, does it follow that too little or too easy work is healthy and stress free? No. The condition of *work underload* can be just as stressful as work overload and equally harmful to one's health.

A study of more than 1,500 executives of a large company found that those under high stress and those under low stress had significantly more health problems than those who experienced a moderate level of stress (French, Caplan, & Van Harrison, 1982). A lack of stimulation can be just as harmful as too much stimulation. Boredom and monotony can be just as stressful as having too much to do.

Paradoxically, then, a complete absence of stress is not beneficial. A certain level of stress is stimulating, invigorating, and desirable. The problem for each individual is to find the optimum stress level under which he or she can function and remain in good health and to avoid those extremes of work overload and underload that cause stress.

Causes of job stress include work overload, change, role conflict, career-development problems, and the responsibility for supervising the work of others.

Another stressor in the workplace is *change*. As we noted, persons who look on change as exciting and challenging are less vulnerable to stress. Those who view change as threatening or frightening are more likely to experience stress from it. Thus, it is the way we perceive or react to change rather than the change itself that is the source of the stress. In general, most people seem to resist change, preferring familiar situations so that they know what to expect. Consider the relationship between an employee and his or her boss. Once such a relationship is established (assuming it is positive), a subordinate feels comfortable with it. The supervisor knows what to expect from the employee and vice versa. The situation is predictable and, therefore, safe and secure. What happens when the supervisor quits or is promoted and the employee faces a new superior? He or she no longer knows what behaviors will be tolerated on the job, how much work is expected, or how he or she will be evaluated. This change in the work environment is threatening and stressful to many people.

Many such changes occur in the workplace. The introduction of a new work procedure may require employees to learn and adapt to different production methods. The purchase of a company by a conglomerate may cause employees to worry about their jobs, their new bosses, or new organizational policies.

A change that has been stressful for older employees is the growing number of young women and ethnic-minority employees on the job who introduce different cultural values, lifestyles, and attitudes. The movement toward participatory democracy is also a stressful change for many employees and managers. Any such change in the organizational climate will result in increased stress effects on those who view change as threatening.

Performance appraisal is a source of stress for a great many people (see Chapter 5). Few people like the experience of being evaluated by someone else, whether at college or at work, because it is a test of one's adequacy and competence relative to others. A poor evaluation affects one's future—it may result in failure to graduate from school or the loss of a job—so it is no wonder that this is a source of stress.

An employee's *role* in the organization can be a source of stress. There are two aspects to a person's role that serve as stressors: role ambiguity and role conflict. *Role ambiguity* arises when the employee's work role—the scope and responsibility of the job and what others expect of him or her—is so poorly structured as to be uncertain and ill defined. The person is not sure exactly what to do in the job. This may be particularly crucial for new employees whose roles are apt to be unclear or confusing. A study of 380 British engineers in their first 3 years of employment found that role ambiguity was responsible for such common problems as difficulties in getting along with superiors and with people in other departments. Role ambiguity was less of a problem by the 4th year of employment (Keenan & Newton, 1987). Adequate socialization techniques for new employees could help reduce the problems associated with role ambiguity. Role ambiguity has been linked to job dissatisfaction, high tension, depression, and increased blood pressure and pulse rate (Howard, Cunningham, & Rechnitzer, 1986; Kahn, Wolfe, Quinn, Snock, & Rosenthal, 1964).

Role conflict arises when there is a disparity among the demands of the job or between the demands of the job and the employee's personal standards, values, or expectations. Consider the situation in which a supervisor is told to allow subordinates more participation in decisions affecting the department and at the same time is put under pressure to increase production. To increase production immediately, the supervisor may have to act in a more authoritarian manner. Yet, he or she has been told to act more democratically. The two demands are in conflict.

Role conflict can also occur when the demands of the job do not live up to the employees' expectations. A study of 377 young British engineers showed a significant relationship between the feeling that their training and abilities were not being used on the job, and role conflict. As a result of the role conflict and the under-utilization of their skills, they also reported a high degree of work underload (Newton & Keenan, 1987).

Role conflict can also occur when the job demands certain behaviors that run counter to a person's morals or values. Suppose an employee is pressured to bribe a local political figure who is in a position to award a company a lucrative contract. If the person's value structure deems bribery to be immoral, he or she will experience a role conflict and, hence, stress. Another example is a salesperson asked to sell a product he or she knows to be inferior or dangerous. Of course, the person in such a role conflict can quit, but the threat of unemployment may be a greater stress than the conflict itself. This source of job stress has been related to low job satisfaction, increased heart rate and blood pressure, and reduced job performance (Jackson & Schuler, 1985).

Problems of *career development* may lead to stress at work. Stress can arise when an employee fails to receive an anticipated promotion. In this case, the employee's personal and career aspirations are not being satisfied, and the resulting frustration can be intense. The opposite condition, overpromotion, can also be stressful. Here a person has been promoted beyond his or her level of competence and ability to a position with which he or she cannot cope. The fear of failure can induce a great deal of stress.

Being responsible for other people is a major source of difficulty for some supervisors and managers. Having to evaluate subordinates for a pay raise, promotion, or dismissal; provide them with incentives and satisfactions; and manage them on a day-to-day basis can lead to stress. These managers are much more likely to experience the physical complaints of stress than are persons such as accountants whose responsibilities do not include managing others.

Contact with a *stress carrier* is, not surprisingly, a cause of stress. Even a person who is otherwise free of stress on the job can be "infected" by someone who is highly stressed. The tension, anxiety, irritability, and other consequences of stress exhibited by one employee can easily affect others.

Assembly-line work has been associated with stress because it is characterized by repetition and monotony, high-speed and routine work, lack of challenge and participation, and, often, high noise levels. Some studies have linked assembly-line work with heart disease and poor mental health. A study of more than 5,000 postal workers demonstrated that machine-paced assembly-line work produced high levels of stress for both men and women workers, although women were affected more strongly (Hurrell, 1985).

Some of the *physical conditions of work* are common sources of stress on the job. Factors such as excessive noise, heat, or cold; poor lighting; shift work; and pollution have been identified as potential stressors.

Two aspects of working with computers—the pacing and the monitoring of the work—are new sources of stress in the workplace. Machine pacing on the assembly line can lead to stress, as we noted earlier. Computer technology applied to the sorting of mail and to other clerical jobs has brought machine pacing into many offices along with increased work pressure. Research clearly demonstrates high levels of absenteeism, turnover, muscle fatigue, and stress among workers who must perform routine, repetitive, simplified keyboard-based tasks (Gomer, Silverstein, Berg, & Lassiter, 1987).

The computer monitoring of every keystroke and every moment the operator is away from the work station is a growing source of stress for millions of computer operators. As we saw in Chapter 5, computer monitoring is like having an unblinking, ever-alert supervisor constantly looking over your shoulder. A survey of VDT employees whose work was continuously monitored showed that they experienced higher levels of stress-related illnesses than other office employees whose work was not computer-monitored (Office of Technology Assessment, 1987).

The pay system known as *piecework* can cause stress. Psychologists studied a group of women clerical workers who changed from a fixed-pay system to the piecework system. Production improved, but the stress on the workers increased. After a brief period on piecework, the employees felt mentally and physically exhausted, and their excretion of adrenalin rose by a dramatic 40% (McLean, 1979).

We mentioned earlier that, for the most part, it is the minor annoyances of everyday life on the job that cause so much stress because there are so many of them and they tend to accumulate. Petty disagreements with co-workers and frequent deadlines are major sources of stress, particularly for office workers. Before getting to work, however, many people experience problems at home that may make them less able to cope with stress in the workplace. Worries about family, health, and finances or concerns about one's pet, house, car, or stereo system, for example, can be constant irritants. These incidents may occur so frequently that they are considered by some psychologists to be more harmful to mental and physical health than are major traumatic events. The latter, for most people, are rare.

A psychologist at the University of California at Berkeley asked 100 white middle-aged and middle-class men and women to keep an accounting of their minor hassles for a period of one year (Lazarus, 1981). The most frequently mentioned items were concern about weight; health problems of a family member; the rising prices of consumer goods; home maintenance and yard work; having too many things to do; misplacing or losing things; worries about property, investments, and taxes; crime; and concern about one's physical appearance.

Overall, then, each person must confront and deal with a large and recurring number of stress-producing events every day both at home and at work. Although most of us experience at least some of the harmful effects of stress at one time or another, most people, fortunately, do manage to cope.

Effects of Stress at Work

We have already discussed the long-term health consequences of stress, the psychosomatic disorders that arise from prolonged exposure to stressful conditions. In addition, there are long-term psychological consequences of stress, including tension, depression, irritability, anxiety, low self-esteem, resentment, psychological fatigue, and general neuroticism. Research has also linked work-related stress with spouse abuse. Research on husbands who had physically abused their wives has associated that behavior with stressful work events such as failure to obtain a promotion or losing one's job (Barling & Rosenbaum, 1986).

In this section, we shall deal with more immediate effects of stress on health, behavior, and job performance. One of the most ambitious studies on the effects of stress focused on 2,000 key members of a large Canadian company (Zaleznik, Kets de Vries, & Howard, 1977). The management asked a team of psychologists to study important personnel in management, staff, and operations jobs who were showing signs of stress. The stress reactions appeared shortly after the company had undergone a sweeping organizational change (itself a well-recognized source of stress). The investigators found a wide range and incidence of stress symptoms in five categories: emotional distress, medication use, cardiovascular illness, gastrointestinal disturbance, and allergy respiratory problems. Some of the specific symptoms and their incidence are shown in Table 13-2.

This is a formidable list of symptoms. Some such as those in the emotional distress category appear at an alarming frequency. However, not all of the 2,000 employees studied suffered these symptoms to the same degree. The differences in stress experienced by the three groups—management, staff, and operations—shed light on how stress reactions vary as a function of the type of job.

The most striking finding is that managers showed a very low incidence of stress reactions compared to those in staff and operations positions as a result of the organizational changes. The staff group had the highest incidence of cardiovascular and gastrointestinal disorders. The operations group had the highest incidence of emotional distress, medication use, and allergy respiratory symptoms.

Why were there such differences when all three groups had been exposed to the same stressful organizational changes? Why were managers less vulner-

TABLE 13-2 **Stress Symptoms and Their Frequency of Occurrence**

Symptom	*Percentage reporting symptom*
1. Emotional distress	
Insomnia	24.0
Restlessness and agitation	21.2
Fatigue	19.1
Irritability	13.2
Worry about a nervous breakdown	11.3
Moodiness	11.0
2. Medication use	
Vitamin pills	21.4
Other prescriptions	6.9
Sleeping tablets	3.2
3. Cardiovascular illness	
Rapid heartbeat	7.8
High blood pressure	6.2
4. Gastrointestinal disturbance	
Digestion problems	11.1
Colitis	5.9
Stomach-distress medication	4.5
5. Allergy respiratory problems	
Hay fever	8.5
Respiratory difficulties	3.5

From "Stress reactions in organizations: Syndromes, causes and consequences" by A. Zaleznik, M. F. R. Kets de Vries, & J. Howard, 1977, *Behavioral Science, 22*, p. 154.

able to stress than the others? There are several reasons. Managers are more familiar with organizational processes and have more power, control, and influence over them. The more power a person has, the greater is his or her tolerance for ambiguity. Role ambiguity, as we have seen, is a cause of stress. Having power also enhances self-esteem and one's sense of personal importance and independence, all factors that affect one's vulnerability to stress effects. Staff and operations personnel, in contrast, feel powerless to influence organizational processes and, so, have lower self-esteem and autonomy and less tolerance of ambiguity.

Managers also feel less threatened by objective performance evaluations. Staff and operations personnel, on the other hand, have a high accountability for results, which can be quantified in their performance evaluations. They are responsible for certain functions, yet are powerless to influence how those functions should be carried out. And, then, they are evaluated on their ability to carry out those functions over which they have no control, clearly a stressful situation.

Another investigation of the harmful effects of stress dealt with 135 high-level women executives in England. Table 13-3 shows their physical and psychological stress-related symptoms.

TABLE 13-3   Women Managers Reporting Physical and Psychological Stress Symptoms

Physical	Percentage	Psychological	Percentage
Migraine	27.4	Tiredness	69.6
High blood pressure	9.6	Irritation	60.0
Arthritis and/or		Anxiety	54.4
rheumatoid arthritis	8.1	Tension (neck or back)	42.2
Eczema	5.9	Anger	35.6
Gastric and/or peptic ulcer	4.4	Frustration	34.8
Asthma	2.2	Sleeplessness	34.1
Heart disease	0.0	Dissatisfaction with life or job	34.1
Stroke	0.0	Low self-esteem	25.9
		Depression	23.7

From "The high cost of stress on women managers" by C. L. Cooper & M. J. Davidson, 1982, *Organizational Dynamics, 10*(4), p. 49.

You will notice that there was not a high incidence of physical health problems, with the exception of migraine headaches. However, headaches caused the loss of more days at work every year than did employee strikes. Also, in general, women are three times more likely than men to have headaches. Most of the stress-related symptoms of this sample of executives were psychological. With regard to their health problems, 71% of the women reported that they were related to stress on the job (Cooper & Davidson, 1982).

So far, we have been discussing the effects of stress on white-collar personnel. Let us turn to the factory floor and a stress-produced disorder known as *mass psychogenic illness* or, more popularly, assembly-line hysteria (Schmitt & Fitzgerald, 1982).

This strange malady affects more women than men and strikes suddenly, without warning. It spreads so quickly that an assembly line or an entire plant may have to shut down within days or even hours of the first appearance of the disorder. Consider the experience of an electronics plant in Ohio. One morning a woman worker on the assembly line began to feel dizzy, light-headed, and nauseous. She complained of muscular weakness and difficulty in breathing. In a matter of minutes, some three dozen employees were being treated in the company's dispensary for the same symptoms. The illness spread. Shortly thereafter the plant had to be closed.

Investigators thought it was something in the air—some chemical, gas, virus, or other infectious agent. Physicians, toxicologists, and industrial hygienists conducted an intensive search and found nothing in the plant that could explain the disorder. The cause was assembly-line hysteria, a mass psychogenic illness that spreads by contagion and has no physical origin. It is not uncommon.

On another assembly line in a different part of the country, employees were packing frozen fish in boxes. One employee noticed a strange odor and made a comment about it. Suddenly, the workers began to choke. They had trouble breathing and became dizzy and nauseous. The plant had to be closed, and a team of investigators made an exhaustive search of the building. They found nothing, no toxic agent in the air or the drinking water or in the fish that were being processed. There was no apparent cause for the illness, yet there was no denying that the workers had become physically sick. They were not feigning the symptoms nor were they malingering.

At a third factory, workers assembling aluminum lawn furniture noticed a blue mist hovering in the air above their heads. Some sensed a strong odor around the assembly-line apparatus itself. Almost immediately, complaints were voiced about tightness in the chest, headaches, and a bad taste in the mouth. Concern spread, perhaps with good reason. Twice before, this factory had had a carbon monoxide leak. The employees were sent home, and the investigators descended on the plant. You guessed it. They found nothing that could explain the employees' behavior.

Typical symptoms of this mass psychogenic illness are headaches, nausea, chills, blurred vision, muscular weakness, and difficulty in breathing. The condition seems to be related to physical and psychological stress on the job. Some physical stressors that can produce this illness include the noise and general sensory overload common to assembly lines, poor lighting, and temperature variations, more evidence of the importance of physical conditions of work. Other physical stressors are exhaust fumes or the odors of solvents and glues, almost any strong, unusual aroma. Recall, however, that assembly-line hysteria is a psychological illness; there is nothing toxic in the air to produce the symptoms. Psychological stressors may be more important. Boredom seems to be the key. Monotonous, repetitive work can lead to muscle tension, job dissatisfaction, and depression.

As a rule, the victims of this mass psychogenic illness had come under pressure to increase production. Often this involved considerable overtime work, which most employees are not in a position to refuse. Poor relations between management and employees is also a factor. In all the cases studied, there had been friction between employees and management, there was no formal means for employees to air grievances, and there was little communication or feedback from management. Employees also felt role conflict because they frequently received conflicting orders from their superiors.

Another stressor was social isolation. The victims of this mass psychogenic illness were unable to communicate with others on the job because of the high noise level. As a result, each employee experienced loneliness and isolation on the assembly line and lacked a feeling of social support from co-workers. We shall see that social support can be an effective antidote to stress.

Why does the disorder strike more women than men? Many men work under similar conditions of physical and psychological stress, yet they are not nearly as prone to assembly-line hysteria. One explanation is the sex-role conflict some women experience between the competing demands of job and home, which, as we noted, can serve as a source of stress. Certain aspects of the job—overtime, depression, dissatisfaction, and tiredness—can interfere with what these women perceive as their domestic responsibilities such as child rearing and homemaking. The conflict may produce a type of guilt and frustration (another source of stress) not shared by most men.

Some companies have had more than one outbreak of assembly-line hysteria, which has disrupted production schedules—sometimes for weeks. It is interesting that most victims of this malady feel better once they go home but often become sick again when they return to work. In one case, an employee became ill as soon as she drove into the company parking lot, an indication of the potency of the stress of her job.

One effect of stress on the job resulting from overwork is called *burnout* (Freudenberger, 1977; 1980). Its symptoms are what you would expect from the label. The employee becomes less energetic and less interested in the job. He or she is emotionally exhausted, apathetic, depressed, irritable, and bored; finds fault with everything about the work, including co-workers; and reacts negatively to the suggestions of others. Not surprisingly, the quality of work deteriorates, although not necessarily the quantity. Burnout victims continue to try to work as hard and as fast as they always did. Paradoxically, they also begin to withdraw from work in small ways by leaving early, arriving late, and taking long breaks. Burnout has been found to consist of three components (Jackson, Schwab, & Schuler, 1986).

1. Emotional exhaustion, the feeling of being drained and empty caused by excessive psychological and emotional demands.
2. Depersonalization, a closing off of sensitivity toward others and a feeling of callousness and cynicism.
3. Low personal accomplishment, the feeling that one's actions and efforts are wasted and worthless.

Advanced stages of burnout are characterized by even lower levels of energy, self-esteem, self-efficacy, job satisfaction, participation, and involvement. Not surprisingly, these are accompanied by an increase in physical symptoms of stress, along with lower productivity and poor performance appraisals. The person also shows a greater need for social support, but, paradoxically, tends to withdraw from those who could provide it (Golembiewski, Hilles, & Daly, 1987).

Women managers are significantly higher than men managers in both frequency and intensity of emotional exhaustion ("Stress, Burnout," 1988). Also, single and divorced persons of both sexes are more likely to experience burnout than are married persons. In a study of police officers, the best predictor of emotional exhaustion was the lack of opportunity for promotion. Also, rigidity in work rules correlated positively with the frequency of emotional exhaustion (Gaines & Jermier, 1983).

Employees with burnout also become rigid about their work, following rules and procedures blindly and compulsively because they are too exhausted to be flexible or consider alternative solutions to a problem. Another result of the growing exhaustion is that employees experience physical ailments such as headaches and backaches. They withdraw from other people, both on and off the job, and become social isolates. This withdrawal from social support makes it more difficult for them to deal with their stress. In time, the burnout victim will affect the emotional state and productive efficiency of co-workers and subordinates. An entire department or section can be affected, particularly if the burnout victim is a supervisor.

The Maslach Burnout Inventory was developed to measure this condition (Maslach & Jackson, 1981). It consists of four subscales to measure the three components of burnout—emotional exhaustion, depersonalization, and low personal accomplishment—as well as personal involvement. Research on the Maslach Burnout Inventory has shown it to be highly reliable and valid. High burnout scores have shown a significant positive correlation with larger caseloads for social security agency employees, with marital problems among police officers, and with high staff-child ratios among social workers (Jones & DuBois, 1987).

The cause of burnout is the accumulated stresses of overwork. This is supported by the finding that burnout usually strikes employees who are the most dedicated and committed to their work, the ones who work the most overtime or stay late at the office and take work home. These are the hardest workers, usually the ones who have contributed the most to the success of the organization. An early sign of burnout is that the person starts working harder than before, putting in longer hours but accomplishing less because of his or her rigidity and exhaustion.

Studies suggest that burnout victims may be insecure people whose personal lives are unfulfilling. Because they lack esteem and recognition off the job they try to find it on the job. By working unusually hard and making effective contributions to the organization, they can become esteemed, honored, and rewarded. Through their efforts on the job, they are able to prove to themselves that they are worthwhile and find a needed sense of security (Freudenberger, 1980).

Of course, there is a price to pay for such overwork over a long period of time. Stress accumulates and leads to the psychological and physical ailments described. These people work so hard that they burn away their energy faster than the body can replace it.

Such persons have been described as *workaholics*, employees who are addicted to their work (Machlowitz, 1980). However, recent research shows that not all workaholics strive to perform well because they are driven by anxiety and insecurity. Some workaholics genuinely love their work and derive tremendous inner satisfaction from it. To these people, work is not an unhealthy compulsion that gradually wears them down. Rather, it is a healthy, stimulating center and focus of their life. Some workaholics seem to be happy, well-adjusted persons for whom work is a joyful experience. They seldom take vacations because they feel no need to get away from their work.

It is estimated that about 5% of all employees are workaholics and that the majority of these are contented and happy with their work. Healthy workaholics are likely to have accepting and supportive families, autonomy and variety in their jobs, tasks for which their personal skills and abilities are well suited, and good physical health. Those workaholics who lack one or more of these characteristics tend to be discontented and unhappy with their work. They are susceptible to burnout and the negative effects of stress.

Contented workaholics do not find their work to be stressful, debilitating, or something that robs them of physical energy. On the contrary, it is an exhilarating, life-sustaining, and enhancing experience. Their work is fun. However, although they may suffer no stress from their intense commitment to their work, they can serve as a source of stress to others.

Think what it would be like to live with or work for a workaholic. Family life would suffer because work would always take precedence. Subordinates would be expected to show the same high degree of commitment to the job as the workaholic and to spend long hours on the job. Employees may feel compelled to try to keep up with a workaholic supervisor who, after all, will be evaluating them for pay raises and promotions. These employees face the alternative of quitting or of striving to meet the workaholic's pace, thus risking the effects of the stress of overwork.

Dealing with Stress at Work

The techniques for dealing with stress on the job involve both the prevention of stress and its reduction or elimination. Some methods provided by the organization include altering the organizational climate, providing employee assistance programs (EAPs), and treating victims of stress-related illnesses. Techniques that individual employees can practice on and off the job include relaxation training, biofeedback, and behavior modification.

Organizational Techniques

I/O psychologists have proposed several organizational techniques for managing stress at work (McLean, 1979; Stoner & Fry, 1983).

1. *Emotional climate control.* Because one of the stressors of modern organizational life is change, the organization must provide sufficient support to enable employees to adapt to change. This can be accomplished by providing a climate of esteem and regard for employees and by allowing them to participate in all decisions involving change in their work and in the structure of the organization. Such participation helps employees accept work changes and aids in adaptation to change by allowing the expression of anger and tension about new ways of working. This can help to prevent the stress of a sudden and unexpected change.
2. *Provision of social support.* Social support can reduce one's vulnerability to stress. Organizations can enhance social support by facilitating the cohesiveness of work groups and by training supervisors to be empathetic to, and

supportive of, subordinates. Social support on the job can minimize the harmful physiological effects of stress.

3. *Redefinition of employee roles.* To reduce the stress caused by role ambiguity, managers must clearly state to their subordinates what is expected of them and what the precise scope and responsibilities of their jobs are. Management can reduce role conflict by making sure that none of the demands of a job is in conflict with another and by not expecting employees to behave in ways contrary to their values and standards.

4. *Elimination of work overload and underload.* Proper selection and training, equitable promotion decisions, and fair distribution of work can do much to eliminate these causes of stress. In some instances, management may be able to add staff or reduce the overtime demands on the workers. Management must ensure that job requirements and employee abilities are matched. If not—if the person has too much or too little to do, or if the job is too complex for the employee's skills—stress will result.

5. *Provision of assistance to stressed employees.* More and more organizations today are recognizing the harmful effects that stress can have on employee health and productivity. As a result, they are providing in-house counseling programs that teach individual stress-control techniques and supplying facilities for physical exercise.

Considerable research has been conducted on *social support* and the results consistently show that an increase in social support can alleviate or reduce the effects of stress. The findings are inconsistent, however, in showing how this reduction in the effects of stress takes place. One hypothesis suggests that social support buffers or moderates the impact of stressors on the person's feelings of being under a strain. Another view is that social support reduces the effects of stress by increasing the person's ability to cope. Research to date provides support for both positions (Dooley, Rook, & Catalano, 1987; Ganster, Fusilier, & Mayes, 1986; Kirmeyer & Dougherty, 1988).

Much of the research on social support focuses on the positive role of supervisors in reducing stress among their subordinates. One study, however, involving 102 hospital nurses, found that social support of supervisors actually strengthened the relationship between the stressors of the job and the nurses' feelings of being under stress, quite the reverse of other findings. The psychologists suggested that in some work situations the source of social support may also be a source of stress. "If a supervisor who is causing stress approaches a subordinate to offer support, even this 'friendly' approach may be experienced as stressful—any interaction with the supervisor in this situation would be a stressful stimulus" (Kaufmann & Beehr, 1986, p. 524).

Although supervisors are in an excellent position to provide social support for their subordinates, they are not the only source available to most employees. On the job, co-workers can be supportive, and at home, family and friends can serve in that capacity. A study of 442 British male airline pilots found that they derived virtually all of their social support primarily from their wives and secondarily from their friends. The single most important factor in the pilots' ability to cope with stress was the stability of their home life and their relationships with their wives (Sloan & Cooper, 1986).

Both government and private organizations have been exploring other approaches to helping their stressed employees. A government agency in Nebraska, for example, taught its employees to alter their cognitive interpretations of stressful events at work, that is, to perceive and react to stressful events in less harmful ways (Ganster, Mayes, Sime, & Tharp, 1982). This technique combined with relaxation training led to significant reductions in psychological and physiological reactions to stress.

Psychologists have conducted a great deal of evaluative research on stress-management techniques in EAPs, including relaxation exercises, biofeedback, and altering cognitive skills. The results are, in general, consistent in showing a reduction of the symptoms of stress as a result of these techniques (Bruning & Frew, 1987; Higgins, 1986). Levels of physiological arousal have been reduced, and participants in these programs report less tension, fewer sleep disturbances, and an improved ability to cope with difficulties in the workplace. These organizational programs are not designed to reduce the sources or causes of stress—unlike techniques of emotional climate control or social support, for example—but rather to teach employees more efficient ways of coping with stress. One problem yet to be resolved is the development of ways to measure coping behavior.

Organizations such as New York Telephone, Xerox, and Kimberly-Clark, among others, have instituted stress-management programs, usually as part of an overall EAP. New York Telephone uses various forms of relaxation training and meditation. After an 18-month test period, employees were found to be less depressed and hostile, suffered fewer stress-related disorders, and were absent less frequently (Pelletier, 1984).

The stress-management program at Johnson & Johnson, called "Live for Life," also deals with eating, exercise, and smoking. This voluntary program has enrolled one third of the company's employees at 40 locations in the United States, Puerto Rico, and Europe. A 2-year study of the effects of the program among 4,000 employees found significant increases in general well-being, in the ability to handle job stress, and in satisfaction with personal relationships at work and with working conditions. A significant reduction in the number of sick days taken was also reported (Rosch & Pelletier, 1987).

Most companies have found their employees to be highly receptive to stress-management programs ("Wellness Programs," 1988). These programs have become more popular with employees than psychological counseling programs, perhaps because there is less social stigma attached to learning to deal with stress.

A number of corporate stress-management programs are designed specifically to alter Type A behaviors in the hope of reducing the incidence of heart disease among executives. Xerox has estimated the cost of the loss of an executive to heart disease at $600,000. Stress reduction and behavioral change techniques are considerably less expensive. Techniques to change Type A behaviors include schemes that can be practiced at home such as talking more slowly and not interrupting other people when they are talking. They also encompass management practices such as learning to delegate responsibility, establishing daily goals, setting priorities, and deciding which stress-producing situations are worthwhile and which are not (Smith & Sherman, 1982).

Individual Techniques

Some individual techniques for dealing with stress may be taught in a company stress-reduction program. Others can be learned and practiced by employees on their own such as a program of physical exercise, which can increase stamina and endurance and help to dissipate the increase in emotional energy and tension that results from stress.

Although employees can exercise at their own pace off the job, company-sponsored physical fitness programs are growing and have become the most popular technique for reducing stress in the workplace. Corporations such as General Motors, Kimberly-Clark, and Tenneco have built well-equipped gymnasiums, running tracks, and saunas for their employees and have organized walking and jogging groups, aerobic dancing, and exercise classes. Approximately 25% of all employees use these facilities, but companies are trying to induce more to participate by offering such financial incentives as lower deductibles on health insurance and cash bonuses ("In the Office," 1988).

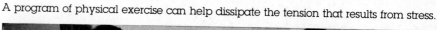

A program of physical exercise can help dissipate the tension that results from stress.

Additional techniques for reducing stress include relaxation training, biofeedback, and behavior modification.

Relaxation Training.   As early as the 1930s, a method of relaxation training was proposed as a way of reducing stress (Jacobson, 1938). Patients were taught to concentrate systematically on one part of the body after another, tensing and then relaxing the muscles. By focusing on the sensations produced by the relaxed state, progressively greater relaxation could be achieved.

Several researchers since that time have proposed refinements of this basic technique. In autogenic training, for example, subjects imagine warmth and heaviness in their limbs to help them relax. Meditation focuses on deep, regular breathing and the repetition of a phrase or sound. The relaxation-response approach combines these techniques and the quieting-reflex approach teaches subjects to achieve the relaxed state more quickly.

Sometimes biofeedback on muscle tension is combined with these approaches. The use of audiotape cassettes providing relaxation instructions along with self-measurement of blood pressure, both before and after the relaxation exercise, are a convenient way of teaching people to lower their blood pressure at home.

Relaxation training is an excellent way of reducing the effects of stress. Meditation has been found to be less successful. Its proponents claim that it results in a deeper and more restorative level of relaxation than merely resting. However, research has demonstrated that meditation may be no more effective in slowing physiological functioning than simply sitting quietly (Holmes, 1984).

A group of 214 Swedish soldiers were exposed to both relaxation and meditation techniques for a period of 8 months. When compared with a control group not exposed to these techniques, the soldiers were found to be better able to handle stressful situations (Larsson, 1987).

Biofeedback.   Biofeedback, a popular technique for dealing with the effects of stress, involves the electronic measurement of internal bodily processes such as heart rate or muscle tension. These measurements are converted into signals—a flashing light or a tone—that provide feedback on how that body process is operating. Using that feedback, we can learn to control internal states.

Suppose that a light flashes whenever our heart is beating at a relaxed rate. We can learn to keep the light on by maintaining that heart rate. Exactly how we learn to do this is not known, but it is beyond question that such control works. After enough practice with a biofeedback device, we can control the physiological function without it.

People have learned to control not only heart rate but also muscle tension, body temperature, brain waves, stomach acid, and blood pressure. Thus, biofeedback can be effective in reducing the effects of stress and preventing the occurrence of stress-related diseases. People working under stress can personally slow the bodily processes that were speeded up by the stress.

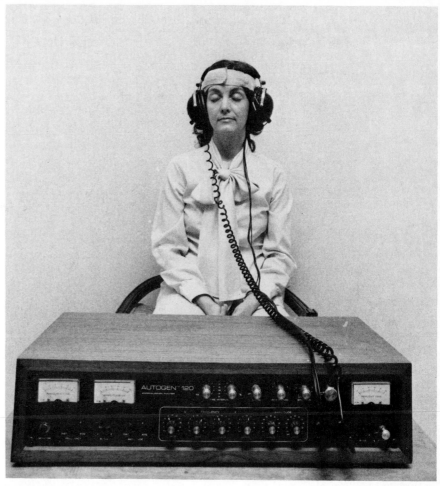

Biofeedback involves the electronic measurement and control of bodily processes such as heart rate and muscle tension.

Behavior Modification. Discussed in earlier chapters, behavior modification has proven effective in rendering Type A persons less vulnerable to stress. Many of the characteristics of the Type A person can be altered by behavior modification, including their intense drives, self-imposed deadlines, and high level of activity. The technique involves learning how to relax (through meditation or some other method), then conditioning positive emotional reactions to stressful events. The Type A person's behavior is modified so that it slows in general, and he or she learns to respond to stressors in a relaxed manner. Results have shown that Type A persons work at a less frantic pace after the behavior modification treatment and that their blood pressure levels drop markedly (Suinn, 1982).

TABLE 13-4   Response Rates to Various Coping Mechanisms

Coping	Never	Sometimes	Often or always
Exercise	20.2%	43.9%	35.9%
Engage in a hobby	26.2	46.6	27.2
Drink alcohol	42.5	42.9	14.6
Take drugs or medicine	70.3	21.5	8.1
Act as though nothing much happened	20.8	49.3	29.9
Keep it to yourself	19.5	45.5	34.9
Apologize even though you were right	38.6	48.0	13.4
Take it out on or blame others	41.2	50.6	8.1
Blow off steam	13.4	53.9	32.7
Talk to a friend	6.1	37.4	56.5
Take action	4.4	45.1	50.5
Smoke cigarettes	70.6	6.8	22.6
Drink more coffee or soda or eat more	17.7	40.2	42.1
Get away from it all	17.3	61.9	20.8

Adapted from "Stress on your job: A major national survey," April 1984, *Ms.*, p. 86.

Less formal individual techniques of dealing with stress include developing stronger social support networks off the job, developing more interests outside work, taking vacations, and leaving a stressful job for a less stressful one. These are commonsense solutions that many people institute on their own. They are not psychological techniques as such, but they can be just as effective.

Different people attempt to cope with stress in different ways and not all approaches, as we have seen, are equally effective. Behaviors such as eating, drinking, and smoking in an effort to ease the feeling of tension may cause more severe health problems than the stress itself. When a nationwide sample of working women were asked what they do to cope with stress, the range of coping mechanisms was varied, as shown in Table 13-4. It is interesting to note that what they do most often is talk to a friend, demonstrating the value of social support in dealing with stress and in maintaining general well-being.

Summary

Stress at work can exert a dramatic effect on employee health and productivity. Stress may disable and even kill many people each year. It lowers productivity and increases absenteeism and turnover. Stress causes damaging **physiological changes** in the human body and can reduce the body's reserves of energy. Prolonged stress may lead to **psychosomatic disorders** such as heart disease, gastrointestinal disorders, arthritis, skin diseases, allergies, headaches, and cancer. These psychosomatic disorders, although physiological in nature, are psychological in origin.

There are individual differences in **vulnerability to stress**. Factors that can reduce the effects of stress on the job include high job satisfaction, high autonomy and power, social support, good physical condition, sufficient ability to perform the job, and certain personality characteristics.

Type A and **Type B** persons differ in their vulnerability to stress and susceptibility to heart attacks. Type A people are highly prone to heart attacks and have a very high competitive drive, a constant sense of time urgency, high levels of hostility and aggression, and much anger and impatience. Type B persons lack these characteristics and are much less vulnerable to the effects of stress. Recent research questions the relationship between Type A behavior and heart disease, and is focusing on anger, hostility, and depression as components of Type A behavior.

People high in **hardiness**, a belief that they can control events in their lives, a deep commitment to work, and a view of change as challenging rather than frightening, are less vulnerable to stress, as are persons high in **internal control**. Some occupations are more stressful than others. High-stress jobs include laborer, secretary, lab technician, police officer, fire fighter, entrepreneur, and jobs in the health care industry. Women managers experience greater stress than men managers.

The **causes of stress** at work include quantitative and qualitative work overload, work underload, changes in the work situation, performance evaluation, role ambiguity and role conflict, career-development problems, contact with a stress carrier, machine-paced assembly-line work, piecework, being responsible for others, and certain physical conditions of work.

The **effects of stress** on the job include the long-term health effects of psychosomatic disorders as well as more immediate effects on health, behavior, and job performance. One study of stress effects revealed five categories of symptoms: emotional distress, medication use, cardiovascular illness, gastrointestinal disturbance, and allergy respiratory problems. Managers were much less affected by stress in an organization undergoing large-scale changes than staff or operations personnel, primarily because of their greater power, tolerance for ambiguity, and autonomy.

Assembly-line hysteria or mass psychogenic illness affects more women than men and spreads quickly to co-workers. It is caused by both physical and psychological stressors, including poor physical working conditions, boredom, pressure for increased production, poor communication with management, role conflict, social isolation, and sex-role conflict.

Burnout results from the stress of prolonged overwork and results in lowered productivity, exhaustion, irritability, rigidity, and social withdrawal. Burnout consists of emotional exhaustion, depersonalization, and low personal accomplishment, and tends to be higher among women, single and divorced employees, and persons who have little opportunity for promotion. Victims of burnout are usually **workaholics** who are compulsively driven to work hard out of insecurity and lack of fulfillment in their personal lives. So-called healthy workaholics derive satisfaction and happiness from their work and are free of the stress effects of burnout. They can cause stress in their subordinates, however.

Organizational techniques for **dealing with stress** include emotional climate control, provision of social support, redefinition of employee roles, elimination of work overload and underload, and provision of assistance to stressed employees. Research confirms the importance of **social support** from supervisors, co-workers, family, and friends, in reducing the effects of stress. Individual techniques for dealing with stress include physical exercise, relaxation training, biofeedback, behavior modification, and commonsense approaches such as taking a vacation or quitting a highly stressful job.

Key Terms

assembly-line hysteria
behavior modification
biofeedback
burnout
hardiness
mass psychogenic
    illness

piecework
psychosomatic
    disorders
relaxation training
role ambiguity
role conflict

social support
stress
Type A/Type B
    personalities
work overload
workaholism

CASE STUDIES

Stress and Job Performance in the Workplace

To investigate the effects on stress of the repetitive performance of routine, computer-based tasks, two groups of experienced employees of the U.S. Postal Service were studied. Their jobs involved the operation of machine-paced mail sorting equipment. Workers in both groups were matched in terms of age, sex, and job experience, and the conditions of the work environment were similar for all employees. Only the work practices of the two groups differed. Employees in the experimental group entered 4-digit codes to sort the mail by machine. The control group entered 3-digit codes, which was considered to be a less stressful task.

Objective data were collected from both groups. These included accuracy rates of job performance, and behavioral and physiological measures of fatigue in the forearm muscles. In addition, self-report measures were obtained: Employees rated the work load they experienced in various aspects of the job and the extent of the discomfort they felt in fingers, hands, wrists, and arms.

On both objective and self-report measures, employees who entered the 4-digit codes showed evidence of greater stress than the 3-digit code group. The behavioral and physiological measures demonstrated significant increases in hand tremor and muscle fatigue. The accuracy rates for the experimental group were lower than for the control group. Workers in the experimental group reported far greater physical discomfort in fingers, hands, wrists, and arms, and rated all aspects of their work load as being objectionably high. Thus, the data from multiple measures were consistent in supporting the effects of the work load on stress.

QUESTIONS

1. What other aspects of working with automated machinery are proving to be stressful?
2. Describe the major sources of stress that result from assembly-line work.
3. What is mass psychogenic illness? Is it likely to be found among postal workers? Among research chemists?
4. What is the difference between quantitative overload and qualitative overload as sources of stress?

Reference: F. E. Gomer, L. D. Silverstein, W. K. Berg, & D. L. Lassiter. (1987). Changes in electromyographic activity associated with occupational stress and poor performance in the workplace. *Human Factors, 29*, 131–143.

A Corporate Fitness Program

In 1982, the Tenneco Company initiated a health and fitness program at its offices in Houston, Texas. A variety of activities, exercises, and classes to promote health awareness were offered in modern, well-equipped facilities. The program was free to all employees. To determine any differences in absenteeism and health care costs between employees who exercised and those who did not, 517 workers selected at random were studied. Approximately half of the subjects participated in fitness center activities. The results showed that these exercisers had lower absenteeism rates for illness than did the nonexercisers, although the difference reached statistical significance only for women employees. Exercisers of both sexes had a significantly lower number of health insurance claims than did nonexercisers.

In addition, the investigation found that the fitness center attracted largely those employees who were already undertaking their own regular program of exercise. Up to 40% of the fitness center participants, however, had not engaged in regular exercise before joining the program. Thus, the health promotion program was considered to be successful in reaching some of those employees who would benefit most from it.

QUESTIONS

1. What other types of company sponsored programs are effective in reducing stress?
2. What is the role of social support in relieving stress?

3. How does biofeedback work as a technique for alleviating stress?
4. Describe the three components of burnout.

Reference: W. B. Baun, E. J. Bernacki, & S. P. Tsai. (1986). A preliminary investigation: Effect of a corporate fitness program on absenteeism and health care cost. *Journal of Occupational Medicine, 28*, 18–22.

Additional Reading

Ivancevich, J. M., & Ganster, D. C. (1987). *Job Stress*. New York: Haworth Press. Also published as the *Journal of Organizational Behavior Management*, 1986, *8*(2). Includes articles covering the measurement of stress, health effects of stress, individual differences in response to stress, organizational factors in stress, and stress management techniques.

Jackson, S. E., Schwab, R. L., & Schuler, R. S. (1986). Toward an understanding of the burnout phenomenon. *Journal of Applied Psychology, 71*, 630–640. Reports on a study of elementary and secondary school teachers relating burnout to (1) emotional exhaustion from unmet expectations, work overload, and role conflict, (2) feelings of low personal achievement, and (3) feelings of depersonalization.

Newton, T. J., & Keenan, A. (1987). Role stress reexamined: An investigation of role stress predictors. *Organizational Behavior and Human Decision Processes, 40*, 346–368. Describes a longitudinal study of college graduates in engineering and the various factors related to stress in their early careers. Covers personal, social, and organizational variables such as personality characteristics, social support, and size of organization.

Wright, L. (1988). The Type A behavior pattern and coronary artery disease. *American Psychologist, 43*, 2–14. Examines the role of time urgency, chronic activity, and anger in the Type A personality and its link with the risk of heart disease.

PART V

Consumer Psychology

Not everyone works for an organization, but all of us are consumers of the products and services of a great many organizations. We buy automobiles, cosmetics, food, and appliances; we vote for political candidates and for issues; we respond to appeals from charities and pressure groups. And we are constantly bombarded by communications from all these organizations—messages from industry, government, or individuals urging us to behave in one way or another. We are influenced by thousands of advertising appeals that appear on television screens, highway billboards, and the pages of our magazines and newspapers.

Consumer psychology is concerned with the interactions between consumers and organizations that affect us all. Advertisers spend billions of dollars each year to influence us, and most of the persuasive techniques they practice were devised by psychologists.

Consumer psychology is also important to you as an employee, particularly if you work for a company that produces consumer goods and services. If people do not buy what your company makes, it will not be in business for long.

Chapter 14 deals with the major facets of the producer/consumer interaction: the research methods of consumer psychologists, the nature of advertising, television programming, and the importance of packaging, product image, and sex in product promotion. On the consumer side, we discuss buying behavior, brand loyalty, and the effects of personality, social class, ethnic-group membership, and age.

Psychology and the Consumer

Introduction

One of the most visible areas in which psychology contributes to organizational life today involves the relationship between the producers of goods and services and the consumers. No matter how high the level of production or the quality of a company's products, the company will not be successful unless the public is made aware of the product and persuaded to buy it. Thus, a company's survival depends on its ability to promote, advertise, and market its product.

For a product, a service, or even a political candidate to sell, people must be made aware and persuaded that they should, indeed, must, have it. This function of persuasion is accomplished by the branch of I/O psychology known as consumer psychology. Psychologists are aided in this endeavor by professionals from other disciplines. To understand fully the complexities of the consumer requires the skills of sociologists, economists, and statisticians as well as copywriters, account executives, filmmakers, and the host of other talents employed by advertising agencies.

Although psychologists may be only a part of the marketing, advertising, and promoting effort, their contribution is unique. They bring to the field a methodology, specific research tools, and the general principles of human behavior gleaned from laboratory and clinical research. The methodology is, of course, the rigorous scientific method with its controls and experimental safeguards applied so successfully in the laboratory and in many different work environments. As noted in Chapter 1, psychologists study human behavior objectively, whether the individual is taking a test, performing a job, or purchasing a new car. In each case, what the person does, how he or she behaves, can be observed and analyzed systematically to determine the nature of the behavior.

Psychologists have developed a number of research tools to enable them to analyze and understand human behavior. These techniques—personality tests, attitude questionnaires, public opinion polls, physiological measurements, and surveys—originally developed for use in the laboratory or the clinic are also useful in the marketplace. The principles that underlie the construction and application of an attitude questionnaire hold, whether it is used to measure job satisfaction or cereal brand preferences. Because of their experience in observing, measuring, and recording human behavior in such a variety of situations, psychologists are also able to develop new research techniques in response to specific needs.

Another contribution of psychologists to consumer psychology is the application of the established principles of human behavior. From a century of study of basic human processes of perception, learning, motivation, and personality, psychologists have learned a great deal that can be applied to people in the marketplace. For example, the research on conditions that facilitate learning can aid in the design of an advertising campaign, the goal of which is to have consumers learn and retain the advertising message so that they are led to a specific product on a supermarket shelf. An understanding of basic principles of human perception can help in promoting the attention-getting value of an advertisement or of the package in which the product is presented. Social/psychological research has revealed factors that make for greater persuasibility of a communication or message.

Consumer behavior has been of interest to I/O psychologists since the beginnings of psychology. Indeed, industrial psychology was formally launched by the work of Walter Dill Scott on advertising and selling in the early years of the 20th century. In 1921, the world-famous founder of the behaviorist school of psychology, John B. Watson, began to apply his ideas to advertising with great success. Forced out of an academic career because of what were, for that time, sensational revelations accompanying his divorce (he was having a love affair with a woman student), and unable to find another academic position, Watson entered the business world instead.

Watson proposed that a person's buying behavior could be conditioned, and therefore predicted and controlled, just like any other kind of behavior. Thus, it could be studied scientifically. He brought the experimental method and the use of surveys to advertising, and he emphasized that advertising should focus on style and image rather than on substance and fact. He also pioneered the use of celebrity endorsements of products (Buckley, 1982). The impact of Watson's efforts on advertising and marketing remain highly influential today.

Vital to industry and necessary for the continuing growth of the economy, consumer psychology is also of practical importance to you as a consumer. Consider all the products you have purchased recently. What led you to buy one brand of deodorant over another? What convinced you in the first place that you needed a deodorant? You were probably persuaded by constant exposure to advertisements. This is something you must have, you were told, to be nice to be near, to be loved, or to get a promotion.

As for the specific brand you purchased, that, too, was probably decided on the basis of the advertising appeal or the image represented by the product, the attractiveness of the package, or its location on the store shelf (this, too, is a carefully planned aspect of a promotional campaign).

Billions of dollars and thousands of hours are expended by companies each year in the effort to get you to notice, want, and purchase their products. It is important to you, then, both as a member of an organization making products and as a consumer, to understand the principles and practices of consumer psychology.

Scope of Consumer Psychology

The study of consumer psychology is growing rapidly, more so now than at any other period in its history. There seems to be no way of escaping the influence of consumer psychology. Pick up a magazine, turn on the radio or television, drive down a highway—almost everywhere you will be bombarded by advertising messages. It is estimated that the average American is exposed to as many as 3,000 ads every day, through one medium or another. Approximately 40,000 television commercials are produced annually, and it is possible for the average viewer to see as many as 190 every day. More than 60 ads for toys are crowded into Saturday morning children's television programming.

It is increasingly difficult to avoid commercial announcements. Major international airlines and cruise-ship lines include advertising on the tax declaration forms that passengers entering the United States must complete. Videotapes of popular films contain commercials. In several major cities advertising has invaded the privacy of rest rooms, with ads hung on the inside of the stall doors (where some irate people have destroyed them).

Advertisers have placed scented strips in magazines so that even if we do not look at the ad for a product, we must smell it. The aromas of perfumes, chocolates, detergents—even the smell of the leather upholstery in a Rolls-Royce automobile—have filled the pages of magazines. In 1983, scent strips were virtually unknown, but by 1988, more than one billion were being used. This has become a severe problem for some people suffering from allergies. The scent market is expected to expand beyond magazines to supermarket aisles and other retail stores (Malcolm, 1988).

Thanks to microchips the size of a grain of salt, it is possible to hear advertisements and to see products in motion by turning a magazine page or touching a designated spot in the ad. In 1987, Absolut Vodka spent $1 million on a magazine ad at Christmastime that played "Jingle Bells" when readers turned the page. The company claimed that the ad produced the largest holiday season sales in its history. Magazine ads that pop up from a page, light up, and sound like the human voice (powered by 3-volt batteries) are under development (Kanner, 1988a).

Of course, we cannot adequately attend to all the messages bombarding us at every turn, nor should we, if we want to maintain our sanity. Many ads are blocked out because they are not perceived. We simply do not see or hear them. In fact, the majority of the daily messages are not received at all. Most people are able to react to only about a dozen of them. But whether or not we see or hear these messages, they are there, cluttering the media. Even if we remain unaware of specific ads, we are most certainly aware that the process of advertising is going on all around us.

Another indication of the scope of consumer psychology is that increasing numbers of Americans are serving as subjects in consumer research. Our buying, viewing, and travel habits are constantly being scrutinized by consumer researchers. We are approached at home, in shopping centers, at the theater, and questioned about the products we use, the programs we watch, or the purchases we plan to make. The Kroger supermarket chain, for example, conducts some 250,000 interviews per year with shoppers in their stores to determine what they like and dislike about shopping there. Sample soaps are delivered to every home in a certain district; if we buy the product when the sample runs out, this is reflected in the area's sales figures. Thus, we are probed and peeked at through consumer research to determine our likes and dislikes, and then prodded or provoked by the advertising messages designed on the basis of this research.

Critics of advertising argue that many people are offended and insulted by advertisements, particularly by those on television. Surveys by advertising agencies have found that 72% of those polled believe that advertising insults their intelligence. Almost 50% feel that advertising offers little useful information (Horovitz, 1987).

Whatever our personal judgment about the credibility, usefulness, and morality of advertising, the fact of its existence on a huge and increasing scale cannot be denied. We shall be better equipped to cope with advertising if we understand what advertisers want to do and how they attempt to do it.

Let us consider some of the functions of the consumer psychologist. Manufacturers must inform and instruct the public about the nature of their product. Potential buyers must know what the product does, why it performs better than its competitor, and how much it costs. There are more than 300,000 brand-name products of all types on the market today. In a typical supermarket, for example, over 15,000 different products are available. In the face of such formidable competition, manufacturers must ensure that their products can be readily recognized and identified. The typical buyer will purchase the item that sounds or looks familiar over one that is unknown.

But communication should not be solely from producer to consumer. A two-way communications link must be established. Manufacturers must be constantly alert for changes in the demand and preference for their products. Ignorance or delayed awareness of such changes can mean losing out to a competitor. Manufacturers must be sensitive to the nature of the market and capable of responding quickly to changes by modifying an advertising campaign, a package design, or the product itself.

The task of defining a potential market is accomplished through studies of consumer needs, desires, buying habits, and attitudes. And these consumer characteristics are influenced by factors such as age, education, socioeconomic level, and ethnic background. This type of market information affects product packaging, displaying, and advertising and also determines production schedules and distribution facilities. Product demand is subject to seasonal variations, general economic and political conditions, and technological innovations in related areas.

Therefore, consumers must continually be studied and industry kept aware of their likes, dislikes, fears, desires, prejudices, and whims. A primary law of survival in the marketplace is to produce what people want to buy or what they can be persuaded they want to buy, and this information is determined only through sound research.

Once the nature and composition of the market for a product have been delimited, consumer psychologists must determine how to reach that market effectively. This is the area of advertising. The type of advertising appeal that will produce maximum sales and the medium through which the advertising should be presented depends on the nature of the market.

A luxury automobile or yacht will only be purchased by a certain segment of the population, and the advertisements must be geared to their level of sophistication and taste and be presented in media known to reach them. More potential buyers for these products will read a magazine such as the *New Yorker* or *Vanity Fair*, rather than *Popular Mechanics*. Similarly, the image created by the ad will not be the same for a $10 watch as for a $500 watch. Many products fail or succeed on the basis of the compatibility of the advertisement with the product market.

Often the product-market/compatibility issue can be decided by a product-testing program. By releasing a new product (or an improved version of an existing product) to a test market area, such as the residents of a particular city, before its release to the general public, it is possible to determine reactions to, and acceptance of, the product. Often this method allows deficiencies to be perceived and corrected before widespread distribution.

In essence, consumer psychology deals with the complex relationship between buyers and sellers. If sellers are to be successful, they must know their buyers, how to appeal to them, and how to persuade them to buy the product. This knowledge comes only through patient, thorough, and expensive research. The scope of consumer psychology is broad, but its effectiveness is limited by the quality of the underlying research.

Research Methods in Consumer Psychology

Several research methods are used by consumer psychologists in their continuing studies of markets, product preferences, and other aspects of consumer-choice behavior. In general, much of the research involves the application of the standard psychological research techniques (discussed in Chapter 2), but additional methods have been developed for special purposes. An analysis of 10 years of advertising studies published in six leading journals showed that experiments and surveys are the most frequently used empirical methods in advertising research. It was also found that 18% of the articles published used college students as subjects, a figure that is lower than for I/O research in general. Women and children were surveyed more often than men (Yale & Gilly, 1988).

Consumer research is conducted in a variety of settings, for example, university laboratories, private homes, street corners, and shopping centers as well as laboratories established by some advertising agencies. Wherever the research is conducted and whatever technique is used, the studies should be performed under the same rigorous and objective conditions required of all psychological research.

Survey and Polling Methods

Most research that deals with consumer preferences, buying behavior, or reactions to new products or new television programs is conducted by some form of survey or public opinion poll. These polls typically are conducted in shopping malls where 58% of all personal interviewing takes place (Dupont,

A consumer researcher conducts a market survey in a shopping center mall in Massachusetts.

1987). The basic premise underlying the use of surveys is simple: Most people can and will articulate their feelings, reactions, opinions, and desires when asked about them.

This assumption holds whether we are trying to determine a person's reactions to a new peanut butter or to a presidential candidate, and it is supported by much research involving careful, thorough, and precise questioning of representative samples of the population whose opinions are at issue. We have only to recall how accurately most pre-election public opinion polls have predicted election results or how successfully many new products have been introduced on the basis of market testing to know that the survey method often does work well.

However, there have also been failures to predict election results accurately or to forecast the success of new products. For example, extensive market research on the specialty ice cream dessert Dove Bars found that they were too large. Few people questioned said they would buy the product. Company executives decided to ignore the survey findings, and the large Dove Bars quickly became a commercial success ("Test for Market Research," 1987).

Part of the difficulty in predicting marketing success is the complex and changeable nature of consumers, who may, for example, tell an interviewer on Friday that they will vote Republican and then vote Democratic on Tuesday because of a sudden downturn in the stock market. Or, the respondents who say that they drink imported beer, but, if the interviewer could open their refrigerators or follow them to the store or examine their trash cans, it would be found that they actually drink a much cheaper brand. They told the consumer researcher that they preferred the more expensive product because they thought it would make them look better. Garbage-can searches have revealed that people actually drink more than twice the amount of beer and liquor than they report to interviewers. Similarly, when people are asked about their debts, they tend to underestimate the dollar amounts. Thus, we tend to tell interviewers what we think will give us a higher status, and on such vagaries elections are lost and manufacturers go bankrupt.

In part for these reasons, Japanese companies do not survey large random samples of consumers to assess their intentions or preferences. Instead, Japanese companies interview only those persons who have actually purchased or used a particular product. When Toyota wanted to find out what American consumers wanted in a small imported car, they surveyed owners of the Volkswagen Beetle (a car similar to the one Toyota was planning) and asked them what they liked and disliked about it (Johansson & Nonaka, 1987).

The problems of surveys, although capable of distorting research results, are not a fault of the survey method but rather of the complexity of human nature. Of course, improper use of research methods can also render the results useless. A poorly constructed questionnaire administered to a nonrepresentative sample will do more harm than good, but, again, that is not a fault of the technique itself. (Specific considerations in developing and applying the survey method are discussed in Chapter 2.)

Figure 14-1 shows a questionnaire used by a shoe manufacturer. It is placed in every box of shoes and is designed to fold to form a postage-paid envelope addressed to the president of the company. Easy and quick to fill out, the questionnaire can supply a great deal of useful information about the type of person purchasing the product.

A more restricted form of survey involves *focus groups*, small samples of consumers who meet in groups of 8 to 12 to describe their reactions to a product, a package, or a commercial. The members of focus groups are usually paid for their participation and are selected to fit the profile of the average user of the product. For example, only pet owners would be selected for a focus group on a dog food ad. Only mothers of infants would be chosen to evaluate a new kind of baby diaper. Focus groups can be selected on the basis of age, income, level of education, or any other variable relevant to the product.

BERNARDO CONSUMER RESPONSE CARD

Congratulations on your Bernardo purchase. To help us continue producing footwear that better satisfies your needs, we would appreciate your answers to the following questions. Thank you.

1. ☐ Mrs. ☐ Ms. ☐ Miss

   First Name _____ Initial _____ Last Name _____

   Street _____ Apt. No. _____

   City _____ State _____ Zip _____

2. Date of purchase, or if gift, date of receipt: Mo._____ Yr._____

3. Telephone No. ( ) _____

4. Bernardo Style Number/Name (see box end): _____

5. Name of Store/Catalog where you purchased this style:

   _____

6. How long have you been wearing Bernardo's?

   _____ Years _____ First Time Buyer

7. How many pairs of Bernardo's have you purchased in the last 12 months? _____

8. Please check the most important factors which influenced your purchase of Bernardo's:

   ☐ Style   ☐ Quality of Workmanship
   ☐ Color
   ☐ Fit   ☐ Quality of Materials
   ☐ Comfort   ☐ All Leather
   ☐ Value for the Price   ☐ Other

9. Please check the 2 most important types of activities for which you plan to use your new Bernardo's:

   ☐ At Home   ☐ Cruise/Resort
   ☐ Working   ☐ Traveling on Vacation
   ☐ Shopping
   ☐ Recreation   ☐ Other

10. Name 3 other footwear brands that you have purchased:

    1. _____
    2. _____
    3. _____

11. Name your 3 most favorite magazines:

    1. _____
    2. _____
    3. _____

12. Which group best describes your age:

    ☐ 25 or under
    ☐ 26 – 35
    ☐ 36 – 45
    ☐ 46 – 55
    ☐ 56 or Over

13. Which group best describes your income:

    ☐ $15,000 – $24,999
    ☐ $25,000 – $34,999
    ☐ $35,000 – $44,999
    ☐ $45,000 – $54,999
    ☐ $55,000 Over

Figure 14-1 Consumer product questionnaire. (Reproduced by permission of Bernardo.)

Usually, the groups are observed through one-way mirrors, but the sessions may also be videotaped so that the potential consumers' comments and reactions can be evaluated more fully at a later time. The data produced by focus group sessions are more qualitative than those from large-scale empirical surveys and questionnaires. Sometimes focus groups are not questioned at all but simply observed as the members try out a product, such as a disposable razor blade. In that instance, observers found that many men cut themselves while shaving because the directions for using the product were not clear.

Focus groups often reveal problems with a product that its developers may not have considered. One businessman planned to start a chain of "dog washes," which would work similarly to car washes. He took the idea to a market research firm to have them survey the reactions of dog owners. A focus group was assembled, and the members quickly brought up a major problem. The dog wash idea itself was fine, but it meant that owners would have to drive home with wet dogs in their cars. Scratch one dog wash!

Research has been conducted on several aspects of focus groups including the interviewing techniques, training, and personality characteristics of the group moderators or leaders; the physical layout of the facilities in which the groups meet; and the size and characteristics of the groups themselves. On the basis of the research results, guidelines for the conduct of focus groups have emerged (Goldman & McDonald, 1987; Nelson & Frontczak, 1988).

In-Depth Methods

We have seen that people may misrepresent themselves to interviewers when asked for their opinions or questioned about the products they use. Because of this potential source of distortion, some consumer psychologists believe that it is not fruitful to ask persons directly for their reactions or attitudes. They contend that the direct question being asked may differ from what the respondents think is being asked. For example, by asking what brand of beer a person drinks, we are, in effect, asking what kind of person he or she is. The respondent may not feel that consumer researchers are asking merely about beer preference. Rather, they are really asking: "Do you drink the cheap stuff or the expensive high-status, snob-appeal brand?" Critics of the survey method say that we cannot uncover true human motivations and feelings by asking direct questions that allow the respondents to distort their feelings.

To probe deeper motivations, in-depth procedures, such as projective techniques (the Rorschach, Thematic Apperception Test, or sentence-completion test, for example) are advocated. These are the same techniques sometimes used for personnel selection, as we discussed in Chapter 4. The theory behind the use of these techniques is the same whether they are applied for selection purposes or for the evaluation of a new product. Presented with an ambiguous stimulus such as an inkblot, it is assumed that personal needs, values, and fears will be projected into the act of interpreting the stimulus.

A classic example of the in-depth approach in consumer research is the instant-coffee study conducted in 1950, an attempt to determine basic attitudes toward Nescafé brand (Haire, 1950). Instant coffee was, at that time, a new product that met with a good deal of consumer resistance. To find out why, the direct-survey approach was tried first. Respondents were asked, "Do you use instant coffee?" If they said no, they were asked what they disliked about it. The researchers suspected that the reasons given by the majority of the noninstant-coffee users concealed other, hidden motives, so the indirect, in-depth approach was attempted.

A shopping list was shown to two groups of women (50 in each group), and they were asked to describe the personality of the homemaker who would make up such a list. The shopping lists were identical except that one list included instant coffee and the other included a "real" coffee (Table 14-1). The approach is a projective technique designed to reveal the respondents' inner feelings about the person who would use either type of coffee. The respondents are not asked directly to reveal their own feelings (at least, as they perceived the situation); in reality, they project their own feelings in their characterization of the fictitious shopper.

On the basis of the type of coffee used (because the other items on the shopping lists were the same), the fictitious shoppers were given totally different personalities by the respondents. Almost half of them described the woman who bought instant coffee as a lazy homemaker who failed to plan household purchases and schedules well. She was described as a spendthrift by 12% and as not being a good wife by 10%.

The real-coffee shopper was described in much less negative terms. No one characterized her as a spendthrift or a poor wife; only a minority described her as lazy.

The descriptions of the two shoppers in this research study apparently reveal why instant coffee took so long to be accepted. The unflattering image of the instant-coffee user was a projection of the consumers' own feelings about the product. Perhaps people were slow to accept instant coffee because they were afraid of being thought of as the lazy kind of person described in the in-depth study.

In the initial consumer survey that asked people directly why they did not like instant coffee, most respondents said they did not like the flavor. But the real motivation may have been that they would feel lazy, failing in their

---

TABLE 14-1 Shopping Lists in Instant-Coffee Study

List 1	List 2
1 can Rumford's Baking Powder	1 can Rumford's Baking Powder
2 loaves Wonder bread	2 loaves Wonder bread
Bunch of carrots	Bunch of carrots
Nescafé instant coffee	1 lb. Maxwell House Coffee (Drip Ground)
Pound and a half of hamburger	Pound and a half of hamburger
2 cans Del Monte peaches	2 cans Del Monte peaches
5 lbs. potatoes	5 lbs. potatoes

Adapted from "Projective techniques in marketing research" by M. Haire, 1950, *Journal of Marketing, 14*, p. 649.

household duties, and wasteful by buying instant coffee, the kind of information difficult to elicit in the direct and formal questionnaire or interview.

Theoretically, the in-depth approach offers the same advantages as projective tests used for personnel selection, that is, the ability to reach unconscious levels of motivation, to determine feeings and desires that could not be reached by direct objective tests and questionnaires. However, many psychologists suggest that this does not work in reality. Further, projective tests have a record of low reliability and validity. Even the most highly trained and experienced clinical psychologists often disagree on the interpretation of projective-test results. This is true even in a clinical setting where the practitioner may devote a great deal of time to a patient and may supplement projective-test results with other tests and examinations. If the method is of doubtful validity in a clinical setting, it must be even more questionable in consumer psychology where the practitioner is often less skilled and devotes less time to securing results.

There have been fruitful uses of projective techniques in consumer research. However, the advertising industry does not publicize its failures, so it is difficult to determine precisely how successful this technique has been.

Behavioral Studies

In both consumer surveys and in-depth research methods, the focus is on opinions, feelings, and motivations; in short, on how people say they react to, and feel about, certain products or experiences. Although these data can be useful in the study of consumer psychology, the methods share one basic weakness: They describe (however accurately) only what people *say* they will do. These expressed intentions do not always coincide with actual behavior.

Some consumer studies do show a positive correlation between expressed intention and actual behavior, but others do not. As noted, people sometimes tell an interviewer that they prefer one brand of a product but buy another brand.

Because of this frequently observed discrepancy, many consumer psychologists believe that the most accurate way to investigate consumer behavior is to observe the behavior itself. Whether in a laboratory or a shopping center, the focus is on what people do when purchasing a product or expressing a preference for one brand over several others.

Purchasing Behavior

Common sense suggests that the best test of the acceptance of a new product or of a new advertising campaign for an existing product is actual sales figures. Surely, if sales for a toothpaste increase by 21% in the 6 months following a new advertising approach, we can conclude that the campaign is successful.

Unless all the variables capable of influencing sales were controlled, we cannot conclude with certainty that the advertising campaign was solely, or even partially, responsible for the boost in sales. The company's aggressive sales staff may have arranged for more prominent counter display of the toothpaste during the 6-month period; this factor alone could be responsible for the higher sales, independent of the new advertising. Or a competitor may have been criticized in a government report for using a new ingredient alleged to be harmful, thus throwing business to all other toothpaste manufacturers.

The point is that sales records can reflect factors other than the one being considered, and, without adequate control over all possible influencing variables, it is impossible to explain exactly what affected the sales figures.

A more direct way of investigating actual purchasing behavior is to place observers at various points throughout shops or supermarkets. In one such study, observers in 20 supermarkets in middle-class and working-class neighborhoods watched the behavior of mothers with young children as they chose a breakfast cereal. In 66% of the cases, the children demanded or asked for a specific cereal. More than half the time the mothers gave in and picked the cereal the child wanted (Atkin, 1978).

You can see how valuable such information can be to a company producing breakfast cereals. It clearly indicates that children, not adults, should be the target of their advertising. Had the mothers been asked in a survey who chose the cereals they purchased, they might well have said they did, not wanting to appear dominated by their children or, perhaps, not realizing the influence of their children on their shopping behavior.

Thus, useful information on actual purchasing behavior can be obtained from on-the-spot observations, but the technique has limitations in addition to the expense and time involved.

One limitation is the problem of adequate sampling of shopping behavior. Stores in different locations—for example, inner city versus suburban—attract different clientele with varying needs and income levels. The nature of the shopper can vary in the same store at different times of the day or week. People forced to shop evenings and weekends may make different purchases than those free to shop during the day. The problem can be handled by making observations in different neighborhoods and at various shopping hours, and this greatly increases the cost of the study.

Another limitation is the lack of suitable experimental control over all possible influencing variables. (This is a weakness of all types of observational research studies). In observing shopping differences between an urban and a suburban supermarket, for example, it is difficult to determine if the differences are a function of social, economic, or ethnic composition of the clientele; of the different product layouts in the stores; or of the availability of some products and not others. Specialty items may not be stocked at stores in low-income neighborhoods; it cannot be determined, therefore, if the product does not sell in that situation because of its cost or simply its lack of availability.

These limitations do not negate the usefulness of the research method, but they do call for special attention in the design and conduct of the investigation.

A more sophisticated way of observing actual purchasing behavior is by electronic means. This technique makes use of *scanner-cable panels* composed of approximately 2,500 shoppers each, people who volunteer to have their food purchases monitored. Each person receives a plastic card containing a numbered code that is given to the supermarket checkout clerk each shopping trip. The card is read by a computerized scanner that identifies the shopper and records the details of the purchase. The information is analyzed even before the shopper finishes paying. Biographical information on the shoppers such as age, income, educational level, ages of children, and type of neighborhood are correlated with the shopping behavior.

This technique is being used in cities with cable-television services to which the members of the scanner-cable panels subscribe. Through the cable system, advertisers can target commercials for different panel members, even during the same network programs. For example, a food manufacturer can send a new commercial for soup to some homes and the old commercial for soup to other homes in the same city. By recording the actual purchases of soup, the manufacturer can determine which commercial may be associated with an increase in the purchase of the product.

Major food manufacturers such as Procter & Gamble, General Foods, General Mills, Kellogg, Campbell Soup, and Nabisco Brands are using scanner-cable panels to study purchasing behavior. The panels have been established in several cities, including Orlando, Florida; Portland, Maine; Marion, Indiana; and Midland, Texas. The cities are demographically representative of the U.S. population as a whole and are not too large, which means they have fewer supermarkets to be equipped with the expensive scanners. The technique is said to cost in excess of $1 million a year for each company, but the results appear to provide more detailed and accurate information than any other approach to the observation of purchasing behavior (Poindexter, 1983).

Brand-Identification and Brand-Preference Research

Research dealing with the ability of consumers to recognize or identify specific product brands is widespread in consumer psychology. The behavior being studied—preference rather than actual purchase—is amenable to study under well-controlled laboratory conditions. Thus, we can have greater confidence in these results than in the results of some observational studies. Even when brand-preference studies are conducted under natural conditions such as in a shopping center, it is relatively easy to control all relevant influencing variables.

Much brand-preference research focuses on consumers' ability to discriminate among competing brands of a product. When all recognizable cues are removed, for example, the product's name or distinctive package or container, can a person distinguish between one kind of cola and a competing brand? This research usually demonstrates that people cannot discriminate among brands. Several studies dealing with cola drinks have shown that people cannot identify the best-known products by taste once distinctive packaging characteristics were removed. Even people who said they would drink only Coca-Cola were not able to distinguish that product from other cola drinks. Similar results have been found for competing brands of cigarettes, whiskey, beer, and margarine (Greenberg & Collins, 1966). Apparently, with some products, consumer preferences and brand loyalty are caused by factors other than the intrinsic qualities of the product itself.

It is essential in brand-identification research that subjects be exposed to the various brands in blindfold fashion with beverages served in identical bottles, product names taped over, and any other distinguishing characteristics such as a unique cigarette filter tip disguised in some way.

Consumer-preference studies are also concerned with testing new products to determine customer reaction in advance of a product's release to the market at large. For example, studies have been performed on the tactual sensations or feel of various clothing fabrics, preferences for shapes of sponges, and perceived crispness of breakfast cereals in different packages. One study showed that consumers believed bread to be fresher when enclosed in a plastic bag than in wax paper alone. Without tasting or feeling the bread itself, consumers judged freshness solely on the basis of the wrappings (Brown, 1962).

These studies can control all variables likely to affect preference except the one under investigation. Such careful research, using subjects representative of the intended market, can provide manufacturers with much information about the reaction to their products. In addition, testing can detect deficiencies or undesirable features that can be corrected before the product is released for sale.

Testing Advertisements

A major research activity of consumer psychologists is testing the effectiveness of advertising and promotional campaigns, especially those presented on television. Approximately 6,000 television ads are tested every year at a cost of almost $60 million. Some 60% of the ads tested are considered to be failures and never appear on television (Young & Robinson, 1987). The tremendous amounts of money spent by business firms on advertising make such research necessary for several reasons: (1) to determine by pretesting advertisements their acceptability and effect before the ad is actually used; (2) to ascertain if a current advertising campaign is reaching the intended audience; (3) to find out if the message transmitted in the ads is the same one being received by the audience; (4) to learn how many of the people in the audience are really attending to the ad. Whether an ad is tested in advance of use or when a campaign is already under way, there are several specific techniques to determine its effectiveness.

The most direct approach is to *ask respondents* for their personal reactions to an ad. People are asked, for example, if the ad really makes them want to buy the product, if they believe the ad, or which of two ads for the same product is the more interesting or attention getting.

A requirement of this method is that the sample consist of a representative group of the same people for whom the product is intended. Using bachelors or elderly people to pretest an ad for baby food would not be wise because their reactions can be expected to differ from those of a young couple rearing a child.

The most frequently used technique of testing advertising effectiveness, particularly for television commercials, is the method of *aided recall*. Designed for any ad in any medium, the method attempts to assess the memorability of an advertisement. Shortly after an ad has appeared in a magazine or been televised, a cross section of consumers is questioned about whether they read that issue of the magazine or saw the program in which the commercial appeared. If they did, they are asked if they read or saw the commercial in question. Those who did see the ad are asked to tell as much of its selling message as they can remember. During this recall, the interviewer asks specific questions about various aspects of the ad, thus aiding the recall.

Another technique for testing the effectiveness of specific advertisements is *recognition*. People who have seen a particular television program or magazine are shown copies of ads that appeared therein and asked questions about them. Did the respondents remember seeing the ad? Did they remember the name of the product? Had they read at least half of the written part of the ad when they first saw it?

There is an unfortunate weakness in the recognition method that is not present with the recall method. People will sometimes say that they have seen an ad, even if they have not. This tendency was verified by using ads in the recognition test that had not yet appeared. Thus, it is possible to detect this kind of response faking.

Laboratory approaches to measuring advertisement reaction use elaborate electronic apparatus. An *eye camera* films the eye movements and fixations of subjects who are able to move their heads freely and read magazines at their own pace, turning the pages at leisure. The film record of eye movement provides much useful information such as which of several ads on the same page attracted attention first or held attention longest, what feature of an ad did a person look at first, in what sequence did the eye explore the various parts of an ad, and how long did the person look at an ad.

Another useful instrument is the *tachistoscope*, which permits short-term exposure of a visual stimulus. The device can be useful in pretesting ads; it makes it possible to determine how much information a person can perceive and recall on the basis of a very short exposure to an ad. Through research using the tachistoscope, it is possible to determine the maximum amount of information that can be presented in an ad.

Some consumer psychologists argue that these laboratory and field approaches provide useful information on how people may feel about an ad and how much of it they remember but that the only meaningful test is whether the ad results in increased sales. We noted the limitations of using sales figures as a criterion of success, but a more experimental approach, *sales tests*, is designed to reduce these deficiencies. It is a test in the sense of exerting experimental control over all influencing variables.

A sales or advertising campaign is introduced in selected cities or geographical areas. Other areas, chosen to be as similar as possible in all respects to the test-market areas, serve as controls; the ads are not seen in the control areas.

Assuming comparability of test and control areas, any resulting increase in sales in the test areas must be attributable to the advertising alone. Scanner-cable panels are one method of conducting such a sales test.

The major advantage of this approach is the control, which can produce conclusive results. The psychologist is not measuring interest in an ad or what people say they remember about an ad or their eye movements when they see it, but whether they actually go out and buy the product solely on the basis of the advertising. Further, the experimental controls assure that purchasing behavior is not caused by extraneous variables that operate independently of the advertising.

This approach to advertising effectiveness is desirable, but it, too, has limitations. An adequate sales test requires great expense, considerable time to arrange, and precise accounting of what large numbers of people do and do not purchase during the period of the study. Another limitation involves the control areas. By not exposing people in the control areas to the new advertising, the manufacturer may lose sales to competitors in those areas. In spite of the difficulties and expense, increasing numbers of advertising agencies are undertaking sales tests because they offer the most accurate method of gauging the impact of advertising effectiveness on sales.

A means of testing magazine and newspaper advertising is through the use of *coupon returns*. For the most part, this is used to gauge reader interest, not actual buying behavior, except in those cases where the coupon is sent to the manufacturer to purchase a product or to receive money back from a purchase (cents-off coupons). In most cases, however, coupons are used to get a sample, a brochure, or to enter a contest. When the inducement to return the coupon is especially attractive, there is the danger of people responding in the absence of any real interest in the product itself. There are also those who will return virtually any coupon simply because they like to receive mail. There is no way of knowing how many coupon returns are from habitual coupon clippers and how many are from people genuinely interested in the product.

The technique of coupon return is in widespread use by many companies. What it may indicate is the attention-getting value of the ad and the attractiveness of the inducement to clip the coupon. Except in the relatively rare case of mail-order sales on the basis of coupons, this method does not provide a direct measure of the effectiveness of an ad in increasing sales.

However, consumer research has demonstrated that coupons are more effective in getting people to change brands than any other kind of promotional activity. Coupons, particularly those offering cents-off the purchase price, are a big business in themselves. It is estimated that the average household in the United States receives close to 3,000 coupons every year (T. Johnson, 1984). According to the *New York Times*, more than 200 billion cents-off coupons were distributed through newspapers and magazines in 1986, an increase of 13% over 1985.

Research has shown that consumer response to a price reduction obtained by returning a coupon is higher than for an equivalent price reduction given in the store. A 15% price reduction on dairy products in supermarkets generated sales increases of 3% to 25%. The same price reduction offered through coupons produced sales increases of 20% to 70%. Studies comparing coupon users and nonusers showed that coupon users were more price conscious than nonusers, placed less value on their time (it does, after all, take time to clip and redeem coupons), and felt a sense of satisfaction in having done something to save money (Babakus, Tat, & Cunningham, 1988).

The rate of return of cents-off coupons varies with their source. People use about 3% of the coupons printed in a newspaper or magazine, 5% of the coupons inserted between the pages of a magazine, 10% of those received in the mail, and 15% to 20% of those attached to a product already purchased. Thus, the most successful use of coupons is with people who already use a particular product (Bridgwater, 1983; Neslin & Clarke, 1987).

There are, then, a variety of methods available to measure the impact of advertisements. Despite the great effort expended in pretesting and posttesting ads, there are still advertising campaign failures. Usually, assuming a worthwhile product, these failures are not an indictment of the methods themselves but of their improper implementation by people insufficiently trained to carry them out or companies unwilling to pay for sound research.

Television Programming Research

Millions of dollars are spent annually to develop television programs that will attract and hold a sizable portion of the viewing audience. Each fall, the widely touted new season opens and the networks compete for the considerable prizes of the advertising dollar. The fact that 90% of all new programs are canceled long before the end of the viewing season attests to the frequency with which television executives are unable to select winning programs.

There are research techniques available that can help to decide in advance of actual programming how successful a new series may be. Also, audience reaction, once a series is under way, can be reviewed periodically. Finally, there are methods to determine not only the size of the audience for a particular program but also its composition. This information is particularly important to sponsors because it will influence the design of commercials.

Predicting Reactions to New Programming.   Often, before a program or series is put on the air, a sample of viewers is invited to view a pilot film of the series. The usual procedure is for the viewers to communicate their reactions continuously throughout the program. Viewers are given a control device with two push buttons. When they are indifferent or neutral toward a scene, they do not press either button, but, when they like a scene, they press the appropriate button; when they dislike a scene, they press the other button.

Each control device is linked to a recorder so that a permanent record of the individual reactions is made for detailed analysis. The advantage of this approach is that it provides a minute-by-minute, scene-by-scene evaluation of all parts of a program, not just a single judgment on the entire program. By analyzing total audience reaction, it is possible to get an overall response to the program as well as the detailed reactions. This can lead to changes in specific scenes of the program before its release to the general public.

This is an excellent technique for predicting program acceptance, assuming that the subjects are a representative sample of the viewing audience. Subject sampling is a crucial factor; if it is not done correctly, all other experimental controls and precautions may be negated.

Unfortunately, most of the samples selected by the television networks are not representative of the total viewing audience. Often the samples are composed of passersby on the street who are persuaded to come into the studio to watch a new program. For example, CBS uses some 80,000 such people in its screening rooms in New York and Los Angeles. People who happen to be walking past the studios at a particular time can hardly be considered representative of the television viewing population as a whole.

Determining Audience Size and Reactions. There are several techniques to measure the ratings of television programs. Telephone surveys are frequently used and follow one of two basic approaches: (1) the interviewer asks the respondents about their television viewing during a recent time period such as the previous day—for example, what programs were seen and which family members watched each program; (2) the interviewer asks respondents what program, if any, is being watched at the moment of the telephone call.

A mechanical technique that eliminates many of the sources of error found in any survey uses a recorder, called an Audimeter, installed in the homes of a viewer sample. The device, unobtrusive and silent, makes a permanent record of exactly when the television set was on and to what channels it was tuned over the course of a day. This kind of device is used to determine the Nielsen ratings, which provide the basis for deciding whether programs will be continued or dropped. Although it provides an accurate record of channel choice for all programming periods, it does not tell which viewers are watching a particular program. Indeed, it cannot tell if anyone is watching. Some people leave a television set on much of the time as a baby-sitter for infants or because they like some sound in the house.

Nielsen Media Research also uses a diary system, in which each member of a household records viewing choices to supplement the ratings obtained by the Audimeter. In 1987, the company introduced the People Meter, a device that looks like a television remote control device. Each member of the household punches in a personal code when watching television, and the program being seen is automatically registered. When the viewer turns off the set or leaves the room, he or she is supposed to push appropriate buttons on the People Meter. Some people tire of this and fail to do it after a while, which obviously distorts the results. Also, some people will punch in the code of another family member as a joke. Research indicates that those most likely to follow the instructions precisely are older people who have only one television set (Deutsch, 1987a).

Other research has demonstrated that over a 4-week period, the statistical reliability of the People Meter is far superior to a diary sample, based on the same number of households (Soong, 1988). Another study found lower ratings of repeat viewing of regular television series when recorded by People Meters rather than by diaries, an average of only 24% repeat viewing on the People Meter and 40% in the diaries (Ehrenberg & Wakshlag, 1987).

The attempt to find a way to record accurately what people are watching on television is becoming increasingly sophisticated and is now focusing on passive techniques, devices that would unobtrusively record viewing habits without the viewers having to do anything to activate them. High-tech research is being conducted on sonar, thermal infrared, and ultrasonic devices that would automatically note when one or more persons entered or left the TV viewing room, and what programs were being aired. Of course, the devices still could not identify who, if anyone, is watching (Lu & Kiewit, 1987).

These attempts to record the size of a television audience are complicated by the finding that a majority of people do not pay full or careful attention to television. A study of the viewing habits of 1,600 people in Springfield, Illinois, showed that for most viewers, television served as little more than a "talking lamp." Of that sample, 40% repeatedly left the room during the course of a program. Up to 75% said they frequently carried on a conversation during a program. In addition, 10% did household chores, 8% read, and 3% talked on the telephone while they reportedly were watching television. Obviously, then, the television advertisers were not receiving the undivided attention of their audience ("When the TV Is On," 1982).

Research on television viewing is also complicated by the fact that viewers have different interests and attitudes toward television. There is no single mass audience for television. Psychologists have identified three types of viewers who react in different ways to television: the *embracers,* the *accommodators,* and the *protesters* (Domzal & Kernan, 1983).

Embracers like television, watch a great deal of it, and enjoy it. They are not discriminating in their viewing habits and will watch nearly everything that is shown for an average of slightly over 30 hours a week. They watch television to relax, to forget their problems, and to be entertained. They identify with the characters they see on television, become highly involved with the plots of various television series, and believe that watching television is a worthwhile way to spend their time. Approximately 49% of the population falls in this category.

Accommodators average 25 hours of television viewing per week. They are more discriminating and are sometimes critical of the programs they watch. They look at television primarily to be sociable with friends and family or to avoid boredom. Despite the number of hours they spend in front of a television set, accommodators believe that much of what is aired is in bad taste and lacks imagination. Little of what they see is acceptable to them. They also report that the more they watch, the less they enjoy it. Accommodators constitute about 27% of the viewing population.

Protesters do not like television, are very critical of it, and are highly selective in what they watch. Their average weekly viewing time is 19 hours. They consider most television programming to be dull, harmful, simple-minded, and boring. They watch primarily news and documentary programs to find out what is going on in the world and to learn something new. This group constitutes about 24% of the viewing audience.

Obviously, then, programming and advertising will appeal to these segments of the viewing population in different ways. Also, they differ from one another in more ways than their attitudes toward television. Educational and income levels, interests, and leisure activities also distinguish these groups. To attract the attention of each segment, advertisers must frame their messages appropriately and perhaps use different media as well.

The Seller

This section deals with the efforts of the sellers of goods to encourage, persuade, stimulate, or manipulate you, the consumer, so that you will buy their products. These numerous activities can be summed up by the label, *advertising*. We examine some of the techniques, tricks, and problems of this sometimes devious art, recognizing also its level of success.

Nature and Scope of Advertising

The influence of advertising can be seen all around us every day. There are more than 4 million firms in the United States, ranging from the corner hardware store to the Fortune 500 corporations, and nearly all of them engage in some form of advertising. There are more than 4,500 advertising agencies that handle about one fourth of all the money spent on advertising each year.

Approximately 75% of the money spent on advertising is devoted to the six major media: newspapers, television, direct mail, magazines, radio, and outdoor (billboards)—in that order of intensity. We may sometimes forget that radio and television programming and most newspapers and magazines are supported primarily by the advertising dollar. Except for cable television subscribers, television viewers do not pay for the expensive programs they watch; without advertising revenue, this programming could not be made available without charge.

The overwhelming majority of advertising is the *direct-sell* type, oriented toward an immediate response on the part of the consumer. Most newspaper and local radio advertising is of this kind, offering sales, coupons, and special purchases.

A second category of advertising is designed to create consumer *awareness* of a new product or model, an improved product or package, or a price change. This type of advertising also tries to reinforce the product's brand name (see Figure 14-2). Because so much purchasing behavior is by brand name,

Figure 14-2 Consumer awareness advertising. (Reproduced by permission of Ford.)

companies spend great sums of money to try to establish and maintain the name of their company or product in the public's awareness.

The third category of advertising attempts to establish an *image* for a product or service. Many products cannot be distinguished from one another in terms of ingredients or quality, so advertisers try to create distinguishable differences in terms of the image or symbol the product represents. For example, an automobile must do more than provide transportation. It must, through its image, make the owner feel younger or sportier or higher in status. The president of a large cosmetics firm said, "In the factory we make cosmetics; in the store we sell hope." And a professor continued, "It is not cosmetic chemicals [people] want, but the seductive charm promised by the alluring symbols with which these chemicals have been surrounded—hence the rich and exotic packages in which they are sold and the suggestive advertising with which they are promoted" (Levitt, 1970, p. 85).

Finally, there is *institutional* advertising, whose goal is to convince the public that an organization is a good neighbor and community benefactor. An example of this is the campaign conducted by an oil company to promote, not their products, but highway safety. Another instance is the ad from a high-technology company that emphasizes its interest in helping people communicate (see Figure 14-3). About 5% of advertising is of this type, and it is conducted mostly by large corporations. In addition to persuading the public of the company's goodwill, institutional advertising can boost sales, help in recruiting professionals, improve employee morale, and increase the price of the company's stock.

Advertising campaigns have three goals: (1) to produce an awareness of, and knowledge about, a company, a product, or a service; (2) to create a positive attitude toward, and preference for, the product; and (3) to stimulate a desire for, and action toward, the product—in other words, to buy it.

Types of Advertising Appeals

The major way in which an advertisement can satisfy these goals is in terms of its appeal, that is, what it promises to do for the potential purchaser. Which human needs or motivations does the product promise to satisfy? We have many drives: innate or primary ones for food, water, shelter, safety, and sexual satisfaction; and a variety of learned or secondary drives that vary from one culture or subculture to another or from one person to another.

Thus, not all segments of the population have a similar need for achievement or for affiliation or for status. These drives depend on a person's past experiences; the experiences of a child growing up in Beverly Hills, California, foster a different set of adult needs than the experiences of a child growing up in Harlem in New York City.

To sell their products, advertisers must gear their messages toward satisfying the right needs, but this is difficult to do because of the group and individual differences in needs as well as the complexity of human motivations.

ONE OUT OF FIVE ADULT AMERICANS IS UNABLE TO READ THIS SENTENCE.

Or a warning label. Or a job application. Or a love letter.

You see, more than 27 million adult Americans are functionally illiterate. And their ranks are swelling by more than two million every year.

As a high-technology maker of America's defense systems, we find this trend more menacing than Soviet missiles.

Experts say curing illiteracy will require the efforts of tens of thousands of us.

That's why General Dynamics has made a grant to help keep the Project Literacy U.S. Hotline operating, toll-free. Call the Hotline, 1-800-228-8813. Find out how you can help someone overcome this terrible handicap.

We think every American ought to be able to read this ad. Don't you?

GENERAL DYNAMICS
A Strong Company For A Strong Country

Figure 14-3 Institutional advertising. (Reproduced by permission of General Dynamics.)

One large-scale study investigated the appeals used in television commercials on the three major networks over a period of 3 months (McNeal & McDaniel, 1984). The products advertised included automobiles, beer and wine, breakfast cereals, deodorants and antiperspirants, fast foods, feminine hygiene products, pet foods, shampoos, and soft drinks. All of the ads contained at least one attempt to appeal to a specific human need. The average was slightly over four needs for each commercial. Many advertisers expected their commercials to satisfy several needs at the same time. For example, an imported beer ad promised to quench thirst and to satisfy the need for status as well.

The primary target of the commercials was the need for affiliation, that is, our desire to be with, and to get along well with, other people. This appeal was contained in 59% of the ads. The second most prominent need, recognized in 47% of the ads, was for positive sensory impressions such as pleasing odors, sights, and sounds or good-tasting food and drink.

The need to avoid embarrassing situations was the focus of 39% of the ads. Also important were the need for achievement; the need for nurturance, that is, to help satisfy the needs of others; and the need to avoid physical discomfort. No matter what need is appealed to, most ads feature attractive people. A study of 115 college women (smokers and nonsmokers) showed that they regarded a cigarette ad as being more persuasive when it contained an attractive model than when it did not (Loken & Howard-Pitney, 1988).

It is not difficult to determine in most ads which need is being appealed to. A mouthwash or shampoo virtually guarantees that its user will be hungrily sought after by the opposite sex. An after-dinner drink being consumed by an expensively dressed couple at a country club assures the drinker of enhanced prestige and status. Almost 10% of the ads to which Americans are exposed contain appeals to status needs. In Japan, twice as many ads appeal to status (Mueller, 1987).

A product endorsed by a celebrity invites the audience to identify with his or her achievements and success. Celebrities are frequently used to sell products, despite the fact that there is little published evidence to show the impact of celebrity endorsements on actual buying behavior. Surveys on consumer attitudes toward celebrity commercials suggest that their appeal may be declining. One study in 1984 found that 26% of the consumers polled expressed a positive opinion about celebrity endorsements. By 1987, however, that figure had dropped to 16%. Another poll showed that 70% of consumers did not believe the comments celebrities were supposed to have made about the products they were endorsing (Kanner, 1988b).

Advertisers continually study consumers to determine their motivations and to slant their messages accordingly. Often, such studies result in a drastic change in the advertising appeal. For example, the theme of an advertising campaign for a well-known household cleaner was its cleaning speed—consumers were told that it worked faster than any other product. Consumer research reported that people who were using the product rarely said they did so because of its alleged speed. Instead, more than half the users said they bought the product because it was gentle to their hands. The wrong appeal was being used, and the situation was quickly remedied.

A choice must be made about the manner in which any appeal should be formulated. Should the message indicate that something pleasant will happen to you if you do use the product (a *positive* appeal)? Or should it show that something unpleasant will happen if you do not use the product (a *negative* appeal)? For example, what is the best way to market a deodorant soap? Do you portray men and women sitting home alone—with no dates or friends—because they do not smell good or fresh or clean? Or do you show them at a party or even getting married because they used the correct product?

The negative appeal has been shown to be effective for certain kinds of products. The negative appeal does not work, however, when the consequences are overly unpleasant such as showing pictures of horrible automobile accidents in a campaign to promote safe driving or pictures of diseased lungs in a campaign to get people to stop smoking. These advertisements distract people from the message. A study of health warnings in cigarette ads showed that specific warnings rendered ads less attractive and less persuasive than did general warnings. Stating that smoking increases the risk of heart disease was less effective, for example, than simply saying that smoking is harmful to your health (Loken & Howard-Pitney, 1988).

A standard approach combines both appeals, first showing the negative consequences of not using the product, then showing the benefits when the consumer began using the product. Both positive and negative appeals can be effective, depending on the product being promoted and on the personal characteristics of the consumer market for that product.

One appeal frequently made in advertising is that of implied superiority, in which the superiority of one product over its competitors is not stated directly but is presented in such a way that it is inferred by the consumer. For example, if all headache remedies take the same amount of time to bring relief, one product may claim that "no pain capsule provides faster relief than Brand A." The claim is true, but the phrasing may cause some consumers to conclude that Brand A is superior to its competitors because it sounds like it works faster. In addition, there is the implied suggestion that some sort of comparative research has been conducted that provides a factual basis for the implied claim that Brand A works faster than all other pain relievers.

Analyses of advertisements show that 70% of the assertions made in airline, beer, deodorant, and shampoo television commercials use claims of implied superiority, and that a majority of viewers believe them. Consumers also tend to exaggerate and expand such claims. In laboratory studies, significant proportions of subjects asserted that claims that had not actually been made had indeed appeared in the advertisements to which they were exposed. As many as 64% of consumers studied believed the claims of implied superiority. Those consumers with less formal education were more likely to believe such claims than persons with more formal education (Wyckham, 1987).

Quality never goes out of style.

Apple Computer, Inc.

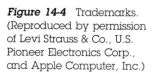

Figure 14-4 Trademarks. (Reproduced by permission of Levi Strauss & Co., U.S. Pioneer Electronics Corp., and Apple Computer, Inc.)

Trademarks

A trademark familiar to most of the consuming public can greatly facilitate advertising effectiveness because it serves as a shorthand symbol of the feelings and images associated with the product through past advertising. Key aspects of the product can come to be identified with and exemplified by the trademark. Most trademarks are simply the name of the product, for example, Coca-Cola, Kleenex, Xerox (see Figure 14-4).

When a trademark is well established in the consumer's vocabulary, it alone—without any other advertising message—can stimulate the person to recall the product and its image.

Consumer psychologists have devoted considerable research to the effectiveness of trademarks and brand names (often the two are synonymous), concerned primarily with their ease of identification and with their meaning. How quickly they can be recognized is usually studied by means of the tachistoscope, flashing trademarks briefly (perhaps one fiftieth of a second) to the subjects to determine what names and symbols can be most readily identified.

Trademark meaning can be studied by using the free association technique in which people respond with the first word that comes to mind when presented with a trademark or brand name as the stimulus word. Considerable effort and large sums of money are devoted to developing product trademarks and names. Specialists called identity consultants have concerned themselves not only with the naming and renaming of products but of companies as well. California Airlines changed its name to AirCal when interviews with focus groups showed that the new name would have greater consumer impact. Allegheny Airlines changed its name to USAir to eliminate the regional connotation of the former name.

Computers are used extensively in developing names because of their capacity for rapidly generating combinations of syllables, sounds, and letters. Consumer psychologists are also conducting research on the emotional impact of product names. A study of college undergraduates found that women were more sensitive to the emotional connotations of product names than were men, and that names with high emotional impact correlated highly with preference for the product (Mehrabian & de Wetter, 1987).

Research can be of great value by informing manufacturers how recognizable the product name is and what that name means to the consuming public. Often such tests lead to a modification in a trademark to make it a more effective advertising cue. This has been especially crucial for U.S. products marketed in other countries. Sometimes a trademark can have an unintended meaning in another language. The Chevrolet Nova, for example, is named for a star that suddenly increases in brightness and energy. In Spanish, however, *no va* means "doesn't go," not a very good name for an automobile. The Coca-Cola Company had to change its product name in China when it was discovered that Coca-Cola meant "bite the wax tadpole." The new name chosen translates as "may the mouth rejoice." Braniff Airlines advertised in Spanish-language newspapers and magazines boasting that their airline seats were leather. In translation, however, the message meant "sit naked."

It took some time for the marketer of Japan's best-selling soft drink to figure out why the product failed when it was introduced to English-speaking consumers. The drink was similar to Gatorade, and the Japanese gave it an English name they thought would emphasize its thirst-quenching qualities. The label they chose was Pocari Sweat, which does not evoke a very appealing image.

Sometimes a trademark can be so effective that it comes to stand for all brands of a certain type of product. For example, kleenex is now used to mean any kind of facial tissue, and xerox any kind of photocopier. When this happens, the company can lose its ready identifiability and share of the market.

Product Image

An integral aspect of advertising is the establishment of a product's image. What ideas, thoughts, and feelings are associated with the product's personality? The development of a successful product image—one with which people will want to identify—has frequently brought companies from obscurity to prosperity.

Indeed, the image of a product can be far more important in selling than the nature of the product itself.

Take the example of Marlboro cigarettes. When first introduced, their packaging and advertising were oriented toward an elegant and essentially feminine personality. Consumer response was not spectacular. In hopes of boosting sales, a new advertising campaign was launched to change the image. Cowboys, ranchers, and other rugged-looking outdoor men, sporting tattoos and riding horses, were used in the advertisements. The Marlboro Man in Marlboro Country became part of our lives, and sales soared.

Sometimes the image of a product is transmitted by a figure or symbol found on the product itself such as the tiny alligator on some popular pullover knit shirts. Such a symbol can represent the image of the person wearing the product. One study compared how a person was perceived by others when wearing a knit shirt with different symbols on it. In three test conditions, the symbols were a fox, an alligator, and a polo player. In the fourth condition, the shirt was plain. When wearing the plain shirt, the person was judged to be self-confident, tolerant, satisfied, and friendly. The same person in the shirt with the fox emblem was described as self-confident, enthusiastic, and a leader. In the polo-player shirt, the person was perceived as less self-confident, less tolerant, less enthusiastic, less satisfied, and less friendly than he was judged to be in any of the other shirts. The image presented by the shirt with the alligator was that of a preppy individual who was neither a leader nor a follower (Swartz, 1983).

The most difficult problem in the development of a product image is not the transmission of the image to the public, but the determination of what that image should be. What will attract potential buyers to one make of automobile or refrigerator or sportswear rather than another? What kind of product personality should be stressed?

There are several methods for studying product image. One technique involves *group interviews* with selected samples of consumers in which they are questioned in detail about their perception of, and feeling toward, various products. This in-depth approach attempts to elicit hidden feelings—positive and negative—about the products in question.

A more objective approach involves the *adjective checklist*. People are asked which of a number of descriptive adjectives or phrases characterize their feelings about a particular product. (This was the technique used in the study about the different symbols on the pullover shirts.) A variation of this approach asks people to apply each adjective in the checklist to one of several products or to their conception of the type of person who would buy those products.

Another study using the adjective checklist involved having 60 college student subjects rank order a list of items describing the personality or the "drama" of several products, including McDonald's fast food and Levi's jeans (Durgee, 1988). The most important product personality factors are shown in Table 14-2.

Based on this kind of research, advertisers can decide which qualities to stress (and which to ignore) in developing an image for the product.

TABLE 14-2   Product Personality Factors

McDonald's fast food	*Levi's jeans*
golden arches sign	casual wear
long thin salty french fries	gray, faded look when old, rugged durability
mushy hamburger, cheese, and bread taste of Big Mac	blue color, shrink to fit, slightly abrasive feel of denim on skin
noises of hissing fries, cooking machines, and people calling orders	leather patch, button fly
counter helpers' striped hats and shirts, plastic hamburger containers	"stove-pipe" cut, tight fit in thighs, copper rivets
Egg McMuffin; beige, orange, brown decor	yellow stitches, small red tag
milkshakes, smell of fry oil and hamburgers, McNuggets	reinforced seams, angle cut pockets

Adapted from "Product drama" by J. F. Durgee, February/March 1988, *Journal of Advertising Research*, p. 46.

The Package

Another important aspect of an advertising and promotional campaign for a product is its package. This is the part of the product that consumers see at the critical moment of decision prior to purchase. When looking for a box of cookies on the supermarket shelf and confronted by a dizzying array of competing brands, shoppers may not remember the commercial they saw the previous night on television. At the moment of purchase, the package may well be the deciding factor. Some consumer psychologists believe that packaging is the single most important element in a consumer's decision to buy a particular product.

The old saying about not being able to judge a book by its cover may be true, but we still tend to make decisions on that basis. How often do we evaluate people on the basis of their clothes or their car? We all tend to categorize others based on their cover. We make similar judgments about many of the things we buy. Psychologists have found many examples where consumers' attitudes about a product are based not on the quality of the product but on the wrapping or package in which it was presented.

In one study, two groups of people were asked about the taste of coffee. One group was served coffee from a modern electric coffee maker and the other group was served from an antique coffee urn. The antique-urn group rated the coffee much better tasting than the modern-coffee-maker group. And the coffee itself? The same in both cases. The container from which the coffee was poured influenced the way in which the people perceived its taste.

In another study, pills of two different sizes were shown to groups of patients and doctors, and they were asked to rate the potency of the drug contained in the pills. Both groups insisted, on the basis of size, that the larger pill was the more potent. In fact, however, the larger pill was less than half as strong as the smaller pill.

We mentioned earlier a study in which bread packaged in a plastic bag was judged to be fresher than the same bread wrapped in wax paper. In addition, American consumers consistently judge white eggs to be superior to brown eggs, even though there is no actual difference between them in taste or quality. European consumers, on the other hand, are willing to pay more for brown eggs because they believe they are superior to white ones. In all these examples, decisions are made on the basis of the package rather than the product itself.

According to a well-known consumer psychologist, a properly designed package must satisfy six criteria (Dichter, 1970).

1. *Convenience*. The package must hold just the right amount of the product to satisfy the average user's needs. It should not be too bulky or heavy.
2. *Adaptability*. The package must fit the space in which such a product is normally kept. For example, medicine bottles should not be too large for a medicine cabinet.
3. *Security*. The package must assure consumers that the product is of high quality.
4. *Status or prestige*. Consumers must feel that the package enables them to express something about themselves. A worthy or desirable personal quality must be stimulated by the package.
5. *Dependability*. The package must cause consumers to feel that they can depend on the product and its manufacturer.
6. *Aesthetic satisfaction*. The design, shape, and color of the package must be aesthetically pleasing.

Overall, the packaging must reinforce the image or personality of the product established by the advertising. A cologne advertised for the virile man should not be packaged in a pink tube with fancy lettering but in a box with bright bold colors.

The design and matching of package and product can be determined through careful research on consumer reactions to existing as well as new packages. Consumers can be asked to examine a package and then to free associate—to tell whatever comes to mind when they see the package—and this research can determine the positive or negative images elicited by the package. Survey and in-depth procedures can also be used to determine packaging impact and preference.

Packaging is an expensive part of the manufacturing and marketing process. Companies spend $55 billion a year on packaging, and this adds considerably to the cost of consumer products. Packaging accounts for more than one third of the price of toiletries, cosmetics, and drugs. When you buy a bottle or can of beer, 30% of the cost goes for the package. Overall, 24% of every dollar spent in supermarkets is for the containers, not for what is in them (Kanner, 1983).

Sex in Advertising

The use of attractive persons, sexual fantasies, and nude or scantily clad models is prominent in advertising. Such illustrations are used to sell everything from spark plugs to perfume. Because the approach is so frequently used, it is natural to assume that its effectiveness as a sales technique is beyond question.

However, its value has been accepted on faith alone with little research support. The research that has been conducted is not optimistic. Sex appeal in ads does seem to have a high attention-getting value for both men and women. Studies of consumers looking at magazines show that, of a variety of ads on a single page, most people immediately look at the one that contains an element of sex. But what then? Ads featuring provocative pictures of women are read more often by women than by men. Men are attracted to this type of illustration, but women read the message along with it. In many cases, this means that the wrong audience is reading the message; usually the attractive woman was included in the ad to seduce men into reading the message.

A similar phenomenon occurs with ads using pictures of attractive men; the messages are more often read by men than by women. Once again, the wrong audience is reading the message.

Even more discouraging is evidence suggesting a very low recall rate for messages accompanying sexy illustrations. One company tried two ads, each with a coupon to return. One ad featured a young woman in a bikini; the other did not. The coupon return was much higher from the ad without the illustration.

Laboratory research verifies the field observations. In one study, men subjects were shown a number of ads, some with and some without sexy illustrations. They were then shown the same ads with the brand names deleted and asked to identify the product or advertiser. When questioned again, 24 hours after seeing them, there was no difference in recall for the sexy and nonsexy ads. After 7 days, however, they had forgotten significantly more of the sexy than the nonsexy ads.

Another study compared the recall of the brand names of ads with pictures of nude women and the same ads with pictures of forests and mountains. The nude ads produced a significantly lower rate of recall of the names of the products involved. Other research has shown that both men and women rated an ad showing a nude woman to be much less appealing than a less sexy ad. The subjects also rated the company as disreputable and the product as low in quality for the nude ad (Peterson & Kerin, 1977).

In summary, the wrong audience reads the messages accompanying sexy advertisements and, although many people enjoy looking at the illustrations, they do not remember the advertising messages that accompany them and think poorly of the companies that produced them.

The Portrayal of Women in Advertisements

Women have frequently been depicted in print advertisements and television commercials as sex objects, homemakers, and mothers. A survey of television commercials in the United States, Mexico, and Australia found that women were consistently less likely than men to be portrayed as employed outside the home (Gilly, 1988). Women are shown primarily at home, seeking fulfillment in a shiny kitchen floor or a clean batch of laundry. Although most commercials still show women in these roles, more and more ads feature them in positions of authority and in business roles, the ways in which men have traditionally been portrayed. This change provides an example of how advertising responds to the changing social climate.

Increasing numbers of women are heads of households and are purchasing items formerly bought by men such as automobile tires and home-repair items. On the other hand, many men in two-career families are purchasing items for cleaning, cooking, and child care. Thus, we have come to see commercials and advertisements for a variety of products aimed at both men and women.

In a laboratory study, two groups of women called "traditional" (homemakers) and "modern" (employed outside the home) were shown commercials depicting women in these two roles (Leigh, Rethans, & Whitney, 1987). The attitudes of each group were more favorable when the role portrayed in the ad was consistent with their own. That is, women in the traditional group were more favorable toward those ads showing women as homemakers and women in the modern group were more favorable toward ads depicting women as employed outside the home. Each group held unfavorable attitudes toward the ads portraying women in the role other than their own.

Another study compared the effectiveness of the traditional and the modern roles for women in commercials (Whipple & Courtney, 1980). The traditional commercial for a floor cleaner showed two women competing in a mopping contest supervised by a man. The modern version showed a husband and wife competing in a mopping contest conducted by a woman. Other commercials showed a women professional and her men assistants on the job and a family fixing breakfast while the mother prepared to go out to work.

Women consumer groups, manufacturers, and advertising agencies viewed the commercials and were interviewed for their reactions. All three groups judged the modern ads to be significantly more effective and less irritating and insulting to women than the traditional ads. The more progressive ads were especially appealing to women under the age of 35, married women, full-time women employees, and women who described themselves as "liberated."

Introducing a New Brand

One frequent business activity is the introduction of new brands of a product. Every year there are new brands of toothpaste, cigarettes, and breakfast cereal, among many others. Some of these new brands succeed and become well established in the marketplace. Others, for a variety of reasons, fail and are withdrawn from the market. And some new brands do not even reach the public; they are doomed by the results of market research tests.

Introducing new brands is an expensive and risky operation. Some 70% to 90% of all new products do not go beyond the test-market stage. An unknown percentage fail (unknown because companies do not generally talk about their failures) even when they had succeeded in the test marketing. Companies spend a great deal of time and money on research that they hope will lead to the development of new products, but only 20% of that effort is successful.

To find out why some new brands succeed and others do not, 100 new food products were studied (Davidson, 1976). Half of them were successful and half were not. Some interesting and significant differences were found between the successes and the failures. Of the successful new brands, 74% offered better quality or performance at the same or even higher prices than competing brands. There was a high correlation between the success of a new brand and its degree of difference from existing brands. Most successful new brands offered an obviously new appearance or performance in a way that was immediately apparent to consumers. Most successful brands represented a dramatically new idea.

On the surface, it may seem simple to ensure the success of a new brand: Offer consumers better value, make sure the product is noticeably different from competing products, and be the first with a new idea. Apparently, most new brands do not meet these criteria.

Success of Advertising Campaigns

We turn now to the most important question of all for the seller: Is the advertising, on which so much money is spent, really effective? Unfortunately, in many cases, neither the advertising agency nor the company whose product is being promoted really knows how successful an advertising campaign has been. Further, when success (or lack of it) is known, it is often kept secret from anyone not directly involved with the company. Understandably, companies do not want to broadcast their failures or have competitors learn of a new technique that has been enormously successful.

The research that has been conducted on the success of advertising presents results that are not very favorable. Consider, for example, viewers' ability to recall a television commercial they had seen only 5 minutes before. In 1965, only 18% of those studied could recall the ad; in 1981, even that low recall rate had dropped to 7% ("Goodbye, Mr. Whipple," 1984).

In another study, viewers at home were surveyed by telephone about commercials they had seen in the previous hour, during which time an average of 19.8 ads had been shown. Some 80% of the people called could not remember a single advertised brand, even when they were given clues about the products that had been advertised. Only 5% could recall more than one brand (Bogart & Lehman, 1983). Another telephone survey found that 85% of those polled could not remember any commercial they had seen in the previous 4 weeks (Kanner, 1987).

Fewer and fewer people in the television-viewing audience are actually watching commercials. They tune out these advertising messages by not paying attention, by leaving the room, by erasing or speeding through them on their video recorders, by switching channels, or by turning off the sound with remote control devices.

Even in test situations, in which subjects watched television commercials without being able to tune them out physically, people misunderstood or forgot approximately 30% of what they had seen when questioned immediately after viewing the ads (Rice, 1983b). One day later, the subjects had forgotten or misunderstood 75% of what they had seen. With magazine ads, the figure is higher; 85% of what was read had been forgotten or misunderstood (Ogilvy & Raphaelson, 1982).

The effectiveness of an ad may depend on the context in which it appears. Although the editorial philosophy or bias of a newspaper or magazine does not appear to have an impact on the effectiveness of the ads contained therein, the emotional tone of a particular television program does seem to affect viewer response to commercials (Appel, 1987; Goldberg & Gorn, 1987). One group of adult subjects viewed a happy program, a segment of the "Real People" show about people trying to teach frogs to improve their self-image. Another group watched a sad program, a "Sixty Minutes" segment about the murder of a child. After the viewings, the subjects were questioned about the commercials that had been shown with the programs. Those viewers watching the happy program demonstrated a higher recall of the content of the commercials and evaluated the commercials as being more effective than those who watched the sad program. However, there was no difference between the two groups in their stated intention to purchase the products advertised.

Repetitions of an ad can influence its effectiveness. In one study, 240 graduate business school students were shown eight different print ads, which varied in complexity, 1 week apart. The repeated exposure had no effect on the simple ads, but did result in a more positive evaluation of the effectiveness of the more complex ads. In addition, the expressed liking for the product being advertised increased substantially with the second exposure to the ad (Cox & Cox, 1988).

Advertising is not seen in isolation, of course. Whether on the pages of newspapers and magazines or on television screens, a great many competing commercials appear, all vying for our attention. Research using both adult and college student subjects viewing magazine ads under laboratory conditions found that the recall of ads was substantially interfered with when the subjects saw ads for competing brands of the same product and ads for other products (Burke & Srull, 1988; Keller, 1987). Perhaps that helps to explain why so few people are able to remember ads, even those seen only a few minutes before.

Other research deals with the effects of advertising in different media on shopping behavior. Slightly over 48% of the adults surveyed reported that their most recent shopping trip was made on the basis of information supplied by advertising. Newspaper advertisements, the most influential information source, were cited by 34% of the respondents. Brochures received by mail were important to approximately 7% of those surveyed, and radio and television commercials accounted for another 6%. These sources were all significantly less important as a guide to shopping than was habit, which influenced approximately 53% of the decisions (Hirschman & Mills, 1980).

These studies indicate what aspects of advertising can influence its effectiveness. You can see that it is difficult to give a simple answer to the question, Is advertising effective? The answer is both yes and no. Under certain conditions, for certain products, and with certain types of people some advertising is effective. For other conditions, products, and people, advertising seems to be of little value.

One analysis identified the following factors as being positively correlated with successful advertising campaigns (Korgaonkar, Moschis, & Bellenger, 1984):

1. The campaign was based on market research techniques.
2. The campaign was backed by adequate financial and management support.
3. The campaign was based on careful media planning.
4. The advertising messages were perceived to be unique and creative.
5. The product was perceived to be unique.

An investigation of more than 800 television commercials showed that the following techniques were effective in persuading people to change brands (Ogilvy & Raphaelson, 1982):

1. Unusual casting, that is, using character actors rather than stereotyped individuals.
2. Humor.
3. Slice-of-life situations in which a doubter is persuaded to use the product.
4. New uses, new ideas, and new information.
5. Candid camera testimonials.
6. Demonstrations of a product in use.

Perhaps the only definitive statement to be made about research on advertising effectiveness is that there should be more of it. Too many advertising campaigns are undertaken in the absence of specific goals and are praised as successful in the absence of supporting empirical evidence.

The Consumer

As the previous data indicate, consumers are not influenced by advertising for all of their purchases. Not everyone is persuaded by appeals to buy a particular brand or even that they need that kind of product or service. There are other factors that can influence buying behavior that have nothing to do with advertising. Even the kind of music that is played in a store can affect behavior, as one 9-week supermarket test demonstrated. On some days, the background music was played at a slow tempo of 60 beats per minute. On other days, a faster tempo of 108 beats per minute was used. Customers bought 38% more goods on the days when the slower music was played. The researcher suggested that the slower music encouraged shoppers to spend more time in the store and to browse. Another interesting finding was that when customers were asked if music had been playing in the store, 29% said no. Another 33% said they were not sure (Milliman, 1982).

Personal factors also influence our buying behavior. Different kinds of consumers constitute different advertising markets. For example, people who purchase luxury cars can be expected to differ from people who buy compact cars. Consumer psychologists study various market segments such as age, marital status, sex, income, level of education, home ownership, and zip code.

The point to be made here is that there are many types of consumers, each with distinct needs, motivations, and values, who can be reached by different kinds of appeals. One consumer analysis dealt with a group of do-it-yourselfers, people who spend $40 billion a year, a figure expected to double in the 1990s (Bush, Menon, & Smart, 1987). There are consumers who repair thier own cars and do many of their own home improvements. Surveys show that this group includes up to 68% of all consumers, a powerful bloc of shoppers for stores that sell tools, lumber, and building supplies.

A survey of 3,910 do-it-yourselfers (DIYs) and non-DIYs found a number of differences between them. The DIYs were significantly more likely to own videocassette recorders and home computers, to read newspapers (including advertising supplements), to listen to classical music on the radio, and to read a variety of magazines. They were significantly less likely to watch cable television. Thus, they constitute a clearly delineated market for advertisers to reach with directed appeals in particular media.

Other personal aspects of consuming, including habit, impulse shopping, product price, social-class and ethnic-group membership, age, and sex can provide a more powerful impetus to buy a particular product than any amount of advertising.

Buying Habits and Brand Loyalty

Many products that are purchased periodically are bought on the basis of habit. As noted, where we shop is also determined primarily by habit. Habitual behavior occurs in nearly everything we do, and there is no reason it should not appear in our shopping behavior as well. Habits represent routine and easy ways of responding to complex situations. Decisions do not have to be made, and alternative behaviors or products do not have to be examined or considered. Once we have decided a product is of sufficient quality for our needs, it is simpler to continue to buy that particular product, especially if it is frequently purchased (such as a food product).

To demonstrate how powerful habits can be in shopping, one supermarket changed the way in which canned soups were displayed on the shelf. The soups had been grouped by brand, but were now changed to an alphabetical arrangement by type of soup. Signs explained the new alphabetical arrangement, but they did not prevent a great deal of confusion. More than 60% of the customers were fooled by the new arrangement. Habit led them to the space on the shelf where they had always obtained the same brand of soup. Half the customers questioned after they had purchased soup said that the soups had been stocked in their usual order and were surprised to find the wrong cans in their shopping basket. Only one fourth of the customers were able to cope with the new arrangement. Nothing about the product's packaging or advertising had been changed, only the location on the supermarket shelf.

Habits lead human behavior in consistent and narrow paths. Once established, it is difficult for an advertising campaign to change them. Also, buying habits seem to persist for a very long time. One study found that a high rate of brand preference persisted over a 20-year period. Of a group of subjects initially contacted between ages 7 and 17 and again 20 years later, one fourth were found to prefer the same products and brands (L. Guest, 1964). A study comparing loyalty to 50 major brands for an 8-year period from 1975 to 1983 found it to be unchanged (T. Johnson, 1984). These results reinforce the importance to advertisers of establishing brand preferences and loyalty in childhood. Once caught, a person may remain loyal to a particular brand for many years.

It is difficult to determine precise differences between buying habits and brand loyalty; both are defined in terms of repeat purchase behavior. Both can make shopping easier, in that the consumer, having selected an agreeable brand, need no longer consider alternative products. No matter whether repeat purchasing behavior is called brand loyalty or buying habit, the result is that the consumer is relatively impervious to advertisements for competing brands.

Impulse Buying

Buying on impulse is widespread over all segments of the consumer population and for many categories of products. Surveys show that as many as 62% of the items purchased in department stores are bought on impulse and often include such so-called big-ticket items as videocassette recorders, microwave ovens, furniture, and vacation cruises. Marketing devices such as telephone credit-card shopping, automatic teller machines, 24-hour retailing, and home shopping cable television programs have made impulse buying easier and more readily available.

Much research has been conducted on impulse buying (Cobb & Hoyer, 1986; Rook, 1987). One survey of 133 adults of both sexes, ranging in age from 18 to 89, analyzed impulsive buying behavior. The results showed that 32% of the subjects reported experiencing a sudden, uncontrollable urge to buy something on the spur of the moment, usually, but not always, triggered by the sight of the product or by some promotion for it. Some people experienced the urge to go out and buy something while they were at home and not in a store or shopping center.

The impulse buyers reported that their urge to buy was a powerful, intense, and compelling need that they felt had to be gratified immediately. Almost 20% of them found the experience to be stimulating and exciting, and they used words such as "thrilling" and "wild" to describe it. Some subjects said they felt hypnotized, drawn toward the product as if in a dream. Some 41% said that impulse buying made them feel good emotionally at the moment of purchase. They described their feelings in such terms as "wonderful," "high," "satisfied," "frivolous," and "naughty."

However, the consequences of impulse buying were negative in some way for more than 80% of the subjects: 56% reported financial problems as a result of their purchases, 37% were disappointed with their purchases, and 19% became the target of disapproval of someone else.

Advertisers have no way of predicting, controlling, or manipulating impulse buying behavior. It is independent of anything they may do.

Price and Consumer Behavior

The price of a product can be an important influence on buying behavior, often independent of advertising or of a product's quality. Consumers frequently use price as an index of quality on the assumption that the more an object costs, the better it must be. Many consumers automatically reach for the product with the higher price. Some manufacturers capitalize on this belief and charge a higher price than their competitors for a product of equal quality. Studies have shown that identical products, differing only in price, will often be judged solely by their price; the most expensive product is rated as the highest in quality (Bettman, 1986).

Another aspect of price in the marketplace is that some consumers do not seem to consider price when shopping for certain items. Observations of supermarket shoppers reveal that most of them do not look for price information when buying breakfast cereals. Also, it has been found that many shoppers are unaware of the current prices charged for certain products. For other products, such as a preferred brand of coffee or soft drink, shoppers can accurately report the current price. Only 12% to 14% of shoppers consistently shop on the basis of price (Woods, 1981).

A popular technique to gain sales when introducing a new product or a new package for an existing product is to charge a low price for a period of time as an introductory offer. The theory behind this is that shoppers will continue to purchase the product out of habit when the price is later raised to the level of competing products. In practice, however, this does not seem to work. Sales are high during the introductory offer period (higher than for the same product selling at its usual price in other stores), but when the price is raised, sales drop sharply and remain lower than in stores that charged the usual price from the outset.

A supermarket shopper compares prices; the more expensive brand may be judged higher in quality based solely on its price.

Another way of offering a price reduction as an inducement to buy is to offer rebates, which have been shown to be extremely effective. A price decrease in the form of a rebate will usually produce higher sales than a direct price reduction of the same amount. A survey of 495 adults found that frequent rebate users bought products they did not need, were highly aware of current prices, and were enticed to buy by a smaller rebate amount than were less frequent rebate users (Jolson, Wiener, & Rosecky, 1987).

One other aspect of product pricing deserves mention. Often, shoppers are unable to determine which of several brands of a product is the best buy because of different package weights or sizes. Is Brand X that sells for $1.82 for a 6-ounce package cheaper than Brand Y at $2.89 for 11 ounces? Observations have shown that most shoppers cannot make these comparisons and seek out the lowest price.

The use of unit pricing, which presents cost-per-serving or cost-per-item information, is popular in supermarkets and is used extensively by all types of shoppers.

Social-Class and Ethnic-Group Characteristics

Considerable research in sociology and social psychology has confirmed important and predictable differences in values, attitudes, and behavior among people of various social classes. The way in which people raise their children, the neighborhood and type of house in which they live, their political attitudes, their prejudices, all vary from lower to middle to upper class.

In view of major differences in lifestyle and values, it is not surprising to find that there are also differences in consumer behavior. For a product to be successful, it must be promoted in such a way to appeal to the social class that represents its best market. Advertising a Rolls-Royce in *Family Circle* magazine (sold in the supermarket) would be a poor matching of a product with its potential market.

In one study of consumer behavior and social class, more than 1,000 women department store customers were interviewed about various aspects of their shopping behavior. The results were compared with their social class (based on occupation, neighborhood, income, and level of education of the head of the family).

Upper-class shoppers used newspaper ads as an aid to shopping much more frequently than did lower-class shoppers. Only 39% of those in the lowest social class looked at newspaper ads; 91% of those in the highest social class did so. Those in the higher classes made many more shopping trips over a year than did those in lower social classes.

Upper-class shoppers preferred department stores and seldom went to discount stores. Half of the lower-class shoppers also shopped in department stores, but more of them shopped in discount stores as well (Schiffman & Kanuk, 1983). One study found that in deciding to purchase a personal computer, families of higher socioeconomic status are far more likely to allow all family members, including children, input in the decision-making process than are families of lower socioeconomic status (Sherman & Delener, 1987).

It must be noted that many social-class consumer differences, once readily identifiable, have now become somewhat blurred. Incomes in the lower and middle classes have risen, and increased affluence (and easy credit) offers the opportunity to emulate the upper classes in buying behavior. Also, many truly wealthy people (particularly of the old-family-money type) tend not to display their wealth; for example, they drive smaller, older cars and put elbow patches on the old tweed jacket. On the other hand, people who are striving for social acceptance would never be seen in such cars or clothing.

Although social-class differences are disappearing to some extent, it is still possible to differentiate among such consumer groups in terms of product and brand preference and purchasing behavior.

Another characteristic that can be used to distinguish among consumers is the ethnic group to which they belong. Blacks, Jews, Italian Americans, Mexican Americans, Asian Americans, and others all have distinct preferences for certain kinds of products, as demonstrated by substantial consumer research.

Blacks, as a group, constitute almost 12% of the population of the United States, but in the large cities often make up more than 90% of the residents. The fact that this represents a large market with a lot of purchasing power has been widely recognized by advertisers since the 1960s. Studies have demonstrated differential purchasing behavior for black and white consumers. For example, blacks spend more money than whites with the same income for clothing, but less for food, housing, and medical care. Blacks tend to have larger and more expensive cars, but they are usually American-made and not imported cars. In general, blacks display greater brand loyalty and buy more milk, soft drinks, and liquor but less tea and coffee. Also, blacks usually favor the leading or most popular brand of a product and do not typically buy private-label products such as a supermarket's own brands (Engel, Blackwell, & Kollat, 1978; Schiffman & Kanuk, 1983).

The second largest ethnic-minority group in the United States is the Spanish subculture, composed primarily of Mexican Americans in the southwestern states, Cubans in Florida, and Puerto Ricans in New York. Like all ethnic groups, Hispanic Americans display distinctive purchasing behaviors. For example, compared to whites, they tend to rent rather than buy homes and they use fewer convenience foods. There are differences in purchasing behavior among Hispanic Americans, too. Puerto Ricans in New York, for example, tend to buy new and different products to a much greater degree than do Mexican Americans or Cubans. Overall, Hispanics seem to strongly prefer major brand-name products (Astor, 1981; "Spanish Speaking," 1973).

Manufacturers and advertisers are constantly studying the preferences of various ethnic groups and shaping their advertising appeals to fit the needs and values of these large and increasingly affluent consumer groups.

Children and Adolescents As Consumers

Children are encouraged to become consumers as early as possible. Studies have shown that most children have begun some form of consuming behavior by age 6 or 7. Initially, children mimic their parents' buying behavior and, later, that of their peer group. Social psychologists report that by the time children are 11 years old, their consumer-behavior patterns are similar to those of adults (see Figure 14-5). This is no surprise. By the time they are 11, they have seen as many as 25,000 television commercials a year.

Marketing to children employs several techniques: placing products that appeal to them on the lower shelves in the supermarket, cartoon commercials on children's television programs, and free distribution in schools of pencils, coloring books, or book covers emblazoned with a product's name.

A substantial portion of the advertising directed toward children appears on television. These commercials have generated a great deal of controversy. Many complaints about the ethics of such advertising have been voiced by parents and consumer groups. A survey of 690 adults found highly negative attitudes toward advertising directed at children. The majority of these adults believed that such advertising stifled creativity, promoted materialism, and encouraged poor nutritional habits (Hite & Eck, 1987).

A major source of concern is that young children may be unaware of the intentions of advertisers. This was demonstrated in one study in which fourth-grade children were less able to distinguish between commercials and regular programs, were less aware of the purpose of commercials, and paid

Figure 14-5 Advertising to children. (Reproduced by permission of Sony Corporation of America.)

more attention to commercials than did eighth-grade children (Roedder, Sternthal, & Calder, 1983). It should be noted, however, that not all research supports this view. Some studies, for example, have shown that children as young as the age of 4 are capable of understanding the content and intent of commercials (Macklin, 1983). Another study demonstrated that 40% of a sample of 5-year-olds understood the purpose of commercials (Macklin, 1987).

There is no disagreement about the effectiveness of television as a medium for reaching older children with advertising messages. Approximately 25% of the population, more than 50 million people, are under the age of 13, and this large audience spends more time watching television than it spends in school. The commercials that they see on television seem to be effective. Both laboratory and observational studies report that television commercials increase children's motivation to acquire many of the products displayed. As noted, children can successfully exert pressure on their parents to buy products shown on television.

In another study, 250 mothers kept diaries for 4 weeks noting each specific request for a product made by her child (Isler, Popler, & Ward, 1987). The mothers were trained to keep accurate records, and were contacted every week to make sure the diaries were being completed correctly. The ages of the children studied were 3–4, 5–7, and 9–11.

Over the 4-week period, the average number of requests per child was 13.5, but the data varied markedly with age, with the greatest number coming from the 3- to 4-year-olds and the smallest number from the 9- to 11-year-olds. This finding may reflect what consumer psychologists call "passive dictation," that is, older children do not have to ask so frequently for a particular product because their parents already know they want it and so buy it regularly.

Most of the requests from the older children were made at home, whereas those of the younger children were made more frequently while shopping, which may, of course, simply reflect the fact that younger children are more likely than older ones to accompany their mothers on a shopping trip. When the mothers were asked the reason for a child's request for a particular item, 26% said the child had seen the product in a store, 21% said the child had seen an ad for the product, and 20% said a sibling or a friend had the product. Most mothers acceded to their child's requests and bought the desired products.

Studies also show that by age 5, some children have developed negative attitudes toward commercials, attitudes that increase as children grow older. The percentage of children who said they liked all TV commercials declined from 69% for first graders to 25% for fourth graders. First, they become annoyed with commercials and, later, they come to distrust them. "They're all lies," a 10-year-old told a group of researchers. By ages 7 to 10, children will reject misleading advertising, feeling that they are being cheated; by then they have learned that many advertising claims are false.

A study of 102 9- and 10-year-olds found a high level of mistrust of ads and an effort to resist advertising's attempts at persuasion. More than 45% of the children had negative thoughts about the ads they saw and expressed these thoughts in such statements as "This ad tricks people," and "Ads don't tell the truth" (Brucks, Armstrong, & Goldberg, 1988).

Eventually, children come to realize that misleading commercials are socially acceptable and thus begin to believe that society sanctions a good deal of hypocrisy. This conflicts with the moral principles they have been taught. By ages 11 or 12, children have begun to accommodate or accept adult values (for example, cheating on income tax returns, lying by politicians, deception by advertisers) and, as a result, develop cynicism. Thus, television advertising plays an important and potentially harmful role in the socialization of our children (Bever, Smith, Bengen, & Johnson, 1975).

The behavior of teenage consumers changed in the 1980s because of the increase in the number of mothers working outside the home. Barely 25% of all teens live in a so-called traditional household in which the mother is a full-time homemaker and the father is employed outside the home. Teenagers spend an estimated $30 billion a year on personal products such as clothing, cosmetics, and audio tapes. However, they spend even more for family purchases such as groceries and basic household items.

Considerable research has been conducted on adolescent buying habits. A study of 16- to 17-year-old girls found that 55% of them bought cookies over a 3-month period. This is no great surprise. What was unusual was that 42% of them also purchased frozen dinners, 39% bought salad dressing, 42% cheese and yogurt, and 28% rice, not the typical teenage snack foods. Other surveys show that 63% of adolescent girls and 39% of adolescent boys do some of the family grocery shopping, 66% help make the family shopping list, and nearly 50% make decisions about specific brands to purchase (Malcolm, 1987).

Advertisers appeal to the teenage market by advertising basic food items on cable television music channels and in magazines read by adolescents. *Seventeen* magazine, which has a monthly circulation of 1.8 million, increased the pages devoted to food ads by 31% in 1986. Teenagers, like younger children, have long influenced their parents' buying decisions, but now they are buying many products themselves that their mothers used to purchase.

Employed Women As Consumers

As another example of how advertisers respond to changing trends in consumer behavior, consider the market created by the large number of women employed outside the home. Not only do these women have more money than the average homemaker but their needs for various products and services also differ.

These women are much more likely than full-time homemakers to have savings accounts, checking accounts, and credit cards. They are more likely to travel, making them a good audience for luggage, travelers checks, airline, and hotel advertising. They are also more apt to buy their own cars. In 1987, 45% of all new car purchases in the United States were made by women.

These working women make fewer food-shopping trips per week and tend to have more brand loyalty than housewives. One impact of this trend is that more men are now shopping for food. In the 1960s, few supermarket shoppers were men; in the 1980s, 40% of them were men. They tend to spend less time and money than women do on each shopping trip, they rarely shop with a list or with cents-off coupons, and they tend to buy by brand name rather than price (Burros, 1987).

It is vital for advertisers to realize that not all employed women represent the same market. There is a difference between those with careers and those who are working to supplement the family income. The spending and purchasing habits of the latter are similar to those of homemakers. It is the career woman who represents the most lucrative portion of the market.

Older Persons As Consumers

Changing demographic trends have produced another important market for advertisers—people over the age of 50—a group ignored for many years. This segment of the market is growing in numbers and in affluence, more than any other age group, and will constitute more than one third of the population by the year 2020. In most cases, people over 50 are no longer rearing children. Often, both spouses are working. Many people in this group believe that it is time to spend more of their 40% share of the nation's income. Advertisers have responded to this behavior by revising the image of older people in advertisements. These people are not so frequently depicted as decrepit or sedentary. For example, Jhirmack markets a silver-gray hair-care product whose ad shows an attractive, sophisticated, woman who is over 50 years old (see Figure 14-6). This group also spends more money on luxury travel, automobiles, clothes, jewelry, restaurants, and theaters, and they are prime targets for ads for spas, health clubs, and cosmetics (Stout, 1988).

One American out of four is now over the age of 50, a group that is the most affluent in the nation. Fully 70% of them own their homes and as a group they account for 80% of the money on deposit in savings-and-loan associations. They represent a $60 billion-a-year market for goods and services. People over 50 buy almost half of all new luxury cars and spend 40% more of their income for health and personal care products than the national average (Coogan, 1984; "Older Consumers," 1984).

Retired persons over the age of 65 are another large and active consumer group. Although their incomes are lower, they purchase many goods and services including travel-related items such as luggage.

Older people tend to read more newspapers and magazines than younger people. Their television preferences run to news and sports programs. They are critical of advertising that suggests that young people are the only ones who have fun, who go to the beach, or who drive expensive cars. However, as a group, they tend to rely on mass media advertising more than do younger people to make purchasing decisions. They also rely more on salespersons than

Figure 14-6 Advertising to older women. (Reproduced by permission of Jhirmack.)

do younger shoppers (Lumpkin & Festervand, 1988). Advertisers have come to recognize the presence and purchasing power of older consumers and the fact that some of them are a more sophisticated and less gullible audience than younger people.

As is true of any segment of the population, not all older consumers are alike. A study of 111 married women over the age of 65 suggests the existence of two types of these consumers: the self-sufficients and the persuadables (Day, Davis, Dove, & French, 1988). Women were chosen as subjects for this study because they constitute some 60% of the over-65 population and are the major purchasers of consumer goods for this age group.

The self-sufficients were found to be high in internal locus of control and were more independent, cosmopolitan, outgoing, and influential in dealing with others. In addition, they were more likely to read books, go shopping, attend concerts and sporting events, and dine out than were the persuadables. The persuadables, on the other hand, were reported to be high in external locus of control and more susceptible to attempts at persuasion. They had little confidence in their own opinions and preferred to stay at home rather than engage in outside activities.

The self-sufficients read more magazines than the persuadables and watched considerably less television. The persuadables watched television much of the day, particularly soap opera programs. The consumer psychologists concluded, therefore, that print ads in magazines would reach more of the self-sufficients, whereas television commercials would be seen by more of the persuadables.

At one time, advertisers were concerned that ads oriented toward older people would have to be presented more frequently than ads for younger people because they believed that older people could not so easily perceive, learn, and recall information that was presented rapidly. Research has shown, however, that this is not the case. One study compared the recall and recognition of nine television commercials for two groups—55 and older, and 35 and younger—and found no differences as a function of age (Stephens & Warrens, 1983).

Sellers must keep up with the changing market and respond accordingly. New markets call for new products and advertising techniques. Consumers must be aware of the sometimes manipulative and deceptive nature of advertising. Above all, you, the consumer, should remember one of the oldest lessons of history: *caveat emptor.* Let the buyer—of ideas, politicians, values, theories, research findings, and even textbooks of psychology—beware.

Summary

Consumer psychology affects all of us. It influences the products we buy and use, the success of the economy, and the survival or failure of the companies for which some of us may work. We are constantly being bombarded with advertisements and frequently being studied to determine their impact.

Consumer psychologists use a variety of research methods. Some of these are standard psychological tools that are also applied in other areas of I/O psychology, and some are developed specifically for the study of consumer behavior. The most frequently used method is the **survey**, in which (through questionnaires and interviews) feelings and attitudes on a variety of topics are investigated. A limited form of survey, the **focus group**, involves a small sample of consumers who meet to discuss their reactions to a product or a commercial. Another method is the **in-depth approach**, which uses projective techniques to attempt to probe hidden motivational aspects of product choice and use.

Consumer psychologists also use **behavioral studies** to investigate how people actually behave in consumer situations. Techniques to study consumer behavior include observations of actual purchasing behavior, scanner-cable panels, research on brand identification and preference, and testing of advertisements by various methods and equipment such as the eye camera and tachistoscope.

Consumer psychologists conduct much research on **television programming** to help develop programs that will attract large audiences. The television networks continually study audience reactions and characteristics for different programs. Panels of representative viewers are used to screen programs in a studio and record their reactions or to watch them at home and respond to mail or telephone surveys or by maintaining a diary of their TV viewing. Another method maintains a mechanical record of when a television set is turned on and off, what channel is selected, and which members of a family are watching. A majority of television viewers do not pay close attention. Further, not all viewers are alike. Research has identified embracers, who watch almost everything shown on television; accommodators, who are more discriminating and critical; and protesters, who are highly critical and selective in their television viewing.

There are four kinds of **advertising**: direct sell, creating an image for a product, creating consumer awareness of a new product, and promoting the organization (institutional advertising).

There are three goals of an advertising campaign: to make consumers aware of, and knowledgeable about, a product; to create a preference for the product; and to get consumers to buy the product. One way to accomplish these goals is through the advertising appeal based on the kind of human need or motivation the product is designed to satisfy. Appeals can be either positive or negative. Television commercials may appeal to more than one human need, but most appeal to the need for affiliation. More than one third of all commercials also appeal to the need for positive sensory impressions, the need to avoid embarrassing situations, and the needs for achievement, nurturance, and the avoidance of physical discomfort. Many ads involve claims of implied superiority, which tend to be believed by most consumers.

Trademarks can become effective advertising aids, as can product **image** (the personality of a product—the thoughts and feelings it produces). The **package** in which the product is presented is also an important selling aid, and it can be very influential at the actual moment of purchase.

Sex in advertisements is a common technique that attracts people to the ads but does not seem to influence how much of the advertising message they will remember.

The changing **role of women** in society has affected the portrayal of women in advertising. Increasingly, they are being shown in positive roles outside the home.

Introducing a **new brand** of a product is a risky operation that fails more often than it succeeds. For the greatest chance of success, a new brand must offer consumers better value, be noticeably different from its competitors, and be the first with a new idea.

Research has shown that advertising campaigns are not always successful. They seem to work for certain products, under certain conditions, and with certain people, but not for other products, conditions, and people.

Television commercials generate a recall rate of only 7%, even when viewers are questioned 5 minutes after seeing an ad. In situations in which subjects watch commercials without being able to tune them out, they forget or misunderstand 30% of what they have just seen. Recall of ads depends on when they are seen, their context and frequency, and the presence of competing ads.

Several factors influence the consumer. **Buying habits** and **brand loyalty** can render buyers immune to advertising for products other than those to which they are loyal. **Impulse buying** is widespread over all segments of the population and may be little affected by advertising. Habit, social class, ethnic-group membership, age, and sex can determine the products that people buy and use, as can the product's **price**. It has been found that some consumers associate higher price with higher quality; some do not examine prices for certain products; others have great difficulty determining the unit price of a product.

Much advertising directed at **children** is effective in persuading them to want the products advertised, but evidence shows that they become increasingly distrustful of advertising as they grow older. **Adolescents** are increasingly purchasing items for the household such as groceries. Other consumer groups toward whom advertising is targeted are **employed women** and **older persons**, who exhibit specific needs and preferences and who represent large, growing, and affluent markets.

Key Terms

advertising	product image	survey research
consumer psychology	public opinion polling	methods
focus groups	sales tests	tachistoscope
impulse buying	scanner-cable panels	trademarks

CASE STUDIES

Predicting Reactions to New Television Programs

A sample of children ages 6 to 11 watched network television programs under standardized viewing conditions. Different groups were exposed to different programs. Observers made ratings of attention every 10 seconds for each subject, based on the percentage of program time during which the child maintained eye contact with the TV screen. After the viewing, the children were asked if they would watch the same program when it was shown on TV the following Saturday morning. These responses were taken as statements of the subjects' intentions.

On Saturday, the children were telephoned at their homes and asked if they were watching TV. If so, they were asked to tell what program they were viewing. Of the 54% of the subjects who said they were watching TV, 37% were tuned to the program they had seen in the testing facility. The children's stated intentions were not related to their choice of program, but their degree of attention during the test viewing was significantly related to program choice. The results indicate that what people say they intend to do does not always agree with their later behavior. Their level of involvement or attention may be a better predictor.

QUESTIONS

1. Could this approach be used to test new consumer products? How would you conduct such a study?
2. What other techniques are used to predict viewer reactions to television programs?
3. What are the limitations of research to determine the size of the audience for a particular television program?
4. Describe the 3 types of viewers and the different ways in which they react to television viewing.

Reference: L. Rust. (1987, April/May). Using attention and intention to predict at-home program choice. *Journal of Advertising Research*, pp. 25–30.

Recall of Commercials

Six new TV commercials for various products were shown to 287 adult subjects at a suburban Chicago, Illinois, shopping mall. The viewers were recruited randomly from among the mall shoppers. They were asked to watch a 50-minute videotape consisting of 4 complete segments of the programs "60 Minutes" and "20/20," including the commercials. Some subjects saw the tape with the commercials in the morning hours, between 9:00 a.m. and 10:00 a.m. Other subjects viewed them between 1:00 and 2:00 in the afternoon, and the rest saw them in the evening between 5:00 p.m. and 6:00 p.m.

Some subjects were tested for their recall of the commercials immediately after the screening. Others were questioned two hours later. Two measures were used: (1) a free, unaided recall test, in which subjects were asked to recall the products and brand names shown in the commercials, and (2) a recognition test, in which subjects were provided with descriptions of the 6 product categories and asked to select from a list the correct brand names and selling points.

Of those viewers who were questioned immediately following their exposure to the commercials, the morning group had the highest recall and the evening group the lowest. Among the viewers questioned two hours after seeing the commercials, the evening group had the highest recall and the morning group the lowest. Thus, how much of a TV commercial is remembered may depend less on the nature of the advertisement itself than on the time of day it is seen.

QUESTIONS

1. What criticisms would you make of the choice of subjects for this research?
2. What weakness is inherent in the recognition method that is not present in the recall method?
3. What other factors have been found to be ca-
pable of influencing the effectiveness of an advertisement?
4. Describe other methods that can be used to test the effectiveness of advertising.

Reference: J. Hornik. (1988). Diurnal variation in consumer response. *Journal of Consumer Research, 14*, 588–591.

Additional Reading

Bettman, J. R. (1986). Consumer psychology. *Annual Review of Psychology, 37*, 257–289. A comprehensive review of recent research on the psychological factors that influence consumer decision making.

Day, E., Davis, B., Dove, R., & French, W. (1988, January). Reaching the senior citizen market(s). *Journal of Advertising Research*, pp. 23–30. Suggests that the over 65 population is greater than the adolescent population, making it a large market segment with a significant amount of purchasing power. Describes the components of this "mature" market and the types of advertising appeals most appropriate for reaching them.

Gilly, M. C. (1988). Sex roles in advertising. *Journal of Marketing, 52*(2), 75–85. Compares the roles assigned to women in television advertising in the United States, Australia, and Mexico. Describes stereotypes of women as defined by their relationship to others (spouse or mother, for example) rather than as independent persons.

O'Shaughnessy, J. (1987). *Why People Buy*. New York: Oxford University Press. Discusses consumer preferences and beliefs, along with the subjective process of choice.

References

Adair, J. G. (1984). The Hawthorne effect: A reconsideration of the methodological artifact. *Journal of Applied Psychology, 69*, 334–345.

Adams, J. S. (1965). Inequity in social exchange. In L. Berkowitz (Ed.), *Advances in experimental social psychology* (Vol. 2). New York: Academic Press.

Adelmann, P. K. (1987). Occupational complexity, control, and personal income: Their relation to psychological well-being in men and women. *Journal of Applied Psychology, 72*, 529–537.

Adler, N. J. (1987). Pacific Basin managers: A *Gaijin*, not a woman. *Human Resource Management, 26*, 169–191.

Adler, S. (1987). Toward the more efficient use of assessment center technology in personnel selection. *Journal of Business and Psychology, 2*, 74–93.

Aerospace labor crunch. (1988, July 18). *Newsweek*.

AIDS #1 workplace issue in 1988. (1988, March). *Administrative Management*, p. 7.

Aikin, O. (1988, May). A positive response to AIDS in the workplace. *Personnel Management*, pp. 52–55.

Albaum, G. (1987). Do source and anonymity affect mail survey results? *Journal of the Academy of Marketing Science, 15*(3), 74–81.

Alderfer, C. (1972). *Existence, relatedness and growth: Human needs in organizational settings*. New York: Free Press.

Alluisi, E. A., & Fleishman, E. A. (1982). *Human performance and productivity: Stress and performance effectiveness*. Hillsdale, NJ: Erlbaum.

Altman, L. K. (1988, June 5). Some who use VDTs miscarried, study says. *New York Times*.

American Psychological Association. (1985). *Standards for educational and psychological testing*. Washington, DC: American Psychological Association.

Anastasi, A. (1986). Evolving concepts of test validation. *Annual Review of Psychology, 37*, 1–15.

Anastasi, A. (1988). *Psychological testing* (6th ed.). New York: Macmillan.

Anderson, G. C., & Barnett, J. G. (1987). Characteristics of effective appraisal interviews. *Personnel Review, 16*(4), 18–25.

Anderson, N., & Shackleton, V. (1986). Recruitment and selection: A review of developments in the 1980s. *Personnel Review, 15*(4), 19–26.

Anderson, R. M., & Bremer, D. A. (1987). Sleep duration at home and sleepiness on the job in rotating twelve-hour shift workers. *Human Factors, 29*, 477–481.

Andrisani, P., & Shapiro, M. (1978). Women's attitudes toward their jobs: Some longitudinal data on a national sample. *Personnel Psychology, 31*, 15–34.

Appel, V. (1987, August/September). Editorial environment and advertising effectiveness. *Journal of Advertising Research*, pp. 11–16.

Appraisal trends. (1988). *Personnel Administrator, 33*(3), 26.

Arbous, A. G., & Kerrich, J. E. (1951). Accident statistics and the concept of accident-proneness. *Biometrics, 7*, 340–432.

Arnold, J. (1986). Getting started: How graduates adjust to employment. *Personnel Review, 15*(1), 16–20.

Arvey, R. D., & Campion, J. E. (1982). The employment interview: A summary and review of recent research. *Personnel Psychology, 35*, 281–322.

Arvey, R. D., Miller, H. E., Gould, R., & Burch, P. (1987). Interview validity for selecting sales clerks. *Personnel Psychology, 40*, 1–12.

Asch, A. (1984). The experience of disability: A challenge for psychology. *American Psychologist, 39*, 529–536.

Ash, R. A., Johnson, J. C., Levine, E. L., & McDaniel, M. A. (1989). Job applicant training and work experience evaluation in personnel selection. In K. M. Rowland & G. R. Ferris (Eds.), *Research in personnel and human resources management* (Vol.7). Greenwich, CT: JAI Press.

Ash, R. A., & Levine, E. L. (1985). Job applicant training and work experience evaluation: An empirical comparison of four methods. *Journal of Applied Psychology, 70*, 572–576.

Ash, R. A., Levine, E. L., & Sistrunk, F. (1983). The role of jobs and job-based methods in personnel and human resources management. *Research in Personnel and Human Resources Management, 1*, 45–84.

Astor, D. (1981, July). The Hispanic market: An in-depth profile. *Marketing Communication*, pp. 15–19.

Athey, T. R., & McIntyre, R. M. (1987). Effect of rater training on rater accuracy: Levels-of-processing theory and social facilitation theory perspectives. *Journal of Applied Psychology, 72*, 567–572.

Atkin, C. (1978). Observations of parent-child interaction in supermarket decision-making. *Journal of Marketing, 42*(4), 41–45.

Atkinson, J. W., & Feather, N. T. (1966). *A theory of achievement motivation*. New York: Wiley.

Axline, L. L. (1987). Identifying and helping the troubled executive. *Personnel, 64*(11), 40–47.

Babakus, E., Tat, P., & Cunningham, W. (1988). Coupon redemption: A motivational perspective. *Journal of Consumer Marketing, 5*(2), 37–43.

Back to the basics. (1987, September 21). *Newsweek*, pp. 54–55.

Backer, T. E. (1988). Managing AIDS at work: Psychology's role. *American Psychologist, 43*, 983–987.

Baldwin, T. T., & Ford, J. K. (1988). Transfer of training: A review and directions for future research. *Personnel Psychology, 41*, 63–105.

Bangert-Drowns, R. L. (1986). Review of the developments in meta-analytic method. *Psychological Bulletin, 99*, 388–399.

Barling, J., & Rosenbaum, A. (1986). Work stressors and wife abuse. *Journal of Applied Psychology, 71*, 346–348.

Barnes, R. M. (1980). *Motion and time study: Design and measurement of work* (7th ed.). New York: Wiley.

Barr, S. H., & Hitt, M. A. (1986). A comparison of selection decision models in manager versus student samples. *Personnel Psychology, 39*, 599–617.

Barrett, G. V., & Kernan, M. C. (1987). Performance appraisals and terminations: A review of court decisions since Brito v. Zia with implications for personnel practices. *Personnel Psychology, 40*, 489–503.

Barrick, M. R., & Alexander, R. A. (1987). A review of quality circle efficacy and the existence of positive-findings bias. *Personnel Psychology, 40*, 579–592.

Bartley, S. H., & Chute, E. (1947). *Fatigue and impairment in man*. New York: McGraw-Hill.

Bartol, K. M., Anderson, C. R., & Schneier, C. E. (1980). Motivation to manage among business students: A reassessment. *Journal of Vocational Behavior, 17*, 22–32.

Bartol, K. M., & Martin, D. C. (1987). Managerial motivation among MBA students: A longitudinal assessment. *Journal of Occupational Psychology, 60*, 1–12.

Bartol, K. M., & Martin, D. C. (1988). Influences on managerial pay allocations: A dependency perspective. *Personnel Psychology, 41*, 361–378.

Baruch, G. K., Biener, L., & Barnett, R. C. (1987). Women and gender in research on work and family stress. *American Psychologist, 42*, 130–136.

Baun, W. B., Bernacki, E. J., & Tsai, S. P. (1986). A preliminary investigation: Effect of a corporate fitness program on absenteeism and health care cost. *Journal of Occupational Medicine, 28*, 18–22.

Bean, E. (1987, February 27). More firms use 'attitude tests' to keep thieves off the payroll. *Wall Street Journal*, p. B1.

Becker, B. E., & Cardy, R. L. (1986). Influence of halo error on appraisal effectiveness: A conceptual and empirical reconsideration. *Journal of Applied Psychology, 71*, 662–676.

Beer, M., & Walton, A. E. (1987). Organization change and development. *Annual Review of Psychology, 38*, 339–367.

Bendix, T., & Bloch, I. (1986). How should a seated workplace with a tiltable chair be adjusted? *Applied Ergonomics, 17*, 127–135.

Benedict, M. E., & Levine, E. L. (1988). Delay and distortion: Tacit influences on performance appraisal effectiveness. *Journal of Applied Psychology, 73*, 507–514.

Ben-Shakhar, G., Bar-Hillel, M., Bilu, Y., Ben-Abba, E., & Flug, A. (1986). Can graphology predict occupational success? Two empirical studies and some methodological ruminations. *Journal of Applied Psychology, 71*, 645–653.

Bensinger, P. B. (1982). Drugs in the workplace. *Harvard Business Review, 60*(6), 48–60.

Berger, C. J., Olson, C. A., & Boudreau, J. W. (1983). Effects of unions on job satisfaction: The role of work-related values and perceived rewards. *Organizational Behavior and Human Performance, 32*, 289–324.

Bergmann, T., & Taylor, M. S. (1984). College recruitment: What attracts students to organizations? *Personnel, 61*(3), 34–46.

Berkowitz, L., Fraser, C., Treasure, F. P., & Cochran, S. (1987). Pay, equity, job gratification, and comparisons in pay satisfaction. *Journal of Applied Psychology, 72*, 544–551.

Bernardin, H. J. (1986). Subordinate appraisal: A valuable source of information about managers. *Human Resource Management, 25*, 421–439.

Bernardin, H. J., & Bulkley, M. R. (1981). Strategies in rater training. *Academy of Management Review, 6*, 205–242.

Bernick, E. L., Kindley, R., & Pettit, K. K. (1984). The structure of training courses and the effects of hierarchy. *Public Personnel Management, 13*, 109–119.

Bettman, J. R. (1986). Consumer psychology. *Annual Review of Psychology, 37*, 257–289.

Bever, T. G., Smith, M. L., Bengen, B., & Johnson, T. C. (1975). Young viewers' troubling response to TV ads. *Harvard Business Review, 53*(6), 109–120.

Beyer, J. M., & Trice, H. M. (1987, Spring). How an organization's rites reveal its culture. *Organizational Dynamics, 15*, 5–24.

Bird, C. P., & Fisher, T. D. (1986). Thirty years later: Attitudes toward the employment of older workers. *Journal of Applied Psychology, 71*, 515–517.

Birnbaum, P. H., Farh, J. L., & Wong, G. Y. Y. (1986). The job characteristics model in Hong Kong. *Journal of Applied Psychology, 71*, 598–605.

Bittel, L. R., & Ramsey, J. E. (1982). The limited, traditional world of supervisors. *Harvard Business Review, 60*(4), 26–36.

Bittel, L. R., & Ramsey, J. E. (1983). New dimensions for supervisory training and development. *Training and Development Journal, 37*(3), 12–20.

Blank, W., Weitzel, J., & Green, S. G. (1986). Situational leadership theory: A test of underlying assumptions. *Proceedings of the Academy of Management*, 384.

Blau, G. (1988). An investigation of the apprenticeship organizational socialization strategy. *Journal of Vocational Behavior, 32*, 176–195.

Blau, G., & Boal, K. (1987). Conceptualizing how job involvement and organizational commitment affect turnover and absenteeism. *Academy of Management Review, 12*, 288–300.

Blocklyn, P. L. (1987). The aging workforce. *Personnel, 64*(8), 16–19.

Blocklyn, P. L. (1988a). Employer recruitment practices. *Personnel, 65*(5), 63–65.

Blocklyn, P. L. (1988b). Preemployment testing. *Personnel, 65*(2), 66–68.

Bogart, L., & Lehman, C. (1983). The case of the 30-second commercial. *Journal of Advertising Research, 23*, 11–19.

Booth-Kewley, S., & Friedman, H. S. (1987). Psychological predictors of heart disease: A quantitative review. *Psychological Bulletin, 101*, 343–362.

Borman, W. C. (1982). Validity of behavioral assessment for predicting military recruiter performance. *Journal of Applied Psychology, 67*, 3–9.

Bourne, B. (1982). Effects of aging on work satisfaction, performance, and motivation. *Aging and Work, 5*, 37–47.

Bouzid, N., & Cranshaw, C. M. (1987). Massed versus distributed word processor training. *Applied Ergonomics, 18*, 220–222.

Boyd, D .P., & Gumpert, D. E. (1983). Coping with entrepreneurial stress. *Harvard Business Review, 61*(2), 44–64.

Bozzi, V. (1987, September). Assertiveness breeds contempt. *Psychology Today*, p. 15.

Bramel, D., & Friend, R. (1987). The work group and its vicissitudes in social and industrial psychology. *Journal of Applied Behavioral Science, 23*, 233–253.

Bray, D. W. (1964). The management progress study. *American Psychologist, 19*, 419–420.

Bray, D. W. (1982). The assessment center and the study of lives. *American Psychologist, 37*, 180–189.

Bray, D. W., Campbell, R. J., & Grant, D. C. (1974). *Formative years in business: A long-term AT&T study of managerial lives*. New York: Wiley.

Brenner, O. C., & Tomkiewicz, J. (1982). Job orientation of black and white college graduates in business. *Personnel Psychology, 35*, 89–103.

Brickner, M. A., Harkins, S. G., & Ostrom, T. M. (1986). Effects of personal involvement: Thought-provoking implications for social loafing. *Journal of Personality and Social Psychology, 51*, 763–769.

Bridgwater, C. A. (1982, August). Inflexible flextimers. *Psychology Today*, p. 13.

Bridgwater, C. A. (1983, April). Redeeming facts. *Psychology Today*, p. 13.

Broad, W., & Wade, N. (1982). *Betrayers of the truth: Fraud and deceit in the halls of science*. New York: Simon & Schuster.

Broadbent, D. E. (1978). Chronic effects from the physical nature of work. In B. Gardell (Ed.), *Man and working life*. New York: Wiley.

Broadbent, D. E., & Little, E. A. J. (1960). Effect of noise reduction in a work situation. *Occupational Psychology, 34*, 133–140.

Brockner, J., Grover, S. L., & Blonder, M. D. (1988). Predictors of survivors' job involvement following layoffs: A field study. *Journal of Applied Psychology, 73*, 436–442.

Brockner, J., & Hess, T. (1986). Self-esteem and task performance in quality circles. *Academy of Management Journal, 29*, 617–623.

Brooks, G. E. (1986). VDTs and health risks: What unions are doing. *Personnel, 63*(7), 59–64.

Broszeit, R. K. (1986). If I had my druthers...A career development program. *Personnel Journal, 65*(10), 84–90.

Brown, R. L. (1962). Wrapper influence on the perception of freshness in bread. *Journal of Applied Psychology, 46*, 393–398.

Brucks, M., Armstrong, G. M., & Goldberg, M. E. (1988). Children's use of cognitive defenses against television advertising: A cognitive response approach. *Journal of Consumer Research, 14*, 471–482.

Bruning, N. S., & Frew, D. R. (1987). Effects of exercise, relaxation, and management skills training on physiological stress indicators: A field experiment. *Journal of Applied Psychology, 72*, 515–521.

Buchanan, D. (1987, May). Job enrichment is dead: Long live high-performance work design! *Personnel Management*, pp. 40–43.

Buckley, K. W. (1982). The selling of a psychologist: John Broadus Watson and the application of behavioral techniques to advertising. *Journal of the History of the Behavioral Sciences, 18*, 207–221.

Buckley, M .R., Kicza, D. C., & Crane, N. (1987). A note on the effectiveness of flextime as an organizational intervention. *Public Personnel Management, 16*, 259–267.

Burke, M. J. (1984). Validity generalization: A review and critique of the correlation model. *Personnel Psychology, 37*, 93–115.

Burke, M. J., & Day, R. R. (1986). A cumulative study of the effectiveness of managerial training. *Journal of Applied Psychology, 71*, 232–246.

Burke, M. J., & Normand, J. (1987). Computerized psychological testing: Overview and critique. *Professional Psychology, 18*, 42–51.

Burke, R. R., & Srull, T. K. (1988). Competitive interference and consumer memory for advertising. *Journal of Consumer Research, 15*, 55–68.

Burke, W. W. (1980). Organization development and bureaucracy in the 1980s. *Journal of Applied Behavioral Science, 16*, 423–428.

Burns, W. (1979). Physiological effects of noise. In C. M. Harris (Ed.), *Handbook of noise control*. New York: McGraw-Hill.

Burros, M. (1987, May 7). Men explore shopping frontier. *St. Petersburg (FL) Times*.

Bush, A., Menon, A., & Smart, D. (1987, October/November). Media habits of the do-it-yourselfers. *Journal of Advertising Research*, pp. 14–20.

Businesses teaching 3 R's to employees in effort to compete. (1988, May 1). *New York Times*.

Butler, R. J., & Yorks, L. (1984). A new appraisal system as organizational change: GE's task force approach. *Personnel, 61*(1), 31–42.

Bycio, P., Hahn, J., & Alvares, K. M. (1987). Situational specificity in assessment center ratings: A confirmatory factor analysis. *Journal of Applied Psychology, 72*, 463–474.

Campbell, T. A., & Campbell, D. E. (1988). 71 percent of employers say they could be part of the child care solution. *Personnel Journal, 67*(4), 84–86.

Campion, M. A., Adams. E. F., Morrison, R. F., Spool, M. D., Tornow, W. W., & Wijting, J. P. (1986). I/O psychology research conducted in nonacademic settings and reasons for nonpublication. *The Industrial-Organizational Psychologist, 24*(1), 44–49.

Campion, M. A., & Mitchell, M. M. (1986). Management turnover: Experiential differences between former and current managers. *Personnel Psychology, 39*, 57–69.

Campion, M. A., Pursell, E. D., & Brown, B. K. (1988). Structured interviewing: Raising the psychometric properties of the employment interview. *Personnel Psychology, 41*, 25–42.

Caplan, R. D., Cobb, S., French, J. R. P., Jr., Van Harrison, R., & Pinneau, S. R., Jr. (1975). *Job demands and worker health*. Washington, DC: National Institute of Occupational Safety and Health.

Carducci, B. J., Deeds, W. C., Jones, J. W., Moretti, D. M., Reed, J. G., Sall, F. E., & Wheat, J. E. (1987). Preparing undergraduate psychology students for careers in business. *Teaching of Psychology, 14*(1), 16–20.

Carey, A. (1967). The Hawthorne studies: A radical criticism. *American Sociological Review, 32*, 403–416.

Carlson, R. C., Thayer, P. W., Mayfield, E. C., & Peterson, D. A. (1971). Improvements in the selection interview. *Personnel Journal, 50*, 268–274.

Carney, L. S., & O'Kelly, C. G. (1987). Barriers and constraints to the recruitment and mobility of female managers in the Japanese labor force. *Human Resource Management, 26*, 193–216.

Carroll, S. J., & Gillen, D. J. (1987). Are the classical management functions useful in describing managerial work? *Academy of Management Review, 12*, 38–51.

Carsten, J. M., & Spector, P. E. (1987). Unemployment, job satisfaction, and employee turnover: A meta-analytic test of the Muchinsky model. *Journal of Applied Psychology, 72*, 374–381.

Carter, R. C., & Biersner, R. J. (1987). Job requirements derived from the Position Analysis Questionnaire and validated using military aptitude test scores. *Journal of Occupational Psychology, 60*, 311–321.

Cascio, W. F. (1984). Contributions of I/O psychologists to the bottom line. *The Industrial-Organizational Psychologist, 21*(3), 21–24.

Cascio, W. F., & Silbey, V. (1979). Utility of the assessment center as a selection device. *Journal of Applied Psychology, 64*, 107–118.

Cederblom, D., Pence, E. C., & Johnson, D. L. (1984). Making I/O psychology useful: The personnel administrator's view. *The Industrial-Organizational Psychologist, 21*(3), 9–17.

Chacko, T. I. (1982). Women and equal employment opportunity: Some unintended effects. *Journal of Applied Psychology, 67*, 119–123.

Chandler, A. D., Jr. (1988). Origins of the organization chart. *Harvard Business Review, 66*(2), 156–157.

Chao, G. T., & Kozlowski, S. W. J. (1986). Employee perceptions on the implementation of robotic manufacturing technology. *Journal of Applied Psychology, 71*, 70–76.

Chapanis, A. (1965). On the allocation of functions between men and machines. *Occupational Psychology, 39*, 1–11.

Chapanis, A., Garner, W., & Morgan, C. (1949). *Applied experimental psychology*. New York: Wiley.

Childs, A., & Klimoski, R. J. (1986). Successfully predicting career success: An application of the biographical inventory. *Journal of Applied Psychology, 71*, 3–8.

Chusmir, L. H. (1982). Job commitment and the organizational woman. *Academy of Management Review, 7*, 595–602.

Chusmir, L. H., & Durand, D. E. (1987). Stress and the working woman. *Personnel, 64*(5), 38–43.

Clark, C. (1975). *Personnel Research and Development Center of the U.S. Civil Service Commission*. Washington, DC: U.S. Civil Service Commission.

Clegg, C., Wall, T., & Kemp, N. (1987). Women on the assembly line: A comparison of main and interactive explanations of job satisfaction, absence, and mental health. *Journal of Occupational Psychology, 60*, 273–287.

Clement, R. W. (1981). Evaluating the effectiveness of management training: Progress during the 1970s and prospects for the 1980s. *Human Resource Management, 20*(4), 8–13.

Clerical staff more at risk from stress. (1988, April). *Personnel Management*, p. 13.

Cleveland, J. N., Murphy, K. R., & Williams, R. E. (1989). Multiple use of performance appraisal: Prevalence and correlates. *Journal of Applied Psychology, 74*, 130–135.

Cliff, R. (1986). *Preventing employee misconduct: A self-defense manual for business.* Lexington, MA: Lexington Books.

Cobb, C. J., & Hoyer, W. D. (1986). Planned versus impulse purchase behavior. *Journal of Retailing, 62*, 67–81.

Coch, L., & French, J. R. P., Jr. (1984). Overcoming resistance to change. *Human Relations, 1*, 512–532.

Cochran, D. J., & Riley, M. W. (1986). The effects of handle shape and size on exerted forces. *Human Factors, 28*, 253–265.

Colarelli, S. M., Konstans, C., & Dean, R. A. (1987). Comparative effects of personal and situational influences on job outcomes of new professionals. *Journal of Applied Psychology, 72*, 558–566.

Condon, M. (1983). Straight talk about robots. *Training and Development Journal, 37*(11), 14–24.

Conger, J. J. (1988). Hostages to fortune: Youth, values, and the public interest. *American Psychologist, 43*, 291–300.

Conley, P. R., & Sackett, P. R. (1987). Effects of using high- versus low-performing job incumbents as sources of job analysis information. *Journal of Applied Psychology, 72*, 434–437.

Coogan, M. H. (1984, Summer). The new maturity market. *University of Maryland Researcher*, pp. 21–24.

Cooper, C. L., & Davidson, M. J. (1982). The high cost of stress on women managers. *Organizational Dynamics, 10*(4), 44–53.

Cooper, G. L., & Smith, M. J. (Eds.). (1986). *Job stress and blue collar work.* New York: Wiley.

Cordes, C. (1985, July). Military waste: The human factor. *APA Monitor*, p. 1.

Cornelius, E. T., III, & Lane, F. B. (1984). The power motive and managerial success in a professionally oriented service industry organization. *Journal of Applied Psychology, 69*, 32–39.

Cornelius, E. T., III, Schmidt, F. L., & Carron, T. J. (1984). Job classification approaches and the implementation of validity generalization results. *Personnel Psychology, 37*, 247–260.

Cotton, J. L., & Tuttle, J. M. (1986). Employee turnover: A meta-analysis and review with implications for research. *Academy of Management Review, 11*, 55–70.

Cotton, J. L., Vollrath, D. A., Froggatt, K. L., Lengnick-Hall, M. L., & Jennings, K. R. (1988). Employee participation: Diverse forms and different outcomes. *Academy of Management Review, 13*, 8–22.

Cowan, T. R. (1987). Drugs and the workplace: To drug test or not to test? *Public Personnel Management, 16*, 313–322.

Cox, D. S., & Cox, A. D. (1988). What *does* familiarity breed? Complexity as a moderator of repetition effects in advertisement evaluations. *Journal of Consumer Research, 15*, 111–116.

Cron, W. L., Dubinsky, A. J., & Michaels, R. E. (1988). The influence of career stages on components of salesperson motivation. *Journal of Marketing, 52*, 78–92.

Cron, W. L., & Slocum, J. W., Jr. (1986). The influence of career stages on salespeople's job attitudes, work perceptions, and performance. *Journal of Marketing Research, 23*, 119–129.

Crouch, A., & Yetton, P. (1988). Manager-subordinate dyads: Relationships among task and social contact, manager friendliness and subordinate performance in management groups. *Organizational Behavior and Human Decision Processes, 41*, 65–82.

Cumming, C. (1988). Linking pay to performance: Why is it so difficult? *Personnel Administrator, 33*(5), 47–52.

Dalton, D. R., & Enz, C. A. (1987). Absenteeism in remission: Planning, policy, culture. *Human Resource Planning, 10*(2), 81–91.

Davidson, J. H. (1976). Why most new customer brands fail. *Harvard Business Review, 54*(2), 117–122.

Davidson, M. J., & Cooper, C. L. (1987). Female managers in Britain: A comparative perspective. *Human Resource Management, 26*, 217–242.

Davis, B. L., & Mount, M. K. (1984). Design and use of a performance appraisal feedback system. *Personnel Administrator, 29*(3), 91–97.

Davis, K. R., Jr. (1984). A longitudinal analysis of biographical subgroups using Owens' developmental-integrative model. *Personnel Psychology, 37*, 1–14.

Davis, T. R. V. (1984). The influence of the physical environment in offices. *Academy of Management Review, 9*, 271–283.

Day, D. V., & Silverman, S. B. (1989). Personality and job performance: Evidence of incremental validity. *Personnel Psychology, 42*, 25–36.

Day, E., Davis, B., Dove, R., & French, W. (1988, December/January). Reaching the senior citizen market(s). *Journal of Advertising Research*, pp. 23–30.

Dean, R. A., & Wanous, J. P. (1984). Effects of realistic job previews on hiring bank tellers. *Journal of Applied Psychology, 69*, 61–68.

Deatherage, B. H. (1972). Auditory and other sensory forms of information presentation. In H. P. Van Cott & R. G. Kinkade (Eds.), *Human engineering guide to equipment design*. Washington, DC: Government Printing Office.

Deets, N. R., & Tyler, D. T. (1986). How Xerox improved its performance appraisals. *Personnel Journal, 65*(4), 50–52.

DeFrank, R. S., & Ivancevich, J. M. (1986). Job loss: An individual level review and model. *Journal of Vocational Behavior, 28*, 1–20.

DeGroot, J. P., & Kamphuis, A. (1983). Eyestrain in VDU users: Physical correlates and long-term effects. *Human Factors, 25*, 409–413.

DeLong, D. (1988, August 21). Computers in the corner office. *New York Times*.

DeMeuse, K. P. (1987). A review of the effects of non-verbal cues on the performance appraisal process. *Journal of Occupational Psychology, 60*, 207–226.

DeNisi, A. S., Cornelius, E. T., III, & Blencoe, A. G. (1987). Further investigation of common knowledge effects on job analysis ratings. *Journal of Applied Psychology, 72*, 262–268.

DeReamer, R. (1980). *Modern safety and health technology*. New York: Wiley.

Design of controls. (1977). Washington, DC: U.S. Air Force Systems Command.

Deutsch, C. H. (1987a, July 26). The battle to wire the consumer. *New York Times*.

Deutsch, C. H. (1987b, November 8). What do people want, anyway? *New York Times*.

Devanna, M. A. (1987). Women in management: Progress and promise. *Human Resource Management, 26*, 469–481.

Dichter, E. (1970). The man in the package. In S. H. Britt (Ed.), *Consumer behavior in theory and in action*. New York: Wiley.

Dickey-Bryant, L., Lautenschlager, G. J., Mendoza, J. L., & Abrahams, N. (1986). Facial attractiveness and its relation to occupational success. *Journal of Applied Psychology, 71*, 16–19.

Dictionary of occupational titles (4th ed.). (1977). Washington, DC: U.S. Government Printing Office.

Dobbins, G. H., & Platz, S. J. (1986). Sex differences in leadership: How real are they? *Academy of Management Review, 11*, 118–127.

Dobbins, G. H., & Russell, J. M. (1986). The biasing effects of subordinate likeableness on leaders' responses to poor performers: A laboratory and a field study. *Personnel Psychology, 39*, 759–777.

Dogging drugs in the office. (1988). *Personnel, 65*(1), 4.

Doll, T. J., & Folds, D. J. (1986). Auditory signals in military aircraft: Ergonomics principles versus practice. *Applied Ergonomics, 17*, 257–264.

Domzal, T. J., & Kernan, J. B. (1983). Television audience segmentation according to need gratification. *Journal of Advertising Research, 23*(5), 37–49.

Donnell, S. M., & Hall, J. (1980). Men and women as managers: A significant case of no significant difference. *Organizational Dynamics, 8*, 60–77.

Donnerstein, E., & Wilson, D. W. (1976). Effects of noise and perceived control on ongoing and subsequent aggressive behavior. *Journal of Personality and Social Psychology, 34*, 774–781.

Donovan, R. J. (1984). Bringing America into the 1980s. *American Psychologist, 39*, 429–431.

Dooley, D., Rook, K., & Catalano, R. (1987). Job and non-job stressors and their moderators. *Journal of Occupational Psychology, 60*, 115–132.

Dorfman, P. W., Stephan, W. G., & Loveland, J. (1986). Performance appraisal behaviors: Supervisor perceptions and subordinate reactions. *Personnel Psychology, 39*, 579–597.

Dossett, D. L., & Hulvershorn, P. (1983). Increasing technical training efficiency: Peer training via computer-assisted instruction. *Journal of Applied Psychology, 68*, 552–558.

Dougherty, T. W., Ebert, R. J., & Callender, J. C. (1986). Policy capturing in the employment interview. *Journal of Applied Psychology, 71*, 9–15.

Downing, J. V., & Sanders, M. S. (1987). The effects of panel arrangement and locus of attention on performance. *Human Factors, 29*, 551–562.

Drazin, R., & Auster, E. R. (1987). Wage differences between men and women: Performance appraisal ratings vs. salary allocation as the locus of bias. *Human Resource Management, 26*, 157–168.

Drury, C. G., & Sinclair, M. A. (1983). Human and machine performance in an inspection task. *Human Factors, 25*, 391–399.

Dube, L. E., Jr. (1986). Employment references and the law. *Personnel Journal, 65*(2), 87–91.

Duffy, E. M., O'Brien, R. M., Brittain, W. P., & Cuthrell, S. (1988). Behavioral outplacement: A shorter, sweeter approach. *Personnel, 65*(3), 28–33.

Dunham, R. B. (1983). Organizational practices. *The Industrial-Organizational Psychologist, 21*(1), 42–47.

Dunham, R. B., & Pierce, J. L. (1983). The design and evaluation of alternative work schedules. *Personnel Administrator, 28*(4), 67–75.

Dunham, R. B., Pierce, J. L., & Castañeda, M. B. (1987). Alternative work schedules: Two field quasi-experiments. *Personnel Psychology, 40*, 215–242.

Dunn, W. N., Pavlak, T. J., & Roberts, G. E. (1987). Cognitive performance appraisal: Mapping managers' category structures using the grid technique. *Personnel Review, 16*(3), 16–19.

Dupont, T. D. (1987, August/September). Do frequent mall shoppers distort mall-intercept survey results? *Journal of Advertising Research*, pp. 45–51.

Durgee, J. F. (1988, February/March). Product drama. *Journal of Advertising Research*, pp. 42–49.

Eberhardt, B. J., & Muchinsky, P. M. (1982). An empirical investigation of the factor stability of Owens' biographical questionnaire. *Journal of Applied Psychology, 67*, 138–145.

Eden, D., & Shani, A. B. (1982). Pygmalion goes to boot camp: Expectancy, leadership, and trainee performance. *Journal of Applied Psychology, 67*, 194–199.

Edmunds, L. (1987, June). Sick buildings. *Johns Hopkins Magazine*, pp. 22–25.

Edwards, M. R., & Goodstein, L. D. (1982). Experiential learning can improve the performance appraisal process. *Human Resource Management, 21*, 18–23.

Ehrenberg, A. S. C., & Wakshlag, J. (1987, February/March). Repeat-viewing with People Meters. *Journal of Advertising Research*, pp. 9–13.

Elton, C. F., & Smart, J. C. (1988). Extrinsic job satisfaction and person-environment congruence. *Journal of Vocational Behavior, 32*, 226–238.

Engel, J. F., Blackwell, R. D., & Kollat, D. T. (1978). *Consumer behavior* (3rd ed.). Hinsdale, IL: Dryden Press.

Ergonomics. (1986). *Personnel Journal, 65*(6), 95–102.

Essex, N. L. (1988). When talk isn't cheap: Steering clear of defamation lawsuits. *Personnel, 65*(5), 44–46.

Exner, J. E., Jr. (1978). *The Rorschach: A comprehensive system, Volume 2. Current research and advanced interpretation*. New York: Wiley.

Exner, J. E., Jr. (1986). *The Rorschach: A comprehensive system, Volume 1. Basic foundations* (2nd ed.). New York: Wiley.

Faley, R. H., Kleiman, L. S., & Lengnick-Hall, M. L. (1984). Age discrimination and personnel psychology: A review and synthesis of the legal literature with implications for future research. *Personnel Psychology, 37*, 327–350.

Farh, J. L., & Werbel, J. D. (1986). The effects of purpose of the appraisal and expectation of validation on self-appraisals leniency. *Journal of Applied Psychology, 71*, 527–529.

Farh, J. L., Werbel, J. D., & Bedeian, A. G. (1988). An empirical investigation of self-appraisal-based performance evaluation. *Personnel Psychology, 41*, 141–156.

Fay, C. H., & Latham, G. P. (1982). Effects of training and ratings scales on rating errors. *Personnel Psychology, 35*, 105–116.

Feeney, E. J. (1972). Performance audit, feedback, and positive reinforcement. *Training and Development Journal, 26*(11), 8–13.

Fein, M. (1974). Job enrichment: A reevaluation. *Sloan Management Review, 15*, 69–88.

Feldman, D. (1988a). Employing physically and mentally impaired employees. *Personnel, 65*(1), 14–18.

Feldman, D. (1988b). The UAW-GM human resource center. *Personnel, 65*(3), 34–36.

Feldman, D. C. (1981). The multiple socialization of organization members. *Academy of Management Review, 6*, 309–318.

Feldman, D. C., & Arnold, H. J. (1983). *Managing individual and group behavior in organizations*. New York: McGraw-Hill.

Feulner, T., & Kleiner, B. H. (1986). When robots are the answer. *Personnel Journal, 65*(2), 44–47.

Fiedler, F. E. (1967). *A theory of leadership effectiveness*. New York: McGraw-Hill.

Fiedler, F. E. (1976). The leadership game: Matching the man to the situation. *Organizational Dynamics*.

Fiedler, F. E. (1978). The contingency model and the dynamics of the leadership process. In L. Berkowitz (Ed.), *Advances in experimental social psychology*. New York: Academic Press.

Fiedler, F. E., & Chemers, M. M. (1984). *Improving leadership effectiveness: The LEADER MATCH concept* (rev. ed.). New York: Wiley.

Fiedler, F. E., & Garcia, J. E. (1987). *New approaches to effective leadership: Cognitive resources and organizational performance*. New York: Wiley.

Fiedler, F. E., & Mahar, L. (1979). The effectiveness of contingency model training: A review of the validation of LEADER MATCH. *Personnel Psychology, 32*, 45–62.

Fiedler, F. E., Wheeler, W. A., Chemers, M. M., & Patrick, D. (1988). Structured management training in underground mining: A five-year follow-up. *Training and Development Journal*.

Field, R. H. (1982). A test of the Vroom-Yetton normative model of leadership. *Journal of Applied Psychology, 67*, 523–532.

Finney, M. I. (1988). The right to be tested. *Personnel Administrator, 33*(3), 74–75.

Fischman, J. (1987a, December). Getting tough: Can people learn to have disease-resistant personalities? *Psychology Today*, pp. 26–28.

Fischman, J. (1987b, July). Graphology: The write stuff? *Psychology Today*, p. 11.

Fischman, J. (1987c, February). Type A on trial. *Psychology Today*, pp. 42–50.

Fisher, C. D., & Thomas, J. (1982). The other face of performance appraisal. *Human Resource Management, 21*, 24–26.

Fisher, H. E. (1988). Make training accountable: Assess its impact. *Personnel Journal, 67*(1), 73–75.

Fisher, K. (1984, April). Behavioral research helps FAA maintain safety in the skies. *APA Monitor*.

Fleishman, E. A. (1953). The description of supervisory behavior. *Journal of Applied Psychology, 37*, 1–6.

Fleishman, E. A., & Harris, E. F. (1962). Patterns of leadership behavior related to employee grievances and turnover. *Personnel Psychology, 15*, 43–56.

Flex hours okayed. (1988). *Personnel Administrator, 33*(1), 20.

Flexitime in the utilities industry. (1984). *Personnel, 61*(2), 42–44.

Fodor, E. M. (1984). The power motive and reactivity to power stresses. *Journal of Personality and Social Psychology, 47*, 853–859.

Fodor, E. M., & Smith, T. (1982). The power motive as an influence on group decision making. *Journal of Personality and Social Psychology, 42*, 178–185.

Fogli, L., Hulin, C. L., & Blood, M. R. (1971). Development of first-level behavioral job criteria. *Journal of Applied Psychology, 55*, 3–8.

Fombrun, C. J., & Laud, R. L. (1983). Strategic issues in performance appraisal: Theory and practice. *Personnel, 60*(6), 23–31.

Ford, J. K., Kraiger, K., & Schechtman, S. L. (1986). Study of race effects in objective indices and subjective evaluations of performance: A meta-analysis of performance criteria. *Psychological Bulletin, 99*, 330–337.

Ford, J. K., & Noe, R. A. (1987). Self-assessed training needs: The effects of attitudes toward training, managerial level, and function. *Personnel Psychology, 40*, 39–53.

Forgionne, G. A., & Peeters, V. E. (1982). Differences in job motivation and satisfaction among female and male managers. *Human Relations, 35*, 101–118.

Foulkes, F. K., & Hirsch, J. L. (1984). People make robots work. *Harvard Business Review, 62*(1), 94–102.

Fox, F. G. (1971). Background music and industrial productivity: A review. *Applied Ergonomics, 2*, 70–73.

Fox, S., & Dinur, Y. (1988). Validity of self-assessment: A field evaluation. *Personnel Psychology, 41*, 581–592.

Foxman, L. D., & Polsky, W. L. (1988). Outplacement must be a partnership. *Personnel Journal, 67*(4), 19–20.

Franke, R.H., & Kaul, J. D. (1978). The Hawthorne experiments: First statistical interpretation. *American Sociological Review, 43*, 623–643.

Franklin, G. M., & Robinson, R. K. (1988). AIDS and the law. *Personnel Administrator, 33*(4), 118–121.

Frayne, C. A., & Latham, G. P. (1987). Application of social learning theory to employee self-management of attendance. *Journal of Applied Psychology, 72*, 387–392.

Fraze, J. (1988). Displaced workers: Okies of the '80s. *Personnel Administrator, 33*(1), 42–51.

French, J. R. P., Jr., Caplan, R. D., & Van Harrison, R. (1982). *The mechanisms of job stress and strain.* New York: Wiley.

French, J. R. P., Jr., & Raven, B. H. (1959). The bases of social power. In D. Cartwright (Ed.), *Studies in social power.* Ann Arbor, MI: Institute for Social Research.

Frese, M., & Semmer, N. (1986). Shiftwork, stress, and psychosomatic complaints: A comparison between workers in different shiftwork schedules, non-shiftworkers, and former shiftworkers. *Ergonomics, 29*, 99–114.

Freudenberger, H. J. (1977). Burn-out: The organizational menace. *Training and Development Journal, 31*(7), 26–27.

Freudenberger, H. J. (1980). *Burnout: The high cost of achievement.* Garden City, NY: Doubleday.

Fried, Y., & Ferris, G. R. (1986). The dimensionality of job characteristics: Some neglected issues. *Journal of Applied Psychology, 71*, 419–426.

Fried, Y., & Ferris, G. R. (1987). The validity of the job characteristics model: A review and meta-analysis. *Personnel Psychology, 40*, 287–322.

Friedman, M., & Rosenman, R. H. (1974). *Type A behavior and your heart.* New York: Knopf.

Fritz, N. R. (1988a). Older employees fight back. *Personnel, 65*(1), 6.

Fritz, N. R. (1988b). Employees help with eldercare. *Personnel, 65*(3), 4–6.

Fritz, N. R. (1988c). Pay for performance doesn't rate a raise. *Personnel, 65*(3), 8.

Fritz, N. R. (1988d). Culture clash. *Personnel, 65*(4), 6–7.

Fritz, N. R. (1988e). A good entry-level employee is hard to find. *Personnel, 65*(5), 10.

Frost, D. E. (1986). A test of situational engineering for training leaders. *Psychological Reports, 59*, 771–782.

Fry, E. H., & Fry, N. E. (1988). Information vs. privacy: The polygraph debate. *Personnel, 65*(2), 57–60.

Fulk, J., & Wendler, E. R. (1982). Dimensionality of leader-subordinate interactions: A path-goal investigation. *Organizational Behavior and Human Performance, 30*, 241–264.

Furtado, T. (1988, March). Training for a different management style. *Personnel Management*, pp. 40–43.

Gable, M., & Hollon, C. (1982). A comparison of retail personnel practices applied to full-time and part-time non-exempt employees. *Personnel Administrator, 27*(2), 62–64.

Gaines, J., & Jermier, J. M. (1983). Emotional exhaustion in a high stress organization. *Academy of Management Journal, 26*, 567–586.

Gallup, G., Jr. (1988). Survey research: Current problems and future opportunities. *Journal of Consumer Marketing, 5*, 27–30.

Gannon, M. J., Norland, D. L., & Robeson, F. E. (1983). Shift work has complex effects on lifestyles and work habits. *Personnel Administrator, 28*(5), 93–97.

Ganster, D. C., Fusilier, M. R., & Mayes, B. (1986). Role of social support in the experience of stress at work. *Journal of Applied Psychology, 71*, 102–110.

Ganster, D. C., Mayes, B., Sime, W. E., & Tharp, G. P. (1982). Managing organizational stress: A field experiment. *Journal of Applied Psychology, 67*, 533–542.

Gardner, D. G., Dunham, R. B., Cummings, L. L., & Pierce, J. L. (1987). Employee focus of attention and reactions to organizational change. *Journal of Applied Behavioral Science, 23*, 351–370.

Garson, B. (1988). *The electronic sweatshop: How computers are transforming the office of the future into the factory of the past*. New York: Simon & Schuster.

Gaugler, B. B., Rosenthal, D. B., Thornton, G. C., III, & Bentson, C. (1987). Meta-analysis of assessment center validity. *Journal of Applied Psychology, 72*, 493–511.

Geis, A. A. (1987). Making merit pay work. *Personnel, 64*(1), 52–60.

Geldard, F. A. (1957). Adventures in tactile literacy. *American Psychologist, 12*, 115–124.

Gemmill, G. R., & Heisler, W. J. (1972). Fatalism as a factor in managerial job satisfaction, job strain, and mobility. *Personnel Psychology, 25*, 241–250.

Gerbert, K., & Kemmler, R. (1986). The causes of causes: Determinants and background variables of human factor incidents and accidents. *Ergonomics, 29*, 1439–1453.

Gerhart, B. (1987). How important are dispositional factors as determinants of job satisfaction? Implications for job design and other personnel programs. *Journal of Applied Psychology, 72*, 366–373.

Gilbreth, F. B. (1911). *Motion study*. Princeton, NJ: D. Van Nostrand.

Gilly, M. C. (1988). Sex roles in advertising: A comparison of television advertisements in Australia, Mexico, and the United States. *Journal of Marketing, 52*(2), 75–85.

Giniger, S., Dispenzieri, A., & Eisenberg, J. (1984). Older workers in speed and skill jobs. *Aging and Work, 7*(1), 7–12.

Gist, M., Rosen, B., & Schwoerer, C. (1988). The influence of training method and trainee age on the acquisition of computer skills. *Personnel Psychology, 41*, 255–265.

Glass, D. C., & Singer, J. E. (1972). *Urban stress*. New York: Academic Press.

Glenn, N. D., & Weaver, C. N. (1982a). Enjoyment of work by full-time workers in the U.S., 1955 and 1980. *Public Opinion Quarterly, 46*, 459–470.

Glenn, N. D., & Weaver, C. N. (1982b). Further evidence on education and job satisfaction. *Social Forces, 61*, 46–55.

Glick, W. H., Jenkins, G. D., & Gupta, N. (1986). Method versus substance: How strong are underlying relationships between job characteristics and attitudinal outcomes. *Academy of Management Journal, 29*, 441–464.

Glickstein, G., & Ramer, D. C. Z. (1988, February). The alternative employment marketplace. *Personnel Administrator, 33*, 100–104.

Goetschin, P. (1987, June). Reshaping work for an older population. *Personnel Management*, pp. 39–41.

Goldberg, M. E., & Gorn, G. J. (1987). Happy and sad TV programs: How they affect reactions to commercials. *Journal of Consumer Research, 14*, 387–403.

Goldman, A. E., & McDonald, S. S. (1987). *The group depth interview: Principles and practice*. Englewood Cliffs, NJ: Prentice-Hall.

Goldstein, I. L. (1986). *Training in organizations: Needs assessment, development, and evaluation* (2nd ed.). Monterey, CA: Brooks/Cole.

Goleman, D. (1983, February). The electronic Rorschach. *Psychology Today*, pp. 36–43.

Goleman, D. (1988, February 7). Why managers resist machines. *New York Times*.

Golembiewski, R. T., Hilles, R., & Daly, R. (1987). Some effects of multiple OD interventions on burnout and work site features. *Journal of Applied Behavioral Science, 23*, 295–313.

Gomer, F. E., Silverstein, L. D., Berg, W. K., & Lassiter, D. L. (1987). Changes in electromyographic activity associated with occupational stress and poor performance in the workplace. *Human Factors, 29*, 131–143.

Gomez-Mejia, L. R., & Balkin, D. B. (1987). Dimensions and characteristics of personnel manager perceptions of effective drug-testing programs. *Personnel Psychology, 40*, 745–763.

Goodale, J. G., & Aagaard, A. K. (1975). Factors relating to varying reactions to the 4-day workweek. *Journal of Applied Psychology, 60*, 33–38.

Goodbye, Mr. Whipple. (1984, March 26). *Newsweek*, pp. 62–64.

Gooding, G. J. (1988). Career moves: For the employee, for the organization. *Personnel, 65*(4), 112–116.

Goodman, P., & Salipante, P., Jr. (1976). Organizational rewards and retention of the hard-core unemployed. *Journal of Applied Psychology, 61*, 12–21.

Goodstein, L. D. (1988). The social psychology of the workplace. In I. S. Cohen (Ed.), *The G. Stanley Hall lecture series* (Vol. 8, pp. 5–46). Washington, DC: American Psychological Association.

Gordon, M. E., & Bowlby, R. L. (1988). Propositions about grievance settlements: Finally, consultation with grievants. *Personnel Psychology, 41*, 107–123.

Gordon, M. E., Cofer, J. L., & McCullough, P. M. (1986). Relationships among seniority, past performance, interjob similarity, and trainability. *Journal of Applied Psychology, 71*, 518–521.

Gordon, M. E., & Miller, S. J. (1984). Grievances: A review of research and practice. *Personnel Psychology, 37*, 117–146.

Gordon, M. E., Slade, L. A., & Schmitt, N. (1986). The 'science of the sophomore' revisited: From conjecture to empiricism. *Academy of Management Review, 11*, 191–207.

Gordon, R. A., Rozelle, R. M., & Baxter, J. C. (1988). The effect of applicant age, job level, and accountability on the evaluation of job applicants. *Organizational Behavior and Human Decision Processes, 41*, 20–33.

Gould, J. D., Alfaro, L., Barnes, V., Finn, R., Grischkowsky, N., & Minuto, A. (1987). Reading is slower from CRT displays than from paper: Attempts to isolate a single-variable explanation. *Human Factors, 29*, 269–299.

Gould, J. D., Alfaro, L., Finn, R., Haupt, B., & Minuto, A. (1987). Reading from CRT displays can be as fast as reading from paper. *Human Factors, 29*, 497–517.

Graen, G. (1976). Role-making processes within complex organizations. In M. D. Dunnette (Ed.), *Handbook of industrial and organizational psychology*. Chicago: Rand McNally.

Graen, G., Novak, M., & Sommerkamp, P. (1982). The effects of leader-member exchange and job design on productivity and satisfaction: Testing a dual attachment model. *Organizational Behavior and Human Performance, 30*, 109–131.

Graen, G., Scandura, T. A., & Graen, M. R. (1986). A field experimental test of the moderating effects of growth need strength on productivity. *Journal of Applied Psychology, 71*, 484–491.

Graen, G., & Schliemann, W. (1978). Leader-member agreement: A vertical dyad linkage approach. *Journal of Applied Psychology, 63,* 206–212.

Graen, G., & Wakabayashi, M. (1986). The Japanese career progress study: A 7-year follow-up. *Journal of Applied Psychology, 69,* 603–614.

Grant, P. (1988a). What use is a job description? *Personnel Journal, 67*(2), 45–53.

Grant, P. (1988b). Rewards: The pizzazz in the package, not the prize. *Personnel Journal, 67*(3), 76–81.

Grant, R. A., Higgins, C. A., & Irving, R. H. (1988). Computerized performance monitors: Are they costing you customers? *Sloan Management Review, 29*(3), 39–45.

Greenberg, A., & Collins, S. (1966). Paired comparison taste tests: Some food for thought. *Journal of Marketing Research, 3,* 76–80.

Greenberg, E. R. (1988). Workplace testing: Results of a new AMA survey. *Personnel, 65*(4), 36–44.

Greenberg, J. (1986). Determinants of perceived fairness of performance evaluations. *Journal of Applied Psychology, 71,* 340–342.

Greenberg, J. (1988). Equity and workplace status: A field experiment. *Journal of Applied Psychology, 73,* 606–613.

Greenhaus, J. H., & Brenner, O. C. (1982). How do job candidates size up prospective employers? *Personnel Administrator, 27*(3), 21–25.

Greenlaw, P. S. (1988). Reverse discrimination: The Supreme Court's dilemma. *Personnel Journal, 67*(1), 84–89.

Grieco, A. (1986). Sitting posture: An old problem and a new one. *Ergonomics, 29,* 345–362.

Guest, L. (1964). Brand loyalty revisited: A twenty-year report. *Journal of Applied Psychology, 48,* 93–97.

Guest, R. H. (1979). Quality of work life: Learning from Tarrytown. *Harvard Business Review, 57*(4), 76–87.

Guglielmino, P. J. (1979). Developing the top-level executive for the 1980s and beyond. *Training and Development Journal, 33*(4), 12–14.

Guion, R. M. (1987). Changing views for personnel selection research. *Personnel Psychology, 40,* 199–213.

Guion, R. M., & Gibson, W. M. (1988). Personnel selection and placement. *Annual Review of Psychology, 39,* 349–374.

Gutek, B. A. (1988). Sex segregation and women at work: A selective review. *Applied Psychology: An International Review, 37*(2), 103–120.

Gutteridge, T. G., & Otte, F. L. (1983). Organizational career development: What's going on out there? *Training and Development Journal, 37*(2), 22–26.

Gyllenhammer, P. G. (1977). *People at work.* Reading, MA: Addison-Wesley.

Hackman, J. R. (1986). The psychology of self-management in organizations. In M. S. Pallak & R. O. Perloff (Eds.), *Psychology and work: Productivity, change, and employment* (pp. 89–136). Washington, DC: American Psychological Association.

Hackman, J. R., & Oldham, G. R. (1975). Development of the Job Diagnostic Survey. *Journal of Applied Psychology, 60,* 159–170.

Hackman, J. R., & Oldham, G. R. (1976). Motivation through the design of work: Test of a theory. *Organizational Behavior and Human Performance, 16,* 250–279.

Hackman, J. R., & Oldham, G. R. (1980). *Work redesign.* Reading, MA: Addison-Wesley.

Hafer, J. C., & Hoth, C. C. (1983). Selection characteristics: Your priorities and how students perceive them. *Personnel Administrator, 28*(3), 25–28.

Haider, M., Koller, M., & Cervinka, R. (Eds.). (1986). *Night and shiftwork: Long-term effects and their prevention*. Bern, Switzerland: Verlag Peter Lang.

Haire, M. (1950). Projective techniques in marketing research. *Journal of Marketing, 14*, 649–656.

Hales, C. (1987). The manager's work in context: A pilot investigation of the relationship between managerial role demands and role performance. *Personnel Review, 16*(5), 26–33.

Halff, H. M., Hollan, J. D., & Hutchins, E. L. (1986). Cognitive science and military training. *American Psychologist, 41*, 1131–1139.

Hall, D. T. (1976). *Careers in organizations*. Pacific Palisades, CA: Goodyear.

Hall, D. T. (1986). *Career development in organizations*. San Francisco: Jossey-Bass.

Hall, K., & Savery, L. K. (1986). Tight rein, more stress. *Harvard Business Review, 64*(1), 160–164.

Hammer, E. G., & Kleiman, L. S. (1988). Getting to know you. *Personnel Administrator, 33*(5), 86–92.

Hammer, T. H., & Turk, J. M. (1987). Organizational determinants of leader behavior and authority. *Journal of Applied Psychology, 72*, 674–682.

Harn, T. J., & Thornton, G. C., III. (1985). Recruiter counselling behaviors and applicant impressions. *Journal of Occupational Psychology, 58*, 57–65.

Harragan, B. L. (1983). Getting ahead: Career priorities. *Working Women, 8*, 38.

Harris, L. (1988). *Inside America*. New York: Vintage.

Harris, M. M., & Fink, L. S. (1987). A field study of applicant reactions to employment opportunities: Does the recruiter make a difference? *Personnel Psychology, 40*, 765–784.

Harris, M. M., & Schaubroeck, J. (1988). A meta-analysis of self-supervisor, self-peer, and peer-supervisor ratings. *Personnel Psychology, 41*, 43–62.

Hartley, D., Roback, H., & Abramowitz, S. (1976). Deterioration effects in encounter groups. *American Psychologist, 31*, 247–255.

Harvey, R. J., & Hayes, T. L. (1986). Monte Carlo baselines for interrater reliability correlations using the Position Analysis Questionnaire. *Personnel Psychology, 39*, 345–357.

Harvey, R. J., & Lozada-Larsen, S. R. (1988). Influence of amount of job descriptive information on job analysis rating accuracy. *Journal of Applied Psychology, 73*, 457–461.

Harwood, K., & Foley, P. (1987). Temporal revolution: An insight into the video display terminal (VDT) "problem." *Human Factors, 29*, 447–452.

Harwood, S., & Briscoe, D. R. (1987). Improving the interview process: A case study. *Personnel, 64*(9), 48–50.

Hassett, J., & Dukes, S. (1986, September). The new employee trainer: A floppy disk. *Psychology Today*, pp. 30–36.

Hatfield, E., & Sprecher, S. (1986). *Mirror, mirror: The importance of looks in everyday life*. Albany: University of New York Press.

Hawk, J. (1986). Real world implications of *g*. *Journal of Vocational Behavior, 29*, 411–414.

Haynes, R. S., Pine, R. C., & Fitch, H. G. (1982). Reducing accident rates with organizational behavior modification. *Academy of Management Journal, 25*, 407–416.

Hebert, H. J. (1988, June 24). Federal government plans to drop written exam for civil service jobs. *St. Petersburg (FL) Times*.

Hedberg, G. (1987). The evaluation of the driver's cab in the Rc5 engine. *Applied Ergonomics, 18*(1), 35–42.

Heilman, M. E., Martell, R. F., & Simon, M. C. (1988). The vagaries of sex bias: Conditions regulating the undervaluation, equivaluation, and overvaluation of female job applicants. *Organizational Behavior and Human Decision Processes, 41*, 98–110.

Helfgott, R. B. (1988). Can training catch up with technology? *Personnel Journal, 67*(2), 67–72.

Heller, P. S. (1986). EEOC standards: What makes for a good test? *Personnel Journal, 65*(7), 102–105.

Helmkamp, J. C., & Bone, C. M. (1987). The effect of time in a new job on hospitalization rates for accidents and injuries in the U.S. Navy, 1977–1983. *Journal of Occupational Medicine, 29*, 653–659.

Helmreich, R. L., Sawin, L. L., & Carsrud, A. L. (1986). The honeymoon effect in job performance: Temporal increases in the predictive power of achievement motivation. *Journal of Applied Psychology, 71*, 185–188.

Henderson, E. (1986). Blacks in corporate America: Is there a future? *Personnel Journal, 65*(1), 12–19.

Heneman, R. L. (1986). The relationship between supervisory ratings and results-oriented measures of performance: A meta-analysis. *Personnel Psychology, 39*, 811–826.

Heneman, R. L., & Cohen, D. J. (1988). Supervisory and employee characteristics as correlates of employee salary increases. *Personnel Psychology, 41*, 345–360.

Hersey, P., & Blanchard, K. (1982). *Management of organizational behavior* (4th ed.). Englewood Cliffs, NJ: Prentice-Hall.

Hersey, R. B. (1932). Rates of production and emotional state. *Personnel Journal, 10*, 355–364.

Herzberg, F. (1966). *Work and the nature of man*. Cleveland: World.

Herzberg, F. (1974). Motivator-hygiene profiles: Pinpointing what ails the organization. *Organizational Dynamics, 3*(2), 18–29.

Herzberg, F. (1987). One more time: How do you motivate employees [a reprint of the original published in 1968, with retrospective commentary by Herzberg]. *Harvard Business Review, 65*(5), 109–120.

Herzog, A. R., & Rodgers, W. L. (1988). Interviewing older adults: Mode comparison using data from a face-to-face survey and a telephone survey. *Public Opinion Quarterly, 52*(1), 84–99.

Hicks, J. (1988, June 5). For the skilled, it's a seller's market. *New York Times*.

Higgins, N. C. (1986). Occupational stress and working women: The effectiveness of two stress reduction programs. *Journal of Vocational Behavior, 29*, 66–78.

Hill, A. B. (1975). Work variety and individual differences in occupational boredom. *Journal of Applied Psychology, 60*, 128–131.

Hill, F. M. (1986). Quality circles in the U.K.: A longitudinal study. *Personnel Review, 15*(3), 25–34.

Hinkin, T. R., & Schriesheim, C. A. (1988). Power and influence: The view from below. *Personnel, 65*(5), 47–50.

Hinrichs, J. R. (1978). An eight-year follow-up of a management assessment center. *Journal of Applied Psychology, 63*, 596–601.

Hirschman, E. C., & Mills, M. K. (1980). Sources shoppers use to pick stores. *Journal of Advertising Research, 20*(1), 47–51.

Hirsh, H. R., Northrop, L. C., & Schmidt, F. L. (1986). Validity generalization results for law enforcement occupations. *Personnel Psychology, 39*, 399–420.

Hirsh, H. R., Schmidt, F. L., & Hunter, J. E. (1986). Estimation of employment validities by less experienced judges. *Personnel Psychology, 39*, 337–344.

Hite, R. E., & Eck, R. (1987, October/November). Advertising to children: Attitudes of business vs. consumers. *Journal of Advertising Research*, pp. 40–53.

Hogan, R. (1985). What every student should know about personality psychology. In V. P. Makosky (Ed.), *G. Stanley Hall lecture series* (Vol. 7, pp. 43–64). Washington, DC: American Psychological Association.

Hogan, R., & Nicholson, R. A. (1988). The meaning of personality test scores. *American Psychologist, 43*, 621–626.

Hollenbeck, J. R., & Klein, H. J. (1987). Goal commitment and the goal-setting process: Problems, prospects, and proposals for future research. *Journal of Applied Psychology, 72*, 212–220.

Hollenbeck, J. R., & Williams, C. R. (1986). Turnover functionality versus turnover frequency: A note on work attitudes and organizational effectiveness. *Journal of Applied Psychology, 71*, 606–611.

Hollie, P. G. (1987, July 12). Why business is barging into the classroom. *New York Times*.

Hollingworth, H. L. (1929). *Vocational psychology and character analysis*. New York: Appleton.

Holloman, C. R. (1968). Leadership and headship: There is a difference. *Personnel Administration, 31*(4), 38–44.

Holman, K. W., Abbasi, S. M., & Murrey, J. H., Jr. (1987). Drug testing: Employers, employees, and the courts. *Industrial Management, 29*(6), 21–27.

Holmes, D. S. (1984). Meditation and somatic arousal reduction: A review of the experimental evidence. *American Psychologist, 39*, 1–10.

Horn, J. C. (1987, July). Bigger pay for better work. *Psychology Today*, pp. 54–57.

Hornik, J. (1988). Diurnal variation in consumer response. *Journal of Consumer Research, 14*, 588–591.

Hornstein, H. A., Heilman, M. E., Mone, E., & Tartell, R. (1987). Responding to contingent leadership behavior. *Organizational Dynamics, 15*, 56–65.

Horovitz, B. (1987, May 13). Today's advertisers leaves 'no bills unposted." *St. Petersburg (FL) Times*.

House, R. J. (1971). A path-goal theory of leader effectiveness. *Administrative Science Quarterly, 16*, 321–338.

House, R. J., & Mitchell, T. (1974). Path-goal theory of leadership. *Journal of Contemporary Business, 3*, 81–97.

House, R. J., & Singh, J. V. (1987). Organizational behavior: Some new directions for I/O psychology. *Annual Review of Psychology, 38*, 669–718.

How to be efficient with fewer violins. (1955). *American Association of University Professors Bulletin, 41*, 454–455.

Howard, A. (1986). College experiences and managerial performance. *Journal of Applied Psychology, 71*, 530–552.

Howard, A., & Bray, D. W. (1988). *Managerial lives in transition: Advancing age and changing times*. New York: Guilford Press.

Howard, A., & Wilson, J. A. (1982). Leadership in a declining work ethic. *California Management Review, 24*(4), 33–46.

Howard, J. H., Cunningham, D. A., & Rechnitzer, P. A. (1986). Role ambiguity, Type A behavior, and job satisfaction: Moderating effects on cardiovascular and biochemical responses associated with coronary risk. *Journal of Applied Psychology, 71*, 95–101.

Howarth, P. A., & Istance, H. O. (1986). The validity of subjective reports of visual discomfort. *Human Factors, 28*, 347–351.

Huchingson, R. D. (1981). *New horizons for human factors in design*. New York: McGraw-Hill.

Hunter, J. E. (1979). An analysis of validity, differential validity, test fairness, and utility for the Philadelphia police officers selection examination prepared by the Educational Testing Service. Report to the Philadelphia Federal District Court, Alvarez v. City of Philadelphia.

Hunter, J. E. (1980). *Validity generalization for 12,000 jobs: An application of synthetic validity and validity generalization to the General Aptitude Test Battery (GATB)*. Washington, DC: U.S. Employment Service.

Hunter, J. E. (1986). Cognitive ability, cognitive aptitudes, job knowledge, and job performance. *Journal of Vocational Behavior, 29*, 340–362.

Hunter, J. E., & Hunter, R. F. (1983). *The validity and utility of alternative predictors of job performance*. Washington, DC: U.S. Office of Personnel Management.

Hunter, J. E., & Hunter, R. F. (1984). Validity and utility of alternative predictors of job performance. *Psychological Bulletin, 96*, 72–98.

Hunter, J. E., & Schmidt, F. L. (1982). The economic benefits of personnel selection using psychological ability tests. *Industrial Relations, 21*, 293–308.

Hunter, J. E., & Schmidt, F. L. (1983). Quantifying the effects of psychological intervention on employee job performance and work-force productivity. *American Psychologist, 38*, 473–478.

Hurrell, J. J., Jr. (1985). Machine-paced work and the Type A behaviour pattern. *Journal of Occupational Psychology, 58*, 15–25.

Hurrell, J. J., Jr. (1987). An overview of organizational stress and health. In L. R. Murphy & T. F. Schoenborn (Eds.), *Stress management in work settings* (pp. 31–45). Washington, DC: National Institute for Occupational Safety and Health.

Huseman, R. C., Hatfield, J. D., & Miles, E. W. (1987). A new perspective on equity theory: The equity sensitivity construct. *Academy of Management Review, 12*, 222–234.

Hutchison, S., & Sowa, D. (1986). Perceived organizational support. *Journal of Applied Psychology, 71*, 500–507.

Idaszak, J. R., & Drasgow, F. (1987). A revision of the Job Diagnostic Survey: Elimination of a measurement artifact. *Journal of Applied Psychology, 72*, 69–74.

IES lighting handbook (5th ed.). (1972). New York: Illuminating Engineering Society.

Imada, A. S. (1982). Social interaction, observation, and stereotypes as determinants of differentiation in peer ratings. *Organizational Behavior and Human Performance, 29*, 397–415.

In the office: See how they run. (1988, January 3). *New York Times.*

Isikoff, M. (1988, June 10). Corporate drug testing on the rise. *Washington Post.*

Isler, L., Popper, E. T., & Ward, S. (1987, October/November). Children's purchase requests and parental responses: Results from a diary study. *Journal of Advertising Research*, pp. 28–39.

It's not who you know. (1988). *Administrative Management, 49*(1), 8.

Ivancevich, J. M. (1982). Subordinates' reactions to performance appraisal interviews: A test of feedback and goal-setting techniques. *Journal of Applied Psychology, 67*, 581–587.

Ivancevich, J. M., & Smith, S. V. (1981). Goal setting interview skills training: Simulated and on-the-job analyses. *Journal of Applied Psychology, 66*, 697–705.

Jackall, R. (1983). Moral mazes: Bureaucracy and managerial work. *Harvard Business Review, 61*(5), 118–130.

Jackson, J. M., & Harkins, S. G. (1985). Equity in effort: An explanation of the social loafing effect. *Journal of Personality and Social Psychology, 49*, 1199–1206.

Jackson, L. H., & Mindell, M. C. (1980). Motivating the new breed. *Personnel, 57*(2), 53–61.

Jackson, S. E., & Schuler, R. S. (1985). A meta-analysis and conceptual critique of research on role ambiguity and role conflict in work settings. *Organizational Behavior and Human Decision Processes, 36*, 16–28.

Jackson, S. E., Schwab, R. L., & Schuler, R. S. (1986). Toward an understanding of the burnout phenomenon. *Journal of Applied Psychology, 71*, 630–640.

Jacobson, E. (1938). *Progressive relaxation*. Chicago: University of Chicago Press.

Jago, A. G., & Ragan, J. W. (1986). The trouble with Leader Match is that it doesn't match Fiedler's contingency model. *Journal of Applied Psychology, 71*, 555–559.

Jago, A. G., & Vroom, V. H. (1980). An evaluation of two alternatives to the Vroom-Yetton normative model. *Academy of Management Review, 23*, 347–355.

Janaro, R. E., Bechtold, S. E., & Klippel, C. F. (1988). A technical note on increasing productivity through effective rest break scheduling. *Industrial Management, 30*(1), 29–33.

Jaroslovsky, R. (1988, July/August). What's on your mind, America? *Psychology Today*, pp. 54–59.

Job satisfaction is number one. (1988). *Personnel Journal, 67*(3), 6.

Jobs OK, pay isn't. (1988). *Personnel Administrator, 33*(3), 30.

Johansson, J. K., & Nonaka, I. (1987). Market research the Japanese way. *Harvard Business Review, 65*(3), 16–22.

Johns, G. (1987, October). The great escape. *Psychology Today*, pp. 30–33.

Johnson, H. E. (1988). Older workers help meet employment needs. *Personnel Journal, 67*(5), 100–105.

Johnson, R., & Heal, L. W. (1976). Private employment agency responses to the physically handicapped applicant in a wheelchair. *Journal of Applied Rehabilitation Counseling, 7*, 12–21.

Johnson, S. L. (1988). Evaluation of powered screwdriver design characteristics. *Human Factors, 30*, 61–69.

Johnson, T. (1984). The myth of declining brand loyalty. *Journal of Advertising Research, 24*(1), 9–17.

Jolson, M. A., Wiener, J. L., & Rosecky, R. B. (1987, February/March). Correlates of rebate proneness. *Journal of Advertising Research*, pp. 33–43.

Jones, E. W., Jr. (1986). Black managers: The dream deferred. *Harvard Business Review, 64*(3), 84–93.

Jones, J. W., & DuBois, D. (1987). A review of organizational stress assessment instruments. In L. R. Murphy & T. F. Schoenborn (Eds.), *Stress management in work settings* (pp. 47–66). Washington, DC: National Institute for Occupational Safety and Health.

Kahle, L. R., Poulos, B., & Sukhdial, A. (1988, February/March). Changes in social values in the United States during the past decade. *Journal of Advertising Research*, pp. 35–41.

Kahn, R. L., Wolfe, D. M., Quinn, R. P., Snock, J. D., & Rosenthal, R. A. (1964). *Organizational stress: Studies in role conflict and ambiguity*. New York: Wiley.

Kainen, T. L., Begley, T. M., & Maggard, M. J. (1983). On-the-job training and work unit performance. *Training and Development Journal, 37*(4), 84–87.

Kane, J. S., & Bernardin, H. J. (1982). Behavioral observation scales and the evaluation of performance appraisal effectiveness. *Journal of Applied Psychology, 35*, 635–641.

Kanner, B. (1983, June 6). Wrapping it up: The new packaging. *New York*, pp. 12–15.

Kanner, B. (1987, April 20). The people's choice. *New York*, pp. 21–22.

Kanner, B. (1988a, September 19). Ads pop up between pages. *New York*, pp. 28–31.

Kanner, B. (1988b, February 8). Are the stars out tonight? *New York*, pp. 22–26.

Kanter, R. M. (1982). The middle manager as innovator. *Harvard Business Review, 60*(4), 95–105.

Kanter, R. M. (1987a). The attack on pay. *Harvard Business Review, 65*(2), 60–67.

Kanter, R. M. (1987b). From status to contribution: Some organizational implications of the changing basis for pay. *Personnel, 64*(1), 12–37.

Karren, R. J., & Nkomo, S. M. (1988). So, you want to work for us. *Personnel Administrator, 33*(4), 88–92.

Katzell, R. A., & Guzzo, R. A. (1983). Psychological approaches to productivity improvement. *American Psychologist, 38*, 468–472.

Kaufman, H. G. (1982). *Professionals in search of work: Coping with the stress of job loss and underemployment.* New York: Wiley.

Kaufmann, G. M., & Beehr, T. A. (1986). Interactions between job stressors and social support: Some counterintuitive results. *Journal of Applied Psychology, 71*, 522–526.

Kaye, S. D. (1987, November). Safety in numbers? *Washingtonian*, p. 334.

Keenan, A., & Newton, T. J. (1987). Work difficulties and stress in young professional engineers. *Journal of Occupational Psychology, 60*, 133–145.

Keller, K. L. (1987). Memory factors in advertising: The effect of advertising retrieval cues on brand evaluations. *Journal of Consumer Research, 14*, 316–333.

Keller, J., & Piotrowski, C. (1987). Career development programs in Fortune 500 firms. *Psychological Reports, 61*, 920–922.

Kelley, H. H. (1973). The processes of causal attribution. *American Psychologist, 28*, 107–128.

Kelly, M. M. (1984). Exploring the potentials of decentralized work settings. *Personnel Administrator, 29*(2), 48–52.

Kelly, N. (1982). Zale Corporation's career development program. *Training and Development Journal, 36*(6), 70–75.

Kemery, E. R., Roth, L., & Mossholder, K. W. (1987). The power of the Schmidt and Hunter model of validity generalization. *Journal of Applied Psychology, 72*, 30–37.

Kerr, W. (1957). Complementary theories of safety psychology. *Journal of Social Psychology, 45*, 3–9.

Kerr, S., Hill, K. D., & Broedling, L. (1986). The first-line supervisor: Phasing out or here to stay? *Academy of Management Review, 11*, 103–117.

King, P. (1984). How to prepare for a performance appraisal interview. *Training and Development Journal, 38*(2), 66–69.

King, L. M., Hunter, J. E., & Schmidt, F. L. (1980). Halo in multidimensional forced-choice performance evaluation scale. *Journal of Applied Psychology, 65*, 507–516.

King, M., Murray, M. A., & Atkinson, T. (1982). Background, personality, job characteristics, and satisfaction with work in a national sample. *Human Relations, 35*, 119–133.

Kingson, J. A. (1988, March 6). Golden years spent under golden arches. *New York Times*.

Kipnis, D. (1976). *The powerholders.* Chicago: University of Chicago Press.

Kirchner, W. K. (1961). The fallacy of accident proneness. *Personnel, 38*(6), 34–37.

Kirk, W. Q., & Maddox, R. C. (1988). International management: The new frontier for women. *Personnel, 65*(3), 46–49.

Kirmeyer, S. L., & Dougherty, T. W. (1988). Work load, tension, and coping: Moderating effects of supervisor support. *Personnel Psychology, 41*, 125–139.

Kizilos, T., & Heinisch, R. P. (1986). How a management team selects managers. *Harvard Business Review, 64*(5), 6–12.

Kleiman, M. P. (1984). Turning career development lip service into action. *Training and Development Journal, 38*(4), 78–79.

Klein, J. A., & Posey, P. A. (1986). Good supervisors are good supervisors—anywhere. *Harvard Business Review, 64*(6), 125–128.

Klein, K. J. (1987). Employee stock ownership and employee attitudes: A test of three models. *Journal of Applied Psychology, 72,* 319–332.

Kleinschrod, W. A. (1988). The trend to electronic training. *Administrative Management, 49*(3), 29–33.

Klimoski, R., & Brickner, M. (1987). Why do assessment centers work: The puzzle of assessment center validity. *Personnel Psychology, 40,* 243–260.

Klotchman, J., & Neider, L. L. (1983). EEO alert: Watch out for discrimination in discharge decisions. *Personnel, 60*(1), 60–66.

Knave, B. (1984). Ergonomics and lighting. *Applied Ergonomics, 15,* 15–20.

Kobasa, S. C. (1979). Stressful life events, personality, and health: An inquiry into hardiness. *Journal of Personality and Social Psychology, 37,* 1–11.

Kobasa, S. C., Maddi, S. R., & Kahn, S. (1982). Hardiness and health: A prospective study. *Journal of Personality and Social Psychology, 42,* 168–177.

Kobasa, S. C., Maddi, S. R., Puccetti, M. C., & Zola, M. C. (1985). Effectiveness of hardiness, exercise and social support as resources against illness. *Journal of Psychosomatic Research, 29,* 525–533.

Kochhar, D. S., & Barash, D. (1987). Status displays in automated assembly. *Applied Ergonomics, 18,* 115–124.

Koelega, H. S., & Brinkman, J. A. (1986). Noise and vigilance: An evaluative review. *Human Factors, 28,* 465–481.

Kohl, G. A. (1983). Effects of shape and size of knobs on maximal hand-turning forces applied by females. *Bell System Technical Journal, 62,* 1705–1712.

Komaki, J. (1986). Toward effective supervision: An operant analysis and comparison of managers at work. *Journal of Applied Psychology, 71,* 270–279.

Komaki, J., Barwick, K. D., & Scott, L. R. (1978). A behavioral approach to occupational safety: Pinpointing and reinforcing safe performance in a food manufacturing plant. *Journal of Applied Psychology, 63,* 434–445.

Komaki, J., Heinzmann, A. T., & Lawson, L. (1980). Effects of training and feedback: Component analysis of a behavioral safety program. *Journal of Applied Psychology, 65,* 261–270.

Komaki, J., Zlotnick, S., & Jensen, M. (1986). Development of an operant-based taxonomy and observational index of supervisory behavior. *Journal of Applied Psychology, 71,* 260–269.

Korgaonkar, P. K., Moschis, G. P., & Bellenger, D. N. (1984). Correlates of successful advertising campaigns. *Journal of Advertising Research, 24*(1), 47–53.

Kossoris, M. D., & Kohler, R. F. (1947). *Hours of work and output.* Washington, DC: Bureau of Labor Statistics.

Kozlowski, S. W., Kirsch, M. P., & Chao, G. T. (1986). Job knowledge, ratee familiarity, conceptual similarity, and halo error: An exploration. *Journal of Applied Psychology, 71,* 45–49.

Kraut, R. E. (Ed.). (1987). *Technology and the transformation of white-collar work.* Hillsdale, NJ: Erlbaum.

Kravitz, D. A., & Martin, B. (1986). Ringelmann rediscovered: The original article. *Journal of Personality and Social Psychology, 50,* 936–941.

Krigsman, N., & Krigsman, R. (1988). How to successfully move an organization. *Personnel Journal, 67*(1), 65–72.

Kryter, K. D. (1970). *The effects of noise on man.* New York: Academic Press.

Kuder, G. F., & Diamond, E. E. (1979). *Kuder Occupational Interest Survey: General manual.* Chicago: Science Research Associates.

Kulik, C. T., Oldham, G. R., & Hackman, J. R. (1987). Work design as an approach to person-environment fit. *Journal of Vocational Behavior, 31,* 278–296.

Kulik, C. T., Oldham, G. R., & Langner, P. H. (1988). Measurement of job characteristics: Comparison of the original and the revised Job Diagnostic Survey. *Journal of Applied Psychology, 73,* 462–466.

Lam, T. H., Lee, P. W. H., Ong, S. G., Wong, C. M., Chow, W. K., & Kleevens, J. W. L. (1987). Mental health and work stress: A comparison of response patterns in executives and clerical workers in Hong Kong. *Journal of Occupational Medicine, 29,* 892–897.

Lambrinos, J., & Johnson, W. G. (1984). Robots to reduce the high cost of illness and injury. *Harvard Business Review, 62*(3), 24–28.

Lance, C. E., & Woehr, D. J. (1986). Statistical control of halo: Clarification from two cognitive models of the performance appraisal process. *Journal of Applied Psychology, 71,* 679–685.

Landers, S. (1987, August). Rising work stress claims hit employers in the pocket. *APA Monitor.*

Landy, F. J. (1985). *Psychology of work behavior* (3rd ed.). Homewood, IL: Dorsey Press.

Larsson, G. (1987). Routinization of mental training in organizations: Effects on performance and well-being. *Journal of Applied Psychology, 72,* 88–96.

Latham, G. P. (1988). Human resource training and development. *Annual Review of Psychology, 39,* 545–582.

Latham, G. P., & Wexley, K. N. (1977). Behavioral observation scales for performance appraisal purposes. *Personnel Psychology, 30,* 255–268.

Latham, G. P., & Wexley, K. N. (1981). *Increasing productivity through performance appraisal.* Reading, MA: Addison-Wesley.

Lawler, E. E., III. (1971). *Pay and organizational effectiveness.* New York: McGraw-Hill.

Lawler, E. E., III. (1986). *High-involvement management: Participative strategies for improving organizational performance.* San Francisco: Jossey-Bass.

Lawler, E. E., III, & Mohrman, S. A. (1987). Quality circles: After the honeymoon. *Organizational Dynamics, 15,* 42–54.

Lawler, E. E., III, & Porter, L. W. (1967). The effect of performance on job satisfaction. *Industrial Relations, 7,* 20–28.

Lawrence, S. (1988). Reduce turnover, promote. *Personnel Journal, 67*(5), 8.

Lawrence, D. G., Salsburg, B. L., Dawson, J .G., & Fasman, Z. D. (1982). Design and use of weighted application blanks. *Personnel Administrator, 27*(3), 47–53.

Lazarus, R. S. (1981, July). Little hassles can be hazardous to your health. *Psychology Today,* pp. 58–62.

Leana, C. R. (1987). Power relinquishment versus power sharing: Theoretical clarification and empirical comparison of delegation and participation. *Journal of Applied Psychology, 72,* 228–233.

Lefkowitz, J. (1970). Effect of training on the productivity and tenure of sewing machine operators. *Journal of Applied Psychology, 54,* 81–86.

Leigh, T. W., Rethans, A. J., & Whitney, T. R. (1987, October/November). Role portrayals of women in advertising: Cognitive responses and advertising effectiveness. *Journal of Advertising Research,* pp. 54–63.

Levine, E. L., Cannon, J. A., & Spector, P. E. (1985). Generalizability of test validities for selection in skilled and semiskilled craft jobs (Tech. Rep.). Bell Communications Research.

Levine, E. L., Sistrunk, F., McNutt, K., & Gael, S. (1988). Exemplary job analysis systems in selected organizations: A description of process and outcomes. *Journal of Business and Psychology, 3,* 3–21.

Levine, E. L., Thomas, J. N., & Sistrunk, F. (1988). Selecting a job analysis approach. In S. Gael (Ed.), *Job analysis handbook for business, industry, and government* (pp. 339–352). New York: Wiley.

Levine, H. Z. (1982). Supervisory training. *Personnel, 59*(6), 4–12.

Levine, H. Z. (1983). Safety and health programs. *Personnel, 60*(3), 4–9.

Levine, H. Z. (1984). Recruitment and selection programs. *Personnel, 61*(1), 4–10.

Levine, H. Z. (1986a). AIDS in the workplace. *Personnel, 63*(3), 56–64.

Levine, H. Z. (1986b). The squeeze on middle management. *Personnel, 63*(1), 62–69.

Levine, H. Z. (1987a). Alternative work schedules: Do they meet workforce needs? Part 1. *Personnel, 64*(2), 57–62.

Levine, H. Z. (1987b). Alternative work schedules: Do they meet workforce needs? Part 2. *Personnel, 64*(4), 66–71.

Levinson, H. (1980). Criteria for choosing chief executives. *Harvard Business Review, 58*(4), 113–120.

Levitt, T. (1970). The morality (?) of advertising. *Harvard Business Review, 48*(4), 85.

Lewin, T. (1988, July 10). Pregnant women increasingly fearful of VDTs. *New York Times.*

Lewis, J. A., & Lewis, M. D. (1986). *Counseling programs for employees in the workplace.* Monterey, CA: Brooks/Cole.

Licker, P. S. (1987). The automated office and performance appraisal. *Personnel, 64*(7), 14–20.

Liden, R. C., & Parsons, G. K. (1986). A field study of job applicant interview perceptions, alternative opportunities, and demographic characteristics. *Personnel Psychology, 39,* 109–122.

Liem, R., & Rayman, P. (1982). Health and social costs of unemployment: Research and policy considerations. *American Psychologist, 37,* 1116–1123.

Lilienthal, R. A. (1980). *The use of reference checks for selection.* Washington, DC: U.S. Office of Personnel Management.

Lo Bosco, M. (1986a). Employee attitude surveys. *Personnel, 63*(4), 64–68.

Lo Bosco, M. (1986b). Safety programs in the workplace. *Personnel, 63*(5), 59–67.

Locke, E. A. (1968). Toward a theory of task motivation and incentives. *Organizational Behavior and Human Performance, 3,* 157–189.

Locke, E. A. (1976). The nature and causes of job satisfaction. In M. D. Dunnette (Ed.), *Handbook of industrial and organizational psychology* (pp. 1297–1349). Chicago: Rand McNally.

Locke, E. A. (1982). The ideas of Frederick W. Taylor: An evaluation. *Academy of Management Review, 7,* 14–24.

Locke, E. A. (Ed.). (1986). *Generalizing from laboratory to field settings: Research findings from industrial-organizational psychology, organizational behavior, and human resource management.* Lexington, MA: Lexington Books.

Locke, E. A., Feren, D. B., McCaleb, V. M., Shaw, K. N., & Denny, A. T. (1980). The relative effectiveness of four methods of motivating employee performance. In K. Duncan, M. Gruneberg, & D. Wallis (Eds.), *Changes in working life.* New York: Wiley.

Locke, E. A., Latham, G. P., & Erez, M. (1988). The determinants of goal commitment. *Academy of Management Review, 13,* 23–39.

Locke, E. A., & Schweiger, D. M. (1978). Participation in decision-making: One more look. In B. M. Staw (Ed.), *Research in organizational behavior.* Greenwich, CT: JAI Press.

Locke, E. A., Shaw, K. N., Saari, L. M., & Latham, G. P. (1981). Goal setting and task performance: 1969–1980. *Psychological Bulletin, 90*, 125–152.

Lodahl, T. M., & Kejner, M. (1965). The definition and measurement of job involvement. *Journal of Applied Psychology, 49*, 24–33.

Loken, B., & Howard-Pitney, B. (1988). Effectiveness of cigarette advertisements on women: An experimental study. *Journal of Applied Psychology, 73*, 378–382.

London, M. (1987). Employee development in a downsizing environment. *Journal of Business and Psychology, 2*, 60–73.

Long, R. J. (1987). *New office information technology: Human and managerial implications*. New York: Croom Helm/Methuen.

Long, R. J. (1988). Factors affecting managerial desire for various types of employee participation in decision making. *Applied Psychology: An International Review, 37*(1), 15–34.

Lord, R. G., DeVader, C. L., & Alliger, G. M. (1986). A meta-analysis of the relation between personality traits and leadership perceptions: An application of validity generalization procedures. *Journal of Applied Psychology, 71*, 402–410.

Lounsbury, J. W., & Hoopes, L. L. (1986). A vacation from work: Changes in work and nonwork outcomes. *Journal of Applied Psychology, 71*, 392–401.

Love, K. G., & O'Hara, K. (1987). Predicting job performance of youth trainees under a Job Training Partnership Act (JTPA) program: Criterion validation of a behavior-based measure of work maturity. *Personnel Psychology, 40*, 323–340.

Lu, D., & Kiewit, D. A. (1987, June/July). Passive people meters: A first step. *Journal of Advertising Research*, pp. 9–14.

Lumpkin, J. R., & Festervand, T. A. (1988, December/January). Purchase information sources of the elderly. *Journal of Advertising Research*, pp. 31–43.

Lutgen, L. (1987). AIDS in the workplace: Fighting fear with facts and policy. *Personnel, 64*(11), 53–57.

Luthans, F., Maciag, W. S., & Rosenkrantz, S. A. (1983). OB Mod: Meeting the productivity challenge with human resources management. *Personnel, 60*(2), 28–36.

Macdonald, W. A., & Cole, B. L. (1988). Evaluating the role of colour in a flight information cockpit display. *Ergonomics, 31*, 13–37.

Machlowitz, M. (1980). *Workaholics: Living with them, working with them*. Reading, MA: Addison-Wesley.

Machlowitz, M. (1987a, May 3). A new take on Type A. *New York Times Magazine*, pp. 40–44.

Machlowitz, M. (1987b, July 19). Without the playground, mothers meet at the office. *New York Times*.

Macklin, M. C. (1983). Do children understand TV ads? *Journal of Advertising Research, 23*(1), 63–70.

Macklin, M. C. (1987). Preschoolers' understanding of the informational function of television advertising. *Journal of Consumer Research, 14*(2), 229–239.

Madlin, N. (1987). Computer-based training comes of age. *Personnel, 64*(11), 64–65.

Magnus, M. (1988a). AIDS: Fear and ignorance still plague the workplace. *Personnel Journal, 67*(2), 28.

Magnus, M. (1988b). What's in a title? Plenty. *Personnel Journal, 67*(3), 23–27.

Majchrzak, A. (1987). *Human infrastructure: Managing successful factory automation*. San Francisco: Jossey-Bass.

Majchrzak, A., & Klein, K. J. (1987). Things are always more complicated than you think: An open systems approach to the organizational effects of computer-automated technology. *Journal of Business and Psychology, 2*, 27–49.

Malcolm, A. H. (1987, November 29). Teenage shoppers: Desperately seeking spinach. *New York Times*.

Malcolm, A. H. (1988, March 27). Overpowering the scent market. *New York Times Magazine*, pp. 56, 66–67.

Mann, F. C., & Hoffman, L. R. (1960). *Automation and the worker*. New York: Henry Holt.

Margolis, B. L., Kroes, W. M., & Quinn, R. P. (1974). Job stress: An unlisted occupational hazard. *Journal of Occupational Medicine, 16*, 659–661.

Marks, M. (1988, June 20). When 40 is too old to find work. *St. Petersburg (FL) Times*.

Marks, M. L. (1986, March). The question of quality circles. *Psychology Today*, pp. 36–46.

Marks, M. L., Mirvis, P. H., Hackett, E. J., & Grady, J. F., Jr. (1986). Employee participation in a quality circle program: Impact on quality of work life, productivity, and absenteeism. *Journal of Applied Psychology, 71*, 61–69.

Marriott, I. A., & Stuchly, M. A. (1986). Health aspects of work with visual display terminals. *Journal of Occupational Medicine, 28*, 833–848.

Martin, D. C. (1986). Performance appraisal, 2: Improving the rater's effectiveness. *Personnel, 63*(8), 28–33.

Masi, D. A. (1987a). AIDS in the workplace: What can be done? *Personnel, 64*(7), 57–60.

Masi, D. A. (1987b). Company responses to drug abuse from AMA's nationwide survey. *Personnel, 64*(3), 40–46.

Maslach, C., & Jackson, S. E. (1981). *The Maslach Burnout Inventory*. Palo Alto, CA: Consulting Psychologists Press.

Maslow, A. (1970). *Motivation and personality* (2nd ed.). New York: Harper & Row.

Mason, R. M. (1984, February 15). Ergonomics: The human and the machine. *Library Journal*, pp. 331–332.

Matthews, K. A. (1982). Psychological perspectives on the Type A behavior pattern. *Psychological Bulletin, 91*, 293–323.

Maurer, S. D., & Fay, C. (1988). Effect of situational interviews, conventional structured interviews, and training on interview rating agreement: An experimental analysis. *Personnel Psychology, 41*, 329–344.

Mayfield, E. C. (1964). The selection interview: A reevaluation of published research. *Personnel Psychology, 17*, 239–260.

McCall, M. W., Jr. (1988). Developing executives through work experiences. *Human Resource Planning, 11*(1), 1–11.

McCall, M. W., Jr., & Lombardo, M. M. (1982). Using simulation for leadership and management research: Through the Looking Glass. *Management Science, 28*, 533–549.

McCall, M. W., Jr., & Lombardo, M. M. (1983, February). What makes a top executive? *Psychology Today*, pp. 26–31.

McClelland, D. C. (1961). *The achieving society*. New York: Free Press.

McClelland, D. C. (1975). *Power: The inner experience*. New York: Irvington.

McClelland, D. C. (1985). *Human motivation*. Glenview, IL: Scott, Foresman.

McClelland, D. C., Atkinson, J. W., Clark, R. A., & Lowell, E. L. (1953). *The achievement motive*. New York: Appleton-Century-Crofts.

McClelland, D. C., & Boyatzis, R. E. (1982). Leadership motive pattern and long-term success in management. *Journal of Applied Psychology, 67*, 737–743.

McClelland, D. C., & Burnham, D. (1976). Power is the great motivator. *Harvard Business Review, 54*(2), 100–110.

McCormick, E. J. (1979). *Job analysis: Methods and applications.* New York: AMACOM.

McCormick, E. J., & Sanders, M. S. (1982). *Human factors in engineering and design* (5th ed.). New York: McGraw-Hill.

McCormick, J., & Powell, B. (1988, April 25). Management for the 1990s. *Newsweek,* pp. 47–48.

McDaniel, M. A., Schmidt, F. L., & Hunter, J. E. (1988). A meta-analysis of the validity of methods for rating training and experience in personnel selection. *Personnel Psychology, 41,* 283–309.

McDonald, A. D., Cherry, N. M., Delorme, C., & McDonald, J. C. (1986). Visual display units and pregnancy: Evidence from the Montreal survey. *Journal of Occupational Medicine, 28,* 1226–1231.

McEnery, J., & McEnery, J. M. (1987). Self-rating in management training needs assessment: A neglected opportunity? *Journal of Occupational Psychology, 60,* 49–60.

McEnrue, M. P. (1988). Length of experience and the performance of managers in the establishment phase of their careers. *Academy of Management Journal, 31,* 175–185.

McEvoy, G. M., & Buller, P. F. (1987). User acceptance of peer appraisals in an industrial setting. *Personnel Psychology, 40,* 785–797.

McEvoy, G. M., Buller, P. F., & Roghaar, S. R. (1988). A jury of one's peers. *Personnel Administrator, 33*(5), 94–101.

McEvoy, G. M., & Cascio, W. F. (1987). Do good or poor performers leave? A meta-analysis of the relationship between performance and turnover. *Academy of Management Journal, 30,* 744–762.

McEvoy, G. M., & Cascio, W. F. (1989). Cumulative evidence of the relationship between employee age and job performance. *Journal of Applied Psychology, 74,* 11–17.

McGarrell, E. J., Jr. (1983). An orientation system that builds productivity. *Personnel, 60*(6), 32–41.

McGee, G. W., & Ford, R. C. (1987). Two (or more?) dimensions of organizational commitment: Reexamination of the affective and continuance commitment scales. *Journal of Applied Psychology, 72,* 638–641.

McGraw, H. W., Jr. (1987). Adult functional illiteracy: What to do about it. *Personnel, 64*(10), 38–42.

McGregor, D. (1960). *The human side of enterprise.* New York: McGraw-Hill.

McGuire, F. L. (1976). Personality factors in highway accidents. *Human Factors, 18,* 433–442.

McGuire, J. B., & Liro, J. R. (1986). Flexible work schedules, work attitudes, and perceptions of productivity. *Public Personnel Management, 15,* 65–73.

McLean, A. A. (1979). *Work stress.* Reading, MA: Addison-Wesley.

McNeal, J. U., & McDaniel, S. W. (1984). An analysis of need-appeals in television advertising. *Journal of the Academy of Marketing Science, 12,* 176–190.

Meglino, B. M., & DeNisi, A. S. (1987). Realistic job previews: Some thoughts on their more effective use in managing the flow of human resources. *Human Resource Planning, 10*(3), 157–167.

Mehrabian, A., & de Wetter, R. (1987). Experimental test of an emotion-based approach to fitting brand names to products. *Journal of Applied Psychology, 72,* 125–130.

Meier, T. K., & Hough, S. (1982). Beyond orientation: Assimilating new employees. *Human Resource Management, 21*(1), 27–29.

Messick, S. (1980). Test validity and the ethics of assessment. *American Psychologist, 35,* 1012–1027.

Meyer, H. H. (1987). Predicting supervisory ratings versus promotional progress in test validation studies. *Journal of Applied Psychology, 72,* 696–697.

Meyer, H. H., & Raich, M. S. (1983). An objective evaluation of a behavior modeling training program. *Personnel Psychology, 36*, 755–761.

Meyer, J. P., & Allen, N. J. (1984). Testing the side-bet theory of organizational commitment: Some methodological considerations. *Journal of Applied Psychology, 69*, 372–378.

Meyer, J. P., Paunonen, S. V., Gellatly, I. R., Goffin, R. D., & Jackson, D. N. (1989). Organizational commitment and job performance: It's the nature of the commitment that counts. *Journal of Applied Psychology, 74*, 152–156.

Middlemist, R. D., & Peterson, R. B. (1976). Test of equity theory by controlling for comparison of worker's efforts. *Organizational Behavior and Human Performance, 15*, 335–354.

Miljus, R. C. (1970). Effective leadership and the motivation of human resources. *Personnel Journal, 49*, 36–40.

Miller, E. C. (1978). GM's quality of work life efforts. *Personnel, 55*(4), 11–23; *55*(5), 64–69; *55*(6), 21–26.

Miller, K. I., & Monge, P. R. (1986). Participation, satisfaction, and productivity: A meta-analytic review. *Academy of Management Journal, 29*, 727–753.

Miller, W., & Suther, T. W., III. (1983). Display station anthropometrics: Preferred height and angle settings of CRT and keyboard. *Human Factors, 25*, 401–408.

Milliman, R. E. (1982). Using background music to affect the behavior of supermarket shoppers. *Journal of Marketing, 46*(3), 86–91.

Miner, J. B. (1984a). From theory to application. *The Industrial-Organizational Psychologist, 21*(2), 9–20.

Miner, J. B. (1984b). The validity and usefulness of theories in an emerging organizational science. *Academy of Management Review, 9*, 296–306.

Miner, J. B., & Smith, N. R. (1982). Decline and stabilization of managerial motivation over a 20-year period. *Journal of Applied Psychology, 67*, 297–305.

Minter, R. L. (1972). Human rights laws and pre-employment inquiries. *Personnel Journal, 51*, 431–433.

Mintz, F. (1986). Retraining: The graying of the training room. *Personnel, 63*(10), 69–71.

Mischkind, L. A. (1986). Is employee morale hidden behind statistics? *Personnel Journal, 65*(2), 74–79.

Mital, A., & Ramanan, S. (1986). Results of the simulation of a qualitative information display. *Human Factors, 28*, 341–346.

Mitchell, J. V., Jr. (Ed.). (1985). *The ninth mental measurements yearbook.* Lincoln, NE: Buros Institute of Mental Measurements.

Mitchell, T. R. (1974). Expectancy models of job satisfaction, occupational preference, and effort: A theoretical, methodological, and empirical appraisal. *Psychological Bulletin, 81*, 1053–1077.

Mitchell, T. R., & Kalb, L. S. (1982). Effects of job experience on supervisor attributions for a subordinate's poor performance. *Journal of Applied Psychology, 67*, 181–188.

Moore, R. W. (1987). Examining the honesty of honesty tests. *Industrial Management, 29*(2), 18–19.

Moos, M. H. (1986). Work as a human context. In M. S. Pallak & R. O. Perloff (Eds.), *Psychology and work: Productivity, change, and employment* (pp. 5–52). Washington, DC: American Psychological Association.

Moos, R. H. (1981). *Work Environment Scale manual.* Palo Alto, CA: Consulting Psychologists Press.

Morrison, A. M., White, R. P., & Van Velsor, E. (1987, August). Executive women: Substance plus style. *Psychology Today*, pp. 18–26.

Morrow, P. C., & Goetz, J. F., Jr. (1988). Professionalism as a form of work commitment. *Journal of Vocational Behavior, 32*, 92–111.

Morrow, P. C., & McElroy, J. C. (1987). Work commitment and job satisfaction over three career stages. *Journal of Vocational Behavior, 30*, 330–346.

Motowidlo, S. J., Packard, J. S., & Manning, M. R. (1986). Occupational stress: Its causes and consequences for job performance. *Journal of Occupational Psychology, 71*, 618–629.

Mount, M. K., & Thompson, D. E. (1987). Cognitive categorization and quality of performance ratings. *Journal of Applied Psychology, 72*, 240–246.

Mowday, R. T., Porter, L. W., & Steers, R. M. (1982). *Employee-organization linkages: The psychology of commitment, absenteeism, and turnover.* New York: Academic Press.

Muczyk, J. P., & Reimann, B. C. (1987). Has participative management been oversold? *Personnel, 64*(5), 52–56.

Mueller, B. (1987, June/July). Reflections of culture: An analysis of Japanese and American advertising appeals. *Journal of Advertising Research*, pp. 51–59.

Mulder, M., de Jong, R. D., Koppelaar, L., & Verhage, J. (1986). Power, situation, and leaders' effectiveness: An organizational field study. *Journal of Applied Psychology, 71*, 566–570.

Münsterberg, H. (1913). *The psychology of industrial efficiency.* Boston: Houghton Mifflin.

Murphy, B. S., Barlow, W. E., & Hatch, D. D. (1988a). Developments in job-related polygraph examinations. *Personnel Journal, 67*(1), 26–27.

Murphy, B. S., Barlow, W. E., & Hatch, D. D. (1988b). Employers required to negotiate drug tests. *Personnel Journal, 67*(1), 27–28.

Murphy, K. R. (1987). Detecting infrequent deception. *Journal of Applied Psychology, 72*, 611–614.

Murphy, K. R., & Constans, J. I. (1987). Behavioral anchors as a source of bias in rating. *Journal of Applied Psychology, 72*, 573–577.

Murray, R. S. (1981). Managerial perceptions of two appraisal systems. *California Management Review, 23*(3), 92–96.

Must part-timers be bottom of the pile? (1988, April). *Personnel Management*, p. 17.

Nagamachi, M. (1986). Human factors of industrial robots and robot safety management in Japan. *Applied Ergonomics, 17*(1), 9–18.

Narayanan, V. K., & Nath, R. (1982). A field test of some attitudinal and behavioral consequences of flexitime. *Journal of Applied Psychology, 67*, 214–218.

Nash, A. N., Muczyk, J. P., & Vettori, F. L. (1971). The relative practical effectiveness of programmed instruction. *Personnel Psychology, 24*, 397–418.

Nathan, B. R., & Alexander, R. A. (1988). A comparison of criteria for test validation: A meta-analytic investigation. *Personnel Psychology, 41*, 517–535.

Naughton, T. J., & Outcalt, D. (1988). Development and test of an occupational taxonomy based on job characteristics theory. *Journal of Vocational Behavior, 32*(1), 16–36.

Nelson, J. E., & Frontczak, N. T. (1988). How acquaintanceship and analyst can influence focus group results. *Journal of Advertising, 17*(1), 41–48.

Neslin, S. A., & Clarke, D. G. (1987, February/March). Relating the brand use profile of coupon redeemers to brand and coupon characteristics. *Journal of Advertising Research*, pp. 23–32.

Nester, M. A., & Sapinkopf, R. C. (1982). *A federal employment test modified for deaf applicants*. Washington, DC: U.S. Office of Personnel Management.

Nevo, B. (Ed.). (1987). *The scientific aspects of graphology: A handbook*. Springfield, IL: Chas. C Thomas.

Newton, T. J., & Keenan, A. (1987). Role stress reexamined: An investigation of role stress predictors. *Organizational Behavior and Human Decision Processes, 40*, 346–368.

Nichols, M. L. (1987). Next question, please [Review of *Generalizing from laboratory to field settings*]. *Contemporary Psychology, 32*, 936–938.

Nicholson, N., & Glynn-Jones, T. (1987, February). Good and bad practices in graduate development. *Personnel Management*, pp. 34–38.

Niebel, B. W. (1972). *Motion and time study* (5th ed.). Homewood, IL: Richard D. Irwin.

Niemcryk, S. J., Jenkins, C. D., Rose, R. M., & Hurst, M. W. (1987). The prospective impact of psychosocial variables on rates of illness and injury in professional employees. *Journal of Occupational Medicine, 29*(8), 645–652.

Night beat. (1988, June). *Psychology Today*, pp. 14–15.

Noble, K. B. (1988, January 10). For OSHA, balance is hard to find. *New York Times*.

Noe, R. A. (1986). Trainees' attributes and attitudes: Neglected influences on training effectiveness. *Academy of Management Review, 11*, 736–749.

Noe, R. A., & Schmitt, D. (1986). The influence of trainee attitudes on training effectiveness: Test of a model. *Personnel Psychology, 39*, 497–523.

Noe, R. A., & Steffy, B. D. (1987). The influence of individual characteristics and assessment center evaluation on career exploration behavior and job involvement. *Journal of Vocational Behavior, 30*(2), 187–202.

Nusbaum, H. J. (1986). The career development program at DuPont's Pioneering Research Laboratory. *Personnel, 63*(9), 68–75.

O'Driscoll, M. P. (1987). Attitudes to the job and the organization among new recruits: Influence of perceived job characteristics and organizational structure. *Applied Psychology: An International Review, 36*(2), 133–145.

Office of Technology Assessment. (1987). *The electronic supervisor: New technology, new tensions*. Washington, DC: Government Printing Office.

Offices of the future. (1984, May 14). *Newsweek*, pp. 72–75.

Ogilvy, D., & Raphaelson, J. (1982). Research on advertising techniques that work—and don't work. *Harvard Business Review, 60*(4), 14–18.

Older consumers *do* have clout. (1984, March 4). *New York Times*.

Oldham, G. R., & Fried, Y. (1987). Employee reactions to workspace characteristics. *Journal of Applied Psychology, 72*, 75–80.

Olian, J. D., Schwab, D. P., & Haberfeld, Y. (1988). The impact of applicant gender compared to qualifications on hiring recommendations: A meta-analysis of experimental studies. *Organizational Behavior and Human Decision Processes, 41*, 180–195.

Olivas, L., & Inman, T. (1983). What concerns today's trainers? *Training and Development Journal, 37*(7), 62–64.

One third of applicants lie about experience. (1987, September 3). *St. Petersburg (FL) Times*.

Ong, C. N., Koh, D., Phoon, W. O., & Low, A. (1988). Anthropometrics and display station preferences of VDU operators. *Ergonomics, 31*, 337–347.

Ong, C. N., Phoon, W. O., Iskandar, N., & Chia, K. S. (1987). Shiftwork and work injuries in an iron and steel mill. *Applied Ergonomics, 18*(1), 51–56.

O'Reilly, C., III, & Chatman, J. (1986). Organizational commitment and psychological attachment: The effects of compliance, identification, and internalization of pro-social behavior. *Journal of Applied Psychology, 71*, 492–499.

Orlansky, J., & String, J. (1981). Computer-based instruction for military training. *Defense Management Journal, 18*(2), 46–54.

Osborne, D. J. (1982). *Ergonomics at work*. New York: Wiley.

Oshima, M., Hayashi, Y., & Noro, K. (1980). Human factors which have helped Japanese industrialization. *Human Factors, 22*, 3–13.

Osipow, S. H. (1986). Career issues through the life span. In M. S. Pallak & R. O. Perloff (Eds.), *Psychology and work: Productivity, change and employment* (pp. 141–168). Washington, DC: American Psychological Association.

Osipow, S. H., & Davis, A. S. (1988). The relationship of coping resources to occupational stress and strain. *Journal of Vocational Behavior, 32*, 1–15.

OSS Assessment Staff. (1948). *Assessment of men: Selection of personnel for the U.S. Office of Strategic Services*. New York: Rinehart.

Ottaway, R. N., & Bhatnagar, D. (1988). Personality and biographical differences between male and female managers in the United States and India. *Applied Psychology: An International Review, 37*(2), 201–212.

Owens, W. A., & Henry, E. R. (1966). *Biographical data in industrial psychology*. Greensboro, NC: Richardson Foundation.

Owens, W. A., & Schoenfeldt, L. F. (1979). Toward a classification of persons. *Journal of Applied Psychology, 65*, 569–607.

Parker, M., & Slaughter, J. (1988, December 4). Behind the scenes at Nummi Motors. *New York Times*.

Parkinson, C. N. (1957). *Parkinson's law and other studies in administration*. Boston: Houghton Mifflin.

Parsons, H. M. (1974). What happened at Hawthorne? *Science, 183*, 922–932.

Parsons, H. M., & Kearsley, G. P. (1982). Robotics and human factors: Current status and future prospects. *Human Factors, 24*, 535–552.

Pate, L. E., & Heiman, D. C. (1987). A test of the Vroom-Yetton decision model in seven field settings. *Personnel Review, 16*(2), 22–26.

Pati, G. C., & Morrison, G. (1982). Enabling the disabled. *Harvard Business Review, 60*(4), 152–168.

Patrick, J., & Moore, A. K. (1985). Development and reliability of a job analysis technique. *Journal of Occupational Psychology, 58*, 149–158.

Patrickson, M. (1986). Adaptation by employees to new technology. *Journal of Occupational Psychology, 59*, 1–11.

Pattan, J. E. (1983). Return on investment: Transferring the results of management training to on-the-job performance. *Personnel, 60*(4), 33–47.

Paunonen, S. V., & Jackson, D. N. (1987). Accuracy of interviewers and students in identifying the personality characteristics of personnel managers and computer programmers. *Journal of Vocational Behavior, 31*, 26–36.

Paunonen, S. V., Jackson, D. N., & Oberman, S. M. (1987). Personnel selection decisions: Effects of applicant personality and letter of reference. *Organizational Behavior and Human Decision Processes, 40*, 96–114.

Paxton, A. L., & Turner, E. J. (1984). The application of human factors to the needs of the novice computer user. *International Journal of Man-Machine Studies, 20*, 137–156.

Pearce, B. (1987, October). The human factor in office design. *Personnel Management*, pp. 56–58.

Pearce, J. L., & Porter, L. W. (1986). Employee responses to formal performance appraisal feedback. *Journal of Applied Psychology, 71*, 211–218.

Pelletier, K. R. (1984). *Healthy people in unhealthy places: Stress and fitness at work*. New York: Delacorte.

Peters, L. H., Hartke, D. D., & Pohlmann, J. T. (1985). Fiedler's contingency theory of leadership: An application of the meta-analytic procedures of Schmidt and Hunter. *Psychological Bulletin, 97*, 274–285.

Petersen, D. J. (1980). Flextime in the United States: The lessons of experience. *Personnel, 57*(1), 21–31.

Petersen, D. J., & Massengill, D. (1988). Childcare programs benefit employees, too. *Personnel, 65*(5), 58–62.

Peterson, R. A., & Kerin, R. A. (1977). The female role in advertisements: Some experimental evidence. *Journal of Marketing, 41*(4), 59–63.

Phillips, J. C., & Benson, J. E. (1983). Some aspects of job satisfaction in the Soviet Union. *Personnel Psychology, 36*, 633–645.

Piccolino, E. B. (1988). Outplacement: The view from HR. *Personnel, 65*(3), 24–27.

Podgursky, M., & Swaim, P. (1987). Duration of joblessness following displacement. *Industrial Relations, 26*(3), 213–226.

Poindexter, J. (1983, May). Shaping the consumer. *Psychology Today*, pp. 64–68.

Pokorny, M. L. I., Blom, D. H. J., Van Leeuwen, P., & Van Nooten, W. N. (1987). Shift sequences, duration of rest periods, and accident risk of bus drivers. *Human Factors, 29*, 73–81.

Pollack, A. (1988, January 10). In spanking-new industry, a search for answers. *New York Times*.

Porter, L. W., & Lawler, E. E., III. (1968a). *Managerial attitudes and performance*. Homewood, IL: Richard D. Irwin.

Porter, L. W., & Lawler, E. E., III. (1968b). What job attitudes tell about motivation. *Harvard Business Review, 46*(1), 118–126.

Portwood, J. D., & Granrose, C. S. (1986). Organizational career management programs: What's available? What's effective? *Human Resource Planning, 9*(3), 107–119.

Posner, B. Z., & Powell, G. N. (1985). Female and male socialization experiences: An initial investigation. *Journal of Occupational Psychology, 58*, 81–85.

Posner, B. Z., & Schmidt, W. H. (1988). Government morale and management: A survey of federal executives. *Public Personnel Management, 17*(1), 21–27.

Powell, G. N. (1987). The effects of sex and gender on recruitment. *Academy of Management Review, 12*, 731–743.

Powell, G. N. (1988). *Women and men in management*. Newbury Park, CA: Sage.

Primoff, E. S. (1975). *How to prepare and conduct job element examinations*. Washington, DC: U.S. Office of Personnel Management.

Puckett, S. B. (1988, January). When a worker gets AIDS. *Psychology Today*, pp. 26–27.

Puffer, S. M. (1987). Prosocial behavior, noncompliant behavior, and work performance among commission salespeople. *Journal of Applied Psychology, 72*, 615–621.

Quayle, D. (1983). American productivity: The devastating effect of alcoholism and drug abuse. *American Psychologist, 38*, 454–458.

Rabinowitz, W., Falkenbach, K., Travers, J. R., Valentine, C. G., & Weener, P. (1983). Worker motivation: Unsolved problem or untapped resource? *California Management Review, 25*(2), 45–56.

Raelin, J. A. (1985). Work patterns in the professional life-cycle. *Journal of Occupational Psychology, 58,* 177–187.

Randall, D. M. (1987). Commitment and the organization: The Organization Man revisited. *Academy of Management Review, 12,* 460–471.

Rassenfoss, S. E., & Kraut, A. I. (1988). Survey of personnel research departments. *The Industrial-Organizational Psychologist, 25*(4), 31–37.

Raynolds, E. H. (1987). Management women in the corporate workplace: Possibilities for the year 2000. *Human Resource Management, 26*(2), 265–276.

Raza, S. M., & Carpenter, B. N. (1987). A model of hiring decisions in real employment interviews. *Journal of Applied Psychology, 72,* 596–603.

Reed, S. (1988, April 10). Job trade-off: Drug test. *New York Times Education Life.*

Reichers, A. E. (1986). Conflict and organizational commitments. *Journal of Applied Psychology, 71,* 508–514.

Reichers, A. E. (1987). An interactionist perspective on newcomer socialization rates. *Academy of Management Review, 12,* 278–287.

Reilly, R. R., Brown, B., Blood, M. R., & Malatesta, C. Z. (1981). The effects of realistic previews: A study and discussion of the literature. *Personnel Psychology, 34,* 823–834.

Reilly, R. R., & Chao, G. T. (1982). Validity and fairness of some alternative employee selection procedures. *Personnel Psychology, 35,* 1–62.

Reilly, B. J., & Diangelo, J. A., Jr. (1988). A look at job redesign. *Personnel, 65*(2), 61–65.

Relieving the stress and strain on VDT operators. (1984). *Personnel, 61*(2), 41–42.

Rendero, T. (1980). Supervisory selection procedures. *Personnel, 57*(2), 4–10.

Revenge of the fired. (1987, February 16). *Newsweek*, pp. 46–47.

Revised JDI: A facelift for an old friend. (1987). *The Industrial-Organizational Psychologist, 24*(4), 31–33.

Rhodes, S. R. (1983). Age-related differences in work attitudes and behavior: A review and conceptual analysis. *Psychological Bulletin, 93,* 328–367.

Rice, B. (1978, June). The new truth machines. *Psychology Today,* pp. 61–77.

Rice, B. (1983a, August). Curing cyberphobia. *Psychology Today*, p. 79.

Rice, B. (1983b, April). Misunderstanding media. *Psychology Today*, p. 21.

Rice, B. (1984, February). Dedicated female managers. *Psychology Today*, p. 17.

Riegle, D. W., Jr. (1982). The psychological and social effects of unemployment. *American Psychologist, 37,* 1113–1115.

Rieland, R. (1988, March). Is your office making you sick? *Washingtonian*, pp. 116–125, 174–181.

Rizzo, A. M., & Mendez, C. (1988). Making things happen in organizations: Does gender make a difference? *Public Personnel Management, 17*(1), 9–20.

Roach, D. E., & Davis, R. R. (1973). Stability of the structure of employee attitudes: An empirical test of factor invariance. *Journal of Applied Psychology, 58,* 181–185.

Robertson, I. T., Gratton, L., & Sharpley, D. (1987). The psychometric properties and design of managerial assessment centres: Dimensions into exercises won't go. *Journal of Occupational Psychology, 60,* 187–195.

Robertson, I. T., & Makin, P. J. (1986). Management selection in Britain: A survey and critique. *Journal of Occupational Psychology, 59,* 45–57.

Robinson, C. P., & Eberts, R. E. (1987). Comparison of speech and pictorial displays in a cockpit environment. *Human Factors, 29,* 31–44.

Roedder, D. L., Sternthal, B., & Calder, B. J. (1983). Attitude-behavior consistency in children's responses to television advertising. *Journal of Marketing Research, 20,* 337–349.

Roethlisberger, F. J., & Dickson, W. J. (1939). *Management and the worker: An account of a research program conducted by the Western Electric Company, Chicago.* Cambridge, MA: Harvard University Press.

Rogers, M. (1988, March 28). Robots find their place. *Newsweek*, pp. 58–60.

Rollins, T. (1988). Pay for performance: Is it worth the trouble? *Personnel Administrator, 33*(5), 42–46.

Romberg, R. V. (1986). Performance appraisal, I: Risks and rewards. *Personnel, 63*(8), 20–26.

Ronco, W. C. (1988). The road to the help trap is paved with good intentions. *Personnel, 65*(2), 44–49.

Rook, D. W. (1987). The buying impulse. *Journal of Consumer Research, 14*, 189–199.

Rooks, B. (1987). Robot growth rate falters in 1986. *Industrial Robot, 14*(3), 149–151.

Rosch, P. J., & Pelletier, K. R. (1987). Designing worksite stress management programs. In L. R. Murphy & T. F. Schoenborn (Eds.), *Stress management in work settings* (pp. 69–91). Washington, DC: National Institute for Occupational Safety and Health.

Rosen, T. H. (1987). Identification of substance abusers in the workplace. *Public Personnel Management, 16*(3), 197–207.

Rosenbaum, L. L., & Rosenbaum, W. B. (1971). Morale and productivity consequences of group leadership style, stress, and type of task. *Journal of Applied Psychology, 55*, 343–348.

Ross, J. E., & Unwalla, D. (1988). Making it to the top: A 30-year perspective. *Personnel, 65*(4), 70–78.

Rothstein, M., & Jackson, D. N. (1980). Decision making in the employment interview: An experimental approach. *Journal of Applied Psychology, 65*, 271–283.

Rotter, J. B. (1966). Generalized expectancies for internal versus external control of reinforcement. *Psychological Monographs, 80*(1, Whole No. 609).

Rotter, J. B. (1975). Some problems and misconceptions related to the construct of internal versus external control of reinforcement. *Journal of Consulting and Clinical Psychology, 43*, 56–67.

Rowe, M. P., Russell-Einhorn, M., & Baker, M. A. (1986). The fear of AIDS. *Harvard Business Review, 64*(4), 28–36.

Russell, J. E. A., & Rush, M. C. (1987). A comparative study of age-related variations in women's views of a career in management. *Journal of Vocational Behavior, 30*, 280–284.

Rust, L. (1987, April/May). Using attention and intention to predict at-home program choice. *Journal of Advertising Research*, pp. 25–30.

Ryan, A. M., & Sackett, P. R. (1987). A survey of individual assessment practices by I/O psychologists. *Personnel Psychology, 40*, 455–488.

Ryland, E. K., & Rosen, B. (1988). Attracting job applicants with flexible benefits. *Personnel, 65*(3), 71–73.

Rynes, S. L., & Boudreau, J. W. (1986). College recruiting in large organizations: Practice, evaluations, and research implications. *Personnel Psychology, 39*, 729–757.

Rynes, S. L., Tolbert, P. S., & Strausser, P. G. (1988). Aspirations to manage: A comparison of engineering students and working engineers. *Journal of Vocational Behavior, 32*, 239–253.

Saal, F. E. (1978). Job involvement: A multivariate approach. *Journal of Applied Psychology, 63*, 53–61.

Saari, L. M., Johnson, T. R., McLaughlin, S. D., & Zimmerle, D. M. (1988). A survey of management training and education practices in U.S. companies. *Personnel Psychology, 41,* 731–743.

Sackett, P. R. (1987). Assessment centers and content validity: Some neglected issues. *Personnel Psychology, 40,* 13–25.

Sales, S. M. (1969). Organizational role as a risk factor in coronary disease. *Administrative Science Quarterly, 14,* 325–336.

Salipante, P., Jr., & Goodman, P. (1976). Training, counseling, and retention of the hardcore unemployed. *Journal of Applied Psychology, 61,* 1–11.

Sartain, A. Q., & Baker, A. W. (1978). *The supervisor and the job* (3rd ed.). New York: McGraw-Hill.

Sashkin, M., & Burke, W. W. (1987). Organizational development in the 1980s. *Journal of Management, 13,* 205–229.

Sauser, W. J., & York, C. M. (1978). Sex differences in job satisfaction: A reexamination. *Personnel Psychology, 31,* 537–547.

Scandura, T. A., & Graen, G. B. (1984). Moderating effects of initial LMX status on the effects of a leadership intervention. *Journal of Applied Psychology, 69,* 428–436.

Scarpello, V., & Campbell, J. P. (1983). Job satisfaction: Are all the parts there? *Personnel Psychology, 36,* 577–600.

Schiemann, W. A. (1987). The impact of corporate compensation and benefit policy on employee attitudes and behavior and corporate profitability. *Journal of Business and Psychology, 2*(1), 8–26.

Schiffman, L. G., & Kanuk, L. K. (1983). *Consumer behavior* (2nd ed.). Englewood Cliffs, NJ: Prentice-Hall.

Schlenker, J. A., & Gutek, B. A. (1987). Effects of role loss on work-related attitudes. *Journal of Applied Psychology, 72,* 287–293.

Schmidt, F. L., & Hunter, J. E. (1978). Moderator research and the law of small numbers. *Personnel Psychology, 31,* 215–232.

Schmidt, F. L., & Hunter, J. E. (1981). Employment testing: Old theories and new research findings. *American Psychologist, 36,* 1128–1137.

Schmidt, F. L., Hunter, J. E., Croll, P. R., & McKenzie, R. C. (1983). Estimation of employment test validities by expert judgment. *Journal of Applied Psychology, 68,* 590–601.

Schmidt, F. L., Hunter, J. E., Outerbridge, A. N., & Trattner, M. H. (1986). The economic impact of job selection methods on size, productivity, and payroll costs of the federal work force: An empirically based demonstration. *Personnel Psychology, 39,* 1–29.

Schmied, L. A., & Lawler, K. A. (1986). Hardiness, Type A behavior, and the stress-illness relation in working women. *Journal of Personality and Social Psychology, 51,* 1218–1223.

Schmitt, N. (1976). Social and situational determinants of interview decisions: Implications for the employment interview. *Personnel Psychology, 29,* 79–101.

Schmitt, N. (1977). Interrater agreement in dimensionality and combination of assessment center judgments. *Journal of Applied Psychology, 62,* 171–176.

Schmitt, N., & DeGregorio, M. (1986). Results of Society surveys. *The Industrial-Organizational Psychologist, 23*(4), 27–34.

Schmitt, N., & Fitzgerald, M. (1982). Mass psychogenic illness: Individual and aggregate data. In M. Colligan, J. Pennebaker, & L. Murphy (Eds.), *Mass psychogenic illness: A social psychological analysis* (pp. 87–100). Hillsdale, NJ: Erlbaum.

Schmitt, N., Ford, J. K., & Stults, D. M. (1986). Changes in self-perceived ability as a function of performance in an assessment centre. *Journal of Occupational Psychology, 59,* 327–335.

Schmitt, N., & Lappin, M. (1980). Race and sex as determinants of the mean and variance of performance ratings. *Journal of Applied Psychology, 65*, 428–435.

Schneider, B. (1987). The people make the place. *Personnel Psychology, 40*, 437–453.

Schneider, B., & Schmitt, N. (1986). *Staffing organizations*. Glenview, IL: Scott, Foresman.

Schultz, D. P. (1979). *Psychology in use: An introduction to applied psychology*. New York: Macmillan.

Schwab, D. P. (1982). Organizational recruiting and the decision to participate. In K. Rowland & G. Ferris (Eds.), *Personnel management: New perspectives*. Boston: Allyn & Bacon.

Scientific validity of polygraph testing: A research review and evaluation. (1983). Washington, DC: U.S. Office of Technology Assessment.

Scott, W. D. (1903). *The theory of advertising*. Boston: Small.

Scott, W. D. (1915). The scientific selection of salesmen. *Advertising and Selling, 25*, 5–6, 94–96.

Seashore, S. E., & Bowers, D. G. (1970). Durability of organizational change. *American Psychologist, 25*, 227–233.

Seers, A., McGee, G. W., Serey, T. T., & Graen, G. B. (1983). The interaction of job stress and social support. *Academy of Management Journal, 26*, 273–284.

Seidel, R. P., & Powell, G. N. (1983). On the campus: Matching graduates with jobs. *Personnel, 60*(4), 66–72.

Sell, R. G. (1977). What does safety propaganda do for safety? A review. *Applied Ergonomics, 8*, 203–214.

Shaffer, G. S. (1987). Patterns of work and nonwork satisfaction. *Journal of Applied Psychology, 72*, 115–124.

Shaffer, G. T., Saunders, V., & Owens, W. A. (1986). Additional evidence for the accuracy of biographical data: Long-term retest and observer ratings. *Personnel Psychology, 39*, 791–809.

Sharf, J. C. (1987). Validity generalization: Round two. *The Industrial-Organizational Psychologist, 25*(1), 49–52.

Shaw, L., & Sichel, H. S. (1971). *Accident proneness: Research in the occurrence, causation, and prevention of road accidents*. New York: Pergamon.

Shea, G., & Berg, D. (1987). Analyzing the development of an OD practitioner. *Journal of Applied Behavioral Science, 23*, 315–336.

Shenkar, O., & Ronen, S. (1987). Structure and importance of work goals among managers in the People's Republic of China. *Academy of Management Journal, 30*, 564–576.

Sheppard, H. L., & Herrick, N. Q. (1972). *Where have all the robots gone?* New York: Free Press.

Sherer, P. D., Schwab, D. P., & Heneman, G., III. (1987). Managerial salary-raise decisions: A policy-capturing approach. *Personnel Psychology, 40*, 27–38.

Sherman, E., & Delener, N. (1987). The impact of demographics on household personal computer purchasing decisions. *Academy of Marketing Science, 15*(2), 25–32.

Shinar, D., & Acton, M. B. (1978). Control-display relationships on the four-burner range: Population stereotypes versus standards. *Human Factors, 20*, 13–17.

Shipper, F. (1983). Quality circles using small group formation. *Training and Development Journal, 37*(5), 80–84.

Shore, L. M., & Thornton, G. C. (1986). Effects of gender on self- and supervisory ratings. *Academy of Management Journal, 29*, 115–129.

Siegel, L. (1982). Paired comparison evaluations of managerial effectiveness by peers and supervisors. *Personnel Psychology, 35*, 843–852.

Sinclair, H. J. (1971). Digital versus conventional clocks: A review. *Applied Ergonomics, 2*, 179–181.

Sinclair, M. A. (1986). Ergonomics aspects of the automated factory. *Ergonomics, 29*, 1507–1523.

Sivak, M. (1987). Human factors and road safety. *Applied Ergonomics, 18*, 289–296.

Sleight, R. (1948). The effect of instrument dial shape on legibility. *Journal of Applied Psychology, 32*, 170–188.

Sloan, S. J., & Cooper, C. L. (1986). Stress coping strategies in commercial airline pilots. *Journal of Occupational Medicine, 28*(1), 49–52.

Smeltzer, L. R., & Kedia, B. L. (1987). Training needs of quality circles. *Personnel, 64*(8), 51–55.

Smith, D. E. (1986). Training programs for performance appraisal: A review. *Academy of Management Review, 11*, 22–40.

Smith, D., & Tarpey, T. (1987). In-tray exercises and assessment centres: The issue of reliability. *Personnel Review, 16*(3), 24–28.

Smith, P. B. (1975). Controlled studies of the outcome of sensitivity training. *Psychological Bulletin, 72*, 597–622.

Smith, P. C., Kendall, L. M., & Hulin, C. L. (1969). *The measurement of satisfaction in work and retirement*. Chicago: Rand McNally.

Smith, R. D., & Sherman, C. (1982, July/August). Change of heart—change of mind. *American Health*, pp. 52–54.

Smith, R. P. (1981). Boredom: A review. *Human Factors, 23*, 329–340.

Smither, J. W., Skov, R. B., & Adler, S. (1986). Attributions for the poorly performing blackjack dealer: In the cards or inability? *Personnel Psychology, 39*, 123–139.

Snizek, W. E., & Bullard, J. H. (1983). Perception of bureaucracy and changing job satisfaction: A longitudinal analysis. *Organizational Behavior and Human Performance, 32*, 275–287.

Society for Industrial and Organizational Psychology. (1983). Bylaws. *The Industrial-Organizational Psychologist, 20*(2), 67–77.

Society for Industrial and Organizational Psychology. (1987). *Principles for the validation and use of personnel selection procedures* (3rd ed.). College Park, MD: The Society.

Solomon, B. A. (1986). New options for more flexible work schedules. *Personnel, 63*(2), 4–6.

Solomon, E. E. (1986). Private and public sector managers: An empirical investigation of job characteristics and organizational climate. *Journal of Applied Psychology, 71*, 247–259.

Soong, R. (1988, February/March). The statistical reliability of People Meter ratings. *Journal of Advertising Research*, pp. 50–56.

Sorcher, M. (1983). Behavior modeling and motivational skills. In J. R. Hackman, E. E. Lawler, III, & L. W. Porter (Eds.), *Perspectives on behavior in organizations* (2nd ed.) (pp. 209–221). New York: McGraw-Hill.

Spanish speaking are $20 billion U.S. market. (1973, November 21). *Advertising Age*, p. 56.

Spector, P. E., & Levine, E. L. (1987). Meta-analysis for integrating study outcomes: A Monte Carlo study of its susceptibility to Type I and Type II errors. *Journal of Applied Psychology, 72*, 3–9.

Spettell, C. M., & Liebert, R. M. (1986). Training for safety in automated person-machine systems. *American Psychologist, 41*, 545–550.

Sproull, L. S. (1986). Using electronic mail for data collection in organizational research. *Academy of Management Journal, 29*, 159–169.

Stagner, R. (1975). Boredom on the assembly line: Age and personality variables. *International Gerontology, 2*, 23–44.

Stagner, R. (1982). Past and future of industrial/organizational psychology. *Professional Psychology, 13*, 892–903.

Stahl, M. J. (1986). *Managerial and technical motivation: Assessing needs for achievement, power, and affiliation.* New York: Praeger.

Staines, G. L., Pottick, K. J., & Fudge, D. A. (1986). Wives' employment and husbands' attitudes toward work and life. *Journal of Applied Psychology, 71*, 118–128.

Stautberg, S. S. (1987). Status report: The corporation and trends in family issues. *Human Resource Management, 26*(2), 277–290.

Staw, B. M. (1984). Organizational behavior: A review and reformulation of the field's outcome variables. *Annual Review of Psychology, 35*, 627–666.

Steele, F. I. (1983). The ecology of executive teams: A new view of the top. *Organizational Dynamics, 2*(4), 65–78.

Steers, R. M., & Porter, L. W. (1983). *Motivation and work behavior* (3rd ed.). New York: McGraw-Hill.

Steffy, B. D., & Jones, J. W. (1988). Workplace stress and indicators of coronary-disease risk. *Academy of Management Journal, 31*, 686–698.

Stephens, N., & Warrens, R. A. (1983). Advertising frequency requirements for older adults. *Journal of Advertising Research, 23*(6), 23–32.

Stockton, W. (1988, June 5). Pilots' fatigue termed threat to safe flying. *New York Times.*

Stone, D. L., & Stone, E. F. (1987). Effects of missing application-blank information on personnel selection decisions: Do privacy protection strategies bias the outcome? *Journal of Applied Psychology, 72*, 452–456.

Stoner, C. R., & Fry, F. L. (1983). Developing a corporate policy for managing stress. *Personnel, 60*(3), 66–76.

Stout, H. (1988, September 11). What's new in marketing to empty nesters. *New York Times.*

Stout, S. K., Slocum, J. W., Jr., & Cron, W. L. (1987). Career transitions of superiors and subordinates. *Journal of Vocational Behavior, 30*, 124–137.

Stout, S. K., Slocum, J. W., Jr., & Cron, W. L. (1988). Dynamics of the career plateauing process. *Journal of Vocational Behavior, 32*, 74–91.

Strauss, G. (1977). Managerial practices. In J. R. Hackman & J. L. Suttle (Eds.), *Improving life at work: Behavioral science approaches to organizational change.* Pacific Palisades, CA: Goodyear.

Stress, burnout high among managers. (1988). *Administrative Management, 49*(3), 7.

Stress on the job. (1988, April 25). *Newsweek*, pp. 40–45.

Stress on your job: A major national survey. (1984, April). *Ms.*, pp. 83–86.

Suinn, R. M. (1982). Intervention with Type A behaviors. *Journal of Consulting and Clinical Psychology, 50*, 933–949.

Summers, L. S. (1983). Stress management in business organizations. *The Industrial-Organizational Psychologist, 20*(3), 29–33.

Sundstrom, E. (1986). *Work places: The psychology of the physical environment in offices and factories.* New York: Cambridge University Press.

Super, D. E., & Hall, D. T. (1978). Career development: Exploration and planning. *Annual Review of Psychology, 29*, 333–372.

Sutton, R. I., & Louis, M. P. (1987). How selecting and socializing newcomers influences insiders. *Human Resource Management, 26*, 347–361.

Sutton, R. I., & Rafaeli, A. (1987). Characteristics of work stations as potential occupational stressors. *Academy of Management Journal, 30*, 260–276.

Sutton, R. I., & Rafaeli, A. (1988). Untangling the relationship between displayed emotions and organizational sales: The case of convenience stores. *Academy of Management Journal, 31,* 461–487.

Swartz, T. A. (1983). Brand symbols and message differentiation. *Journal of Advertising Research, 23*(5), 59–64.

Tagliaferri, L. E. (1988). Taking note of employee attitudes. *Personnel Administrator, 33*(4), 96–102.

Tang, T. L., Tollison, P. S., & Whiteside, H. D. (1987). The effect of quality circle initiation on motivation to attend quality circle meetings and on task performance. *Personnel Psychology, 40,* 799–814.

Tannenbaum, A. S., Kavačič, B., Rosner, M., Vianello, M., & Wieser, G. (1974). *Hierarchy in organizations: An international comparison.* San Francisco: Jossey-Bass.

Taylor, F. W. (1911). *Scientific management.* New York: Harper.

Taylor, G. S., & Zimmerer, T. W. (1988). Personality tests for potential employees: More harm than good. *Personnel Journal, 67*(1), 60–64.

Taylor, M. S., & Bergmann, T. J. (1987). Organizational recruitment activities and applicants' reactions at different stages of the recruitment process. *Personnel Psychology, 40,* 261–285.

Taylor, M. S., & Sackhaim, K. K. (1988). Graphology. *Personnel Administrator, 33*(5), 71–76.

Taylor, M. S., & Schmidt, D. W. (1983). A process-oriented investigation of recruitment source effectiveness. *Personnel Psychology, 36,* 343–354.

Taylor, M. S., & Sniezek, J. A. (1984). The college recruitment interview: Topical content and applicant reactions. *Journal of Occupational Psychology, 57,* 157–168.

Taylor, R. L., & Zawacki, R. A. (1984). Trends in performance appraisal: Guidelines for managers. *Personnel Administrator, 29*(3), 71–80.

Taylor, R. R. (1986). A positive guide to theft deterrence. *Personnel Journal, 65*(8), 36–40.

Taylor, T. O., Friedman, D. J., & Couture, D. (1987). Operating without supervisors: An experiment. *Organizational Dynamics, 15,* 26–38.

Teel, K. W. (1986). Are merit raises really based on merit? *Personnel Journal, 65*(3), 88–95.

Tenopyr, M. L., & Oeltjen, P. D. (1982). Personnel selection and classification. *Annual Review of Psychology, 33,* 581–618.

Test for market research (1987, December 28). *Newsweek,* pp. 32–33.

Tetrick, L. E., & LaRocco, J. M. (1987). Understanding, prediction, and control as moderators of the relationship between perceived stress, satisfaction, and psychological well-being. *Journal of Applied Psychology, 72,* 538–543.

Thacker, J. W., & Fields, M. W. (1987). Union involvement in quality-of-worklife efforts: A longitudinal investigation. *Personnel Psychology, 40,* 97–111.

Thayer, P. W. (1983). Industrial/organizational psychology: Science and application. In C. J. Scheirer & A. M. Rogers (Eds.), *The G. Stanley Hall lecture series* (Vol. 3, pp. 9–30). Washington, DC: American Psychological Association.

Thornton, G. C., III. (1980). Psychometric properties of self-appraisals of job performance. *Personnel Psychology, 33,* 263–272.

Tierney, J. (1988, May 15). Wired for stress. *New York Times Magazine,* pp. 49, 81–85.

Tougas, G., & Nordin, M. C. (1987). Seat features recommendations for workstations. *Applied Ergonomics, 18*(3), 207–210.

Trahiotis, C., & Robinson, D. E. (1979). Auditory psychophysics. *Annual Review of Psychology, 30*, 31–61.

Tsui, A. S., & Barry, B. (1986). Interpersonal affect and rating errors. *Academy of Management Journal, 29*, 586–599.

Tubbs, M. E. (1986). Goal setting: A meta-analytic examination of the empirical evidence. *Journal of Applied Psychology, 71*, 474–483.

Turnage, J. T. (1988). Coverage of I/O psychology in introductory textbooks. *The Industrial-Organizational Psychologist, 25*(2), 45–51.

Tziner, A., & Dolan, S. (1982). Validity of an assessment center for identifying future female officers in the military. *Journal of Applied Psychology, 67*, 728–736.

Vale, C. D., Keller, L. S., & Bentz, V. J. (1986). Development and validation of a computerized interpretation system for personnel tests. *Personnel Psychology, 39*, 525–542.

Vecchio, R. P. (1984). The problem of phony resumes: How to spot a ringer among applicants. *Personnel, 61*(2), 22–27.

Vecchio, R. P. (1987). Situational leadership theory: An examination of a prescriptive theory. *Journal of Applied Psychology, 72*, 444–451.

Vecchio, R. P., & Gobdel, B. C. (1984). The VDL model of leadership: Problems and prospects. *Organizational Behavior and Human Performance, 34*, 5–20.

Vidaček, S., Kaliterna, L., & Radošević-Vidaček, B. (1986). Productivity on a weekly rotating shift system: Circadian adjustment and sleep deprivation effects. *Ergonomics, 29*, 1583–1590.

Vodanovich, S. J., & Reyna, M. (1988). Alternatives to workplace testing. *Personnel Administrator, 33*(5), 78–84.

Vroom, V. H. (1964). *Work and motivation.* New York: Wiley.

Vroom, V. H., & Yetton, P. W. (1973). *Leadership and decision-making.* Pittsburgh: University of Pittsburgh Press.

Wagel, W. H. (1986a). Opening the door to employee participation. *Personnel, 63*(4), 4–6.

Wagel, W. H. (1986b). The safe way to quality. *Personnel, 63*(8), 4–6.

Wagel, W. H. (1986c). Building excellence through training. *Personnel, 63*(9), 5–10.

Wagel, W. H. (1986d). A positive approach to alcohol and drug abuse. *Personnel, 63*(12), 4–11.

Wagel, W. H. (1987). Working (and managing) without supervisors. *Personnel, 64*(9), 8–11.

Wagner, R. (1949). The employment interview: A critical summary. *Personnel Psychology, 2*, 17–46.

Wahba, M. A., & Bridwell, L. G. (1976). Maslow reconsidered: A review of research on the need hierarchy theory. *Organizational Behavior and Human Performance, 15*, 212–240.

Waldman, D. A., & Avolio, B. J. (1986). A meta-analysis of age differences in job performance. *Journal of Applied Psychology, 71*, 33–38.

Wall, T. D., Kemp, N. J., Jackson, P. R., & Clegg, C. W. (1986). Outcomes of autonomous workgroups: A long-term field experiment. *Academy of Management Journal, 29*, 280–304.

Wallin, L., & Wright, I. (1986). Psychosocial aspects of the work environment: A group approach. *Journal of Occupational Medicine, 28*(5), 384–393.

Walsh, J. P., Weinerg, R. M., & Fairfield, M. L. (1987). The effects of gender on assessment centre evaluations. *Journal of Occupational Psychology, 60,* 305–309.

Wanous, J. P. (1980). *Organizational entry: Recruitment, selection and socialization of newcomers.* Reading, MA: Addison-Wesley.

Wanous, J. P. (1983). The entry of newcomers into organizations. In J. R. Hackman, E. E. Lawler, III, & L. W. Porter (Eds.), *Perspectives on behavior in organizations* (2nd ed.) (pp. 159–167). New York: McGraw-Hill.

Wanous, J. P., & Zwany, A. (1977). A cross-sectional test of need hierarchy theory. *Organizational Behavior and Human Performance, 18,* 78–97.

Warm, J. S., & Dember, W. N. (1986, April). Awake at the switch. *Psychology Today,* pp. 46–49, 52–53.

Watts, L. R., & White, H. C. (1988). Assessing employee turnover. *Personnel Administrator, 33*(4), 80–85.

Weaver, C. N. (1978). Black-white correlates of job satisfaction. *Journal of Applied Psychology, 63,* 255–258.

Weaver, C. N., & Holmes, S. L. (1975). A comparative study of females with full-time employment and full-time housekeeping. *Journal of Applied Psychology, 60,* 117–118.

Weaver, C. N., & Matthews, M. D. (1987). What white males want from their jobs: Ten years later. *Personnel, 64*(9), 62–65.

Weber, M. (1947). *The theory of social and economic organization.* New York: Oxford University Press.

Weekley, J. A., & Gier, J. A. (1987). Reliability and validity of the situational interview for a sales position. *Journal of Applied Psychology, 72,* 484–487.

Wehrenberg, S. B. (1988). Train supervisors to measure and evaluate performance, *Personnel Journal, 67*(2), 77–81.

Weiss, R. M. (1987). Writing under the influence: Science versus fiction in the analysis of corporate alcoholism programs. *Personnel Psychology, 40,* 341–356.

Weiss, D. J., Dawis, R. V., England, G. W., & Lofquist, L. H. (1967). *Manual for the Minnesota Satisfaction Questionnaire.* Minneapolis: University of Minnesota.

Wellness: A new concept in health care. (1982, January). *American Pharmacy,* pp. 42–46.

Wells, A. S. (1987, October 11). The rising market in educating executives. *New York Times.*

Wells, B. W. P. (1965). Subjective responses to the lighting installation in a modern office building and their design implications. *Building Science, 1,* 57–68.

Wernimont, P. F., Toren, P., & Kapell, H. (1970). Comparison of sources of personal satisfaction and of work motivation. *Journal of Applied Psychology, 54,* 95–102.

Weston, D. J., & Warmke, D. L. (1988). Dispelling the myths about panel interviews. *Personnel Administrator, 33*(5), 109–111.

Wexley, K. N. (1984). Personnel training. *Annual Review of Psychology, 35,* 519–551.

Wexley, K. N., & Baldwin, T. T. (1986). Posttraining strategies for facilitating positive transfer: An empirical exploration. *Academy of Management Journal, 29,* 503–520.

Wexley, K. N., & Klimoski, R. (1984). Performance appraisal: An update. In K. M. Rowland & G. R. Ferris (Eds.), *Research in personnel and human resources management* (Vol. 2, pp. 35–79). Greenwich, CT: JAI Press.

Wexley, K. N., & Latham, G. P. (1981). *Developing and training human resources in organizations.* Glenview, IL: Scott, Foresman.

Wexley, K. N., & Youtz, M. A. (1985). Rater beliefs about others: Their effects on rating errors and rater accuracy. *Journal of Occupational Psychology, 58,* 265–275.

Wexley, K. N., Yukl, G. A., Kovacs, S. Z., & Sanders, R. E. (1972). Importance of contrast effects in employment interviews. *Journal of Applied Psychology, 56,* 45–48.

When managers must play parent. (1986, April 6). *St. Petersburg (FL) Times.*

When the mean and the median diverge. (1986, May 18). *New York Times.*

When the TV is on, who's watching. (1982, October 18). *Newsweek.*

Whipple, T. W., & Courtney, A. E. (1980). How to portray women in TV commercials. *Journal of Advertising Research, 20*(2), 53–59.

Whitney, E. (1988, January 17). The real laggards: White-collar workers. *St. Petersburg (FL) Times.*

Wiersma, U., & Latham, G. P. (1986). The practicality of behavioral observation scales, behavioral expectation scales, and trait scales. *Personnel Psychology, 39,* 619–628.

Williams, K., Harkins, S. G., & Latané, B. (1981). Identifiability as a deterrent to social loafing: Two cheering experiments. *Journal of Personality and Social Psychology, 40,* 303–311.

Wing, J. F. (1965). *A review of the effects of high ambient temperature on mental performance.* Washington, DC: U.S. Department of the Air Force.

Winstanley, N. B. (1980). How accurate are performance appraisals? *Personnel Administration, 25*(8), 53–58.

Wogalter, M. S., Godfrey, S. S., Fontenelle, G. A., & Desaulniers, D. R., Rothstein, P. R., & Laughery, K. P. (1987). Effectiveness of warnings. *Human Factors, 29,* 599–612.

Wokoun, W. (1963). *Vigilance with background music.* Aberdeen Proving Ground, MD: U.S. Army Human Engineering Laboratories.

Wolinsky, J. (1982, December). Beat the clock. *APA Monitor.*

Wood, R. E., Mento, A. J., & Locke, E. A. (1987). Task complexity as a moderator of goal effects: A meta-analysis. *Journal of Applied Psychology, 72,* 416–425.

Woods, W. A. (1981). *Consumer behavior: Adapting and experiencing.* New York: Elsevier.

Work gossip. (1987, August 4). *St. Petersburg (FL) Times.*

Work in America: Report of a special task force to the Secretary of Health, Education, and Welfare. (1973). Cambridge, MA: MIT Press.

Would you quit your job? (1988, May 7). *St. Petersburg (FL) Times.*

Wright, L. (1988). The Type A behavior pattern and coronary artery disease. *American Psychologist, 43,* 2–14.

Wright, M. (1986). Helping employees speak out about their jobs and the workplace. *Personnel, 63*(9), 56–60.

Wrogg, S. G. (1961). The role of emotions in industrial accidents. *Archives of Environmental Health, 3,* 519.

Wyckham, R. G. (1987, February/March). Implied superiority claims. *Journal of Advertising Research,* pp. 54–63.

Yale, L., & Gilly, M. C. (1988). Trends in advertising research: A look at the content of marketing-oriented journals from 1976 to 1985. *Journal of Advertising, 17*(1), 12–22.

Yankelovich, D. (1979). Work, values, and the new breed. In C. Kerr & J. M. Rosow (Eds.), *Work in America: The decade ahead.* New York: Van Nostrand Reinhold.

Yoder, D., & Staudohar, P. D. (1984). Testing and EEO: Getting down to cases. *Personnel Administrator, 29*(2), 67–74.

Young, C. E., & Robinson, M. (1987, June/July). Guideline SM: Tracking the commercial viewer's wandering attention. *Journal of Advertising Research,* pp. 15–22.

Yukl, G., & Taber, T. (1983). The effective use of managerial power. *Personnel, 60*(2), 37–44.

Zalesny, M. D. (1988). Work and organizations in the 1990s: What's a union to do? *The Industrial-Organizational Psychologist, 24*(4), 45–51.

Zalesny, M. D., & Farace, R. V. (1987). Traditional versus open offices: A comparison of sociotechnical, social relations, and symbolic meaning perspectives. *Academy of Management Journal, 30*, 240–259.

Zaleznik, A., Kets de Vries, M. F. R., & Howard, J. (1977). Stress reactions in organizations: Syndromes, causes and consequences. *Behavioral Science, 22*, 151–162.

Zedeck, S., & Cascio, W. F. (1984). Psychological issues in personnel decisions. *Annual Review of Psychology, 35*, 461–518.

Zedeck, S., Jackson, S.E., & Summers, E. (1983). Shift work schedules and their relationship to health, adaptation, satisfaction, and turnover intention. *Academy of Management Journal, 26*, 297–310.

Zippo, M. (1982). The U.S. executive: Underutilized and restless. *Personnel, 59*(3), 42–43.

Zohar, D. (1980). Safety climate in industrial organizations: Theoretical and applied implications. *Journal of Applied Psychology, 65*, 96–102.

Zuboff, S. (1988). *In the age of the smart machine: The future of work and power*. New York: Basic Books.

Photo Credits

Index